GUSTAV STICKLEY'S CRAFTSMAN HOMES AND BUNGALOWS

Gustav Stickley

Skyhorse Publishing

Skyhorse Publishing books may be purchased in bulk at special discounts for sales promotion, corporate gifts, fund-raising, or educational purposes. Special editions can also be created to specifications. For details, contact the Special Sales Department, Skyhorse Publishing, 555 Eighth Avenue, Suite 903, New York, NY 10018 or info@skyhorsepublishing.com.

www.skyhorsepublishing.com

10 9 8 7 6 5 4 3 2 1

Library of Congress Cataloging-in-Publication Data

Stickley, Gustav, 1858-1942.
    [Craftsman homes and bungalows]
    Gustav Stickley's Craftsman homes and bungalows / Gustav Stickley.
        p. cm.
    ISBN 978-1-60239-303-5 (alk. paper)
1. Stickley, Gustav, 1858-1942. 2. Architecture, Domestic--United States--Designs and plans. 3. Arts and crafts movement--United States. I. Title.
    NA737.S65A4 2009
    728'.370973--dc22

                                                2008029730

Printed in Canada

TABLE OF CONTENTS

Craftsman Bungalows *413*

GUSTAV STICKLEY: ORIGINATOR OF CRAFTSMAN HOUSES AND CRAFTS-
MAN FURNITURE: FOUNDER AND EDITOR OF THE CRAFTSMAN MAGAZINE.

CRAFTSMAN HOMES

"THE SIMPLIFICATION OF LIFE:" A CHAPTER FROM EDWARD CARPENTER'S BOOK CALLED "ENGLAND'S IDEAL"

WHEN we remember the sincere reformers of the world, do we not always recall most gladly the simple men amongst them, Savonarola rather than Tolstoi, Gorky rather than Goethe, and would it not be difficult to associate this memory of individual effort for public good with consciously elegant surroundings. Could we, for instance, picture Savonarola with a life handicapped, perhaps, by eager pursuit of sartorial eccentricities, with a bias for elaborate cuisine and insistence upon unearned opulence, or the earning of luxury at the sacrifice of other's lives or happiness? It does not somehow fit into the frame. In remembering those who have dedicated their lives to the benefit of their own lands, we inevitably picture them as men of simple ways, who have asked little and given much, who have freed their shoulders from the burdens of luxury, who have stripped off from their lives the tight inflexible bandages of unnecessary formalities, and who have thus been left free for those great essentials of honest existence, for courage, for unselfishness, for heroic purpose and, above all, for the clear vision which means the acceptance of that final good, honesty of purpose, without which there can be no real meaning in life.

Such right living and clear thinking cannot find abiding place except among those whose lives bring them back close to Nature's ways, those who are content to be clad simply and comfortably, to accept from life only just compensation for useful toil, who prefer to live much in the open, finding in the opportunity for labor the right to live; those who desire to rest from toil in homes built to meet their individual need of rest and peace and joy, homes which realize a personal standard of comfort and beauty; those who demand honesty in all expression from all friends, and who give in return sincerity and unselfishness, those who are fearless of sorrow, yet demand joy; those who rank work and rest as equal means of progress—in such lives only may we find the true regeneration for any nation, for only in such simplicity and sincerity can a nation develop a condition of permanent and properly equalized welfare.

By simplicity here is not meant any foolish whimsical eccentricity of dress or manner or architecture, colonized and made conspicuous by useless wealth, for eccentricity is but an expression of individual egotism and as such must inevitably be short-lived. And what our formal, artificial world of today needs is not more of this sort of eccentricity and egotism, but less; not more conscious posing for picturesque reform, but greater and quieter achievement along lines of fearless honesty; not less beauty, but infinitely more of a beauty that is real and lasting because it is born out of use and taste.

From generation to generation every nation has the privilege of nourishing men and women (but a few) who think and live thus sincerely and beautifully, and who so far as possible strive to impress upon their own generation the need of such sincerity and beauty in daily life. One of the rarest and most honest of these sincere personalities in modern life is Edward Carpenter, an Englishman who, though born to wealth and station, has stripped his life of superfluous social paraphernalia and stepped out of the clumsy burden of tradition, up (not down) to the life of the simple, common people, earning his living and that of his family as a cobbler (and a good one, too) and living in a peaceful fashion in a home planned and largely constructed by himself. His life and his work are with the people. He knows their point of view, he writes for them, lectures for them, and though a leader in modern thought in England and a man of genius, he is one with his daily associates in purpose and general scheme of existence. In all his present writings the common man and his relation to civilization, is Mr. Carpenter's theme, and he deals with the great problems of sociology in plain practical terms and with a straightforward thought born of that surest knowledge possible, experience.

From the beginning of the endeavor of THE CRAFTSMAN to aid in the interests of better art, better work and a better and more reasonable way of living, the work of Edward Carpenter has been an inspiration and an ideal, born out of that sympathy of purpose which makes men of whatever nation brothers and comrades. We have from time to time in the magazine quoted from Mr. Carpenter's books at length, feeling that he was expressing our own ideal as no words of ours could, and particularly have we felt a oneness of purpose with him in his book called "England's Ideal," in which he publishes a chapter on the "Simplification of Life," which with its honesty, sincerity, its high courage and rare judgment should make clear the pathway for all of those among us who are honestly interested in readjusting life on a plane of greater usefulness and higher beauty. In this essay which we purpose here to quote at length, Mr. Carpenter begins by speaking of his own method of readjusting his life as follows:

"IF YOU do not want to be a vampire and a parasite upon others, the great question of practical life which everyone has to face, is how to carry it on with as little labor and effort as may be. No one wants to labor needlessly, and if you have to earn everything you spend, economy becomes a very personal question—not necessarily in the pinching sense, but merely as adaptation of means to the end. When I came some years ago to live with cottagers (earning say £50 to £60 a year) and share their life, I was surprised to find how little both in labor and expense their food cost them, who were doing far more work than I was, or indeed the generality of the people among whom I had been living. This led me to see that the somewhat luxurious mode of living I had been accustomed to was a mere waste, as far as adaptation to any useful end was concerned; and afterward I had decided that it had been a positive hindrance, for when I became habituated to a more simple life and diet, I found that a marked improvement took place in my powers both of mind and body.

"The difference arising from having a small piece of garden is very great, and makes one feel how important it is that every cottage should have a plot of ground attached. A rood of land (quarter acre) is sufficient to grow all potatoes and other vegetables and some fruit for the year's use, say for a family of five. Half an acre would be an ample allowance. Such a piece of land may easily be cultivated by anyone in the odd hours of regular work, and the saving is naturally large from not having to go to the shop for everything of this nature that is needed.

"Of course, the current mode of life is so greatly wasteful, and we have come

THE SIMPLIFICATION OF LIFE

to consider so many things as necessaries—whether in food, furniture, clothing or what not—which really bring us back next to no profit or pleasure compared with the labor spent upon them, that it is really difficult to know where the balance of true economy would stand if, so to speak, left to itself. All we can do is to take the existing mode of life in its simpler forms, somewhat as above, and work from that as a basis. For though the cottager's way of living, say in our rural districts or in the neighborhood of our large towns, is certainly superior to that of the well-to-do, that does not argue that it is not capable of improvement. * * * *

"NO DOUBT immense simplifications of our daily life are possible; but this does not seem to be a matter which has been much studied. Rather hitherto the tendency has been all the other way, and every additional ornament to the mantelpiece has been regarded as an acquisition and not as a nuisance; though one doesn't see any reason, in the nature of things, why it should be regarded as one more than the other. It cannot be too often remembered that every additional object in a house requires additional dusting, cleaning, repairing; and lucky you are if its requirements stop there. When you abandon a wholesome tile or stone floor for a Turkey carpet, you are setting out on a voyage of which you cannot see the end. The Turkey carpet makes the old furniture look uncomfortable, and calls for stuffed couches and armchairs; the couches and armchairs demand a walnut-wood table; the walnut-wood table requires polishing, and the polish bottles require shelves; the couches and armchairs have casters and springs, which give way and want mending; they have damask seats, which fade and must be covered; the chintz covers require washing, and when washed they call for antimacassars to keep them clean. The antimacassars require wool, and the wool requires knitting-needles, and the knitting-needles require a box, the box demands a side table to stand on and the side table involves more covers and casters—and so we go on. Meanwhile the carpet wears out and has to be supplemented by bits of drugget, or eked out with oilcloth, and beside the daily toil required to keep this mass of rubbish in order, we have every week or month, instead of the pleasant cleaning-day of old times, a terrible domestic convulsion and bouleversement of the household.

"It is said by those who have traveled in Arabia that the reason why there are so many religious enthusiasts in that country, is that in the extreme simplicity of the life and uniformity of the landscape there, heaven—in the form of the intense blue sky—seems close upon one. One may almost see God. But we moderns guard ourselves effectually against this danger. For beside the smoke pall which covers our towns, we raise in each household such a dust of trivialities that our attention is fairly absorbed, and if this screen subsides for a moment we are sure to have the daily paper up before our eyes so that if a chariot of fire were sent to fetch us, ten to one we should not see it.

"However, if this multiplying of the complexity of life is really grateful to some people, one cannot quarrel with them for pursuing it; and to many it appears to be so. When a sewing machine is introduced into a household the simple-minded husband thinks that, as it works ten times as quick as the hand, there will now be only a tenth part of the time spent by his wife and daughter in sewing that there was before. But he is ignorant of human nature. To his surprise he finds that there is no difference in the time. The difference is in the plaits and flounces—they put ten times as many on their dresses. Thus we see how little external reforms avail. If the desire for simplicity is not really present, no labor-saving appliances will make life simpler.

"As a rule all curtains, hangings, cloths and covers, which are not absolutely necessary, would be dispensed with. They all create dust and stiffness, and all entail trouble and recurring expense, and they all tempt the housekeeper to keep out the air and sunlight—two things of the last and most vital importance. I like a room which looks its best when the sun streams into it through wide open doors and windows. If the furnishing of it cannot stand this test—if it looks uncomfortable under the operation—you may be sure there is something unwholesome about it. As to the question of elegance or adornment, that may safely be left to itself. The studied effort to make interiors elegant has only ended—in what we see. After all, if things are in their places they will always look well. What, by common consent, is more graceful than a ship—the sails, the spars, the rigging, the lines of the hull? Yet go on board and you will scarcely find one thing placed there for the purpose of adornment. An imperious necessity rules everything; this rope could have no other place than it has, nor could be less thick or thicker than it is; and it is, in fact, this necessity which makes the ship beautiful. * * * *

"WITH regard to clothing, as with furniture and the other things, it can be much simplified if one only desires it so. Probably, however, most people do not desire it, and of course they are right in keeping to the complications. Who knows but what there is some influence at work for some ulterior purpose which we do not guess, in causing us to artificialize our lives to the extraordinary extent we do in modern times? Our ancestors wore woad, and it does not at first sight seem obvious why we should not do the same. Without, however, entering into the woad question, we may consider some ways in which clothing may be simplified without departing far from the existing standard. It seems to be generally admitted now that wool is the most suitable material as a rule. I find that a good woolen coat, such as is ordinarily worn, feels warmer when unlined than it does when a layer of silk or cotton is interposed between the woolen surface and the body. It is also lighter; thus in both ways the simplification is a gain. Another advantage is that it washes easier and better, and is at all times cleaner. No one who has had the curiosity to unpick the lining of a tailor-made coat that has been in wear a little time, will, I think, ever wish to have coats made on the same principle again. The rubbish he will find inside, the frettings and frayings of the cloth collected in little dirt-heaps up and down, the paddings of cotton wool, the odd lots of miscellaneous stuff used as backings, the quantity of canvas stiffening, the tags and paraphernalia connected with the pockets, bits of buckram inserted here and there to make the coat "sit" well—all these things will be a warning to him. * * * *

"And certainly, nowadays, many folk visibly are in their coffins. Only the head and hands are out, all the rest of the body clearly sickly with want of light and air, atrophied, stiff in the joints, strait-waistcoated, and partially mummied. Sometimes it seems to me that is the reason why, in our modern times, the curious intellect is so abnormally developed, the brain and the tongue waggle so, because these organs alone have a chance, the rest are shut out from heaven's light and air; the poor human heart grown feeble and weary in its isolation and imprisonment, the liver diseased and the lungs straitened down to mere sighs and conventional disconsolate sounds beneath their cerements.

"There are many other ways in which the details and labor of daily life may be advantageously reduced, which will occur to anyone who turns practical attention to the matter. For myself I confess to a great pleasure in witnessing the Economics of Life—and how seemingly nothing need be wasted; how the very stones that offend the spade in the garden become invaluable when foot-paths have to be laid out or drains to be made. Hats that are past wear get cut up into strips for nailing creepers on the wall; the upper leathers of old shoes are useful for the same purpose. The under garment that is too far gone for mending is used for patching another less decrepit of its kind, then it is torn up into strips for bandages or what not; and when it has served its time thus it descends to floor washing, and is scrubbed out of life—useful to the end. When my coat has worn itself into an affectionate intimacy with my body, when it has served for Sunday best, and for week days, and got weather-stained out in the fields with the sun and rain—then faithful, it does not part from me, but getting itself cut up into shreds and patches descends to form a hearthrug for my feet. After that, when worn through, it goes into the kennel and keeps my dog warm, and so after lapse of years, retiring to the manure-heaps and passing out on to the land, returns to me in the form of potatoes for my dinner; or being pastured by my sheep, reappears upon their backs as the material of new clothing. Thus it remains a friend to all time, grateful to me for not having despised and thrown it away when it first got behind the fashions. And seeing we have been faithful to each other, my coat and I, for one round or life-period, I do not see why we should not renew our intimacy—in other metamorphoses—or why we should ever quite lose touch of each other through the æons.

"In the above sketch my object has been not so much to put forward any theory of the conduct of daily life, or to maintain that one method of living is of itself superior to another, as to try and come at the facts connected with the subject. In the long run every household has to support itself; the benefits and accommodations it receives from society have to be covered by the labor it expends for society. This cannot be got over. The present effort of a large number of people to live on interest and dividends, and so in a variety of ways on the labor of others, is simply an effort to make water run up hill; it cannot last very long. The balance, then, between the labor that you may consume and the labor that you expend may be struck in many different ways, but it has to be struck; and I have been interested to bring together some materials for an easy solution of the problem."

"THE ART OF BUILDING A HOME": BY BARRY PARKER AND RAYMOND UNWIN

S A nation we do not easily submit to coercion. We want a hand in the government, national or local. We are pretty direct if we do not like a senator or a governor, and express our opinion fully of our ministers and college presidents. In more intimate matters of courtship and marriage we regard ourselves as more independent than any other nation. We marry usually whom we please, and live where we please, and work as we please—but when it comes to that most vital matter—building a home, individuality and independence seem to vanish, and we are browbeaten alike by architect, builder, contractor, interior decorator, picture dealer and furniture man. We live in any old house that anyone else has discarded, and we submit to all manner of tyrannies as to the size, style and finish of our houses, impertinences that we would not permit in any other detail of life. We not only imitate foreign ideals in our architecture, but we have become artificial and unreal in all the detail of the finish and fittings of our homes. How many of us would dare to rise up and assert sufficient individuality to plan and build a house that exactly suited our personal ideal of comfort and beauty, and represented our station in life?

And to what extent can we hope for finer ideals in a country that is afraid to be sincere in that most significant feature of national achievement—the home. We are a country of self-supporting men and women, and we cannot expect to develop an honest significant architecture until we build homes that are simple, yet beautiful, that proclaim fine democratic standards and that are essentially appropriate to busy intelligent people.

That this same state of affairs prevails somewhat in other lands (though nowhere to the same extent as in America) we realize from the writing of two well-known English architects, Barry Parker and Raymond Unwin, who in a series of lectures published under the title of "The Art of Building a Home" have entered a plea for greater honesty in architecture and greater sincerity in decoration which ought to strike a responsive chord in the heart of every American who has contemplated the foolish, unthinking, artificial structures which we have vainly called homes.

In the introduction to this vital valuable little book Messrs. Parker and Unwin take up the question of lack of thought in architecture in so simple, straightforward and illuminating a fashion that it has seemed wise to present it to the readers of CRAFTSMAN HOMES as expressing our creeds and establishing more fully our own ideals!

"THE way we run in ruts is wonderful: our inability to find out the right principles upon which to set to work to accomplish what we take in hand, or to go to the bottom of things, is simply astonishing: while the resignation with which we accept the Recognized and Usual as the Right and Inevitable is really beautiful.

"In nothing is this tendency more noticeable than in the art of house-building. We begin by considering what, in the way of a house, our neighbors have; what they would expect us to have; what is customary in the rank of life to which we belong; anything, in fact, but what are our actual needs. About the last thing

THE ART OF BUILDING A HOME

we do is to make our home take just that form which will, in the most straight-forward manner, meet our requirements. * * * *

"The planning having been dictated by convention, all the details are worked out under the same influence. To each house is applied a certain amount of meaningless mechanical and superficial ornamentation according to some recognized standard. No use whatever is made of the decorative properties inherent in the construction and in the details necessary to the building. These are put as far as possible out of sight. For example, latches and locks are all let into the doors leaving visible the knobs only. The hinges are hidden in the rebate of the door frame, while the real door frame, that which does the work, is covered up with a strip of flimsy molded board styled the architrave. All constructional features, wherever possible, are smeared over with a coat of plaster to bring them up to the same dead level of flat monotony, leaving a clear field for the erection of the customary abominations in the form of cornices, imitation beams where no beams are wanted, and plaster brackets which could support, and do support, nothing. Even with the fire the chief aim seems to be to acknowledge as few of its properties and characteristics as possible; it is buried as deep in the wall and as far out of sight and out of the way as may be; it is smothered up with as much uncongenial and inappropriate "enrichment" as can be crowded round it; and, to add the final touch of senseless incongruity, some form of that massive and *apparently* very constructional and essential thing we call a mantelpiece is erected, in wood, stone or marble, towering it may be even to the ceiling. If we were not so accustomed to it, great would be our astonishment to find that this most prominent feature has really no function whatever, beyond giving cause for a lot of other things as useful and beautiful as itself, which exist only that they may be put upon it, 'to decorate it.' * * * *

"The essence and life of design lies in finding that form for anything which will, with the maximum of convenience and beauty, fit it for the particular functions it has to perform, and adapt it to the special circumstances in which it must be placed. Perhaps the most fruitful source whence charm of design arises in anything, is the grace with which it serves its purpose and conforms to its surroundings. How many of the beautiful features of the work of past ages, which we now arbitrarily reproduce and copy, arose out of the skilful and graceful way in which some old artist-craftsman, or chief mason, got over a difficulty! If, instead of copying these features when and where the cause for them does not exist, we would rather emulate the spirit in which they were produced, there would be more hope of again seeing life and vigor in our architecture and design.

"WHEN the architect leaves the house, the subservience to convention is not over. After him follow the decorator and the furnisher, who try to overcome the lifelessness and vapidity by covering all surfaces with fugitive decorations and incongruous patterns, and filling the rooms with flimsy stereotyped furniture and nick-nacks. To these the mistress of the house will be incessantly adding, from an instinctive feeling of the incompleteness and unsatisfactoriness of the whole. Incidentally we see here one reason why the influence of the architect should not stop at the completion of the four walls, but

THE ART OF BUILDING A HOME

should extend to the last detail of the furnished house. When his responsibility ceases with the erection of the shell, it is natural that he should look very little beyond this. There is no inducement for him to work out any definite scheme for a finished room, for he knows that if he had any aim the decorator and furnisher would certainly miss it and would fail to complete his creation. If, when designing a house, the architect were bearing in mind the effect each room would have when finished and furnished, his conceptions would be influenced from the very beginning, and his attitude toward the work would tend to undergo an entire change. At present he but too readily accepts the popular idea of art as a thing quite apart from life, a sort of trimming to be added if funds allow.

"It is this prevalent conception of beauty as a sweetmeat, something rather nice which may be taken or left according to inclination after the solid meal has been secured, which largely causes the lack of comeliness we find in our houses. Before this idea can be dispelled and we can appreciate either the place which art should hold in our lives or the importance of rightly educating the appreciation of it, we must realize that beauty is part of the necessary food of any life worth the name; that art, which is the expression of beauty as conceived and created by man, is primarily concerned with the making of the useful garments of life beautiful, not with the trimming of them; and that, moreover, in its higher branches art is the medium through which the most subtle ideas are conveyed from man to man.

"Understanding something of the true meaning of art, we may set about realizing it, at least in the homes which are so much within our control. Let us have in our houses, rooms where there shall be space to carry on the business of life freely and with pleasure, with furniture made for use; rooms where a drop of water spilled is not fatal; where the life of a child is not made a burden to it by unnecessary restraint; plain, simple, and ungarnished if necessary, but honest. Let us have such ornament as we do have really beautiful and wrought by hand, carving, wrought metal, embroidery, painting, something which it has given pleasure to the producer to create, and which shows this in every line—the only possible work of art. Let us call in the artist, bid him leave his easel pictures, and paint on our walls and over the chimney corner landscapes and scenes which shall bring light and life into the room; which shall speak of nature, purity, and truth; shall become part of the room, of the walls on which they are painted, and of the lives of us who live beside them; paintings which our children shall grow up to love, and always connect with scenes of home with that vividness of a memory from childhood which no time can efface. Then, if necessary, let the rest of the walls go untouched in all the rich variety of color and tone, of light and shade, of the naked brickwork. Let the floor go uncarpeted, and the wood unpainted, that we may have time to think, and money with which to educate our children to think also. Let us have rooms which once decorated are always decorated, rooms fit to be homes in the fullest poetry of the name; in which no artificiality need momentarily force us to feel shame for things of which we know there is nothing to be ashamed: rooms which can form backgrounds, fitting and dignified, at the time and in our memories, for all those little scenes, those acts of kindness and small duties, as well as the scenes of deep emotion and trial, which make up the drama of our lives at home."

A CRAFTSMAN HOUSE FOUNDED ON THE CALIFORNIA MISSION STYLE

E have selected for presentation here what we consider the best of the houses de-signed in The Craftsman Workshops and published in THE CRAFTSMAN during the past five years. Brought together in this way into a closely related group, these designs serve to show the development of the Craftsman idea of home building, decoration and furnishing, and to make plain the fundamental principles which underlie the planning of every Craftsman house. These principles are simplicity, durability, fitness for the life that is to be lived in the house and harmony with its natural surroundings. Given these things, the beauty and comfort of the home environment develops as naturally as a flowering plant from the root.

As will be seen, these houses range from the simplest little cottages or bungalows costing only a few hundred dollars, up to large and expensive residences. But they are all Crafts-man houses, nevertheless, and all are designed with regard to the kind of durability that will insure freedom from the necessity of frequent repairs; to the greatest economy of space and material, and to the securing of plenty of space and freedom in the interior of the house by doing away with unnecessary partitions and the avoidance of any kind of crowding. For interest, beauty, and the effect of home comfort and welcome, we depend upon the liberal use of wood finished in such a way that all its friendliness is revealed; upon warmth, rich-ness, and variety in the color scheme of walls, rugs and draperies, and upon the charm of structural features such as chimneypieces,

window-seats, staircases, fireside nooks, and built-in furnishings of all kinds, our object being to have each room so interesting in itself that it seems complete before a single piece of furniture is put into it.

This plain cement house has been selected for presentation at the head of the list chiefly because it was the first house designed in The Craftsman Workshops and was published in THE CRAFTSMAN for January, 1904, for the benefit of the newly formed Home Builders' Club. Therefore it serves to furnish us with a starting point from which we may judge whether or not any advance has since been made in the application of the Craftsman idea to the planning and furnishing of houses.

It was only natural that our first expression of this idea should take shape in a house which, without being exactly founded on the Mission architecture so much used in Cali-fornia, is nevertheless reminiscent of that style, this effect being given by the low broad proportions of the building and the use of shallow, round arches over the entrance and the two openings which give light and air to the recessed porch in front. The thick cement walls are left rough, a primitive treatment that produces a quality and texture difficult to obtain by any other method and to which time and weather lend additional interest. The roof, which is low pitched and has a fairly strong projection, is covered with un-glazed red Spanish tile in the usual lap-roll pattern with ridge rolls and cresting. The house, as it stands, is a fair example of the way in which the problem of the exterior has been solved by the combination of three fac-tors: simplicity of building materials, em-ployment of constructive features as the only

Published in The Craftsman, January, 1904

A CRAFTSMAN HOUSE BUILT OF CEMENT OR CONCRETE AFTER THE CALIFORNIA MISSION STYLE, WITH LOW-PITCHED TILED ROOF, ROUND ARCHES AND STRAIGHT MASSIVE WALLS. THE DECORATIVE EFFECT DEPENDS ENTIRELY UPON COLOR, PROPORTIONS AND STRUCTURAL FEATURES.

A CRAFTSMAN HOUSE IN CALIFORNIA MISSION STYLE

decoration, and the recognition of the color element which is so necessary in bringing about the necessary harmony between the house and its surroundings. In this case the walls are

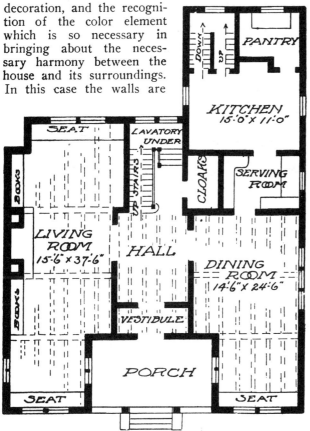

FIRST STORY FLOOR PLAN.

treated with a pigment that gives a soft warm creamy tone, almost a biscuit color, and the roof is dull red,—a scheme that is excellently suited to the prevailing color in California or in the South, where yellows, browns and violets abound. For the colder coloring of the northern or eastern landscape, the cement walls might either be left in the natural gray, or given a tone of dull green, which, applied unevenly, gives an admirable effect upon rough cast plaster. Or, for that matter, the house might be built of brick, stone, or of any one of the various forms of concrete construction. And the roof could be of tile, heavy shingles, or, if given a steeper pitch, of heavy, rough slate. In fact, the design as shown here is chiefly suggestive in its nature, making clear the fundamental principles of the Craftsman house and leaving room for such variation of detail as the owner may desire.

It will be noted that the foundation is not visible and that the turf and shrubbery around it appear to cling to the walls of the house,—a circumstance that is apparently slight and yet has a good deal to do with the linking of a house to the ground on which it stands. This effect would be greatly heightened by a growth of vines over the large plain wall spaces, which would lend themselves admirably to a natural drapery of ivy or ampelopsis.

The treatment of the interior is based upon the principles already laid down, the object being to obtain the maximum effect of beauty and comfort from materials which are few in number and comparatively inexpensive. Although we have not space here for illustration of the interior features, a description of the color scheme employed and of the use made of woodwork and built-in furnishings may serve to give some idea of its character. While the outside of the house is plain to severity, the inside, as we have designed it, glows with color and is rich in suggestion of home comfort. As in all Craftsman houses, wood is abundantly used in the form of beams, wainscots and numerous built-in furnishings.

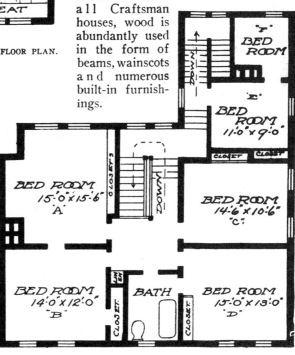

SECOND STORY FLOOR PLAN

AN OLD-FASHIONED HOUSE WITH THE DINING ROOM AND KITCHEN IN ONE

Published in The Craftsman, May, 1905.

VIEW OF HOUSE FROM THE FRONT SHOWING DORMERS, ENTRANCE PORCH AND GROUPING OF WINDOWS.

UPON looking over the plan of this compact little dwelling, it occurs to us that possibly some people might like the general idea of the house and yet not find it convenient to go into the simple life to such an extent as to have the dining room and kitchen in one, as suggested here. Personally we like very much the homely comfort and good cheer which belongs to the big, old-fashioned kitchen which is exquisitely kept and which has in it room for the dining table. But in order to make such an arrangement a suc-

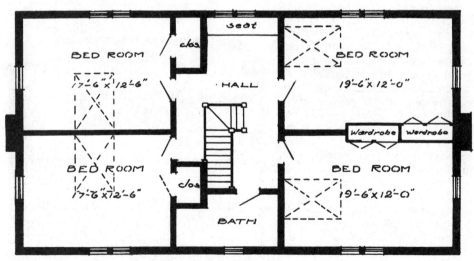

SECOND STORY FLOOR PLAN.

AN OLD-FASHIONED HOUSE

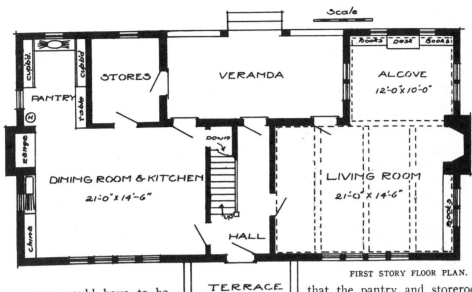

FIRST STORY FLOOR PLAN.

cess, a woman would have to be the sort of a housekeeper her grandmother probably was, and take a personal interest in her cupboard shelves and the brilliancy of her copper and brass cooking utensils, which few women nowadays have time to do.

For those who prefer a separate dining room and a kitchen proper, we would suggest that the pantry and storeroom be thrown into one and used for a kitchen. The chimney built for the range would serve equally well for a fireplace in the dining room, and the range, if set in the adjoining corner, could easily be connected with the same flue. One of the pleasantest features is the veranda at the back, which can be enclosed with glass in winter.

RECESSED VERANDA AT THE BACK OF THE HOUSE, WHICH MAY BE USED AS A DINING PORCH IN SUMMER AND GLASSED IN FOR A CONSERVATORY OR SUN ROOM IN WINTER.

AN OLD FASHIONED HOUSE

LIVING ROOM, SHOWING FIREPLACE OF SPLIT BOULDERS; NOOK WITH BUILT-IN BOOKCASES AND WRITING DESK; DIVISION OF WALL SPACES BY WAINSCOTING, STENCILED PANELS AND FRIEZE, AND EFFECT OF CASEMENTS SET HIGH IN THE WALL ABOVE THE WAINSCOT.

KITCHEN AND DINING ROOM COMBINED, SHOWING RANGE SET IN A RECESS AND HOODED TO CARRY OFF COOKING ODORS; THE DECORATIVE EFFECT OF AN OLD-FASHIONED CUPBOARD BUILT INTO THE WALL AND THE PLACING OF THE DINING TABLE BENEATH A GROUP OF FOUR WINDOWS.

A SMALL COTTAGE THAT IS COMFORTABLE, ATTRACTIVE AND INEXPENSIVE

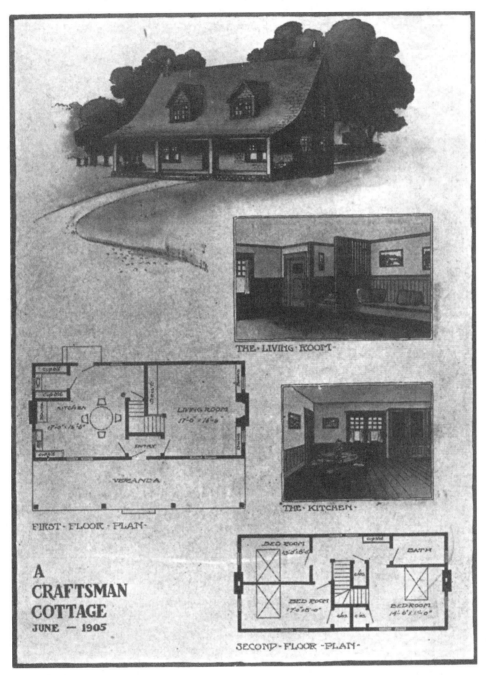

THE · LIVING · ROOM ·

THE · KITCHEN ·

FIRST · FLOOR · PLAN ·

A CRAFTSMAN COTTAGE JUNE — 1905

SECOND · FLOOR · PLAN ·

NOTE THE DIVISION OF SPACE SO THAT THE GREATEST AMOUNT OF FREEDOM AND CONVENIENCE IS OBTAINED WITHIN A SMALL AREA. THE ILLUSTRATIONS OF THE INTERIOR SERVE TO SHOW HOW THE STRUCTURAL FEATURES, ALTHOUGH SIMPLE AND INEXPENSIVE, GIVE TO EACH ROOM AN INDIVIDUAL BEAUTY AND CHARM. THE KITCHEN IS ARRANGED TO SERVE ALSO FOR A DINING ROOM.

A PLAIN HOUSE THAT WILL LAST FOR GENERATIONS AND NEED BUT FEW REPAIRS

Published in The Craftsman, July, 1905.

EXTERIOR VIEW SHOWING STRUCTURAL USE OF TIMBERS ON UPPER STORY AND EFFECT OF BUNGALOW ROOF.

MOST of the Craftsman houses are designed for an environment which admits of plenty of ground or at least of a large garden around them, but this one,—while of course at its best in such surroundings,—would serve admirably for a dwelling to be built on an ordinary city lot large enough to accommodate a house thirty feet square. Seen from the exterior, the house shows a simplicity and thoroughness of construction which makes for the greatest durability and minimizes the necessity for repairs. Also the rooms on both floors are so arranged as to utilize to the best advantage every inch of space and to afford the greatest facility for communication; a plan that tends to lighten by many degrees the burden of housekeeping.

In looking over the plan of the interior, we would suggest one modification which is more in accord with the later Craftsman houses. It will be noticed that the doors leading from the hall into the living room and dining room are of the ordinary size. We have found the feeling of space and freedom throughout the rooms intended for the common life of the family so much more attractive than the shutting off of each room into a separate com-

partment, so to speak, that were we to revise this plan in the light of our later experience, we would widen these openings so that the partitions would either be taken out entirely or else be suggested merely by a panel and post extending only two or three feet from the wall and open at the top after the fashion of so many of the Craftsman interiors. This device serves to break the space pleasantly by the introduction of a structural feature which is always decorative and yet to leave unhampered the space which should be clear and open.

While we advocate the utmost economy of space and urge simplicity as to furnishing, we nevertheless make it a point to render impossible even a passing impression of barrenness or monotony. As we have said, this is partly a matter of woodwork, general color scheme and interesting structural features that make each room a beautiful thing in itself, independent of any furnishing. But also we realize the never ending charm of irregularity in arrangement, that is, of having the rooms so placed and nooks and corners so abundant that the whole cannot be taken in at one glance.

In this case the simple oblong of the living room is broken by the window seat on one

A PLAIN HOUSE THAT WILL LAST FOR GENERATIONS

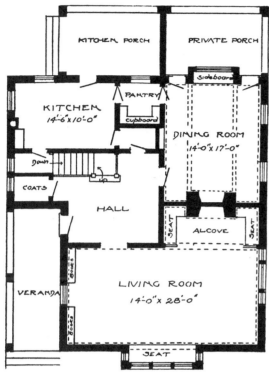

FIRST STORY FLOOR PLAN.

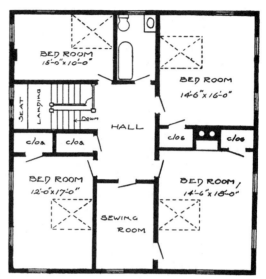

SECOND STORY FLOOR PLAN.

side and the alcove with its chimneypiece and fireside seats on the other. Just beside the alcove is a group of casement windows set high in the wall, so that the sill comes just on a level with the top of an upright piano. The same line is carried all around the room, which is wainscoted preferably with oak or chestnut.

END OF DINING ROOM, SHOWING EFFECT OF BUILT-IN SIDEBOARD, PICTURE WINDOW AND GLASS DOORS. A BUILT-IN CUPBOARD APPEARS AT THE SIDE OF THE ROOM.

A PLAIN HOUSE THAT WILL LAST FOR GENERATIONS

FIRESIDE NOOK IN THE LIVING ROOM, SHOWING ARRANGEMENT OF SEATS AND THE PLACING OF A CRAFTSMAN PIANO JUST BELOW A GROUP OF CASEMENTS. THE DECORATIONS IN THE WALL PANELS ARE STENCILED ON ROUGH PLASTER IN COLORS THAT ARE MEANT TO ACCENT THE GENERAL COLOR SCHEME.

BEDROOM SHOWING A TYPICAL CRAFTSMAN SCHEME FOR DECORATING AND FURNISHING A SLEEPING ROOM. NOTE THE DIVISION OF WALL SPACES INTO PANELS BY STRIPS OF WOOD. THE PANELS ARE COVERED WITH JAPANESE GRASS-CLOTH.

A COTTAGE OF CEMENT OR STONE THAT IS CONVENIENTLY ARRANGED FOR A SMALL FAMILY

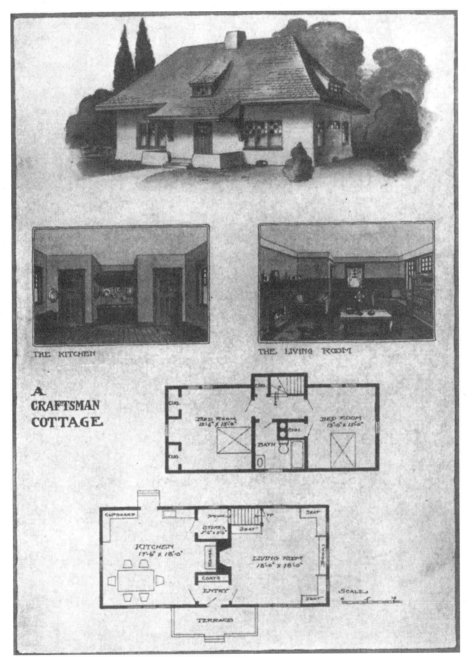

THE KITCHEN

THE LIVING ROOM

A CRAFTSMAN COTTAGE

Published in The Craftsman, April, 1905.

THE DRAWING OF THE EXTERIOR SHOWS THE GRACEFUL LINES AND PROPORTIONS OF THE COTTAGE. THE GLIMPSES GIVEN OF THE INTERIOR SHOW HOW A HOODED RANGE IS PLACED IN A RECESS AND THEREFORE OUT OF THE WAY IN THE ROOM WHICH SERVES AS KITCHEN AND DINING ROOM, AND ALSO HOW A LIVING ROOM MAY BE MADE INDIVIDUAL AND CHARMING AT VERY LITTLE COST.

SUBURBAN HOUSE DESIGNED FOR A LOT HAVING WIDE FRONTAGE BUT LITTLE DEPTH

Published in The Craftsman, September, 1905.

HOW THE HOUSE LOOKS WITH AMPLE GROUNDS AROUND IT AND A SETTING OF TREES FOR A BACKGROUND.

THIS house was designed primarily for use in the suburbs and the plan was adapted to a lot with wide frontage, but no great amount of depth. Of course, it would be better to have such a building surrounded by plenty of lawn, trees and shrubs; but if ground space were limited, a great deal could be made even of a meager allowance for front and back yards.

While the design admits the use of other materials which may be better suited to a given locality or considered more desirable by the owner, our plan was to have the house built of stone and shingles, the lower story and chimneys being of split field stone laid up in dark cement, and the upper story of cedar or rived cypress shingles, so finished that they are given a soft gray tone in harmony with the prevailing color of the stones. We have suggested that the shingle roof be stained or painted a soft moss green.

We regard the arrangement of these verandas as being especially comfortable and convenient, for although none of them are large, they serve admirably to supplement the inner rooms by furnishing what are practically outdoor rooms for general use. The front veranda, which is partially recessed, is

sheltered from the street by the parapets and flower boxes. As doors open from this veranda into the hall, dining room and living room, it is much more closely connected with the house proper than is the case with the usual entrance porch, and is well fitted to serve as an outdoor sitting room. The veranda at the back of the house opens from the dining room and is meant to be used as a dining porch in summer time. Another door opening into the pantry makes it easy to serve meals out there. In winter this porch can easily be glassed in and used as a conservatory or sun room, and if heated, would make a very pleasant place for the serving of afternoon tea or for any such use. A third veranda opens from the kitchen and is meant especially for the comfort and convenience of the servants.

We would suggest here also that the openings from the hall into the dining room and living room be very much wider—a thing which could be easily done and which is now a feature of all the Craftsman houses. A glance at the floor plan will suggest the charm of such an arrangement, as it would allow a long vista from one fireplace to the other and would add much to the comfort and charm of the house as a whole. As will be noted, the liv-

SUBURBAN HOUSE FOR WIDE LOT WITH LITTLE DEPTH

ing room fireplace is flanked on either side by a built-in bookcase with a casement window above, and in the dining room the same arrangement furnishes two china closets surmounted by casements set high in the

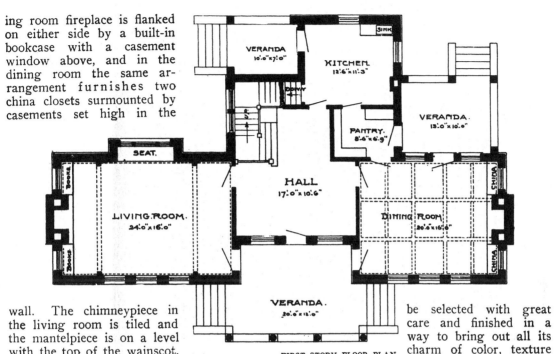

wall. The chimneypiece in the living room is tiled and the mantelpiece is on a level with the top of the wainscot, which runs around the room; but in the dining room the straight, massive brick chimneypiece runs to the ceiling, thus affording a pleasant variation in what otherwise might be too even a balance in the arrangement. The most decorative structural feature in the hall is the staircase, which is lighted by two casements set high above the lower landing and having wide sills, so that they afford an admirable place for plants.

The hall and dining room are wainscoted and the wall spaces in the living room are divided into panels by broad stiles of wood. As the woodwork is so essential in the decorative plan, it should be selected with great care and finished in a way to bring out all its charm of color, texture and grain. The general arrangement and style of the house would seem to demand some strong fibred, richly marked wood, which always seems best suited to rooms intended for general use.

The color scheme always is a matter of individual choice, but a safe rule to follow is to select some wood of rich and quiet coloring for the woodwork, and develop from that the color of the wall spaces, rugs and draperies.

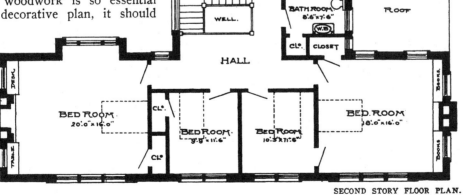

SECOND STORY FLOOR PLAN.

SUBURBAN HOUSE FOR WIDE LOT WITH LITTLE DEPTH

PARTIALLY RECESSED ENTRANCE PORCH, SO SHIELDED BY PARAPETS AND FLOWER BOXES THAT IT MAY BE USED AS AN OUTDOOR LIVING ROOM.

CORNER OF THE LIVING ROOM, SHOWING STRUCTURAL EFFECT OF FIREPLACE AND THE BUILT-IN BOOKCASES SET FLUSH ON EITHER SIDE SO THAT THE TOPS ARE PRACTICALLY AN EXTENSION OF THE MANTEL.

A VERY SIMPLE AND INEXPENSIVE COTTAGE BUILT OF BATTENED BOARDS

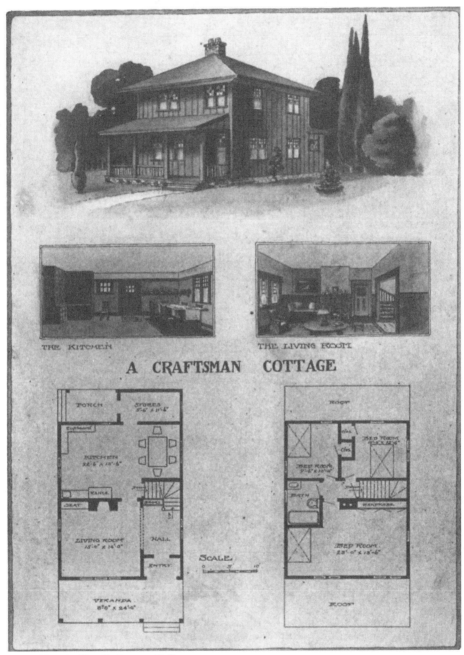

A CRAFTSMAN COTTAGE

Published in The Craftsman, April, 1905.

AN ILLUSTRATION OF THE DECORATIVE POSSIBILITIES OF SIMPLE BATTENED BOARDS. THE INTERIOR VIEWS CONTAIN ANOTHER SUGGESTION FOR THE ARRANGEMENT OF A COMBINED KITCHEN AND DINING ROOM AND ALSO SHOW HOW A VERY PLAIN LIVING ROOM MAY BE MADE COMFORTABLE AND HOMELIKE.

A CEMENT HOUSE THAT SHOWS THE DECORATIVE USE OF CONCRETE AS A FRAMEWORK

Published in The Craftsman, January, 1907.

EXTERIOR VIEW. NOTE EFFECT OF RAISED FRAMEWORK OF CONCRETE AGAINST ROUGH-CAST PANELS.

ONE or the other of the more massive forms of construction seems to be called for by the design of this house, which was meant to be built either of concrete or of hollow cement blocks, and so is planned especially with a view to the use of one or the other of these materials, although the design would be equally well suited to stone or brick. Believing that a house built of cement or concrete should be exceedingly simple in design, with plain straight lines and unbroken wall surfaces, we have carried out this idea as consistently as possible.

No timbers are used on the outside of the house, but the form of the framework is

A CEMENT HOUSE FRAMED IN SMOOTH CONCRETE

revealed in the heavy corner-posts, uprights and horizontal bands of smooth concrete which span the walls and break up the broad plain surfaces. As the walls are given a rough pebble-dash finish, this framework of smooth concrete, which projects slightly from the surface of the wall proper, gives a contrasting effect which adds much to the interest of the design. The concrete may either be left in the natural gray, or the coldness of this tint may be modified by an admixture of coloring which will give it a tone of deeper gray, a suggestion of green, or one of the buff or biscuit shades, according to the color effect that harmonizes best with the surroundings. If the house should be built of stone or brick, the color effect, of course, would be much more decided.

The roof is of slate—not the smooth, thin, lozenge-shaped slates with which we are so familiar, but a much more interesting form of this durable roofing material. The slates we have in mind are large and as rough on surface and edge as split paving-stones. They come in very interesting colors, dull red and slate-color with green and purplish tones which are much like the varied colorings found in stone. If red slate should be chosen for the roof, a pleasant repetition of the color could be obtained by flooring the verandas with square cement blocks of a dull brick red, which give the same effect as the much more expensive Welsh tiles.

Ample provision is made in this house for the healthful outdoor living that is now regarded as so necessary. A wide veranda extends across the entire front and at the back is a large square recessed porch that looks out over the garden at the rear of the house and is used as an outdoor living room where meals can be served if desired. This porch is exposed to the weather on one side only and this can easily be glassed in for the severest days of winter. With a southern exposure, though, it might be open nearly all winter, except on inclement days, for a sun room is pleasant when a room completely walled in is chilly and gloomy and in this case the

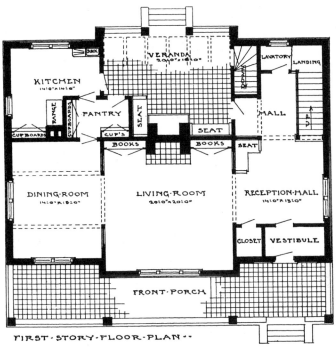

FIRST·STORY·FLOOR·PLAN

warmth of the sun would be supplemented by the comfort of the open fire, for the veranda is provided with an outdoor fireplace big enough to hold a pile of good sized logs. As this veranda has so much the character of a living room, the walls are treated in a way that connects it closely with the interior of the house. A high wainscot of cypress runs around all three sides and built-in fireside seats of the same wood afford a comfortable place for those who are minded to enjoy the fresh air and the warmth of the blazing logs at the same time. A fairly large table placed out here would serve all requirements for both living room and dining room out of doors, and a few comfortable easy chairs would make it a most inviting lounging place. The red cement floor would best be covered by a thick Indian blanket or two, or any rug of sturdy weave and primitive color and design. The wooden ceiling of the porch is heavily beamed and from the beams hang lanterns enough to make the place cheerful by night as well as by day. The color of the floor is repeated in the massive fireplace of hard-burned red brick and the plain mantel-shelf is made of a thick cypress plank.

Just above the sun room is an open-air sleeping room of the same size and general

A CEMENT HOUSE FRAMED IN SMOOTH CONCRETE

LIVING ROOM, SHOWING FIREPLACE AND BUILT-IN BOOKCASES WITH PANELS ABOVE. THE USE OF SPINDLES APPEARS IN THE GRILLES AND BALUSTRADE AND THE IDEA IS FURTHER DEVELOPED IN THE FURNITURE.

arrangement, except that it has no fireplace. On this upper porch the balustrade is replaced by a solid parapet made of the wall of the house. Like the sun room, this sleeping porch can be glassed in when necessary for protection from driving storms. But under ordinary circumstances no protection from the weather is needed even in winter, as nothing is better for the average housed-up human being than sleeping out of doors under plenty of covers.

The plan of the interior is an excellent example of the Craftsman method of arranging the divisions so as to secure at once the greatest possible amount of space, freedom and convenience within a given area and also to keep the construction as inexpensive as possible. The only fireplace is in the living room and is so placed that it may use the same chimney as the veranda fireplace. The arrangement of the rooms, however, is so open that both dining room and reception hall share the benefit of the fireplace. Draughts from the entrance are cut off by a small vestibule which opens into the reception hall and the space beside it is occupied by a coat closet which receives wraps, overshoes and all those articles which are such a problem to dispose of in a hall that is part of the living room.

Ceiling beams are used only to indicate the divisions into rooms, but around the ceiling angle runs a broad beam and all three rooms are wainscoted to the height of six feet with oak paneling. We have suggested oak for the interior woodwork in this house, as the effect of it is both rich and restful and the color mellows with every passing year. Our idea would be to finish it in a rich nut-brown tone, which has much to do with giving a mellow sunny effect to the whole decorative

A CEMENT HOUSE FRAMED IN SMOOTH CONCRETE

scheme, for color goes far toward creating the cheery atmosphere that rightly belongs to a home. The rough plaster of the shallow wall spaces above the wainscot might be done in a warm tawny yellow and the whole decorative scheme developed from this foundation of walls and woodwork.

The structural feature that is most prominent in the living room is the fireplace, with the bookcase built in on either side. These bookcases are about four feet in height, so that the upper panels of the wainscot show above them. One decorative structural feature that is seen in all these rooms is the use of spindles wherever they would be effective. They appear in the balustrade of the staircase, in the open spaces above the panels, in the little partitions, in the continuation of these into grilles above the doors, in the built-in seats and even in the furniure.

On the second story there are three large bedrooms in the front of the house and the open-air bedroom at the back. The staircase with its well occupies the space at one side of the sleeping porch, and the bath room is at the other. The upper hall, though not large, is so designed as to give a feeling of open arrangement and free communication, and the closets are concentrated at the center, where they are easy of access and do not interfere with the space required for the sleeping rooms. The plan of this house, as well as its decoration and interior arrangement, admit of very free interpretation and may be modified greatly to meet personal tastes and requirements.

VERANDA THAT IS FITTED UP AS A LIVING ROOM, SHOWING OUTDOOR FIREPLACE, WAINSCOTING, BUILT-IN SEATS AND USE OF LANTERNS, WITH SUGGESTIONS FOR SUITABLE FURNISHINGS.

CEMENT HOUSE SHOWING LAVISH USE OF HALF-TIMBER AS A DECORATION

Published in The Craftsman, January, 1909.

CRAFTSMAN HOUSE AT NASSAU, LONG ISLAND. NOTE THE EFFECT OF SLOPING FOUNDATION AND PARAPETS.

THE house illustrated on this page was not only designed in The Craftsman Workshops, but built largely under our own supervision, so that Craftsman ideas as to plan and construction have been carried out with only such modifications as were suggested by the individual tastes and needs of the owner. It is definitely a suburban residence and its site is as desirable as it well could be for the home of a man who wishes to have plenty of space and freedom in his surroundings and yet be within convenient reach of the city. The owner, a New York business man, is keenly desirous of making the part of Long Island which he has chosen for his home one of the most delightful places within the immediate neighborhood of New York: thus his interest has not been limited merely to the building of a desirable house, but has extended to the planning of its surroundings so that the place shall be beautiful as a whole.

The site is large enough to allow for extensive grounds, which are being laid out with direct reference to the plan of the house. There is a slope of about fifteen feet from the rear of the lot down to the front. This slope is terraced at the highest part and the house is built well to the rear, allowing for a large lawn and shrubbery in front. The terrace at the back is used for a vegetable garden and the rest of the lot is left so far as is possible in its natural shape.

The rising ground upon which the house is situated affords an extensive view over the hills and meadows of Long Island. The house faces directly southeast and at the west end is a terrace, covered with a pergola, which commands a view of the main road,—a busy thoroughfare that is usually thronged with carriages and automobiles. At the opposite end of the house is a porch which looks directly toward the neighboring golf links. This porch is connected with the dining room by double French doors so that in summer it can be used as an outdoor dining room, especially as it will be protected all around with screens. In winter the screens will be replaced with glass, so that the porch may be used as a sun room or as a breakfast room on mild days. The small front porch serves to shelter the entrance.

These porches and the pergola greatly relieve the severity of the plan. As the house is built of cement, the construction naturally calls for straight lines and massive effects; but while these are preserved in their entirety, all sense of coldness or bareness is avoided by the liberal use of half-timber and by such structural features as we have just described. The floors of the pergola, the entrance porch, the dining porch, and the small kitchen porch

CEMENT HOUSE WITH HALF-TIMBER DECORATION

at the rear of the house are all of dull red cement divided into squares so that they have more the appearance of Welsh quarries. All the exterior woodwork is cypress darkened to a warm tone of brown by the chemical process which is described fully in the chapter dealing with wood finishes.

Long shallow dormers on either side of the house serve to break the straight lines of the roof. The roof itself has widely overhanging eaves supported on heavy

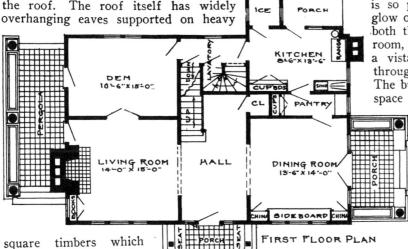

FIRST FLOOR PLAN

square timbers which project slightly and the whole upper story overhangs at the ends of the house, the weight being supported upon the projecting timbers. The line of demarcation between the upper and lower stories is emphasized by a wide timber which runs completely around the house. Above this are the smaller timbers which divide the cement wall into panels.

As the house is intended for a small family of three, with office accommodation for the owner, the interior arrangement is very simple. The entrance door leads directly into a central hall that opens into the dining room on one side and into the living room on the other, both openings being so wide that there is hardly any sense of division. The staircase is at the back of the hall, where a small coat closet is provided in a little nook taken off the space allowed for the butler's pantry.

Both living room and din-

ing room are closely connected with out of doors; the dining room, as we have already said, opening upon the screened porch and the living room upon the pergola. Just back of the living room is the den, which is the owner's special retreat and work-room. For this reason, double doors divide it from the living room instead of the usual broad opening. The big fireplace in the living room is so placed that the cheery glow of the fire is seen from both the hall and the dining room, as it forms one end of a vista which goes straight through to the dining porch. The built-in bookcase fills the space between this fireplace and the corner on one side, and on the other side is the door leading to the pergola. The entire front of the dining room is taken up with a built-in sideboard, flanked on either side by a china closet. Directly over this sideboard is the group of three windows which lights the dining room from the southeast.

The woodwork in the hall, living room and dining room is all of chestnut, fumed to a rich brown tone and given the soft dull finish that makes the surface appear fairly to radiate color. The fact that the woodwork is alike throughout these three rooms emphasizes the close connection between them and makes them appear almost like different parts of one room that is furnished harmoniously throughout.

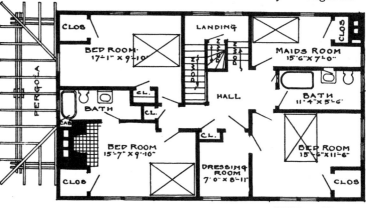

SECOND FLOOR PLAN.

CEMENT HOUSE SHOWING CRAFTSMAN IDEA OF HALF-TIMBER CONSTRUCTION

Published in The Craftsman, August, 1906.

EXTERIOR VIEW SHOWING STRUCTURAL USE OF TIMBERS AND THE WAY WINDOWS ARE BANDED TOGETHER.

A house that typifies to rather an unusual degree the Craftsman idea of construction is shown here. It is a perfect square in plan and is designed with the utmost simplicity. There are no bays, recesses or projections on the outside, the attractiveness of the exterior depending entirely upon the proportions of mass and spacing. It is a building which should attain the maximum of durability for cement con-

CEMENT HOUSE SHOWING HALF-TIMBER CONSTRUCTION

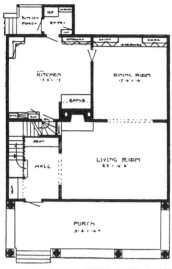

FIRST STORY FLOOR PLAN.

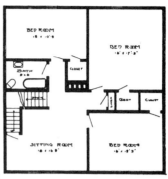

SECOND STORY FLOOR PLAN.

struction, as there is nothing to invite decay or render repairs necessary.

The walls are built of cement plaster and metal lath, the half-timber construction being used to break up the severely plain wall spaces into panels that are more agreeable to the eye. As originally designed the rough-finished cement was left in its natural gray color and the roof of white cedar shingles was merely oiled and left to weather to a harmonizing tone of silvery gray. The necessary color accent as well as the emphasis of form is given by the wood trim, which should be of cypress so treated that the brown color of the wood is fully brought out. The rafters of the porch as well as those supporting the widely overhanging roof are left uncased, carrying out the effect of solid construction which distinguishes the entire building and emphasizing the decorative use made of wood.

CORNER OF LIVING ROOM SHOWING FIREPLACE SET FLUSH WITH THE WALL AND HAVING PANEL OF DULL FINISHED PICTURE TILE. NOTE THE DECORATIVE EFFECT OF OPENINGS IN THE SPINDLE GRILLE WHICH APPEARS IN THE HALL, ALSO THE PLACING OF THE SEAT AND THE ARRANGEMENT OF THE STAIRCASE.

A COMFORTABLE AND CONVENIENT HOUSE FOR THE SUBURBS OR THE COUNTRY

Published in The Craftsman, May, 1907.
VIEW OF THE FRONT, GIVING A GOOD IDEA OF THE EFFECT OF BRICK AND CEMENT WALLS WITH TILED ROOF.

BELIEVING as we do that the happiest and healthiest life is that in the country, we take especial pleasure in designing houses that are definitely meant to be surrounded by large grounds that slope off into the fields, meadows and orchards all around. Such a house has always the effect of taking all the room it needs, and this will be found important when we come to analyze the elements that go toward making the restful charm of a home. The sense of privacy and freedom from intrusion that is conveyed by English homes with their ample gardens and buildings placed well back from the street is a quality which we badly need in our American home life as a relief from the rush and crowding outside.

Although the form of this house is straight and square, its rather low, broad proportions and the contrasting materials used in its construction take away all sense of severity. The walls of the lower story and the chimneys are of hard-burned red brick and the upper walls are of Portland cement plaster with half-timber construction. The foundation, steps and porch parapets are of split stone laid up in dark cement and the roof is tiled. Of course, this is only a suggestion for materials, as the house would be equally well adapted to almost any form of construction, from stone to shingles. The coloring also may be made rich and warm or cool and subdued, as demanded by the surroundings. One feature that is especially in accordance with Craftsman ideas is the way in which the half-timbers on the upper story are used. While we like half-timber construction, it is an article of faith with us that it should be made entirely "probable"; that is, that the timbers should be so placed that they might easily belong to the real construction of the house. In a building that is entirely designed by ourselves we adhere very strictly to this rule, varying it only when the taste of the owner requires a more elaborate use of timbers, such as is shown in the house illustrated on page 28 Another feature of typical Craftsman construction is well illustrated in the windows used in this house. It will be noted that they are double-hung in places where they are ex-

A COMFORTABLE AND CONVENIENT SUBURBAN HOUSE

posed to the weather and that casements are used when it is possible to hood them or to place them where they will be sheltered by the roof of the porch.

The arrangement of the interior of this house is simplicity itself, as the living room and dining room, which have merely the suggestion of a dividing partition, occupy the whole of one side. The arrangement of kitchen, hall and staircase on the other side of the house is equally practical and convenient, as it utilizes every inch of space and provides many conveniences to lighten the work of the housekeeper.

The entrance door opens into a small vestibule that serves to shut off draughts from the hall, especially as the entrance from the vestibule to the hall is at right angles to the front door instead of being directly opposite, mak-

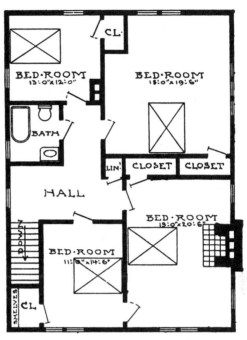

SECOND STORY FLOOR PLAN.

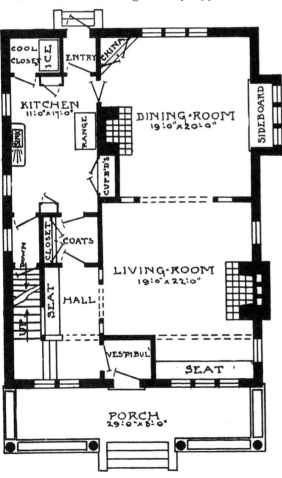

FIRST STORY FLOOR PLAN.

ing the danger from draughts so small that this opening might easily be curtained and a second door dispensed with. The broad landing of the staircase is opposite this opening from the vestibule and in the angle where the stair runs up a large hall seat is built. The vestibule jutting into the living room leaves a deep recess at the front, in which is built a long window seat just below the triple group of casements that appears at the front of the house. The fireplace is in the center of the room just opposite the hall, and another fireplace in the dining room adds to the comfort and cheer.

In a recess in the dining room somewhat similar to that at the front of the living room the sideboard is built in so that the front of it is flush with the wall and three casement windows are set just above it. The china cupboards built in on the opposite side are shown in two ways in the plan and illustration. In one the cupboard is built straight with the wall and in the other across the corner. Either way would be effective and the choice depends simply upon personal preference and convenience.

The tone of the woodwork would depend largely upon the position of the house and consequent exposure of the rooms. If they

A COMFORTABLE AND CONVENIENT SUBURBAN HOUSE

DETAIL OF ENTRANCE PORCH SHOWING HEAVY ROUND PILLARS, DECORATIVE USE OF REVEALED CONSTRUCTION IN THE ROOF, AND THE USE OF FLOWER BOXES.

are bright and sunny nothing could be better than the rich nut-brown of oak or chestnut with its strong sugggestion of green, as this gives a somewhat grave and subdued effect that yet wakes into life in a sunshiny room and shows the play of double tones of green and brown under a sheen that makes them seem almost luminous. If the rooms are fairly well shaded so that the effect of warmth would be desirable in the color, the woodwork might be of cypress, as its strong markings take on deep shades in the softer parts and beautiful autumn tints in the grain when treated by the Craftsman process that emphasizes so strongly the natural quality of the wood and brings out all its color.

A COMFORTABLE AND CONVENIENT SUBURBAN HOUSE

CORNER OF DINING ROOM SHOWING TILED CHIMNEYPIECE WITH COPPER HOOD; BUILT-IN CUPBOARD AND THE GROUPING OF WINDOWS AT THE SIDE.

LIVING ROOM WITH HALL BEYOND, SHOWING TYPICAL CRAFTSMAN DIVISION BETWEEN THE TWO ROOMS BY MEANS OF HEAVY SQUARE POSTS AND PANELS OPEN AT THE TOP.

A CRAFTSMAN CITY HOUSE DESIGNED TO ACCOMMODATE TWO FAMILIES

Published in The Craftsman, October, 1907.

VIEW OF FRONT AND SIDE, INDICATING THE SIMILARITY IN ARRANGEMENT OF UPPER AND LOWER FLOORS.

SOME little time ago a problem was brought to us which proved interesting, not only in itself but on account of its application to a condition which in city life is almost universal. It was this: A man living in Brooklyn, who owned a lot thirty feet wide by a hundred feet deep, desired to build within this space a Craftsman house which should not only show a departure from the usual design of the city house in such matters as economy of space, arrangement of rooms, and interesting structural features that would serve as a basis for interior decorations and furnishing, but would accommodate two families who desired to live independently of one another, as they would in separate houses.

It had often been brought to our attention by people living in cities that most of our plans were for detached dwellings in the country or the suburbs, where the houses could have the environment of ample grounds and be given all the room necessary to carry out any idea of arrangement that might seem desirable. This method of living in the open with plenty of room and green growing things all around has always been so much more in accordance with the Craftsman idea of a home environment than any house cramped to fit the dimensions of a city lot, that our suggestions for house building have as a rule naturally taken the form of dwellings best fitted for the country. The number and frequency, however, of the requests which have come to us from time to time for city houses made the problem shown here one that we took much interest in working out.

As the owner desired a detached house with a walk on either side it was necessary to bring the dimensions of our plan within a very narrow space. Accordingly the width of the

A CRAFTSMAN CITY HOUSE DESIGNED FOR TWO FAMILIES

house was fixed at twenty-five feet, with a depth of sixty-eight feet, including a front porch nine feet in width. The first story is occupied by a tenant, the owner reserving the second floor for himself and his family.

It will be noticed by looking carefully at the floor plans that only the front porch, the vestibule and the rear entrance can be used in common by both families. There is no connection between the two apartments. One door from the vestibule opens to the stairway which leads to the second story and the other opens into the hall of the first story. Both stories are the same in arrangement and are planned to secure the greatest possible open-

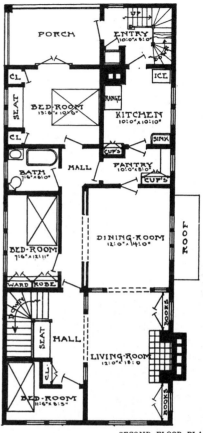

SECOND FLOOR PLAN.

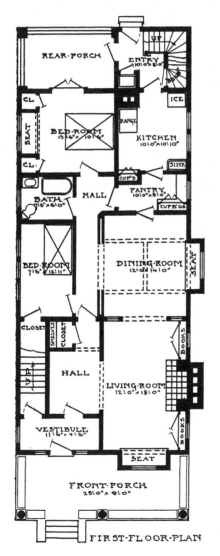

FIRST·FLOOR·PLAN

ness and freedom of space in the living rooms. The large bedrooms at the back of the house open upon rear porches, which are glassed in for the winter and screened in summer to serve as outdoor sleeping rooms.

The floor plans themselves give the best idea of the arrangement of space in the apartments. Both kitchens are provided with gas stoves and individual boilers for hot water. A dumbwaiter runs from the cellar to the attic for the convenience of the upper apartment. The cellar contains individual store rooms and coal bins, and a big laundry with a set of three tubs and a stove was installed, together with a hot water heating system for the entire house. The attic is divided in a way that provides two rooms in the dormer for the servants of both apartments, as well as a large room facing the front that can be used as a dry room in inclement weather or as a play-room for children. The cellar walls are of concrete faced with split field stone.

A CRAFTSMAN FARM HOUSE THAT IS COMFORT-ABLE, HOMELIKE AND BEAUTIFUL

Published in The Craftsman, June, 1906.

VIEW FROM THE FRONT, SHOWING DORMER, GABLE AND RECESSED PORCH. NOTE THE EFFECT OF THE BROAD LOW PROPORTIONS, THE GROUPING OF WINDOWS AND THE DECORATIVE USE OF TIMBERS.

A HOMELIKE AND BEAUTIFUL CRAFTSMAN FARMHOUSE

IF there is any one style of house that we enjoy planning more than others, it is a farmhouse,—a home that shall meet every practical requirement of life and work on the farm, and yet be beautiful, comfortable and homelike. This is our first farmhouse and we endeavored to make it characteristic in design, plan, decoration and the materials used for building. As a rule, we do not advocate the use of clapboards for sheathing the walls of a frame house, for the reason that the small, thin, smoothly planed and painted boards generally used for this purpose give a flimsy, unsubstantial effect to the structure and a characterless surface to the walls. However, clapboards are often preferred, especially in building a farmhouse, and it is quite possible to use them so that these objections may be removed. In this building the clapboards are unusually broad and thick, giving to the walls a sturdy appear-

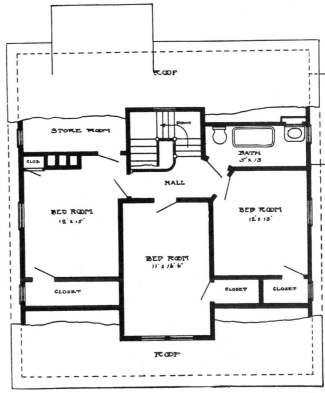

SECOND FLOOR PLAN.

ance of permanence. They may be of pine, cedar, or cypress, and may be stained or painted according to individual taste and the character of the environment. If the house is to be rather dark and quiet in color, the boards might be given a thin stain of moss green or brown; or a delightful color effect may be obtained by going over the boards with a wash of much diluted sulphuric acid. With either one of these colors a good effect would be obtained by painting the timbers of the framework a light cream so that the structural features are strongly accented.

We regard this house as having in a marked degree the comfortable and inviting appearance which seems so essentially to belong to a home,—particularly to a farm home. It is wide and low, with rather a shallow pitch to the broad roof, the line of which is unbroken by the large dormers set at different

FIRST FLOOR PLAN.

A HOMELIKE AND BEAUTIFUL CRAFTSMAN FARMHOUSE

CORNER OF LIVING ROOM, SHOWING TREATMENT OF WALL SPACES BY A VERY SIMPLE USE OF THE WOODWORK, WHICH IS USED TO GIVE THE EFFECT OF A BROAD, PLAIN FRIEZE. NOTE THE MANNER IN WHICH THE WINDOW AND DOOR FRAMINGS ARE RELATED TO THE LOWER BEAM OF THIS FRIEZE.

heights. The entrance porch, which is of ample size, is recessed to its full width. The timbers which accent the construction give special interest to the interior, as they are so placed as to add to the apparent width of the house, and are arranged so as to avoid, by means of the prominent horizontal lines of the beams, any possible "spotty" effect which might result if the vertical lines of the framework were not so relieved. This device is especially apparent in the grouping of the three windows which light the gable. The plan of the house makes it necessary that these be rather far apart, but they are built together by the beams so as to form a symmetrical group rather than to give the impression of

three separate windows in a broad wall space. The same effect is preserved throughout the lower story by the massive beam which extends the entire width of the house, not only defining the height of the lower story but serving as a strong connecting line for the window and door framings which all spring from the foundation to the height of this beam.

A small vestibule, which serves to cut off draughts that might come from the entrance door, opens into the central hall which forms a connecting link between the living room on one side and the library and dining room on the other. The staircase, which is opposite the entrance, is placed well toward the back

A HOMELIKE AND BEAUTIFUL CRAFTSMAN FARMHOUSE

CORNER OF DINING ROOM SHOWING SIDEBOARD BUILT INTO A RECESS, WITH GROUP OF WINDOWS AND DISH CUPBOARD.

of the house, giving as much width as possible to the hall. A small coat closet occupies a few feet of space that has been made available between the vestibule and the living room, so that the lines of both hall and living room are uninterrupted.

The living room has the advantage of every ray of sunshine which strikes that side of the house, as it is not sheltered by the porch. It is quite a long room in proportion to its width and the entire end at the rear is taken up by the fireplace and the two seats which, extending from it at right angles, give the effect of a deeply recessed fireside nook. A single chimney is made to do service for the entire house, as it is arranged to accommodate three flues.

HOUSE WITH COURT, PERGOLAS, OUTDOOR LIVING ROOMS AND SLEEPING BALCONIES

Published in The Craftsman, January, 1909.

HOUSE DESIGNED FOR OUTDOOR LIFE IN A WARM CLIMATE.

LIFE in a warm country, where there is much sunshine and where it is possible to be out of doors during the greater part of the time, was specially taken into consideration in the designing of this house, for the plan makes as much account of the terraces, porches and the open paved court as it does of the rooms within the walls of the building. Such a plan would serve admirably for a dwelling in California or in the Southern States, but would be advisable only for specially favored spots in the North and East, as its comfort and charm necessarily depend very largely upon the possibility of outdoor life.

As originally planned, the walls of the lower story are to be built of cement or of stucco on metal lath. The upper walls are shingled. The roof is of red tile and the foundation and parapets are of field stone. As with all these houses, though, the materials used are entirely optional and can be varied according to the taste of the owner, the requirements of the landscape or the limitations of the amount to be expended, as the building would look quite as well if constructed of concrete or of brick, and with clapboards in the place of shingles. If a

wooden house should be preferred, the walls from top to bottom could either be shingled or sheathed with wide clapboards, while the roof is equally well adapted to tiles, slates or shingles. The first of the perspective drawings gives a view of the whole house as seen from the rear, showing the pergola at the back and the design of the roof, which we consider specially attractive. The second drawing shows the side of the house instead of the front, as by taking this view it is possible to include both porch and court and also show the balcony and outdoor sleeping room on the upper story. A broad terrace runs across the front of the house and continues around the side, where it forms a porch which is meant to be used as an outdoor living room. This porch is nearly square in shape and is either tiled with Welsh quarries or, if a less expensive flooring be desired, is paved with red cement marked off into squares that measure about nine inches each way. This floor has a close resemblance to one made of Welsh quarries and is dry and durable. In flooring a porch of this kind it is always better to avoid the use of plain brick, as this porous material gathers and holds moisture to such an extent that the floor is seldom dry.

HOUSE WITH COURT, PERGOLAS AND OUTDOOR ROOMS

The entrance door opens from this porch into the hall, which is separated from the living room only by two panels open at the top after the usual Craftsman fashion, the wood running only a little above the height of the two bookcases, which may either be built in or movable, as desired. Directly opposite this entrance is the large fireplace, which is recessed so as to form a fireside nook. Seats are placed on either side and the tiled hearth extends the full length of these. Back of them, in the small recesses left on either side of the fireplace, are built-in bookcases with casement windows set above. A square bay window, below which is a broad window seat, looks out upon the terrace, and double glass doors from both living room and hall bring this part of the house into very close communication with the outside world; an important feature in the planning of a house intended for life in a warm climate where there is little rain.

The dining room has every appearance of being merely a large square recess in the living room, as the division between them is only indicated and the dining room is just large enough to afford comfortable accommodation for a good-sized dining table and the necessary furniture. The sideboard, which is built in, occupies the entire end of the room and a group of three casement windows are set in the wall just above it.

The floor plan shows the convenient arrangement of the hall, staircase and closets, everything being grouped within a small compass so that not an inch of space is wasted. The arrangement of pantry and kitchen is equally convenient and plenty of cupboard room is provided for dishes and the necessary kitchen utensils.

The chimney that is used for the kitchen range has space also for a flue leading from the fireplace on the porch outside. We are greatly in favor of these outdoor fireplaces, because there are many days and evenings when it is almost warm enough to stay out of doors, and yet without a fire it is not quite comfortable. Also, a fire in the open air has always something of the charm of a camp fire. The placing of this one is peculiarly

desirable, as it not only makes a pleasant sitting room of the porch, but also has much of the charm of a garden, as from the porch one steps down into the court, which is surrounded on the outside by a vine-covered pergola and which may be paved or not, as desired. Even when these courts are paved they often hold growing trees or a fountain, so that both shade and the nearness of green, growing things are possible, while the court itself seems merely an extension of the porch. The den, which can be closed off by doors from the rest of the house in case privacy is desired for work or reading, has double doors leading to the square entrance porch and also to the court.

On the second floor there are three large bedrooms, plenty of closet room and three baths. One of these is for the exclusive use of the maids and opens from the maids' room at the back. The other two are placed so

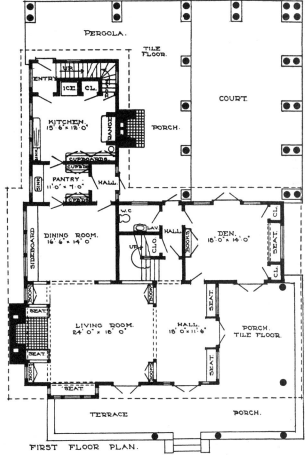

FIRST FLOOR PLAN.

HOUSE WITH COURT, PERGOLAS AND OUTDOOR ROOMS

CORNER OF HOUSE SHOWING PERGOLA AND SLEEPING PORCH.

that each one is accessible from two bedrooms, counting the outdoor sleeping room as one. The linen and clothes closets are so placed that they occupy the least possible amount of space. The central hall is more in the nature of a corridor running around the four sides of the staircase well, and at the back is a long window seat built beneath a group of windows that look out over the court and pergola.

The matter of interior woodwork and general scheme of color and decoration would depend very largely upon the part of the country in which the house is built. Its design is primarily that of a California house and reflects the spirit which rules the new architecture that is springing up in that country. Therefore it would seem quite in keeping to suggest that the inside of the house be finished after the well-known California style, because no other would be so completely in harmony with the plan of the exterior.

Living so much out of doors, the Californians almost instinctively make the transition between outdoors and indoors as little marked as possible by finishing the interior of their houses in the most natural way.

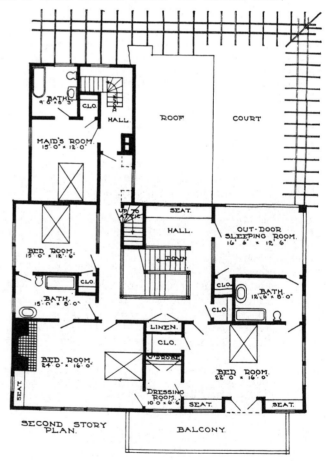

SECOND STORY PLAN.

THE CRAFTSMAN'S HOUSE: A PRACTICAL APPLICATION OF OUR THEORIES OF HOME BUILDING

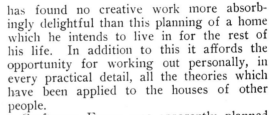

Fireplace in Open Air Dining Room

WHILE all the houses illustrated in this book are of Craftsman design, the dwelling shown here is perhaps the most complete example in existence of the Craftsman idea, for the reason that it is to be built by the founder and editor of The Craftsman at "Craftsman Farms," his estate in New Jersey, and will be used there as his own home. Therefore in this case the tastes of the designer are one with the tastes and needs of the owner, who

has found no creative work more absorbingly delightful than this planning of a home which he intends to live in for the rest of his life. In addition to this it affords the opportunity for working out personally, in every practical detail, all the theories which have been applied to the houses of other people.

Craftsman Farms was apparently planned by nature for the site of just such a house. It has heavily wooded hills, little wandering brooks, low-lying meadows and plenty of garden and orchard land; and the house will be built on a natural terrace or plateau half way up the highest hill. The building faces toward the south, overlooking the partially cleared hillside, which runs down to the orchard and meadows at the foot and which needs very little cultivation to develop it into a beautiful sloping greensward with here and there a clump of trees or a mass of shrubbery. There is a friendliness about the natural conformation of the land which makes it seem homelike before one stone is laid upon another or one bit of underbrush is cleared away, for the combination of sheltering hills and woods with a sheltered swale or meadowland gives interesting

Entrance to Craftsman Farms

Published in The Craftsman, October, 1908.

FRONT VIEW OF THE HOUSE AT "CRAFTSMAN FARMS", SHOWING PERGOLA AND RECESSED ENTRANCE PORCH AND AT THE SIDE THE OUTDOOR DINING ROOM WITH FIREPLACE AND CHIMNEY BUILT AT THE END. THE PLASTER PANELS BETWEEN THE SEVERAL GROUPS OF WINDOWS ARE TO BE FILLED WITH LARGE PICTURE TILES SYMBOLIZING FARM LIFE AND INDUSTRIES.

THE CRAFTSMAN'S HOUSE

variety in the immediate surroundings, while the view of the whole country from the hilltop through the gaps in the surrounding hills does away with any sense of being shut in.

In designing the house, the first essential naturally was that it should be suited exactly to the requirements of the life to be lived in it; the second, that it should harmonize with its environment; and the third, that it should be built, as far as possible, from the materials to be had right there on the ground and left as nearly as possible in the natural state. Therefore the foundation and lower walls of the building are of split field stone and boulders taken from the tumbledown stone fences and loose-lying rocks on the hillsides. The timbers are cut from chestnut trees growing on the land, and the lines, proportions and color of the building are designed with a special view to the contour of the ground upon

DETAIL OF LIVING ROOM SHOWING PIANO, PICTURE WINDOW AND BOOKCASES.

which it stands and the background of trees which rises behind it.

The hillside site, affording, as it does, well nigh perfect drainage, makes it possible to put into effect a favorite Craftsman theory,—that a house should be built without a cellar and should, as nearly as possible, rest directly on the ground with no visible foundation to separate it from the soil and turf in which it should almost appear to have taken root. The house is protected against dampness by making the excavation for the foundation down to clear hard soil, filling it in partly with the smaller pieces of stone that were rejected from the walls and placing on this a thick layer of broken stone leveled off with an equally thick layer of Portland cement and concrete, making it level and smooth like a pavement. All of this foundation is drain-tiled both inside and out. On the top of the cement floor is a double layer of damp-proofing, which extends without a break up the wall, and a thick layer of tar and sand, in which the floor timbers are bedded. Another layer of waterproof paper covers this; and then comes the floor itself— as completely protected from moisture as if it were on the top story of the building. The heating plant and laundry are provided for in a separate building and the stone storage

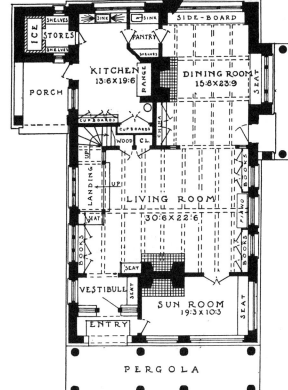

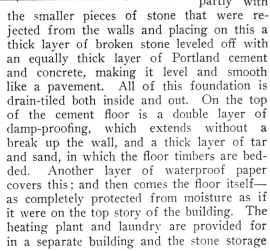

FIRST STORY FLOOR PLAN.

END OF LIVING ROOM, ILLUSTRATING HOW THE STAIRCASE WITH ITS LANDING MAY BE MADE THE PROMINENT STRUCTURAL FEATURE OF A ROOM.

vaults for vegetables and the like are sunk into the side of the hill.

No effort has been made to give the appearance of a grade line, the ground being allowed to preserve its natural contour around the stone walls of the first story. The upper walls are of plaster and half-timber construction. The plaster is given a rough pebble-dash finish and a tone of dull brownish green brushed off afterward so that the color effect varies with the irregularity of the surface. In each one of the large panels ultimately picture tiles will be set, symbolizing the different farm and village industries,—for example, one will show the blacksmith at his forge; another a woman spinning flax; others will depict the sower, the plowman and such typical figures of farm life. These tiles will be very dull and rough in finish and colored with dark reds, greens, blues, dull yellows and other colors which harmonize with the tints of wood and stone.

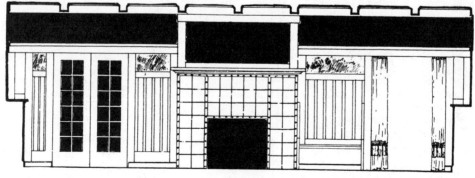

DETAIL OF LIVING ROOM SHOWING FIREPLACE, DOORS INTO SUN ROOM AND ENTRANCE TO VESTIBULE.

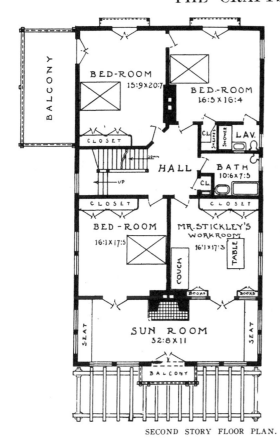

SECOND STORY FLOOR PLAN.

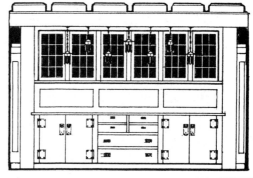

DETAIL OF DINING ROOM SHOWING
BUILT-IN SIDEBOARD AND WINDOWS.

proper, but is merely the expression of an individual fancy for an outdoor dining room and a sort of camp cooking place. At the end is built an outdoor fireplace and a big rough chimney. The detail of this fireplace, with its hobs, crane, and two brick ovens, is given in the first illustration.

The timbers are not applied to the outside of the house for the purpose of ornamentation, but are a part of the actual construction, which is thus frankly revealed. They are peeled chestnut logs squared on either side and with the face left rounded in the natural shape of the tree, hewn a little here and there to keep the lines from being exaggerated in their unevenness. These timbers are stained to a grayish brown tone that, from a little distance, gives the same effect as the bark. The lines of the red-tiled roof are low and broad, with an overhang of four feet on the ends and three feet at the sides.

The pergola is made of peeled cedar logs left in their natural shape and color, and the floor, which is almost on a level with the ground, is a dull red vitrified brick laid in herring-bone pattern at right angles. Extending from the side of the house is a roofed pergola,—if such a thing may be,—for while the timbers and the flooring are those of a pergola, it has a tiled roof like that of the house. This is not a part of the construction

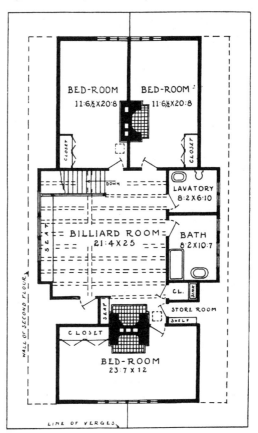

THIRD STORY FLOOR PLAN.

A SMALL SHINGLED HOUSE THAT SHOWS MANY INTERESTING STRUCTURAL FEATURES

Published in *The Craftsman, February, 1907.*

EXTERIOR VIEW FROM THE FRONT.

WE have suggested the use of shingles for the walls of this plain little cottage because they seem the best adapted to the peculiarities of its construction. They should, however, be laid in double course, the top ones being well exposed and the under ones showing not much over an inch below. This not only gives an interesting effect of irregularity as to the wall surface, but adds much to the warmth of the house. All the lines of the framework are simple to a degree, but the plainness is relieved by the widely overhanging eaves and rafters of the roof, the well-proportioned porch, which is balanced by the extension to the rear, the heavy beams which

run entirely around the walls with a slight turn of the shingles above and the effective grouping of the windows. The little house is

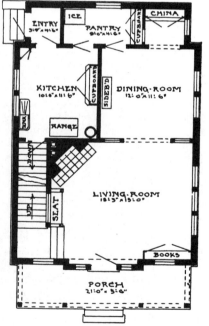

FIRST STORY FLOOR PLAN.

·WINDOW·SEAT·IN·LIVING·ROOM·

A SMALL SHINGLED HOUSE

·INTERIOR·ELEVATION·OF·LIVING·ROOM·
·FACING·FRONT·OF·HOUSE·

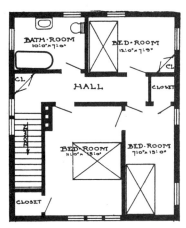

SECOND STORY FLOOR PLAN.

built to stand rough weather and this sturdiness is the direct cause of the wealth of attractive structural features. The roof of the porch projects two and a half feet, which affords protection even in a driving storm. Also for protection, all the exposed windows are capped by little shingled hoods which come up from the walls and which, in addition to their usefulness, form one of the most charming features of the whole construction. The eaves of the main roof project over the front for two and a half feet, and the weight is supported by purlins placed at the peak of the roof and at this connection with each of the side walls. This widely projecting roof gives a most comfortable effect of shelter and homelikeness, an effect which is heightened by the way in which the quaint little casement windows on the second story seem to hide under its wing. The view of the living room shown in the illustration is that which would be seen by anyone looking through the triple casement on the side wall. The first thing seen by one entering from the porch would be the fireplace, which is thrown diagonally across the corner with a small built-in seat between it and the landing of the staircase. The fireplace is made of rough red brick, with a stone mantel-shelf set on a line with the wainscot.

LIVING ROOM SHOWING CORNER FIREPLACE, BUILT-IN SEAT AND STAIR LANDING, WITH A VIEW OF THE ENTRANCE DOOR AT THE SIDE.

A ROOMY, INVITING FARMHOUSE, DESIGNED FOR PLEASANT HOME LIFE IN THE COUNTRY

Published in The Craftsman, December, 1908.

VIEW SHOWING FRONT PORCH, OUTSIDE KITCHEN AND DORMER.

BELIEVING that no form of dwelling better repays the thought and care put upon it than does the farmhouse, we give here a design for the kind of house that is meant above all things to furnish a pleasant, convenient and comfortable environment for farm life and farm work.

The house is low, broad and comfortable looking in its proportions and exceedingly simple in design and construction. The walls are sheathed with clapboards and rest upon a foundation of field stone that is sunk so low as to be hardly perceptible, so that the house, while perfectly sanitary and well drained, seems very close to the ground. The clapboards are eight or ten inches wide and should be at least seven-eighths of an inch thick. Although they are to be laid like all clapboards, the thickness of the boards will necessitate a small triangular strip between each board and the joist to which it is nailed. This support prevents the boards from warping or splitting, as they might do if nailed directly to the joist without any support between.

The grouping of the windows is one of

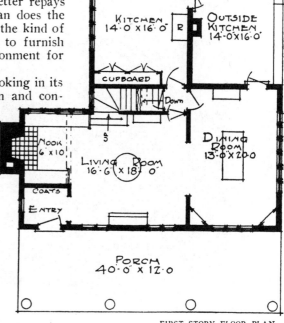

FIRST STORY FLOOR PLAN.

A ROOMY, INVITING FARMHOUSE

the most attractive features of the house as seen from the outside. They are all casements made to swing outward and are grouped in long horizontal lines that harmonize admirably with the low-pitched roof and the wide low look of the house as a whole. The shutters are made of wide clapboards like those used on the walls, four boards to each shutter, with a heart-shaped piercing cut out of the two central boards before they are fitted together. These shutters are wide enough to cover the whole window when closed. The windows that give light to the three front bedrooms upstairs are grouped into one long dormer, the casements being divided by two plaster panels, behind which come the ends of the partitions between the bedrooms. This dormer adds greatly to the effect of the whole building, as it breaks the long sweep of the roof without introducing a false line.

The plan of the interior is simple to a degree, as the rooms are arranged with a view to making the work of the household as light as possible. The greater part of the lower floor is taken up by the large living room, which practically includes the dining room, as the division between them is so slight as to be hardly more than the sug-

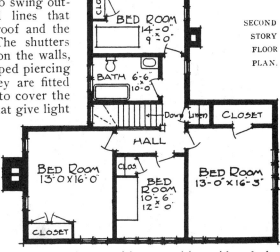

gestion of a partition on either side of the wide opening. The front door opens into an entry or vestibule which is divided from the living room by a curtain and, where provision is made, for hanging up hats and coats and for keeping other outdoor belongings.

LIVING ROOM OF THE FARMHOUSE SHOWING FIREPLACE NOOK WITH BUILT-IN SEATS AND CASEMENT WINDOWS; THE ENTRY APPEARS AT ONE SIDE OF THE NOOK.

A SIMPLE, STRAIGHTFORWARD DESIGN FROM WHICH MANY HOMES HAVE BEEN BUILT

Published in The Craftsman, January, 1909.

EXTERIOR VIEW, SHOWING WELL-BALANCED PROPORTIONS AND SIMPLE TREATMENT OF WINDOWS AND WALL-SPACES.

FIREPLACE IN LIVING ROOM, SHOWING THE BUILT-IN BOOKCASES AND CASEMENTS ON EITHER SIDE.

A SIMPLE, STRAIGHTFORWARD DESIGN

THIS has been one of the most popular of the Craftsman house designs and as shown here it has been modified somewhat from the first plan, the modifications and improvements having been suggested by the different people who have built the house, so that they are all valuable as the outcome of practical experience. Although the illustration shows plastered walls and a foundation of field stone, the design lends itself quite as readily to walls of brick or stone, or even to shingles or clapboards, if a wooden house be desired.

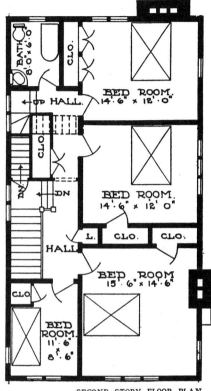

SECOND STORY FLOOR PLAN.

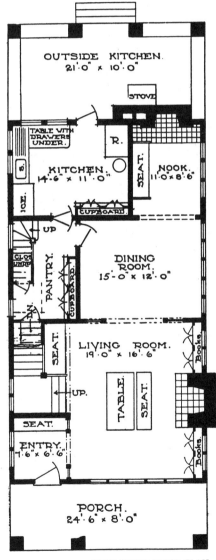

FIRST STORY FLOOR PLAN.

The outside kitchen at the back is recommended only in the event of the house being built in the country, because in town it would hardly be needed. In a farmhouse such an outside kitchen is most convenient as it affords an outdoor place for such work as washing and ironing, canning, preserving and other tasks which are much less wearisome if done in the open air. The position of the chimney at the back of the house makes it possible for a stove to be placed upon this porch for the use mentioned. The house is so designed that this outside kitchen may be added to it or omitted, as desired, without making any difference to the plan as a whole. The plan of the lower story shows the usual open arrangement of the Craftsman house. The entrance door opens into a small entry screened from the living room by heavy portiéres, so that no draught from the front door is felt inside. On the outside wall of the living room is the arrangement of fireplace and bookcases, as shown in the illustration. A large table might be placed in the center, with a settle back to it and facing the fire.

A CRAFTSMAN HOUSE IN WHICH TOWER CONSTRUCTION HAS BEEN EFFECTIVELY USED

Published in The Craftsman, September, 1906.

FRONT VIEW OF HOUSE SHOWING TOWERS AND VERANDAS IN FRONT AND PERGOLA AT THE SIDE.

SOMETHING of a departure is made from the usual style of the Craftsman house in planning this one, which we regard as one of the most completely successful house plans ever published in THE CRAFTSMAN. It is not a large house, yet it gives the impression of dignity and spaciousness which usually belongs only to a large building; it is in no sense an elaborate house, yet it is decorative,—possessing a sort of homely picturesqueness which takes away all appearance of severity from the straight lines and massive walls. This is largely due to the square tower-like construction at the

A CRAFTSMAN HOUSE WITH TOWER CONSTRUCTION USED

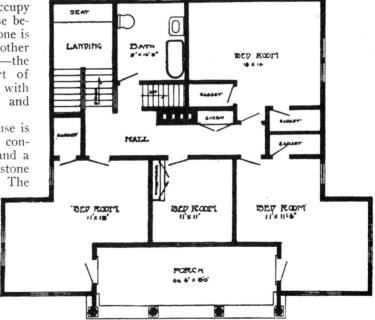

FIRST STORY FLOOR PLAN.

All the exterior wood trim is of cypress very much darkened by the chemical process which we use. In this house the exterior woodwork is especially satisfying in its structural form, being decorative in its lines and the division of wall spaces and yet obviously an essential part of the structure. The horizontal beams serve to bind together the lines of the whole framework, and the uprights are simply corner-posts and continuations of the window frames. The roof of dull red tiles gives life and warmth to the color scheme of the exterior, and the thick round pillars painted white lend a sharp accent that emphasizes the whole.

The entrance door is at the left end of the porch which, by this device, is made to seem less like a mere entrance and more like a pleasant gathering place where outdoor life may go on. This porch is illustrated in detail on page ninety-nine as a typical Craftsman front porch.

two corners in front and to the upper and lower verandas, both ample in size and deeply recessed, which occupy the whole width of the house between the towers. Of these, one is the entrance porch and the other an outdoor sleeping room,—the latter a very essential part of every house that is built with special reference to health and freedom of living.

As suggested here, the house is of cement and half-timber construction with a tiled roof and a foundation of local field stone carefully split and fitted. The foundation is carried up to form the parapets that shelter the recessed porches on the lower story, and the copings are of gray sandstone. The walls are of cement plaster on metal lath, the plaster being given the rough gravel finish and colored in varying tones of green.

SECOND FLOOR PLAN. STORAGE-ROOM AND SERVANTS ROOM IN ATTIC.

A CRAFTSMAN HOUSE WITH TOWER CONSTRUCTION

ALCOVE IN THE DINING ROOM MADE BY THE TOWER CONSTRUCTION. THIS LITTLE NOOK IS FITTED UP FOR A SMOKING ROOM OR DEN AND HAS ALL THE ADVANTAGES OF A BAY WINDOW OR SMALL SUN ROOM, AS THE WINDOWS ON EITHER SIDE ADMIT FLOODS OF SUNSHINE, PROVIDED THE HOUSE IS SO PLACED AS TO GIVE THIS TOWER A SOUTHERN OR WESTERN EXPOSURE. NOTE THE CONSTRUCTION OF THE OVERHEAD BEAMS.

A CRAFTSMAN HOUSE WITH TOWER CONSTRUCTION

A CORNER OF THE LIVING ROOM, LOOKING INTO THE DINING ROOM SO THAT THE POST-AND-PANEL CONSTRUCTION WHICH INDICATES A DIVISION BETWEEN THE TWO ROOMS IS PLAINLY SHOWN. THE CHIMNEYPIECE IS MADE OF LARGE SQUARE TILES, MATT-FINISHED IN A DULL TONE OF BROWNISH YELLOW AND BOUND AT THE CORNERS WITH STRIPS OF EITHER COPPER OR IRON. THE FIREPLACE HOOD IS OF COPPER AND THE ANDIRONS OF WROUGHT IRON. COMBINED WITH THE BROWN OF THE OAK OR CHESTNUT WOODWORK, THIS WOULD FORM THE BASIS OF A RICH AND QUIET COLOR SCHEME.

A CONCRETE COTTAGE DESIGNED IN THE FORM OF A GREEK CROSS TO ADMIT MORE LIGHT

Published in The Craftsman, February, 1907.

FRONT VIEW OF THE COTTAGE SHOWING THE TWO SMALL ENTRANCE PORCHES.

CONCRETE or hollow cement block construction were what we had in mind in the designing of this cottage. Therefore the form of it is especially adapted to the use of this material, although, like the others, the general plan admits of the use of brick or stone, clapboards or shingles, if desired. As we have shown it here, the side walls are broken into panels by raised bands of concrete, which bind the corners and also run around the entire structure at the connection of the roof and again between the first and second stories. These bands are smooth-surfaced, but the walls are made very rough by the simple process of washing off the surface with a brush and plenty of water immediately after the form is removed and while the material is set but still friable. If this is done at exactly the right time, the washing-brush can be so applied as to remove the mortar to a considerable depth between the blocks, leaving them in relief and producing a rough coarse texture that is very interesting.

The plan of this house is not unlike a Greek cross, the rooms being so arranged that the greatest possible allowance of space is made

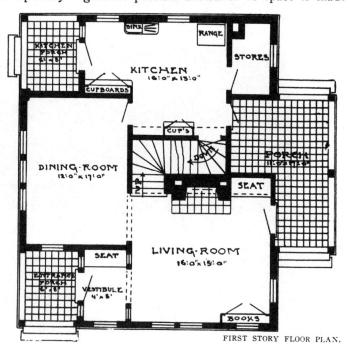

FIRST STORY FLOOR PLAN.

A CONCRETE COTTAGE

available and also an unusual amount of light and air. The foundation is of concrete and is continued upward on a gentle slant from the ground to a line at the base of the windows on the first floor, which gives a continuous horizontal line on a level with the parapets of the porches that are placed on either side of the front wing.

The main entrance porch is at the right of the house, as shown in the half-tone illustration, while the kitchen is entered from the porch on the left. The rear porch is recessed and extends the whole width of the wing, being large enough to serve as a very comfortable dining room. For this style of house we would recommend that all the porches be floored with red cement divided into squares. As shown in the illustration of the interior, the rooms on the first floor are separated with the open post-and-panel construction, which merely indicates a division between them.

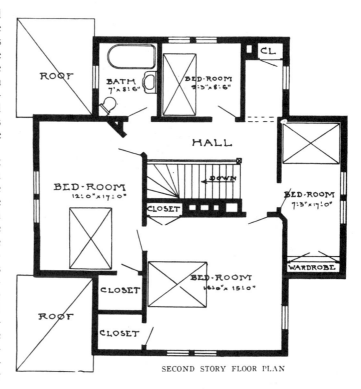

SECOND STORY FLOOR PLAN

A SECTION OF THE LIVING ROOM, SHOWING ENTRANCE HALL, STAIRWAY, CHIMNEYPIECE, FIRESIDE SEAT AND A GLIMPSE OF THE DINING ROOM. NOTE THE WAY THE WOODWORK IS USED TO CARRY THE SAME STRUCTURAL IDEA THROUGHOUT THE WHOLE LOWER FLOOR.

A BUNGALOW OF IRREGULAR FORM AND UNUSUALLY INTERESTING CONSTRUCTION

Published in The Craftsman, April, 1907

VIEW OF THE BUNGALOW SHOWING COURT AND PERGOLA, DINING PORCH AND SLOPE OF THE HILL.

THE plans and drawings of this bungalow, while partly our own, are adapted from rough sketches sent us by one of our subscribers, Mr. George D. Rand, of Auburndale, Mass. Mr. Rand is an architect who has retired from active work, and these sketches were made for his own bungalow, which is situated in the mountain region of New Hampshire. In sending us the sketches, Mr. Rand kindly gave us permission to use the idea as outlined by him, with such alterations as seemed best to us. In accordance with this permission, we make quite a number of minor modifications in the original design, and many of the suggestions for construction are our own.

The house is somewhat irregular in design, but is so admirably proportioned and planned that the broken lines impress one as they do when seen in some old English house that has grown into its present shape through centuries of alteration in response to changing needs. It seems above all things to be a house fitted to crown a hilltop in the open country, especially where the slope is something the same as indicated in the site here shown. The line from the back of the roof down to the boat landing comes as near to being a perfect relation of house and ground as is often seen, and this relation is of the first importance in the attempt to suit a house to its environment.

The exterior walls and the roof are of shingles, and the foundations, parapets, columns and chimneys are of split stone laid up in dark cement. The construction of the roof is admirable and, with all the irregularity, there is a certain ample graciousness and dignity in line and proportion. At the front

AN UNUSUALLY INTERESTING BUNGALOW

of the house between the two gables is a recessed court, paved with red cement cut into squares like tiles and roofed over with a pergola of which the beautiful construction is shown in the detail given of this court.

The large porch at the side of the house is intended for an outdoor living and dining room and corresponds closely in arrangement with the rooms which open upon it. Its construction is the same as that of the court, except that it is sheltered by a wide-eaved roof instead of a pergola and is so arranged that it can be easily closed in for cold or stormy weather. At the end next the living room there is a large fireplace built of split stone, which exactly corresponds with the fireplace in the indoor living room. A good fire of logs on this outdoor hearth gives the same effect of warmth and cheer as a camp fire. If casements were placed all around the porch so that it could be entirely closed in time of storm and cold, it might be an excellent idea to floor it smoothly with wood for dancing; but if

it is to be exposed to the weather, the cement floor would be more durable, as sun

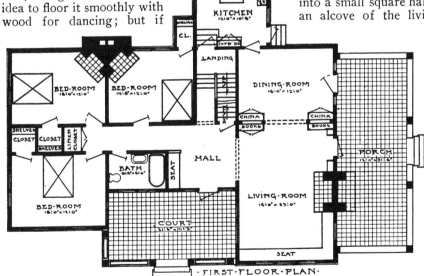

•SECOND·FLOOR·AND·ROOF·PLAN•

•FIRST·FLOOR·PLAN•

and wind soon roughen the best wood floor.

The house is rich in fireplaces, for not only are there the large chimneypieces, in the living room and on the porch adjoining, but two of the bedrooms on the lower floor have corner fireplaces. As the kitchen is so placed as to be practically detached from the remainder of the house, another flue is necessary for the kitchen range.

From the court the entrance door opens into a small square hall, which is practically an alcove of the living room and which connects by a narrow passage with the bedrooms at the opposite side of the house. The bathroom is placed almost in the center of the house, which might be undesirable if it were not completely shut off from the living rooms by the plan of the hall and by the same plan made easily accessible to the three bedrooms.

AN UNUSUALLY INTERESTING BUNGALOW

DETAIL OF THE COURT, SHOWING CONSTRUCTION OF THE PERGOLA AND THE USE OF VINES, SHRUBS AND FLOWER BOXES. THE GLASS DOOR IS THE MAIN ENTRANCE DOOR OF THE HOUSE.

The construction of the living room is very interesting, as everything is revealed up to the ridge pole and rafters of the roof. The roof itself has such a long sweep that there would be danger of its sagging, were it not for the trusses that brace it in the center. These trusses, in addition to their use, add much to the decorative effect of the structure. Across the front and down the side of the living room to the fireplace is a built-in seat paneled below and backed with a wainscot of V-jointed boards. If desired, the top of this seat can be hinged in sections, making the lower part a place for storing things. The window above the seat in front gives an unusually interesting effect, as there is a group of double casements on what in an ordinary house would be the lower floor, and another group of single casements, the center one higher than the sides, just above the frieze and beam. Another casement set high in the wall is placed opposite the fireplace, corresponding in position to the door which opens upon the porch.

Extending to a point half way across the opening into the hall is the balcony which forms the upstairs sitting room; this is divided from the living room only by a railing. The floor of this balcony forms the ceiling of the dining room, which is separated from the living room only by double cupboards made to be used as bookcases on one side and china closets on the other. These cupboards extend to the same height as the window-sills and mantel, carrying this line around the room. The space above is open and hung with small curtains. This effect of a small low dining room recessed from a living room that runs clear to the roof is delightful in the sense it gives of homelike comfort, as the effect is that of a snug little retreat devoted to good cheer.

A BUNGALOW OF IRREGULAR FORM

CORNER OF THE LIVING ROOM, SHOWING UPPER AND LOWER WINDOWS AT THE FRONT OF THE HOUSE, THE SEAT WHICH SERVES BOTH AS WINDOW AND FIRESIDE SEAT AND THE FORM AND CONSTRUCTION OF THE FIREPLACE.

A PORTION OF THE LIVING ROOM, LOOKING INTO THE DINING ROOM. THE CEILING OF THE LATTER IS FORMED BY THE FLOOR OF THE BALCONY ABOVE, SO THAT IT HAS THE APPEARANCE OF A LOW-CEILED RECESS, AND THE BOOKCASES MAKE THE PARTITION. THE BALCONY IS USED AS AN UPSTAIRS SITTING ROOM.

A ROOMY, HOMELIKE FARMHOUSE FOR LOVERS OF PLAIN AND WHOLESOME COUNTRY LIFE

Published in The Craftsman, March, 1909.

FRONT VIEW SHOWING PORCH, DORMER AND SLEEPING BALCONY.

BOTH in exterior seeming and in interior arrangement and finish, this building is essentially a farmhouse,—not of the comfortless type that we have been accustomed to of late years, but one that is reminiscent of earlier days, when a farmhouse was in very truth the homestead and as such was large, substantial, comfortable and inviting. The design is very simple, with clapboarded or shingled walls and a broad sheltering roof, the straight sweep of which is broken by a large dormer on either side. The wide veranda in front is recessed, forming a sheltered porch that could be used for much outdoor life. The windows as suggested here are all casements, those on the upper story being protected from the weather by the broadly overhanging roof and the lower ones sheltered by hoods. At the front of the house the dormer is extended to form a good-sized sleeping porch and at the back it accommodates the bathroom.

As the general effect of the house is broad and low, it is fitting that very little of the foundation should be visible. A far better effect is given if no attempt is made to establish too strict a grade line, as the house seems to fit the

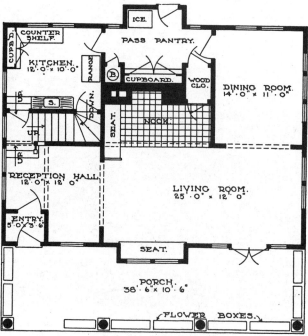

FIRST STORY PLAN

A ROOMY, HOMELIKE FARMHOUSE

ground much better if the foundation is accommodated to the natural irregularities and if the floor of the porch is very little elevated above the turf.

The interior arrangement, while simplicity itself, is very convenient. There is hardly anything to mark the divisions between the reception hall, living room and dining room, so that these names rather serve to indicate the uses to which the different parts of this one large room may be put than to imply that they are separate rooms. In the very center of the house is the large fireplace nook which naturally forms the center of interest and attraction, with its ample chimneypiece of the split field stone and the comfortable fireside seat beside the hearth. Were it not for the arrangement of this large open space, there might be a sense of bareness; but this is entirely obviated by the shape of the room, the prominence given to the fireside nook, and the liberal use of wood in the form of beams, wainscots, seats and such built-in fixtures as may be necessary.

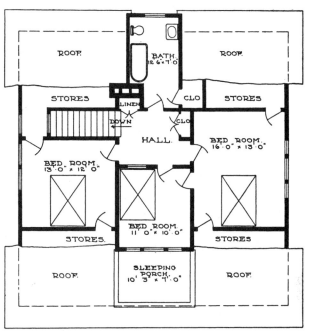

SECOND STORY PLAN.

FIRESIDE NOOK, GIVING AN IDEA OF THE BROAD CHIMNEYPIECE BUILT OF SPLIT FIELD STONE AND OF THE FIRESIDE SEAT, WHICH IS MADE OF WIDE BOARDS V-JOINTED.

A PLASTER HOUSE UPON WHICH WOOD HAS BEEN LIBERALLY USED

Published in The Craftsman, December, 1906.

FRONT OF THE HOUSE, SHOWING EFFECT OF PORCHES WITH WOODEN BALUSTRADES.

WE have always found the combination of rough-finished plaster with plenty of exterior woodwork to be very attractive, and this house is a good example of the way in which we relieve the severity of the plain plaster. The design of the house is not as straight and massive as is usual with the Craftsman cement or plaster houses, yet it is very simple, and the exterior features are such as to make for great durability.

The foundation of the house as shown is of very hard and rough red brick as to the visible part. Should this brick not be easily obtainable or too costly in the local market, a quarry-faced, broken-joint ashlar or some

A PLASTER AND TIMBER HOUSE

darker stone would be very effective with either gray or green cement. As to the woodwork, we would suggest cypress, which is inexpensive, durable and beautiful in color and grain when finished according to the process we describe elsewhere in this book. The color under this treatment is a rich warm brown which, when used for the half-timber construction, window framings and balustrades, would look equally well with plaster either left in the natural gray or given a tone of biscuit color or of dull green.

Some idea of the interior woodwork is given in the detail drawings. A great deal of wood is used in the form of wainscoting, grilles and

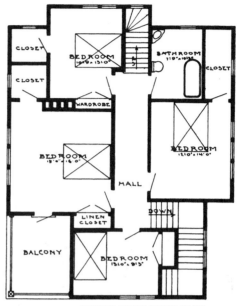

SECOND STORY FLOOR PLAN.

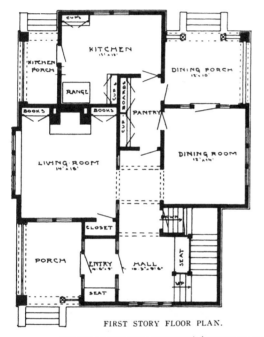

FIRST STORY FLOOR PLAN.

the like, and the whole scheme of decoration and furnishing naturally is founded on this use of wood. It would be best to treat the upper walls and ceilings of the hall, living room and dining room alike, as the object is to give a sense of space, dignity and restfulness to the part of the house that is most lived in and this effect is best obtained by having no change in the background. The rooms open into each other in such a way as to suggest one large room irregularly shaped and full of recesses, and any marked difference in the treatment of the walls is apt to produce an effect of patchiness as well as the restlessness that comes from marked variations in our home surroundings.

DETAIL DRAWING SHOWING CONSTRUCTION AND PLACING OF WAINSCOT, DOOR, STAIRCASE AND LANDING.

A FARMHOUSE DESIGNED WITH A LONG, UN-BROKEN ROOF LINE AT THE BACK

Published in The Craftsman, January, 1909.

FRONT VIEW, SHOWING RUSTIC PERGOLA AND INTERESTING CONSTRUCTION THAT SUPPORTS THE OVERHANG.

REAR VIEW SHOWING WIDE SWEEP OF ROOF AT THE BACK IN PLACE OF THE CUSTOMARY "LEAN-TO."

A FARMHOUSE WITH A LONG ROOF LINE

WE feel that the design for this farmhouse is one of the most satisfactory that we have ever done, not only because the building, simple as it is, is graceful in line and proportion, but because the interior is so arranged as to simplify the work of the household and to give a good deal of room within a comparatively small area.

The plan is definitely that of a farmhouse, and in this frank expression of its character and use lies the chief charm of the dwelling. The walls might be covered with either shingles or clapboards, according to the taste and means of the owner. If the beauty of the building were more to be considered than the expense of construction, we should recommend the use of rived cypress shingles, as these are not only very durable but have a most interesting surface. The only difficulty is that they cost about double the price of the ordinary shingles. As the construction of the house in front is such that a veranda

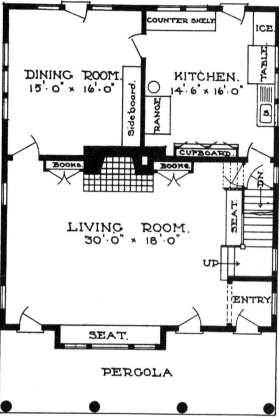

FIRST STORY FLOOR PLAN.

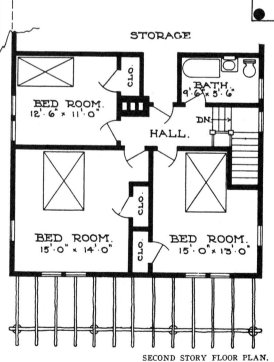

SECOND STORY FLOOR PLAN.

would be rather a disfigurement than an improvement, we have supplied its place by a terrace covered with a pergola. The terrace would naturally be of cement or vitrified brick and the construction of the pergola should be rustic in character. One great advantage of such a pergola is that the vines that cover it afford sufficient shade in summer, while in winter there is nothing to interfere with the air and sunlight, which should be admitted as freely as possible to the house. We have allowed the roof to come down in an unbroken sweep toward the back because of the beauty and unusualness of this long roof line as compared with the usual square form of a house with the lower roof of a porch or lean-to at the back. Furthermore, by this device there is considerable space for storage left over the kitchen and dining room. The entry opens into the living room at right angles with the entrance door and this opening might be curtained to avoid draughts.

TWO INEXPENSIVE BUT CHARMING COTTAGES FOR WOMEN WHO WANT THEIR OWN HOMES

IT has always seemed to us that if there is one kind of dwelling that is more generally needed than another, it is the small and inexpensive, yet comfortable and homelike, cottage that can be built almost for the year's rent of a flat, or even of room and board in a boarding house, and that would serve as a home for two or three people. Especially is this sort of a house needed by women of limited means,—women who either work at home or possibly in an office or shop and who need all the home comfort they can get, instead of dragging out an existence in a boarding house or facing the bugbear of rent day in a flat.

These cottages each would serve to accommodate a group of three or four and the number might even be stretched to six in case of very congenial people who did not mind

Published in The Craftsman, March, 1904.

STONE COTTAGE WITH RECESSED PORCH.

sharing their rooms. The houses as represented here are built of field stone, but the designs would serve equally well for concrete,—a form of construction that would greatly lessen the cost,—or for frame houses covered with shingles, clapboards, or even with plain boards and battens. In fact, after the initial cost of the lot in some suburb not too far away from the place of employment, it should be a very easy matter for two or three women who felt that they would like to make a home for themselves to combine their resources and build one of these little houses. Even the cost of the lot might be very greatly lessened if it were possible to build in a village near the city or right out in the country. It is the woman who is stranded in some forlorn hall bedroom, or who is forced to feel that she is a superfluous member of someone else's family, who would most welcome the dignity and content that would be found

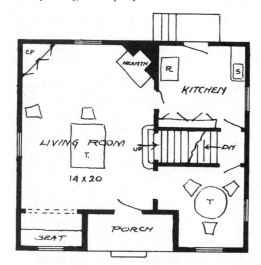

FIRST STORY FLOOR PLAN.

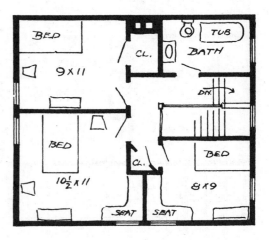

SECOND STORY FLOOR PLAN.

TWO INEXPENSIVE BUT CHARMING COTTAGES

in a home of her own,—a home which might be shared by a relative or close friend in similar circumstances.

The chief value of these little houses lies in the fact that although they are but the simplest of cottages, they nevertheless possess a beauty and individuality which is lacking in many a residence that costs ten times as much. We feel that in exterior attractions they are fitted to take rank with any of the houses designed in The Craftsman Workshops, and that the interior arrangement is compact and comfortable to a degree. The chief difference between them, as regards the exterior, lies in the fact that in the case of the first one the porch is recessed and, in the second, is extended to the dimensions of a good-sized veranda that runs the whole width of the house. In interior arrangement they are much alike, the living room in each case occupying the whole of one side of the house and

Published in The Craftsman, March, 1904.

STONE COTTAGE WITH VERANDA. NOTE THE EFFECT OF SQUARE BUNGALOW ROOF AND OF CASEMENT WINDOWS HIGH UNDER THE EAVES.

opening into a dining alcove which takes about half of the other side. The kitchen occupies the remaining corner and, if this be fitted with convenient cupboards, work table and the like, there would be no necessity for a pantry. Upstairs also the arrangement of the two cottages is somewhat similar, as in each case the space is divided into three bedrooms and a bathroom, with plenty of closet room tucked away into nooks and corners.

As to the interior woodwork and furnishing, these need not be costly in order to be attractive. Some inexpensive native wood, such as pine, or cypress, or that grade of chestnut known to builders as "sound wormy," would, if finished properly, give the most delightful effect when used for interior trim, built-in seats, cupboards, balustrades for the stairways, and for wainscoting,—providing the sum set aside for the house admitted such a luxury as the last. The remaining wall spaces and the ceilings could be left in the rough sand-finished plaster, tinted in any color desired, and the fireplace would naturally be of brick or field stone and of the simplest design. Given such a foundation, the question of furnishing would adjust itself.

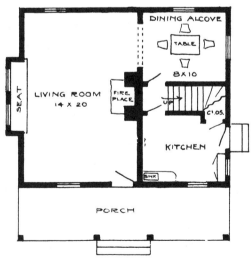

FIRST STORY FLOOR PLAN.

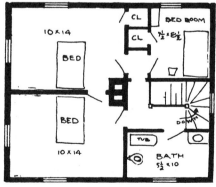

SECOND STORY FLOOR PLAN.

A LOG HOUSE THAT WILL SERVE EITHER AS A SUMMER CAMP OR A COUNTRY HOME

Published in The Craftsman, March, 1907.

EXTERIOR OF LOG HOUSE, SHOWING DECORATIVE USE OF THE PROJECTING ENDS OF PARTITION LOGS.

SO many people like log houses for summer homes that we give here a design that would harmonize with the most primitive surroundings. At the same time it is so carefully planned and so well constructed that it could be used as a regular dwelling all the year round. While the lines of the building are simple to a degree, all the proportions are so calculated and the details of the construction so carefully observed that, with all this simplicity and freedom from pretense, there is no suggestion of bareness or crudity. It is essentially a log house for woodland life, and it looks just that; yet it is a warm, comfortable, roomy building perfectly drained and ventilated and, with proper construction, ought to last for many generations.

As the first step towards securing good drainage and also saving the lower logs of the wall from decay, there is an excellent foundation built of stone or cement,—according to the material most easily and economically obtained,—and this foundation is quite as high as it would be in any dwelling built of the conventional materials in the conventional way. But as the appearance of such a foundation would spoil the whole effect of the house by separating it from the ground on which it stands, it is almost entirely concealed by terracing the soil up to the top of it and therefore to the level of the porch floors. The first log of the walls rest directly upon this foundation and is just far enough above the ground to prevent rotting. By this device perfect healthfulness is secured so far as good drainage is concerned, and at the same time the wide low house of logs appears to rest upon the ground in the most primitive way.

The logs used in building should have the bark stripped off and then be stained to a dull grayish brown that approaches as closely as possible to the color of the bark that has been removed. This does away entirely with the danger of rotting, which is unavoidable when the bark is left on, and the stain removes the raw, glaring whiteness of the peeled logs and restores them to a color that harmonizes with their surroundings. The best logs for this purpose are from trees of the second growth, which are easily obtained almost anywhere. They should be from nine to twelve inches in diameter and should be carefully

A LOG HOUSE

selected for their straightness and symmetry.

The wide porches that extend all along both sides of the house afford plenty of room for outdoor living. As shown in the picture, one end of the porch at the front of the house is recessed to form a square dining porch, which opens into the kitchen and also into the big room. This is a combined living room and indoor dining room, to be used for the latter purpose only in chilly or stormy weather, if the house is meant for a summer camp.

The general effect of this room is in exact harmony with the exterior of the house. The door from the porch opens into an entry which on one side gives access to the two bedrooms at the front of the house and on the other leads by a wide opening into the main room. The walls and partitions are of logs and the ceiling is beamed with logs flattened on the upper side to support the floor above. The fireplace, like the chimney outside, is built of split stone, a material especially suited to this house, and is in a nook or recess that is formed, not by the shape

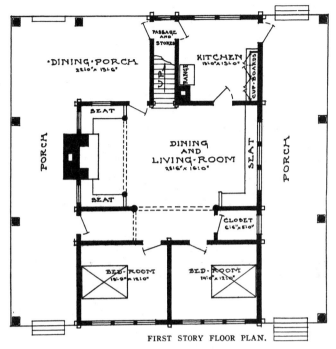

FIRST STORY FLOOR PLAN.

of the room, but by the suggestion of a division made by the two logs placed one above the other across the ceiling logs, and the two posts that form the ends of the fireside seats.

VIEW OF LIVING ROOM, SHOWING THE LOG CONSTRUCTION WHICH SEPARATES THE FIREPLACE NOOK FROM THE REST OF THE ROOM, AND ALSO GIVING AN IDEA OF THE EFFECT TO BE OBTAINED BY THE USE OF LOG PARTITIONS.

A PLEASANT AND HOMELIKE COTTAGE DESIGNED FOR A SMALL FAMILY

Published in The Craftsman, February, 1905.

VIEW OF COTTAGE FROM THE FRONT.

FIREPLACE AND SEAT IN THE LIVING ROOM, WITH GLIMPSE OF HALL AND STAIRCASE.

COTTAGE FOR A SMALL FAMILY

THIS design for a cottage is best suited for the suburbs or for a village, as the shape of the building is such that it needs plenty of ground around it. If it were built in the open country, it would look particularly well on a large lot where there are plenty of trees, as for example the site of an old apple orchard, as the gnarled trunks and low spreading branches would give the ideal setting to a house like this.

In the event of the house being built in a locality where field stone could easily be obtained, it would be advisable to use this material for the first story, as suggested in the illustration. The gables and roof are shingled and an admirable effect could be produced by using rived cypress shingles darkened by the application of diluted sulphuric acid. This brings out all the color in the wood and also brings it into complete harmony with the stone.

The porch at the front of the house is eight feet wide, permitting the use of a hammock and such rustic furniture as is needed for veranda life in the summer. The second and smaller porch at the rear of the house opens into the dining room and may be used as an outdoor dining room during the warm months.

The vestibule inside the entrance door is very small, serving merely to cut off the draught from the door. This is one of our earlier plans and has narrower openings between the rooms. Were we to make it over now, we would suggest that the partition between the hall and the living room on the side

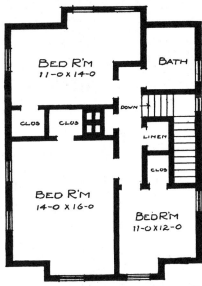

SECOND STORY FLOOR PLAN.

toward the front be taken away as far as the vestibule, making the hall a part of the living room. The narrow passage between the fireside seat and the staircase could remain unaltered, or the post-and-panel construction might be put across, making a doorway in which could be hung a portiere. Although the doorway between the living room and the dining room is very wide, yet the division is indicated sufficiently to separate the space into two distinct rooms. If this arrangement should be preferred, the opening could be left just as it is and either curtained with heavy portiéres, or partially filled with a large screen which could be spread across or removed at will. It would, however, be more in accordance with the later Craftsman arrangement to remove even these slight partitions, leaving only the chimneypiece to mark the division between the rooms.

FIRST STORY FLOOR PLAN.

Published in The Craftsman, December, 1908.

VIEW OF THE CLUBHOUSE AT CRAFTSMAN FARMS, SHOWING DECORATIVE EFFECT OF LOG CONSTRUCTION ON THE LOWER STORY AND THE PLASTER PANELS ABOVE. NOTE THE GROUPING OF THE WINDOWS AND THE DECORATED PANELS BETWEEN THE CASEMENTS IN THE DORMER. THE SLOPE OF THE HILL AT THE BACK SHOWS THE POSSIBILITY OF BUILDING THE BASEMENT ROOMS AS DESCRIBED.

A COUNTRY CLUBHOUSE THAT IS BUILT LIKE A LOG CABIN

WE have given the design of the Clubhouse at Craftsman Farms for the use of country clubs that may find such a plan desirable. As we use it ourselves, it will be the general assembly house of the whole colony, so planned that meals may be served either indoors or out on a big veranda, according to the weather, and where meetings, lectures and entertainments of all kinds may be held by the people staying at the Farms and accommodation provided for guests invited from the outside. For our own purpose, no form of building is so suitable and desirable as a low, roomy house built of logs, and we imagine that many a country club will find that similar uses and surroundings seem to demand a building of this character.

As will be seen by comparison of the exterior view of the house with the plan of the lower floor, there are three main divisions in the building, indicated in the perspective drawing by the projecting ends of the logs which form the log partition between the reception room and sitting room

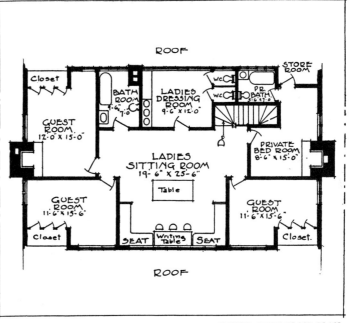

SECOND STORY FLOOR PLAN.

FIRST STORY FLOOR PLAN.

and kitchen on the one side, and serve as the outer wall of the house on the porch side. The width of this porch is the same as the width allowed for the sitting room and kitchen and the center of the building for the whole length is taken up by the reception room, which will be used for the assembly room or the indoor dining room, as seems necessary. The porch will be used as an outdoor living room or dining room, as the case may be, and the little sitting room at the back is meant for guests who may wish some place apart from the general assembly room for a quiet chat with a few friends.

The upper floor is divided into guest rooms, with a comfortable sitting room for ladies

A COUNTRY CLUBHOUSE

and a dressing room and two bathrooms, so that there is not only accommodation for transient guests but room for a few guests who may wish accommodation over night or for several days at a time.

The smoking room and dressing room for men are placed below the main floor, as in the case of the building at Craftsman Farms the ground slopes sufficiently away from the back of the house to allow ample accommodation for these basement rooms. This slope is sufficiently steep to expose the stone foundation to a depth of seven or eight feet, so that anyone entering the smoking room from the outside comes in on a level instead of going down as into a basement. Flower boxes placed between the pillars around this end of the porch will afford some protection where the slope is most abrupt.

As will be seen, the design of the house is very simple, the effect of comfort and of ample spaces depending entirely upon its proportions. The big sweep of the low pitched, widely overhanging roof is broken by the broad shallow dormers, which not only give sufficient additional height to make the greater part of the upper story habitable, but also adds much to the structural charm of the building. As the walls of the upper story are of plaster, the logs being used after the manner of half-timber construction, the ends of the dormers are also of plaster and plaster panels divide the groups of casement windows.

These plaster panels form one of the most interesting features of the house because they put into effect our idea of a form of exterior decoration that shall be symbolic of the house itself and the environment in which it stands. Roughly modeled in low relief, are figures symbolizing the life and industries of the farm. Dull colored pigments will be used to emphasize these figures and to add a definite color accent to the house, but the pigments will in all cases come into harmony with the natural tones of wood, stone and earth. These panels form the sole decoration that exists purely for the sake of decoration. For the rest, the beauty of the house depends entirely upon structural features; upon the casement windows, which are all uniform in size and are so arranged as to form long horizontal lines; upon the use of the logs and of stone in the foundation and the chimneys and upon the color harmony of the whole in relation to the prevailing tones of the landscape.

UPSTAIRS SITTING ROOM, SHOWING THE WRITING TABLE AND SEATS IN THE DORMER.

A PLAIN LITTLE CABIN THAT WOULD MAKE A GOOD SUMMER HOME IN THE WOODS

Published in The Craftsman, November, 1908.

VIEW OF THE FRONT AND SIDE, SHOWING CASEMENTS HIGH IN THE WALL.

ONE of the features at Craftsman Farms is the housing of guests, students and workers in small bungalows or cabins scattered here and there through the woods and over the hillside, standing either singly or in groups of three and four in small clearings made in the natural woodland. Therefore they are designed especially for such surroundings and are most desirable for those who wish to build inexpensive summer or week-end cottages for holiday and vacation use. Of course, any one of the plans would serve perfectly well for a tiny cottage for two or three people to live in, but the design and general character of the buildings is hardly adapted to the ordinary town lot and would not be so effective in conventional surroundings as in the open country.

The cottages built at Craftsman Farms are meant first of all to live in and next to serve as examples of a variety of practical plans for small moderately priced dwellings designed on the general order of the bungalow. They will be built of stone, brick, or any one of a number of our native woods suitable for such construction and will be as comfortable, beautiful and interesting as we can make them, each one being specially planned for its own use.

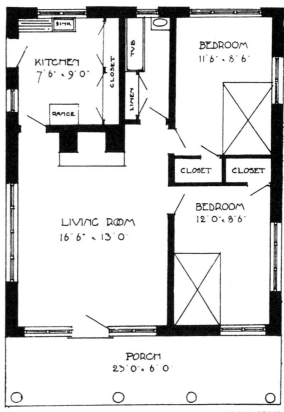

FLOOR PLAN.

Published in The Craftsman, July, 1904.

A BUNGALOW BUILT AROUND A COURTYARD FACING THE WATER: VIEW OF THE FRONT, SHOWING ENTRANCE, TERRACE AND CHIMNEYS, AND THE RELATION OF THE HOUSE TO ITS SITE.

A BUNGALOW BUILT AROUND A COURTYARD FACING THE WATER

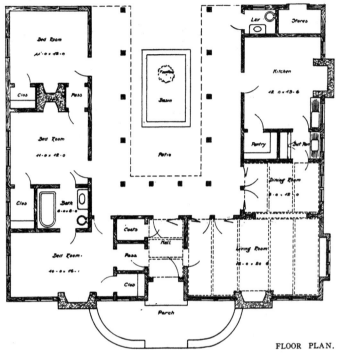

FLOOR PLAN.

ONE of our earliest designs is shown in this bungalow, which has proven very popular for summer homes, especially where they are built on the shore of a lake or river; for the chief characteristic of the design is an inner court, or *patio,* which looks directly out upon the water. The bungalow is built around three sides of this courtyard,—an arrangement which carries with it a suggestion of the old Mission architecture of California.

The original design was for a house with shingled walls, but the construction is equally suitable for stone, brick, or concrete. The material chosen, of course, would depend entirely upon the locality and the taste of the owner. Were we designing it now, we would probably suggest concrete, as the form of the house, with its straight walls and simple lines, is well suited to this material, and also because this method of construction is comparatively inexpensive as well as substantial and durable. If the walls were finished with rough plaster or pebbledash surface, the effect would be admirable, especially for the woods, if a little dull green pigment were brushed on irregularly, giving a general tone of green that yet is not a solid smooth color.

The central court as shown here is paved with stone, but this would be only in case of stone or shingle construction. For either brick or concrete it would be best to pave the court with cement colored a dull red and marked off into squares. This has much the appearance of Welsh quarry tiles and is much less expensive. Provision has been made in the center of the court for a basin, in the middle of which a pile of rocks affords opportunity for a fountain or trickling cascade, while the pool furnishes an admirable place for the growth of aquatic plants. The court can either be paved clear up to the pool as shown in the picture, or the pavement may stop just outside the pillars, leaving the center of the courtyard for turf. In either case the *patio* is meant to be furnished for use as an outdoor living room, such as is so frequently seen in the courtyards of California houses. If the house is built for a camp in the woods, the pillars around this courtyard would best be made of peeled logs left in the natural shape and stained back to the color of the bark. For more conventional use, heavy round pillars of concrete or of wood painted white would naturally be used. These details, however, are always ruled by the locality, the materials used for building and the taste of the builder.

The arrangement of the interior is very simple, as from the entrance hall one turns toward the right into the living room, which occupies half the front of the building. Just back of the living room in the wing is the dining room and back of this again is the kitchen. Turning to the left from the hall, a small passage leads to one of the bedrooms, and the other two bedrooms and the bathroom occupy the whole length of the wing. All of these rooms open out upon a central court and all are lighted from the outside by casements set high in the wall. Fireplaces are plentiful, the chimneys being so arranged that one is allowed for each bedroom and one for the living room. This being almost opposite the dining room, or rather alcove, serves for that room as well.

VIEW OF THE COURTYARD LOOKING OUT UPON THE WATER. THIS MIGHT BE USED AS AN OUTDOOR LIVING ROOM AND FURNISHED WITH TEA TABLE, CHAIRS, HAMMOCKS AND RUGS. BEING SO COMPLETELY SHELTERED FROM THE WIND IT SHOULD MAKE A VERY PLEASANT AFTERNOON LOUNGING PLACE IN WARM WEATHER.

A RUSTIC CABIN THAT IS MEANT FOR A WEEK-END COTTAGE OR A VACATION HOME

Published in The Craftsman, November, 1908.

FRONT VIEW OF CABIN, SHOWING DECORATIVE USE OF TRUSS IN THE GABLE.

THIS is another example of the cottages built at Craftsman Farms and is somewhat larger than the stone cabin shown on page 81, as it contains a bathroom and a recessed porch which serves as an open air dining room, in addition to the living room, two bedrooms and kitchen provided in the smaller cottage.

The walls are sheathed with boards eight or ten inches wide and seven-eighths of an inch thick. A truss of hewn timber in each gable, projecting a foot and a half from the face of the wall, not only gives added support to the roof, but forms a decorative feature that relieves the extreme simplicity of the construction. The casement windows are all hung so they will swing outward and are mostly small and set rather high in the wall. At the ends of the building these casements are protected by simple shutters, each one

made of two wide boards with either heart shaped or circular piercing. These solid shutters provide ample shelter in severe weather.

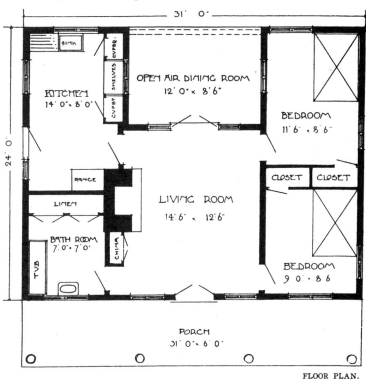

FLOOR PLAN.

A BUNGALOW DESIGNED FOR A MOUNTAIN CAMP OR SUMMER HOME

Published in The Craftsman, March, 1905.

REAR VIEW OF BUNGALOW, WITH VERANDA LOOKING TOWARD THE WATER.

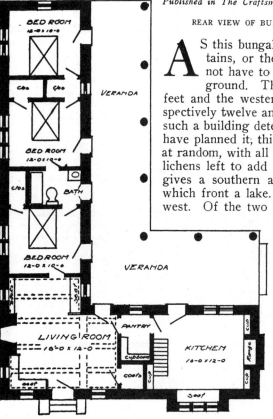

FLOOR PLAN.

AS this bungalow is meant either for the woods, the mountains, or the open country, where the cost of land does not have to be considered, it spreads over a good deal of ground. The eastern wing has a frontage of sixty-four feet and the western of forty-four feet, the verandas being respectively twelve and ten feet. Also the probable environment of such a building determines the character of the exterior. As we have planned it; this bungalow is built of rugged field stones set at random, with all the weather stains and accretions of moss and lichens left to add to the color value. The site suggested here gives a southern and western exposure to the wide verandas which front a lake. The building itself faces toward the northwest. Of the two wings, the eastern, containing the bedrooms, extends into the wooded portion of the land in order to insure protection and coolness; while the west wing looks toward the lake.

The interior of this bungalow is divided into a living room, a kitchen and three bedrooms. The living room is large and comfortably arranged, the idea being to give it a character in harmony with the plan, purpose and exterior effect of the building.

The kitchen is planned so that meals may be served in it in bad weather. Ordinarily the meals would be served in the sheltered corner of the veranda. The whole eastern wing is given up to the bedrooms which are all entered from the veranda, and overhead is a large storage attic.

A MOUNTAIN CAMP OR SUMMER HOME

FRONT VIEW OF BUNGALOW, SEEN FROM THE LAND.

CHIMNEYPIECE AND FIRESIDE NOOK IN THE LIVING ROOM. NOTE THE USE OF LOGS FOR OVERHEAD BEAMS AND OF WIDE V-JOINTED BOARDS FOR THE WALLS AND SEAT.

A CONVENIENT BUNGALOW WITH SEPARATE KITCHEN AND OPEN AIR DINING ROOM

Published in the Craftsman, April, 1906.

FRONT AND REAR VIEWS OF COTTAGE. THE FIRST SHOWING RECESSED ENTRANCE PORCH AND THE SECOND THE OPEN AIR DINING ROOM WHICH SEPARATES THE KITCHEN FROM THE MAIN PART OF THE HOUSE.

A BUNGALOW WITH OPEN-AIR DINING ROOM

FOR any place, whether mountain or valley, that is really " in the country," the best form of summer home is the bungalow. It is a house reduced to its simplest form, where life may be carried on with the greatest amount of freedom and comfort and the least amount of effort. It never fails to harmonize with its surroundings, because its low broad proportions and absolute lack of ornamentation give it a character so natural and unaffected that it seems to sink into and blend with any landscape. It may be built of any local material and with the aid of such help as local workmen can afford, so it is never expensive unless elaborated out of all kinship with its real character of a primitive dwelling. It is beautiful, because it is planned and built to meet simple needs in the simplest and most direct way; and it is individual for the same reason, as no two families have tastes and needs alike.

The bungalow illustrated here is designed on the purest Craftsman lines. The material we have suggested is cedar shingles throughout with a foundation and chimney of rough gray stone. No cellar is provided, but the walls have a footing below the frost line and space under the floor for ventilation. The building is in the form of a T the main portion covering a space twenty-four by forty feet and the extension at the back fourteen by thirty-six feet. The low-pitched, widely overhanging roof gives a settled, sheltered look to the building, and this is emphasized even more by the deeply recessed porch in front, which is meant to be used by a small outdoor sitting room. The porch be-

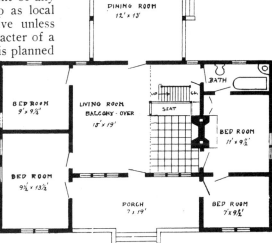

FLOOR PLAN.

tween the kitchen and the main part of the house is really a portion of the extension left with open sides and is intended for an outdoor dining room that shall be sufficiently sheltered

RECESSED ENTRANCE PORCH, SHOWING DOOR WITH THUMB LATCH AND HEAVY STRAP HINGES OF WROUGHT IRON; ALSO THE INTERESTING USE OF HEAVY TIMBERS IN THE DOOR AND WINDOW FRAMING, WHERE THE BEAM ACROSS THE TOP BINDS THE ENTIRE GROUP INTO A UNIT.

A BUNGALOW WITH OPEN-AIR DINING ROOM

END OF LIVING ROOM, SHOWING BALCONY, FIRESIDE NOOK WITH CHIMNEYPIECE AND ARRANGEMENT OF STAIRCASE.

ARRANGEMENT OF CUPBOARDS, WORK SHELF AND WIN-DOWS IN KITCHEN.

from storms to allow the outdoor life to go on through any sort of weather.

The living room occupies the whole center of the house, except for the recessed porch in front, and it is one of the best examples of the Craftsman idea of the decorative value that lies in revealing the actual construction of the building. Everyone knows the sense of space and freedom given by a ceiling that follows the line of the roof. It seems to add materially to the size of the room and when it is of wood it gives the keynote for a most friendly and restful color scheme. In this case the whole room is of wood, save for the rough gray plaster of the walls and the stone of the fireplace. A balcony runs across one side, serving the double purpose of recessing the fireplace

A BUNGALOW WITH OPEN-AIR DINING ROOM

OPEN-AIR DINING ROOM: NOTE CONSTRUCTION OF THE ROOF AND PROPORTION OF THE SIDE OPENINGS AND PARAPET.

into a comfortable and inviting nook, and of affording a small retreat which may be used as a study or lounging place, or as an extra sleeping place in case of an overflow of guests, or even as a storage place for trunks. Its uses are many, but its value as an addition to the beauty of the room is always the same.

The sleeping rooms, four in number, occupy the two ends of the main building. They are all of ample size for camp life, and are plastered, walls and ceiling. The dining porch is one of the most distinctive features of the bungalow. It occupies just half of the extension and completely separates the kitchen from the main part of the house. The kitchen is well open to air and light. Instead of a pantry the whole of one side is occupied by cupboards amply supplied with shelves and drawers.

AN OPEN FIRE IN ONE OF THE BEDROOMS.

A COTTAGE PLANNED WITH A SPECIAL IDEA TO ECONOMICAL HEATING

Published in The Craftsman, March, 1905.

NOTE THE USE OF THE BAY WINDOW ON THE LOWER FLOOR AND THE DORMER ABOVE TO ADD TO THE STRUCTURAL INTEREST OF THIS PLAIN LITTLE DWELLING. THE INTERIOR IS CAREFULLY PLANNED TO GIVE THE MOST CONVENIENT ARRANGEMENT OF ROOMS AND TO UTILIZE ALL THE SPACE, SO THAT THERE IS MORE ROOM IN THE HOUSE THAN MIGHT BE EXPECTED FROM THE SPACE OCCUPIED, WHICH IS THIRTY FEET FRONT BY TWENTY-TWO FEET DEEP.

A COTTAGE THAT COMES WITHIN THE LIMITS OF VERY MODERATE MEANS

THE LIVING ROOM

Published in The Craftsman, March, 1905.

A COTTAGE WITH A FRONTAGE OF THIRTY-FOUR FEET AND A DEPTH OF TWENTY-FOUR FEET AND ARRANGED SO THAT THE ROOMS ARE A TRIFLE LARGER THAN THOSE IN THE COTTAGE SHOWN ON THE PRECEDING PAGE. AS NO SPACE IS TAKEN OFF FOR A VERANDA. THE COST OF THE TWO BUILDINGS IS ABOUT THE SAME AND COMES WITHIN VERY MODERATE MEANS.

Published in The Craftsman, July, 1903.

EXTERIOR VIEW OF MOUNTAIN CAMP, SHOWING RELATION TO SURROUNDINGS, USE OF ROUGH TIMBERS AND SLABS FOR CONSTRUCTION, WIDE OVERHANG OF ROOF AND DEEPLY RECESSED LOGGIAS FOR OUTDOOR SLEEPING ROOMS.

A COUNTRY HOUSE THAT WAS ORIGINALLY PLANNED FOR A MOUNTAIN CAMP

ALTHOUGH this house would serve anywhere as a country dwelling for people who like this style of building, it was originally intended for a camp in the Adirondacks, the object of the design being to build a house that would be permanent, and at the same time would have the openness and freedom of a tent, where the family could live out of doors and yet have immunity from flies, mosquitoes and kindred pests. Being a camp, it is naturally not an expensive building, as the plan is simple and the materials about the site would naturally be used. Our constant dwelling upon this point might seem superfluous, but the fact that not long ago a noted architect built a house of stone in the clay-bearing State of Virginia and another of brick in the granite-ribbed State of Maine.

The word camp is suggestive, causing the mind instantly to revert to a large parade ground, with the orderly arrangement of kitchens in the rear, the radial axis, and the sense of order and openness. Therefore the arrangement of this camp has been made with this in mind; the great hall serves for the place of general gathering,— the place where, when the duties or pleasures of the day are over, all may meet on common ground. This, with the kitchen and dining room in the rear, makes for convenience, largeness and economy of

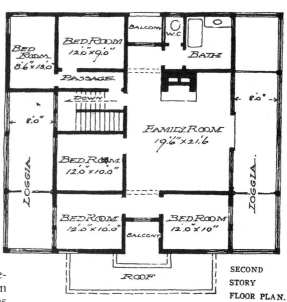

SECOND STORY FLOOR PLAN.

space. There is an upstairs; as sleeping rooms, if in direct connection with the rooms and arrangements already mentioned, would interfere and be interfered with seriously. Economy also has its part, for the roof which covers one story will serve equally well to cover two. In laying out the floors below, no account has been taken of privacy for the immediate family. Therefore on the upper floor there is a large room provided for with the sleeping rooms grouped about it.

The floor plans give a clear idea of the arrangement. The dropping back of the outside walls to form second story balconies or loggias takes up a good deal of the floor space on the second story, so that the bedrooms are rather small. This, however, is hardly to be considered a fault in a building of this kind, because the loggias are screened to serve as sleeping porches: It is also quite possible to screen or partition each loggia to make four separate outdoor sleeping rooms, or they could be divided in part and the rest used for an outside sitting room. These screens should be removable at will, so that they can be stored during the winter months.

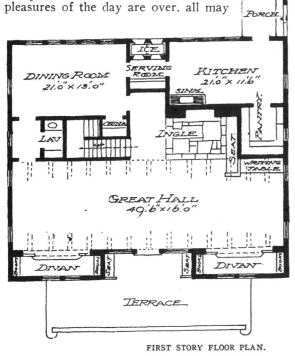

FIRST STORY FLOOR PLAN.

Published in The Craftsman, July, 1903.

GREAT HALL OF MOUNTAIN CAMP, SHOWING RECESSED FIREPLACE AND LONG FIRESIDE SEAT AND GIVING SOME IDEA OF THE WAY IN WHICH HEAVY TIMBERS ARE USED IN THE CONSTRUCTION.

PORCHES, PERGOLAS AND TERRACES: THE CHARM OF LIVING OUT OF DOORS

IN these days when the question of light and air is of so much importance in the planning of the home, the tendency is more and more toward the provision of ample room for as much open-air life as possible. In all the Craftsman houses, as well as in the best modern dwellings of other styles, the veranda, whether open in summer or enclosed for a sun room in winter, is one of the prominent features. Partly for convenience in enclosing with glass if desired, but mainly to insure the pleasant sense of privacy that means such a large part of the comfort of home, these porches or verandas are usually recessed so that they are partially protected by the walls of the house and are further sheltered by the copings and flower boxes. In a front porch which must serve for a sitting room as well as an entrance, the coping, surmounted by flower boxes, acts as a screen and, with the aid of a generous growth of vines, serves as a very satisfactory shelter from the street. Where there is also a garden veranda it can be made into a charming outdoor living or dining room

both for summer and for mild days in winter by being so recessed and protected that it is like a summer house or an outdoor room always open to the sun and air.

Outdoor living and dining rooms. to be homelike and comfortable, should be equipped with all that is necessary for daily use so as to avoid the carrying back and forth of tables, chairs and the like, as when the veranda is used only occasionally. It goes without saying that the furniture should be plain and substantial, fitted for the rugged outdoor life and able to stand the weather. Indian rugs or Navajo blankets lend a touch of comfort and cheer, and the simple designs and primitive colors harmonize as well with trees and vines and the open sky as they do with their native wigwams. Willow chairs and settles seem to belong naturally to life in the garden, and with a few light tables, a book rack or two and plenty of hammocks, the veranda has all the sense of peace and permanency that should belong to a living room, whether indoors or out, that is habitually used by the family.

Published in The Craftsman, June, 1905.

COURTYARD AND PERGOLA, SHOWING DECORATIVE EFFECT OF THE CENTRAL SQUARE OF TURF WITH ITS FOUNTAIN, SHRUBS AND ROCKS AND THE COMFORT OF THE VINE-SHADED PORCH WHEN FURNISHED FOR USE AS AN OUTDOOR LIVING ROOM.

Published in The Craftsman, November, 1906.

PORCH THAT NOT ONLY SERVES AS A DESIRABLE ENTRANCE BUT GREATLY INCREASES THE STRUCTURAL INTEREST OF THE FRONT OF THE HOUSE. THE WINDOWS ON EITHER SIDE PROJECT SLIGHTLY FROM THE WALL IN A SHALLOW BAY AND THE ENTRANCE DOOR WITH ITS CASEMENTS ON EITHER SIDE PROJECTS STILL FARTHER. THE PORCH IS COMPARATIVELY NARROW AND THE ROOF IS SUPPORTED BY TWO HEAVY PILLARS OF WOOD PAINTED WHITE, WHICH SERVE TO GIVE ACCENT TO THE DARKER TONES OF THE SHINGLES, EXTERIOR WOODWORK AND STONE FOUNDATION. THE WALLS ARE SHEATHED WITH CYPRESS SHINGLES THAT ARE OILED AND LEFT TO WEATHER, AND THE WOOD-WORK OF THE ROOF, DOOR AND WINDOW FRAMINGS AND BALUSTRADE IS IN A DARKER TONE OF BROWN. THE USE OF SPINDLES FOR EXTERIOR WOODWORK IS SHOWN IN THE BALUSTRADE.

PORCHES, PERGOLAS AND TERRACES

Published in The Craftsman, September, 1906.

ENTRANCE PORCH FITTED UP FOR AN OUTDOOR LIVING ROOM. FLOOR OF WELSH QUARRIES COVERED WITH A LARGE RUG INTENDED TO STAND ROUGH USAGE AND EXPOSURE TO THE WEATHER. THE BEAMED CEILING IS FORMED BY THE EXPOSED RAFTERS AND THE PORCH IS PARTIALLY SHELTERED BY THE PARAPET.

PORCHES, PERGOLAS AND TERRACES

Published in The Craftsman, May, 1906.

ENTRANCE PORCH TO A HOUSE BUILT OF ROUGH CAST CEMENT. THE WOODEN PILLARS ARE PAINTED PURE WHITE AND ARE VERY THICK AND MASSIVE IN PROPORTION TO THEIR HEIGHT. THE RAFTERS ARE LEFT IN VIEW WHERE THEY SUPPORT THE ROOF AND A HEAVY BEAM RUNNING THE LENGTH OF THE PORCH SERVES TO UPHOLD THE RAFTERS. SQUARE MASSIVE CROSS-BEAMS EXTEND FROM THE PILLARS TO THE WALL, WHERE THE ENDS ARE SUNK IN THE FRAMING OF THE HOUSE. THE FLOOR AND STEPS ARE OF CEMENT COLORED A DARK RED AND MARKED OFF IN BLOCKS LIKE TILES.

PORCHES, PERGOLAS AND TERRACES

Published in The Craftsman, November, 1904.

RECESSED PORCH AT REAR OF HOUSE, SHOWING RELATION OF THE PORTION THAT IS SHELTERED TO THE OPEN TERRACE THAT EXTENDS BEYOND THE ROOF AND GIVES SUFFICIENT SPACE FOR AN OUTDOOR LIVING ROOM THAT IS PARTLY OPEN TO THE SKY.

Published in The Craftsman, August, 1905.

RECESSED ENTRANCE PORCH FURNISHED AS AN OUTDOOR LIVING ROOM THAT IS PARTLY SHELTERED BY THE WALLS AND PARTLY SCREENED BY VINES.

THE EFFECTIVE USE OF COBBLESTONES AS A LINK BETWEEN HOUSE AND LANDSCAPE

IN the building of modern country homes there seems to be no end to the adaptability of cobblestones and boulders in connection with the sturdier kinds of building material, for, if rightly placed with regard to the structure and the surroundings, they can be brought into harmony with nearly every style of architecture that has about it any semblance of ruggedness, especially if the surrounding country be hilly and uneven in contour and blessed—or cursed—with a plentiful crop of stones.

effect of a loose pile of stones. Very few houses that are possible for modern civilized life,—outside of the mountain camp—are sufficiently rough and primitive in construction to be exactly in harmony with the use of cobbles, and always there is a slight sense of effort when they are brought into close relation with finished structure.

Nevertheless the popularity of cobblestones and boulders for foundations, pillars, chimneys and even for such interior use as chimneypieces, is unquestioned and in many cases the

Published in The Craftsman, November, 1908, Hunt & Eager, Architects.

CEMENT PAVED TERRACE OF A CALIFORNIA HOUSE, SHOWING EFFECT OF COBBLESTONES IN WALLS AND PILLARS, AND THE WAY THEY HARMONIZE WITH THE ROUGH SHINGLE AND TIMBER CONSTRUCTION.

We have never specially advocated the use of cobblestones in the building of Craftsman houses, for as a rule we have found that the best effects from a structural point of view can be obtained by using the split stones instead of the smaller round cobbles. Splitting the stone brings into prominence all the interesting colors that are to be found in field rubble and it is astonishing what a variety and richness of coloring is revealed when the stone is split apart so that the inner markings appear. Also a better structural line can be obtained when foundation and pillars are clearly defined instead of having somewhat the

effect is very interesting. There is growing up in this country, especially on the Pacific Coast, a style of house that seems to come naturally into harmony with this sort of stone work, and there is no denying that when the big rough stones and cobbles are used with taste and discrimination, they not only give great interest to the construction, but serve to connect the building very closely with the surrounding landscape.

The fact that we have found the best examples of this natural use of boulders and cobbles in California seems to be due largely to the influence of Japanese architecture over

THE EFFECTIVE USE OF COBBLESTONES

Published in The Craftsman, November, 1908, Hunt & Eager, Architects.

VERANDA AND TERRACE OF THE SAME HOUSE, GIVING A GOOD IDEA OF THE WAY COBBLESTONES MAY SERVE TO LINK THE HOUSE WITH THE SURROUNDING LANDSCAPE. THE EFFECT OF THE RUGGED FORM OF PILLARS AND PARAPET IN CONNECTION WITH THE SHINGLES OF THE WALL AND THE LACY FOLIAGE OF THE TREE IS ESPECIALLY STRIKING.

THE EFFECTIVE USE OF COBBLESTONES

Published in The Craftsman, July, 1907, Greene & Greene, Architects.

A CALIFORNIA HOUSE MODELED AFTER THE JAPANESE STYLE, WITH HIGH RETAINING WALL IN WHICH THE USE OF COBBLESTONES HAS PROVEN ESPECIALLY DECORATIVE.

danger of incongruity, and on the other hand the stone is usually employed in a way that brings the entire building into the closest relationship with its environment.

The cobblestones used for the houses of this kind are of varying sizes. To give the best effect they should be neither too small nor too large. Stones ranging from two and one half inches in diameter for the minimum size to six or seven inches in diameter for the maximum size are found to be most generally suitable. Such stones, which belong of course to the limestone variety, and are irregularly rounded, can usually be obtained without trouble in almost any locality where there are any stones at all, picked up from rocky pasture land or a dry creek bottom. The tendency of builders is to select the whitest stones and the most nearly round that are obtainable.

This, however, applies only to the regular cobblestone construction as we know it in the East. In California the designers are much more daring, for they are fond of using large mossy boulders in connection with both brick and cobbles. The effect of this is singularly interesting both in color and form, for the warm purplish brown of the brick contrasts delightfully with the varying tones of the boulders covered with moss and lichen, and the soft natural grays and browns of the more or less primitive wood construction that is almost invariably used in connection with cobbles gives the general effect of a structure that

the new building art that is developing so rapidly in the West. In these buildings the use of stone in this form is as inevitable in its fitness as the grouping of rocks in a Japanese garden, for on the one hand the construction of the house itself is usually of a character that permits such a use of stone without

THE EFFECTIVE USE OF COBBLESTONES

Published in The Craftsman, April, 1908, Grosvenor Atterbury, Architect.

PERGOLA, PORCH AND ENTRANCE OF A COUNTRY HOUSE AT RIDGEFIELD, CONNECTICUT. THE FOUNDATION AND FIRST STORY OF THE HOUSE ARE OF FIELD RUBBLE SET IN CEMENT, AND THE SECOND STORY IS BUILT OF OVER-BURNED BRICK WITH HALF-TIMBER CONSTRUCTION, GIVING A DELIGHTFUL COLOR EFFECT. THE HOUSE AND GARDEN ARE SO LINKED TOGETHER THAT THE FIRST IMPRESSION IS THAT OF PERFECT HARMONY AND CLOSE RELATIONSHIP, AN IMPRESSION THAT IS GREATLY HEIGHTENED BY THE USE MADE OF THE LOCAL STONE.

THE EFFECTIVE USE OF COBBLESTONES

Published in The Craftsman, July, 1907, Greene & Greene, Architects.

CONSTRUCTION OF THE PERGOLA AND ESPLANADE LEADING TO THE ENTRANCE OF A CALIFORNIA HOUSE. NOTE THE COMBINATION OF LARGE MOSSY BOULDERS WITH HARD-BURNED CLINKER BRICK SET IRREGULARLY IN DARK MORTAR.

in the illustration on page 105, where hard-burned brick and natural wood are most effectively combined with big rugged boulders and the large round slabs of stone that serve as steps. These stones, by their very conformation, proclaim themselves as belonging to New England, and the manner in which they are used is as definitely Eastern as the construction of the California houses is Western.

The Western method is admirably illustrated in the three different views given of the California house that so strongly reflects the influence of Japanese architecture. Here, instead of sharp-edged granite, we have big comfortable looking boulders with all the edges and corners worn off during the ages when they have rolled about in the mountain torrents, and the way they are wedged helter-skelter among the irregular, roughly laid bricks of the walls, pillars and chimneys is as far from the conventional use of stone as is a Japanese garden from our own trim walks and flower beds. Such a combination as in shown in these pictures almost demands the suggestion of Japanese architecture in the house itself, and yet the whole thing belongs entirely to California.

has almost grown up out of the ground, so perfectly does it sink into the landscape around it.

The same effect is being sought more and more in the East by certain daring and progressive architects who, without regard to style and precedent, are building houses suited to the climate, the soil and the needs of life in this country. An excellent example of this is shown

The harmony of this house with its surroundings will be understood when we say that it is situated on high ground overlooking the wild gorge of the Arroyo Seco and that the trees close to it are gnarled, hoary oaks, towering eucalyptus, widespreading cottonwoods, tall, slim poplars and sycamores.

THE EFFECTIVE USE OF COBBLESTONES

Published in The Craftsman, November, 1907.

A HOUSE NEAR PASADENA, CALIFORNIA, SHOWING THE STRIKING EFFECT GAINED BY THE USE OF COBBLESTONES AND BOULDERS IN THE FOUNDATION, CHIMNEY AND YARD WALL.

Published in The Craftsman, November, 1907.

A CALIFORNIA HOUSE WHERE THE USE OF COBBLESTONES IN THE STRUCTURE ITSELF IS REPEATED IN THE LOW PILLARS THAT MARK THE ENTRANCE OF WALK AND DRIVEWAY AND IN THE GARDEN WALL, THUS DRAWING CLOSER THE RELATIONSHIP BETWEEN HOUSE AND GROUND.

THE EFFECTIVE USE OF COBBLESTONES

Published in The Craftsman, July, 1907, Greene & Greene, Architects.

A HOUSE IN SOUTHERN CALIFORNIA THAT SHOWS STRONG TRACES OF JAPANESE INFLUENCE, AS EVIDENT IN THE USE OF COBBLESTONES AND BOULDERS IN COMBINATION WITH BRICK, AS IN THE STRUCTURE ITSELF.

Published in The Craftsman, July, 1907, Greene & Greene, Architects.

AN EXCELLENT EXAMPLE OF THE RIGHT USE OF COBBLES AND BOULDERS. ANOTHER VIEW OF THE SAME HOUSE, SHOWING THE WAY IN WHICH THE GRACEFUL LINE OF THE CHIMNEY RISES FROM THE WALL OF BRICK AND STONE, AND ALSO THE MANNER IN WHICH THE STONE IS CARRIED PART WAY UP THE CHIMNEY SO THAT IT SHOWS IRREGULARLY HERE AND THERE.

BEAUTIFUL GARDEN GATES: THE CHARM THAT IS ALWAYS FOUND IN AN INTERESTING APPROACH TO AN ENCLOSURE

FEW people realize how much depends upon the approach to any given place. A pleasant entrance that rouses the interest and conveys some impression of individuality seems an earnest of pleasant things to come and is always associated in the memory with the anticipation that came from that first impression. Especially is this true of a garden gate, which for most of us holds a suggestion of sentiment and poetry because it is in its own way a symbol; it leads out to greater spaces or inward to more intimate beauty. Even to the most prosaic it always holds something of a promise of the peaceful and pleasant place that lies within. Thus it seems right that a garden gate should have a charm and grace all its own; that it should be embowered with trailing vines and blooming flowers in summer time and should always hold forth the inviting suggestion of pleasure and welcome beyond.

The illustrations given here are all of very simple garden gateways that are made attractive by the method of construction, by the placing of vines and flowers or by some graceful conceit in outline and relation to the surroundings. The hooded gate shown on this page forms a charming link between garden and garden. One may rest a moment within its shade and it seems to bind together the two plots of green divided by the fence. The trellised arbor and archway which spans the flower walk in an English garden is illustrated here because of the charming suggestion it contains for making a division between two parts of the same garden. The "pergola gate" shown below is illustrated without the vines that are meant to clothe it, because we desire to give a clear idea of the construction. The finely planned proportions of the heavy timbers and the straight unornamented lines suggest an inspiration from Japan. The vine covered rustic arbor which arches over the walk leading to the entrance of the house beyond is hardly a garden gate, yet it comes within the same class because it furnishes a most attractive approach to house and garden.

Published in The Craftsman, June, 1908.

A HOODED GATEWAY LEADING FROM ONE GARDEN TO ANOTHER. NOTE INTERESTING CONSTRUCTION OF THE ROOF AND THE WAY THE IDEA IS CARRIED OUT IN THE GATE AND THE FENCE.

Courtesy of John Lane Company.

ARBOR AND FLOWER WALK IN AN ENGLISH GARDEN, AFFORDING NOT ONLY A PLEASANT SUMMER RETREAT BUT ALSO A MOST ATTRACTIVE VISTA THROUGH THE LARGE GROUNDS.

Published in The Craftsman, June, 1908.

GATE WITH PERGOLA CONSTRUCTION OVERHEAD MEANT TO SERVE AS A SUPPORT FOR CLIMBING VINES

Published in The Craftsman, March, 1907.

HOMEMADE RUSTIC ARBOR, COVERED WITH CLIMBING ROSES AND HONEYSUCKLE, PLACED AT THE ENTRANCE OF THE WALK LEADING TO THE FRONT DOOR. ONE SUCH STRUCTURAL FEATURE AS THIS WOULD SERVE AS THE CENTRAL POINT OF INTEREST IN AN ENTIRE GARDEN.

Published in The Craftsman, March, 1907.

A VERY SIMPLE RUSTIC GATEWAY MADE OF TWO UPRIGHTS WITH CROSS-PIECES THAT SERVE AS A SUPPORT FOR VINES, AND A PEAKED HOOD OF THE SAME CONSTRUCTION, THE FENCE AND GATE ARE ALSO OF RUSTIC CONSTRUCTION. SUCH AN ENTRANCE ADDS A TOUCH OF DIGNITY AS WELL AS PICTURESQUENESS TO THE SIMPLEST GARDEN.

THE NATURAL GARDEN: SOME THINGS THAT CAN BE DONE WHEN NATURE IS FOLLOWED INSTEAD OF THWARTED

MAKING a garden is not unlike building a home, because the first thing to be considered is the creation of that indefinable feeling of restfulness and harmony which alone makes for permanence. Therefore, in planning a garden that we mean to live with all our lives, it is best to let Nature alone just as far as possible, following her suggestions and helping her to carry out her plans by adjusting our own to them, rather than attempting to introduce a conventional element into the landscape.

We have already explained in detail the importance of building a house so that it becomes a part of its natural surroundings; of planning it so that its form harmonizes with the general contour of the site upon which it stands and also of the surrounding country, and of using local materials and natural colors, wherever it is possible, so that the house may be brought into the closest relationship with its natural surroundings. But no matter how well planned the house may be, or how completely in keeping with the country, the climate and the life that is to be lived in it, the whole sense of home peace and comfort is gone if the garden is left to the mercy of the average gardener, whose chief ambition usually is to achieve trim walks, faultless flower-beds and neatly barbered shrubs, and whose appreciation of wild natural beauty is small.

To give a real sense of peace and satisfaction a garden must be a place in which we can wander and lounge, pick flowers at our will and invite our souls, and we can do none of these if we have the feeling that trees, shrubs and flowers were put there arbitrarily and according to a set, artificial pattern, instead of being allowed to grow up as Nature meant them to do. Therefore, knowing the vital importance of the right kind of garden to the general scheme, we have given here some examples of the natural treatment of moderate-sized grounds, trusting that they may be suggestive to home builders. The house shown in the illustrations was built by an artist out in a pasture lot and the garden that has been encouraged to grow up around it has more of the

Published in The Craftsman, January, 1908.

A HOME WHERE THE SURROUNDINGS HAVE BEEN LEFT AS NEARLY NATURAL AS POSSIBLE; THE DWELLING OF MR. FREDERICK STYMETZ LAMB.

Published in The Craftsman, June, 1908.

A FLIGHT OF STEPS WHICH HAVE BEEN CUT OUT FROM THE SIDE OF A HILL AND REINFORCED WITH HEAVY BOARDS ROUNDED AT THE EDGE. THE CURVING LINE OF THE STEPS, WHICH CONFORMS TO THE CONTOUR OF THE HILL, AND THE DRAPERY OF VINES AND NATURAL UNDERGROWTH THAT COVERS THE RUSTIC RAILING ON EITHER SIDE GIVES TO THIS APPROACH A RARE AND COMPELLING CHARM.

Published in The Craftsman, January, 1908.

AN EXAMPLE OF THE EFFECT PRODUCED BY THE LAVISH USE OF VINES UPON A HOUSE WHERE THEY NATURALLY BELONG. THE CONSTRUCTION OF COBBLESTONE AND ROUGH CEMENT SEEMS TO DEMAND JUST SUCH GRACIOUS DRAPERY TO BRING IT INTO STILL CLOSER RELATIONSHIP WITH ITS SURROUNDINGS.

Published in The Craftsman, January, 1908.

A GARDEN THAT HAS MUCH OF THE SIMPLE CHARM OF A PASTURE LOT. TREES ARE LEFT TO GROW ALMOST AS THEY WILL. ROCKS LIE ABOUT HERE AND THERE AS ON A HILLSIDE AND THE FLOWERS ARE OF THE RUGGED HARDY VARIETY THAT ARE QUITE AT HOME IN THIS CLIMATE.

THE NATURAL GARDEN

feeling of free woods and meadows than of a primly kept enclosure. The trees were thinned out just enough to allow plenty of air and sunshine and the sense of space that is so necessary, and, for the rest, were permitted to grow as they would. As Nature never makes a mistake in her groupings, the different varieties of trees fall into the picture in a way that could never be achieved by the most ingenious planting. Such shrubs and flowers as have been set out are of the more hardy varieties that belong to the climate and to the soil, and the vines that clamber over the low stone garden walls and curtain the walls of the house seem more to belong to the wild growths of the hillside than to have been planted by man. Where there is a path or a flight of steps the course of it is ruled by the contour of the ground so that the whole impression is that of Nature smoothed down in places and in others encouraged to do her very best.

These pictures, of course, are only suggestive, for in the very nature of things this kind of a garden cannot be made by rule, as no two places require or will admit the same treatment. The only way to obtain the effect desired is to cultivate the feeling of kinship with the open country and with growing things, and so to learn gradually to perceive the original plan. After that, all that is needed is to let things alone so far as arrangement goes, and to work in harmony with the thing that already exists.

Most fortunate is the home builder who can set his house out in the open where there is plenty of meadowland around it and an abundance of trees. If the ground happens to be uneven and hilly, so much the better, for the gardener has then the best of all possible foundations to start from and, if he be wise, he will leave it much as it is, clearing out a little here and there, planting such flowers and shrubs as seem to belong to the picture and allowing the paths to take the directions that would naturally be given to footpaths across the meadows or through the woods,—paths which invariably follow the line of the least resistance and so adapt themselves perfectly to the contour of the ground.

In connection with these garden pictures we give several illustrations of the effect of an abundant growth of vines over the walls of the house and around its foundations, and also show in one picture the result that can be obtained by allowing a fast growing vine to form a leafy shade to the porch that is used as an outdoor living room. The lattice construction of the roof admits plenty of sunlight.

Published in The Craftsman, December, 1907.

VINE COVERED PORCH THAT IS USED AS AN OUTDOOR LIVING ROOM AND THAT SEEMS MORE A PART OF THE GARDEN THAN OF THE HOUSE.

Published in The Craftsman, March, 1907.

AN OPEN SUMMER HOUSE WITH QUAINT THATCHED ROOF THAT FORMS AN INEXPENSIVE BUT MOST PICTURESQUE FEATURE IN A LARGE GARDEN, AND ALSO SERVES AS A PLAYHOUSE FOR THE CHILDREN.

WHAT MAY BE DONE WITH WATER AND ROCKS IN A LITTLE GARDEN

WE have to acknowledge our indebtedness to the Japanese for more inspiration in matters of art and architecture than most of us can realize, and in no department of art is the realization of subtle beauty that lies in simple and unobtrusive things more valuable to us as home makers than the suggestions they give us as to the arrangement of our gardens. With our national impulsiveness, we are too apt to go a step beyond the inspiration and attempt direct imitation, which is a pity, because the inevitable failure that must necessarily attend such mistaken efforts will do more than anything else to discourage people with the idea of trying to have a Japanese garden. But if we once get the idea into our heads that the secret of the whole thing lies in the exquisite sense of proportion that enables a Japanese to produce the effect of a whole landscape within the compass of a small yard, there is some hope of our being able to do the same thing in our own country and in our own way.

Our idea of a garden usually includes a profusion of flowers and ambitious-looking shrubs, but the Japanese is less obvious. He loves flowers and has many of them, but the typical Japanese garden is made up chiefly of stones, ferns, dwarf trees and above all water. It may be only a little water,—a tiny, trickling stream not so large as that which would flow from a small garden hose. But, given this little stream, the Japanese gardener,—or the American gardener who once grasps the Japanese idea,—can do wonders. He can take that little stream, which represents an amount of water costing at the outside about three dollars a month, and can so direct it that it pours over piles of rocks in tiny cascades, forming pool after pool, and finally shaping its course through a miniature river into a clear little lake. If it is a strictly Japanese garden, both river and lake will be bridged and the stream will have as many windings as possible, to give a chance for a number of bridges. Also it will have temple lanterns of stone, bronze storks and perhaps a tiny image of Buddha.

But in the American garden we need none of these things, unless indeed we have space enough so that a portion of the grounds may be devoted to a genuine Japanese garden like the one shown in the illustrations. This indeed might have been picked up in Japan and transplanted bodily to America, for it is the garden of Mr. John S. Bradstreet, of Minneapolis, who is a lover of all things Japanese and has been in Japan many times. This garden occupies a space little more than one hundred feet in diameter, and yet the two illustrations we give are only glimpses of its varied charm. They are chosen chiefly because they illustrate the use that can be made of a small stream of water so placed that it trickles over a pile of rocks. The effect produced is that of a mountain glen, and so perfect are the proportions and so harmonious the arrangement that there is no sense of incongruity in the fact that the whole thing is on such a small scale.

Where people have only a small garden, say in the back yard of a city home or in some nook that can be spared from the front lawn, an experiment with the possibilities of rocks, ferns and a small stream of water would bring rich returns. We need no temple lanterns or images of Buddha in this country, but we do need the kind of garden that brings to our minds the recollection of mountain brooks, wooded ravines and still lakes, and while it takes much thought, care and training of one's power of observation and adjustment to get it, the question of space is not one that has to be considered, and the expense is almost nothing at all.

The thing to be most avoided is imitation either of the Japanese models from which we take the suggestion for our own little gardens or of the scenery of which they are intended to remind us. It is safest to regard such gardens merely as an endeavor on our part to create something that will call into life the emotion or memory we wish to perpetuate.

All these suggestions are for a small garden such as would naturally belong to a city or suburban house, but if such effects can be produced here in a corner and by artificial means, it is easy to imagine what could be done with large and naturally irregular grounds, say on a hillside, or where a natural brook wound its way through the garden, giving every opportunity for the picturesque effects that could be created by very simple treatment of the banks, by a bridge or a pool here and there and by a little adjustment of the rocks lying around.

Courtesy of Country Life in America.

A PART OF A JAPANESE GARDEN OWNED BY MR. JOHN S. BRADSTREET, OF MINNEAPOLIS. AN EXCELLENT EXAMPLE OF HOW ROCKS, DWARF TREES AND A TINY STREAM OF WATER MAY BE USED TO MAKE A HIGHLY DECORATIVE EFFECT.

Courtesy of Country Life in America.

ANOTHER PART OF MR. BRADSTREET'S GARDEN, SHOWING BRIDGES MADE OF WATER-WORN TEAKWOOD TAKEN FROM AN OLD JUNK. THE FOUNTAIN, PILE OF ROCKS AND DWARF TREES ARE SEEN FROM A DIFFERENT ANGLE.

Courtesy of Country Life in America.

EXAMPLE OF WHAT MAY BE DONE WITH A VERY SMALL SUPPLY OF WATER. THE POOL HERE IS FED SOLELY BY A TINY STREAM WHICH ISSUES FROM THE DRAGON'S MOUTH AND FORMS A SLENDER CASCADE OVER THE ROCKS.

Courtesy of Country Life in America.

REST HOUSE AND POOL IN MR. BRADSTREET'S JAPANESE GARDEN, SHOWING TEMPLE LANTERN, SMALL IMAGE OF BUDDHA AND THE EFFECT OF ROCKS AROUND THE MARGIN FRAMING THE AQUATIC PLANTS IN THE POOL.

Published in The Craftsman, October, 1904.

VIEW OF THE GARDEN ENTIRE, SHOWING WHAT A SMALL SPACE IN THE YARD IS OCCUPIED BY AN ARRANGEMENT WHICH GIVES THE AMAZING EFFECTS SHOWN IN THE PRECEDING ILLUSTRATIONS.

HALLS AND STAIRWAYS: THEIR IMPORTANCE IN THE GENERAL SCHEME OF A CRAFTSMAN HOUSE

WITH the general adoption of the simpler and more sensible ideas of house building that have come to the front in late years, the hall seems to be returning to its old-time dignity as one of the important rooms of the house. Instead of the small dark passageway, with just room enough for the hat tree and the stairs, that we have long been familiar with in American houses, we have now the large reception hall with its welcoming fireplace and comfortable furnishings,—as inviting a room as any in the house. There is even a suggestion of the "great hall of the castle," where in bygone days all indoor life centered, in the ever-increasing popularity of the plan which throws hall, living room and dining room into one large irregular room, divided only by the decorative post-and-panel construction that we so frequently use to indicate a partition, or by large screens that serve temporarily to shut off one part or another if privacy should be required. In this main room all guests are received, all the meals are served and the greater part of the family life is carried on. Even where this plan is not adopted and the rooms of the lower story are completely separated from one another, the large reception hall is still counted as one of the principal rooms of the house, and what used to be considered the entrance or stair hall is now either absent entirely or treated as a vestibule; generally curtained off from the reception hall or living room into which it opens in order to prevent drafts from the entrance door.

Whether it be a large or small reception hall, or an entrance only large enough for the stairs and the passageway from the front door to the other rooms in the house, the hall is always worthy of careful consideration as to structural features and color scheme, for it gives the first impression of the whole house. It is the preface to all the rest and in a well planned house it strikes the keynote of the whole scheme of interior decoration. Above all things, the hall ought to convey the suggestion of welcome and repose. In a cold climate, or if placed on the shady side of the house, it is worth any pains to have the hall well lighted and airy and the color scheme rich and warm. It is the first impression of a house that influences the visitor and the sight of a cheerless vista upon entering chills any appreciation of subsequent effects. With a sunny exposure, or in a country where heat has to be reckoned with for the greater part

Published in The Craftsman, January, 1906.

A TYPICAL CRAFTSMAN STAIRWAY WITH LANDING USED AS A STRUCTURAL FEATURE OF THE RECEPTION HALL. THIS IS AN EXCELLENT EXAMPLE OF THE POST-AND-PANEL CONSTRUCTION WHICH IS SO OFTEN USED TO INDICATE THE DIVISION BETWEEN TWO ROOMS.

Published in The Craftsman, November, 1906.

AN UPPER HALL WHICH IS FITTED UP FOR USE AS A SEWING ROOM, STUDY, OR PLAYROOM, ACCORDING TO THE USE FOR WHICH IT IS MOST NEEDED. SUCH AN UPSTAIRS RETREAT IS DELIGHTFUL IN A HOUSE WHERE THE ARRANGEMENT OF THE WHOLE LOWER STORY IS OPEN, AS IT AFFORDS A MORE OR LESS SECLUDED PLACE FOR WORK OR STUDY AND YET HAS THE FREEDOM AND AIRINESS OF A LARGE SPACE.

HALLS AND STAIRWAYS

of the year rather than cold, an effect of restful shadiness and coolness is quite as inviting in its way, although it is always safe to avoid a cold color scheme for a hall, as the suggestion it conveys is invariably repellent rather than welcoming.

In England the large hall designed for the general gathering place of the family is a feature in nearly every moderately large house, particularly in the country. These English halls are always roomy and comfortable and in many cases are both picturesque and sumptuous in effect, having a certain rich stateliness that seems to have descended in direct line from the great hall of old baronial days. In this country the hall is more apt to be a part of the living room, and, while quite as homelike and inviting, is simpler in style.

The illustration on page 125 shows the part of a Craftsman reception hall that contains the stairway. A small den or lounging room is formed by the deep recess that appears at one side of the staircase, which is central in position and is completely masked, excepting the lower steps and the landing, by the post construction above the solid wainscot that surrounds it. This wainscot turns outward to the width of a single panel at either side of the stair, one sheltering the end of the seat built in at the right side and the other partially dividing off the recess to the left. So arranged, the staircase forms an important part of the decorative treatment of the room.

The second illustration shows an upstairs hall, which has somewhat the effect of a gallery, as it is open to the stairway except for a low balustrade. This nook in the upper hall takes the place of a sewing room or an upstairs sitting room, and is infinitely more attractive because of the freedom and openness of the arrangement. While not in any sense a separate room, it still allows a certain seclusion

Published in The Craftsman, January, 1906.

A STAIRWAY THAT RUNS DIRECTLY UP FROM THE LIVING ROOM AND IS USED AS A PART OF THE STRUCTURAL DECORATION. NOTE THE LAMP ON THE NEWEL POST WHICH GIVES LIGHT TO THE SEAT BELOW AND THE WAY IN WHICH THE WINDOW ON THE LANDING CARRIES OUT THE LINE OF THE UPPER WALL SPACE.

Published in The Craftsman, January, 1906.

RECEPTION HALL AND STAIRCASE WHERE THE LANDING PROJECTS INTO THE ROOM ALMOST DIRECTLY OPPOSITE THE ENTRANCE DOOR. THIS HALL IN MOST CRAFTSMAN HOUSES IS LITTLE MORE THAN A NOOK IN THE LIVING ROOM.

for anyone who wishes to read, work or study.

The third illustration shows another Craftsman reception hall in which the staircase is the prominent structural feature. The double casements light stair and landing and also add considerably to the light in the room. Just below the stair is a comfortable seat with the radiator hidden below, and a coat closet fills the space between the seat and the wall.

A larger hall that is emphatically a part of the living room is seen in the last illustration. Here there is no vestibule and the wide entrance door with the small square panes in the upper part belong to the structural decoration of the room. Additional light is given from the same side by the row of casements recessed to leave a wide ledge for plants. The ceiling is beamed and the whole construction of the room is satisfying, although interest at once centers upon the staircase as the prominent structural feature. This is in the center of the room and has a large square landing approached by three shallow steps. The stairs run up toward the right at the turn and the space between steps and ceiling is filled with slim square uprights, two on each step, which give the effect of a grille, very open and very decorative. Opposite the stair on the landing is a railing about the height of a wainscot with posts above. Treated in this manner, the staircase seems intended as much for beauty as for utility, and so fulfills its manifest destiny in the Craftsman decorative scheme.

In a small house there are often many considerations which prevent the use of the hall as a living room. Many people object to the draughts and waste of heat entailed by the open stairway and prefer a living room quite separate from the entrance to the house. In this case it is better to omit the reception hall and to have merely a small entrance hall, rather than the compromise that contains no possibility of comfort and yet is crammed with all the features that belong in the larger hall intended for general use. An entrance hall of this kind may be made very attractive and inviting by the wise selection of the woodwork and color scheme and by care in the designing of the stairway, which of course is the principal structural feature in any hall.

THE LIVING ROOM: ITS MANY USES AND THE POSSIBILITIES IT HAS FOR COMFORT AND BEAUTY

UNQUESTIONABLY the most important room in the house is the living room, and in a small or medium sized dwelling this room, with the addition of a small hall or vestibule and a well-planned kitchen, is all that is needed on the first floor. A large and simply furnished living room, where the business of home life may be carried on freely and with pleasure, may well occupy all the space that is ordinarily partitioned into small rooms conventionally planned to meet supposed requirements. It is the executive chamber of the household, where the family life centers and from which radiates that indefinable home influence that shapes at last the character of the nation and the age. In the living room of the home,

more than in almost any other place, is felt the influence of material things. It is a place where work is to be done and it is also the haven of rest for the worker. It is the place where children grow and thrive and gain their first impressions of life and of the world. It is the place to which a man comes home when his day's work is done and where he expects to find himself comfortable and at ease in surroundings that are in harmony with his daily life, thought and pursuits.

In creating a home atmosphere, the thing that pays and pays well is honesty. A house should be the outward and visible expression of the life, work and thought of its inmates. In its planning and furnishing, the station in life of its owner should be expressed in a

Published in The Craftsman, April, 1907.

CHIMNEYPIECE AND FIRESIDE SEATS IN A TYPICAL CRAFTSMAN LIVING ROOM. THE CHIMNEYPIECE IS PANELED WITH DULL-FINISHED GRUEBY TILES BANDED WITH WROUGHT IRON HELD IN PLACE BY COPPER RIVETS. THE FIREPLACE HOOD IS OF COPPER AND THE PANELING OF SEATS AND WAINSCOT IS IN FUMED OAK.

Published in The Craftsman, December, 1905.

A LIVING ROOM WHICH IS ALSO USED FOR LIBRARY AND WORK ROOM. NOTE THE WAY IN WHICH THE DESK WITH ITS DRAWERS AND PIGEON HOLES IS BUILT INTO THE WALL SO THAT IT FORMS A PART OF THE BOOKCASE. THE LONG ROW OF CASEMENTS WITH THE WINDOW SEAT BELOW NOT ONLY FLOODS THE ROOM WITH LIGHT BUT FORMS A DECORATIVE FEATURE OF THE CONSTRUCTION.

THE LIVING ROOM

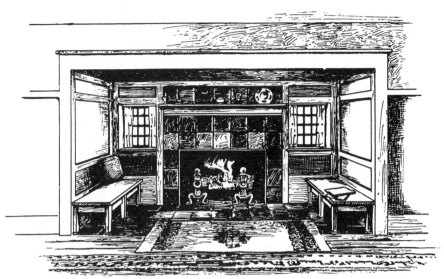

Published in The Craftsman, December, 1905.

A FIRESIDE NOOK THAT IS DEEPLY RECESSED FROM THE LIVING ROOM. THE CEILING OF THE NOOK IS MUCH LOWER THAN THAT OF THE MAIN ROOM, GIVING AN EFFECT OF COMFORT THAT IS HARD TO OBTAIN IN ANY OTHER WAY.

dignified manner, not disguised. If servants cannot be afforded without too heavy a tax upon the family finances, build the house so that it is convenient to get along without them. It is astonishing how easy the care of a house can be made by the simple process of eliminating unnecessary things. The right kind of a home does not drag out all that there is in a man to keep it going, nor is the care of it too heavy a burden upon a woman. It should be so planned that it meets, in the most straightforward manner, the actual requirements of those who live in it, and so furnished that the work of keeping it in order is reduced to a minimum.

It is the first conception of a room that decides whether it is to be a failure or a success as a place to live in, for in this lies the character that is to be uniquely its own. In every house, however, modest, there can be a

Published in The Craftsman, December, 1905.

CORNER OF A LIVING ROOM THAT IS ALSO USED AS A WORK ROOM. THE PANELING ON EITHER SIDE OF THE CHIM-NEYPIECE EXTENDS TO THE CEILING SO THAT THE ENTIRE WALL SPACE IS LINED WITH WOOD.

Published in The Craftsman, July, 1906.

CHIMNEYPIECE IN A MODERATE SIZED LIVING ROOM WHERE THE WALL TREATMENT ALLOWS THE INTRODUCTION OF A SHADOWY LANDSCAPE FRIEZE. THIS BEING SO DEFINITELY DECORATIVE, THE WALL SPACES BELOW ARE LEFT ABSOLUTELY PLAIN AND THE STRUCTURAL FEATURES ARE ALSO SEVERELY SIMPLE IN CHARACTER.

THE LIVING ROOM

living room that shows an individuality possessed by no other, an individuality that is actually a part of the place, if the room be planned to meet the real needs of those who are to live in it and to turn to the best advantage the conditions surrounding it. These conditions are as many as there are rooms. The situation and surroundings of the plot of ground on which a house is built has much to do with the position of the living room in the plan of that house. As

Published in The Craftsman, February, 1902.

A RECESSED WINDOW SEAT THAT WOULD SERVE FOR ANY ROOM IN THE HOUSE.

it is the principal room, it should have an exposure which insures plenty of sunlight for the greater part of the day and also the pleasantest outlook possible to the situation. Both of these considerations, as well as the best arrangement of wall spaces, govern the placing of the windows and of outside doors, which may open into the veranda, the sun room, or the garden.

The structural variations of the living room are endless, as they are dominated by the tastes and needs of each separate family. If

the room is to be a permanently satisfying place to live in, nothing short of the exercise of individual thought and care in its arrangement will give the result. But one thing must be kept in mind if the room is to be satisfactory as a whole, and that is, to provide a central point of interest around which the entire place is built, decorated and furnished, for it gives the keynote both as to structure and color scheme. It may be a well planned fireplace, either recessed or built in the ordinary manner, with fireside seats, bookcases,

Published in The Craftsman, October, 1905.

A RECESSED FIREPLACE NOOK IN A ROOM WHERE THE WOODWORK IS LIGHT AND FINE AND THE PANELED WALL SPACES ARE COVERED WITH SOME FABRIC SUCH AS SILK, CANVAS, OR JAPANESE GRASS CLOTH.

THE LIVING ROOM

Published in The Craftsman, February, 1907.

A CHARACTERISTIC CRAFTSMAN INTERIOR, SHOWING THE ENTRANCE HALL, STAIRCASE AND LANDING AND A PART OF THE LIVING ROOM. NOTE THE WAY IN WHICH THE LINE OF THE MANTEL SHELF IS CARRIED THE WHOLE LENGTH OF THE WALL BY THE TOPS OF THE BUILT-IN BOOKCASES AND HOW IT IS FINISHED BY THE BALUSTRADE OF THE STAIR LANDING. ALSO NOTE THE MANNER IN WHICH THE ENTRANCE HALL IS DIVIDED FROM THE LIVING ROOM SO THAT ITS SEPARATENESS IS INDICATED WITHOUT DESTROYING THE SENSE OF SPACE WHICH MEANS SO MUCH TO THE BEAUTY OF THE MAIN ROOM.

Published in The Craftsman, November, 1905.

BUILT-IN CHINA CLOSETS ON EITHER SIDE OF THE FIREPLACE IN A LIVING ROOM WHICH IS ALSO USED AS A DINING ROOM. BY A SLIGHT DIFFERENCE IN ARRANGEMENT THE CUPBOARDS ABOVE COULD BE MADE TO SERVE AS BOOKCASES AND THOSE BELOW AS STORAGE PLACES FOR PAPERS, MAGAZINES AND THE LIKE.

THE LIVING ROOM

cupboards, shelves, or high casement windows so arranged as to be an integral part of the structure. The chimneypiece strikes a rich color-note with its bricks or tiles and glowing copper hood, and the woodwork, wall spaces and decorative scheme are naturally brought into harmony with it. Or perhaps the dominant feature may be the staircase, with its broad landing and well-designed balustrade; or it may be a group of windows so placed that it makes possible just the right arrangement of the wall spaces and commands the best of the view. Or if living room and dining room are practically one, the main point of interest may be a sideboard, either built into a recess or, with its cupboards on either side and a row of casement windows above, occupying the entire end of the room.

Any commanding feature in the structure of the room itself will naturally take its place as this center of interest; if there are several, the question of relative importance will be easily settled, for there can be only one dominant point in a well planned room. The English thoroughly understand the importance of this and the charm of their houses depends largely upon the skilful arrangement of interesting structural features around one center of attention to which everything else is subordinate. Also the English understand the charm of the recess in a large room. Their feeling regarding it is well expressed by a prominent English architect of the new school who writes: "Many people have a feeling that there is a certain cosiness in a small room entirely unattainable in a large room; this is a mistake altogether; quite the reverse has been my experience, which is, that such a sense

Published in The Craftsman, April, 1907.

FIREPLACE IN A LIVING ROOM. THE SQUARE MASSIVE CHIMNEYPIECE IS BUILT OF HARD-BURNED RED BRICK LAID UP IN DARK MORTAR WITH WIDE JOINTS. THE MANTEL SHELF AS ILLUSTRATED HERE IS OF RED CEMENT, BUT A THICK OAK PLANK WOULD BE EQUALLY EFFECTIVE. THE HOOD IS OF COPPER AND THE FIREPLACE IS BANDED WITH WROUGHT IRON. THE PANELING ABOVE THE BOOKCASES GIVES AN INTERESTING DIVISION OF THE WALL SPACES.

THE LIVING ROOM

of cosiness as can be got in the recesses of a large room can never be attained in a small one. But if your big room is to be comfortable, it must have recesses. There is a great charm in a room broken up in plan, where that slight feeling of mystery is given to it which arises when you cannot see the whole room from any one place in which you are likely to sit; when there is always something around the corner."

Where it is possible, the structural features that actually exist in the framework should be shown and made ornamental, for a room that is structurally interesting and in which the woodwork and color scheme are good has a satisfying quality that is not dependent upon pictures or bric-a-brac and needs but little in the way of furnishings.

Only such furniture as is absolutely necessary should be permitted in such a room, and that should be simple in character and made to harmonize with the woodwork in color and finish. From first to last the room should be treated as a whole. Such furniture as is needed for constant use may be so placed that it leaves plenty of free space in the room and when once placed it should be left alone. Nothing so much disturbs the much desired home atmosphere as to make frequent changes in the disposition of the furniture so that the general aspect of the room is undergoing continual alteration. If the room is right in the first place, it cannot be as satisfactorily arranged in any other way. Everything in it should fall into place as if it had grown there before the room is pronounced complete.

Published in The Craftsman, January, 1906.

WINDOW SEAT IN A LIVING ROOM. THE GROUP OF WINDOWS WITH THE SEAT BELOW EXTENDS ACROSS THE ENTIRE END OF THE ROOM AND THE TWO ENDS OF THE SEAT ARE FORMED BY THE SMALL SQUARE BOOKCASES BUILT INTO THE CORNERS.

THE DINING ROOM AS A CENTER OF HOSPITALITY AND GOOD CHEER

NEXT to the living room the most important division of the lower floor of a house is the dining room. The living room is the gathering place of the household, the place for work as well as for pleasure and rest; but the dining room is the center of hospitality and good cheer, the place for in a carefully planned house the work of the household is made as easy as possible. Hence it goes without saying that the dining room should be placed in such relation to the kitchen that the work of serving meals goes on with no friction and with as few steps as possible. A noiseless and well fitted swing

Published in The Craftsman, January, 1906.

CRAFTSMAN DINING ROOM WITH SIDEBOARD BUILT INTO A RECESS AND SURMOUNTED BY FOUR CASEMENT WINDOWS. NOTE HOW THE GROUPING OF THE WINDOWS IS REPEATED AT THE END OF THE ROOM.

that should hold a special welcome for guests and home folk alike. Instead of being planned to fulfil manifold functions like the living room, it has one definite use and purpose and no disturbing element should be allowed to creep in.

In planning a dining room two considerations take equal rank,—convenience and cheerfulness. Convenience must come first, door serves as a complete bar against sounds and odors from the kitchen, even if the connection be direct. If a butler's pantry should be preferred for convenience in serving, it would naturally be placed between the kitchen and the dining room. Much time and many steps are saved also if the principal china cupboard is built in the wall between the dining room and kitchen or butler's pantry, with

THE DINING ROOM

Published in The Craftsman, October, 1905.

DINING ROOM WITH DISH CUPBOARD BUILT INTO THE WALL SO THAT THE DOORS ARE FLUSH WITH THE SURFACE. THE SIDEBOARD IN THIS CASE IS MOVABLE AND THE REMAINDER OF THE WALL SPACE BELOW THE FRIEZE IS TAKEN UP BY A PICTURE WINDOW IN WHICH ARE ACCENTED THE COLORS THAT PREVAIL IN THE DECORATION OF THE ROOM.

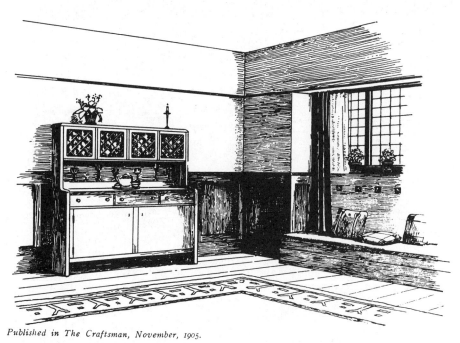

Published in The Craftsman, November, 1905.

RECESSED WINDOW AND SEAT IN A DINING ROOM. AN UNUSUALLY QUAINT EFFECT IS GIVEN BY THE SMALL LEADED PANES OF GLASS AND THE BROAD WINDOW LEDGE FOR HOLDING PLANTS.

THE DINING ROOM

Published in The Craftsman, December, 1905.

SIDEBOARD BUILT INTO A RECESS WITH DISH CUPBOARDS ON EITHER SIDE. SQUARE MATT-FINISHED TILES ARE USED TO FILL IN THE PANELS ABOVE THESE CUPBOARDS AND THE SPACE BETWEEN THE TOP OF THE SIDEBOARD AND THE WINDOW LEDGE.

Published in The Craftsman, November, 1905.

WINDOW EXTENDING THE WHOLE WIDTH OF A DINING ROOM AND INTENDED FOR AN EXPOSURE WHERE THERE IS AN ESPECIALLY FINE VIEW.

THE DINING ROOM

doors opening on both sides so that dishes may be put away after washing without the necessity of carrying them into the dining room. Such an arrangement results in a great saving of broken china as well as in added convenience. This kind of a china cupboard may be made very decorative by putting small-paned or leaded glass doors on the dining room side and treating the wooden doors at the back like the wood trim of the room, which makes an effective setting for the china.

of cheerfulness may be given by the warmth of color in the room. A richness and decision of wall coloring that would grow wearisome in a room lived in all the time has all the pleasant and enlivening effects of a change when seen occasionally in a dining room. If the dining room is to be a part of the living room, it is well to plan it as one would a large recess. In that case the color scheme should, of course, be in close harmony with that of the living room; but even then it may strike a stronger

Published in The Craftsman, November, 1905.

ANOTHER FORM OF BUILT-IN SIDEBOARD WITH LINEN DRAWERS ON EITHER SIDE. THIS IS INTENDED TO FILL THE WHOLE SPACE ACROSS THE END OF THE DINING ROOM.

If possible, the dining room should have an exposure that gives it plenty of light as well as air. The windows play such an important part in the decoration of a room that a pleasant outlook is greatly to be desired. The brilliance of a sunny exposure may always be tempered by a cool and restful color scheme in walls and woodwork. On the other hand, if the room has a shady exposure and threatens to be somber on dark days, an atmosphere

and more vivid note in the walls, while the woodwork remains uniform throughout. A large screen placed in the opening of the recess may be made very decorative if it serve as a link in the color scheme as well as the leading element in that pleasant little sense of mystery that always accompanies a glimpse of something partially unseen.

Nowhere more than in the dining room is evidenced the value of structural features.

THE DINING ROOM

Almost all the decorative quality of the room depends upon them. In addition to wainscot and ceiling beams,—or instead of them if the room be differently planned,—the charm of well placed windows, large and small; of built-in cupboards, sideboards and cabinets for choice treasures of rare china or cut glass; of shelves and plate rack; of window ledge and window seat; and above all of a big cheery fireplace, is as never-ending as the ingenuity which gives to each really beautiful room exactly what it needs. And always it should be remembered that, in the dining room as in the living room, there should be one central structural feature which dominates all the rest.

Some examples of these ruling features are given in the accompanying illustrations. In one there is the wide sideboard built into a recess surmounted by three casement windows and flanked by a small china cupboard on either side. In another a wide window is recessed, giving a broad ledge for the growing things that always add beauty and life to a room. Still another recessed window shows a row of small-paned casements with plant ledge and a well cushioned seat below.

Published in The Craftsman, July, 1906.

A GROUP OF CRAFTSMAN SHOWER LIGHTS SWINGING FROM A BEAM OVER A LONG DINING TABLE. THIS IS ONE OF THE MOST EFFECTIVE METHODS WE HAVE FOUND OF MANAGING THE LIGHTS IN A DINING ROOM.

A CONVENIENT AND WELL-EQUIPPED KITCHEN THAT SIMPLIFIES THE HOUSEWORK

EACH room in the house has its distinct and separate function in the domestic economy. Therefore it should be remembered that before any room can attain its own distinctive individuality everything put into it must be there for some reason and must serve a definite purpose in the life that is to be lived and the work that is to be done in that room. Take for example the kitchen, where the food for the household must be prepared and where a large part of the work of the house must be done. This is the room where the housewife or the servant maid must be for the greater part of her

good fortune to associate such a room with their earliest recollections of home. No child ever lived who could resist the attraction of such a room, for a child has, in all its purity, the primitive instinct for living that ruled the simpler and more wholesome customs of other days. In these times of more elaborate surroundings the home life of the family is hidden behind a screen and the tendency is to belittle that part of the household work by regarding it as a necessary evil. Even in a small house the tendency too often is to make the kitchen the dump heap of the whole household, a place in which to do what cooking and

Published in The Craftsman, September, 1905.

CORNER OF THE KITCHEN SHOWING BUILT-IN CUPBOARD AND SINK.

time day after day, and the very first requisites are that it should be large enough for comfort, well ventilated and full of sunshine, and that the equipment for the work that is to be done should be ample, of good quality and, above all, intelligently selected. We all know the pleasure of working with good tools and in congenial surroundings; no more things than are necessary should be tolerated in the kitchen and no fewer should be required.

We cannot imagine a more homelike room than the old New England kitchen, the special realm of the housewife and the living room of the whole family. Its spotless cleanliness and homely cheer are remembered as long as life lasts by men and women who have had the

dishwashing must be done and to get out of as soon as possible. In such a house there is invariably a small, cheap and often stuffy dining room, as cramped and comfortless as the kitchen and yet regarded as an absolute necessity in the household economy. Such an arrangement is the result of sacrificing the old-time comfort for a false idea of elegance and its natural consequence is the loss of both.

In the farmhouse and the cottage of the workingman, where the domestic machinery is comparatively simple, cheerful and homelike, the kitchen,—which is also the dining room of the family and one of its pleasantest gathering places,—should be restored to all its old-time comfort and convenience. In

A CONVENIENT AND WELL-EQUIPPED KITCHEN

planning such a house it should come in for the first thought instead of the last and its use as a dining room as well as a kitchen should be carefully considered. The hooded range should be so devised that all odors of cooking are carried off and the arrangement and ventilation should be such that this is one of the best aired and sunniest of all the rooms in the house.

Where social relations and the demands of a more complex life make it impossible for the house mistress to do her own work and the kitchen is necessarily more separated from the rest of the household, it may easily be planned to meet the requirements of the case without losing any of its comfort, convenience, or suitability for the work that is to be done in it. Modern science has made the task very easy by the provision of electric lights, open plumbing, laundry conveniences, and hot and cold running water, so that the luxuries of the properly arranged modern kitchen would have been almost unbelievable a generation ago. Even if the kitchen is for the servant only, it should be a place in which she may take some personal pride. It is hardly going too far to say that the solution of the problem of the properly arranged kitchen would come near to being the solution also of the domestic problem.

The properly planned kitchen should be as open as possible to prevent the accumulation of dirt. Without the customary "glory holes" that sink and other closets often become, gen-

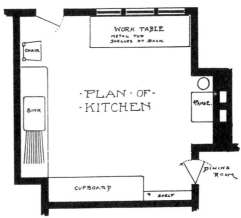

FLOOR PLAN.

uine cleanliness is much easier to preserve and the appearance of outside order is not at all lessened. In no part of the house does the good old saying, "a place for everything and everything in its place," apply with more force than in the kitchen. Ample cupboard space for all china should be provided near the sink to do away with unnecessary handling and the same cupboard, which should be an actual structural feature of the kitchen, should contain drawers for table linen, cutlery and smaller utensils, as well as a broad shelf which provides a convenient place for serving. The floor should be of cement and the same material may be used in tiled pattern for a high wainscot, giving a cleanly and pleasant effect.

Published in The Craftsman, September, 1905.

RANGE SET IN A RECESS TO BE OUT OF THE WAY AND WORK TABLE PLACED JUST BELOW A GROUP OF WINDOWS.

THE TREATMENT OF WALL SPACES SO THAT A ROOM IS IN ITSELF COMPLETE AND SATISFYING

SO much of the success of any scheme of interior decoration or furnishing depends upon the right treatment of the wall spaces that we deem it best to take up this subject more in detail than it has been possible to do in the general descriptions of the houses or even of the separate rooms.

It goes without saying that we like the friendly presence of much wood and are very

practical value in the life of the household, as such furnishings mean great convenience, economy of space and the doing away with many pieces of furniture which might otherwise be really needed, but which might give the appearance of crowding that is so disturbing to the restfulness of a room.

When the walls are rightly treated, it is amazing how little furniture and how few or-

Published in The Craftsman, October, 1904.

A HIGH WAINSCOT MADE WITH RECESSES TO HOLD CHOICE BITS OF METAL OR EARTHENWARE. THIS IS ESPECIALLY BEAUTIFUL IF CARRIED OUT IN CHESTNUT OR GUMWOOD TREATED IN THE CRAFTSMAN MANNER.

sensible of the charm of beams, wainscots and built-in furnishings which are a part of the house itself and so serve to link it closer to the needs of daily life. Bare wall spaces, or those covered with pictures and draperies which are put there merely for the purpose of covering them, are very hard to live with. But wall spaces that provide bookcases, cupboards, built-in seats for windows, fireside and other nooks are used in a way that not only gives to them the kind of beauty and interest which is theirs by right, but makes them of

naments and pictures are required to make a room seem comfortable and homelike. The treatment of wall spaces in itself may seem but a detail, yet it is the keynote not only of the whole character of the house but of the people who live in it. We hear much criticism of the changing and remodeling which is deemed necessary every year or two because a house must be "brought up to date" or because the owners "grow so tired of seeing one thing all the time." Yet both of these reasons are absolutely valid so far as they go, for the

THE TREATMENT OF WALL SPACES

majority of houses are in themselves so uninteresting that it is little wonder that the people who live in them have always a sense of restlessness and discontent, and that they are always doing something different in the hope that eventually they may find the thing which satisfies them.

We believe that the time to put thought into the decoration of a home is when we first begin to draw up the plans, and that the first consideration in each room should be the adjustment of the wall spaces so that there is not a foot of barren or ill-proportioned space in the entire room. It is true that utility and the limitations of the plan are necessarily the first considerations; that the ceilings of all the rooms on one story must be of uniform height in a house where the expense of construction is a thing to be considered; that windows must be placed where they will admit the most light and that doors are meant to serve as means of communication between rooms or with the outer world. Yet working strictly within these limitations, it is quite possible to adjust the height of each room so

Published in The Craftsman, June, 1905.
WALL DIVIDED INTO PANELS BY STRIPS OF WOOD.

that, no matter what may be its floor space, to all appearances its proportions are entirely harmonious; to place doors and windows so that, instead of being mere holes in the wall, they become a part of the whole structural scheme, and to see that in shape and proportions as well as in position they come into entire harmony with the rest of the room.

Published in The Craftsman, October, 1907.

LOW WAINSCOT WITH BROAD PANELS. NOTE THE PLACING OF THE WINDOW SO THAT IT REALLY FORMS A DECORATIVE PANEL IN THE WALL SPACE ABOVE.

THE TREATMENT OF WALL SPACES

Published in The Craftsman, June, 1905.

ATTRACTIVE TREATMENT OF WALLS IN A BEDROOM OR WOMAN'S SITTING ROOM.

Naturally, in considering the treatment of the wall spaces, the most important feature is the woodwork, especially if the room is to be wainscoted. Where this is possible, we would always recommend it, particularly for the living rooms of a house, as no other treatment of the walls gives such a sense of friendliness, mellowness and permanence as does a generous quantity of woodwork. The larger illustra-

tions reproduced here give some idea of what we mean and of what may be done with wall spaces when it is possible to use much wood in the shape of wainscot and beams. It will be noted that in each case the wall is of the same height; yet owing to the treatment of the spaces, each one appears to be different. Also note the way in which windows, doors and fireplace form an integral part of the structural scheme and how they are balanced by the wall spaces around them so that the whole effect is rather that of a well planned scheme of structural decoration than of the introduction of a purely utilitarian feature.

When we speak of the friendliness of woodwork, however, we mean woodwork that is so finished that the friendly quality is apparent, —which is never the case when it is painted or stained in some solid color that is foreign to the wood itself, or is given a smooth glassy polish that reflects the light. When this is done the peculiar quality of woodiness, upon which all the charm of interior woodwork depends, is entirely destroyed and any other material might as well be used in the place of it. In a later chapter we purpose to deal more

Published in The Craftsman, October, 1907.

TREATMENT OF WAINSCOTED WALL IN A LIVING ROOM WHERE THE PANELING IS REPEATED IN THE FRIEZE AND THE FIREPLACE IS PERFECTLY PROPORTIONED IN RELATION TO THE WALL SPACES ON EITHER SIDE.

THE TREATMENT OF WALL SPACES

Published in The Craftsman, August, 1905.

TREATMENT OF WALLS IN A NURSERY. PLAIN ROUGH PLASTER BELOW AND A SHADOWY SUGGESTION OF A FOREST IN THE FRIEZE. BY THIS ARRANGEMENT THE SURFACE OF THE LOWER WALL IS EASILY KEPT CLEAN AND YET ALL APPEARANCE OF BARRENNESS IS AVOIDED.

Published in The Craftsman, August, 1905.

ANOTHER SUGGESTION FOR THE TREATMENT OF NURSERY WALLS, SHOWING A PICTURE DADO ILLUSTRATING NURSERY TALES AND A BLACKBOARD BUILT INTO THE WAINSCOT WITHIN EASY REACH OF THE LITTLE ONES.

THE TREATMENT OF WALL SPACES

fully with the question of finishing interior woodwork so that all its natural qualities of color, texture and grain are brought out by a process which ripens and mellows the wood as if by age without changing its character at all. Here it is sufficient to say that any of our native woods that have open texture, strong grain and decided figure,—such as oak, chestnut, cypress, ash, elm or the redwood so much used on the Pacific coast,—are entirely suitable for the woodwork of rooms in general use, and that each one of them may be so finished that its inherent color quality is brought out and its surface made pleasantly smooth without sacrificing the woody quality that comes from frankly revealing its natural texture.

The first illustration (page 144) shows a wainscot that is peculiarly Craftsman in design. The panels are very broad and what would be the stiles in ordinary paneling are even broader. At the top of each panel is a niche in which may be set some choice bit of pottery or metal work that is shown to the best advantage by the wood behind it and that serves to give the accents or high lights to the whole color scheme of the room. The

Published in The Craftsman, June, 1905.
TREATMENT OF PLAIN WALLS WITH LANDSCAPE FRIEZE.

wall space above is of plain sand-finished plaster that may either be left in the natural gray or treated with a coat of shellac or wax which carries the color desired. The rough texture of the plaster has the effect of seeming to radiate color, while it absorbs the light instead of reflecting it as from a smoothly polished surface, and when the color is put on lightly enough to be a trifle uneven instead of a dead solid hue without variation of any sort, there is a chance for the sparkle and play of light which at once adds life and interest.

Published in The Craftsman, October, 1907.
WALL WITH A HIGH WAINSCOT IN WHICH THE DOOR AND WINDOW ARE MADE A PART OF THE STRUCTURAL DECORATION: THE LEADED PANELS IN WINDOW AND DOOR ADD MUCH TO THE BEAUTY OF THE ROOM.

FLOORS THAT COMPLETE THE DECORATIVE SCHEME OF A ROOM

ONE of the most important elements in the success of a room designed to be beautiful as a whole in structure and color scheme, is the floor. Whether it be a more or less elaborate parquet floor or one made simply of plain boards, it must be in harmony with the color chosen for the wood trim of the room. Also it should invariably be at least as dark as the woodwork, if the effect of restfulness is to be preserved. A floor that strikes a higher note of color than the woodwork above it, even if it be otherwise harmonious in tone, gives the room a topheavy, glaring effect that no furniture or decoration will remove.

Full directions for finishing floors will be given later in the chapter on wood finishes. While the Craftsman method of finishing woodwork differs widely from others, it does not apply so much to the floor, for here a filler should be used for precisely the same reason that it should be avoided in the treatment of furniture and woodwork, as it destroys the texture of the wood by covering it with a glassy, smooth and impervious surface. Texture is not needed in the wood of a floor, which should be entirely smooth and non-absorbent.

The first of the three floors illustrated here is meant to complete the color scheme of a room in which the woodwork is of silver-gray maple and the furniture and decorations are in delicate tones such as would naturally harmonize with gray. The floor is very simple in design, having a plain center of silver-gray maple that is finished exactly like the woodwork of the room. Around the edge is a wide border of "mahajuà," a beautiful Cuban hardwood, close and smooth in grain and left in its natural color, which is a greenish gray slightly darker than the finish of the maple.

The second floor is made of quartered oak in the natural color, and the boards are bound together with keys of vulcanized oak. Where the floor is stained to match the woodwork in tone, the color value of boards and keys will remain the same, as the vulcanized oak keys will simply show a darker shade of whatever color is given the boards of plain oak. The last illustration shows a floor of quartered oak in the natural color combined with vulcanized oak and white maple to form a border in which a primitive Indian design appears.

Published in The Craftsman, October, 1905.

A FLOOR OF SILVER-GRAY MAPLE AND MAHAJUA.

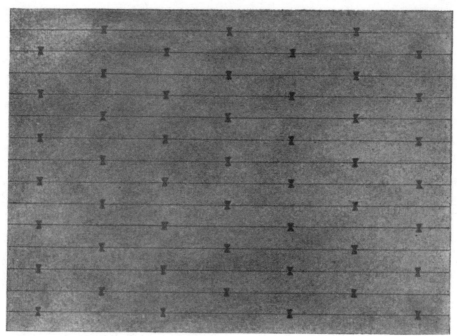

Published in The Craftsman, October, 1905.

FLOOR OF NATURAL OAK INLAID WITH KEYS OF VULCANIZED OAK.

Published in The Craftsman, October, 1905.

FLOOR OF OAK INLAID WITH MAPLE.   BORDER IN INDIAN DESIGN.

AN OUTLINE OF FURNITURE-MAKING IN THIS COUNTRY: SHOWING THE PLACE OF CRAFTSMAN FURNITURE IN THE EVOLUTION OF AN AMERICAN STYLE

THIS book is meant to give a comprehensive idea of the elements that go to make up the typical Craftsman home. Therefore at least one chapter must be devoted to Craftsman furniture, for in the making of this we first gave form to the idea of home building and furnishing which we have endeavored to set forth. For this reason, and because the furniture has so far remained the clearest concrete expression of the Craftsman idea, we are here illustrating a few of the most characteristic pieces that

scope of their experience, for, after the first primitive days of the Pilgrim Fathers in New England and the earliest settlers in the South, the life of the Colonists was modeled closely upon that of the old country and this life naturally found expression in their dwellings and household belongings. Therefore the Colonial style was so close to the prevailing style of the eighteenth century that it may be regarded as practically the same thing.

After the end of the Colonial period, and during the swift expansion that followed the

ONE OF THE LARGEST AND MOST MASSIVE OF THE CRAFTSMAN SETTLES; MADE OF FUMED OAK; SOFT LEATHER SEAT.

serve to show all the essential qualities of the style.

In order that the reader may understand clearly the reasons which led to the making of Craftsman furniture, and its place in the evolution of a distinctively American style that bids fair eventually to govern the great majority of our dwellings and household belongings, we will first briefly review the history of furniture making in this country. With the older styles, such as the English and the Dutch Colonial, we have little to do. They were importations from older civilizations, as were the Colonists themselves, and they expressed the life of the mother country rather than that of the new. When we first began to make furniture in this country, the cabinetmakers naturally followed their old traditions and made the kind of furniture which most appealed to them and which came within the

Revolution, there was inevitably a return to the primitive. Importations from the old world were no longer popular and while the houses of the wealthy were still furnished with the graceful spindle-legged mahogany pieces of earlier days, most of the people were forced to content themselves with much plainer and more substantial belongings. Little chair factories sprang up here and there, especially in Maine, Vermont and Massachusetts, and these supplied the great demand for the plain wooden chairs that we now call kitchen chairs, and the cane-seated chairs which were usually reserved for use in the best room. As the demand increased with the increasing population, the alert and resourceful New Englander began to invent machinery which would increase his output. As a consequence, the business of chair making made rapid growth, but the primitive

FURNITURE MAKING IN THIS COUNTRY

AN ARM-CHAIR AND ROCKER THAT ARE BUILT FOR SOLID COMFORT AS WELL AS DURABILITY.

beauty of the hand-made pieces was lost. The Windsor chairs, with their perfect proportions, subtle modeling and slender legs shaped with the turning lathe, became a thing of the past, for in the factories it was necessary from a business point of view to effect the utmost savings in material and also to consider the limitations of the machinery of that day. The object of the manufacturer naturally was to turn out the greatest possible quantity of goods with the least possible amount of labor and expense, and the result was so many modifications of the original form that the factory-made chairs soon become commonplace. When machines were invented to take the place of hand turning and carving, it was inevitable that vulgarity should be added to the commonplaceness, be-

LARGE CRAFTSMAN LOUNGING CHAIR.

cause it is so easy to disguise bad lines with cheap ornamentation.

Side by side with these chair factories another furniture industry was springing up, mainly in the Middle West because that was the black walnut country and black walnut was the material most in demand for the more elaborate furniture. At the same time that the New Englander was evolving from the artisan who carried on his work with the aid of a little water mill, to a manufacturer who owned a chair factory run by machinery, a number of German cabinetmakers who had settled in Indiana and the neighboring states were accumulating, by means of industry and thrift, enough means to set up general

LARGE OCTAGONAL TABLE, TOP COVERED WITH HARD LEATHER. DESIGNED FOR LIBRARY OR LIVING ROOM.

furniture factories, which supplied the country with black walnut "parlor suits," upholstered with haircloth, repps or plush, while the New Englander remained content to furnish it with dining room and kitchen chairs.

This period in our furniture corresponds with the architectural phase in this country which has aptly been termed the "reign of terror," but we are in some measure consoled for the hideous bad taste of it all by the reflection that it was contemporary with the early and mid-Victorian period in England, a term that everywhere stands for all that is ugly, artificial and commonplace in household art. It was succeeded by the first of the Grand Rapids furniture, which was in some measure a change for the better. Tempted by the success of the German furniture makers, the

FURNITURE MAKING IN THIS COUNTRY

shrewd New England manufacturers, with their superior knowledge of machinery, managed to plant themselves in the Middle West and to distance their competitors. The center of these new manufacturing interests was then in Grand Rapids, Michigan, so that the new style of furniture which was produced came to be known as Grand Rapids furniture. It

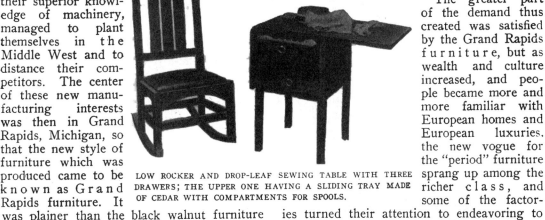

LOW ROCKER AND DROP-LEAF SEWING TABLE WITH THREE DRAWERS; THE UPPER ONE HAVING A SLIDING TRAY MADE OF CEDAR WITH COMPARTMENTS FOR SPOOLS.

was plainer than the black walnut furniture and was fashioned more after the Colonial models, but the best features were speedily lost in the ornamentation with which it was overlaid, as well as in the modification and adaptation of the earlier forms by a new generation of designers, who had studied foreign furniture and so gained a smattering of the traditional styles which they proceeded to apply to the creation of "novelties." About this time the large department stores sprang up and, as they very soon became the principal retailers, they naturally assumed control of the furniture that was made. The demand for novelties was unceasing and the designer was at the beck and call of the traveling salesman, who in his turn was compelled to supply a ceaseless stream of new attractions to the head of the furniture department,—whose business it was constantly to whet the public

appetite for further novelties.

The greater part of the demand thus created was satisfied by the Grand Rapids furniture, but as wealth and culture increased, and people became more and more familiar with European homes and European luxuries. the new vogue for the "period" furniture sprang up among the richer class, and some of the factories turned their attention to endeavoring to duplicate the several styles of French and English furniture of the seventeenth and eighteenth centuries. These factories are still running, some of them being employed in turning out the closest imitation they can make of the "period" furniture and others in reproducing Colonial models.

While we were doing these things in America, Ruskin and Morris had been endeavoring to establish in England a return to handicrafts as a means of individual expression along the several lines of the fine and industrial arts. This gave rise over there to the Arts and Crafts movement, which was based chiefly upon the expression of untrammeled individualism. Much furniture was made,— some of it good, but a great deal of it showing the eccentricities of personal fancy un-

ROUND TABLE THAT IS WELL ADAPTED TO GENERAL USE.

CHESS OR CHECKER TABLE HAVING TOP COVERED WITH HARD LEATHER MARKED OFF INTO SQUARES FOR THE BOARD.

FURNITURE MAKING IN THIS COUNTRY

A BOOKCASE THAT IS A GOOD EXAMPLE OF THE DECORATIVE USE OF PURELY STRUCTURAL FEATURES.

permanent style in English furniture for the reason that they have striven for a definite and intentional expression of art that was largely for art's sake and had little to do with satisfying the plain needs of the people. Although the founders of the movement held and preached the doctrine that all vital art necessarily springs from the life of the people, it is nevertheless recognized even by their followers that in practice such expression as they advocate belongs to the artist alone and that the people care very little about it.

A LIGHT WRITING TABLE FOR A LIVING ROOM OR SMALL SITTING ROOM.

modified by any settled standards. It was a move in the right direction because it meant a return to healthy individual effort and a revolt from the dead level established by the machines. But the Arts and Crafts workers have not succeeded in establishing another

It was during this same period that the movement called *L'Art Nouveau* sprang up in France and for a time attained quite a vogue under the leadership of Bing. Belgium followed suit with a rather heavier and more pronounced interpretation of the distinctive features of this style and for a few years the plant forms and swirling lines that distinguished *L'Art Nouveau* productions were very popular. In Germany and Austria the art students and others of the more restless spirits who were constantly in revolt from the established styles determined to outdo the French and accordingly established government schools for the teaching of a definite style, which was called New Art or Secessionist and which

RUSH SEATED CHAIR AND DROP LEAF TABLE WITH SEPARATE WRITING CABINET.

FURNITURE MAKING IN THIS COUNTRY

contained some of the features of *L'Art Nouveau* and others that were borrowed from the English Arts and Crafts and also from ancient Egyptian forms of art. The French school has already failed in the efforts to establish a permanent style, and the indications are that the efforts of the German and Austrian Secessionists will prove equally futile, because in both cases the workers have merely attempted to do something different; to evolve a new thing by combining the features of the old. In other words, they began at the top instead of beginning at the bottom and allowing the style to develop naturally

A LARGE WRITING DESK FOR THE LIBRARY OR WORKROOM.

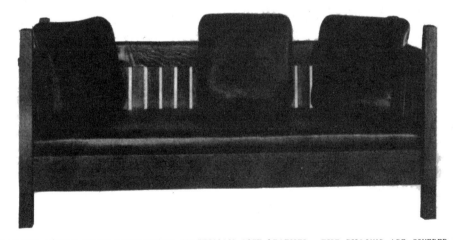

A TYPICAL CRAFTSMAN LOUNGING CHAIR.

from the sure foundation of real utility. The leaders succeeded in making things that, whatever their relative merits, were a new departure; but this once made, it stood as a completed achievement that might be imitated, but could hardly be developed, as it lacked the beginnings of healthy growth.

But during the same period in this country things were on a different basis. Out of the chaos of ideals and standards which had naturally resulted from the rapid growth of the young nation, a vigorous and coherent national spirit was being developed, and amid the general turmoil and restlessness attendant upon swift progress and expansion, it became apparent that we were evolving a type of people distinct from

A LARGE OAKEN SETTLE UPHOLSTERED WITH CRAFTSMAN SOFT LEATHER. THE PILLOWS ARE COVERED WITH THE STILL SOFTER AND MORE FLEXIBLE SHEEPSKIN.

all others,—a type essentially American. And the distinguishing characteristic of this type is the power to assimilate so swiftly the kind of culture which leads to the making of permanent standards of life and art that it is hardly to be compared with what might seem to be the corresponding class in other countries. Such Americans have fundamental intelligence and the power of discrimination, and the direct thinking that results from these qualities inevitably produces a certain openness of mind that responds very quickly to

ness alone. In this country, where we have no monarchs and no aristocracy, the life of the plain people is the life of the nation; therefore, the art of the age must necessarily be the art of the people. Our phases of imitation and of vulgar desire for show are only a part of the crudity of youth. We have not yet outgrown them and will not for many years; but as we grow older and begin to stand on our own feet and to cherish our own standards of life and of work and therefore of art, we show an unmistakable tendency to

A GROUP OF CRAFTSMAN SPINDLE FURNITURE. THIS IS QUITE AS STRONG AND DURABLE AS THE MORE MASSIVE PIECES BUT IS A LITTLE LIGHTER IN APPEARANCE.

anything which seems to have a real and permanent value.

This quality was shown in the immediate recognition and welcome accorded to Craftsman furniture when we first introduced it ten years ago. Like the Arts and Crafts furniture in England, it represented a revolt from the machine-made thing. But there was this difference: The Arts and Crafts furniture was primarily intended to be an expression of individuality, and the Craftsman furniture was founded on a return to the sturdy and primitive forms that were meant for useful-

get away from shams and to demand the real thing.

And to an American the real thing is something that he needs and understands. The showroom quality is all very well when it comes to proving how much money he has or to establishing a reputation for owning things that are just as good as his neighbor's. But for use he wants the things that belong to him,—the things that are comfortable to live with; that represent a good investment of his money and have no nonsense about them. Furthermore the true American likes to know

FURNITURE MAKING IN THIS COUNTRY

how things are done. His interest and sympathy are immediately aroused when he sees something that he really likes and knows to be a good thing, if he is able to feel that, if he wanted it and had the time, he could make one like it himself.

So strong is this national characteristic that it is hardly overstating the case to say that in America any style in architecture or furniture would have to possess the essential qualities of simplicity, durability, comfort and convenience and to be made in such a way that

A BIG DEEP CHAIR THAT MEANS COMFORT TO A TIRED MAN WHEN HE COMES HOME AFTER THE DAY'S WORK.

takes on trust the word of the dealers, and every year brings us more abundant proof that they do not in any way represent the real tastes and standards of the people. All machine-made imitations of furniture which belonged to another country and another age and represented the life of a totally different people, are alike to the average American. If he can get them cheap, he has at least the satisfaction of feeling that they make a pretty good outward show for the money; if they are expensive, there is something in being able to afford them and to know that his house has in it rooms which are fairly

SMALL WRITING DESK FOR A WOMAN'S SITTING ROOM OR FOR THE LIVING ROOM

the details of its construction can be readily grasped, before it could hope to become permanent. We are not so many generations removed from our pioneer forefathers that we have grown entirely out of their way of getting at things. We may not always stop to think about them, but when we do our thought is apt to be fairly sound and direct. The prevalence of cheap, showy, machine-made things in our houses is due chiefly to the lack of thought that

NO BETTER EXAMPLES OF THE CRAFTSMAN STYLE CAN BE FOUND THAN ARE SHOWN IN THIS CHAIR AND ROCKER.

FURNITURE MAKING IN THIS COUNTRY

CRAFTSMAN SIDEBOARD WHERE WROUGHT IRON PULLS AND HINGES ARE USED IN A DECORATIVE WAY.

successful imitations of the rooms in French or English palaces two or three hundred years ago. But in all this there is no real thought and nothing that approaches it. It is only when a thing has the honest primitive quality that reveals just what it is, how it is made and what it is made for, that it comes home to us as something which possesses an individuality of its own. It is not an elaborate finished thing made by machinery with intricate processes which we cannot understand and about which we do not care in the least; it

is something that we might make with our own hands. Therefore it is something that sets us to thinking and establishes a point of contact from which springs the essentially human qualities of interest and affection. Understanding just how it is made, we are in a position to appreciate exactly what the artisan has done and how well he has done it. From this understanding comes the personal interest in good work that alone gives the vital quality which we know as art.

Many people misunderstand the meaning of the word primitiveness, mistaking it for crudeness, but the word is used here to express the directness of a thing that is radical instead of derived. In our understanding of the term, the primitive form of construction is that which would naturally suggest itself to a workman as embodying the main essentials of a piece of furniture, of which the first is the straightforward provision for practical need. Also we hold that the structural idea should be made prominent because lines which clearly define their purpose appeal to the mind with the same force as does a clear concise statement of fact. This principle is the basis from which the Craftsman style of furniture has been developed. In the beginning there was no thought of creating a new style, only a recognition of the fact that we should have in our homes something better suited to our needs and

CRAFTSMAN DINING TABLE AND TWO OF THE MORE MASSIVE DINING CHAIRS, ONE UPHOLSTERED IN HARD LEATHER STUDDED WITH DULL BRASS NAILS AND THE OTHER MADE OF PLAIN OAK WITH A HARD LEATHER SEAT.

FURNITURE MAKING IN THIS COUNTRY

SERVING TABLE AND TWO OF THE LIGHTER DINING CHAIRS, SUITABLE FOR A DINING ROOM TOO SMALL TO TAKE THE MORE MASSIVE FURNITURE: UPHOLSTERED WITH LEATHER.

more expressive of our character as a people than imitations of the traditional styles, and a conviction that the best way to get something better was to go directly back to plain principles of construction and apply them to the making of simple, strong, comfortable furniture that would meet adequately everything that could be required of it.

Because Craftsman furniture expresses so clearly the fundamental sturdiness and directness of the true American point of view, it follows that in no other country and under no other conditions could it have been produced at the present day. The history of art shows us that a new form of expression never develops from the top and that nothing permanent is ever built upon tradition. When a style is found to be original and vital it is a certainty that it has sprung from the needs of the plain people and that it is based upon the simplest and most direct principles of construction. This is always the beginning and a style that has in it sufficient vitality to endure, will grow naturally as one worker after another feels that he has something further to express. In making Craftsman furniture we went back to the beginning, seeking the inspiration of the same law of direct answer to need that animated the craftsmen of an earlier day, for it was suggested by the primitive human necessity of the common folk. It is absolutely plain and unornamented, the severity of the style marking a point of departure from which we believe that a rational development of the decorative idea will ultimately take place.

LARGE SIDEBOARD THAT IS USUALLY MADE IN OAK FINISHED IN A VERY LIGHT TONE OF BROWN, WITH PULLS AND HINGES IN DULL, BROWNISH COPPER, FORMING A DECORATIVE EFFECT.

WILLOW CHAIRS AND SETTLES WHICH HARMONIZE WITH THE MORE SEVERE AND MASSIVE FURNITURE MADE OF OAK

AN ARM CHAIR OF WOVEN WILLOW.

a part of the general impression, instead of standing out as a separate article.

In the Craftsman houses we do away with a great deal of the movable furniture by the use in its place of built-in fittings, which are made a part of the structure of the house. As these include window seats, fireside seats, settles, bookcases, desks, sideboards, china cupboards and many other things, it will easily be seen that their presence not only adds to the structural interest and beauty of the room itself, but makes it possible to dispense with much of the furniture which would otherwise be needed. For the rest, we use Craftsman furniture where it is necessary to have pieces of wood construction, but we relieve any possible severity of effect by a liberal use of willow settles and chairs which afford the best possible foil to the austere lines, massive forms and sober coloring of the oak. We select willow for this use rather than rattan, because, while all such furniture is necessarily handmade, the rattan pieces are usually patterned after the elaborate effects that we have learned to associate with machine-made goods, and so have none of the natural interest that is a part of something which grows under the hand and is shaped as simply as possible to meet the purpose for which it is intended.

THE opinion is frequently expressed with regard to Craftsman furniture that it is all very well for the library, den or dining room, but that an entire house furnished with it would be apt to appear too severe and monotonous in its general effect. While naturally we feel that Craftsman furniture is equally suitable for every room in the house, we are aware that there is precisely the same element of truth in this criticism that it holds when applied to any kind of furniture. The point is that too much of any one thing is apt to be monotonous, and the way we avoid that fault in a Craftsman house is to make the furniture entirely a secondary thing and keep it as little obtrusive as possible, so that each piece sinks into its place in the picture and becomes merely

The charm of willow is that it is purely a handicraft, and obviously so. A rattan chair or settle may be twisted into any fan-

A HIGH-BACK SETTLE OF WILLOW THAT HARMONIZES ADMIRABLY WITH THE GENERAL CHARACTER OF CRAFTSMAN FURNITURE.

WILLOW CHAIRS AND SETTLES

tastic form, but willow furniture is essentially of basket construction. Our idea in making the kind of willow furniture illustrated here was to gain something based upon the same principles of construction that characterize our oak furniture; that is, to secure a form that should suggest the simplest basket work and the flexibility of lithe willow branches and yet be as durable as any of the heavy oak furniture which is emphatically of wood construction.

Consequently these pieces are basketry pure and simple and have an elastic spring under the pressure of the body that suggests the flexibility of baskets such as are woven by the fireside or on the back porch at the edge of the garden. The making of willow furniture as a handicraft is rather a hobby with us, for willow is a material beloved of the craftsman and the work is very interesting and comparatively easy to do. The trouble is that so many people are inclined to overdo it and to make out of woven willow the kind of furniture that demands wood construction. Seat furniture alone is permissible in willow and yet we frequently see tables, racks and stands of various kinds, and even the front of a bureau or a dresser, made of this material. Such misuse is a pity, the more that it tends to create a prejudice again against willow furniture as a whole.

The pieces shown here hold in their beauty of form and color evidences of the personal interest of the worker. The willow has been so finished that the surface has the sparkle seen in the thin branches of the growing tree as it becomes lustrous with the first stirring of the sap. This natural sparkle on the surface of willow has all

WILLOW CHAIR MADE ON A LOWER AND BROADER MODEL.

the intangible silvery shimmer of water in moonlight. This is lost absolutely when the furniture made of it is covered with the usual opaque enamel, which not only hides the luster of the surface but gives the effect of a stiff uncompromising construction in which the pliableness of the basket weave is entirely obliterated and all the possible interesting variations of tone are lost under the smooth surface.

We finish our willow furniture in two colors; one gives the general impression of green, but it is really a variation of soft wood tones, brown and green, light and dark, as the texture of the withes has been smooth or rough. In this way the silvery luster of the willow is left undisturbed and the color beneath is like that of fresh young bark. The other color is golden brown in which there is also a suggestion of spring-like gray and green.

VERY LARGE WILLOW SETTLE MADE AFTER A DESIGN THAT WE HAVE FOUND MOST SATISFACTORY IN RELATION TO THE REGULAR CRAFTSMAN FURNITURE OF OAK.

CRAFTSMAN METAL WORK: DESIGNED AND MADE ACCORDING TO THE SAME PRINCIPLES THAT RULE THE FURNITURE

IN a room decorated according to Craftsman ideas,—especially if it be furnished with Craftsman furniture,—it is of the utmost importance that the metal accessories should be of a character that fits into the picture. We found out very soon after we began to make the plain oak furniture that even the best of the usual machine-made and highly polished metal trim was absurdly out of place, and that in order to get the right thing it was necessary to establish a metal-work department in the Craftsman Workshops where articles of wrought metal in plain rugged designs and possessing the same structural and simple quality as the furniture could be made. We began with such simple and necessary things as drawer and door pulls, hinges and escutcheons, but with a work so interesting and so full of possibilities as this one thing inevitably leads to another, and our metal workers were soon making in hand-wrought iron, copper and brass all kinds of household fittings, such as lighting fixtures, fire sets, and other articles that were decorative as well as

LARGE LANTERN THAT IS BEST FITTED FOR USE IN AN ENTRANCE HALL OR VERANDA.

useful, and that showed the same essential qualities as the furniture.

Since then we have not only made all manner of metal furnishings ourselves, but through the pages of THE CRAFTSMAN we have warmly encouraged amateur workers to do the same thing and have given for their use a number of models as well as full directions regarding methods of working and the necessary equipment for doing all kinds of simple metal work at home. Under the inspiration of these suggestions and directions, a number of readers of THE CRAFTSMAN have set up little home workshops and have succeeded in making many pieces that show originality and merit. In fact, metal work is one of the most interesting of the crafts to the home worker who possesses skill and taste and, above all, a genuine interest in making for himself the things that are needed either for use or ornament at home, and anyone who takes it up and discovers its possibilities is likely to go on with it indefinitely. Instruction in the technicalities is easily obtained from any blacksmith who can teach the rudiments of handling iron, or from any working jeweler or coppersmith who is able to give the necessary personal supervision to the first efforts of a worker in brass or copper. Given even a little ingenuity and handiness with tools, it

COPPER-FRAMED LANTERN THAT IS INTENDED TO HANG FROM A BRACKET ATTACHED TO THE WALL.

CRAFTSMAN METAL WORK

might be possible to dispense even with this instruction and to work out each problem as it comes up; learning by doing, in the simple way of the handicraftsman of old.

It ought to be possible for such home workers to make everything necessary for the fireplace, including shovels and tongs, andirons, fenders, coal buckets and even fireplace hoods, although the last named might be a fairly ambitious undertaking for an amateur. One needs but little imagination to realize the interest and charm that would attach to a comfortable fireside nook that had been furnished in this way, and the same principle applies to every one of the smaller articles of furniture in the home. For example, it is not at all hard to make from either brass or copper a tray or an umbrella stand, a simple vase or metal jug

niére, and the quality of really won- is, if the care to con- to simple

or a jardi- decorative such things is derful; that worker takes fine himself

SMALL SQUARE LANTERN MEANT TO HANG FROM THE CEILING OR AN OVERHEAD BEAM.

SQUARE LANTERN WITH AN UNUSUALLY DECORATIVE COPPER FRAME.

possible the need for which the just as well as he can, keeping mon to metal workers of artifi- wrought" effect by putting ham- business to be, leaving the exaggerating into crudity the if rightly used, give to a terest and charm. Much of way the metal is finished. wrought-iron work is

good designs that meet as directly as article is made, and then makes it free from the temptation so com- cially heightening the "hand- mer dents where they have no edges rough and generally traces of workmanship which, piece such a human in- the effect depends upon the For example, all of our finished in a way that has

ELECTROLIER IN FUMED OAK AND HAMMERED COPPER, ESPECIALLY DESIGNED FOR HANGING RATHER LOW OVER A DINING TABLE.

ONE OF THE LITTLE LANTERNS THAT IS FREQUENTLY USED WITH THE SHOWER LIGHTS.

long been known in England as "armor bright." This is a very old process used by the English armorers, whence it derives its name, and its peculiar value is that it finishes the surface is a way that brings out all the black, gray and silvery tones that naturally belong to iron, and also prevents it from rusting. This method applies to both wrought iron and sheet iron and is the only thing we know that accomplishes the desired result. The process itself is very simple. After the iron is hammered it should be polished on an emery belt; or if this is not at hand and it is not convenient to borrow the use of one in some thoroughly equipped metal shop, emery

ELECTRIC LANTERN DESIGNED AS A FINIAL TO A NEWEL POST.

CRAFTSMAN METAL WORK

cloth—about Number O—may be used in polishing the surface by hand.

Then the iron must be smoked over a forge or in a fireplace, care being taken to avoid heating it to any extent during this process, as the object is merely to smoke it thoroughly. It should then be allowed to cool naturally and the surface rubbed well with a soft cloth dipped in oil. Naturally, the more the iron is polished the brighter it will be, especially in the higher parts of an uneven surface, which take on almost the look of dull silver. After this the piece must be well wiped off so that the oil is thoroughly removed, and the surface lacquered with a special iron lacquer.

To give the copper the deep mellow brownish glow that brings it into such perfect harmony with the fumed oak, the finished piece should be rubbed thoroughly with a soft cloth dipped in powdered pumice stone, and then left to age naturally. If a darker tone is desired, it should be held over a fire or torch and heated until the right color appears. Care should be taken that it is not heated too long, as copper under too great heat is apt to turn black. We use no lacquer on either copper or brass, age and exposure being the only agents required to produce beauty and variety of tone. All our brass work is made of the natural unfinished metal, which has a beautiful greenish tone and a soft dull surface that harmonizes admirably with the natural wood. Like copper, it darkens and mellows with age.

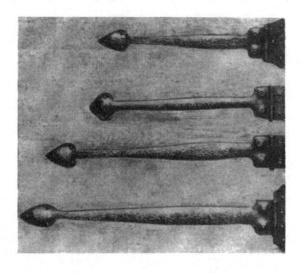

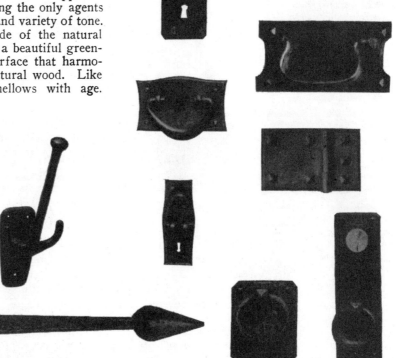

CHARACTERISTIC CRAFTSMAN HINGES, DOOR AND DRAWER PULLS, KNOCKERS AND COAT HOOKS, ALL DESIGNED TO HARMONIZE WITH CRAFTSMAN FURNITURE.

THE KIND OF FABRICS AND NEEDLEWORK THAT HARMONIZE WITH AND COMPLETE THE CRAFTSMAN DECORATIVE SCHEME

WE have traced in this book the development of the Craftsman scheme of building and interior decoration, beginning with the house as a whole and thence working back to an analysis of the different rooms, the wall spaces, struc-

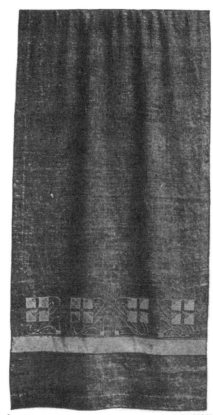

PORTIÈRE OF CRAFTSMAN CANVAS WITH PINE CONE DESIGN IN APPLIQUÉ.

tural features, furnishings and metal work, all of which must be considered separately as essential parts of the complete structure, including the decorative scheme. In doing this we have reversed the process by which we worked out the idea in the first place, for we began ten years ago with the furniture; the metal work followed as a matter of course because it was the next thing needed; then the dressing of leathers to harmonize with the style of the furniture and the wood of which it was made. Then came the finding of suit-

able fabrics and the kind of decoration most in keeping with them, and from all these parts was naturally developed the idea of the Craftsman house as a whole.

At first it was very difficult to find just the right kind of fabric to harmonize with the Craftsman furniture and metal work. It was not so much a question of color, although of course a great deal of the effect depended upon perfect color harmony, as it was a question of the texture and character of the fabric. Silks, plushes and tapestries, in fact delicate and perishable fabrics of all kinds, were utterly out of keeping with Craftsman furniture. What we needed were fabrics that possessed sturdiness and durability; that were made of materials that possessed a certain rugged and straightforward character of fiber, weave and texture,—such a character as

PORTIÈRE OF CRAFTSMAN CANVAS WITH CHECKERBERRY DESIGN IN APPLIQUÉ.

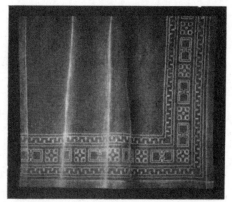

SASH CURTAIN OF TEA-COLORED NET DARNED IN AN OPEN PATTERN WITH SILVER-WHITE FLOSS.

SASH CURTAIN OF CASEMENT LINEN WITH FRETWORK DESIGN IN SOLID DARNED WORK.

would bring them into the same class as the sturdy oak and wrought iron and copper of the other furnishings. Yet they could not be coarse or crude, for that would have taken them as far away from the quality of the furniture on the one side, as plushes and brocades were on the other.

For upholstering the furniture itself we had found leather more satisfying than anything else, especially as by constant experimenting we had succeeded in developing a method of dressing that preserved all the leathery quality in much the same way that we were able to preserve the woody quality of the oak, so that the leather maintained its own sturdy individuality, at the same time possessing a softness and flexibility and a sub-

tlety of coloring that proved wonderfully attractive. This was especially the case with sheepskin, which we finished in all the subtle shades of brown, biscuit, yellow, gray, green, and fawn, but always with the leathery quality predominant under the light surface tone. These leathers accorded so well with the plain oak furniture and metal work that for a time they became almost too popular, for they were used by many people for table covers, portiéres and the like, in rooms where rugged effects were considered desirable. In fact, the fad ran to such lengths that it fortunately wore itself out and leather was allowed to return to its proper uses.

This was made easier by the discovery of certain fabrics that harmonize as completely as leather with the general Craftsman scheme. These are mostly woven of flax left in the natural color or given some one of the nature hues. There are also certain roughly-woven, dull-finished silks that fit into the picture as

SCARF OF HAND-WOVEN LINEN WITH PINE CONE DESIGN IN DARNED WORK.

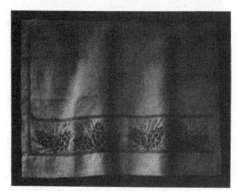

SASH CURTAIN OF CASEMENT LINEN WITH ANOTHER FORM OF PINE CONE DESIGN DONE IN DARNED WORK.

TABLE SCARF OF UNBLEACHED HAND-WOVEN LINEN WITH DRAGONFLY DESIGN DARNED IN PERSIAN COLORS.

TABLE SCARF WITH GINKGO DESIGN IN APPLIQUÉ OF DEEP LEAF GREEN UPON HOMESPUN LINEN.

well as linen, and for window curtains we use nets and crepes of the same general character. A material that we use more than almost any other for portiéres, pillows, chair cushions,—indeed in all places were stout wearing quality and a certain pleasant unobtrusiveness are required—is a canvas woven of loosely twisted threads of jute and flax and dyed in the piece,—a method which gives an unevenness in color that amounts almost to a two-toned effect because of the way in which the different threads take the dye. This unevenness is increased by the roughness of the texture, which is not unlike that of a firmly woven burlap. The colors of

the canvas are delightful. For example, there are three tones of wood brown,—one almost exactly the color of old weather-beaten oak; another that shows a sunny yellowish tone; and a third that comes close to a dark russet. The greens are the foliage hues,—one dark and brownish like rusty pine needles, another a deep leaf-green; the third an intense green like damp grass in the shade; and a fourth a very gray-green with a bluish tinge like the eucalyptus leaf.

Our usual method of decorating this canvas is the application of some bold and simple design in which the solid parts are of linen appliqué in some contrasting shade and the connecting lines are done in heavy outline stitch or couching with linen floss. This sim-

TABLE SCARF OF HOMESPUN LINEN WITH PINE CONE DESIGN IN APPLIQUÉ.

PILLOW COVERED WITH CRAFTSMAN CANVAS AND ORNAMENTED WITH PINE CONE DESIGN IN APPLIQUÉ.

CRAFTSMAN FABRICS AND NEEDLEWORK

TABLE SCARF FOR A BEDROOM, WITH POPPY DESIGN IN DARNED WORK.

taste in the selection of materials, designs and color combinations, there is no reason why any woman should not, with comparatively little time and labor, make her home interesting with beautiful and characteristic needlework that is as far removed from the "fancy work" which too often takes the place of it, as any genuine and useful thing is removed from things that are unnecessary.

For scarfs, table squares, luncheon and dinner sets and the like, we find that the most suitable fabrics in connection with the Craftsman furnishings are the linens, mostly in the natural colors and the rougher weaves.

SAME POPPY DESIGN AS APPLIED TO A BEDSPREAD OF HOMESPUN LINEN.

plicity is characteristic of all the Craftsman needlework, which is bold and plain to a degree. We use appliqué in a great many forms, especially for large pieces such as portières, couch covers, pillows and the larger table covers. For scarfs, window curtains and table furnishings of all kinds we are apt to use the simple darning stitch, as this gives a delightful sparkle to any mass of color. For the rest we use the satin stitch very occasionally when a snap of solid color is needed for accenting now and then a bit of plain hem-stitching or drawn work. It is the kind of needlework that any woman can do and, given the power of discrimination and

We use hand-woven and homespun linens in many weights and weaves, and a beautiful fabric called Flemish linen, which has a matt finish and is very soft and pliable to the touch. Some of these come in the cream or ivory shades and all of them in the tones of cream gray and warm pale brown natural to the unbleached linen. We find, as a rule, that the finer and more delicate white linens do not belong in a Craftsman room any more than silks, plushes and tapestries in delicate colorings belong with the Craftsman furniture. The whole scheme demands a more robust sort of beauty,—something that primarily exists from use and that fulfils every requirement. The charm that it possesses arises from the completeness with which it answers all these demands and the honesty which allows its natural quality to show.

POPPY DESIGN CARRIED OUT IN APPLIQUÉ TO ORNAMENT THE CORNER OF A COUCH COVER.

CABINET WORK FOR HOME WORKERS AND STUDENTS WHO WISH TO LEARN THE FUNDAMENTAL PRINCIPLES OF CONSTRUCTION

IN the brief sketch we have already given of furniture making in this country we made the statement that one of the chief elements of interest in Craftsman furniture is the fact that its construction is so simple and direct and so clearly revealed that any one possessing even a rudimentary knowledge of tools and of drawing and some natural skill of hand could easily make for himself many pieces of furniture in this style. Believing this thoroughly, and also realizing fully the interest that cabinetwork holds for most people and the means it affords of developing the constructive and creative faculties, we have given in THE CRAFTSMAN a number of designs solely for the benefit of home workers. For a year or two we published, in connection with these designs, full working drawings and also mill bills for the necessary lumber; but we were forced to abandon that on account of lack of space and to give only the drawings showing the finished pieces, for which the working drawings and mill bills were easily obtainable upon application.

We illustrate here a number of these designs, most of which are for pieces that are fairly easy to make and that have a definite use as household furnishings. While the designs of course show the exact models of the pieces they represent, we intend them to have also a suggestive value and to stimulate thought and experiment along the lines of designing and making plain substantial furniture. It has been proven beyond question that the most powerful stimulus to well-defined constructive thought is found in the direction of the mind to some form of creative work. Therefore if a man or a boy has any aptitude along these lines, it is a foregone conclusion that he will not have

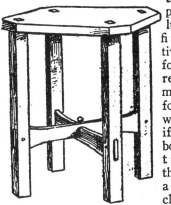

FIGURE ONE.—SQUARE TABOURET.

made many pieces after given models before he begins to think for himself and to make or modify designs to meet his own demands and to afford an opportunity for working out his own problems. Furthermore, as his experience grows, he will naturally discover new ways of doing things that may be better for him to follow than any of the stereotyped rules. We approve thoroughly of the freedom of spirit that leads to such experimenting, for, although we originated the Craftsman furni-

FIGURE TWO.—A ROUND TABOURET.

ture, it is just such interest and work on the part of other people that will ultimately develop it into a national style. One warning, however, we would like to give to all amateur workers: that is, that one's own whims must no more be followed than the whims of other people. We will find plenty of interest and occupation in making things that are actually needed and plenty of exercise for all our creative power in designing them to fulfil as adequately as possible the purpose for which they are intended. So long as this is done there is no danger of the work degenerating into a fad; instead, it is likely not only to give much pleasure and profit to individuals, but to grow until the whole nation once more reaps the benefit that comes from the intelligent exercise of the creative powers in some interesting form of handicraft.

Every one knows the relief to brain workers and to professional men that is found in this kind of work. It not only affords a wholesome change of occupation but brings into play a different set of faculties and so proves both restful and stimulating. A professional or business man who can find relief from his regular work in some such pursuit,

CABINET WORK FOR HOME WORKERS

FIGURE THREE.—HALL BENCH WITH CHEST.

peals to him instead of being taught sound principles of design and construction and so guided by a competent worker that all his own work is based upon these principles and is thoroughly done. If the work is m e r e l y regarded as play, the theoretical attitude toward the expression of individuality is all right; but if it is regarded as a preparation for the serious business of later life, the result shows that it unfits the student for real work in just such measure as he shows an aptitude for play work.

which he takes up as a recreation, does better work in his own vocation because he is a healthier and better balanced man and his interest in his home grows more vivid and personal with every article of furniture that he makes with his own hands and according to his own ideas.

As for the means of education afforded by this kind of work, we have no better proof than is shown by the widespread belief in the efficacy of manual training in our public schools, although to a practical craftsman there would seem to be plenty of room for improvement, both as to methods of teaching and the quality of workmanship that is required from the students. W h e r e manual training is taken up purely on account of the mental development it affords, there is a tendency to make it entirely academic. The teachers for the most part rely almost wholly upon theory and have very little practical knowledge of the t h i n g they teach. The result is that a boy is encouraged to "express his own individuality" in designing and making the thing that ap-

The introduction of the Craftsman style has practically revolutionized manual training in our public schools, because it has placed at the disposal of the teachers designs of such simplicity and clearness of construction that the work of teaching has been made much easier and the field of manual training has been greatly broadened. Before the introduction of Craftsman furniture, manual training in the schools rested chiefly upon sloyd, which was confined to the making of small articles entirely for the sake of the mental development afforded by the intelligent use of the hands. Now, however, the students of manual training are learning to

FIGURE FOUR.—CHILD'S OPEN BOOKCASE.

FIGURE FIVE.—CHESS OR CHECKER TABLE.

CABINET WORK FOR HOME WORKERS

make furniture after such models as we show here and the very necessary element of usefulness is added to the things they make. The only difficulty is that the craft itself is not well enough understood by the teachers to be imparted to the students in such a way that they derive any permanent benefit from it. The teaching is, as we have said, largely theoretical and the object of the whole training is mental development along general lines rather than the moral development that comes from learning to do useful work thoroughly and well. As cabinet-work is handled in the manual training departments of the schools, it is distinctly a side issue, and exhibitions of the work to which public attention is frequently invited show ambitious pieces of furniture that are wrongly proportioned, badly put together and finished in a slovenly way, thus producing exactly the opposite effect upon the pupil from what is intended. If the State or municipal authorities would see to it that manual training in the form of wood-working of all kinds, and especially the making of furniture, were placed under the charge of thoroughly skilled craftsmen who understood and were able to teach all the principles of construction, the moral and educational effect of such work would be almost incalculable.

In order to make the training of any real value, it is absolutely necessary that the student begin simultaneously with mechanical drawing and the application of its principles

FIGURE SEVEN.—PORTABLE CABINET FOR WRITING TABLE.

to his work as he goes along. If he began with simple models to which could be applied the elementary lessons in mechanical drawing, the laying out of plans, the reading of detail drawings and the like, and would also afford a chance to demonstrate lessons in the use of the square, the level, the saw and the plane;—a good foundation would be laid not only for the understanding of right principles of construction but for the accurate use of tools. A boy trained in this way would be able in future years to put his knowledge to almost any use that was needed. Instead of this the students endeavor to make something that is interesting and that shows well at home or in an exhibition. In fact, the situation now is very much as it would be if a student of music were to take two or three lessons in the rudiments and then endeavor to play a more or less elaborate composition. There is no question as to the benefit that boys, and girls too, derive from being taught to work with their hands; but it is better not to teach them at all than to give them the wrong teaching. No one expects a schoolboy or an amateur worker of any age to make elaborate furniture that would equal similar pieces made by a trained cabinet-maker. But if the student be taught to make small and simple things and to make each one so that it would pass muster anywhere, he learns from the start the fundamental principles of design and proportion and so comes naturally to understand what is meant by thorough workmanship.

There is no objection to any worker, however inexperienced, attempting to express his own

FIGURE SIX.—PIANO BENCH, STRONGLY MADE WITH SOLID ENDS.

FIGURE EIGHT.—CHILD'S WRITING DESK.

and construction as carefully as he would be grounded in mathematics or classical literature, he might safely be trusted to produce something that would express his own individuality, for then, if ever, he would have developed an individuality that was worth while. And this principle applies as well to amateur workers of all kinds as it does to the students in the public schools, for it is the basis of all work that is worthy to endure.

One great advantage of taking up cabinetmaking at home as well as in the schools, is that it could be made not only a means of amusement or mental development to the individual, but could be expanded into a home or neighborhood handicraft that might be carried on in connection with small farming, upon a basis that would insure a reasonable financial success. Handicrafts, as practiced by individual arts and crafts workers in the studio, do not afford a sufficient living to craft workers as a class, but that is largely because these very principles of sound construction and thorough workmanship are not always observed or even comprehended, so that it is difficult for the individual worker to produce anything that has a definite and permanent commercial value. This kind of furniture, on the contrary, has a very well defined and thoroughly established commercial value, as our own experience has proven; and yet it is so simple in design and construction that it can be made at home or on the farm during the idle months of winter or by a group of

individuality, but the natural thing would be for him to express it in more or less primitive forms of construction that are, so far as they go, correct, instead of attempting something that, when it is finished, is all wrong because the student has not understood what he was about. Unquestionably there are certain principles and rules as to design, proportion and form that are as fundamental in their nature as are the tables of addition, subtraction, division and multiplication, with relation to mathematics, or as the alphabet is as a basis to literature, but they are not yet formulated for general use. The trained worker learns these things by experience and comes to have a sort of sixth sense with regard to their application, but this takes strong direct thinking, keen observation and the power of initiative that is possessed only by the very exceptional and highly skilled workman.

Nevertheless it surely is as easy to begin work in the right way as in the wrong way. It would be better if all our teaching of manual training were based upon some text book carefully compiled by a master workman and kept within certain well defined limits. After the student had thoroughly learned all that lay within these limits and was grounded in the principles of design

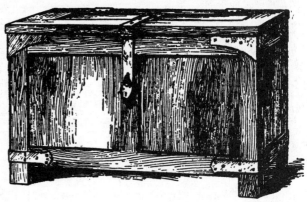

FIGURE NINE.—BRIDE'S CHEST.

CABINET WORK FOR HOME WORKERS

FIGURE TEN.—BOOK CABINET.

have much more individual interest because of this very feature, for then it would be possible to select certain pieces of wood for special uses and to develop to the utmost all the natural qualities of color and grain that might prove interesting when rightly used and in the right place. It is by these very methods and under similar conditions that the Japanese have gained such world-wide fame as discriminating users of very simple and inexpensive woods. A Japanese regards a piece of wood as he might a picture and his one idea is to do something with it that will show it to the very best advantage, as well as gain from it the utmost measure of usefulness.

Among the cabinet woods native to this country and easily obtained are white oak, brown ash, rock elm, birch, beech and maple. Chestnut, cypress, pine, redwood and gumwood, while all excellent for interior trim,

workers in a village,—in fact under almost any conditions where it would seem advantageous to do such work, especially under the guidance of a competent cabinetmaker.

Whether regarded as one of the forms of a profitable handicraft that might be depended upon as a means of support,—or at least of adding to the income obtained from a small farm,—or whether regarded merely as a means of recreation for a busy man during his leisure hours at home, cabinetmaking is likely to prove a most interesting pursuit. One distinct advantage is that furniture made in this way, if well done, would be better than any that could possibly be made in a factory, because the work would naturally be more carefully done. Also the interest that attaches to the right use of wood could be developed to a much greater degree than is possible where the work is done on a large scale, because judgment and discrimination could be applied to the selection of lumber that is without any special market value according to commercial standards, but that has in it certain flaws and irregularities that make it far more interesting than the costlier lumber necessary for purely commercial work. This one item would be a great advantage as lumber grows scarcer and harder to obtain. Also, the furniture itself would

FIGURE ELEVEN.—BOOKCASE WITH ADJUSTABLE SHELVES.

FIGURE TWELVE.—SMALL STAND FOR USE IN A BEDROOM.

are not hard enough to give satisfactory results when used for the making of furniture. Of those first mentioned, white oak is unquestionably the best for cabinetmaking and, indeed, it is a wood as well suited to the Craftsman style of furniture as the Spanish mahogany was to the French, English and Colonial furniture of the eighteenth century. Spanish mahogany is very rare now and the modern mahogany, or baywood, is very little harder than whitewood and so cannot be considered particularly desirable as a cabinet wood. The old mahogany was a hard, close-grained, fine-textured wood that lent itself naturally to the slender lines, graceful curves and delicate modeling of the eighteenth century styles. In addition to this the wood itself was so treated as to ripen to the utmost the quality of rich and mellow coloring, which was one of its distinctive characteristics. The boards were kept for months, and some of them for years, in the courtyards of the cabinet shops, where sun and rain could give them the mellowness of age. Then the finished pieces were treated with linseed oil and again put out into the sunshine to oxidize, this process being repeated until the wood gained just the required depth of color and perfection of finish. The slowness of this process and the care and skill required to produce the results that were aimed at makes fine mahogany furniture almost an impossibility today, except to the craftsman who may be able to afford selected pieces of this rare and almost extinct wood, and who has sufficient leisure and love of the work to treat it according to the methods of the old cabinetmakers. Even then it is not suitable for the plain massive furniture that

we show here as models for home workers. The severely plain structural forms that we are considering now demand a wood of strong fiber and markings, rich in color, and possessing a sturdy friendly quality that seems to invite use and wear. The strong straight lines and plain surfaces of the furniture follow and emphasize the grain and growth of the wood, drawing attention to instead of destroying the natural character that belonged to the growing tree. As the use of oak would naturally demand a form that is strong and primitive, the harmony that exists between the form and construction of the furniture and the wood of which it is made is complete and satisfying.

We will then assume that oak is the wood that would naturally be selected by the home cabinetmaker and for large surfaces such as table-tops and large panels, quarter-sawn oak is deemed preferable to plain-sawn, as the first method, which makes the cut parallel with the medullary rays that form the peculiar wavy lines seen in quarter-sawn oak, not only brings out all the natural beauty of the markings, but makes the wood structurally stronger, finer in grain and less liable to check and warp than when it is straight-sawn. Care should then be taken to see that the wood is thoroughly dried, otherwise the best work might easily be ruined by the checking, warping, or splitting of the lumber. Quarter-sawn oak is the hardest of all woods to dry and requires the longest time, so that it would hardly be advisable for the amateur cabinetmaker to attempt to use other than selected kiln-dried wood that is ready for the saw and plane.

FIGURE THIRTEEN.—ROUND TABLE.

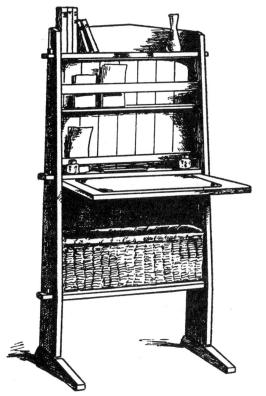

FIGURE FOURTEEN.—WRITING DESK WITH WILLOW WASTE BASKET.

The work of construction must all be done before the wood is given its final finish; but in this connection we will outline briefly the best method of finishing oak, as the sturdy wooden quality of the furniture depends entirely upon the ability of the worker to treat the wood so that there is little evidence of an applied finish. Oak should be ripened as the old mahogany was ripened by oil and sunshine, and this can be done only by a process that, without altering or disguising the nature of the wood, gives it the appearance of having been mellowed by age and use. This process is merely fuming with ammonia, which has a certain affinity with the tannic acid that exists in the wood, and it is the only one known to us that acts upon the glossy hard rays as well as the softer parts of the wood, coloring all together in an even tone so that the figure is marked only by its difference in texture. This result is not so good when stains are used instead of fuming, as staining leaves the soft part of the wood dark and the markings light and prominent.

The fuming is not an especially difficult process, but it requires a good deal of care, for the piece must be put into an air-tight box or closet, on the floor of which has been placed shallow dishes containing aqua ammonia (26 per cent). The length of time required to fume oak to a good color depends largely upon the tightness of the compartment, but as a rule forty-eight hours is enough. When fuming is not practicable, as in the case of a piece too large for any available compartment or one that is built into the room, a fairly good result may be obtained by applying the strong ammonia directly to the wood with a sponge or brush. In either case the wood must be in its natural condition when treated, as any previous application of oil or stain would keep the ammonia from taking effect. After the wood so treated is thoroughly dry from the first application it should be sandpapered carefully with fine sandpaper, then a second coat of ammonia applied, followed by a second careful sandpapering.

Some pieces fume much darker than others, according to the amount of tannin left free to attract the ammonia after the wood has

FIGURE FIFTEEN.—TABLE DESK.

FIGURE SIXTEEN.—LIBRARY TABLE.

ened by the addition of a small quantity of the stain used in touching up. Care must be taken, however, to carry on the color so lightly that it will not grow muddy under the brush of an inexperienced worker. The danger of this makes it often more advisable to apply two coats of lacquer, each containing a very little color. If this is done, sandpaper each coat with very fine sandpaper after it is thoroughly dried and then apply one or more coats of prepared floor wax. These directions, if carefully followed, should give the same effects that characterize the Craftsman furniture.

Sometimes a home cabinetworker does not find it practicable or desirable to fume the oak. In such a case there are a number of good stains on the market that could be used on oak as well as on other woods.

Oak and chestnut alone are susceptible to the action of ammonia fumes, but in other ways the oak, chestnut, ash and elm come into one class as regards treatment, for the reason that they all have a strong, well-defined grain and are so alike in nature that they are affected in much the same way by the same method of finishing. For any one of these woods a water stain should never be used, as it raises the grain to such an extent that in sandpapering to make it smooth again, the color is sanded off with the grain, leaving an unevenly stained and very unpleasant surface. The most satisfactory method we know, especially for workers who have had but little experience, is to use a small amount of color carried on in very thin

been kiln-dried. Where any sap wood has been left on, that part will be found unaffected by the fumes. There is apt also to be a slight difference in tone when the piece is not all made from the same log, because some trees contain more tannic acid than others. To meet these conditions it is necessary to make a "touch-up" to even the color. This is done by mixing a brown aniline dye (that will dissolve in alcohol) with German lacquer, commonly known as "banana liquid." The mixture may be thinned with wood alcohol to the right consistency before using. In touching up the lighter portions of the wood the stain may be smoothly blended with the darker tint of the perfectly fumed parts, by rubbing along the line where they join with a piece of soft dry cheese-cloth, closely following the brush. If the stain should dry too fast and the color is left uneven, dampen the cloth very slightly with alcohol. After fuming, sandpapering and touching up a piece of furniture, apply a coat of lacquer, made of one-third white shellac and two thirds German lacquer. If the fuming process has resulted in a shade dark enough to be satisfactory, this lacquer may be applied clear; if not, it may be dark-

FIGURE SEVENTEEN.—LARGE LIBRARY TABLE.

CABINET WORK FOR HOME WORKERS

shellac. If the commercial cut shellac is used it should be reduced with alcohol in the proportion of one part of shellac to three of alcohol. This is because shellac, as it is ordinarily cut for commercial purposes, is mixed in the proportion of four pounds to a gallon of alcohol, so that in order to make it thin enough it is necessary to add sufficient alcohol to obtain a mixture of one pound of shellac to a gallon of alcohol. If the worker does his own cutting he will naturally use the proportion last mentioned,—

FIGURE NINETEEN.—PLATE RACK TO BE PLACED OVER A SIDEBOARD.

one pound of shellac to a gallon of alcohol. When the piece is ready for the final finish, apply a coat of thin shellac, adding a little color if necessary; sandpaper carefully and then apply one or more coats of liquid wax. These directions are entirely for the use of home workers. The method we use in the Craftsman Workshops differs in many ways, for we naturally have much greater facilities for obtaining any desired effect than would be possible with the equipment of a home worker.

For lighter pieces of furniture suitable for a bedroom or a woman's sitting room, where dainty effects are desirable, we find maple the most satisfactory, in both color and texture, of our native woods, for the reason that it is

hard enough to be used for all kinds of furniture. Gumwood is equally beautiful, but is not hard enough for chairs. For built-in furniture, however, and for tables, dressers and the like, gumwood is one of the most beautiful woods we have, as it takes on a soft, satin-like texture with variable color effects not unlike those seen in the finest Circassian walnut. We find that the best effect in both maple and gumwood is obtained by treating the wood with a solution of iron-rust made by throwing iron filings or any small pieces of iron into acid vinegar or a weak solution of acetic acid. After forty-eight hours the solution is drained off and diluted with water until the desired color is obtained. The wood is merely brushed over with this solution,—wetting it thoroughly,—and left to dry. This is a process that requires much experimenting with small pieces of wood before attempting to treat the furniture, as the color does not show until the application is completely dry. By this treatment maple is given a beautiful tone of pale silvery gray and the gumwood takes on a soft pale grayish brown, both of which colors harmonize admirably with dull blue, old rose, straw color, or any of the more delicate shades so often used in furnishing a bedroom or a woman's sitting room.

As to the actual construction of the pieces shown here, it is in most cases very simple. By a careful study of the different models it will be noted that the only attempt at decoration lies in the emphasizing of the actual structural features, such as posts, panels, tenons with or without the key, the dovetail joint and the key as

FIGURE EIGHTEEN.—SMALL SIDEBOARD.

CABINET WORK FOR HOME WORKERS

it is used to strengthen and emphasize the joining of two boards. For the rest, the beauty of each piece depends wholly upon the care with which the wood is selected, the proportions and workmanship of the piece, and the attention that is given to the delicate details of construction and to the finish of the wood.

In Figures 1 and 2 we illustrate two of the simplest models we have ever offered for the use of home cabinetworkers. They are two designs for small tabourets and were selected to illustrate the first article on home training in cabinetwork, published in THE CRAFTSMAN in April, 1905. Therefore from the point of view of their precedence in the series, no less than their fitness as models for the beginner, they have been chosen to head the illustrations for this article. In the case of both of them the construction shows for itself. The tenons of the legs are visible through the top of the table, where they are firmly wedged and then planed flush with the top. This not only strengthens the table very considerably, but the difference in the grain of the wood gives the effect of four small square inlays in each table top. Also it is well to note that, in cutting the mortises for the stretchers of the square tabouret, there is half an inch difference in the heights of the two stretchers. A dowel pin three-eighths of an inch in diameter

FIGURE TWENTY-ONE.—SMALL LETTER AND PAPER FILE.

runs all the way through the legs and holds firm the tenons of the stretchers, making it practically impossible for the table to rack apart. These pins are planed off flush with the sides of the legs.

Figures 3 and 6 illustrate companion pieces, the first being a hall bench and the second a piano bench. Both are simple to a degree, yet the proportions are so contrived that the effect of each is individual and decorative. The outward slope of the solid end pieces gives an appearance of great strength that does full justice to the real strength of both benches. The severity of these end pieces is rather lightened by the curved opening at the bottom and by the openings at the top, meant in each case for convenience in moving the bench. These openings, with the slight projections of the tenons at the ends, form the only decoration. In the case of the hall bench, a shallow box takes the place of the curved brace that appears under the seat in the piano bench. This box can be used to hold all sorts of things that ordinarily accumulate in the hall and the hinged seat lifts like a lid over it. The bench can be made in any desired length to fit any wall space without interfering with its construction or proportions.

Figure 4 shows a small open bookcase that is intended for the use of children. All housewives know that one of the greatest difficulties in keeping a tidy nursery often arises because there is no place where children can easily put things away themselves. Closet doors are hard to open and the shelves too high to be of use, while shelves and brackets are usually purposely out of reach and the nursery table is apt to be full. This little bookcase is planned especially to meet just such a nursery problem. There are no

FIGURE TWENTY.—COMBINATION TABLE AND ENCYCLOPEDIA BOOKCASE.

doors and the shelves are broad and

CABINET WORK FOR HOME WORKERS

low enough to be within the reach of very little children. The shelves are not adjustable but are put in stoutly with tenon and key so that they are never out of place and never need attention.

Figure 5 shows a small table that would prove a convenient piece of furniture in a household where either chess or checkers happens to be a favorite game. The legs are slightly tapering, sloped outward and are made firm with bracket supports below, which would interfere with the comfort of the players sitting at the table, are not needed. The rails under the top are tenoned to the legs. In a case like this, where two or more rails meet with the ends opposite each other, short tenons must be used with two dowel pins in each one to hold it in place. These pins are placed near the edge of the table legs so that they may not interfere with the tenoning of the side rails. It is a good plan to dowel the bracket supports first to the legs and then to the top of the table, in addition to the glue which holds them in place. The small drawer is made in the regular way, being hung from the top instead of running on a center guide as do most of the wider drawers in Craftsman furniture. The checks on the table top may be burned into the wood or a dye or stain may be used for the dark checks.

Figure 7 shows a small portable cabinet that may be placed on the top of any writing table. It is provided with little compartments which are protected by doors with flat key locks and with a shelf and pigeon-holes for papers and books. The piece is perfectly plain except for the slight decorative touch given by the dovetailing at the end, but if the wood is well chosen and the cabinet carefully finished, it will be found an attractive as well as a convenient bit of furniture.

Figure 8 illustrates a child's desk, the making

FIGURE TWENTY-TWO.—SMALL REVOLVING BOOK-RACK.

of which would be an especially pleasant piece of work for the home craftsman, because there is no article of miniature furniture which affords the children so much delight as a desk where they can work like grown-up folks and have pads and pencils never to be loaned or lost. This little desk is so simple that the small members of the family might even help to make it and so gain some understanding of the pleasure of making their own belongings. The construction has the same general features that have already been described and the only touch of decoration is the projection of the two back posts above the small upper shelf.

Figure 9 suggests a useful and desirable present for a bride, for it is a cedar-lined chest

FIGURE TWENTY-THREE.—COMBINATION BOOKCASE AND CUPBOARD.

FIGURE TWENTY-FOUR.—A HALL CLOCK.

intended for the storing of linen and clothing,—just the same sort of chest as the German maidens use for storing away the linen they weave during their girlhood. In making the chest the legs are first built up, then the front and back fastened in; the ends and bottom are put in at the same time, fitting in grooves. The top is simply made, with two panels divided by a broad stile which affords support for the iron strap-hinge that extends down the side to be fastened with hasp and padlock. The inside of the chest is lined with cedar boards, so desirable for their pleasant aromatic odor and for their moth - preventing properties. This lining should be put in after the chest is made. The iron work can be made by any blacksmith from the drawing, or even made at home if the amateur cabinetworker also possesses a forge.

Figure 10 shows a book cabinet which would be convenient in a workroom, where it might stand near the desk or table of the worker and provide a place for the few books of reference that are in constant use, as well as for papers, drawings and so forth, that might otherwise be mislaid or scattered in confusion about the room. The cabinet is easy to make and is very satisfying in line and proportion. The shelf that covers half the top offers room for a small paper rack or any of the many things that have to be within reach and yet not in the way.

Figure 11 gives a model for a bookcase having two drawers below for papers or magazines and three adjustable shelves that can be moved to any height simply by changing the position of the pegs that support the shelves. If the books are small, an additional shelf might be put in if required. The frame of the bookcase is left plain, the smooth surface of the sides being broken only by the slightly projecting tenons at the top and bottom. The edges of these tenons are chamfered off and carefully sandpapered so that they have a smooth rounded look. Inside the ends of the bookcase holes about half an inch in diameter are bored about halfway through the thickness of the plank, affording places for the pegs that hold the adjustable shelves.

Figure 12 shows a small table primarily chosen for use in a bedroom, to stand near the bed and hold a lamp or candle and one or two books, but it is convenient in any place where a small stand is needed. The top of the back is to be doweled in place with three half-inch dowel pins and the top itself is fastened to the sides by table fasteners placed under a wide overhang. The drawers should be dovetailed together at the corners and all edges slightly softened by careful sandpapering.

Figure 13. The round table shown here embodies in its construction the same general features as the large square library table shown in Figure 17, only modified to such a degree that the effect is light rather than massive. The braces, top and bottom, are crossed and the four legs are wide and flat, with openings following the lines of the outside. The tenons, which have a bold projection and are fastened with wooden keys, are used as a distinctively decorative feature.

Figure 14 gives a very good idea of a desk which looks hard to make but is not so difficult as might appear at the first glance. The lid can be made first, then the sides and shelves carefully fitted and a quarter-inch iron pin inserted between the sides and the lid so that all

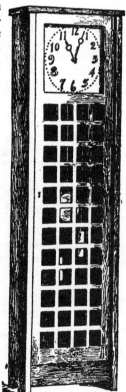

FIGURE TWENTY-FIVE— A HALL CLOCK.

are fastened together at once. Then the back is put in and is held in place by small blued oval-headed screws. After this the letter and blotter rack may be sprung into place and, with a little button at the top under which is a leather washer, the desk is complete except for the basket, which should be woven of willow withes to fit the shelf.

Figure 15 shows a simple desk or writing table for the library or living room. The two little upper drawers with the letter file between give a very convenient arrangement for stowing away letters, writing paper, etc. This is a piece which might easily be made crude and heavy, by just a little awkwardness in getting the right proportions and lack of skill in the use of tools; but if carefully made and well finished it possesses a sturdy attractiveness that is very interesting.

Figure 16. This design for a library table should not be attempted until experience in woodwork has taught the worker how to use his tools and materials well. Everything depends upon care both in construction and finishing and especial attention should be given toward maintaining in their integrity all the lines and proportions, as these details have everything to do with making or marring the design. The end pieces, while massive in effect, are relieved from over-heaviness by the use of slats and the shaping of the broad strips on the outside. The top of the table is fastened firmly with table irons so that it is quite solid. Where the shelf tenons come through the end pieces there is a

projection of three-sixteenths of an inch and the edges are chamfered off to give a smooth rounded effect. The tenon itself should be wedged and glued so that it cannot be pulled out. The dovetailing on the drawer may need a little practice before it is successfully executed, but if it is well done it will be a satisfactory evidence of the cleverness of the worker.

Figure 17 shows a large library table that is practically a companion piece to the round table illustrated in Figure 13. In this case, however, the natural massiveness of the construction is emphasized rather than modified, although the severity of the solid ends is softened by the curved lines and open spaces which serve to take away all appearance of clumsiness. The projecting tenons and keys form a suitable structural decoration and add to the strength of the piece. A strong brace just beneath the top keeps the ends firm while the lower shelf acts as another brace.

Figure 18. The lines and proportions of this small sideboard make it an unusually satisfying piece for the home worker to try his skill on because, if it is well made, it is a piece

FIGURE TWENTY-EIGHT.—RUSTIC BENCH WITH SLAB TOP.

books near at hand. It is meant to hold a complete set of books, with additional space for a dictionary. The plans are so simple that they can be understood and applied by a beginner in cabinetwork and the usefulness of the piece is such as to make it one of the most interesting models we have ever designed for the use of home workers.

Figures 21 and 22 show two most convenient little pieces for a library table. The first is a small letter file with four compartments for note paper, envelopes and letters, making it very useful for the home bookkeeper. The second is a small revolving book rack, made in the form of a swastika, which revolves upon a flat round stand that raises it about an inch from the table. It is meant to hold small books that are needed for constant reference. Both these pieces show to the best advantage the decorative use of the dovetail as a joint. This bit of structural decoration is a favorite with us because we consider the hand-made dovetail to be one of the most interesting structural features used in joinery, as well as the strongest joint. This, of course, applies only to pieces where the strength of the structure depends upon the strength of the corner, for it is purely a corner joint. For example, in the case of this little book-rack the use of the dovetail is almost inevitable, for without it the corners would not only be less perfectly

of furniture that would add much to the beauty of a dining room. The construction, though on a larger scale and in some ways more complicated than in any of the preceding pieces, is no more difficult and no trouble will be found in putting it together. The back is to be screwed into place and is put on last. The top can be doweled on or fastened with table irons. The latter will be safer if there is any doubt as to the thorough seasoning of the wood, as the irons will admit of a slight shrinkage or swelling without cracking the wood. All the edges should be slightly softened with sandpaper just before the finish is applied.

Figure 19. This plate rack is meant to be hung by chains, cords, or heavy picture wire just above the sideboard, although it also serves as a stein rack for a den. The construction speaks for itself and is so simple that nothing need be said about it except that the brackets are fastened with screws from the back. If chains are used to hang it from the rail above, it would be better to have them fairly heavy. Plain round link chains can be bought ready made, together with the hooks, or they can be made to order by any blacksmith.

Figure 20 shows a combination table and encyclopedia bookcase designed especially for the student who wishes to have his reference

FIGURE TWENTY-NINE.—RUSTIC TABLE THAT CAN BE TAKEN APART AT WILL.

CABINET WORK FOR HOME WORKERS

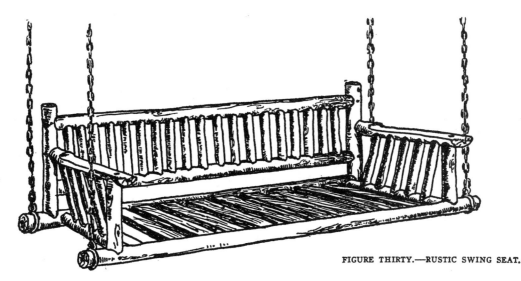

joined as regards strength, but the piece would lose its greatest claim to structural interest.

Figure 23 shows a combination bookcase and cupboard with an open shelf in the middle for such books as are most used. The sides have small-paned glass doors and are shelved for books; the central cupboard with the wooden doors is meant to hold papers, magazines and the like.

Figures 24 and 25 show two hall clocks, of the type usually known as the "grandfather's clock." Given a moderate skill in the handling of tools, the home worker can easily make a clock that will prove a quaint and satisfactory

bit of furnishing and will have all the charm of an individual piece of handicraft made for the place it is to fill. Oak is the most appropriate wood for the cases of both these clocks, and the construction is very simple. The face may be made of wood with the figures burned in, or of a twelve-inch plate of brass with figures of copper. If the latter is used, holes should be drilled in the plate to receive the pins which rivet on the figures. These pins are simply bent over after the figures are in place. In both cases the door at the back should have a silk panel in it so that the sound may easily pass through.

Figure 26 shows a child's high-chair designed in the typical Craftsman style. In building this chair put everything together except the arms and when the glue is dry the arm dowels are fitted and the back ones shoved into place. Then by pressure the front will spring into its proper position. All the dowels should be well glued. Care should be used in the joining of the seat rails and it should also be noted that three-eighths of an inch is cut from the bottom of the back post after the chair is put to-

FIGURE THIRTY-ONE.—RUSTIC BED FOR LOG CABIN OR MOUNTAIN CAMP.

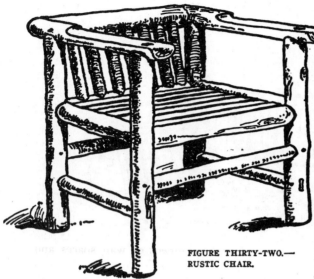

FIGURE THIRTY-TWO.— RUSTIC CHAIR.

gether. This makes a little slant back to the seat and gives a comfortable position to the sitter. The back slats of the chair are slightly curved—a thing that can be done by thoroughly wetting or steaming the wood and pressing it into shape and then allowing it to dry. The arms of the adjustable tray are cut from a single piece of wood and the back ends are splined by sawing straight in to a point beyond the curve and inserting in the opening made by the saw a piece of wood cut with the grain and well glued. This device gives strength to a point that otherwise would be very weak.

Figure 27 shows a screen which is very easy to make, yet most decorative, owing to the proportion of the leaves, the curving of the top and the use of keys to hold together the broad V-jointed boards of the lower part. The upper part may be of silk, leather, or any material that is preferred.

Figures 28 and 29 show a rustic bench and table

meant for a log cabin or mountain camp. The legs of the bench are made of small logs which are hewn or planed at four angles, leaving the round surface and the wane, so that the piece has in it some of the irregularity of the trunk of the growing tree. The top of the bench is made of a split log planed only at the upper side, the under side being stripped of its bark and left in the natural shape. The horses for the table are made in the same way as the legs of the bench. The table top is in two pieces, the wide thick planks of which it is made being finished as carefully as for any well-made table. These table boards are locked together underneath so that there is no danger of their parting when in use and they can easily be taken apart when it is necessary to move or set aside the table. The great convenience of this table is that it can be taken to pieces and used anywhere, indoors or out.

Figures 30, 31, 32 and 33 show some substantial pieces of rustic furniture designed for country or camp life or for outdoor use. The first is a swinging seat for the veranda or lawn; the second, a bedstead for use in a log cabin or camp; the third is a rustic chair and the fourth a rustic couch for outdoor use. The value of this rustic furniture is not wholly that it is durable and capable of weathering sun and rain alike, but that it makes a special appeal to the amateur carpenter, as its rough exterior hides defects in joining and there is not the special need of well seasoned and carefully prepared lumber that is so essential to the success of the finer pieces.

FIGURE THIRTY-THREE.—COUCH FOR VERANDA OR LAWN.

OUR NATIVE WOODS AND THE CRAFTSMAN METHOD OF FINISHING THEM

SO much of the success of the whole Craftsman scheme of building and decoration depends upon the right selection and treatment of the woodwork, which forms such an important part of the structural and also of the decorative scheme, that we have considered it worth while to devote an entire chapter to such information and instruction as we are able to give concerning some of our native woods that we consider most desirable for this purpose. We are taking up only the woods that are native to this country, for the reason that they are nearest at hand and because, when finished by our method, they reveal the beauty of color and grain that forms the basis of the whole Craftsman idea of interior decoration. These vary widely, as each wood possesses strongly marked characteristics as to color, texture and grain; but all the woods we mention here are desirable for interior trim and the use of them is much more in accordance with the Craftsman scheme of decoration than are the elaborate and more or less exotic effects obtained by the use of expensive foreign woods. This does not mean that we claim greater beauty for the native woods, but merely that, when properly treated, they are quite as interesting as any of the more costly woods imported from other countries and have the great advantage of being easily obtainable at moderate cost.

We need not dwell upon the importance of using a generous amount of woodwork to give an effect of permanence, homelikeness and rich warm color in a room. Anyone who has ever entered a house in which the friendly natural wood is used in the form of wainscoting, beams and structural features of all kinds, has only to contrast the impression given by such an interior with that which we receive when we go into the average house, where the plain walls are covered with plaster and paper and the conventional door and window frames are of painted or varnished wood, in order to realize the difference made by giving to the woodwork its full value in the decorative scheme. No care bestowed on decoration, or expense lavished on draperies or furniture, can make up for the absence of wood in the interior of a house. This is a truth that has long been understood and applied in the older countries, especially in England, whose mellow friendly old houses are the delight and despair of Americans; but it is only a few years since

we began to apply it to the building and furnishing of our own homes. With us the realization of the possibilities of natural wood when used as a basis for interior decoration first took root in the West, particularly on the Pacific Coast, where the delightful atmosphere of rooms that were wainscoted, ceiled and beamed with California redwood gave rise to a new departure in the finishing and decoration of our homes, and stirred the East to follow suit.

In recommending the generous use of woodwork, however, we would have it clearly understood that we mean the use of wood so finished that its individual qualities of grain, texture and color are preserved so far as possible, and such treatment of wall spaces and structural features that they are not made unduly prominent, but rather sink quietly into the background and become a part of the room itself, forming a friendly unobtrusive setting for the furniture, draperies and ornaments, instead of coming into competition with them. To this end the woodwork should be so finished that its inherent color quality is deepened and mellowed as if by time and its surface made pleasantly smooth without sacrificing the woody quality that comes from frankly revealing its natural texture. When this is done, the little sparkling irregularity of the grain allows a play of light over the surface that seems to give it almost a soft radiance,—a quality that we lose entirely in woodwork that is filled, stained to a solid color, varnished and polished so that the light is reflected from a hard unsympathetic surface.

It is interesting also to note how much the character of a room depends upon the kind of wood we use in it. For example, the impression given by oak is strong, austere and dignified, suggesting stability and permanence such as would naturally belong to a house built to last for generations. It is a robust, manly sort of wood and is most at home in large rooms which are meant for constant use, such as the living room, reception hall, library or dining room. Chestnut, ash and elm,—although each one has an individual quality of color and grain that differentiates it from all the others,—all come into the same class as oak, in that they are strong-fibered, open-textured woods that find their best use in the rooms in which the general life of the household is carried on. The finer-textured woods,

WOODS AND HOW WE FINISH THEM

such as maple, beech, birch and gumwood, are more suitable for the woodwork in smaller and more daintily furnished rooms that are not so roughly used, such as bedrooms or small private sitting rooms. Aside from this general classification, the choice of wood for interior woodwork naturally must depend upon the taste of the home-builder, the requirements of the decorative scheme planned for the house as a whole, and the ease with which a particular kind of wood may be obtained. .

In considering the relative value of our native woods for interior woodwork, we are inclined to give first place to the American white oak, which possesses not only strength of fiber and beauty of color and markings, but great durability, as its sturdiness and the hardness of its texture enables it to withstand almost any amount of wear. In this respect it is far superior to the other woods, such as chestnut, ash and elm, which we have mentioned as being in the same general class of open-textured, strong-fibered woods; although these, under the right treatment, possess a color quality finer than that of oak, in that they show a greater degree of that mellow radiance which counts so much in the atmosphere of a room. This is especially true of chestnut, which is so rich in color that it fairly glows. But in addition to its dignity and durability, there is something about oak that stirs the imagination. Not only is it suggestive of the rich somber time-mellowed rooms of old English houses which have seen generation after generation live and die in them, but it is the wood we are accustomed to associate with nearly all the magnificent carved work of earlier days. In fact, oak has come to stand as a symbol of strength and permanence, and a great part of our affection for it comes from the romance and the rare old associations with which its very name is surrounded.

There are many varieties of oak in this country, but of these the white oak is by far the most desirable, both for cabinetmaking and for interior woodwork. One reason for this is the deep, ripened color it takes on under the process we use for finishing it,—a process which gives the appearance of age and mellowness without in any way altering the character of the wood. We refer to the fuming with ammonia, which we have already described in the preceding chapter. The fact that ammonia fumes will darken new oak was discovered by accident. Some oak boards stored in a stable in England were found after a time to have taken on a beautiful mellow brown tone and on investigation this change in color was discovered to be due to the ammonia fumes that naturally are present in stables. This ripening, so essential to the beauty of oak woodwork, takes a long time when left to the unaided action of air and sunlight, and the fact that the wood darkened very quickly when it was stored in a stable led to experimenting with the effect of ammonia fumes upon various kinds of oak. The reason for this effect was at first unknown and, to the best of our belief, it was not discovered until the experiments with fuming made in The Craftsman Workshops established the fact that the darkening of the wood was due to the chemical affinity existing between ammonia and tannic acid, of which there is a large percentage present in white oak. This being established, preparations were at once made for using ammonia fumes in a practical way, which we have already described in a preceding chapter. The process mentioned there, however, is practicable only when furniture is to be fumed, as it is quite possible to construct an air-tight compartment sufficiently large to hold one or more pieces of furniture, but when it comes to fuming the woodwork of a whole room it is not so easy. The fuming boxes we use in The Craftsman Workshops are made of tarred canvas stretched tightly over large light wooden frames which are padded heavily around the bottom so that no air can creep in between the box and the floor. The box is drawn to the ceiling by means of a rope and pulley; the furniture is piled directly below and shallow dishes are set around the edges inside the line that marks the limits of the compartment. The box is then lowered almost to the floor; very strong aqua ammonia (26 per cent.) is quickly poured into the dishes and the box dropped at once to the floor. The strength of the ammonia used for this purpose may be appreciated when one remembers that the ordinary ammonia retailed for household use is about 5 per cent.

Of course, for fuming interior woodwork, the air-tight compartment is hardly practicable; but a fairly good substitute for it may be obtained by shutting up the room in which the woodwork is to be fumed, stuffing up all the crevices as if for fumigating with sulphur and then setting around on the floor a liberal number of dishes into which the ammonia is poured last of all. It is hardly necessary to say that the person to whom the pouring of the ammonia is entrusted will get out of the room as quickly as possible after the fumes are released.

Another way of treating oak with ammonia is to brush the liquid directly on the wood, but owing to the strength of the fumes this is not a very comfortable process for the worker and it is rather less satisfactory in its results. The ammonia being in the nature of water, it naturally raises the grain of the wood. Therefore, after the application, it should be allowed to dry over night and the grain carefully sandpapered down the next day. As this is apt to leave the color somewhat uneven, the wood should again be brushed over with the ammonia and sandpapered a second time after it is thoroughly dry. This method of getting rid of the grain is by no means undesirable, for the wood has a much more beautiful surface after all the loose grain has been raised and then sandpapered off. Where paint or varnish is used there is no necessity for getting rid of the grain, as it is held down by them. But with our finish, which leaves the wood very nearly in its natural state, it is best to dispose of the loose grain once for all and obtain a natural surface that will remain permanently smooth.

We find the finest white oak in the Middle West and Southwest, especially in Indiana, which has furnished large quantities of the best grade of this valuable wood. Like so many of our natural resources, the once bountiful supply of our white oak has been so depleted by reckless use that it is probable that ten or fifteen years more will see the end of quartered oak, and possibly of the best grades of plain-sawn oak as well. The popularity of quarter-sawn oak,—a very wasteful process of manufacture,—is one of the causes of the rapid depletion of our oak forests. We append a small cut showing the cross-section of a tree trunk marked with the lines made by quarter-sawing. As will be seen, the trunk is first cut into quarters and then each quarter is sawn diagonally from the outside to the center, naturally making the boards narrower and increasing the waste. There is some hope to be derived from the fact that great stretches of oak timberland are now being reforested by the Government, but at best it will be a generation or two before these slow-growing trees are large enough to furnish the best

quality of lumber. There is no question as to the greater durability of quarter-sawn oak for uses which demand hard wear and also where the finer effects are desired, as in furniture, but for interior woodwork plain-sawn oak is not only much less expensive than quarter-sawn but is quite as desirable in every way. The markings are stronger and more interesting, the difference between the hard and soft parts of the grain is better defined, and the openness of texture gives the wood a mellower color quality than it has when quarter-sawn. The distinguishing characteristic of quarter-sawn oak is the presence of the glassy rays,—technically called medullary rays,—which bind the perpendicular fibers together and give the oak tree its amazing strength. In quarter-sawing, the cut is made parallel with these

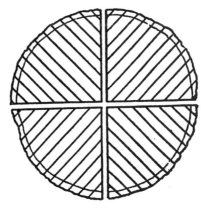

Cross-section of tree-trunk, showing method of quarter-sawing

medullary rays instead of across them, as is done in straight sawing, so that they show prominently, forming the peculiar wavy lines that distinguish quarter-sawn oak. The preservation of the binding properties of these rays gives remarkable structural strength to the wood, which is much less liable to crack, check or warp than when it is plain-sawn. This, of course, makes a difference when it comes to making large panels, table tops, or anything else that shows a large plain surface, and for these uses quarter-sawn oak is preferable merely because it "stands" better. But for the woodwork of a room, we much prefer the plain-sawn oak on account of its friendliness and the delightful play of light and shade that is given by the boldness and color variation of the grain. When quarter-sawn oak is used for large stretches of woodwork, the effect is duller and more austere because the

WOODS AND HOW WE FINISH THEM

color of the wood is colder and more uniform and it shows a much harder and closer texture.

In the final finishing of oak woodwork, the method that we find most practicable differs somewhat from that described in the directions we have already given for finishing furniture. As the woodwork in a room is not called upon to stand the hard wear that is necessarily given to the furniture, we do not need the shellac, and after the right tone has been obtained by fuming, the wood may be given several coats of prepared floor wax and then rubbed until the surface is satin smooth. If, however, a darker shade of brown is desired, the fumed wood may be given one or more coats of thin shellac, with a little color carried on in each coat, and then finished with wax after the manner described in the directions given for finishing furniture. This method of finishing is one that we have adopted after years of experimenting and it has become so identified with the Craftsman use of oak that it has been very generally taken up by other makers of this style of furniture and by decorators who advocate the Craftsman treatment of interior woodwork.

Next in rank to oak for use in large rooms comes chestnut, which is equally attractive in fiber and markings, has a color quality that is even better, and is plentiful, easily obtained and very reasonable as to cost. While it lacks something of the stateliness and durability of oak, chestnut is even more friendly because of the mellowness and richness of its color, which under very simple treatment takes on a luminous quality that seems to fill the whole room with a soft glow like that of the misty color that is radiated from trees in autumn. Chestnut takes even more kindly than oak to the fuming process, because it contains a greater percentage of tannin and the texture of the wood itself is softer and more open. But unless a deep tone of brown is desired, fuming may be dispensed with, because the wood is so much richer in the elements from which color can be produced that a delightful effect may be obtained merely by applying a light stain of nut brown or soft gray, under which the natural color of the wood appears as an undertone. The staining is very easy to do, but care should be taken to have only a very little color in each coat because the wood takes the stain so readily that a mere trifle of superfluous color will give a thick muddy effect that destroys the clear luminous quality which is

the chief charm. In the case of our Craftsman houses, we find it easier to fume chestnut woodwork than to stain it, and this process is the more to be recommended because chestnut takes the fumes of ammonia very quickly and easily. Also because of this, the ammonia should never be brushed directly on the wood, which is so porous that the moisture is sure to raise the grain to such an extent that the amount of sanding required to smooth it down again destroys the natural surface. One great advantage of chestnut,—aside from its charm of color, texture and markings,—is that it is very easy to work, stays in place readily and is so easy to dry that the chances of getting thoroughly dry lumber are much greater than they would be if oak were used.

Next to chestnut, in our opinion, comes rock elm,—a wood that is fairly abundant, not expensive, and easily obtainable, especially in the East. Rock elm is not affected by the fumes of ammonia and, so far as our experiments go, we have never been able to obtain the right color effect by the use of chemicals. Therefore, in order to get a good color, this wood has to be stained. The colors which are most in harmony with its natural color are brown, green, and gray, particularly in the lighter shades. The distinguishing peculiarity of rock elm is its jagged or feathery grain. Also, the difference in color between the hard and softs parts of the wood is very marked, giving, under the right treatment, a charming variation of tone. If one has the patience to experiment with stains on small pieces of rock elm, some unexpectedly good effects may be obtained. Care must be taken, however, that the stain is light enough to show merely as an over-tone that modifies the natural color of the wood, as the interplay of colors in the grain is hidden by too strong a surface tone. Elm is excellent for interior woodwork where the color effect desired is lighter than that given by either oak or chestnut and also it is hard enough to make pretty good furniture. This last is a decided advantage, especially in a room containing many built-in pieces which naturally form a part of the woodwork. In the earlier days of our experimenting with Craftsman furniture we made a good many pieces of elm and found them, on the whole, very satisfactory.

Brown ash comes into the same class with rock elm, as it is good for furniture as well as interior woodwork. It has a texture and color very similar to elm and should be treated in the same way with a very light stain of either brown, gray or green, all of which blend perfectly with the color quality inherent in the wood. Unfortunately, however, brown ash is no longer plentiful, having been wasted in the same reckless way that we have wasted other excellent woods. Some years ago it was used in immense quantities for making cheap furniture, agricultural implements and the like, and as it was used not only freely but wastefully, the supply is today very nearly exhausted.

In considering all these woods in connection with interior woodwork, it is well to keep in mind that each one of them harmonizes admirably with all the others while retaining, to the full, its own individuality. Therefore, in finishing the rooms on the first floor of a house, it is merely a matter of personal choice as to whether or not the same wood should be used throughout, or each room finished in a different wood. We have often recommended that one wood be used because in a Craftsman house there are practically no divisions or partitions between the rooms, and in this case the effect is so much like that of one large room with many nooks and corners that it would seem the natural thing to use one kind of wood for the interior woodwork throughout. However, if a variation should be desired,—and especially if the separation between the rooms were a little more clearly defined,—the use in different rooms of the different woods we have mentioned would be most interesting, as by this means variety in the woodwork could be obtained without any loss of harmony.

In buildings where it seems desirable to show in the woodwork the bold, strikingly artistic effects such as we associate with Japanese woods, we can heartily recommend cypress, which is plentiful, easily obtained and not expensive. For bungalows, mountain camps, seaside cottages, country clubs and the like, where strong and somewhat unusual effects are sought for, cypress will be found eminently satisfactory, as it is strong and brilliant as to markings and possesses most interesting possibilities in the way of color. Cypress is a soft wood belonging to the pine family and we get most of it from the cypress swamps in the Southern States. It is very like the famous Japanese cypress, which gives such a wonderful charm to many of the Japanese buildings and which is so identified with the Japanese use of woods. Over there they bury it for a time in order to get the color quality that is most desired,—a soft gray-brown against which the markings stand out strongly and show varying tones. This method, however, did not seem expedient in connection with our own use of the wood and after long experimenting we discovered that we could get much the same effect by treating it with sulphuric acid.

This process is very simple, as it is merely the application of diluted sulphuric acid directly to the surface of the wood. The commercial sulphuric acid should be used rather than the chemically pure, as the first is much cheaper and is quite as good for this purpose. Generally speaking, the acid should be reduced with water in the proportion of one part of acid to five parts of water, but the amount of dilution depends largely upon the temperature in which the work is done. Conditions are best when the thermometer registers seventy-five degrees or more. If it is above that, the sulphuric acid will stand considerably more dilution than it will take if the air is cooler. Of course, in the case of interior woodwork, it is possible to keep the room at exactly the right temperature by means of artificial heat, but when exterior woodwork or shingles are given the sulphuric acid treatment, it is most important to take into consideration the temperature and state of the weather. Exposure to the direct rays of the sun darkens the wood so swiftly that a much weaker solution is required than when the work is done in the shade. In any case, it is best to do a good deal of experimenting upon small pieces of wood before attempting to put the acid on the woodwork itself, as it is only by this means that the exact degree of strength required to produce the best effect can be determined. After the application of the acid the wood should be allowed to dry perfectly before putting on the final finish. For interior woodwork this last finish is given by applying one or two coats of wax; for the exterior, one or two coats of raw linseed oil may be used. If the wood threatens to become too dark under the action of the acid, the burning process can be stopped instantly by an application of either oil or wax, so that the degree of corrosion is largely under the control of the worker. A white hog's-bristle brush should be used for applying the acid, as any other kind of brush would be eaten up within a short time. Also great care should be taken to avoid getting acid on the face, hands, or clothing.

In connection with the subject of cypress for interior woodwork, we desire to say something concerning its desirability for outside use, such as half-timbering and other exterior woodwork. It is one of the most attractive of all our woods for such use because of its color quality and markings and it has the further advantage of "standing" well, without either shrinking or swelling. Naturally the sulphuric acid treatment that we have just described applies to this wood whether it is used indoors or out.

Another use of cypress is found in the rived cypress shingle which give us some of the most interesting effects in exterior wall surfaces. These shingles are the product of one of our few remaining handicrafts, and our sole source of supply depends upon the negroes in the Southern swamps. These negroes are adepts at splitting or riving shingles, and when they get the time or need a little extra money, they split up a few cypress logs into shingles and carry them to a lumber merchant in the nearest town. Consequently, the quantity that is available in the market varies, as no merchant has any great or steady supply of rived shingles and has to accumulate them by degrees and store them, in order to be able to fill any large order. Being hand-rived, these shingles cost about twice as much as the machine-sawn shingles, but they are well worth the extra outlay if one desires a house that is beautiful, individual and durable. The sawn shingle, unless oiled or stained in the beginning, is apt to get a dingy, weather-beaten look under the action of sun and rain and to require renewing early and often. But the rived shingle has exactly the surface of the growing tree from which the bark has been stripped; or, to be more exact, it shows the split surface of a tree trunk from which a bough has been torn, leaving the wood exposed. This surface, while full of irregularities, preserves the smooth natural fiber of the tree, and this takes on a beautiful color quality under the action of the weather, as the color of the wood ripens and shows as an undertone below the smooth silvery sheen of the surface,—an effect which is entirely lost when this natural glint is covered with the "fuzz" left by the saw. These rived shingles are also made of juniper, which is as good in color as cypress and has proven itself even more durable.

All cypress woodwork, whether interior or exterior, takes stain well; and if staining is preferred to the sulphuric acid treatment, very good effects may be gained in this way. We wish, however, to repeat the caution against using too strong a stain, as the effect is always much better if a very little color is carried on in each coat. We cannot too strongly urge the necessity of preliminary experimenting with small pieces of wood in order to gain the best color effects, and we also recommend that in finishing the woodwork of the room itself a very light color be put on at first, to be darkened if a deeper color is found necessary to give the desired effect. The reason for this is that a color which may be considered perfect upon a small piece of wood that is examined closely and held to the light, may prove either too strong or too weak when it is seen on the woodwork as a whole. Much of the effect depends upon the lighting of the room, and therefore it is best to go slowly and "work up" the finish of the woodwork until exactly the right effect is gained. After staining cypress woodwork it should be given either a coat of shellac or wax, or of wax alone, if the amount of wear does not necessitate shellac.

California redwood, when used for interior woodwork, gives an effect as interesting as that obtained by the use of cypress; but redwood does not respond well to the sulphuric acid treatment, which darkens and destroys its beautiful cool pinkish tone. In fact, redwood is best when left in its natural state and rubbed down with wax, as it then keeps in its purity the color quality that naturally belongs to it. Except for this slight finish and protection to the surface, it is a good wood to let alone, as either oil or varnish gives it a hot red look that is disquieting to live with and does not harmonize with any cool tones in the furniture; stains disguise the charm of its natural color and the chemical treatment brings out a purplish tone and gives a darkened and rather muddy effect.

While hard pine is fairly plentiful and lends itself well either to the sulphuric acid treatment or to simple staining, we do not recommend it for interior woodwork, as it costs no less than other woods we have mentioned and is less interesting in color and grain. But if it should be preferred, we would recommend that it be treated with the sulphuric acid, which gives a soft gray tone to the softer parts of the wood and a good deal of brilliancy to the markings.

In considering the woods that are most desirable for woodwork in rooms where light colors and dainty furnishings are used, birch comes first on the list, as it is nearest in character to the open-textured woods we have just described. Of the several varieties, red birch is best for interior woodwork. It is easily obtained all over the East, the Middle West and the South and costs considerably less than the other woods we have mentioned. When left in its natural state and treated with sulphuric acid, red birch makes really beautiful interior woodwork, as the acid deepens its natural color and gives it a mellowness that is as fine in its way as the mellowness produced in oak or chestnut by fuming. Some such treatment is absolutely necessary, for if red birch is left in its natural state, its color fades instead of ripening, so that it gets more and more of a washed-out look as time goes on. In using the acid on birch it is necessary to have a stronger solution than is required in the case of cypress; one part of acid to three parts of water should give it about the required strength. One advantage of birch is its hardness, for after the acid treatment it needs only waxing and rubbing to give it the final finish. The good qualities of birch, treated in this way and used for interior woodwork, are very little known, because it is the wood which has been used more than any other to imitate mahogany. The grain of birch is very similar to that of the more expensive wood, and when it has been given a red water stain and finished with shellac and varnish it bears a close resemblance to mahogany finished in the modern way,—which is by no means to be confused with the rare old Spanish mahogany of the eighteenth century.

Another excellent wood for use in a room that should have comparatively fine and delicate woodwork is maple, which can either be left in its natural color or finished in a tone of clear silver gray. As is well known, the natural maple takes on with use and wear a tone of clear pale yellow. This is not considered generally desirable, but if it should be needed to complete some special color scheme, it can be given to new maple by the careful use of aqua fortis, which should be diluted with water and used like sulphuric acid. The same precautions should be observed in using it, as it is a strong corrosive. Maple is generally

considered much more beautiful when finished in the gray tone, as this harmonizes admirably with the colors most often used in a daintily furnished room,—such as dull blue, old rose, pale straw color, reseda green and old ivory. It is not at all difficult to obtain this gray finish, for all that is needed is to brush a weak solution of iron rust on the wood. This solution is not made by using oxide of iron,—which is commonly but erroneously supposed to mean the same thing as iron rust,—but is obtained by throwing iron filings, rusty nails or any small pieces of iron into acid vinegar or a weak solution of acetic acid. After a couple of days the solution should be strained off and diluted with water until it is of the strength needed to get the desired color upon the wood. It is absolutely necessary in the case of this treatment to experiment first with small pieces of wood before the solution is applied to the woodwork as a whole, because otherwise it would be impossible to judge as to the strength of solution needed to give the desired effect. The color does not show at all until the application is thoroughly dry. If it is too weak, the wood will not be gray enough, and if it is too strong, it will be dark and muddy looking, sometimes almost black. After the woodwork so treated is perfectly dry and has been carefully sandpapered with very fine sandpaper, it should be given a coat of thin shellac that has been slightly darkened by putting in a few drops of black aniline (the kind that is soluble in alcohol); then it is given the final finish by rubbing with wax. These are the only methods we know that give good results on maple. We have tried the sulphuric acid treatment upon this wood, but have not found it satisfactory.

Beech, which is a little darker than maple and of a similar texture and grain, is equally desirable for the same uses. It may be treated either with iron rust or aqua fortis, following the same directions given in the case of maple. This wood is cheap and abundant and is usually found in the same regions which produce birch and maple. Poplar also does very well for the woodwork in a room that is not subjected to hard wear, as it is a very soft wood and will not stand hard usage. The best finish is simply a brown or green stain thin enough to allow the natural color of the wood to show through it. This natural color has in it a strong suggestion of green, so that it affiliates with the green stain and modifies the brown.

One wood that hitherto has been very little known, but that is coming more and more into prominence for the finer sorts of interior woodwork, is gumwood, which is obtained from the red gum that grows so abundantly in the Southern States and on the Pacific Coast. It is a pity that this beautiful wood should have been so little used that most people are unfamiliar with it, because for woodwork where fine texture, smooth surface and delicate coloring are required, quarter-sawn gumwood stands unsurpassed among our native woods. The best effects are obtained from gumwood by treating it with the iron-rust solution used in the way already described in connection with maple; but much more diluted, as the color of gumwood needs only the slightest possible mellowing and toning to make it perfect. When treated with a very weak iron-rust solution it bears a close resemblance to Circassian walnut, and the surface, which is smooth and lustrous as satin, shows a delightful play of light and shade. Sulphuric acid may be used on gumwood, but should be much more diluted than for any other wood, the proportion of acid being not more than one part to eight parts of water. This treatment gives a pinkish cast to the natural gray-brown tone of the wood, and while this does not harmonize as readily with most colors as does the pure gray-brown, it is very effective with certain decorative schemes.

Other woods that are valuable for interior woodwork, although much less plentiful than those we have named, are black walnut, butternut, quartered sycamore and several other woods that come naturally into the same class. Our American black walnut, although one of the standard woods in Europe, has been in a great measure spoiled for us because of its abuse during what we now speak of as the "black walnut period," which has come to mean over-ornamentation, distorted shapes and general bad taste. We have no forests of black walnut left, but there are still single trees, so that if this wood is especially desired, it may be obtained without much difficulty. The characteristics of butternut are much the same as those of black walnut, but it is rather lighter in color and not so hard.

Many people prefer white enameled woodwork for daintily furnished rooms. When this is used, the best kinds of wood for the purpose are poplar and basswood, preferably poplar. One thing should be remembered in connection with white woodwork, and that is that it should be treated in an entirely different way from the typical Craftsman woodwork, which depends for its effect upon the beauty of color and grain and therefore emphasizes these by means of simple forms, straight lines and plain surfaces. When white enameled woodwork is used, the style of it should be more elaborate, as all the interest that naturally belongs to the wood is hidden, and the only way to obtain the play of light and shade necessary to break up the monotony of the white surface is to use moldings, beadings and similar ornamentation, after what is called the Adam style, which we find in the best of our Colonial houses.

In considering interior woodwork one point should not be forgotten; that is the great interest that may be obtained by the right use of what, from a commercial point of view, is faulty wood. We all know the interest and charm of paneling and other woodwork that displays irregularities in the grain, such as knots, knurls and all sorts of queer twists. One of the best examples is found in the "curly" redwood, which is so greatly sought after in California. While the use of such pieces adds greatly to the beauty of a room, the selection of them requires much taste and judgment and absolutely demands that the personal attention of the owner or decorator be given to the work. It is never safe to trust the selection of faulty wood to the lumber merchant or its placing to the carpenter. The necessity of this care is rather an advantage than otherwise, because it is upon just such touches as these that much of the individuality of a decorative scheme depends.

We have treated fully the selection and coloring of the wood, but one practical detail that should be remembered by all who desire beautiful woodwork is that particular attention should be paid to having all the wood thoroughly kiln-dried. Even more important is the necessity of having the house free from dampness before the woodwork is put in, because no wood, however dry and well seasoned, will stand against the dampness of a newly plastered house. In fact, the effect upon the woodwork in such a case is almost worse than when the wood itself is not thoroughly seasoned, for in the latter case it will merely shrink, while dampness in the house will cause it to swell and bulge. The drying of wood not only needs close attention but the aid of some experienced person, as kiln-dried lumber is very apt to be uneven, and there is need of very careful watching while the wood is in the kiln to insure the even drying of all the boards, or the woodwork will be ruined.

Another thing that is worth watching is the final smoothing of the wood before it is put into place. After it leaves the planing machines in the mill it has to be made still smoother, and so most mills that furnish interior trim have installed sandpapering machines. These are convenient and labor-saving, but give a result that is very undesirable for fine woodwork, as the rotary sanding "fuzzes" the grain and, under the light finish we use, it is apt to be raised and roughened by moisture absorbed from the atmosphere. This does not matter when the woodwork is varnished, because the varnish holds it down, but where the natural surface of the wood is preserved great care should be used in the treatment of the grain. The popularity of Craftsman furniture and interior woodwork has created a demand for a surface that shows the sheen of the knife rather than the fuzz of the sanding machine, and some mills have met this demand by putting in scraping machines. These give better results than the sanding machines, but nothing equals the surface that is obtained by smoothing the wood by hand just before it is put into place. For this we use the hand scraper and a smoothing plane that is kept very sharp, as by this method the fiber is cut clean instead of being "cottoned out" and the sheen that naturally belongs to the wood is unimpaired. Although this means hand work, it is not very expensive because of the inconsiderable quantity of wood that is used in a house. Also the Craftsman method of finishing afterward costs so little that the slight extra care and expense incurred in obaining just the right surface is well worth while.

In connection with the woodwork in a house it is necessary to give some attention to the floors, which come into close relation with the treatment of the walls. The best wood for flooring is quartered oak, which all lumber merchants keep in stock in narrow widths, tongued and grooved. We find, however, that a more interesting floor can be made by using wider boards of uneven width, as this gives an effect of strength and bigness to the room. These wide boards need not be tongued and grooved, but may be put together with butt joints and the boards nailed through the top by using brad-head nails that can be countersunk and the holes puttied up so that they are almost invisible. When very wide boards are used it is best to build the floor in "three ply," like paneling. Plain-sawn oak is also good for flooring, but it is more likely to warp and sliver than quartered oak and it does not lie so flat. An oak floor, whether plain or quarter-sawn, must always be filled with a silex wood filler so that its surface is made smooth and non-absorbent. The color should be made the same as that of the woodwork, or a little darker; and after the stain is applied, the floor should be given one coat of shellac and then waxed. In rooms where the color schemes permit a slightly reddish tone in the floor, we would suggest that either birch or beech be used for flooring, as these may be finished by the sulphuric acid process,—a method which is better than stain because it darkens the wood itself and therefore does not wear off with use. If a gray floor should be desired, we would suggest maple treated with the iron-rust solution. In either case a coat of thin shellac should be applied after the chemical has been thoroughly dried,—say twenty-four hours after the first application,— and then waxed in the regular way. For ordinary floors a good wood to use is comb-grained pine, which receives its name from the method of sawing that leaves the grain in straight lines, not unlike the teeth of a comb. This does not warp or sliver and is very durable; it may be treated with stain and then given the regular finish of shellac and wax.

THE CRAFTSMAN IDEA OF THE KIND OF HOME ENVIRONMENT THAT WOULD RESULT FROM MORE NATURAL STANDARDS OF LIFE AND WORK

IN this book we have endeavored to set forth as fully as possible the several parts which, taken together, go to make up the Craftsman idea of the kind of home environment that tends to result in wholesome living. We have shown the gradual growth of this idea, from the making of the first pieces of Craftsman furniture to the completed house which has in it all the elements of a permanently satisfying home. But we have left until the last the question of the right setting for such a home and the conditions under which the life that is lived in it could form the foundation for the fullest individual and social development.

There is no question now as to the reality of the world-wide movement in the direction of better things. We see everywhere efforts to reform social, political and industrial conditions; the desire to bring about better opportunities for all and to find some way of adjusting economic conditions so that the heart-breaking inequalities of our modern civilized life shall in some measure be done away with. But while we take the greatest interest in all efforts toward reform in any direction, we remain firm in the conviction that the root of all reform lies in the individual and that the life of the individual is shaped mainly by home surroundings and influences and by the kind of education that goes to make real men and women instead of grist for the commercial mill.

That the influence of the home is of the first importance in the shaping of character is a fact too well understood and too generally admitted to be offered here as a new idea. One need only turn to the pages of history to find abundant proof of the unerring action of Nature's law, for without exception the people whose lives are lived simply and wholesomely, in the open, and who have in a high degree the sense of the sacredness of the home, are the people who have made the greatest strides in the development of the race. When luxury enters in and a thousand artificial requirements come to be regarded as real needs, the nation is on the brink of degeneration. So often has the story repeated itself that he who runs may read its deep significance. In our own country, to which has fallen the heritage of all the older civilizations, the course has been swift, for we are yet close to the memory of the primitive pioneer days when the nation was building, and we have still the crudity as well as the vigor of youth. But so rapid and easy has been our development and so great our prosperity that even now we are in some respects very nearly in the same state as the older peoples who have passed the zenith of their power and are beginning to decline. In our own case, however, the saving grace lies in the fact that our taste for luxury and artificiality is not as yet deeply ingrained. We are intensely commercial, fond of all the good things of life, proud of our ability to "get there," and we yield the palm to none in the matter of owning anything that money can buy. But, fortunately, our pioneer days are not ended even now and we still have a goodly number of men and women who are helping to develop the country and make history merely by living simple natural lives close to the soil and full of the interest and pleasure which come from kinship with Nature and the kind of work that calls forth all their resources in the way of self-reliance and the power of initiative. Even in the rush and hurry of life in our busy cities we remember well the quality given to the growing nation by such men and women a generation or two ago and, in spite of the chaotic conditions brought about by our passion for money-getting, extravagance and show, we have still reason to believe that the dominant characteristics of the pioneer yet shape what are the salient qualities in American life.

To preserve these characteristics and to bring back to individual life and work the vigorous constructive spirit which during the last half-century has spent its activities in commercial and industrial expansion, is, in a nut-shell, the Craftsman idea. We need to straighten out our standards and to get rid of a lot of rubbish that we have accumulated along with our wealth and commercial supremacy. It is not that we are too energetic, but that in many ways we have wasted and misused our energy precisely as we have wasted and misused so many of our wonderful natural resources. All we really need is a change in our point of view toward life and a keener perception regarding the things that count and the things which merely burden us. This being the case, it would seem obvious that the place to begin a readjustment is in the home, for it is only natural that the relief from friction which would follow the ordering of our lives along more simple and reasonable lines would not only assure greater comfort, and therefore greater efficiency, to the workers of the nation, but would give the children a chance to grow up under conditions which would be conducive to a higher degree of mental, moral and physical efficiency.

THEREFORE we regard it as at least a step in the direction of bringing about better conditions when we try to plan and build houses which will simplify the work of home life and add to its wholesome joy and comfort. We have already made it plain to our readers that we do not believe in large houses with many rooms elaborately decorated and furnished, for the reason that these seem so essentially an outcome of the artificial conditions that lay such harassing burdens upon modern life and form such a serious menace to our ethical standards. Breeding as it does the spirit of extravagance and of discontent which in the end destroys all the sweetness of home life, the desire for luxury and show not only burdens beyond his strength the man who is ambitious to provide for his wife and children surroundings which are as good as the best, but taxes to the utmost the woman who is trying to keep up the appearances which she believes should belong to her station in life. Worst of all, it starts the children with standards which, in nine cases out of ten, utterly preclude the possibility of their beginning life on their own account in a simple and sensible way. Boys who are brought up in such homes are taught, by the silent influence of their early surroundings, to take it for granted that they must not marry until they are able to keep up an establishment of equal pretensions, and girls also take it as a matter of course that marriage must mean something quite as luxurious as the home of their childhood or it is not a paying investment for their youth and beauty. Everyone who thinks at all deplores the kind of life that marks a man's face with the haggard lines of anxiety and makes him sharp and often unscrupulous in business, with no ambition beyond large profits and a rapid rise in the business world. Also we all realize regretfully the extrava-

THE CRAFTSMAN IDEA

gance and uselessness of many of our women and admit that one of the gravest evils of our times is the light touch-and-go attitude toward marriage, which breaks up so many homes and makes the divorce courts in America a by-word to the world. But when we think into it a little more deeply, we have to acknowledge that such conditions are the logical outcome of our standards of living and that these standards are always shaped in the home.

That is why we have from the first planned houses that are based on the big fundamental principles of honesty, simplicity and usefulness,—the kind of houses that children will rejoice all their lives to remember as "home," and that give a sense of peace and comfort to the tired men who go back to them when the day's work is done. Because we believe that the healthiest and happiest life is that which maintains the closest relationship with out-of-doors, we have planned our houses with outdoor living rooms, dining rooms and sleeping rooms, and many windows to let in plenty of air and sunlight. The most cursory examination of the floor plans given in this book will show that we have put into practical effect our conviction that a house, whatever its dimensions, should have plenty of free space unencumbered by unnecessary partitions or over-much furniture. Therefore we have made the general living rooms as large as possible and not too much separated one from the other. It seems to us much more friendly, homelike and comfortable to have one big living room into which one steps directly from the entrance door,—or from a small vestibule if the climate demands such a protection,—and to have this living room the place where all the business and pleasure of the common family life may be carried on. And we like it to have pleasant nooks and corners which give a comfortable sense of semi-privacy and yet are not in any way shut off from the larger life of the room. Such an arrangement has always seemed to us symbolic of the ideal conditions of social life. The big hospitable fireplace is almost a necessity, for the hearth-stone is always the center of true home life, and the very spirit of home seems to be lacking when a register or radiator tries ineffectually to take the place of a glowing grate or a crackling leaping fire of logs.

Then too we believe that the staircase, instead of being hidden away in a small hall or treated as a necessary evil, should be made one of the most beautiful and prominent features of the room, because it forms a link between the social part of the house and the upper regions which belong to the inner and individual part of the family life. Equally symbolic is our purpose in making the dining room either almost or wholly a part of the living room, for to us it is a constant expression of the fine spirit of hospitality to have the dining room, in a way, open to all comers. Furthermore, such an arrangement is a strong and subtle influence in the direction of simpler living because entertainment under such conditions naturally grows less elaborate and more friendly,—less alien to the regular life of the family and less a matter of social formality.

Take a house planned in this way, with a big living room made comfortable and homelike and beautiful with its great fireplace, open staircase, casement windows, built-in seats, cupboards, bookcases, sideboard and perhaps French doors opening out upon a porch which links the house with the garden; fill this room with soft rich restful color, based upon the mellow radiance of the wood tones and sparkling into the jeweled high lights given forth by copper, brass, or embroideries; then contrast it in your own mind with a house which is cut up into vestibule, hall, reception room, parlor, library, dining room and den,—each one a separate room, each one overcrowded with furniture, pictures and bric-a-brac,—and judge for yourself whether or not home surroundings have any power to influence the family life and the development of character. If you will examine carefully the houses shown in this book, you will see that they all form varying expressions of the central idea we have just explained, although each one is modified to suit the individual taste and requirements of the owner. This is as it should be, for a house expresses character quite as vividly as does dress and the more intimate personal belongings, and no man or woman can step into a dwelling ready made and decorated according to some other person's tastes and preferences without feeling a sense of strangeness that must be overcome before the house can be called a real home.

It will also be noticed in examining the plans of the Craftsman houses that we have paid particular attention to the convenient arrangement of the kitchen. In these days of difficulties with servants and of inadequate, inexperienced help, more and more women are, perforce, learning to depend upon themselves to keep the household machinery running smoothly. It is good that this should be so, for woman is above all things the home maker and our grandmothers were not far wrong when they taught their daughters that a woman who could not keep house, and do it well, was not making of her life the success that could reasonably be expected of her, nor was she doing her whole duty by her family. The idea that housekeeping means drudgery is partly due to our fussy, artificial, overcrowded way of living and partly to our elaborate houses and to inconvenient arrangements. We believe in having the kitchen small, so that extra steps may be avoided, and fitted with every kind of convenience and comfort; with plenty of shelves and cupboards, open plumbing, the hooded range which carries off all odors of cooking, the refrigerator which can be filled from the outside,—in fact, everything that tends to save time, strength and worry. In these days the cook is an uncertain quantity always and maids come and go like the seasons, so the wise woman keeps herself fully equipped to take up the work of her own house at a moment's notice, by being in such close touch with it all the time that she never lays down the reins of personal government. The Craftsman house is built for this kind of a woman and we claim that it is in itself an incentive to the daughters of the house to take a genuine and pleasurable interest in household work and affairs, so that they in their turn will be fairly equipped as home makers when the time comes for them to take up the more serious duties of life.

WE HAVE set forth the principles that rule the planning of the Craftsman house and have hinted at the kind of life that would naturally result from such an environment. But now comes one of the most important elements of the whole question,—the surroundings of the home. We need hardly say that a house of the kind we have described belongs either in the open country or in a small village or town, where the dwellings do not elbow or crowd one another any more than the people do. We have planned houses for country living because we firmly believe that the country is the only place to live in.

THE CRAFTSMAN IDEA

The city is all very well for business, for amusement and some formal entertainment,—in fact for anything and everything that, by its nature, must be carried on outside of the home. But the home itself should be in some place where there is peace and quiet, plenty of room and the chance to establish a sense of intimate relationship with the hills and valleys, trees and brooks and all the things which tend to lessen the strain and worry of modern life by reminding us that after all we are one with Nature.

Also it is a fact that the type of mind which appreciates the value of having the right kind of a home, and recognizes the right of growing children to the most natural and wholesome surroundings, is almost sure to feel the need of life in the open, where all the conditions of daily life may so easily be made sane and constructive instead of artificial and disintegrating. People who think enough about the influence of environment to put interest and care into the planning of a dwelling which shall express all that the word "home" means to them, are usually the people who like to have a personal acquaintance with every animal, tree and flower on the place. They appreciate the interest of planting things and seeing them grow, and enjoy to the fullest the exhilarating anxiety about crops that comes only to the man who planted them and means to use them to the best advantage.   Then again, such people feel that half the zest of life would be gone if they were to miss the fulness of joy that each returning spring brings to those who watch eagerly for the new green of the grass and the blossoming of the trees. They feel that no summer resort can offer pleasures equal to that which they find in watching the full flowering of the year; in seeing how their own agricultural experiments turn out, and in triumphing over each success and each addition to the beauty of the place that is their own. Few of these people, too, would care to miss the sense of peace and fulfilment in autumn days, when the waning beauty of the year comes into such close kinship with the mellow ripeness of a well-spent life that has borne full fruit. And what child is there in the world who would spend the winter in the city when there are ice-covered brooks to skate on, the comfort of jolly evenings by the fire and the never-ending wonder of the snow? And all the year round there are the dumb creatures for whom we have no room or time in the city,—the younger brothers of humanity who submit so humbly to man's dominion and look so placidly to him for protection and sustenance.

THANK heaven, though, we are not so far away from our natural environment that it needs much to take us back to it. We have many evidences of the turning of the tide of home life from the city toward the country. Even workers in the city are coming more and more to realize that it is quite possible to maintain their place in the business world and yet give their children a chance to grow up in the country. Also the economic advantage of building a permanent home instead of paying rent year after year is gaining an ever-increasing recognition, so that in a few years the American people may cease to deserve the reproach of being a nation of flat-dwellers and sojourners in family hotels. The instinct for home and for some tie that connects us with the land is stronger than any passing fashion, and although we have in our national life phases of artificiality that are demoralizing they affect only a small percentage of the whole people, and when their day is over they will be forgotten as completely as if they had never existed. Psychologists talk learnedly of "Americanitis" as being almost a national malady, so widespread is our restlessness and feverish activity; but it is safe to predict that, with the growing taste for wholesome country life, it will not be more than a generation or two before our far-famed nervous tension is referred to with wonder as an evidence of past ignorance concerning the most important things of life.

And when we have turned once more to natural living instead of setting up our puny affairs and feverish ambitions to oppose the quiet, irresistible course of Nature's law, we will not need to turn hungrily to books for stories of a bygone Golden Age, nor will we need to deplore the vanishing of art and beauty from our lives, for when the day comes that we have sufficient courage and perception to throw aside the innumerable petty superfluities that hamper us now at every turn and the honesty to realize what Nature holds for all who turn to her with a reverent spirit and an open mind, we will find that art is once more a part of our daily life and that the impulse to do beautiful and vital creative work is as natural as the impulse to breathe.

Therefore it is not idle theorizing to prophesy that, when healthful and natural conditions are restored to our lives, handicrafts will once more become a part of them, because two powerful influences will be working in this direction as they have worked ever since the earliest dawn of civilization. One is the imperative need for self-expression in some form of creative work that always comes when the conditions of life are such as to allow full development and joyous vigor of body and mind. The other is that which closer relationship with Nature seems to bring; a craving for greater intimacy with the things we own and use. Machine-made standards fall away of themselves as we get away from artificial conditions. It is as if wholesome living brought with it not only quickened perceptions but also a sense of personal affection for all the familiar surroundings of our daily life. It is from such feeling that we get the treasured heirlooms which are handed down from generation to generation because of their associations and what they represent.

Naturally the primitive conditions of pioneer life in any nation include handicrafts as a matter of course, from the simple fact that people had to make for themselves what they needed or go without. We realize that in this age of invention and of labor-saving machinery it is neither possible nor desirable to return to such conditions, but we believe that it is quite possible for a higher form of handicrafts to exist under the most advanced modern conditions and that achievements as great as those of the old craftsmen who made famous the Mediæval guilds are by no means out of the reach of modern workers when they once realize the possibilities that lie in this direction. Our theory is that modern improvements and conveniences afford a most welcome and necessary relief from the routine drudgery of household and farm work by disposing quickly and easily of what might much better be done by machinery than by hand, and that therefore there should be sufficient leisure left for the enjoyment of life and for the doing of work that is really worth while, which are among the things most essential to all-round mental and moral development. Almost the greatest drawback to farm life as it is today is the lack of interest and of mental alertness.

THE CRAFTSMAN IDEA

Especially is this the case during the winter months, when work on the farm is slack and much time is left to be spent in idleness or in some trifling occupation. Consider what the effect would be if it were made possible at such times to take up some form of creative work that would not only bring into play every atom of interest and ability, but would also serve a practical purpose by adding considerably to the family income!

WE HAVE given a great deal of consideration to the practical side of such a combination of handicrafts and farming, and we realize of course that the great difficulty in the way of making such a thing possible by making it profitable is the question of obtaining a steady market for the products of such crafts as might be practiced in connection with country life. It is often urged as an argument against handicrafts that hand-made goods could not possibly compete with factory-made goods, and that it would be absurd for people to waste time in making things for which there would be no sale. This does not seem to us to be the case, for the reason that there is no competition between the products of handicrafts and factory-made goods, because they are not measured by the same standard of value nor do they appeal to the same class of consumer. Hand-made articles have a certain intrinsic value of their own that sets them entirely apart from machine-made goods. This value depends, not upon the fact that the article is made entirely by hand or with appropriate tools,—that is not the point,—but upon the skill of the workman, his power to appreciate his own work sufficiently to give it the quality that appeals to the cultivated taste and the care that he gives to every detail of workmanship, from the preparation of the raw material to the final finish of the piece. We are not urging that handicrafts be cultivated in connection with farming for the purpose of competing with the factories for the same class of trade, for, with the demand that necessitates the immense production of goods of all kinds, the labor-saving machinery and efficient methods of the factories are absolutely essential, just as they are essential in the general economic scheme because they furnish employment to thousands of workers who ask nothing better than to be allowed to tend a machine with a certainty of so much a day coming to them at the end of the week. The place of home and village industries on the economic side, is to supplement the factories by producing a grade of goods which it is impossible to duplicate by machinery,—and which command a ready market when they can be found,—and to give to the better class of workers a chance not only to develop what individual ability they may possess, but to reap the direct reward of their own energy and industry in the feeling that they are free of the wage system with all its uncertainties and that what they make goes to maintain a home that is their own, to educate their children and to lay up a sufficient provision against old age.

We do not deny that handicrafts, as practiced by individual arts and crafts workers in studios, fall very short of affording a sufficient living to craft workers as a class, and also we do not deny that small farming as carried on in our thinly populated districts is neither interesting, pleasant, nor profitable. But we do assert that it is possible to connect the two and to carry them on upon a basis that will insure not only peace and comfort in living, and a form of industry that affords the greatest opportunity for all-round development, but also a permanent competence. To bring about such a condition is the end and aim of the whole Craftsman idea. We call it by that name because we have been the first to formulate it in this country. But it is in the air everywhere. It is taking shape in several of the European countries in the form of government appropriations for the reëstablishment and encouragement of handicrafts among the people, government schools for the teaching of various crafts, and government exchanges to look after the question of a steady market. In Great Britain and Ireland the same thing is being done by private enterprise, partly as a matter of social reform and partly as an effort of philanthropy. But in this country conditions are different. We have no peasant class and almost the only people in need of social reform, or of philanthropic efforts in their behalf are the vast hordes of immigrants who pour into the country each year and too often find it difficult to adjust their lives to American conditions.

THE people to whom the Craftsman idea makes its appeal are the better class farmers who own their farms, workers in the city who are able to get together a little place in the country and build up a permanent home, and the better class of artisans who desire to escape from the routine of factory work. That such people are taking a keen interest in the question of life in the country and that farming is rapidly being restored to its former status as a desirable occupation is evidenced by the encouragement given to the widespread activities of the Department of Agriculture, which is doing so much to bring about better and more economical methods of cultivating the soil. We have plenty of proof that these efforts do not fall short in the matter of results, for all over the country there is a growing appreciation of the possibilities that lie in intensive agriculture and a desire to learn something of modern scientific farming. We most heartily endorse all that is being done along these lines; but we go a step farther because we maintain that the whole standard of living must be changed before there can be a return of natural conditions to our lives. For example, we have been accustomed of late years to an artificial scale of income and expenditure, and the prices of the most ordinary necessities of life have risen so high that it takes all the average man can do to make ends meet. This is both wrong and unnecessary, but a natural consequence of artificial conditions, and we maintain that the only way to correct it is to put ourselves in a position to realize that, in permitting our lives to be ruled by false standards and inflated values, we have lost sight of the principle that economy means wealth. When we regain this simple and reasonable point of view, we will find no difficulty in admitting that comfort and happiness in living do not depend upon the amount of money we can make and spend, but upon pleasant surroundings and freedom from the pressure of want and apprehension; and when this truth is brought home to the affairs of daily life, the work of establishing natural standards is done.

Therefore we advocate a return to cultivating the soil as a means of obtaining the actual living,—that is, of looking to garden, grain-patch, orchard, chicken yard and pasture for the vegetables, fruits, cereals, eggs and meat consumed by the family. If properly cared for and cultivated according to the modern methods that are now everybody's for the learning, a little farm of five or ten acres can be made not only to yield a living for its owner and his family but a handsome surplus for the markets, thus serving the double purpose of stopping the outflow and adding to the income of actual money as well as providing home comfort and healthful working surroundings. The farm home once established, its owner is free of any steady expense save for taxes and repairs, so that everything that is done is constructive and cumulative in its effects.

This, in brief, is the whole idea of the Craftsman home,—a pleasant comfortable dwelling situated on a piece of ground large enough to yield, under proper cultivation, a great part of the food supply for the family. Such a home, by its very nature, would be permanent and, with the right kind of education and healthful occupation for the children, would do much to stop the flow of population into the great commercial centers and to insure a more even division of prosperity throughout the land. In many instances the home is an established fact, but the education and the occupation are yet to come. It is with a view to solving this problem that we advocate individual handicrafts in the home and industries to be carried on upon a more extended scale in the neighborhood or the village. The very fact of a thorough training in any useful craft would insure to a boy or girl the right groundwork for an education, so that the solution of one problem is practically a solution of both.

Naturally, the greatest field for home handicrafts lies in the making of household furnishings, wearing apparel and articles of daily use. For example, there is a large and steady demand for hand-woven, hooked and hand-tufted rugs in good designs and harmonious colorings, especially when they can be had at reasonable prices. That there would be a market for good hand-made rugs in this country is shown by the demand for similar rugs that are made abroad by peasant labor. This is, of course, much cheaper than any class of labor in this country. Nevertheless, the same grade of rugs could be made here by home and farm workers and sold at a profit at the same price that must be demanded for the imported rugs, after the high import duty on this class of goods has been added to the original cost. Also cabinetmaking, considered as a handicraft, opens a field of unusually wide and varied interest, as the making of things so closely associated with our daily life and surroundings is a form of work that is both delightful and profitable. Iron work is equally interesting, and a preliminary training in good hard blacksmithing not only offers an excellent foundation for the doing of good things in structural iron work and articles for household use, but it equals wood work in developing any creative power that may be latent in the worker. Weaving and needlework come into the first rank of interesting and profitable crafts, and among the lighter industries that offer a chance for individual expression and at the same time pay pretty well, are basketry, block printing, dyeing, lace making, bookbinding and the like.

EVER since its first publication in nineteen hundred and one, THE CRAFTSMAN Magazine has, in one form or another, been advocating this idea; and we have most satisfactory proof in the growth and standing of the magazine that a great many people in this country are thinking along the same lines. When THE CRAFTSMAN was founded it was with the intention of making it a magazine devoted almost solely to the encouragement of handicrafts in this country. We believed, then, as we believe now, in the immense influence for good in the development of character that is exerted merely by learning to use the hands. One needs only to look at any part of the history of handicrafts to realize how much strength, sincerity and genuine creative thought went into the work of the old craftsmen who were also such solid and substantial citizens. We have always felt that it is not the making of things that is important, but the making of strong men and women through the agency of the sound development that begins when the child learns to use its hands for shaping to the best of its ability something which is really needed either for its own play or for the comfort and convenience of others in the home. It is going back in spirit to the primitive beginning of handicrafts,—which marks the beginning of civilization, and is so important a factor in the growth of character that upon it depends nearly every quality of heart and brain that goes into what we may call the craftsmanship of life. But, as THE CRAFTSMAN grew and step by step attained a wider outlook, the question of the study of handicrafts as an end in itself gradually sunk to a position of minor importance in the policy of the magazine. Our belief that in it lay the foundation of all growth was no less, but the field was so broad that the record and discussion of all constructive work in the larger affairs of life came gradually to take first place.

As we began to design houses and to shape the idea of the Craftsman country home as we have here tried to describe it, we took up the subjects of architecture and interior decoration, doing our best to promote the establishment of the right standards and to offer all the aid in our power toward the development of a national spirit in our architecture. This naturally led to other forms of art, and THE CRAFTSMAN became a magazine for painters and sculptors as well as for architects, interior decorators and craftsmen. Along these lines it has always been progressive and rather radical, aiming always to discover and bring to the front any notable achievement that seemed to indicate the blazing of a new trail. The magazine has also taken the deepest interest in all social, industrial and political reforms and in the question of industrial education along practical lines that would fit any boy or girl to earn a living under any and all circumstances. In fact, taken altogether, THE CRAFTSMAN has been the outward and visible expression of the more philosophic side of the Craftsman idea, just as the houses and their furnishings have put into form its more concrete phases.

We have also paid a good deal of attention to agriculture in THE CRAFTSMAN, taking it up along very general lines. But we have felt that this is a field which required much more exhaustive treatment than we are able to give it in the pages of a magazine of this character. So to meet this need, we are about to establish a second magazine that will be called "THE YEOMAN" and that will be devoted entirely to the interests of farming, the possibilities of life in rural communities and to the handicrafts that might profitably be carried on in connection with agriculture.

THE time has come, however, to test out all the principles we have been advocating and give them the most practical and comprehensive demonstration within our power. Therefore we are this year opening a country place, where everything we have said can be put to the test of practical experience.

THE CRAFTSMAN IDEA

This place is called "Craftsman Farms" and it serves as a most complete exposition of the Craftsman idea as a whole. "Craftsman Farms" is situated in the hill country of New Jersey, and our intention is to make it a summer home and school for students of farming and handicrafts. While grown people are welcome, the chief object of the school's existence is to provide an opportunity for the instruction of boys and girls whose parents desire for them a method of training that will enable them to earn a living in whatever circumstances they may happen to be placed. In other words, we purpose to teach them to work with their hands,—not to hoe, dig, plow, or chop wood in a mechanical way,—but to do the kind of constructive work which requires direct thought and which will train them to cope with all the practical problems of life. In fact, the plan of the school is not only a return to the old system of apprenticeship, where the student learned his trade by mastering its difficulties one by one under the guidance of a master craftsman, but it is apprenticeship on improved lines because, instead of working for the benefit of the master, the student acquires by working solely for the sake of his own thorough training and the development in himself not merely skill but initiative and self-reliance.

The instruction will be in the form of lectures and informal talks from the teachers, who will not only give in this way such theoretical knowledge as seems to be required but will answer all questions and respond to all suggestions, so that the student's brain is necessarily made alert by his being forced to take an active part in his own training. The method of instruction will be the same throughout, whether the subject be agriculture, landscape gardening, house building, designing, or any one of the handicrafts. In the latter, students will work side by side with experienced craftsmen, so that every lesson will be the solving of some problem and the doing of actual work according to the methods employed by the best workmen.

For example, every man, sooner or later, hopes or intends to build himself a home. Imagine what that home might be if, as a boy, he had been trained to have a practical working knowledge of drawing, of construction, of the quality and use of different woods, of finishing these woods so that their full value would be brought out and of laying out the grounds surrounding his house so that the most harmonious environment would be a matter of course. As the thing stands now, most men hire some one else to do this sort of thing, which practically amounts to hiring some one else to think for them in matters that most intimately concern their personal life and surroundings.

It is now being very generally acknowledged that our present methods of education fail to a serious degree in the vital work of educating boys and girls toward the larger business of life,—toward the understanding of how to do, and the ability to do, those things upon which our physical existence depends. It does not by any means follow that training along lines of practical work will confine the future activities of the boy to manual labor or to the necessity of doing things for himself. He may use his abilities in as many other directions as he can, but we believe that learning to do the actual work of daily life in the country gives him a kind of ability that may be applied to any form of work, mental or manual, with the best effect, and also that any one possessing it may at any time get back to first principles and start afresh. It has always seemed to us that

THE CRAFTSMAN IDEA

the great disintegrating force in our modern way of living lies in the system by which everything is done by rote,—and largely by machinery,—and where labor of all kinds is so specially divided that a man, whether he be workman or director, has very little chance to cope with problems outside of his own particular line of work. The great purpose in life and work is the development of character and it naturally follows that true development can come only by the training and use of all the faculties in coping with all the problems that may come up in the ordinary course of life.

In addition to the instruction given at "Craftsman Farms," the conditions of life there will be such as to carry out the same idea. The students, whether young or old, will be housed in small hamlets scattered about the neighborhood in places chosen on account of their fitness for the several things to be done. Each group of cottages will be under the care of a house mother and an instructor and the student will go from hamlet to hamlet until, at the end of the course, he is not only master of the trade he has chosen to learn but also has a general knowledge of related trades and of farming. For example, most of the cottages in which the students live will be designed and built with their active assistance, as the students will be invited to use their own brains and creative ability in designing houses and cottages that they would like to live in or that seem suited to the place. In doing this, of course, they will work directly with the corps of architects that has in charge the designing of the cottages, and in the actual building the students will be allowed to work side by side with experienced carpenters, stone masons, wood finishers, cabinetmakers, blacksmiths and coppersmiths, so that every lesson will be the doing of actual work in the way it is done by competent workmen.

Aside from the educational feature of this enterprise, one of the main objects in carrying it out along the lines indicated is to put to a practical test our favorite theory of a farming community grouped around a central settlement where all social interchange and recreation are as full and convenient as they would be in the city and where every house is within easy reach of the farm lands that belong to it.

If the experiment should prove a success, we confidently look to see it put into practice by many other people; and if it should not, at least we shall have discovered its weak points and have learned something by experience. In any case, the school is meant to complete the work begun by the magazine and to give to the world the result of all the experience we have gained since the first inception of the Craftsman idea ten years ago. If it should have ever so little influence in bringing about the development of our national life along the lines laid down by the men who founded the Republic, it will have fulfilled its mission, because a truth which one man finds courage to utter today is echoed and applied by thousands tomorrow.

MORE CRAFTSMAN HOMES

A WORD ABOUT CRAFTSMAN ARCHITECTURE

FROM the beginning of my work as a craftsman my object has been to develop types of houses and house furnishings that are essentially cheerful, durable and appropriate for the kind of life I believe the intelligent American public desires. It comes to me every day of my life that a home spirit is being awakened amongst us, that as a nation we are beginning to realize how important it is to have homes of our own, homes that we like, that we have been instrumental in building, that we will want to have belong to our children. And, of course, this means that the homes must be honest and beautiful dwellings; they must be built to last; they must be so well planned that we want them to last, and yet they must be within our means. The delusion that a really beautiful home is within the reach of only the very rich is losing ground, as is its sister delusion that only by the slavish imitation of foreign models is æsthetic satisfaction to be achieved. People are also awakening to the fact that beauty in a building is not merely a matter of decoration, a something to be added at will, but is inherent in the lines and masses of the structure itself.

The point of view of the New England farmer, whose instructions to the architect were: "I'll build my house, and you fetch along your architecture and nail it on," is no longer typical. Today if you find a farmer who is thinking about building a home, the chances are that he and his family and the town builder spend a lot of evenings around the farm dining table, poring over plans and blue prints, and probably sketches which the farmer himself has made. There is no suggestion about an Italian villa or a French chateau, but the farmer is probably saying, "We want a large room to live in; we want an open fire in it because it looks cheerful and the children like it; we want a kitchen that my wife won't mind working in, and we want the house light and warm and pretty." This is a great change from the old days, and is in line with the theory on which Craftsman architecture is founded,—namely, a style of building suited to the lives of the people, having the best possible structural outline, the simplest form, materials that belong to the country in which the house is built and colors that please and cheer.

The Craftsman type of building is largely the result not of elaboration, but of elimination. The more I design, the more sure I am that elimination is the secret of beauty in architecture. By this I do not mean that I want to think scantily and work meagerly. Rather, I feel that one should plan richly and fully, and then begin to prune, to weed, to shear away everything that seems superfluous and superficial. Practically every house I build I find, both in structural outline and in the planning and the adjustment of the interior space, that I am simplifying, that I am doing away with something that was not needed; that I am using my spaces to better advantage. All of this means the expenditure of less money and the gain of more comfort and beauty.

It is only when we to an extent begin at the beginning of these things that we come to know how much that is superfluous we have added to life, and how fearful we have been to be straightforward and honest in any artistic expression. Why may we not build just the house we want, so that it belongs to our lives and expresses them? I have, all too slowly, begun to realize that it is right to build houses as people wish them, to cut away ornament, to subordinate tradition,

A WORD ABOUT CRAFTSMAN ARCHITECTURE

and to put into the structure and into the interior finish the features that the occupants will find comfortable and convenient, and which almost inevitably result in beauty for them. It seems to me that every man should have the right to think out the plan for his house to suit himself, and then the architect should make this plan into a reasonable structure; that is, the outline should be well-proportioned and the different parts should be brought together so that the structural perfection will result in decorative beauty. If, added to this simple reasonable structure, the materials for the house are so far as possible those which may be found in the locality where the house is built, a beauty of fitness is gained at the very start. A house that is built of stone where stones are in the fields, of concrete where the soil is sandy, of brick where brick can be had reasonably, or of wood if the house is in a mountainous wooded region, will from the beginning belong to the landscape. And the result is not only harmony but economy. Why should the man who lives on a hillside bring brick from a long distance when the most interesting of modern dwellings, the log house, is at his hand? Or, if the brick could be had from the kiln a few miles away, why seek logs which are made expensive by the long freight haul from far-away mountains, and which would not seem in any way harmonious with the country where trees are scarce?

Once having settled upon the style of house which must suit the lie of the land and the happiness of the owner, the arrangement of floor spaces is next in significance. First of all, do away with any sense of elaboration and with the idea that a house must be a series of cells, room upon room, shut away from all others. Have a living room, the "great room" of the house that corresponds to the old "great hall" of ancient dwellings. This space is the opportunity for people to come together, to sit around the fireplace, for there must always be an open fire. It is the room where people read or study or work evenings, or play or dance, as the case may be,—the place where the elderly members of the family will have the greatest comfort and contentment, and where the children will store up memories that can never die. This great room must be well lighted, it will have groups of windows that furnish cheerful vistas in the daytime, and it must be so planned that seats or divans circle the fireplace and bring, by the very structure of the house, the family into intimate, happy relationship. It is wise, of course, that the entrance to this room from out of doors should be through an entry way or vestibule, in order that drafts may not be felt and to furnish coat room and opportunities for the putting aside of heavy wraps, umbrellas, etc. This should be borne in mind especially in cold climates where the whole comfort of the room may be sacrificed to a too abrupt connection with out of doors.

In the planning of this first floor and the adjustment of the spaces I have as few entrances and doorways as possible. They are expensive; they use up space, prevent a look of coziness and lessen the opportunities for building in of interesting fittings. It is also economical and picturesque to group the windows, and always the built-in fittings, the bookcases, the corner seats should be adjusted to the light from the windows as well as the fireplace. But here, as in the outside structure, I find the process of elimination must be always borne in mind. I do away with everything that does not contribute to comfort and beauty. This is a safe rule. The charm of the living room can be greatly enhanced by

A WORD ABOUT CRAFTSMAN ARCHITECTURE

the alcove dining room, a greater sense of space is added and all the things that are put in the dining room to make it beautiful contribute to the pleasure of the people who are sitting in the living room. Also, the pleasure in the dining room is enhanced by glimpses of the living room, its spaces, its open fires, its grouped windows. This does away also with one partition; it furnishes opportunity for the interesting use of screens, or for the half-partition, on top of which may be placed lines of books or jars of ferns, not expensive ornaments for the house, and adding greatly to the beauty of color and to the homelike quality.

The question of built-in fittings is one that I feel is an essential part of the Craftsman idea in architecture. I have felt from the beginning of my work that a house should be live-in-able when it is finished. Why should one enter one's dwelling and find that it is a barren uninviting prisonlike spot, until it is loaded with furniture and the walls hidden under pictures and picture frames? I contend that when the builder leaves the house, it should be a place of good cheer, a place that holds its own welcome forever. This, of course, can only be accomplished by the building in of furnishings that are essentially structural features, and by the planning of the finishing of the walls and the woodwork so that they are a part of the inherent beauty of the home, and not mere backgrounds for endless unrelated decorations. In my own houses I study the color of the interior when I am designing the house. I plan the woodwork so that it embraces the built-in fittings, so that every bookcase or corner seat is a part of the development of the woodwork. In no other way can a house be made beautiful, or the architecture of the interior be complete and homelike.

You cannot make your house and your furnishings two separate schemes of attractiveness and expect an harmonious whole. The reason that this has been so much done in America is because people have not owned their homes. Usually their furniture alone belongs to them, and *that* they have tried to select so that it would be pleasant and well related. They have adjusted it to the houses that they have chanced to live in as well as they could, until they have grown to feel that a house is one thing and furnishings quite another. This is especially true in city apartments, where people expect to remain only a few years before they move on to another set of inconveniences. The furniture which in one house was adjusted to mahogany and green walls is later on adjusted to yellow oak and pink walls. And so families have gone from one set of torturing surroundings to another, until it seems a miracle that any sense of color and proportion in house furnishings should survive.

As for my own houses, I realize that they more or less demand the sort of furniture that I have been in the habit of planning for them. Not because I hold to one narrow outlook of beauty, but because I cannot but see that most of the imitation antiques as well as the types of modern furniture made purely for department store sales are not adjusted to simple practical artistic home surroundings. In the planning of my houses I have so eliminated the superfluous in structure, in floor plans, in interior fittings, that furniture which is not well planned or is overornamented must of necessity seem out of place.

"More Craftsman Homes," which is the second book of houses that I have published, stands for my own ideal of house building. In other words, it shows the extent to which I have been able in my own, perhaps small, way, to achieve

A WORD ABOUT CRAFTSMAN ARCHITECTURE

beauty in architecture through this process of elimination. It makes clear how I feel about houses which are built on economical principles, on good structural lines, always with the ideal of beauty, always insisting upon the utmost comfort and convenience. The edition (20,000) of the first book, "Craftsman Homes," which was published over two years ago, is now exhausted. And so great has been the demand for a book of Craftsman houses that we have found it necessary, in order to meet the response of the people who are interested in this kind of architecture, to get out within the last few months the book to which this little talk forms the introduction. This book in some respects is scarcely more than a catalogue. It is merely a straightforward presentation of my more recent designs in Craftsman houses suited for building in concrete, in stone, in brick and in wood. Many of these houses have already been built and have been found most satisfactory by their owners. Several of them have been built on Craftsman Farms, my own home place in New Jersey. I feel that every time a Craftsman house is built I verify in my own mind my ideal of architecture; that is, beauty through elimination.

There can be no doubt in my mind that a native type of architecture is growing up in America. I am not prepared to say to what extent the Craftsman idea has contributed to it, but I do know, from a very wide correspondence, that people all over the country are asking for houses in which they may be comfortable, houses which will be appropriate backgrounds for their own lives and right starting points for the lives of their children. It is my own wish, my own final ideal, that the Craftsman house may so far as possible meet this demand and be instrumental in helping to establish in America a higher ideal, not only of beautiful architecture, but of home life.

THE RELATION OF CRAFTSMAN ARCHITECTURE TO COUNTRY LIVING

IN THE development of Craftsman architecture I have had in mind especially the need of better dwellings for suburbs and country, and although I have also designed houses for city and town, most of the plans are intended for a rural environment. I believe that on the right use of the land depends much of our national welfare, and that therefore farm life should be made not only effective and profitable but also pleasant. I realize that the normal existence is one which includes an all-round development of the faculties, a wholesome proportion of manual and mental labor, opportunities for spiritual growth; and so I believe that a form of building which makes for simplicity of housekeeping and provides ample chance for outdoor working and living will help to increase the health, happiness and efficiency of the people.

My effort, therefore, has been directed toward something that will make country life more interesting. I see no reason why people should not build comfortable houses in the country, and make for themselves the kind of surroundings that will prove an incentive and inspiration, instead of the ugly buildings, tawdry furnishings and the many inconveniences which now make farm life so unattractive. Why should the advantages of our civilization be confined to the cities and towns? If they are to be of real value to the people at large, is it not imperative that they should be shared by the guardians of those natural resources from which the city draws its strength? And is it not an inadequate and one-sided sort of progress which gives to one set of workers those comforts and conveniences which modern science has devised, and leaves the others in conditions of discomfort and drudgery?

This lack of balance, I believe, can be adjusted to a great extent by the right kind of rural architecture. In the case of the farm, not only is it possible to plan the buildings and arrange the work on a basis of economy and convenience, but it is also possible to make the interior of the house so attractive that the housewife as well as the farmer will find it a place of daily pleasure and contentment. But it is essential for this that we simplify most of our present complicated ideals of cooking, ornament, apparel and furnishing; that we construct more convenient and comfortable homes; that we employ labor-saving devices for the house as well as for the barns and the fields. Especially is this needed for the woman who now turns in disgust from the overwork and isolation of the country to the city with its artificial amusements. By the use of labor-saving devices, by more scientific methods of housekeeping, by the simplifying of ways of living and thinking, what is now a heartbreaking drudgery can be made a source of joy and pride.

The house can be so planned that it will be a factor in the growth and happiness of the people. The large living room with its central fireplace will form the nucleus of home life, a place for rest and entertainment, for the gathering of the family and the planning of whatever industries are being developed on the farm. The piazza at the back will serve to connect house and garden and encourage outdoor living, and a dining porch will permit the joy of meals served in the open. The provision of a summer kitchen will bring fresh air and brightness to many tasks that would be wearisome indoors. The laundry tubs may be placed here instead of down cellar, thus saving time and steps and making labor less irksome. Here also can be done the cooking, preserving and canning of fruits and vegetables, the cleaning of milk cans, the preparing of food for the stock. In short, both house and housework can be so adjusted as to make labor a pleasure and the country home a center of interest.

And with the bettering of conditions in home and farm a new spirit will enter into our tasks. We shall readjust our attitude toward work. Instead of submitting to it as one of life's necessary evils, we shall welcome it with courage and with joy, as the thing through which we get our greatest development.

Not only does such a type of architecture as that which we advocate form an incentive and inspiration to country living, but it tends to promote a coöperative spirit. People are willing to coöperate if they can get more comfort into their lives, and keep better in touch with progress. And in the necessary development of rural life, problems of lighting, water supply, sewerage, farm machinery, motive power, etc., as well as of social and educational needs, will have to be solved by coöperation. Then with the increase of common material interests there will come a strengthening of spiritual ties. In place of the old feeling of rural isolation we shall find a quickening of the recreative and intellectual life of the people. Community spirit and community pride will become factors in the betterment of rural conditions, until every dweller of township, village, farm and open country will enjoy a share in the responsibilities and privileges of happy community life, and so contribute to the progress of the nation.

It was with this point of view that I started to organize Craftsman Farms, to demonstrate what could be done to bring interest, efficiency and beauty into country living. While we have a number of buildings there already, we expect later on to have a good many more, and from time to time we shall publish in THE CRAFTSMAN pictures, plans and descriptions of the houses, stables and shops we may build. The illustrations and plans of the Log House which we are showing on page 147 will give some idea of what we have accomplished in this direction, and the latch string is always out for anyone who is planning to build or who cares to see what we are doing.

G. S.

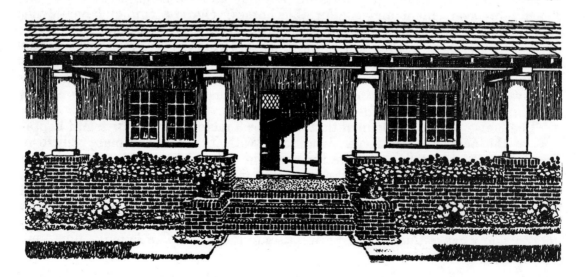

THE HOUSE OF THE DEMOCRAT: BY WILLIAM L. PRICE

"And what wealth then shall be left us when
    none shall gather gold,
To buy his friend in the market, and pinch and
    pine the sold?

"Nay, what save the lovely city, and the little
    house on the hill,
And the wastes and the woodland beauty and
    the happy fields we till."

MY DEFINITION of Democracy is a state wherein there is no special privilege; my definition of a democrat is one who of his own impulse can truly say with Walt Whitman, "By God, I will not have anything that every man may not have the counterpart of on like terms." Not the "Thou shalt not" of extraneous force, but the "I will not" of self-control and brotherliness.

And the House of the Democrat? It must need no special privilege for its gaining, and it must not oppress by its possession.

I once built a house for a Democrat,—a man who left a money-making partnership when he believed he had as much money as he could employ profitably to his fellowmen,—and his one concern for this house was not that it should cost too much, but that it should in no wise embarrass his friends: ample enough to contain them; simple enough to leave them unoppressed; yet with artistry to please and to lead them, if they would, to do likewise. Some of his friends were not well enough off to afford such a house, some of them were rich enough to build palaces; yet his house was not to make the one envious or the other contemptuous.

But such a house is only possible to the real Democrat, the man who demands equality of opportunity without desiring an *impossible* equality of attainment. A man may, perhaps I should say, must be a stately gentleman to be such a Democrat. His possessions may be many or few and his house great or small, but to have arrived at the dignity of democracy is to have arrived at stateliness. To have in your possession nothing that is not by right your own, to ask no favor but comradeship, to demand no rights but equal rights, to produce and get the equivalent, to be able to give of yourself rather than of your goods, —this were an achievement that would gild a cottage, or make simply human the stateliest habitation.

But no man can be a Democrat by himself, however many sturdy steps he may take toward it or however his heart may swell with the hope of it. "We be of one flesh, you and I," and we neither live to ourselves nor build to ourselves nor by ourselves. A man may by a wish set the feet of the whole world toward democracy, but the house of the democrat can only be built by the willing hands of democrats, so as there are few democratic architects and few democratic craftsmen there are few democratic houses.

Look at your own houses, my friends, the houses of your friends, and the houses that line your roadways. You may find, here and there, an old farmhouse springing out of the soil, built by village carpenter and mason and smith, with low roofs and wide-spreading porches that mothers its human brood as the hen its tired chicks,—and when you find it, your heart will yearn to it; you will feel that a Jefferson might have spoken his noblest thoughts under its rooftree and the simplest yeoman his simplest hopes for tomorrow's crops with an equal dignity and an even fitness.

THE HOUSE OF THE DEMOCRAT

I do not mean the pillared porticoes of the stately mansions of Colonial days; they speak of pomp, of powdered wig, of brocade gown, of small clothes and small sword, of coach and four, of slavery or serfdom; nor do I speak of the lesser imitations of such houses. When Jefferson and Washington spoke of democracy, they spoke not of what was, but of what *was to be;* they spoke of democrats in spite of kings, of democracy in spite of palaces.

AND we who have built up privileges and powers and potentates in the the name of democracy, we who have reëstablished the power of dead men and their deeds over the living, we who have repudiated Jefferson's "The earth belongs in usufruct to the living," we who in this civilization of stupid waste play shuttlecock to the barbaric battledores of roaring Hells and stifling pens,—what should we know of the house of the democrat? We are fastening tighter the rule of the past in the name of education and taste; we are forging chains of "wisdom" and knowledge and riveting them on the arms of Prophecy; setting up styles in art at the mandates of established orders of taste, just as our "Supreme Courts" are binding the hands of Tomorrow with the precedents of yesterday, as if there were any supreme court but the people whose hands they vainly try to bind, or any canon of taste more holy than fitness. Our laws are like our houses, cluttered up with imitations of the outworn junk of other days.

There is scarcely a molding in your house that is not stupidly copied or perverted from some lost meaning expressed by men of other days in the building of temple or palace; no stupid, dirty, wooden baluster that had not its inception in crook-kneed debasement to an unhallowed state, no ornament that does not reek of the pride of place and power; shield and wreath, festoon and torch, they speak no word to us at all, and if they could speak would tell only of the pomps and prides of other days, of an order that has passed in the flesh even in those old lands where the people still hang the remnants and insignia of powers gone on their sham princes and powerless potentates, and even the spirit of that false pride is dead, for they produce no new emblems, no new visible manifestations of rank and power, but are content to paw over the tawdry finery of the past.

And, however, with our lips we have repudiated those shams—in our spirits we still kiss the feet of place and pomp; we still glorify hereditary power; we still hold up its hands to our own undoing, and we still copy so far as we can its vainglorious essays at expression. Our dress at a few cents the yard must ape their gorgeousness, our models must come from Paris even if our goods come from Kensington, and are made up in loathsome sweat-shops. Our furnishings, tossed out by machines and held together by the grace of imitation varnish, and our houses tacked together, putty-filled, mean in workmanship and mean in design, lick the feet of a pompous past, bow down in worship of a time that, at least, had the conviction of its sins, and openly elected to be lorded over by privileged classes.

WHEN at last we build the house of the democrat, its doors shall be wide and unbarred, for why should men steal who are free to make? It shall be set in a place of greenery, for the world is a large place and its loveliness mostly a wilderness; it shall be far enough away from its next for privacy

THE HOUSE OF THE DEMOCRAT

and not too far for neighborliness; it shall have a little space knit within a garden wall; flowers shall creep up to its warmth, and flow, guided, but unrebuked, over wall and low-drooped eaves. It shall neither be built in poverty and haste, nor abandoned in prosperity; it shall grow as the family grows; it shall have rooms enough for the privacy of each and the fellowship of all. Its arms shall spread wide enough to gather in a little measure of the common earth, for your democracy will provide leisure and your democrat will not only pluck flowers but will grow them, not only eat the fruits of the earth but will find joy in planting, in "seed time and harvest," and all the myriad days of growth between will look to the sundial rather than the timetable for the ordering of his day.

The rooms of his house shall be ample, and low, wide-windowed, deep-seated, spacious, cool by reason of shadows in summer, warm by the ruddy glow of firesides in winter, open to wistful summer airs, tight closed against the wintry blasts: a house, a home, a shrine; a little democracy unjealous of the greater world, and pouring forth the spirit of its own sure justness for the commonwealth.

Its walls shall be the quiet background for the loveliness of life, hung over with the few records of our own and others' growth made in the playtime of art; its furnishings the product of that art's more serious hours; its implements from kitchen-ware to dressing table touched by the sane and hallowing hand of purpose and taste.

This is the house of the Democrat, and of such houses shall the democracy be full: none so humble that it may not touch the hem of art; none so great that the hand of art, whose other name is service, shall have passed it by.

When the tale of our hours of labor is a tale of hours of joy; when the workshop has ceased to be a gloomy hell from which we drag our debased bodies for a few hours of gasping rest; when the workshop shall rather be a temple where we joyously bring our best to lay it on the shrine of service; when art shall mean work and work shall mean art to the humblest,—then democracy shall be real; then shall our hours be too short for the joy of living; then patiently shall we build up a civilization that shall endure; then shall we laugh at the slips of our eagerness, and no more remember the horrid gorgon-headed monster, privilege, whose merest glance turned the hearts of men to stone, set nation against nation, armed man's heels to crush his fellows, fenced our coast from our fellow men, built strong portaled prisons, armed ships to kill, filled our hearts with devastating fear, clouded our clear sight and spilled the lives and hopes of the many, and stole their hard-bought wealth for the bedecking of her snaky tresses— then shall we build the house of the Democrat.

And when the Democrat has built his house, when free men have housed themselves to meet their present need and have no fear that the need of tomorrow shall cry at their doors unmet,—then shall men and women and little children, out of the fulness of their lives, out of the free gift of their surplus hours, build for each and for all, such parks and pleasure places, such palaces of the people, such playhouses, such temples, as men have not yet known. And the men and women and children shall find playtime to use them; find time and powers out of their work to write plays and play them, to write poems and sing them, to carve, to paint, to teach, to prophesy new philosophies and new sciences; to make, to give, to live.

I believe that the keynote of life is work, and that upon the honesty of work depends all that is worthy and lasting in art and in life.

G. S.

PRACTICAL CRAFTSMAN CEMENT HOUSE PLANNED FOR BEAUTY AND CONVENIENCE

IN the houses shown in this book we have endeavored to embody certain features essential to beauty and usefulness, the important elements for which every homemaker is seeking, the happy blending of which will create that homelike quality desired by whoever contemplates building. The usefulness of a house depends upon the arrangement of the space enclosed within its outer walls, and in designing Craftsman houses the floor plans receive first attention. From these the remainder of the house is worked out. The exterior thus becomes the outward expression of the inner purpose.

A study of the floor plans of the cement house which we have shown on pages 12 and 13, will serve to illustrate how close is the relation between a practical arrangement of rooms and a comfortable and beautiful home. The approach to the living room is an especially interesting feature. In addition to the recessed porch, which always gives a peculiarly intimate sense of inner seclusion and comfort, there is a little hall with an inviting window seat facing the stairway. The first view of the living room is stamped with the genial welcome of the open fireplace and the convenient proximity of the well-chosen fireside friends—the books. A good book and a glowing hearth are closely associated in the minds of most home-loving people, and it is fitting that they should be allowed an intimate alliance in the plan of the house.

The perspective drawing of the living room gives some idea of the decorative quality which results from a careful handling of the structural features of the interior. The ornamental use of Tapestry brick in the chimneypiece, the frank simplicity which characterizes the beams and woodwork, the treatment of the windows, and the placing of the staircase so that one gets a glimpse of its simple construction through the wide living room entrance, as well as from the dining room, all these things combine to form a quiet and dignified background for the more personal furnishings of the house. The convenient placing of the dining room in relation to the kitchen and to the living room, and the placing of the kitchen where the odors of the coming meal will not reach the waiting guests long before the meal is served, are in keeping with the rest of the carefully considered plan. A secluded dining porch is to be seen within easy access of the kitchen, so that during summer months meals could be served there with little additional work.

Upstairs the arrangement is as simple as it is compact, four good-sized bedrooms, a bathroom, and plenty of closet room being provided. The square space at the end of the upper hallway, directly above the lower entrance, could be used as a tiny sewing room, or it could be transformed into a most inviting nook with a comfortably cushioned window seat.

Cement on metal lath was chosen for the construction of this house, because these materials have proven themselves to be both durable and inexpensive. Though the original cost is more, the continued necessity for repairs is done away with, which makes it cheaper in the end. The lines of the building, as projected from the floor plans, lend themselves especially to the use of cement or concrete, for they are essentially simple. There is a decorative quality in this severe simplicity of line, and any possibility of severity being

CEMENT HOUSE, WITH SEVEN ROOMS AND DINING PORCH

Published in The Craftsman, December, 1911.

CRAFTSMAN CEMENT HOUSE: NO. 12

carried to extreme is obviated by the grouping of the small-paned, double-hung windows, and by the use of vines about the chimney and pillars of the porches, and by the plants at the base of the walls. The stone chimneys add an element of picturesqueness to the exterior, and the Ruberoid roof, which may be red or green as preferred, is pleasantly broken

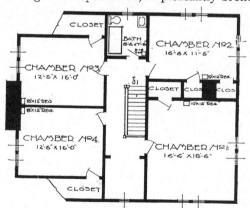

CEMENT HOUSE NO. 125: FIRST FLOOR PLAN.

HOUSE NO. 125: SECOND FLOOR PLAN.

CEMENT HOUSE, WITH SEVEN ROOMS AND DINING PORCH

by the long dormer which allows ample height for the rooms of the upper story.

The rooms on the first floor may be finished in stained chestnut, and the floors may be maple finished with vinegar and iron rust, which gives a rich tone to the whole room. The entire upper part of the house may be finished in red gumwood, with maple floors.

Important and interesting features of the house are the Craftsman fireplace-furnaces, which are so constructed that they not only furnish the joy and companionship of an open fire, but heat and ventilate the whole house as well.

In furnishing this house various Craftsman fittings could be used that would harmonize with the treatment of the interior as well as add to its comfort. In the living room, for instance, we have shown two lanterns from the Craftsman workshops, the design of which is

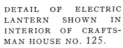

DETAIL OF ELECTRIC LANTERN SHOWN IN INTERIOR OF CRAFTSMAN HOUSE NO. 125.

illustrated more clearly in a detail cut. These ceiling lights could be supplemented by a bracket lantern such as the one shown here, which could be fastened to the wall at any convenient height.

CRAFTSMAN ELECTRIC BRACKET LANTERN.

In the wide openings between the entrance and the living room and dining room, portières could of course be hung to obviate any possibility of draft from the front door, adding at the same time to the general comfort of the interior and securing a greater sense of privacy. These hangings would also serve to soften the straight lines of the woodwork, and would naturally carry out, in color and design, the decorative scheme of the rooms.

Long, comfortably cushioned seats might also be placed in the living room on each side of the fireplace—one against the wall at the left, and the other beneath the windows. These would contribute much to the homelike quality of the place, and would transform that end of the room into a sort of inglenook. Or, a long settle might be placed directly in front of the hearth, with a table of the same length at the back so that the light from a reading lamp would fall over one's shoulder at a convenient angle. In fact, the room affords many possibilities of arrangement, and the details could be planned according to personal taste.

LIVING ROOM IN HOUSE NO. 125, SHOWING FIREPLACE-FURNACE AND GLIMPSE OF STAIRWAY.

CEMENT HOUSE SHOWING INTERESTING ROOF TREATMENT AND ROOMY HOMELIKE INTERIOR

Published in The Craftsman, November, 1909.

CRAFTSMAN CEMENT HOUSE WITH EIGHT ROOMS AND THREE PORCHES: NO. 79.

LONG, sloping roofs of shingle or slate, in which dormers are broken out to give the necessary height to the chambers, make the exterior of this cement house especially charming. The building is strongly constructed upon truss metal laths, and every care has been taken to avoid the possibility of leakage. The cement is brought close about the windows, which are so grouped as to break the wall into pleasing spaces.

The rooms are fitted with ample closets and are well lighted with large windows, both casement and double-hung. The amount of furniture that is built into the house will make quite a difference in the expense of furnishing it. In the kitchen there is a long dresser and a sink fitted with drip boards. A sideboard, flanked by china closets, is built into the dining room beneath the group of five small casements. The living room shows a

long seat beneath the front windows, with built-in bookshelves on either side, and seats beside the piano in the opposite wall; but the most attractive feature is the deep inglenook which runs out between the twin porches that are connected with the room by means of

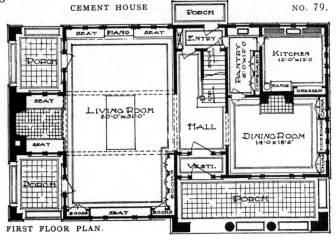

CEMENT HOUSE   NO. 79.

FIRST FLOOR PLAN.

CEMENT HOUSE, WITH EIGHT ROOMS AND THREE PORCHES

long glass doors. The chimneypiece is of split field stone with rough tile hearth. On either side are two long settles with high wainscoted backs splayed out a little for greater comfort, and casement windows above. The ceiling within the nook is lower than that of the living room, being dropped to a level with the top of the heavy lintel across the entrance, adding a greater air of seclusion. From this lintel could be suspended Craftsman lanterns of hammered copper with amber glass. The nook, in fact, affords many opportunities for those little individual touches, in color, texture and detail, which can bring such comfort and beauty into an interior. And when the firelight plays over the warm tones of the woodwork and the soft varied colors of the stone, glinting upon a bit of metal above the mantelpiece, or upon the brighter colors of the cushions, the inglenook becomes truly the heart of the house, the center of interest of the home.

Turning to the floor plan of the upper story, we find that this is also worth studying, for it shows an unusually pleasant arrangement of the bedrooms. These are all light and airy,

HOUSE NO. 79: SECOND FLOOR PLAN.

and the windows, with their small panes, add greatly to the charm of the interior, and at the same time give a decorative touch to the outer walls. The most attractive feature of this plan is the built-in window seats which are seen in little nooks in four of the bedrooms, and which add so much to the comfort and cheerfulness of the rooms. The various corners, moreover, that break up the walls afford unique possibilities of furnishing.

VIEW OF THE FIREPLACE NOOK IN THE LIVING ROOM, SHOWING CHIMNEYPIECE OF SPLIT FIELD STONE, ROUGH TILE HEARTH AND SETTLES WITH WAINSCOTED BACKS ON EITHER SIDE.

THREE-STORY CRAFTSMAN BUNGALOW SUITABLE FOR A HILLSIDE SITE

Published in The Craftsman, January, 1911.

THREE-STORY BUNGALOW FOR HILLSIDE SITE: NO. 105.

A THREE-STORY bungalow is unusual, yet the Craftsman house illustrated here shows a distinct bungalow form of construction. Stone is used for the foundation and lower walls, cement for the walls above, boards for the gable, and slates for the roof. The main floor contains the kitchen, living room and two bedrooms, with room in the attic for three additional bedrooms if required. The basement is divided into a large billiard room, laundry, furnace and fuel room, and storeroom, so that, although the house does not look very large, there is really a great deal of space in it.

As pictured here, the house is built upon irregular ground, so that the foundation wall varies in height. The entrance to the house is approached by a terrace which leads to the square entrance porch. At the opposite side a straight road runs directly into the garage, which occupies all the space under the porch that is sheltered by the pergola. This placing of the garage is specially convenient, as it not only gives the best possible shelter to the motor car, but enables its occupants to descend within the house itself—a great advantage in stormy weather—and to go directly into the billiard room, from which a stairway leads up to the living room. The garage is fourteen feet broad, giving ample room for the motor car and also for a workbench, which is placed just below the line of casement windows. The billiard room, which is very large, is lighted by the three groups of casement windows that appear in the lower wall at the front of the house. A large fireplace in the middle of the

THREE-STORY BUNGALOW FOR HILLSIDE SITE

BUILT-IN SIDEBOARD, CLOSETS, WINDOW SEAT, DESK AND BOOKSHELVES IN LIVING ROOM OF HOUSE NO. 105.

opposite wall gives warmth and cheer to the room, and its construction is sufficiently rugged to allow a bold and rather primitive form of decoration and furnishing, suitable to such a basement playroom for men. The interior view given below may be helpful in its suggestion of the corner seat, willow chair, and Craftsman hanging and bracket lights. Just back of the billiard room is seen the very convenient arrangement of the stairway, which has a double landing, giving a means of communication between the living room and the billiard room

and also between the kitchen and the furnace room. This lies just behind the fireplace, and the coal cellar joins it. The oblong space in the corner is not excavated, nor is the corresponding space at the corner of the billiard room; but if more room were required in the basement it would be an easy matter to excavate and utilize these spaces. The laundry is a square room large enough to hold the necessary conveniences for washing.

On the main floor the entrance leads directly into the large living room, one end of which is

CORNER OF BILLIARD ROOM ON GROUND FLOOR OF THREE-STORY CRAFTSMAN BUNGALOW NO. 105.

THREE-STORY BUNGALOW FOR HILLSIDE SITE

to be used as a dining room. A glass door from this end opens upon the porch that is covered by the pergola, and another leads to the dining porch, which is roofed in so that it may be used in all moderately warm weather,

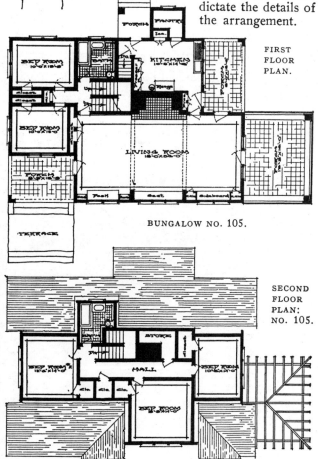

CRAFTSMAN BUNGALOW.   NO. 105.

GROUND FLOOR PLAN.

whether stormy or not. A large fireplace, with a massive chimneypiece, occupies the center of the inner wall space, the staircase being placed on one side and the doors leading to the kitchen and the dining porch upon the other. The entire front of the long room, although treated as a unit, contains three separate built-in features. In the center is a large window seat occupying the space below the main group of windows. At one side of this is a large built-in writing desk, with bookshelves on either side and double windows above, and on the other side, in the part of the room that is meant to be used as a dining room, is a built-in sideboard with china closets. Treated in this way, the whole end of the room is made interesting and decorative, while it serves all purposes of utility and convenience. There is opportunity for a generous display of woodwork, and the line of wainscoting that runs around the whole room is preserved unbroken by the tops of the bookshelves, china closets and the high ends and back of the window seat.

According to this arrangement there is ample space left on the main floor for two bedrooms with the necessary closet room at the end of the house just back of the entrance porch. A bathroom occupies the square space in rear of the stairs and the kitchen is placed directly

behind the big fireplace in the living room, so that the flue may be utilized for the kitchen range, thus doing away with the necessity for a second chimney. The service porch, pantry and ice-box form an extension at the back of the house. In case a different arrangement is preferred, the space given to the two bedrooms and the bath could easily be used for a workroom, a library or den, as the three bedrooms in the attic would be enough to accommodate a small family.

These three rooms are of good size and are well lighted and ventilated. Plenty of space is given to closets, and there is also a bathroom. Our own idea was to have these upper bedrooms serve for guest rooms and possibly a servant's room, leaving the two rooms on the main floor for the family; but, of course, the necessities of each individual case would dictate the details of the arrangement.

FIRST FLOOR PLAN.

BUNGALOW NO. 105.

SECOND FLOOR PLAN: NO. 105.

CRAFTSMAN CEMENT DWELLING INSPIRED BY OLD-FASHIONED NEW ENGLAND FARMHOUSE

Published in The Craftsman, September, 1909.

CRAFTSMAN CEMENT FARMHOUSE: NO. 74.

ALTHOUGH built according to a very modern method—cement on metal lath—this building will be seen to follow the salient structural features of the so-called New England farmhouse, varied, however, by the big dormer which breaks the long, sloping roof at the back to admit more light and air to the second story. The four-foot overhang at the eaves, with the deep brackets that support it, the large cement chimneys at either end, the porch at the corner and the pergola over the front door give interest to the exterior.

This pergola is better seen in the detail view of the building, on the next page. Instead of using the customary single heavy beam in the roof supports, we have shown here two smaller beams, thus making a lighter structure while taking nothing away from the strength of it. The pillars are of cement. The vine over the pergola and the flower-boxes set between the pillars add a note of grace and hospitality to the entrance, and seem to knit the house more closely to its surroundings. Vines could also be grown at the sides of the house, to soften

the long straight lines of the two chimneys.

The entrance door, with its long metal hinges and knocker, and its row of small lights in the upper part of the panels, is as simple as it is decorative, and is quite in keeping with the rest of the construction. The casements on either side of the door serve to light the hall within, and at the same time add another note of welcome to the exterior.

The interior of the house, of course, meets the modern standards of comfort. The placing of the stairs, however, suggests the old New England arrangement; the landing is raised only a few steps above the living room and a railing runs along its edge so that the effect of a balcony is given. From the landing the stairs continue to the second story behind a partition of spindles, making them a part of both living room and hall, thus turning a necessary feature of the house into a most artistic one.

The large living room is well lighted by the window groups at the front and rear, and by the two large windows on each side of the

CRAFTSMAN CEMENT FARMHOUSE

DETAIL VIEW OF CRAFTSMAN CEMENT FARMHOUSE NO. 74, SHOWING FRONT ENTRANCE WITH CEMENT PILLARS AND PERGOLA CONSTRUCTION ABOVE. THE SIMPLE BUT EFFECTIVE TREATMENT OF THE DOOR AND SMALL CASEMENTS ON EITHER SIDE IS ALSO WORTH NOTICING.

fireplace. A glass door leads onto the sheltered porch at the back, where meals may be served whenever the weather is warm enough. This porch also connects with the dining

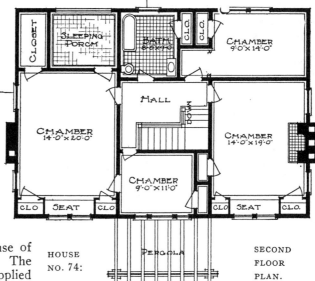

HOUSE NO. 74:
FIRST FLOOR
PLAN.

room, which is provided with a built-in sideboard and communicates with the kitchen through a convenient pantry. The kitchen, it will be noticed, has ready access to the staircase, hall and entrance door. In fact the arrangement and relation of all the rooms has been made as simple and direct as possible in order to facilitate the work of housekeeping.

In one corner of the hall a coat closet is provided, and a wide opening at the right leads into a little den or library. In here is another open fireplace which utilizes the same chimney as the kitchen range, and on either side of the chimneypiece are built-in bookcases.

The upper floor plan gives one a sense of compactness and spaciousness combined. The rooms are large and airy, and amply supplied with closets. Two of the front bedrooms have built-in window seats—a feature which always adds much to the comfort and charm of an interior—and the bedroom to the right has the additional attraction of an open fire-

place which uses the same chimney as that of the den below. The large chamber on the left communicates with a sleeping porch at the rear which, being sheltered on three sides, is protected from the weather, and could be used practically the year round by those who believe in the healthfulness of outdoor sleeping. The large bedroom also communicates with the smaller central bedroom in front, which can also be entered from the hall. This little bedroom could be used as a dressing room, if desired, in connection with the adjoining room at the left. The bathroom is large and is provided with a linen closet.

All through the house, it will be noticed, in both the exterior and the interior, there is an entire absence of affectation or superfluous ornament. The treatment of the whole is extremely simple, and whatever decorative quality the building and the rooms possess will be found to be the outcome of necessary elements of the construction, handled in such a manner as to combine practical architectural features with

HOUSE
NO. 74:

PERGOLA

SECOND
FLOOR
PLAN.

comfort and usefulness of arrangement and harmony of proportion and line. Like all the houses shown here, the plans could be adapted to meet individual requirements.

SIMPLE CEMENT COTTAGE FOR A SMALL FAMILY

Published in The Craftsman, June, 1910.

SIMPLE CEMENT CRAFTSMAN COTTAGE: NO. 91.

A SMALL cement cottage is illustrated here such as we find coming more and more into favor as the possibilities of this excellent building material are developed. The compact floor plans, which are practically square, result in a very simple exterior. The walls and foundation of this house are built of cement on metal lath, and the hood over the entrance door is of the same material. The shape and structure of this hood express the limitations and possibilities of cement, and reveal the method of construction as frankly as do the beams and brackets used in wood construction. The severity of the plain cement walls is relieved by the grouping and placing of the windows, and by the use of wide V-jointed boards in the gables, the lower ends of

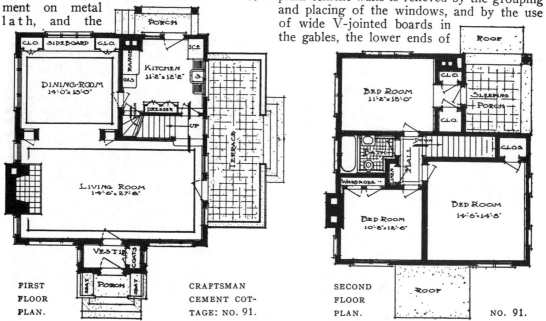

FIRST FLOOR PLAN.

CRAFTSMAN CEMENT COTTAGE: NO. 91.

SECOND FLOOR PLAN.

NO. 91.

CEMENT COTTAGE FOR A SMALL FAMILY

the boards resting against a wide beam that marks the upper termination of the cement wall. The roof is of Ruberoid, the lengths of the material being brought down from the ridge-pole to the heavy roll at the eaves, and each joint being covered with a strip of wood which caps the rafter to which the roofing is fastened.

A cement seat is built at either side of the entrance porch, and the front door opens into a small vestibule with a coat closet at one end. This vestibule leads directly into the living room, which extends across the entire front of the house, with a big fireplace at one end and a glass door at the other leading to the terrace at the side. This living room is wainscoted to the height of the frieze with wide V-jointed boards.

The staircase and landing occupy the greater part of the wall between the living room and kitchen, and the remainder of the wall space is taken up by the wide opening into the dining room. This is finished in the same way as the living room, as the intention is to throw the two into one large room, the division between them being merely suggested. The entire end of the dining room is taken up by a built-in sideboard, with a group of three casement windows set high in the wall above,

and a good-sized china closet on either side.

The kitchen is arranged to simplify housework as much as possible.

The upper floor is divided into three bedrooms, a bathroom, plenty of closets, and a good-sized sleeping porch which can be screened in summer and glassed in winter if desired. The bathroom and this sleeping porch, as well as the terrace below, may be floored with cement.

This cottage admits of the use of many interesting furnishings and fixtures, such as the lamp fitted to the newel-post of the staircase in the view of the living room shown below. This lamp, which comes in hammered copper or wrought iron, with amber glass, seems especially in keeping with the general treatment of the interior, and while simple in design, is decorative as well as useful.

DETAIL OF NEWEL-POST LAMP SHOWN IN INTERIOR VIEW OF HOUSE NO. 91.

CORNER OF LIVING ROOM IN CRAFTSMAN CEMENT COTTAGE NO. 91, SHOWING STAIRCASE WITH NEWEL-POST LAMP, AND DOOR LEADING ONTO THE TERRACE AT THE SIDE OF THE HOUSE.

INEXPENSIVE ONE-STORY BUNGALOW WITH EFFECTIVE USE OF TRELLIS

Published in The Craftsman, September, 1911. CEMENT AND CLAPBOARD ONE-STORY BUNGALOW: NO. 123.

ONE END OF THE LIVING ROOM IN BUNGALOW NO. 123, SHOWING CRAFTSMAN FIREPLACE-FURNACE WITH DECORATIVE USE OF TAPESTRY BRICK.

CEMENT AND CLAPBOARD ONE-STORY BUNGALOW

PLANNED for a small family and designed for a narrow suburban lot, this little bungalow may be inexpensively and yet substantially built. Cement plaster with boarded gable and slate roof are the materials shown here, although concrete foundation and shingled sides and roof might be used; but the durability of cement would more than compensate for its greater initial cost.

The veranda floor may be of concrete, and the pillars of concrete or rough hand-hewn logs. The trellis and the pergola entrance add a decorative note which is pleasing both before the vines have grown and when they are leafless during winter.

The floor plan shows a small but comfortable interior, comprising a large sitting room to be used as a dining room, and two bedrooms, a bathroom and kitchen. Ample closet space is allowed and the kitchen is equipped with all the necessary conveniences. The bungalow can be well warmed and ventilated by the centrally located Craftsman fireplace-furnace, the illustration of which shows an effective use of Tapestry brick.

On each side of this fireplace, with its decorative chimney and tiled hearth, are paneled doors, one of which leads into the kitchen, and the other into the hall. Each door has small square lights set in the upper portion, and these, together with the well-balanced groups of windows in the front and side walls, add to the structural interest of the room. The simple treatment of the woodwork, while possessing a certain decorative quality, will form a restful and unobtrusive background for the furnishings. The built-in window seats in the nooks formed by the vestibule will also prove welcome features of the interior.

A similar seat is seen in the recess between the closets in one of the bedrooms, with small windows above it overlooking the porch. The other bedroom is also a fair size and is well lighted by windows at the back and side. The small hallway, with its closet in one corner, takes up as little space as possible, and communicates with each room of the bungalow.

The plan of the house is one which lends itself to a light form of housekeeping, and if simply furnished the work of the household could be reduced to a minimum.

The porch, being recessed and sheltered on two sides, would serve as a pleasant outdoor living room during warm weather, and it could be glassed in during the winter if de-

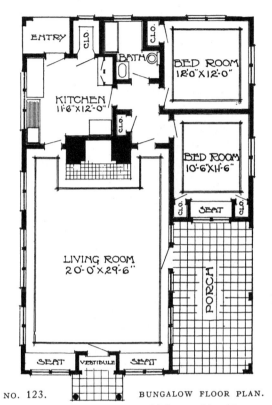

NO. 123.   BUNGALOW FLOOR PLAN.

sired,—an arrangement which would add considerably to the space within the bungalow. In any case, it could be easily furnished with a few willow pieces,—chairs, table and swinging seat with comfortable cushions,—and if screened from the street in summer by a plentiful growth of vines, it would be a very serviceable as well as a very charming feature of the house.

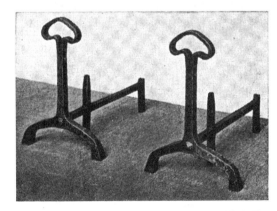

ANDIRONS OF WROUGHT IRON WHICH MIGHT BE USED ON THE OPEN HEARTH IN ANY CRAFTSMAN INTERIOR.

SMALL ONE-STORY CEMENT BUNGALOW WITH SLATE ROOF, DESIGNED FOR A NARROW LOT

Published in The Craftsman, September, 1911.

CEMENT BUNGALOW FOR NARROW LOT: NO. 124.

THIS one-story bungalow is a small, simply-arranged dwelling, intended for a narrow lot, and planned economically to afford the greatest possible comfort within a limited space. Cement plaster would be suitable for the walls and slate for the roof.

The most attractive feature of the exterior is the long porch which extends across the front of the house. This is enclosed by a low parapet of cement from which rise the hewn log pillars which support the pergola roof. Against this parapet is placed trelliswork, and from the trellis vines may be trained up the pillars and over the beams of the pergola above. Thus a very pleasant entrance will be formed, and even in winter, when the vines are leafless, the trelliswork and pergola construction overhead will still lend a distinctly decorative note to the exterior, softening by their graceful details the severity of what would otherwise be a plain cement building.

A touch of interest is also given to the side of the house by the extension of the main roof over the kitchen entrance, with its vine-encircled pillars rising from the cement floor.

Since the use of trelliswork is found to hold such charm, it might even be carried out further, and used in the entrance to the garden at the front of the house. The line drawing shown here gives a suggestion for such treatment, which would make a very effective gateway and would link the house more closely to its surroundings. Another factor in relieving the plainness of the bungalow walls is the use of small panes in all the windows. This not only breaks up the surface in a pleasing way, but at the same time seems to carry out the effect of the trelliswork.

The front door opens from the pergola porch directly into the ample living room, which is well lighted by the groups of windows on three sides, and is provided with an open fireplace. The latter, if a Craftsman fireplace-furnace, will serve to heat and ventilate the entire bungalow.

The kitchen and two bedrooms, though of moderate dimensions, will be large enough for a small family, and the whole plan is one that will lend itself to simple housekeeping.

The illustration of one of the rooms in this

CEMENT BUNGALOW FOR A NARROW LOT

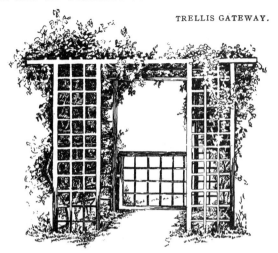

TRELLIS GATEWAY.

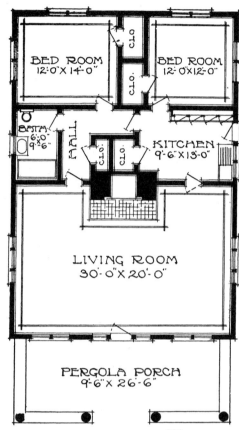

FLOOR PLAN OF BUNGALOW NO. 124.

bungalow will give some impression of the effective simplicity of Craftsman bedroom furniture. The plain lines and restful proportions of the bed and bureau are thoroughly in keeping with the treatment of the woodwork, and the small square lights set in the paneled door form a pleasant relief to the flat surface of the walls. In the interior of this bungalow, as in other Craftsman houses, it will be found that much of the interest comes from the thoughtful handling of necessary architectural details, and the more carefully these are worked out, the easier will be the task of furnishing the home.

BEDROOM IN CEMENT BUNGALOW, NO. 124, WITH CRAFTSMAN FURNITURE.

CEMENT HOUSE WITH PERGOLA, SLEEPING BALCONY AND PRACTICAL INTERESTING INTERIOR

Published in The Craftsman, September, 1910.

CRAFTSMAN TWO-STORY CEMENT HOUSE WITH EIGHT ROOMS AND RECESSED SLEEPING BALCONY: NO. 97.

THIS cement house is simply built, with a low-pitched roof showing a wide overhang. The roof is Ruberoid stretched over the rafters and battened down as usual, but instead of the roll at the eaves we have brought it down to the inside of the cypress gutter. The rafters are hollowed out, and the gutter let into the curve so that it forms a continuous trough, as shown in the diagram. The pergola in front is supported on massive cement pillars, and the timber construction above is ornamental as well as sturdy and enduring. Over this pergola is a partly recessed sleeping porch, ending in a balcony that is supported on the extended timbers of the second floor. A group of six windows and a glass door in the back of this porch give plenty of light to the bedroom which opens upon it.

The living room extends across the whole

DIAGRAM OF CYPRESS GUTTER USED IN HOUSE NO. 97.

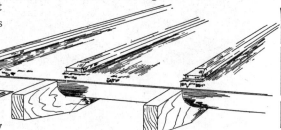

front of the house, and at one end is a large chimneypiece extending to the ceiling, the space on either side being filled with bookcases. A square den opens out of the living room at one side of the staircase, and at the other side is the dining room with a second fireplace flanked with combination sideboards and china closets.

This house has one bedroom on the lower floor with a small private bath attached. On the second floor is a large square bathroom, and the closets also are unusually big. Two large storerooms are provided.

CEMENT HOUSE WITH EIGHT ROOMS AND SLEEPING BALCONY

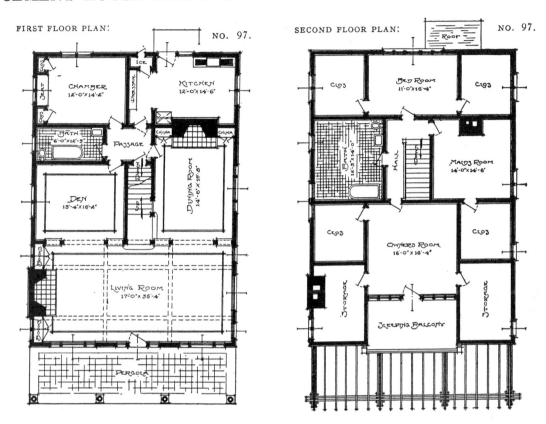

FIRST FLOOR PLAN: NO. 97.   SECOND FLOOR PLAN: NO. 97.

END OF DINING ROOM IN HOUSE NO. 97, SHOWING FIREPLACE AND BUILT-IN CHINA CLOSETS.

PLASTER DWELLING FOR TOWN OR COUNTRY

Published in The Craftsman, January, 1909.   PLASTER HOUSE WITH TYPICAL CRAFTSMAN INTERIOR: NO. 58.

THE house shown here is suitable for either an ordinary lot in a town or village, or for the open country. It has plastered or stuccoed walls, foundation of field stone, and shingled roof. The design, however, lends itself quite as readily to shingled or clapboarded walls.

The outside kitchen at the back is recommended only in the event of the house being built in the country, because in town it would hardly be needed.

The plan of the lower story shows the usual Craftsman arrangement of rooms opening into

STONE FIREPLACE AND BUILT-IN BOOKCASES IN LIVING ROOM OF HOUSE NO. 58.

PLASTER HOUSE WITH TYPICAL CRAFTSMAN INTERIOR

one another with only suggested divisions. The entrance door opens into a small entry, screened by portières from the living room so that no draught from the front door is felt inside. On the outside wall of the living room is the arrangement of fireplace and bookcases, as shown in the detail illustration. The chimneypiece is built of split field stone laid up in cement and runs clear to the ceiling. A bookcase is built in on either side and above each one of these are two small double-hung windows. The tops of the bookcases serve admirably as shelves for plants.

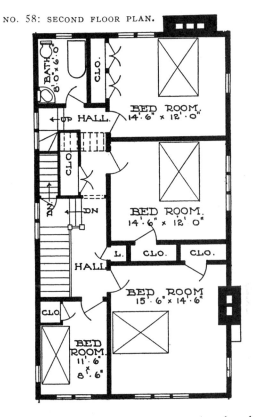

HOUSE NO. 58: FIRST FLOOR PLAN.

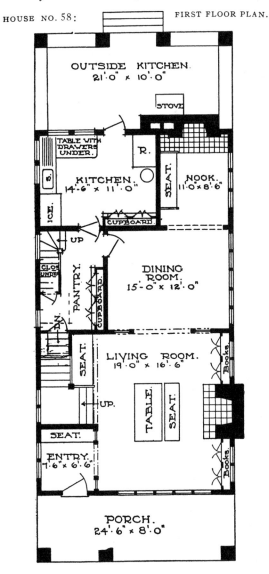

In the center of the room may be placed a large table with a settle of exactly the same length placed back to it and facing the fire, so that it affords an ideal arrangement for anyone who wishes to sit facing the fire with the light from a reading lamp falling over the shoulder. The back of the seat would be on a level or a little below the top of the table, so that the two seem almost to be one piece of furniture. This is usually found to be a pleasant and comfortable arrangement.

The dining room is simply a continuation of the living room, from which it is divided only by posts and panels with open spaces in the upper part, as shown in the illustration of the fireplace. Beyond this dining room again is a nook, the end of which is completely filled by a large fireplace using the same chimney as the kitchen range and the stove in the outside kitchen. The seat in this nook is not built in, but a broad bench or settle would be very comfortable if placed as suggested in the plan.

The kitchen though not large is compactly planned, and the work is greatly simplified by the small space and convenient arrangement.

COMMODIOUS CEMENT HOUSE WITH TERRACE, PORCHES AND SLEEPING BALCONIES

Published in The Craftsman, August, 1910.

CRAFTSMAN CEMENT HOUSE: NO. 95.

HERE is a substantial and moderate-sized cement house. The lines are all rather straight and severe, the pillars and parapets being plain and the walls broken only by the groups of windows. All look of bareness in the upper part of the house is taken away by the effect of the widely overhanging roof with its exposed rafters, heavy beams and the large brackets which support it. The roof itself is of Ruberoid, finished at the eaves with a wood gutter. Below, the square outline of the house is broken by a veranda that is partly open to the sky and partly roofed in. This veranda may be floored with red cement marked off in squares, and in front has much the appearance of a terrace, as it is shielded only by a low parapet crowned with flower-boxes. At either side of the house the veranda is sheltered by a roof which forms the floor of the sleeping balcony above. These balconies are also shielded by para-pets surmounted with flower-boxes, so that the cots or low beds are concealed from view.

The balconies are open to the sky, but could be covered with awnings if desired. The exposed win-

HOUSE NO. 95.

FIRST FLOOR PLAN

COMMODIOUS CRAFTSMAN CEMENT HOUSE

dows and entrance door are sheltered by cement hoods constructed like the walls and extending outward in a graceful sweep that not only protects the windows and door, but adds a distinctly decorative feature to the walls. These hoods are supported upon heavy timber brackets. Beneath the balconies the timber construction is left exposed as it is in the roof.

The house is arranged in the typical Craftsman way, the entrance hall being merely suggested as a division between the dining room and living room. As a matter of fact, the whole lower part of the house is open, with the exception of the kitchen and pantry at the back and the den at one side of the living room. The staircase, although apparently in the entrance hall, is really a part of the living room, which is divided from the hall only by a massive overhead beam. There is a coat closet in one corner and plenty of space for a built-in seat in the recess formed by the stairway. The living room is very plain as regards woodwork and other finish, but if the wood be properly selected and treated the room will have a greater beauty than could be

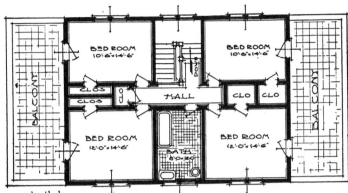

HOUSE NO. 95: SECOND FLOOR PLAN

given by a more elaborate arrangement. The walls are wainscoted with wide V-jointed boards to the height of the frieze, and the big square chimneypiece of Tapestry brick extends only to the same line, which thus runs unbroken all around the room. Above this line the chimneypiece is plastered like the ceiling and frieze with rough sand-finished plaster, tinted to harmonize with the woodwork.

On the opposite side of the entrance hall is the dining room, lighted in front with a group of windows like that in the living room. A glass door opens on the porch and on either side of this door are china closets.

TAPESTRY BRICK FIREPLACE IN LIVING ROOM OF CRAFTSMAN CEMENT HOUSE NO. 95.

CEMENT HOUSE, COMPACT YET SPACIOUS, SUITABLE FOR A CITY STREET

Published in The Craftsman, May, 1909.

TEN-ROOM CEMENT HOUSE: NO. 66.

CORNER OF LIVING ROOM IN HOUSE NO. 66, WITH SUGGESTION FOR PLACING OF TABLE AND FIRESIDE SEAT.

TEN-ROOM CEMENT HOUSE SUITABLE FOR A CITY STREET

THIS house is built entirely of cement on a stone foundation, and requires a frontage of not less than fifty feet. The entrance of the porch is roofed over and the rest is pergola construction.

The cement chimney, which is built in three widths, forms an interesting variation at the side of the house, and the grouping of the windows with their large and small panes helps to break up the plain cement surface into well-proportioned spaces, while adding at the same time to the charm of the interior.

The interior view shows casement windows in the dining room and above the built-in bookcases on each side of the living-room fireplace. The chimneypiece is built of rough bricks of varied colors,—old blue, burnt sienna, dull yellow and many tan and salmon shades, and when rightly arranged the result is beautiful, especially if the colors are repeated in the decorative scheme of the room. The shelf is

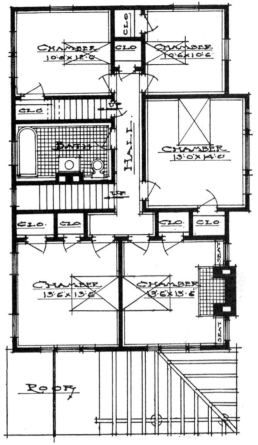

HOUSE NO. 66: SECOND FLOOR PLAN.

a thick board, of whatever wood is selected for the finishing of the room.

The dining room is wainscoted and is separated only by narrow partitions from the living room. The sideboard is built in and the space between it and the rear wall is filled by a china closet. In the corresponding space between the sideboard and the front wall a swinging door leads into a roomy butler's pantry. The kitchen has several cupboards and also two big pantries, one of which contains the icebox. A few steps leading from a landing on the main stairway connect the kitchen with the upper part of the house. It will be noticed that the servant's sleeping room and bath are on the first floor. The large garret, which may be additionally lighted by skylights, would make a splendid billiard hall, or could be broken up into smaller rooms to be used for various purposes, such as storerooms or extra bedrooms.

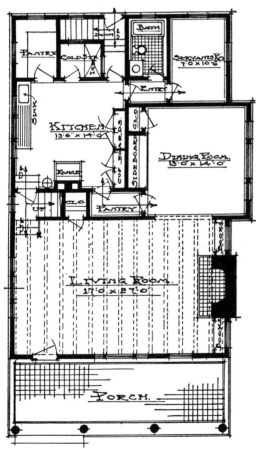

HOUSE NO. 66: FIRST FLOOR PLAN.

LARGE CEMENT HOUSE FOR TOWN OR COUNTRY

Published in The Craftsman, February, 1909.

CRAFTSMAN CEMENT HOUSE: NO. 60.

DESIGNED on simple lines that harmonize with almost any surroundings, this cement house is suitable for town, village or country site. The walls are of vitrified terra cotta blocks, the plastering being laid directly on the blocks both outside and inside. The foundation and parapet of the little terrace are of field stone.

Above the entrance door the wall runs up straight to the second story, where it terminates in a shallow balcony. Provision is made here for a flower-box, as the severity of the wall seems to demand the relief in color and line afforded by a cluster of plants and drooping vines. At the back of the house is a similar construction, for in place of a roof above the dining porch and part of the kitchen, is a large open balcony which may be used as a sleeping porch. This balcony is partially shielded by the cement parapet, but otherwise is open to the weather.

The roof, which has a wide overhang, is covered with rough heavy slates supported on strong beams and girders. The little roof over the bay window in the reception hall is also covered with slates and serves to break the straight lines of the wall. All the windows are casements and their grouping forms one of the distinctly decorative features of the construction.

The dining room opens with double glass doors upon the porch at the back of the

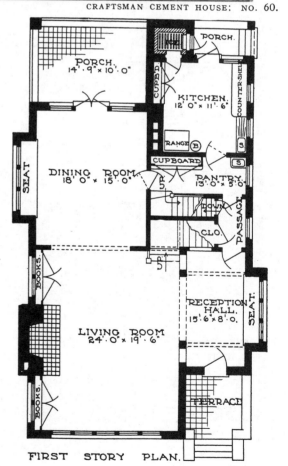

FIRST STORY PLAN.

LARGE CEMENT HOUSE FOR TOWN OR COUNTRY

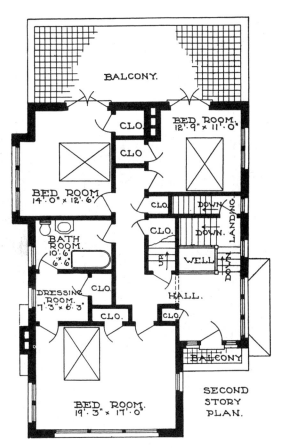

DETAIL OF LANTERN SHOWN IN INTERIOR OF HOUSE NO. 60

house, which may be left open or screened in summer, and closed in winter for a dining porch or sun room. Built-in bookcases, wide inviting window seats and a big fireplace add to the comfort and structural interest of the rooms.

High wainscots are used throughout the reception hall, living room and dining room in this house, and the general effect of the divisions between the rooms and the arrangement of the staircase and landing is shown by the view of the interior given below. The woodwork in all these rooms would, of course, be the same, and the choice and treatment of it gives the keynote to the whole decorative scheme. Craftsman fittings, such as the hanging lanterns and newel-post lamp suggested here, seem especially appropriate.

The kitchen is compact and convenient, as are also the bedrooms, bathroom and closets on the second floor, and the little hall that opens out upon the balcony is admirably adapted for use as an upstairs sitting room. On the third floor are the billiard room and bedroom for the maid.

SECOND STORY PLAN.

GLIMPSE OF ENTRANCE HALL AND STAIRCASE IN HOUSE NO. 60, AS SEEN FROM THE LIVING ROOM.

CONCRETE OR PLASTER HOUSE OF MODERATE SIZE AND SIMPLE DESIGN

Published in The Craftsman, February, 1910.

SIMPLY PLANNED CONCRETE OR PLASTER HOUSE WITH RECESSED ENTRANCE PORCH AND BALCONY: NO. 83.

EITHER concrete or plaster on metal lath may be used for this house, which is of moderate size, simply planned and comparatively inexpensive as to the cost of building. The severity of the straight lines and broad surfaces is relieved by the grouped windows, the arched openings of the entrance porch and the large dormer which occupies the inner angle of the L-shaped building.

No foundation is visible, the cement walls rising from a level with the ground. The chimneys are of concrete and the roof is covered with heavy rough slates which are much the same as the English flat tiles and which are not only fireproof and practically indestructible, but also give an admirable effect. The color of these slates would depend upon the color of the concrete walls. The slates come in gray, dull red, moss green and a variegated purplish tone, and upon the selection of the right color to blend with the walls and harmonize with the general tone of the landscape

will depend much of the beauty of the house.

The wide low openings of the recessed entrance porch show a suggestion of the California Mission architecture in the flattened arches and massive concrete square pillars. The porch floor may be paved with Welsh quarries, or dull red cement marked off in squares, either material being durable, attractive and thoroughly in keeping with cement construction.

Perhaps the most individual of the exterior features is the group of dormer windows placed in the angle of the house. These serve to light and ventilate the two large bedrooms and the upper hall. A great part of the decorative effect of the windows of this house depends upon the use of rather small square panes and the grouping of the windows themselves in twos and threes in such a way as to give a massive rather than a scattered arrangement of openings in the wall.

The entrance door opens into a small vesti-

SIMPLY PLANNED HOUSE OF CONCRETE OR PLASTER

bule or entry which serves as a focal point for the arrangement of the rooms. The openings on either side are so broad as to leave only the merest suggestion of a partition, and the staircase may be regarded as a decorative structural feature common to both living room and dining room, rather than as a necessity to be relegated to the hall. This staircase leads up to a small square landing that is almost opposite the entrance door, and a door at the back of the open vestibule leads into a small enclosed passage which communicates with the kitchen and from which the stairs go down to the cellar.

Both living room and dining room are heated with large fireplaces, that in the dining room being placed

WILLOW CHAIR WHICH WOULD ADD TO THE COMFORT OF A CRAFTSMAN INTERIOR.

frieze at the top, while in the living room the walls might be of plaster divided into broad panels by stiles and plate rail of the same wood. The plaster would be most attractive if left rather rough and matt-finished in some pale tone.

On the upper floor the arrangement of rooms is much the same as it is below, three bedrooms occupying the same space as the living room, dining room and kitchen, with the bath directly over the pantry, and the hall a duplicate of the entry beneath. This makes a great saving in the cost of construction.

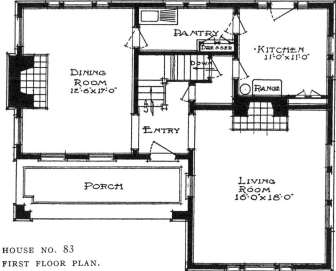

HOUSE NO. 83
FIRST FLOOR PLAN.

in the outside wall, while the one in the living room uses the same chimney as the kitchen range. We would suggest that the same woodwork and same general color scheme be used for the dining room and living room, thereby increasing the apparent space as well as the restfulness of the rooms. This does not at all imply monotony, for the same woodwork may be used in different ways and the arrangement of the wall spaces may convey a sense of variation that is interesting and yet entirely harmonious. For instance, if the woodwork were chestnut, dull-finished in a soft grayish brown, the dining room might be wainscoted high enough to leave only a plaster

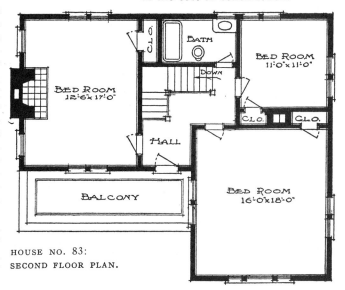

HOUSE NO. 83:
SECOND FLOOR PLAN.

INEXPENSIVE CEMENT AND SHINGLE COTTAGE

Published in The Craftsman, February, 1910.

SEVEN-ROOM COTTAGE: NO. 84.

THIS is a simple little house intended for a small family, and the plan has purposely been arranged so that the construction shall be as inexpensive as is compatible with durability and safety. The shingled roof has a steep pitch and its line is broken by two shallow dormers on either side which afford plenty of light to the bedrooms and add to the interest of the exterior. The walls of the lower story are of cement on metal lath and the upper walls are shingled. A very satisfactory effect could be obtained by giving a rough, pebble-dash finish to the cement and brushing on enough pigment to give it a tone of dull grayish green, varied by the inequalities in the surface of the cement. It would pay to use rived cypress shingles for the upper walls, as these are much more interesting and durable than the ordinary sawn shingles, and possess a surface that responds admirably to the treatment with diluted sulphuric acid which we have found most successful with this wood. The roof could be either moss green or grayish brown, a little darker than the shingles of the upper walls. Four heavy cement pillars support the roof of the porch, which is also of shingles the same color as the main roof of the house. The porch floor may

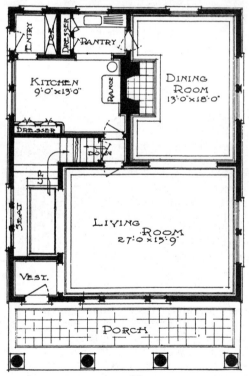

HOUSE NO. 84: FIRST FLOOR PLAN.

SEVEN-ROOM COTTAGE OF CEMENT AND SHINGLE

be paved with cement, or the outside edge might be plain cement of the same color as the walls, and the long strip down the center might be Welsh quarries or red cement marked off in squares.

The entrance door is at one end of the porch and opens into a small vestibule which leads directly into the living room, the opening being at right angles to the entrance door. A small partition separates the entrance from the stairway beyond, which is placed in a nook at the end of the living room. The entire end of this nook is occupied by a group of windows and a window seat. There is no fireplace in the living room, but in the dining room a large open fireplace uses the one central chimney which also serves for the kitchen range. The opening between the living room and the dining room is so broad that the fireplace serves equally well for both.

A small passageway leads from the kitchen to the living room, affording access to the entrance door, and in this passage is also the door leading to the cellar stairs. The kitchen is small and the pantry is little more than a nook in the larger room. Two large built-in china closets give plenty of room for the dishes, and the sink is placed in the pantry. Usually this arrangement would mean many additional steps, but the kitchen is so small that the distance from the range to the sink is no more than it would be in an ordinary room. An entry at the back of the kitchen communi-

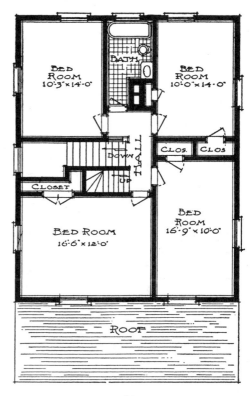

HOUSE NO. 84: SECOND FLOOR PLAN.

case in the center and the bathroom at the back.

On the whole, the interior of the cottage is one which would lend itself to simple housekeeping, and if tastefully furnished should prove both comfortable and attractive. The entrance could be made even more pleasant by the use of flower-boxes between the cement pillars of the porch, and vines planted along the side walls would add to the charm of the exterior and link the house more intimately to its surroundings.

The willow settle shown here would be a comfortable addition to this or any other interior, and would lighten up the general effect of the darker and heavier Craftsman oak furniture. The finish of soft green or deep golden brown would be a pleasant note in almost any color scheme, and the cushion coverings could be varied according to the material, color and design preferred.

LARGE WILLOW SETTLE WHICH HARMONIZES WELL WITH CRAFTSMAN OAK FURNITURE.

cates with a door leading to the outside, and furnishes a cool place for the ice box. A door from the pantry opens into the dining room.

The arrangement of the upper floor is very simple, as the four bedrooms occupy the four corners of the building with the hall and stair-

CRAFTSMAN HOUSE DESIGNED FOR NARROW LOT

Published in The Craftsman, May, 1909.

CEMENT AND SHINGLE HOUSE WITH SIX ROOMS, PORCHES AND BALCONY FOR NARROW LOT: NO. 67.

THIS cement and shingle house, being only nineteen feet wide, can be built on the ordinary town lot. It is as compact and comfortable as possible for winter use, and still not without certain advantages in spring and summer which are quite lacking in the usual town block. Front and rear porches and a balcony that may be shaded by an awning will do much toward making the summer heat endurable.

The lower story of the house is of cement on a low foundation of split field stone, and the second story is covered with hand-split shingles.

The suggestion of pergola at the rear of the house is merely a three-foot projection on a porch running under the second story and is built of the exposed timbers of the house supported by pillars. It not only adds to the attractiveness of that corner as seen from the street, but, covered with vines, would give a lovely outlook for the dining-room windows, and, since a door connects it with the kitchen, may be used itself as a dining room in warm weather.

The stone chimney, instead of running up at an even depth from the foundation to the roof and narrowing above the fireplace on the

ground floor, keeps its same width almost to the eaves, but slants in at the second story to about half the original depth. This does away with the monotonous line of the ordinary outside chimney and gives a fireplace upstairs as wide, although not so deep, as the one on the ground floor.

All the exposed windows on the second story are hooded to protect them from driving storms. It is an attractive feature in the construction, especially in connection with the window group—a long French casement flanked on either side by a double-hung window, looking out upon the balcony. The floor of this balcony and the timbers that support it form the ceiling of the porch. The ends of these exposed supports, projecting beyond the beam on which they rest, emphasize the line between the porch and the balcony and are at once decorative and economical, for the open construction does away with much repairing of the sort occasioned by the action of dampness upon timbers sheathed in.

The entrance door, which is very simple in design, opens from the front porch directly into the large living hall. Here, on each side of the open fireplace, we find built-in book-

CEMENT AND SHINGLE HOUSE PLANNED FOR NARROW LOT

cases, with small casements set in the wall above. The room is also made light and cheerful by the window groups in the opposite wall and on each side of the entrance door, as well as by the wide opening into the dining room.

The view of the interior is made from a point just in front of the living room hearth and shows the use of spindles between the rooms and in the high balustrade that screens the two or three steps which lead up from the dining room, and are intended for the use of the servants. The meeting of these stairs with those from the living room makes an odd little corner that offers many possibilities for decorative effects. The dining room is wainscoted to the plate rail. The sideboard is built in and suggests the old-time dresser with its platter rail and side cupboards. There is a small pantry between the dining room and the kitchen, and the latter is fitted with the usual conveniences.

The upper floor plan shows a simple arrangement of the three bedrooms and bathroom.

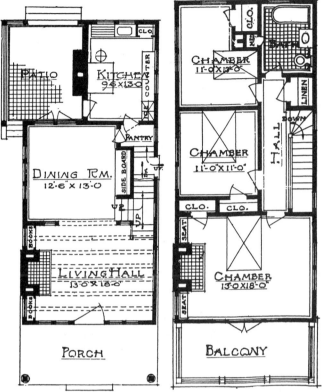

HOUSE NO. 67: FIRST AND SECOND FLOOR PLANS.

INTERIOR OF HOUSE NO. 67, SHOWING ONE CORNER OF THE LIVING HALL WITH GLIMPSE OF STAIRS AND DINING ROOM. THE DECORATIVE HANDLING OF WOODWORK AND STRUCTURAL FEATURES IS WORTH STUDYING.

SMALL TWO-STORY CEMENT HOUSE WITH RE-CESSED PORCH AND BALCONY

ALTHOUGH this house is a small one, its good proportions and the decorative quality of its structural features combine in producing a homelike and dignified impression. The severity of the building is broken by the recessed porch and sleeping balcony above, and the plain surfaces of the walls are relieved by the small hooded entrance and the design and grouping of the windows. The walls are cement on metal lath—a form of construction which we have found most satisfactory—and the gables are sheathed with wide V-jointed boards which form a pleasant variation to the plainness of the cement below. The low-pitched roof, with its revealed rafters and purlins, offers no corners to collect moisture and induce rot under the action of the weather. The solid construction seen in the timbers is used in the hood over the entrance door. The round cement pillars of the lower porch are repeated in the balcony above, where they support the purlins that hold up the roof, thus carrying out the idea of massive construction in appearance as well as in actuality.

Much of the charm of this house would depend upon its color and the finish of the walls. The best effect would be gained by having the cement mixed with coarse brown sand and simply troweled on without any other finish, rough or smooth. A beautiful color effect would be gained by giving the cement a soft indeterminate tone of brown that would blend with the brown wood tones of the boards in the gable and the shingles on the roof.

The porch and balcony, the living-room hearth, and also the bathroom might be paved with dull red cement. The shower bath in the corner of the bathroom is separated from the rest of the room by a partition like the outer walls extending part way to the ceiling.

Published in The Craftsman, March, 1910.

SEVEN-ROOM CEMENT HOUSE: NO. 85.

CRAFTSMAN CEMENT HOUSE, SIMPLE, COMFORTABLE AND SPACIOUS

Published in The Craftsman, July, 1910.

CRAFTSMAN CEMENT HOUSE, CONVENIENTLY PLANNED, WITH NINE ROOMS AND RECESSED DINING PORCH: NO. 94.

SEVEN-ROOM CRAFTSMAN CEMENT HOUSE

The small entry at the corner of the house opens into the living room; the opening being at right angles to the entrance door in order to shut off the draught. The stair, which is separated from the entry by a partition, leads directly out of the living room, so that the first three steps and the landing form an attractive structural feature of the room. Between the staircase and the doorway leading into the small passageway to the kitchen, is a wide seat which is thus recessed from the main room. The spaces on either side of the chimneypiece are filled with built-in bookshelves.

Owing to the arrangement of this house, the living room and dining room are more definitely separated than is usual in a Craftsman interior. Both rooms are of the same size and are nearly square, and the arrangement

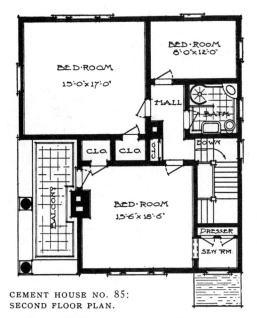

CEMENT HOUSE NO. 85:
SECOND FLOOR PLAN.

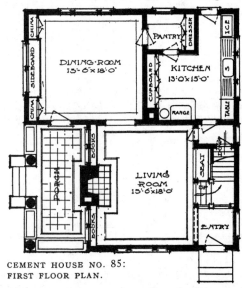

CEMENT HOUSE NO. 85:
FIRST FLOOR PLAN.

of chimneypiece and bookshelves in the living room is repeated by the built-in sideboard and china-cupboards that occupy the whole corresponding side of the dining room. The door from the dining room leads to the porch, where the table may be set in warm weather, and which provides a pleasant outdoor sitting room. There is no direct communication between the dining room and the kitchen, but swing doors from both rooms lead into the pantry, which occupies a corner of the space allotted to the kitchen. The kitchen itself is small, but very conveniently arranged, with cupboards, table, dressers, etc.

As the plan shows, the furnishing of the

first floor of this house would be a comparatively simple matter, as so many pieces are built in. The handling of the woodwork and the various details of the construction could also be made an effective and important factor in the decoration of the rooms, and by a thoughtful study of the general arrangement a comfortable and homelike effect could be obtained.

Upstairs there are three bedrooms of convenient size and amply lighted, leading out of the small hall. The front bedroom opens upon the sleeping balcony at the side. Next to this room and just above the entry is a small sewing room provided with a convenient dresser.

LOW CRAFTSMAN ROCKER AND DROP-LEAF SEWING TABLE
WHICH COULD BE USED IN THE LITTLE SEWING ROOM IN
HOUSE NO. 85.

CEMENT HOUSE WITH NINE ROOMS AND DINING PORCH

INTERIOR OF CEMENT HOUSE NO. 94, SHOWING DINING-ROOM SIDEBOARD AND CASEMENT WINDOWS ABOVE. THE SIMPLE TREATMENT OF THE HIGH WAINSCOTED WALL FORMS AN EXCELLENT BACKGROUND FOR THIS INTERESTING PIECE OF CRAFTSMAN FURNITURE.

THE walls of this house are of cement on metal lath and the roof is of red Ruberoid. The small roof over the entrance porch is of cement on metal lath like the walls, but the rafters that support it are of wood, and it rests upon heavy wooden beams. A variation in the color is given by the use of split field stone for the chimneys, one of which is revealed for its whole length, breaking the broad space at the end of the house. The severity of the wall in front is relieved by the spacing and grouping of the windows, and also by the recessed dining porch with its low parapet and row of blooming plants that are placed along the top.

The entrance door is entirely of glass and with the windows on either side lights the front of the living room. Another group appears at the back, and the whole side wall is occupied by casements set high over bookshelves on either side of the central fireplace.

The division between living room and dining room is marked by the closets at either end. Casement windows are set high above the sideboard in the dining room, and in the wall at right angles to it. A glass door opens into the garden, and double glass doors with windows lead to the dining porch in front, which, being so effectually sheltered from the

DETAIL OF HAMMERED COPPER CHAFING DISH SHOWN IN INTERIOR VIEW OF HOUSE NO. 94.

DETAIL OF CIDER SET OF MARBLE-HEAD POTTERY AND COPPER TRAY SHOWN IN INTERIOR VIEW ABOVE.

THESE PIECES ARE ESPECIALLY SUITABLE, IN WORKMANSHIP, MATERIAL AND DESIGN, FOR CRAFTSMAN HOME.

CEMENT HOUSE WITH NINE ROOMS AND DINING PORCH

weather, could be used as an outdoor living room during a great part of the year. In winter it could be readily glassed in if desired, and would thus form an appreciable addition to the livable space within the house.

Perhaps one of the most interesting features

ful craftsmanship and pleasing color and form.

The kitchen and servant's bedroom are placed in the one-story addition, so that they are entirely separated from the general plan of the house. The kitchen facilities are most conveniently contrived, and a storeroom and lavatory take up the space on either side of the hall that leads to the servant's bedroom. This arrangement is especially desirable, for the reason that it gives the maid her own quarters where she

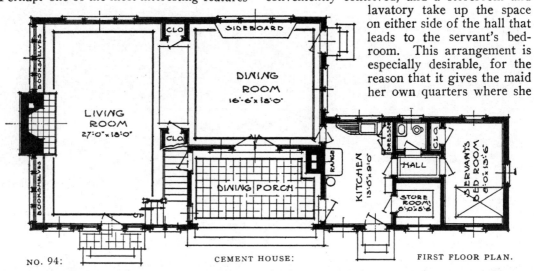

NO. 94:   CEMENT HOUSE: FIRST FLOOR PLAN.

of this construction is the simple but effective handling of the woodwork and wall spaces. As shown in the view of the dining room on the preceding page, the walls are wainscoted to the height of the frieze with V-jointed boards, finished in Craftsman style. This adds to the restfulness and unity of the interior, and forms a quiet and appropriate background for the furnishings, hangings and various details in the rooms. The treatment of the woodwork as shown here is especially in keeping with Craftsman furniture, and it will be noticed how the lines of the sideboard shown in the illustration carry out those of the general structural scheme. This piece of furniture, in fact, gives one a good idea of the satisfying effect that can be obtained by the thoughtful working out of a sturdy, practical and well-balanced design; and the larger details of the chafing dish and the set of pottery suggest, by their simple proportions, how much can be added to the beauty of a room by the choice of things which combine utility with care-

can come and go as she pleases without disturbing the rest of the house.

The second story has five bedrooms and a bath, grouped about a small central hall. The bathroom is floored with red cement marked off into squares, a plan that we usually follow in the Craftsman houses because it is attractive as well as sanitary and is very easy to keep clean.

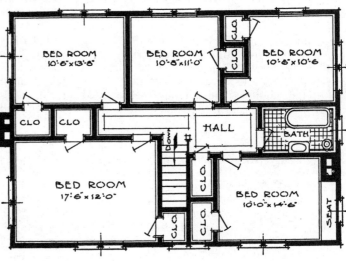

HOUSE NO. 94: SECOND FLOOR PLAN.

SMALL BUT ROOMY ONE-STORY CEMENT BUNGA-LOW PLANNED FOR SIMPLIFIED HOUSEKEEPING

Published in The Craftsman, May, 1910.

ONE-STORY CEMENT BUNGALOW: NO. 90.

THIS one-story bungalow is meant for a small family, as it has room for only two bedrooms, but the arrangement of the interior is so compact that the maximum of room is afforded within the space enclosed by the outer walls. These are of cement on metal lath, with a roof of rough red slate and ridges of tile. The low, broad, sturdy effect is heightened by the use of buttresses which support the wide-eaved roof and give strength and dignity to the lines of the wall. The house has ample window space. Two small recessed porches at one end serve respectively as entrance porch and outdoor dining room. A glass door leads from the entrance porch directly into the living room.

The whole front of this room is taken up with the central group of windows and the casements set high on either side. A window seat is built below the middle group and bookcases occupy the remainder of the wall space to the height of the casements, and open shelves are built in on either side of the fireplace. The dining room, as is nearly always the case in a Craftsman house, is really a recess

in the living room. A sideboard occupies the whole of the outside wall, with three casement windows set high above it. A glass door leads to the front porch, and the whole of the rear wall is taken up by casement windows and another glass

DETAIL OF CRAFTSMAN RECLINING CHAIR WITH ADJUSTABLE BACK AND SPRING CUSHION SEAT, SHOWN ON THE NEXT PAGE IN INTERIOR VIEW OF BUNGALOW.

SMALL BUNGALOW PLANNED FOR SIMPLE HOUSEKEEPING

CORNER OF LIVING ROOM IN ONE-STORY BUNGALOW NO. 90, SHOWING OPEN SHELVES ON EACH SIDE OF THE FIREPLACE, AND EFFECTIVE USE OF CRAFTSMAN FURNISHINGS.

door leading to the rear porch. The room is thus well lighted and cheerful.

A tiny hall opening from the other end of the living room gives access to the two bedrooms and also to the kitchen, which by this means is entirely shut off from the remainder of the house. The bath is so placed that it is accessible from both bedrooms and from the kitchen.

The arrangement of this cottage is such that the house-mistress is practically independent of servants, for the compactness of the floor plan, the directness of the communication between the several rooms, and the convenient placing of the tables, closets, dressers, etc., in the kitchen and pantry, all help to minimize the necessary household work.

Another important factor is the presence of the several built-in pieces — sideboard, seat and bookshelves. These not only reduce the amount of furniture needed for the living room and dining room, but add considerably to their comfort and charm.

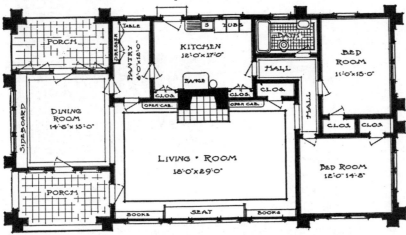

FLOOR PLAN OF ONE-STORY BUNGALOW: NO. 90.

CONCRETE COTTAGE WITH COMFORTABLE INTERIOR, DESIGNED TO ADMIT AMPLE LIGHT

Published in The Craftsman, February, 1907.   SEVEN-ROOM CONCRETE COTTAGE WITH THREE PORCHES: NO. 47.

IN designing this cottage we had in mind concrete or hollow cement block construction. Therefore the form of it is especially adapted to the use of such material, although the general plan admits of the use of brick or stone.

As we have shown it here, the side walls are broken into panels by raised bands of concrete which bind the corners and also run around the entire structure at the connection of the roof and between the first and second stories. These bands are smooth-surfaced, but the walls are made very rough by the simple process of washing off the surface with a brush and plenty of water immediately after the form is removed and while the material is set but still friable. If this is done at exactly the right time, the washing-brush can be so applied as to remove the mortar to a considerable depth between the aggregates, leaving them in relief and producing a rough texture that is very interesting.

The plan of this house is not unlike a Greek cross, the rooms being so arranged that the greatest possible space is available and also an unusual amount of light and air. The foundation is of concrete and is continued upward on a gentle slant from

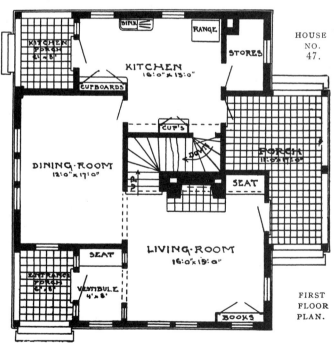

HOUSE NO. 47.

FIRST FLOOR PLAN.

INTERIOR VIEW OF CONCRETE COTTAGE NO. 47, SHOWING A CORNER OF THE LIVING ROOM, AND GLIMPSES OF THE VESTIBULE, DINING ROOM AND STAIRCASE. THE BUILT-IN SEATS AND DECORATIVE HANDLING OF THE WOODWORK ARE ESPECIALLY INTERESTING.

the ground to a line at the base of the windows on the first floor, which gives a continuous horizontal line on a level with the parapets of the corner porches.

The rear porch is recessed and extends the whole width of the wing, being large enough to serve as a very comfortable outdoor dining room. For this style of house we would recommend that all the porches be floored with red cement divided into squares.

The interior of the cottage is somewhat unique in plan, and the arrangement of the rooms is unusually convenient. The built-in seat in the vestibule and beside the living room hearth, the built-in bookshelves above the latter seat, and those in the opposite corner of the room, add to the comfort as well as the homelike appearance of the whole, and the way in which the woodwork is handled is distinctly decorative and will prove a helpful factor in the task of furnishing. The paneled wainscot, the spindles above the openings between the living room and the dining room and vestibule, and the pleasant handling of wall spaces can be seen in the sketch of the interior on this page. The various details, of course, would be worked out to suit the taste and convenience of the owner, and the illustration and floor plan may serve to suggest many delightful possibilities of decoration.

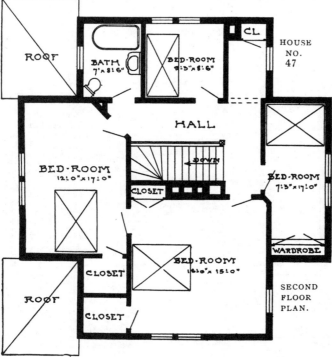

HOUSE NO. 47

SECOND FLOOR PLAN.

INEXPENSIVE CEMENT CONSTRUCTION FOR SUMMER AND WEEK-END ONE-STORY BUNGALOW

ALTHOUGH so simple in construction that the owner can assist in building it, this little bungalow will prove a well-planned, serviceable and attractive dwelling. The walls sunshine to each one of the five rooms within.

In spite of the extreme simplicity of its construction and lay-out of the interior—or perhaps we should rather say because of this

Published in The Craftsman, December, 1909.

INEXPENSIVE CEMENT BUNGALOW: NO. 80.

and partitions are of cement mortar upon metal lath. The girders of the house are supported upon concrete piers, less expensive than a stone foundation. The base of the chimney runs to the depth of the piers. The porch floor may be of cinder concrete, the same as used for sidewalks, slightly slanted so that it will drain easily, and the porch roof supports are of logs. The rafters are sheathed with V-jointed boards, dressed, and finished on the under side. These boards make the only ceiling to the cottage, and above them are laid strips of Ruberoid roofing. Within, all the structural beams are left exposed and are smoothed and stained.

The big chimney in the living room contains also the flue of the kitchen range. Besides these two rooms there are two bedrooms, a bathroom and many convenient closets, the arrangement, as the floor plan shows, being both compact and convenient.

The groups of windows with their small square panes not only add a touch of interest to the plain cement walls of the building, but give ample air and simplicity—the bungalow, when comfortably and tastefully furnished, should make a very charming little summer home, and would certainly permit a minimizing of all housework

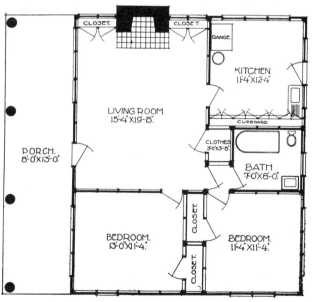

FLOOR PLAN OF CEMENT BUNGALOW: NO. 80.

TWO-STORY CEMENT BUNGALOW WITH AMPLE PORCH ROOM AND COMFORTABLE INTERIOR

Published in The Craftsman, December, 1909.

TWO-STORY CEMENT BUNGALOW WITH FIVE ROOMS AND PORCH: NO. 81.

WHILE this cottage is more elaborate in design than the one-story bungalow shown on the preceding page, the same general construction is used, cement mortar upon metal lath being chosen for the walls, stone for the chimney, logs for the pillars of the porch and cinder concrete for the porch floor. In this cottage, however, the roof is shingled. The exterior, though quite unpretentious, is pleasing in line and proportion, with its well-placed windows, sloping dormer and sheltered angle of the long, roomy porch.

VIEW OF STONE FIREPLACE IN LIVING ROOM OF TWO-STORY BUNGALOW, NO. 81. THE WOODWORK SHOWN IN THIS INTERIOR IS SIMPLY THE STRUCTURAL BEAMS OF THE BUILDING.

The illustration of the living room will also furnish an idea of the appearance of the living room of the previous bungalow, inasmuch as the main structural beams are the same. Indeed, all the woodwork in the living room, with the exception of the baseboard, which is cut in between the studs, is simply the necessary structural beams. The stairs lead up from the right, and a curtain may be hung to shield those about the hearth from any draught that may come from the upper rooms.

A door from one corner of the living room

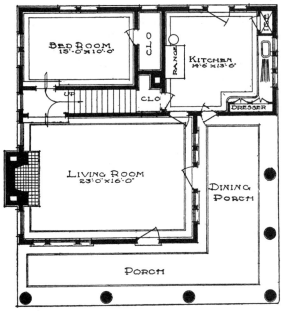

CEMENT BUNGALOW NO. 81: FIRST FLOOR PLAN.

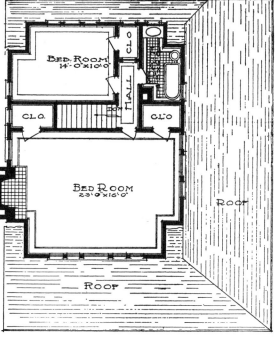

BUNGALOW NO. 81: SECOND FLOOR PLAN.

leads into the kitchen, which is large, well lighted and conveniently arranged. On the first floor there is also a bedroom provided with a large closet. The smaller closet beside it opens into the kitchen.

On the upper floor are two bedrooms and a bath, leading out of a small hall. The front bedroom is a large, cheerful apartment, with plenty of windows, and provided with an open fireplace which uses the same chimney as the one in the living room just below. Two good-sized closets are placed at opposite corners. Both this bedroom and the one in the rear could be made charming and comfortable by the use of window or corner seats and simple furnishings.

The arrangements of the rooms on each floor are so simple and compact that it would be an easy matter to keep them in order, and the accommodation would be quite sufficient for a small family.

Both this bungalow and the one previously described are intended exclusively for summer use. Either of them, however, could be built with an inside wall which would fit them also for winter, but this, of course, would add greatly to the expense. One of the chief advantages of both constructions shown is that when closed for the winter there is no place in which mice would build their nests or mildew collect. Every part of the cottage is open to the air. Returning in the spring, the owner needs only to brush down the cobwebs and wipe away the dust to find himself settled and at home for the summer.

CANDLESTICK, ANDIRONS AND BOWL FOR A CRAFTSMAN INTERIOR.

THESE FITTINGS ARE SO SIMPLE AND ARTISTIC THAT THEY WILL HARMONIZE WITH ANY FURNISHINGS.

TWO-STORY HOUSE FOR VILLAGE CORNER PLOT

A VILLAGE corner plot of average size (60 x 150) is the site for which the house was designed, keeping in mind the usual restrictions which limit the building line to within forty feet of the front street, fifteen feet of the side street, and five feet of the side line. The walls are covered with cement stucco and the roof is of slate. The chimney is carried up full size, and being in the center of the house, forms an apex for the four corners of the roof. The two balconies and the various groups of windows, the broad veranda

tween them opening onto the dining porch at the back of the house. From the dining room, swing doors lead through the large pantry, with its ice-box and ample shelves, into the kitchen, which communicates in turn with the laundry at the rear.

A small square den is provided off one side of the living room, and next to this the staircase goes up to the landing and thence to the second floor. This staircase, as the interior view indicates, forms an interesting part of the living room, and the Craftsman newel-post

Published in The Craftsman, April, 1911.   CEMENT HOUSE WITH NINE ROOMS AND DINING PORCH: NO. 113.

with its cement floor, and the end flower-boxes which serve at the same time as screens, are all pleasant exterior features.

In the lay-out of the rooms we have considered the particular requirements of a family living in the suburbs. The entrance is through a vestibule in which is the coat closet. The living room is a large cheerful apartment, lighted by groups of windows on two sides, and provided with an open fireplace. A wide opening leads into the dining room beyond, through which a pleasant vista is given by the windows at the end and glass door be-

lamp is a useful as well as a decorative feature. This house may be heated with a Craftsman fireplace-furnace, the living room, dining room and two rear bedrooms being heated by warm air, and the other rooms having hot-water heat, both supplied from the fireplace-furnace.

We have located the laundry on the first floor, as it will serve as a summer kitchen during the hot days, and also is a suitable place for preparing vegetables, canning fruit, etc. The rear porch may be screened for use as an open-air dining room in the summer, and the screens can be replaced with sash to provide

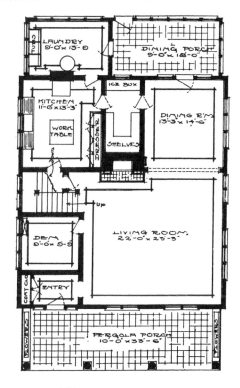

HOUSE NO. 113: FIRST FLOOR PLAN.

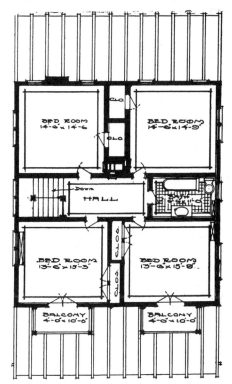

HOUSE NO. 113: SECOND FLOOR PLAN.

a cheerful sun room during winter months.

The upper rooms are very simply arranged, with a square bedroom at each corner of the floor plan, opening out of the central hall. Each bedroom is lighted with windows on two sides, and is provided with a closet. The two front rooms are especially pleasant, as each has double glass doors giving access to a small balcony placed over the roof of the pergola porch.

GLIMPSE OF LIVING ROOM IN CEMENT HOUSE, NO. 113, SHOWING TILED CHIMNEYPIECE AND DECORATIVE TREATMENT OF DOORS, WOODWORK AND WALL SPACES.

MODERATE-SIZED CRAFTSMAN HOUSE COMBINING BOTH PRIVACY AND HOSPITALITY

Published in The Craftsman, April, 1911.

NINE-ROOM CEMENT HOUSE WITH PORCHES AND SLEEPING BALCONIES: NO. 114.

THIS house is planned for a middle lot on a village street. Cement stucco is used for the walls of the building, and the roof is of slate. The recessed porches in the front and the large sleeping balcony in the rear are interesting exterior features. The floor plans are worked out with the idea of economy in space, and yet nothing has been sacrificed in comfort or convenience.

The living room and dining room are separated by the entry; no vestibule has been provided, as the entrance door is well protected by the recessed porch. The coat closet and stairs are located in the entry, and the fireplace is screened by bookshelves built in between the supporting posts of the overhead beams.

The large living room has a direct opening on the rear veranda, and on either side of this is a long built-in bookcase with a group of three win-

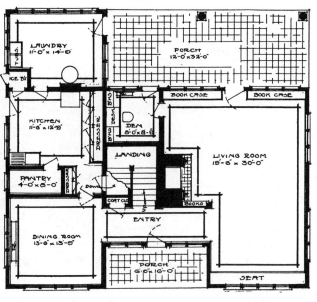

HOUSE NO. 114: FIRST FLOOR PLAN

ROOMY CEMENT HOUSE, WITH PORCHES AND BALCONIES

dows set in the wall above, overlooking the porch. There are two more window groups in the side wall, and another in the recess at the front, where a long window seat is built in. The irregular shape of the room, with its various nooks and corners, and the interest derived from the careful handling of the necessary structural features, combine to make an unusually charming interior. The sketch shown here of the fireplace corner gives one some impression of the general effect, and suggests many delightful possibilities in the way of furnishing. In fact, with a few simple pieces, chosen for comfort and beauty, with a carefully worked-out color scheme, and the addition of those little individual touches in furnishing and decoration which must always be left to the personal taste of the owner, the apartment could be made very homelike and hospitable.

The small den communicates directly with the living room and rear veranda, and here too the built-in bookcases and a desk add to the comfort. Ample closet and pantry room are provided in the kitchen, and a built-in icebox is planned with outside door for putting in ice. The open laundry may be screened in summer and glazed in winter, and serves also as a summer kitchen. If a Craftsman fire-

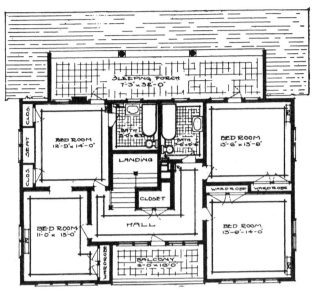

HOUSE NO. 114: SECOND FLOOR PLAN.

place-furnace is used, as shown here, the cellar may be omitted.

The recessed balcony under the roof is a delightful addition to the upper rooms. Two of the bedrooms are arranged so that they may be used *en suite* with private bath.

CORNER OF LIVING ROOM IN CRAFTSMAN HOUSE NO. 114: THE USE OF TILES FOR THE FIREPLACE-FURNACE, THE PLACING OF THE BOOKSHELVES AND THE LONG WINDOW SEAT, AND THE GLIMPSE OF THE WELL-LIGHTED ENTRY, SUGGEST AN UNUSUALLY INTERESTING INTERIOR.

CRAFTSMAN HOUSE DESIGNED FOR CITY OR SUBURBAN LOT

Published in The Craftsman, June, 1911. COMPACTLY PLANNED, EIGHT-ROOM CEMENT HOUSE: NO. 117.

CEMENT stucco on metal lath is used for this house, which is intended for a city or suburban lot. The wide pergola and balcony, the stone and brick chimneys and groups of casements present a homelike and pleasing appearance. Purposely we have set the house down so as to show only a suggestion of the foundation. Instead of having a cellar, we prefer to level up the space between the walls of the foundation with earth, topping this with cinders and cinder concrete to a level of the foundation walls, and using 2 x 4's embedded in this for the first floor beams.

The interior has been arranged to eliminate all unnecessary partitions, and the stairs lead up directly from the living room. A den or workroom has been provided off the living room. Seats are built in beside each fireplace, and the one in the dining room has been so placed as to serve in connection with the table. Placing the table in this position allows ample space around the fireplace and does not give an appearance of being crowded, so often the case when fireplaces are built in the dining room. The house may be heated and ventilated by using Craftsman fireplace-furnaces.

The view of the fireplace end of the living room, with its corner seat, built-in bookshelves, and casement windows above, gives some idea of the general effect of the interior. The treatment of woodwork and wall spaces is simple but effective, and serves as a restful background for the various furnishings. The tiled hearth, the decorative placing of the bricks in the chimneypiece, and the recess above the shelf, add to the attraction of the inglenook, which, with its comfortable seats and inviting books, naturally becomes the center of interest of the room. The walls could be left plain or could be stenciled as suggested in the illustration with some design that would help to carry out the general color scheme of the interior. The woodwork of the staircase in the opposite corner of the living room could also be handled in such a way as to give structural beauty to this necessary feature.

COMPACTLY PLANNED, EIGHT-ROOM CEMENT HOUSE

CORNER OF LIVING ROOM IN CRAFTSMAN CEMENT HOUSE NO. 117, SHOWING THE FIREPLACE-FURNACE AND BUILT-IN SEAT AND BOOKSHELVES IN THE INGLENOOK.

The second floor is quite simple in arrangement, a bedroom occupying each of the four corners of the plan, with the bathroom between the smaller bedrooms on one side. Three of the bedrooms open into the hall, which is wide and cheerful and terminates a few steps down on the stair landing at the rear. From this landing several steps lead up to the other back chamber. All four of the bedrooms have windows on two sides, and ample closet room is provided.

Perhaps one of the most attractive features of this upper floor plan is the little balcony in the front over the pergola porch. Part of this balcony is open, protected by a railing, and part is recessed, as shown.

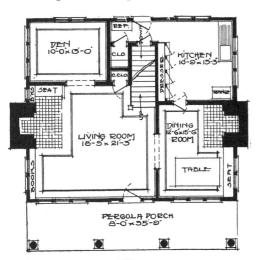

CEMENT HOUSE NO. 117: FIRST FLOOR PLAN.

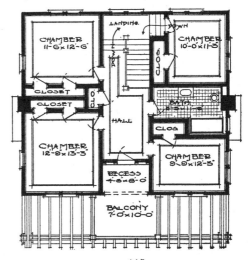

HOUSE NO. 117: SECOND FLOOR PLAN.

CEMENT COTTAGE FOR A NARROW TOWN LOT

Published in The Craftsman, June, 1911.

CRAFTSMAN CEMENT COTTAGE NO. 118.

THIS cement cottage is planned for a narrow lot and is only a story and a half high. It has a long roof line broken with flat dormers front and rear. The groups of windows are most interesting, all being casement except the large plate glass picture window of the front group, which is stationary. No front veranda has been provided; but the entry is recessed and the graceful arch emphasizes the cement construction. Hollyhocks would be especially charming against the plain walls.

On entering, you find the hall space has been included in the living room, with an open stair conveniently located near the entrance. A partition dividing dining and living room is only suggested—an arrangement which permits of a vista from living room through dining room and across the rear porch. Open bookshelves break up the long wall of the living room and a space has been left for the piano, which will give it an appearance of being built in.

The Craftsman fireplace-furnace is large and generous, and with the inviting seat nearby becomes at once the center of interest. The

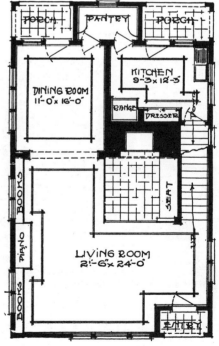

HOUSE NO. 118: FIRST FLOOR PLAN.

CEMENT COTTAGE FOR A NARROW TOWN LOT

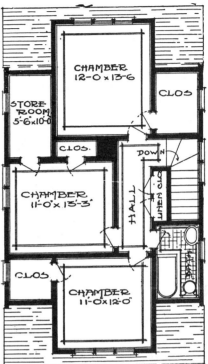

fireplace is built of common brick and is plastered, while color may be introduced by the use of tile porcelain for the inside panel on which the hammered copper hood is placed.

The view which is given below of one corner of the living room, with its fireplace, fireside seat and glimpse of the stairway behind, suggests an interesting method of handling the woodwork, and gives a general impression of the treatment of the various structural features of the interior. As is usual in a Craftsman house, these possess decorative quality without being in the least elaborate, and while they add to the beauty of the rooms they also help to minimize the task of furnishing.

CRAFTSMAN LANTERN WHICH COULD BE USED IN THE INTERIOR SHOWN BELOW.

The kitchen, which is a convenient size, communicates with the dining room through the pantry, which is built out between the two corner porches at the rear. A door from the kitchen also opens upon the adjacent porch.

The second floor is conveniently arranged with three bedrooms, ample closets and a large storeroom, the closets being built under the roof and not being full height except at the front. The storeroom and the large closets

CRAFTSMAN CEMENT COTTAGE: SECOND FLOOR PLAN.

against the outer walls are lighted by small windows. The staircase is also well lighted.

ONE CORNER OF THE LIVING ROOM IN CEMENT COTTAGE NO. 118, SHOWING ARRANGEMENT OF THE CRAFTSMAN FIREPLACE-FURNACE, WITH BUILT-IN SEAT AND STAIRWAY BEHIND IT.

INEXPENSIVE AND HOMELIKE COTTAGE OF STONE AND SHINGLE, FOR SIMPLE HOUSEKEEPING

IN the cottage shown here, split stone is used for the walls and for the parapet and pillars of the front porch. The steps and floor of this porch are of cement. The gables are shingled with split cypress shingles, and the roof is also shingled, with the rafters left exposed at the widely overhanging eaves.

The interior of this cottage is very compactly and conveniently arranged, the idea being to make it easy for the mistress of the house to do her own work if she so desires. At one end there are two bedrooms and a good-sized bathroom, shut off from the rest of the house by a small hall that affords access to five rooms—the dining room and kitchen as well as the bedrooms and the bath. It also separates the kitchen from the dining room, so that all odors of cooking are shut off from the front part of the house. The dining room is placed directly in front with the two high windows above the sideboard looking out upon the front porch. The room itself is small, but there is no feeling of being cramped for space because the wide opening into the sitting room makes it to all intents and purposes a recess in the larger room. The sitting room, with the large fireside nook at the back, occupies the whole end of the house. Like the sitting room, this nook is wainscoted with chestnut to the height of the broad beam that marks the angle of the ceiling, so that the whole wall is of wood. The large chimneypiece of split field stone extends to the ceiling, and the recesses on either side are filled with bookshelves. Seats are built in on each side of the nook, the panels at the ends serving the double purpose of suggesting a separation from the main room and furnishing the seat ends. The ceilings are tinted to a tone that harmonizes with the soft greenish brown of the chestnut.

Published in The Craftsman, July, 1910.
INEXPENSIVE COTTAGE OF STONE AND SHINGLE, PLANNED FOR SIMPLE HOUSEKEEPING: NO. 93.

INEXPENSIVE CRAFTSMAN COTTAGE OF STONE AND SHINGLE

INGLENOOK IN SITTING ROOM OF CRAFTSMAN COTTAGE, NO. 93, SHOWING STONE CHIMNEYPIECE WITH BUILT-IN BOOKSHELVES AND SEAT ON EITHER SIDE, AND GLIMPSE OF STAIRWAY WITH NEWEL-POST LAMP AT THE RIGHT.

In the view of this inglenook a glimpse of the staircase to the right is also seen. This forms an interesting part of the structural woodwork of the interior, and if the newel post is fitted with a lamp as suggested in the illustration a very decorative effect is obtained.

In the front bedroom which opens out upon the porch, there is a built-in seat beneath the window, occupying the recess formed by the small corner closets on either hand. The cottage, on the whole, is one which would require very little movable furniture to make it ready for its occupants, and in addition to the economical advantage of the built-in pieces, they add to the unity of the interior by the way in which they carry out the general effect of the rest of the woodwork,—wainscot, beams, etc.

—giving the rooms an air of permanency and repose that is very homelike.

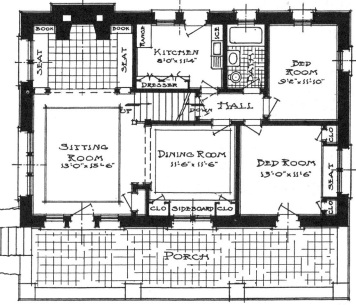

FLOOR PLAN OF STONE AND SHINGLE COTTAGE: NO. 93.

STONE AND SHINGLE HOUSE, WITH SEVEN ROOMS AND RECESSED ENTRANCE PORCH

Published in The Craftsman, December, 1911.

SEVEN-ROOM STONE AND SHINGLE HOUSE: NO. 126.

THE foundation, chimneys and lower walls of this house are of split stone; above this, hand-split cypress shingles are used for the walls and sawed red cedar shingles for the roof.

One of the most attractive features of the exterior is the recessed entrance porch, better

shown in the enlarged detail view on the next page. The simple lines of the stonework, the low curve of the arch, broken by the graceful touch of vines, the wide Dutch door with small square lights set in the upper half, the window and bracket lantern on each side, and the bench beneath the dining-room window,—

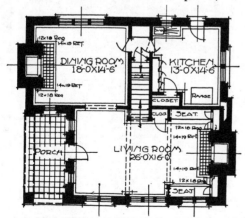

CRAFTSMAN HOUSE NO. 126: FIRST FLOOR PLAN.

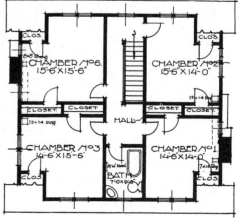

HOUSE NO. 126: SECOND FLOOR PLAN.

SEVEN-ROOM HOUSE WITH RECESSED PORCH

all combine to make the approach to the house especially inviting, indicating at the same time by the simple sincerity of treatment, the prevailing characteristic of the home within.

One enters from the porch directly into the living room, which is large, light and hospitable, and the interest centers at once in the pleasant inglenook at the farther end. Tapestry brick is used for the chimneypiece of the Craftsman fireplace-furnace, which, with the one in the dining room, serves to heat and ventilate the whole building. Front and rear dormers give ample height to the four bedrooms and bath on the second story.

CORNER OF INGLENOOK IN LIVING ROOM OF HOUSE NO. 126, SHOWING FIREPLACE-FURNACE, BOOKSHELVES AND SEAT.

ROOMY CRAFTSMAN HOUSE IN WHICH STONE, CEMENT AND WOOD ARE USED

Published in The Craftsman, August, 1909.

TWO-STORY CRAFTSMAN HOUSE: NO. 72.

STONE, cement and wood are used in the construction of this two-story house, the foundation and lower walls being of stone and the upper walls shingled. The roof is broken into a dormer, and is covered, like the porch, with a composition roofing. The rafters and purlins are left exposed. The base of the chimney is of split field stone like the parapet, but brick is used toward the upper part, as shown.

The windows of the second story are hooded and are both casement and the double-hung variety. The double-hung window has a single pane of glass in the lower sash, and six small panes in the upper sash. This contrast makes a very attractive effect seen from the outside, and also obviates looking out through small panes, which some people dislike. Throughout the lower story window groups are used, consisting of a double-hung window made in the fashion of those on the second story, with a single casement set on either side.

The detail view of the exterior on the opposite page shows the pergola at one end of the porch, and the bay window of the dining room. The roof of the pergola, as well as that of the porch, is supported upon a wood beam resting upon pillars of cement. These pillars stand upon the stone posts of the parapet, between which run cement flower-boxes. The steps and parapet are of split field stone.

The side entrance under the pergola leads into a big open hall between the dining room and living room; the front entrance opens into a vestibule leading into another open hallway between the living room and den. At the rear of this is a landing raised about two steps, and from this landing the stairs go up to the second story. A railing separates the landing from the big side hall and makes a very interesting background to the room as one enters from the pergola. The lower story is very open, with the exception of the kitchen which is sufficiently separated to prevent any odor of cooking penetrating the rest of the house. It is well fitted with shelves and closets, and connects with the dining room through a butler's pantry. At the end of another closet two steps lead up to the landing so that the maid has a direct passage from the kitchen to the door. The upstairs plan explains itself. A flight of stairs leads to the attic where two rooms may be finished for use if desired.

ROOMY TWO-STORY CRAFTSMAN HOUSE

HOUSE NO. 72: DETAIL OF PERGOLA PORCH SHOWING INTERESTING VARIETY OF BUILDING MATERIALS.

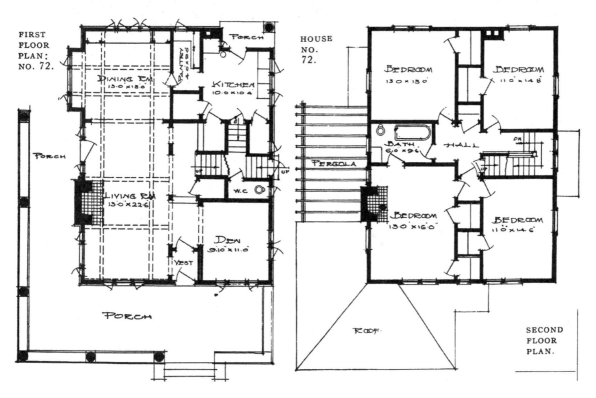

FIRST FLOOR PLAN: NO. 72.

PORCH

DINING RM 13·0"X18·0"

KITCHEN 10·0"X10·4"

PANTRY

PORCH

W.C.

LIVING RM 13·0"X22·6"

DEN 9·10"X11·0"

VEST

PORCH

HOUSE NO. 72.

BEDROOM 13·0"X13·0"

BEDROOM 11·0"X14·8"

BATH 6·0"X9·6"

HALL

DN

PERGOLA

BEDROOM 13·0"X16·0"

BEDROOM 11·0"X14·6"

ROOF

SECOND FLOOR PLAN.

CRAFTSMAN STONE HOUSE WITH PRACTICAL BUILT-IN FITTINGS

Published in The Craftsman, July, 1909.

REAR VIEW OF STONE HOUSE, NO. 71.

ALTHOUGH we have shown this house of stone, with heavy timber lintels and composition roofing, the design could be worked out in other materials. Glass doors open from dining room and living room upon a terrace with parapet and posts of stone, cement floor and flower-boxes. The railing of the sleeping balcony above is supported upon the exposed timbers of the house. This and the two casements on either side form practically a dormer construction.

The house is entered from the front through a hallway with doors leading to the living room, dining room and kitchen. On each side of the

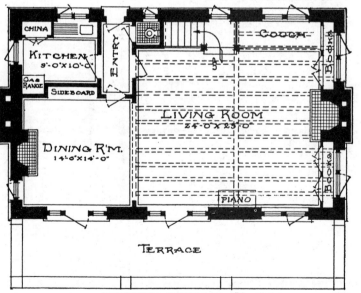

CRAFTSMAN HOUSE, NO. 71: FIRST FLOOR PLAN

STONE HOUSE WITH PRACTICAL BUILT-IN FITTINGS

living-room fireplace, with its hood of hammered copper, are built-in bookcases with convenient drawers below and windows above. The dining room is separated from the living room only by a shallow grille running along the ceiling, and the sideboard is built into the room. The kitchen is connected with the dining room by the entry.

On the second floor the small hall gives access to the bathroom, two large bedrooms and a smaller one between. The bedroom at the right has a big open fireplace which uses the same chimney as that in the living room below, and on either side of this are casement windows. In each corner of the room is a closet, and beneath the windows in the recess formed by the closets is a built-in seat. In the bedroom on the opposite side of the house there is a somewhat smaller fireplace and a similar arrangement of corner closets and recessed window seat in front. Each of the bedrooms has a door opening out onto the sleeping balcony.

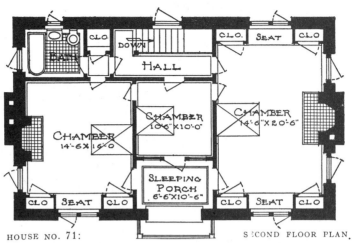

HOUSE NO. 71:   SECOND FLOOR PLAN.

As the drawings and description indicate, the interior is one which could be very easily furnished, for there are already so many built-in pieces that the rooms seem hospitably ready to be occupied even before the owner has moved in his personal possessions. The simple but effective treatment of the woodwork and the interest derived from the frank handling of the many structural features are full of suggestions for the arranging of the more intimate details in the furnishing of a home.

INTERIOR OF HOUSE NO. 71: CORNER OF LIVING ROOM WITH FIREPLACE AND BUILT-IN FITTINGS.

ROUGH STONE HOUSE COMBINING COMFORT AND PICTURESQUENESS

Published in The Craftsman, June, 1909.

STONE HOUSE WITH SEVEN ROOMS, BREAKFAST PORCH AND RECESSED SLEEPING BALCONY: NO. 69.

STONE HOUSE COMBINING COMFORT AND PICTURESQUENESS

ROUGH stone is the material used for this house. The timbers are left exposed, making a rugged finish consistent with the stone exterior. The dormers, gracefully proportioned and in harmonious relation to the slope of the roof, are fitted with simple casements opening upon garden boxes. In the windows of the lower story, the middle section is a stationary panel of glass, and the two outside sections are outward-opening casements. On the sides of the house are smaller windows, similar in shape, which have a double casement in place of the glass panel.

The interior view on page 74 shows a rear corner of the living room. The chimneypiece suggests

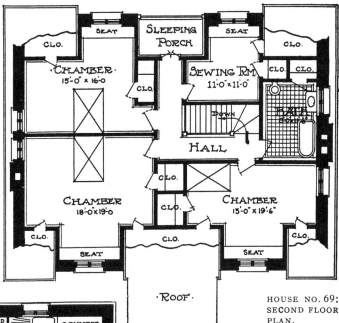

HOUSE NO. 69: SECOND FLOOR PLAN.

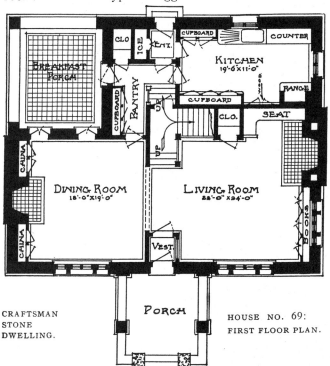

CRAFTSMAN STONE DWELLING.

HOUSE NO. 69: FIRST FLOOR PLAN.

piece are built-in bookcases with casement windows above. There is a convenient closet between the fireside seat and the staircase, and the latter is accessible from both living room and pantry. A wide opening leads into the dining room which is also provided with an open fireplace with built-in china closets on each side. Doors lead from the dining room to the corner breakfast porch at the rear, which can also be reached from the kitchen through the swinging doors of the pantry.

On the second floor there are three good-sized bedrooms, and a small sewing room, each of which is fitted with a comfortable built-in window seat in the recess formed by the dormer. Under the slope of the roof, in front and at the four corners of the house, closets are provided, and there are also closets between the interior walls. One end of the L-shaped hall leads onto a small recessed sleeping porch at the rear. This, being protected by walls on three sides, is sufficiently sheltered to be of use in practically all sorts of weather, and the front could be further screened with an awning if necessary.

the exterior of the house because it is of the same material, bringing the whole into closer relation. The seat in the wainscoted inglenook is as useful as it is attractive. By lifting up the top, one finds the logs for the hearth fire, placed there through a little door from the kitchen. On the other side of the chimney-

STONE HOUSE COMBINING COMFORT AND PICTURESQUENESS

See Pages 72 and 73.

CORNER OF LIVING ROOM IN STONE HOUSE NO. 69, SHOWING ARRANGEMENT OF FIREPLACE, BUILT-IN CORNER SEAT AND BOOK-CASES WITH CASEMENT WINDOWS ABOVE.

EIGHT-ROOM BUNGALOW OF STONE AND CEMENT

Published in The Craftsman, April, 1909.

EIGHT-ROOM CRAFTSMAN BUNGALOW: NO. 65.

IN this bungalow, which is suitable for either country or suburbs, we have used split field stone for the walls of the lower story and for the square pillars of the porch. The gables are plastered, with half-timber construction, and the roof is shingled.

This kind of building lends itself admirably to the use of heavy timbers such as appear all around the walls at the top of the first story, and in keeping with this effect are the exposed rafters and girders which support the widely overhanging roof. Especially decorative is the construction over the recess in the middle of the porch, the beams being raised as shown in the illustration, admitting more light to the living room.

Just above is the sleeping porch, also recessed for a part of its depth, and protected by a heavy wooden balustrade. This porch affords ample room for two beds, and it would be easy to throw a partition across the center, dividing it into two outdoor sleeping rooms,—an arrangement made the more practicable by the two glass doors which lead to this

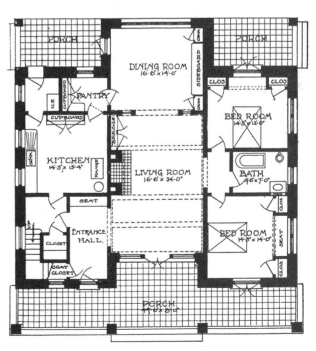

BUNGALOW NO. 65: FIRST FLOOR PLAN

EIGHT-ROOM BUNGALOW OF STONE AND CEMENT

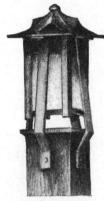

CRAFTSMAN NEWEL-POST LAMP WHICH COULD BE USED IN ANY INTERIOR.

porch from the upper hall.

The floor plan shows a typical Craftsman interior, the details of which could be adapted to the owner's needs. The door from the porch opens into an entrance hall with closets and staircase on one side and an inviting seat built into the wall directly opposite the front door. A wide opening on the right leads into the large living room with its open fireplace, built-in bookcase, and glass door opening onto the front porch. The dining room is in the rear running out between two corner porches, onto one of which it opens. There is a group of four windows at the back of the room, and built-in sideboard and china closets along one side. Between the dining room and living room post and panel construction is used, the wide opening accentuating the space of the lower story. Swinging doors through the pantry lead from the dining room into the kitchen, which is fitted with every convenience for housekeeping, and from which access can also be had to the adjacent corner porch. A door leads also from the kitchen to the lower stairway hall and entrance hall in front.

On the other side of the floor plan are two bedrooms and a bath, somewhat separated from the rest of the house by a small private hall. In both bedrooms there are two corner closets and in the front room there is also a built-in window seat. Each room has long double glass doors opening out onto the front and rear porches respectively.

On the second floor is another bedroom, also fitted with corner closets and built-in window seat. On the other side of the hall is the maid's room, and at the back a billiard room with long seats at each end and a group of

CRAFTSMAN CHAIR OF SIMPLE DESIGN.

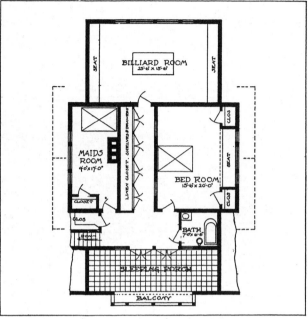

BUNGALOW NO. 65: SECOND FLOOR PLAN.

windows in the rear wall. In the hall is a long and very convenient linen closet with shelves and drawers. A small bathroom is also provided on this floor, and doors lead from the hall onto the sleeping balcony, as previously described.

The pieces from the Craftsman workshops shown on this page, being simple in design, sturdily made, and harmonizing with the woodwork of a Craftsman interior, suggest the style of furniture best adapted for these rooms.

WRITING DESK WHICH WOULD FORM A USEFUL AND INTERESTING PART OF THE FURNISHINGS OF A CRAFTSMAN HOME.

CRAFTSMAN COTTAGE OF STONE, SHINGLE AND SLATE: A PRACTICAL AND COMFORTABLE HOME

Published in The Craftsman, March, 1911.

COTTAGE OF STONE, SHINGLE AND SLATE, WITH SEVEN ROOMS, DINING PORCH AND SLEEPING BALCONIES: NO. 111.

THE attractiveness of the design, the harmonious colors of the different building materials used, and the well-arranged floor plans combine to make this house especially interesting. The exterior is of stone, rived shingles and slate. The open construction of the roof, together with the rough texture of the stone, will be found sufficiently rustic to be in keeping with the surrounding hills and woods.

Care should be taken in selecting the building stone. Field stone, when split and laid up in irregular shapes and sizes, forms the most pleasing effect.

The entry and fireplace nook are wainscoted with V-jointed boards, but all other walls and ceilings are plastered. The broad surfaces are broken up in panels by extending the door and window casings from baseboard to frieze, and by the large beams on the ceiling.

The fireplace is laid up of split stone, the same as used for exterior walls, but in the selection of this more care has to be exercised. The hammered copper hood harmonizes with the variegated surfaces of the stone. The Craftsman fireplace-furnace is shown installed here, furnishing heat and ventilation for the entire house.

The living room is large and well lighted

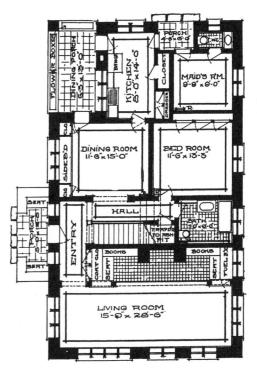

COTTAGE NO. 111: FIRST FLOOR PLAN.

CRAFTSMAN COTTAGE OF STONE, SHINGLE AND SLATE

with several groups of casement windows. The illustration below shows one corner of this room, with the stone fireplace, built-in bookshelves on either side, and wainscoted seats of the inglenook. The simple decorative treatment of the woodwork with its post and panel construction, the charm of the small-paned casement windows, and the glimpse of the entry on the right and the bottom of the staircase with its newel-post lamp, suggest something of the general appearance of the interior, and give one an idea of the homelike quality that results from this frank handling of the various structural features.

Built-in sideboard and china closets occupy the entire end of the dining room, and the open dining porch, slightly screened in with flowers, affords a delightful place for outdoor meals. The floor of this porch is of cement. The owner's bedroom and bath, as well as the room for the maid, are located on the first floor. The kitchen is large, well lighted and so arranged as to be easily accessible from the dining room, dining porch and maid's room, while not connecting directly with the latter. The little recessed kitchen porch serves also as a porch for the maid.

On the second floor only two bedrooms and a bath are provided. These rooms, although in the attic, are worked out with full-height ceilings, and by the aid of dormers cross-ventilation is provided which renders them as comfortable and livable as though the house were full two stories.

A charming feature of these bedrooms is the

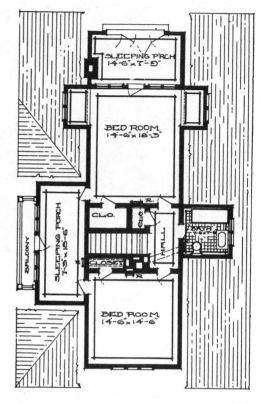

COTTAGE NO. 111: SECOND FLOOR PLAN

sleeping porches. While the end of each one is left open, provision has been made to shut out bad weather, and since they are built within the house they may be glassed in, making delightful sunrooms for winter days.

INTERIOR OF COTTAGE NO. 111, SHOWING LIVING-ROOM INGLENOOK WITH CRAFTSMAN FIREPLACE-FURNACE, BUILT-IN BOOKSHELVES AND SEATS. AT THE LEFT IS A GLIMPSE OF STAIRCASE FITTED WITH NEWEL-POST LAMP.

BRICK COTTAGE WITH CONVENIENT BUILT-IN FURNISHINGS AND AMPLE PORCH ROOM

Published in The Craftsman, March, 1911.

BRICK COTTAGE WITH SIX ROOMS, DINING PORCH AND PERGOLA: NO. 112.

BRICK on a stone foundation is used for this cottage. The common dark-colored, hard-burned brick (laid up in Dutch bond with half-inch joints) blends in texture and color with the rived shingles and rough slates of gables and roof. A section of the roof on either side is raised up, forming a flat dormer which accentuates the low bungalow effect. An interesting feature is found in the pergola porch, the ends being carried up about three feet and flower-boxes built into the walls.

The entry is provided with conveniently arranged coat closet, and is one step higher than the living room. The living room and the dining room are planned as one, the latter being merely an alcove raised a step above the living room proper. The fireplace nook is large and is shown provided with the Craftsman fireplace-furnace.

In the dining alcove is a built-in corner seat big enough to accommodate four or five at the table, and the dining porch is easily accessible from dining room and kitchen. The latter is large, well lighted and ventilated, and equipped with ample pantry and storage closets, built-in refrigerator and screened entry porch.

The bedrooms, three in number, are located in the attic, but by the use of dormers they are all arranged with full-height ceilings. They are good-sized and have plenty of closet room. The bath and hall linen closet complete the design and form a very compact floor plan.

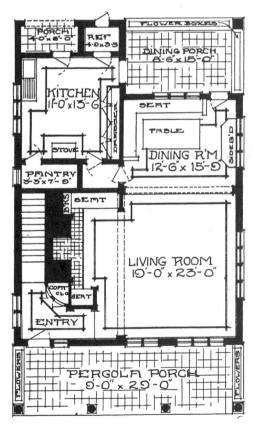

COTTAGE NO. 112: FIRST FLOOR PLAN.

BRICK COTTAGE WITH CONVENIENT BUILT-IN FURNISHINGS

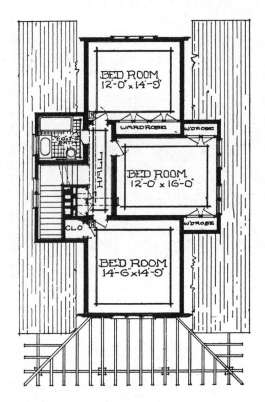

CRAFTSMAN BRICK COTTAGE, NO. 112:
SECOND FLOOR PLAN.

The house may be trimmed throughout the first floor in chestnut, stained a nut brown. The second floor we would trim in gumwood. This wood is beautifully marked with a fine grain, and when stained shows various shades of brown with slight traces of delicate buff and green. Maple floors might be used throughout, finished in a soft shade of gray-brown, a permanent color obtained by the use of vinegar and iron rust, covered with two coats of thin shellac and then waxed.

The view of the interior shown below gives one a good idea of the interesting and somewhat unique arrangement of the living room and dining room. The hospitable charm of the fireside nook with its tiled chimneypiece, built-in bookshelves and seats; the glimpse through the arched alcove of the dining room, with its table and corner seat, and the simple but effective way in which the woodwork, doors and wall spaces are treated,—all these features show what a friendly and homelike atmosphere results from the careful working out of the various structural details. The introduction, too, of Craftsman furnishings and fittings, such as the tables, lamp, hanging and bracket lanterns shown, helps to carry out the effect. Portières which harmonize in color and design with the general decorative scheme of the rooms might be hung across the opening between the living room and entry, to shut off any possible draft from the front door.

LIVING ROOM OF CRAFTSMAN BRICK COTTAGE, NO. 112: GLIMPSE OF FIRESIDE NOOK AND DINING ALCOVE BEYOND.

TWO-STORY HOUSE OF STONE, BRICK AND CEMENT, WITH TYPICAL CRAFTSMAN INTERIOR

Published in The Craftsman, May, 1907.   TWO-STORY CRAFTSMAN HOUSE: NO. 51.

ALTHOUGH the form of this house is straight and square, its rather low, broad proportions and the contrasting materials used in its construction take away all sense of severity. The walls of the lower story and the chimneys are of hard-burned red brick, and the upper walls are of cement plaster with half-timber construction. The foundation steps and porch parapets are of split stone laid up in dark cement, and the roof is tiled. Cement is used for the pillars and also for the floor of the porch.

This is only a suggestion for materials, as the house would be equally well adapted to different forms of construction. The coloring also may be made rich and warm or cool and subdued, as demanded by the surroundings.

One feature that is especially in accordance with Craftsman ideas is the way in which the half-timbers are used. While we do not generally advocate half-timber construction, we believe that when it is used it should be made entirely "probable;" that is, that the timbers should be so placed that they might easily belong to the real construction of the house. Another feature of typical Craftsman con-

struction is illustrated in the windows. It will be noted that they are double-hung in places where they are exposed to the weather, and that casements are used when it is possible to hood them or to place them where they will be sheltered by the roof of the porch.

The arrangement of the interior of this house is very simple, as the living room and dining room, which have merely the suggestion of a dividing partition, occupy the whole of one side. The arrangement of kitchen, hall and staircase on the other side of the house is equally practical, as it utilizes every inch of space and provides many conveniences to lighten the work of the housekeeper.

The entrance door opens into a small vestibule that serves to shut off draughts from the hall, especially as the entrance from the vestibule to the hall is at right angles to the front door instead of being directly opposite, making the danger from drafts so small that this opening might easily be curtained and a second door dispensed with. The broad landing of the staircase is opposite the opening from the vestibule, and in the angle where the stair runs up a large hall seat is built.

TWO-STORY HOUSE WITH TYPICAL CRAFTSMAN INTERIOR

DETAIL OF ENTRANCE PORCH: HOUSE NO. 51.

The vestibule jutting into the living room leaves a deep recess at the front, in which is built a long window seat just below the group of casements that appears at the front of the house. The fireplace is in the center of the room just opposite the hall, and another fireplace in the dining room adds to the comfort and cheer.

In a recess in the dining room, somewhat similar to that at the front of the living room, the sideboard is built in so that the front of it is flush with the wall and three casement windows are set just above it. The china cupboards built in on the opposite side are shown in two ways in the plan and illustration. In the former the cupboard is built across the corner, and in the latter it is straight with the wall. Either way would be effective and the choice depends simply upon personal preference and convenience.

CORNER OF LIVING ROOM IN HOUSE NO. 51, AND GLIMPSE OF HALL AND STAIRCASE.

CORNER OF DINING ROOM IN HOUSE NO. 51: THE BUILT-IN FEATURES AND TREATMENT OF WOODWORK MAKE THE INTERIOR OF THIS HOME ESPECIALLY INTERESTING.

TWO-STORY HOUSE WITH TYPICAL CRAFTSMAN INTERIOR

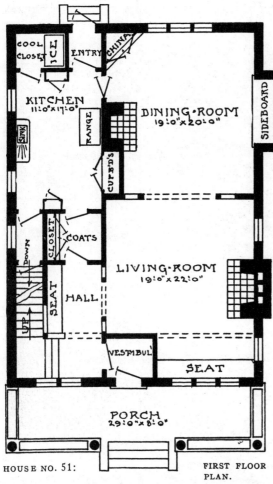

HOUSE NO. 51: FIRST FLOOR PLAN.

the kitchen. The tiles of the chimneypiece and hearth and the panels of the woodwork seem to carry out still further this unity of effect. In fact, the interior of this house is one which lends itself especially to unusual and interesting treatment of structural features, and a study of the floor plans will reveal many delightful possibilities of furnishing and decoration.

A swinging door leads from the dining room to the kitchen, which is large and provided with ample closet room, including a cool place for the ice-box. A small entry leads to the back door. Between the kitchen and the front hall there is a long closet and plenty of room for coats, umbrellas, etc.

The plan of the second story shows three bedrooms and a bath opening out of the upper hall, which has a small linen closet in one corner. A closet is also provided in each bedroom, and one of the rooms has an open fireplace which utilizes the same chimney that serves for the living room. The two front bedrooms communicate and could be used together if desired, the smaller one serving as dressing room. Or the bedroom with the fireplace could be used as an upstairs sitting room if preferred.

The two views of the living room and dining room shown on page 83 show how effectively the woodwork of the house is used, and how full of friendliness and charm are the various built-in features of the rooms. The paneled wainscot, the simple wall spaces and beams, the post and panel construction between the living room and hall, with the small open space at the top and ledge for plants or pottery, the spindles of the staircase and the small square panes of the casement windows —all harmonize admirably with the Craftsman furniture and fittings shown. The hanging lanterns suspended from the ceiling beam across the recess in the living room are particularly pleasing. In the illustration of the dining room the small panes in the upper portion of the windows are repeated by the doors of the built-in sideboard in the corner, and by the lights in the top of the door leading to

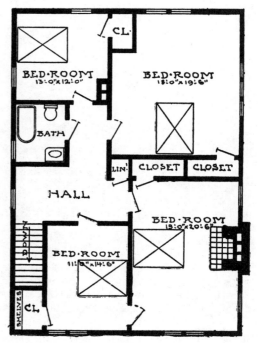

HOUSE NO. 51: SECOND FLOOR PLAN.

CRAFTSMAN HOUSE OF TAPESTRY BRICK WITH PORCHES, BALCONY AND SPACIOUS INTERIOR

VERY interesting is the use of Tapestry brick in this house. The center of the building, with its balcony of wood, is considerably recessed, leaving the two ends in the form of wings. The floor of this recess may

dining room is filled in the same way with the built-in sideboard and china closets, so that there is hardly a foot of wall space in these rooms that is not treated in a useful and decorative way. At the back of both rooms French

Published in The Craftsman, January, 1911.

TEN-ROOM BRICK HOUSE: NO. 106.

be of dull red cement, and the roof of red slate with tiles at the ridges and angles. At the back of the house are two pergola-covered porches, opening from the living room and the dining room.

The interior view shows an unusually attractive reception hall. Across its entire width runs a huge fireplace nook with a built-in seat at either end. The central fireplace with its copper hood, the tiled walls and floor, the cabinets and recesses above, and the small cupboards with glass doors above the end seats, are all typically Craftsman in effect.

Another fireplace occupies the middle of the outer wall of the living room, and on either side the wall spaces below the casement windows are shelved for books. The end of the

doors open upon the porches, and as windows are placed on either side in the dining room it will be seen that there is ample provision for light and air.

The one-story addition between the two porches at the back of the house gives room for the kitchen, pantry and maid's room, so that the servant's domain is complete in itself and practically cut off from the rest of the house. The service porch is built on the back of the kitchen which is equipped with every convenience for doing housework swiftly and easily.

On the second story the staircase leads into a large central hall lighted from the front by the group of windows which look out upon the balcony and by the glass doors which lead

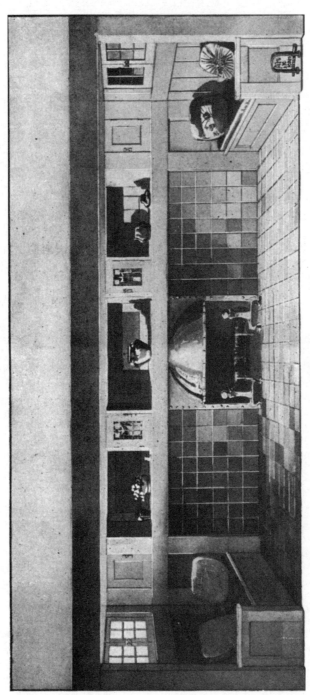

TILED INGLENOOK IN RECEPTION HALL OF CRAFTSMAN BRICK HOUSE, NO. 106: SHOWING BUILT-IN SEATS AT EITHER END, AND DECORATIVE USE OF WALL SPACES FOR CABINETS AND SHELVES.

TEN-ROOM CRAFTSMAN HOUSE OF TAPESTRY BRICK

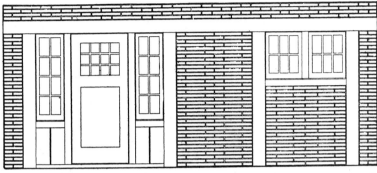

DETAIL ELEVATION OF FRONT WALL AND ENTRANCE DOOR OF BRICK HOUSE, NO. 106.

to it. At the back of this hall is a fireplace nook which, though smaller than the one below, is still large enough to accommodate two comfortable built-in seats. The remainder of the space is occupied by the two bathrooms, one of which serves for the guest chambers at one end of the house, and the other as a private bath for the owner's suite of chamber and dressing room. Such a suite was required in this particular house, but the arrangement might easily be modified to allow two bedrooms instead, as the only al-

HOUSE NO. 106. **FIRST FLOOR PLAN.**

teration needed would be the omission of the connecting door and the adding of closets between, as in the case of the guest chambers.

An impression of the general effect of the interior of this house can be gained from the illustration on page 86. This shows the tiled inglenook in the reception hall, with its built-in seats and decorative use of wall spaces for cabinets and shelves. Also, a definite idea of the construction of the outer walls of the house and the placing of the doors and window groups, is given by the detail elevation above, which shows the recessed entrance door and the windows on either side. The use of small panes is especially effective, and adds considerably to the interest of the exterior.

A study of the floor plans indicate what a simple task the furnishing of this house would be. The built-in fittings, both upstairs and down, are so numerous that comparatively little movable furniture is required. This not only makes for economy, but simplifies the labor of housekeeping, and adds greatly to the charm of the interior. There is an air of quiet intimacy, of durability and repose about built-in furnishings which brings a restful atmosphere into the home. In this particular case, moreover, the arrangement seems especially typical of the Craftsman ideal. The rooms have a certain spacious hospitality which characterizes most of the Craftsman designs, and at the same time there is plenty of opportunity for privacy when desired. The three large fireplaces, of course, focus much of the interest and increase the comfort of the house, while the porches and balcony permit outdoor life.

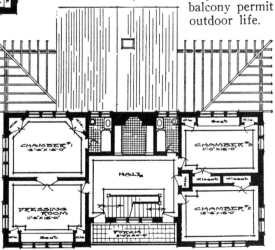

HOUSE NO. 106: SECOND FLOOR PLAN.

BRICK HOUSE WITH MANY HOMELIKE FEATURES

Published in The Craftsman, June, 1909.
REAR VIEW OF BRICK HOUSE WITH SEVEN ROOMS, PERGOLA PORCH AND SLEEPING BALCONIES: NO. 68.

VIEW IN LIVING ROOM OF BRICK HOUSE, NO. 68, SHOWING ARRANGEMENT OF ENTRY AND STAIRCASE.

BRICK HOUSE WITH MANY HOMELIKE FEATURES

THIS house is of brick, with slate roof, exposed rafters and purlins, and pergola-covered porch. The walls of each wing are carried up to form the parapet of a little balcony, fitted with flower-boxes. All the windows in the lower story of the house and those above the roof over the door are casements, opening out.

One enters the house through a vestibule, on one side of which is a toilet, on the other a coat closet, and from the vestibule three steps go up to the living room. The difference in floor levels allows the stairs to the second story to run up over the vestibule, thus economizing space. This arrangement, at once useful and decorative, is clearly shown by the floor plan and the interior view. The latter suggests an interesting use of structural features which, frankly and simply treated, have a distinct decorative value, and become an important factor in the general effectiveness of the rooms. The plain lines of the woodwork, the unpretentious charm of the entrance door, with the small windows on either side, the bench beside the staircase, the lamp of the newel post,—all these features convey an idea of the general treatment of the rest of the interior.

The living room is large and is lighted by groups of windows and a glass door which gives access to the long porch at the rear of the house. Beyond the living room, in the wing, is the den, which is provided, like the living room, with an open fireplace. A long seat is built in beside the hearth and below the rear windows, as the floor plan shows.

On the opposite side of the living room is the dining room with its open fireplace and built-in group of sideboard and china closets. Swing doors lead through the pantry to the kitchen, which is compact and convenient in arrangement.

There are three bedrooms on the second floor, two of them having open fireplaces, and one, built-in seats.

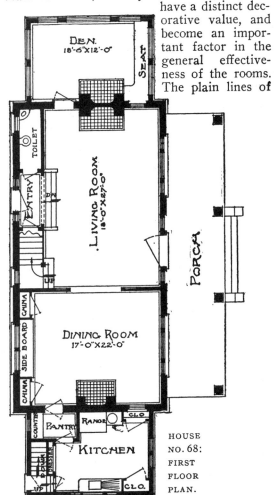

HOUSE NO. 68: FIRST FLOOR PLAN.

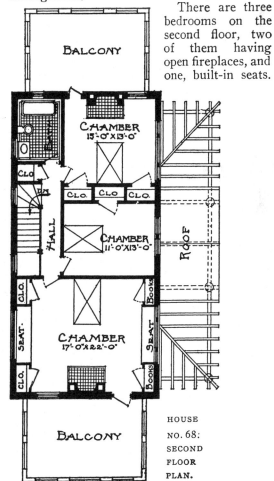

HOUSE NO. 68: SECOND FLOOR PLAN.

CITY HOUSE WITH INTERESTING FAÇADE AND SLEEPING BALCONY, AND HOMELIKE INTERIOR

WE are showing here a house of Craftsman construction with open, simple interior and yet adapted to a restricted space and suited to life in the city. The house is planned to be built on a long, narrow lot, 25 feet wide. As the floor plans show, the building is semi-detached, having on one side a party wall, while on the other the windows are arranged to overlook a side court or alley. The arrangement of the rooms, therefore, is considerably modified by the limited space allowed and the necessarily long, narrow shape of the building, and the exterior is modified to an even greater degree, because, as the house is not intended to be built on a corner lot, the façade is all that can be seen from the street.

As it was manifestly impossible to introduce any of the features that make up the beauty and comfort of a country house, we have sought a new expression of our basic architectural principles.

Richly-colored, rough-surfaced Tapestry bricks are used, laid in darkened mortar with wide joints. The main roof, the dormer roof, the hood over the entrance door and the upper part of the pilasters are all dull green matt-glazed tile. The porch is screened by flower-boxes.

Published in The Craftsman, October, 1910.

THREE-STORY CRAFTSMAN HOUSE FOR THE CITY, WITH SLEEPING BALCONY AND HOMELIKE INTERIOR: NO. 99.

THREE-STORY CRAFTSMAN HOUSE FOR THE CITY

ONE END OF A BEDROOM IN HOUSE NO. 99, SHOWING TREATMENT OF WOODWORK, DOORS AND WINDOWS.

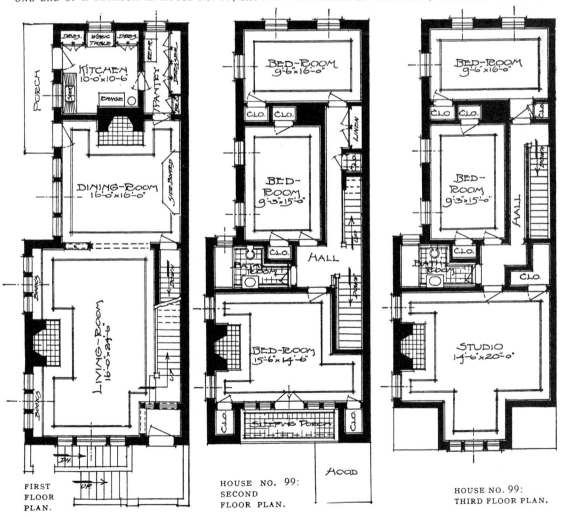

FIRST FLOOR PLAN.

HOUSE NO. 99: SECOND FLOOR PLAN.

HOUSE NO. 99: THIRD FLOOR PLAN.

CRAFTSMAN CITY HOUSE WITH SECOND-STORY PORCH AND THIRD-STORY SLEEPING BALCONY

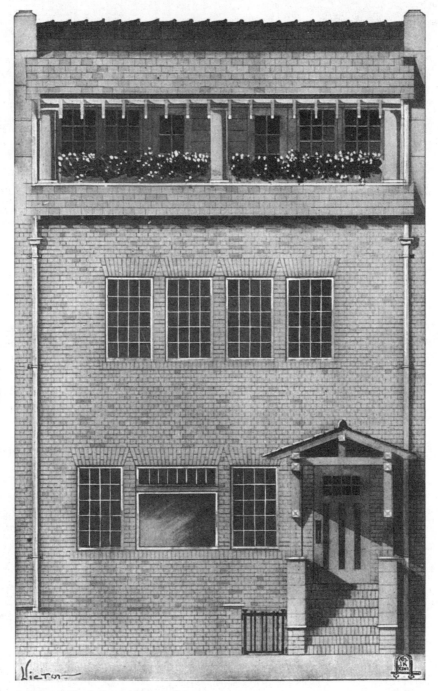

Published in The Craftsman, October, 1910.

CRAFTSMAN BRICK HOUSE FOR THE CITY, WITH ELEVEN ROOMS AND TWO SLEEPING PORCHES: NO. 100.

ELEVEN-ROOM CITY HOUSE, WITH TWO SLEEPING PORCHES

LIKE the house shown on pages 91 and 92, this building is also planned for a 25-foot city lot. But the restrictions in this case are even greater, for instead of facing an alley on one side the central portion of this house obtains light and ventilation from an interior court or air-shaft on which the windows of library, dining room, bathroom and several bedrooms open. Notwithstanding this fact, the careful planning of the interior insures light and air for all the rooms.

Plain red hard-burned brick is used for the façade, the uniform dark red being varied by the darker purplish tones of the arch brick which are introduced wherever they will be effective. The roof and the hood over the entrance door are of dull red tile.

The object being to get a good design and construction as inexpensively as possible, the sleeping porch is placed on the third story just under the tiled roof. The rafters of the roof are emphasized, projecting sufficiently to give a suggestion of a pergola and affording a support for vines that might be grown in the flower-boxes.

The half-tone illustration of the staircase in the living room shows the way in which the stairs are screened by a high-backed seat and an arrangement of slats above. The fireplace in the large back bedroom is also shown, with

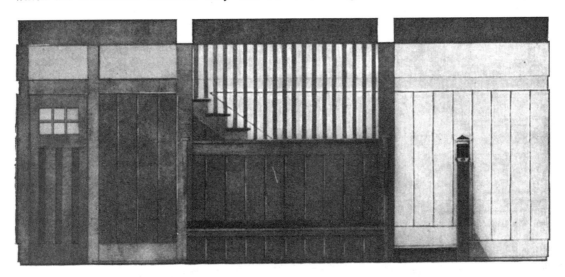

TWO VIEWS OF INTERIOR OF CITY HOUSE, NO. 100. THE FIRST SHOWS STAIRWAY GOING UP FROM LIVING ROOM, WITH BUILT-IN SEAT AND SPINDLES ABOVE; THE SECOND SHOWS FIREPLACE END OF ONE OF THE BEDROOMS, WITH GLASS DOORS ON EACH SIDE LEADING TO SLEEPING PORCH.

ELEVEN-ROOM CITY HOUSE, WITH TWO SLEEPING PORCHES

the glass doors on either side opening upon the rear porch.

The floor plans show the front entrance door opening directly into the living room, which has a large open fireplace on one side. By placing corner seats or long settles beside the hearth a very comfortable inglenook could be formed. Beyond this room is the library, with a window group in one wall overlooking the interior court, and on the opposite side are built-in bookshelves with windows set high in the wall above. Beyond the library is the dining room with its open fireplace, on the right

of which is a swing door leading to the conveniently arranged kitchen in the rear.

The second floor contains three bedrooms and bath, with ample closet room. On each side of the fireplace in the back bedroom are doors leading to the porch. On the third floor are four bedrooms and a bath. Here also there are plenty of closets. The two front rooms open upon the recessed sleeping porch, with its pleasant screen of flower-boxes. This porch has a partition across the center as shown, and is so sheltered from the weather that it could be used practically all the year round.

While city restrictions have not permitted a typical Craftsman dwelling, still the house reveals many possibilities for the making of a comfortable and homelike interior.

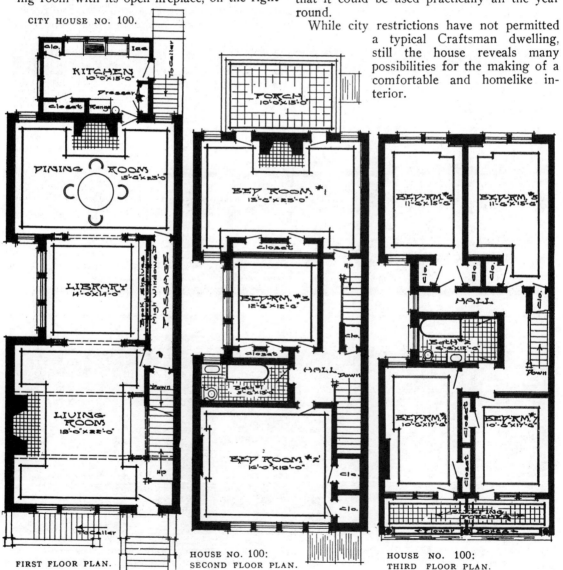

CITY HOUSE NO. 100.

FIRST FLOOR PLAN.

HOUSE NO. 100: SECOND FLOOR PLAN.

HOUSE NO. 100: THIRD FLOOR PLAN.

INEXPENSIVE COTTAGE FOR A SMALL FAMILY

Published in The Craftsman, December, 1910.   COTTAGE OF BRICK, CLAPBOARD AND SHINGLE: NO. 103.

WHILE the cost has been carefully kept down to the minimum for a properly built Craftsman house, this little dwelling is solidly made as well as comfortable and attractive. It is planned for a family of not more than two or three people. It would be entirely suitable for the first home of a newly married couple just starting in life, or for a man and wife whose children are all married and gone and who wish to pass the remainder of their lives in a snug little home that gives the least possible trouble to the housekeeper. Or, it would be convenient for two self-supporting women who might revolt at the ordinary flat or boarding-house existence and pool their resources to build a home of their own.

The walls of this house are built of brick according to a method of construction which is both economical and practically fireproof. The gables are sheathed with wide cypress boards, V-jointed and darkened so that they show the natural reddish brown color and strong markings of the wood. The square pillars of the front porch are made of brick like the wall, and the main roof is shingled and

stained to a warm brown tone that harmonizes with the brick and with the boarding of the gables. The roof of the dormer, being neces-

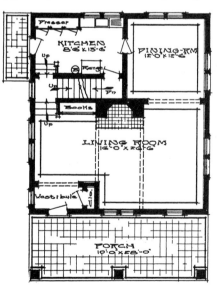

COTTAGE NO. 103: FIRST FLOOR PLAN.

sarily much flatter than the main roof in order to allow head room in the chambers on the

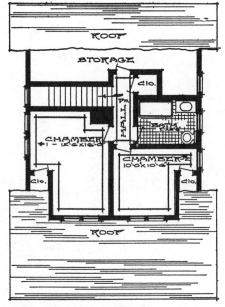

NO. 103: SECOND FLOOR PLAN.

upper floor, is not sufficiently steep in pitch to be shingled; therefore, it is covered with Ruberoid, the upper edge of which runs to the ridge-pole beneath the top courses of shingles which extend the entire length of the roof, forming a finish at the top for the dormer roof. This Ruberoid is painted the same color as the roof shingles, and may be battened or not according to taste. The rafters supporting it are left exposed.

The front door opens into a small vestibule which is little more than a recess in the living room. The end of this vestibule serves to hold a coat closet and the partition wall gives to the living room a "jog" that breaks up what would be otherwise a plain square in shape. The fireplace is directly in the center and the dining room is as much a part of the main room as is usual in a Craftsman house.

The kitchen, though very small, is equipped with conveniences which should make the housework easy to handle. Upstairs there are two bedrooms, a bathroom and a large storage room under the slope of the roof at the back of the house.

CORNER OF DINING ROOM IN CRAFTSMAN BRICK COTTAGE, NO. 103.

MODERATE-SIZED BRICK HOUSE, WITH RECESSED PORCH AND PLEASANT, HOMELIKE ROOMS

Published in The Craftsman, December, 1910.

SEVEN-ROOM BRICK HOUSE: NO. 104.

THE walls of this house are of brick, constructed in such a manner that they are both economical and practically fireproof. The gables show a sheathing of V-jointed boards. The round pillars of the porch are painted white, serving with the window sash to relieve the subdued color scheme of the house.

One interesting structural feature is seen in the posts which frame the entrance door and form the corners of the small vestibule. These are solid square timbers and the bricks between are laid up just as they are in the walls, giving a construction that is really what it appears to be instead of the ordinary half-timber construction which shows merely strips of wood nailed on the outside. The roof is of rough-finished slate, preferably dark red in color, and the ridge-pole is of tile. The porch, which extends down one side, is floored with cement.

The whole end of the living room is occupied by the big fireplace nook shown in the illustration. This forms the chief structural

feature of the house and also gives the keynote of color. The hearth, which extends over the entire nook, is paved with red tiles, and built-in

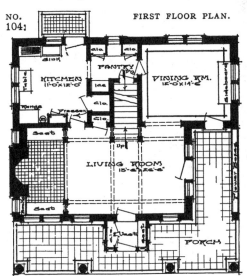

COMPACT SEVEN-ROOM HOUSE, WITH RECESSED PORCH

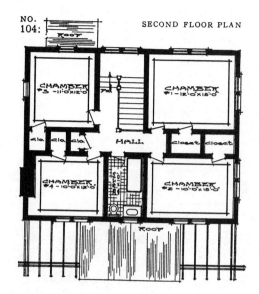

seats on either side offer a delightful suggestion of home comfort, particularly as the wall spaces flanking the chimneypiece are shelved for books, and the whole nook is lighted by small casement windows set high in the wall. The chimneypiece up to the mantelshelf is hard-burned red brick with cement above, finished in a tone that harmonizes with both the brick and the walls. The walls in this room are wainscoted up to the ceiling with chestnut boards, and the ceiling is crossed by massive beams.

The stairs lead up from the living room, with closet and kitchen door on one side, and on the other a wide opening into the dining room. The latter is lighted by two double casement windows and a glass door leading onto the sheltered porch. A similar door, with windows on either side, leads from the porch into the living room. This recessed corner of the porch, which is further screened by a side parapet and flower-boxes, would make a delightful outdoor dining room.

Both kitchen and pantry are compactly arranged, with ample closet room, and the kitchen range uses the same chimney as the living-room fireplace.

The upper floor affords space for four chambers, with plenty of closet room and a bath. These rooms are of moderate size and very simple in shape, being arranged to afford the greatest amount of space possible in a house of these dimensions.

VIEW OF RECESSED INGLENOOK IN HOUSE NO. 104, WITH BRICK AND CEMENT CHIMNEYPIECE, TILED HEARTH. BUILT-IN BOOKSHELVES AND SEATS AND CASEMENT WINDOWS.

RURAL ONE-STORY BUNGALOW OF FIELD STONE

ONE-STORY CRAFTSMAN BUNGALOW: NO. 55.

Published in The Craftsman, November, 1908.

THIS little cottage is planned and constructed on simple and practical lines. The walls and chimney are built of field stone. There is a regular bungalow roof, low-pitched, square in line and widely overhanging. This extends in front of the house without a break over the porch and is supported by the log pillars that belong so definitely to this type of building.

The entrance door leads directly from the porch into the living room, which is a comfortable size and is provided with an open fireplace so placed that it serves to warm the adjacent rooms. There are windows on each side of the entrance door as well as along the other outer wall of the living room, and the two bedrooms and kitchen are also well lighted and ventilated. Each of these latter rooms is provided with a closet, and a linen closet is also included in the bathroom. As in the other bungalows, the arrangement here is as simple as it is convenient.

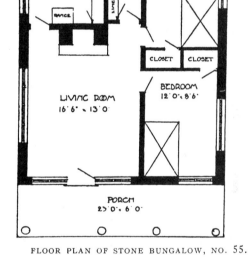

FLOOR PLAN OF STONE BUNGALOW, NO. 55.

The detail view given here of the entrance to the bungalow shows what effective charm lies in this simple construction. The stone walls, the plain wood door, with its long iron hinges, the small-paned casement windows on either hand, the square-tiled floor of the porch and the flower-boxes at the side, all seem perfectly in keeping with the character and purpose of this little rural home.

The cost of construction would be comparatively low.

DETAIL OF ENTRANCE TO BUNGALOW, NO. 55.

ONE-STORY CRAFTSMAN BUNGALOW PLANNED ON SIMPLE AND ECONOMIC LINES

Published in The Craftsman, September, 1909.

FIVE-ROOM BUNGALOW: NO. 75.

THE bungalow shown here seems particularly suitable for a rural site. Split field stone is used for the foundation and for the walls of the porch. The sides of the building above this are shingled, and the gables are covered with V-jointed boards. The round pillars supporting the porch are shown of cement, but posts of hewn wood might be used instead. The harmonious variety of these materials, the ample porch, the interesting windows and broad slope of the roof give the exterior an air of hospitality and repose that is very homelike.

The plans show the rooms to be conveniently arranged so that, although on the same floor, the bedrooms are completely separated from the kitchen and living room. The latter serves also as the dining room and is a large apartment occupying almost one-third of the whole bungalow. It opens upon the porch by a glass door, on either side of which is a window group consisting of two single casements with a stationary glass panel between. Above these windows are transoms set with small panes— a very attractive arrangement and an additional method of ventilation. A large portion of the end wall is devoted to windows, and indeed so much light and sunshine come to the room that it is almost a sun parlor.

The interior of this bungalow, which was

built in nineteen hundred and nine, was decorated in Craftsman style. The tones in hammered copper seemed best to sum up the light and shade that were needed in the rooms, and our color scheme accordingly resolved itself into an analysis of these hues.

The walls were left in brown plaster with no finishing surface applied. Against this tone were the girders, the built-in sideboard and all the stationary woodwork of chestnut, the sunny, variegated browns of which furnished a transition from the light tone of the walls to the deep red-brown of the fumed oak furniture, upholstered in leather of the same shade. The wood furniture was varied by occasional pieces of brownish green willow which blended the brown of the furniture and walls with the green rug on the floor. The design in the rug was worked out in dull amber and red-brown, and these shades were repeated in the lanterns of hammered copper set with amber glass and suspended by chains from the girders. The china-closet doors had panes of this same glass, and, like the sideboard, the trim was of hammered copper. The chimneypiece was of split field stone, with a thick board shelf, and the hearth was set with square, rough-textured tiles blending with the color of the rug and of the stone.

The large bedroom in the front of the bun-

TYPICAL ONE-STORY CRAFTSMAN BUNGALOW

LIVING ROOM IN BUNGALOW NO. 75: A HOMELIKE CRAFTSMAN INTERIOR.

galow has two corner closets with a seat built into the recess formed between them. Over the seat is a group of windows which overlook the porch,—a stationary panel in the center and an outward opening casement on each side. The other two bedrooms are each provided with a closet, and there is also one in the small hall beside the bathroom. The kitchen is compactly planned, with range and dresser on one side and tubs, sink and drainboard on the other. On one side of the rear entry is the ice-box, and on the other the door to the cellar stairs.

The view of the interior will serve to give

some impression of the homelike and artistic quality of the rooms of this little bungalow.

BUNGALOW FLOOR PLAN: NO. 75.

CRAFTSMAN CANDLESTICK SHOWN IN INTERIOR OF BUNGALOW NO. 75.

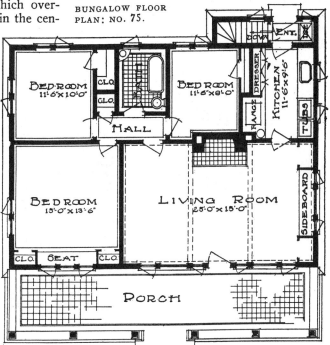

TWO-STORY COUNTRY BUNGALOW MADE COMFORTABLE WITH MUCH BUILT-IN FURNITURE

Published in The Craftsman, October, 1909.

SEVEN-ROOM BUNGALOW: NO. 76.

IN planning this two-story bungalow a variation of ten feet was found in the elevation of the site, and this has been met by a series of rough terraces in keeping with the rugged character of the vicinity. Although designed for a hillside situation, the broad low lines of the structure adapt it equally well to a level suburban site. The foundation is of stone, the siding is of rived shingles left to weather, and the roof of rough slate with a tile ridge.

As the object has been to bring as much outdoor feeling as possible into the house, especial attention has been given to the windows, of which there are a great many.

The living room occupies the center of the house. The rear end is used as the dining room, with double French doors leading out under a pergola. On either side are casement windows, so that the end of the room is largely glass. Beneath the casements two useful pieces of furniture are constructed: combination sideboards and china closets. The front wall of the room is also chiefly windows, and the proportions of the big stationary panel with its ventilating transom of small panes

contrast pleasantly with the sizes of the casements. This end of the room projects between twin porches and is connected with them by French doors.

The chimneypiece in this room is one of its chief beauties. It is of split field stone with a rough tiled hearth and board shelf. The opening for the fire is five feet high, so that the logs may be stood upon end, and the effect of

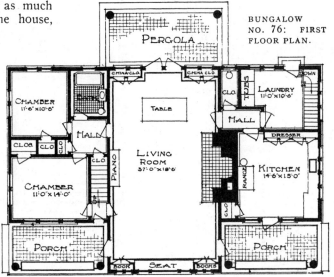

BUNGALOW NO. 76: FIRST FLOOR PLAN.

TWO-STORY COUNTRY BUNGALOW

ONE END OF LIVING ROOM IN BUNGALOW NO. 76. ON EACH SIDE OF THE GLASS DOORS THAT LEAD OUT ONTO THE PERGOLA ARE BUILT-IN CHINA CLOSETS AND DRAWERS, WITH CASEMENT WINDOWS ABOVE.

the firelight upon the depth of the chimney-piece is very beautiful and unusual. We have rarely designed a room that could be so effectively furnished with so little trouble.

On one side of the fireplace is a door leading to a small hallway which communicates with closet, laundry and kitchen. The latter opens onto the corner porch. On the other side of the living room is a second hall, communicating with two bedrooms and the bathroom. Each bedroom has a closet and there are also two in the hall.

As the floor plans show, this arrangement of the rooms is very practical, the service portion of the house being grouped on one side of the central living room, quite apart from the rest, and the sleeping apartments being equally separate on the opposite side of the bungalow. Thus there is the greatest possible convenience and privacy, and at the same time the large middle room furnishes a hospitable gathering place for family and guests. So far as this room is concerned, the built-in fittings will help to minimize both the cost of furnishing and the amount of housework need to keep it in order,

besides adding to the general comfort of the interior by its air of permanence and repose.

The view of the living room gives a general idea of the interior, and it will be noticed that the use of small panes in the long glass doors, casement windows and cabinet doors gives a pleasant effect of trelliswork in the room.

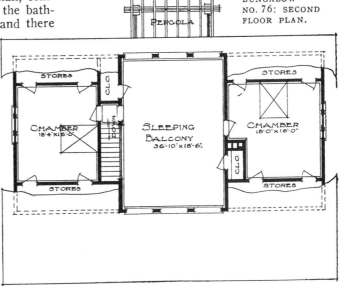

BUNGALOW NO. 76: SECOND FLOOR PLAN.

TWO-STORY COUNTRY BUNGALOW

THIS SKETCH SHOWS ARRANGEMENT OF FRONT WALL OF LIVING ROOM IN BUNGALOW NO. 76, WITH LONG BUILT-IN WINDOW SEAT BETWEEN THE BOOKCASES, AND GLASS DOOR AT THE LEFT OPENING ONTO ONE OF THE FRONT PORCHES.

The sleeping balcony is intended to be used in all sorts of weather, and a flight of stairs connects it directly with the chamber on the first floor and with the living room. On either side of the sleeping balcony, which is protected by dormer roofs, are two large rooms which may be fitted with hammocks and bunks or finished into the more usual style of sleeping room. There is ample closet room beneath the slope of the roof, both in front and rear.

CHIMNEYPIECE OF SPLIT FIELD STONE AND ROUGH TILED HEARTH IN LIVING ROOM OF BUNGALOW NO. 76.

SHINGLED HOUSE WITH SPACIOUS LIVING ROOM AND SHELTERED PORCHES

THIS house is of shingle construction and the whole of one end is taken up with the recessed porch and sleeping balcony above. The small entrance porch is sheltered by a shingled hood supported on brackets, and small across the wide opening of the living room, and the posts that define the opening into the dining room. The walls in both rooms are wainscoted to the height of the frieze with V-jointed boards, and the frames of doors

Published in The Craftsman, June, 1910

SEVEN-ROOM SHINGLED HOUSE: NO. 92.

hoods appear over each of the windows that are exposed to the weather, and also over the openings at the ends of the upper and lower porches.

This building is simple in form and the arrangement of the lower story is very open, giving the effect of more space than would seem possible, considering the size of the house. The living room occupies the whole depth of the building. A big chimneypiece is built in the middle of the outside wall, the chimney projecting on both porch and balcony. On either side of this chimneypiece is a glass door leading to the porch, with windows on each side. Grouped windows also appear at either end of the room, so that it is well lighted and cheerful. The entrance door opens into a small vestibule, which leads in turn into a hallway connecting the dining room and living room. The position of this hallway is hardly more than indicated by the staircase, the ceiling beam

and windows are so planned that they appear merely to emphasize the construction of the wainscot. The living

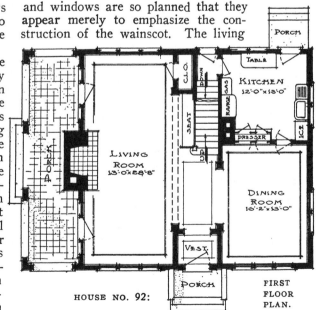

HOUSE NO. 92:

FIRST FLOOR PLAN.

SEVEN-ROOM SHINGLED HOUSE WITH SHELTERED PORCHES

room is also fitted with a closet and a long built-in seat beside the staircase.

The interior view below gives some impression of the generous dimensions of this room, and the sense of light and airiness that results from the numerous and pleasantly grouped windows. The stone fireplace in the center of the long wall adds a homelike and hospitable note.

From the dining room a swing door leads into the kitchen, which includes among its furnishings a dresser to which access may be had from both these rooms.

The second floor is divided into four bedrooms, bathroom and hall, each room, as well as the hall, being provided with a closet. The hall and stairs are lighted by a window in the rear wall of the house just above the landing.

The two bedrooms at the right have double windows in both outer walls, and the two rooms on the opposite side of the house, in addition to the windows in front and rear, have glass doors opening onto the long sleeping balcony which extends across the side of the house above the lower porch. This balcony is well sheltered from the weather, and if further protected with awnings could be used practically all the year. If desired, of course, a parti-

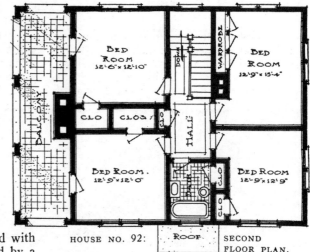

HOUSE NO. 92: SECOND FLOOR PLAN.

tion could be placed across the center to divide it into two private outdoor sleeping apartments.

This house, unlike most of the Craftsman designs, shows very few built-in fittings, the furnishing being left to the taste of the owner. The lower floor plan, however, could be very comfortably arranged, with fireside seats either in front of the hearth or on either side of it, and bookcases in the corners of the room. In the dining room there is plenty of space left for sideboard and china closets, and a window seat could also be included.

INTERESTING EXAMPLE OF DOOR AND WINDOW GROUPING IN LIVING ROOM OF HOUSE NO. 92.

COMFORTABLE SHINGLED HOUSE WITH BUILT-IN FITTINGS AND SLEEPING PORCHES

Published in The Craftsman, November, 1910.

CRAFTSMAN SHINGLED HOUSE NO. 101.

A SHINGLED house with Ruberoid roof is shown here—simple in design, compact in arrangement, and comparatively inexpensive as regards the cost of construction. The interior is economical to a degree, the floor space being utilized to the best advantage and the plumbing and heating facilities planned to cost as little as possible. One large central chimney serves for the whole house.

The wide porch, floored with cement, extends across the front of the building. The living room also extends the whole width of the house, and is entered by two glass doors. The wall space between these doors is occu-

BUILT-IN TABLE IN LIVING ROOM: HOUSE NO. 101.

LIVING-ROOM FIREPLACE IN HOUSE NO. 101.

pied by two small coat closets which project into the room, and in the recess between these closets a table is built, with a shelf below and windows in the wall above. Directly opposite is the big recessed fireplace of split stone.

Illustrations are given on page 107 of both the built-in table and the fireplace. The view of the former shows the compactness of arrangement, the effective treatment of wainscot and paneled doors, and the use of small square panes in the upper portion of the latter, repeating the larger panes of the windows. The view of the fireplace shows how much is added to the charm of the stonework by the arched recess with its long shelf. A comfortable seat could be placed directly opposite the fireplace, or if preferred, settles might be used on either side of the hearth, thus forming a sort of inglenook.

Turning again to the floor plans, at the left of the living room we find the entire wall filled by a wide couch beneath the windows and built-in bookcases on either side. Besides being a very comfortable and convenient arrangement, this adds much to the structural interest of the interior. The wainscot is of V-jointed boards to the height of the frieze, and the ceiling beams extending across the room from the fireplace to the closets in the opposite wall emphasize the frankness and simplicity of the construction, and at the same time give one a slight sense of separation be-

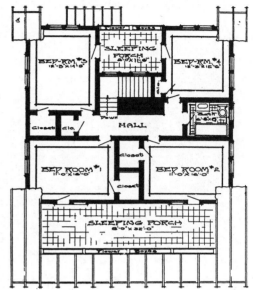

HOUSE NO. 101: SECOND FLOOR PLAN.

tween the fireplace portion and the ends of the room. Each end of the living room is lighted with a group of windows, and at the right of the fireplace the opening into the dining room is so wide that it allows only the post and panel construction on either side.

Almost the entire side of the dining room is occupied by a group of windows like that in the living room, and the whole end is filled with built-in china closets and sideboard. The staircase goes up from the dining room just back of the fireplace, a rather unusual arrangement made necessary by the plan of the house. A large pantry, well equipped, is placed between the dining room and kitchen, and the latter, though rather small, affords all facilities for housework.

Each one of the four bedrooms communicates with a sleeping porch. The front porch is open to the sky except for the slight shelter afforded by the eaves of the dormer. Yet it is so shielded by being sunk, as it were, in the main roof, that it is wholly sheltered from observation below. Flower-boxes along the front add to this sense of privacy, and the rise of the roof serves all the purposes of a wall at either end. The recessed and sheltered porch at the back could be easily glassed in for a sun room during winter, and if properly heated such a room would make a delightful sewing room or upstairs sitting room—almost a necessity in a house like this, where the lower story is so open.

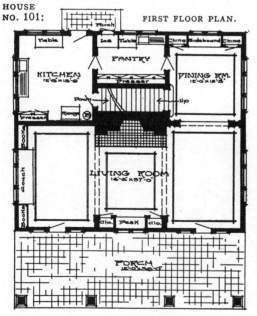

HOUSE NO. 101: FIRST FLOOR PLAN.

SHINGLED HOUSE WITH AMPLE PROVISION FOR OUTDOOR LIVING

Published in The Craftsman, November, 1910.

NINE-ROOM SHINGLED HOUSE: NO. 102

IN this house shingles are used for the walls and Ruberoid for the roof. There is a comparatively small porch covered by a pergola in front of the house, but at the back there is plenty of room for outdoor life. The porch opening from the living room is as large as the room itself, and is intended to be used as an outdoor living room in summer and as a sun room in winter. The other porch might be used as an outdoor dining room or given over to the maid, whose room looks out upon it. The maid's room in this house is placed next to the kitchen, because we have had so many requests from housekeepers for such an arrangement. The room connects with both the kitchen and the pantry, and through the pantry with the porch.

The front door opens directly into the large central hall, but is screened by the arrangement shown in the elevation. On the floor plan this is called an entry, but all that separates it from the living room is a high-backed seat with a screen of spindles above extending to the ceiling. This gives the same effect as a sofa or settle set out into the room, and yet shuts off the front door as much as is necessary. This seat faces the fireplace, and heavy beams running across the ceiling bind

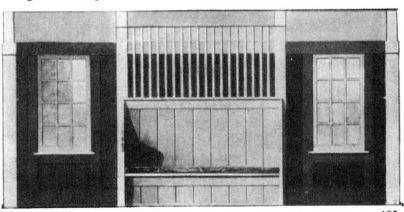

WAINSCOTED AND SPINDLED SEAT FACING HALL FIREPLACE IN HOUSE NO. 102.

SHINGLED HOUSE WITH AMPLE ROOM FOR OUTDOOR LIVING

FIREPLACE AND GLIMPSE OF STAIRWAY BEHIND, IN HALL OF HOUSE NO. 102.

with a row of windows set high, and bookshelves are built below. At the opposite end of the vista appear the sideboard and china closets, which occupy the whole end of the dining room. Wide groups of windows light both rooms from the front, and both open with glass doors to the porches in the rear.

There are four bedrooms on the second floor and two sleeping porches which may be used for outdoor bedrooms in mild weather and glassed in during the winter. These porches are open only at one end.

In the two front bedrooms there is an especially convenient arrangement of closets and window seat, the closets occupying the corners and the seat being built in the recess formed between them. One of these rooms has a private bath, the other bathroom opening out of the hall. In this hall two linen closets are provided.

This floor plan, of course, could be modified to suit various requirements. For instance, if a second bath were not needed, the space could be used for a small dressing room in connection with the corner bedroom. Or it could be included in the middle room.

the two together and define the intention of the arrangement. Two other beams serve to mark the division from the living room on one side and from the dining room on the other, but the openings into both these rooms are so wide that the effect is that of one long room. At one side of the fireplace is a coat closet, with the door concealed in the wainscot, and on the other side is the stair landing. The staircase itself runs up back of the fireplace. An arrangement that is especially convenient is the carrying of the smoke-pipe from the kitchen range underneath this staircase in a terra cotta flue. This prevents any possibility of danger, utilizes the central chimney for the range as well as the fireplace, and does away with any disfigurement.

The entire end of the living room is lighted

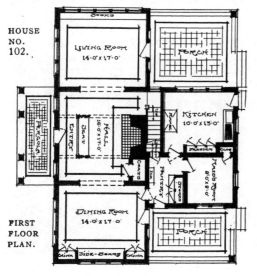

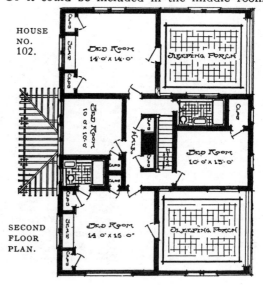

SHINGLED COTTAGE SUITABLE FOR COUNTRY, SEASIDE OR SUBURBAN LIFE

Published in The Craftsman, November, 1909.

SEVEN-ROOM SHINGLED COTTAGE: NO. 78.

THIS little cottage, ideal for the seaside but adapted also to suburban or country building, is covered with rived shingles. Where the windows are not sheltered by the overhanging roof they are protected by springing the shingles out over the head of the windows into the form of a hood which acts as a watershed and prevents the rain and moisture from lodging about the casings.

The shingles, if of split cypress, may be left to weather to the silvery gray color of driftwood, or given a wash of diluted sulphuric acid which will slightly burn the surface to a dull brown. In the chimney the varying tones of the field stone and the red of the brick will add color and interest to the exterior, and the roof may be stained a dull green or red, giving a touch of brightness to the landscape.

The interior is very compactly planned. The living room with its big stone fireplace occupies one whole side of the house. The ceiling shows two of the heavy structural beams. At the rear end of the room is a

low bookcase and at the opposite end a long, deep seat is built in beneath the windows. The dining room, as shown in the

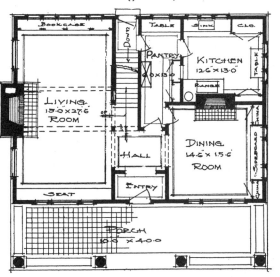

COTTAGE NO. 78: FIRST FLOOR PLAN.

COTTAGE FOR COUNTRY, SEASIDE OR SUBURBS

drawing of the interior, contains a built-in sideboard with a cupboard, and a china closet on either side. The stairs lead up from the rear of the hall, which is practically a part of the living room. Note the opening with a lattice frame which makes an attractive setting for a pot of flowers. At the foot of the stairs a door is seen which opens into a rear hall, connecting with a large and convenient pantry. The kitchen is well fitted with closets and a big dresser. The second floor is divided into four airy bedrooms with a bath at the end of the hall. One of these bedrooms has an open fireplace with a closet on one side, and in the recess formed by the front dormer there is a long seat built in beneath the window group. A similar seat is provided in the dormer nook in the other front bedroom, and also in one of the rooms at the rear. The front bedroom on the left has ample closet room beneath the slope of the roof, and the other rooms have closets against the interior walls. There is also a linen closet in the hall.

The somewhat irregular shape of the bedrooms will add to the interest of their furnishing.

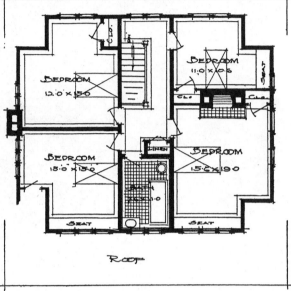

COTTAGE NO. 78: SECOND FLOOR PLAN.

VIEW FROM LIVING ROOM OF COTTAGE NO. 78, WITH GLIMPSE OF STAIRCASE, HALL AND DINING ROOM BEYOND.

PRACTICAL SIX-ROOM SHINGLED COTTAGE

Published in The Craftsman, March, 1910.

THE walls and roof of this cottage are shingled, the porch pillars are peeled and hewn logs, and the porch floor is cement.

The open hearth and fireside seat, the built-in sideboard in the dining room and the bookcases between the rooms are pleasant features of the interior.

Upstairs the dormer nook in each front bedroom is so deep that it might even serve as a small extra room, for the couch built in below the window is meant to serve as a bed if needed. Or the bedroom proper might be arranged as a sitting room, and the couch in the nook used regularly as a bed.

FIRST FLOOR PLAN: NO. 86.

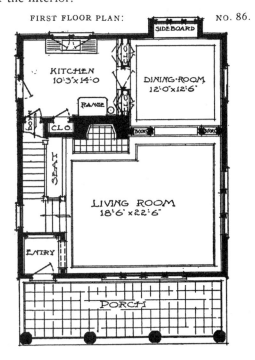

SECOND FLOOR PLAN: NO. 86.

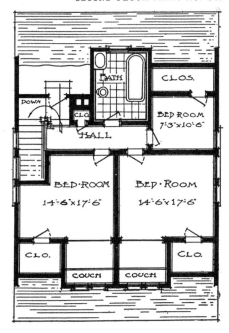

SMALL CRAFTSMAN FARMHOUSE OF STONE AND SHINGLES, SIMPLE AND HOMELIKE IN DESIGN

Published in The Craftsman, February, 1909.

SIX-ROOM FARMHOUSE: NO. 61

VILLAGE or open country would be the environment most suitable for this little house. The walls are shingled and the low foundation is of field stone, sunk into a site that has not been too carefully leveled off. This irregularity of the ground is utilized in a practical way, the slope at the back being sufficient to allow space for the cellar windows, while at the front it is high enough to bring the cement floor of the porch almost upon a level with the lawn. Instead of parapets, the spaces between the pillars of the porch are filled with long flower-boxes which serve as a slight screen and add a note of color to the house. The roof extends over the porch and the sweep of it is broken by the dormer with its group of casements which give light to both bedrooms and the sewing room.

The entrance door at the corner of the porch opens directly into a little nook in the living room. Directly opposite the door is the stairway which runs up three steps to a square landing and then turns and goes up behind the wainscoted wall of the room. The whole wall on this side is taken up by the long fireside seat. The chimneypiece of split field stone occupies the space between the wall and the opening into the dining room. This little ingle-

nook is shown in the illustration which gives some idea of the treatment of the wainscot, posts and beams. A decorative note is added by the Craftsman hanging lanterns above. Behind the dining room is a small, conveniently arranged kitchen.

Upstairs there are two bedrooms, a tiny sewing room, bathroom and hall. Both bedrooms communicate with the sewing room which is placed between them and is provided with a wardrobe. There is ample closet room at each corner beneath the slope of the roof, and one of the bedrooms also has a closet with shelves against the inner wall beside the central chimney. Seats are built into the front recesses beneath the windows.

The house is a small one, having only five rooms and bath, but the compactness of its arrangement and the sense of space given by the openness of the lower floor plan result in a very homelike interior.

For the farmer who is planning to build a home of his own, the farmhouse shown here, as well as those on other pages of the book, should prove full of practical and helpful suggestions in arrangement and design. We have endeavored to keep the plans as simple and inexpensive as possible, and at the same

SMALL CRAFTSMAN FARMHOUSE OF STONE AND SHINGLES

STONE FIREPLACE IN CORNER OF LIVING ROOM OF FARMHOUSE NO. 61, WITH FIRESIDE SEAT AND GLIMPSE OF STAIRCASE.

time to secure the greatest possible comfort and beauty, both in the exterior of the building and the rooms within. For the farmer has tolerated too long the discomfort and bareness of the average farmhouse. He needs a home for himself and his family which is both comfortable and cheerful, a place where he may find rest and recreation after the day's work, and in which the necessary labor of the household may be done under conditions which make it as light as possible.

When our farmhouses are designed from this standpoint of utility and beauty, we shall no longer regard the work within their walls as a round of drudgery, a necessary evil. Instead, the so-called "menial" tasks of cooking, sweeping, sewing, will be a source of pleasure and pride, and in place of the old weary attitude toward work we shall find ourselves laboring with interest, with enthusiasm,—qualities which are inevitable in the building up of the ideal home.

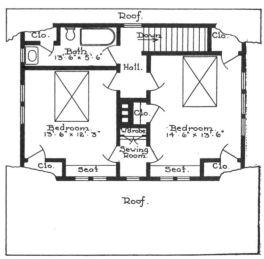

FARMHOUSE NO. 61: FIRST FLOOR PLAN.

FARMHOUSE NO. 61: SECOND FLOOR PLAN.

CRAFTSMAN RURAL DWELLING COMBINING BEAUTY, COMFORT AND CONVENIENCE

Published in The Craftsman, March, 1909.

CRAFTSMAN SHINGLED FARMHOUSE: NO. 63.

THIS farmhouse is designed with simple lines, clapboarded or shingled walls and a broad sheltering roof, the straight sweep of which is broken by a large dormer on either side. The interior arrangement is very simple, as there is hardly anything to mark a division between the reception hall, the long living room with its fireplace nook, and the dining room. The arrangement of space avoids all sense of bareness, and if wood in the form of beams and wainscots is liberally used the effect will be friendly and homelike. The kind of wood selected would naturally depend upon the locality, and a safe rule to follow in nearly every case is the use of local materials so far as practicable. The color scheme, of course, would be based upon the tone of the wood.

The front door, which is extremely simple in design, opens from the porch into a small entry which in turn opens into the wide reception hall. The center of interest of the room is, of course the wide inglenook with its stone chimneypiece and fireside seat.

The interior view shows the arrangement of this nook and its solid construction. The frank use of beams and posts emphasizes the structural lines and seems particularly appropriate in a farmhouse or rural dwelling. The V-jointed boards of the wainscot, the lintel and recessed shelf of the stone chimneypiece, and

the tiled hearth, are all pleasant features, and the three panels which form the end of the seat serve to shield it from possible draft and at the same time add to the privacy of the inglenook. The Craftsman lantern, a glimpse of which is shown suspended from the ceiling, suggests other possibilities in decorative fittings for the various rooms.

In the recess in the living room there is a built-in seat and double glass doors flanked by casement windows open onto the porch, which is edged with flower-boxes placed between the cement pillars supporting the sloping roof.

On one side of the living-room fireplace is the door of a wood closet which can also be reached from the pantry in the rear. This pantry, which is fitted with an ice-box and a long cupboard, serves as a passageway between the dining room and the kitchen. Steps lead up from the kitchen to the staircase landing, which is also accessible from the reception hall.

The upper floor, which is divided into three bedrooms with a bathroom in the dormer at the back, is arranged with a view to the greatest possible economy of space, and there is plenty of store room and closet room under the slope of the roof. The sleeping porch in front is sheltered by the parapets and is open to the

FIREPLACE NOOK IN LIVING ROOM OF FARMHOUSE, SHOWING FRANK HANDLING OF BEAMS AND WAINSCOTING.

sky, so that believers in the efficacy of outdoor sleeping will be able to get the full benefit of the breeze without being exposed to the view of passersby. Opening as it does from a bedroom, it can be used even in the severest weather, as all dressing is, of course, done indoors. Flower-boxes similar to those around the lower porch could be placed along the edges of the parapet, and would add a welcome note of color to the house.

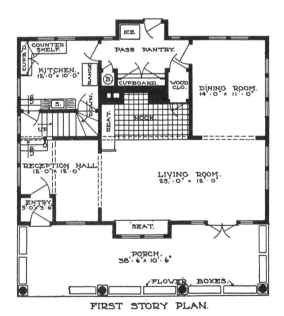

FIRST STORY PLAN.

SECOND STORY PLAN.

FARMHOUSE DESIGNED FOR UTILITY AND COMFORT

THIS farmhouse is simple in design and construction, planned to be built entirely of stock material, and the owner can attend to the superintending of the construction, the ordering of the material, etc., without the aid or expense of an architect.

The house is shingled with sawn shingles. This is the most satisfactory of the cheaper materials for exterior walls and can be finished with the ordinary shingle stains. The roof is Ruberoid, battened, and as this roofing is made

an average sized family. The large living room with its broad fireplace will suffice at once as a place for entertainment and the gathering of the family to plan and discuss the work and management of the farm. The opening to the dining room is left wide and a dining porch is provided so that meals may be served in the open.

The laundry tubs have been placed in the summer kitchen—an arrangement which practically takes the work out of the house and at

Published in the Craftsman, February, 1911.

EIGHT-ROOM CRAFTSMAN FARMHOUSE, WITH CONVENIENT SUMMER KITCHEN AND ROOMY PORCHES: NO. 107.

in colors, harmonizing effects can be secured between roof and walls. We specially recommend this roofing material not only because of its cheapness, but because it is practically fireproof—a condition well worth considering in building in the country, where fire protection is often inadequate. With the open construction of the overhanging roof, the hewn log posts for porches and balcony, and the stone foundation, the house will be rustic enough in effect to make the exterior suitable for almost any location in the country.

The interior is planned to meet the needs of

the same time saves the time and labor involved when the laundry is down cellar.

This summer kitchen is one of the delights of the plan, as it provides a place in summer where such tasks as cooking, preserving and canning can be done with much more comfort and under less tiring conditions than in the house. In winter it serves as a convenient place for cooking food for the stock, the cutting-up and preparing of meats, and so forth. Four large bedrooms, bath and sewing room are provided on the second floor. There are plenty of closets and the bedrooms are well

FARMHOUSE DESIGNED FOR UTILITY AND COMFORT

ONE CORNER OF LIVING ROOM IN FARMHOUSE NO. 107: THE CRAFTSMAN FIREPLACE-FURNACE AND THE STAIR-
CASE ARE INTERESTING FEATURES OF THIS COMMODIOUS AND SIMPLY ARRANGED INTERIOR.

lighted, having double-hung windows on two sides. A door from the sewing room opens onto the long sleeping porch at the rear, which is sheltered by an extension of the roof. This porch may be edged with flower-boxes, which will serve somewhat as a screen and add a welcome note to the exterior. Vines may also be trained about the pillars of the front and dining porches.

The house may be heated and ventilated by using the Craftsman fireplace-furnace shown in the view of the interior. This will serve for all the rooms, the arrangement of the pipes for the upper rooms being indicated by dotted lines in the floor plan of the second story.

Some idea of the general appearance of the interior and the treatment of woodwork and wall spaces, is given by the illustration above.

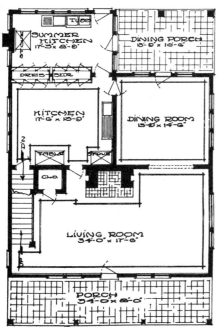

FARMHOUSE NO. 107: FIRST FLOOR PLAN.

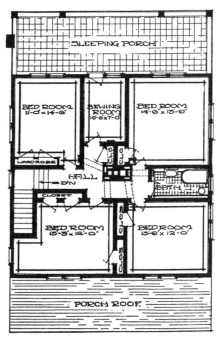

FARMHOUSE NO. 107: SECOND FLOOR PLAN.

COMFORTABLE, CONVENIENT, HOMELIKE FARM-HOUSE WITH CONNECTED WOODSHED AND BARN

Published in The Craftsman, February, 1911.

FARMHOUSE WITH WOODSHED AND BARN: NO. 108.

BUILT on a stone foundation, with walls of sawn shingles, with roof of Ruberoid, and hewn log posts supporting the roofs of pergola, porches and balcony, this farmhouse presents a simple but attractive exterior. The building is planned especially for convenience and economy of labor, and is heated and ventilated by a Craftsman fireplace-furnace. Coal and wood closets are provided where fuel can be stored, easily accessible to fireplace and kitchen. A summer kitchen is also provided containing stove and laundry tubs, while an outdoor dining room, its long table and benches enclosed from the yard by a curved hedge, forms a most charming place for serving meals during the summer.

ONE SIDE OF LIVING ROOM IN FARMHOUSE NO. 108, SHOWING RECESSED FIREPLACE AND EFFECTIVE SIMPLICITY OF WALL TREATMENT.

FARMHOUSE WITH CONNECTED WOODSHED AND BARN

The woodshed provides a passage under shelter to the barn and sufficiently isolates the barn from the house to remove any objectionable features. The barn is not intended to accommodate much stock, but a box stall and one single stall have been planned for horses, and a separate room large enough for three or four cows has been partitioned off with a solid wall. This stall has an outside entrance.

We located the feed bins in the loft and convey the feed to the first floor through metal chutes. A hay chute is also provided. Ample room for carriage, wagon and farm tools is arranged for on the first floor. The corn crib is constructed of slats as shown; this should be lined on all sides, top and bottom, with a fine mesh wire to keep out rats or mice.

One of the great advantages of the fireplace-furnace being located on the first floor is the fact that there is no heat in the cellar. Fruit and vegetables can be stored in the cellar and will keep nicely all the winter.

The second floor plan shows a very simple arrangement. There are four bedrooms of convenient size, and a bathroom, all opening out of the small central hall. Plenty of closets are provided. The two bedrooms at the right have glass doors lead-ing to the sleeping porch which runs across the side of the house and is sheltered by the roof extension.

The illustration of the living room suggests a simple but interesting treatment of woodwork and walls, and the use of small panes in the windows always adds a decorative note to the interior. The recessed hearth is a somewhat unusual feature, and increases the homelike air of the long cheerful room.

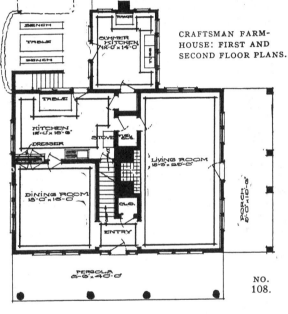

CRAFTSMAN FARM-HOUSE: FIRST AND SECOND FLOOR PLANS.

NO. 108.

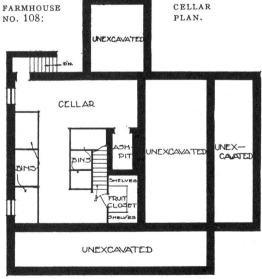

FARMHOUSE NO. 108: CELLAR PLAN.

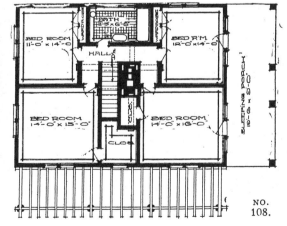

NO. 108.

COMPACTLY BUILT CRAFTSMAN FARMHOUSE

Published in The Craftsman, January, 1909.

SIX-ROOM SHINGLED FARMHOUSE, NO. 59.

THE plan of this building is so arranged as to simplify greatly the work of the household and to give a great deal of room within a comparatively small space.

The design is definitely that of a farmhouse, and in this frank expression of its character and use lies the chief charm of the dwelling. The walls are covered with shingles or clapboards, according to the taste or means of the owner. If the beauty of the building were more to be considered than the expense of construction, we should recommend the use of rived cypress shingles. But the ordinary sawn shingle oiled and left to weather, or stained to some unobtrusive tone of green or brown, would give a very good effect.

The roof, of course, would be shingled, and for the sake of durability would be painted rather than stained. As the construction of the house in front is such that a veranda would be rather a disfigurement than an improvement, we have supplied its place by a terrace covered with a pergola. The terrace, of course, would be of cement or vitrified brick, and the construction of the pergola would naturally be rustic in character, especially in the case of a shingled house. One great advantage of the pergola is that the vines which cover it afford sufficient shade in summer, while in winter there is nothing to interfere with the air and sunlight which should be ad-

mitted as freely as possible to the house. We have allowed the roof to come down in an unbroken sweep toward the back because of the

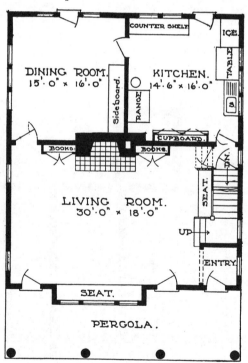

FARMHOUSE NO. 59: FIRST FLOOR PLAN.

COMPACTLY BUILT CRAFTSMAN FARMHOUSE

beauty and uniqueness of it. By this device there is considerable space for storage left over the kitchen and dining room.

The entry opens into the living room. The big chimney being in the middle of the house, the fireplace in the living room is connected with it on one side and with the kitchen range on the other. The fireplace has a bookcase built in on either side, and these bookcases with the two built-in seats form the nucleus of the furnishings.

The dining room is separated from the living room by a door of the usual width. A built-in sideboard is the chief piece of furniture in this room, and a door communicates directly with the kitchen, where there is every convenience combined with the greatest economy of space.

On the second story the arrangement is as convenient and economical as it is below. The upper hall, that communicates with all three of the bedrooms, bathroom and the storage place under the roof, is made small so that all the space possible may be utilized for the rooms. The big sweep of the roof at the back affords a large place for storage, though the walls are not high enough to permit of its being used for any other purpose.

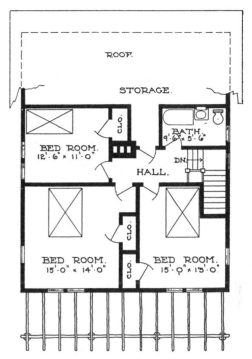

FARMHOUSE NO. 59: SECOND FLOOR PLAN.

REAR VIEW OF CRAFTSMAN SIX-ROOM SHINGLED FARMHOUSE NO. 59.

PRACTICAL, INEXPENSIVE ONE-STORY BUNGALOW

THIS small bungalow is a characteristic Craftsman home. We would use split cypress shingles for the walls and split field stone for the foundation. A broad terrace, open to the sky, takes the place of a veranda in front, and the vestibule projects upon this terrace. The roof, which has a very wide overhang, is made of Ruberoid battened at the joints, and its line is broken by the broad low dormer with its group of casement windows— a feature that adds greatly to the structural interest of the building.

The small vestibule, which has a seat on one side and a coat closet on the other, is lighted by casements set high in the wall and also by the lights in the upper part of the door. The framing of door and windows is unusual and very effective, as it brings out the whole front of the vestibule into one structural group. This vestibule opens into a small passageway from which a door on one side leads to a den shut off from the rest of the house, and an open doorway on the other side communicates with the living room. The arrangement of living room and dining room is spacious and open, while the fireplace occupies a deep recess in the living room. The latter, as shown, is wainscoted to the height of the frieze, and the windows and door openings are so placed that the line around the room is unbroken. The top of the wainscot is finished with a square beam instead of a plate rail, and the partition between dining room and living room is indicated by post and panel construction. There is only one group of windows in the living room, but that is so large that almost the entire front wall appears to be of glass.

In the dining room the walls are wainscoted clear to the ceiling, and a group of windows similar to that in the living room gives plenty of light and a pleasant sense of airiness. The combined sideboard and china closets built in below a row of casement windows occupy the whole end of the room. The china closets extend to the ceiling, and the sideboard, which is fifteen feet long, projects several inches beyond the closets.

All the rooms are on one floor, the two bedrooms and a good-sized bathroom occupying the greater part of the space at the rear of the house. The kitchen is small but well equipped, and a large pantry adds greatly to the convenience of the housekeeping arrangements.

There is a closet in each bedroom as well as

Published in The Craftsman, August, 1910.

SIX-ROOM SHINGLED BUNGALOW: NO. 96.

PRACTICAL, INEXPENSIVE ONE-STORY BUNGALOW

PART OF LIVING ROOM OF BUNGALOW NO. 96, WITH VIEW OF DINING ROOM AND BUILT-IN FITTINGS.

in the den, and a good-sized linen closet in the hall. The stairs lead up from the hall to the attic which may be used for storage purposes, and which is lighted by two small windows in each gable and a row of four windows in the low dormer in front. From the pantry stairs lead down to the cellar.

The arrangement of the rooms of this bungalow will be found especially convenient, both for economy of housework and the convenience and privacy of the various members of the household. The sleeping apartments are kept quite separate from the service part of the house and from the living and dining rooms, and while the latter are open and hospitable, serving as a place for the gathering of family and guests, the smaller den provides opportunity for privacy when desired.

All the rooms are of convenient size and are well lighted, the small panes of the casement windows adding to the interest of the exterior as well as of the rooms within, as shown by the illustration of the liv-

ing and dining rooms given above. This view also shows the treatment of the woodwork, the boarded wainscot, the open arrangement of the post and panel construction between the rooms, and the effect of the built-in fittings.

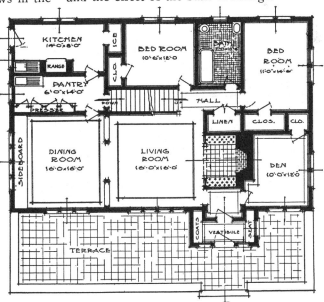

FLOOR PLAN OF SHINGLED BUNGALOW: NO. 96.

SEVEN-ROOM SHINGLED CRAFTSMAN COTTAGE

Published in The Craftsman, January, 1912.

SHINGLES are used for the walls and roof of this cottage. Pillars of hewn logs are used to support the roof where it slopes over the porch. The windows are all double-hung, with a single lower pane and small panes above. The grouping of these windows, the long lines of the roof and the dormer which breaks it give interest to the exterior of this unpretentious and homelike little dwelling.

Both the dining room and the large living room have fireplaces, and if Craftsman fireplace-furnaces are used they will heat and ventilate the whole house. The effective treatment of the long wall of the living room, with its built-in seat and bookcases, is shown in a perspective view. Kitchen, pantry and a large

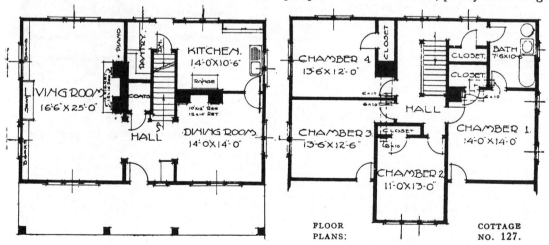

SEVEN-ROOM SHINGLED CRAFTSMAN COTTAGE

FIREPLACE CORNER OF DINING ROOM IN COTTAGE NO. 127, SHOWING CRAFTSMAN FITTINGS AND FURNITURE.

coat closet occupy the remainder of the lower floor plan. Upstairs there are four bedrooms and bath, opening out of the hall which is lighted by three windows in the rear. There are several interior closets as well as storage space beneath the slope of the front roof. The compactness of the rooms of the cottage will make the household work very light.

SIDE OF LIVING ROOM IN COTTAGE NO. 127: A NOTABLE EXAMPLE OF USEFUL AND DECORATIVE WALL TREATMENT

SHINGLED COTTAGE WITH RECESSED PORCHES

Published in The Craftsman, January, 1912.

CRAFTSMAN SHINGLED COTTAGE: NO. 128.

BRICK is used for the foundation and chimney of this cottage and the walls and roof are shingled. The windows are double-hung, small square panes being used in the upper portion. It will be noticed that where the windows are not sheltered by the porch recess or by the overhanging roof they are hooded at the top by springing outward a row of shingles to protect them from storms. These window groups, the recessed corner porch and the trelliswork over the front wall are pleasant features of the exterior; and the vines trained over the trellis, up the corner pillar of the porch, against the chimney at the side, and the small shrubs planted along the base of the walls, all help to knit the little cottage more closely to its surroundings and at the same time break up the straight lines of the building.

The entrance door opens directly into the living room, which is a long and spacious apartment with windows on three sides and a

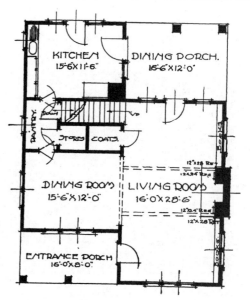

COTTAGE NO. 128: FIRST FLOOR PLAN

door opening onto the corner dining porch at the rear. In the center of the side wall is a Craftsman fireplace-furnace which serves to heat and ventilate the whole cottage. The chimneypiece is of Tapestry brick, and low built-in bookcases fill the wall space on either side. A wide opening leads from the living room into the dining room, which is practically a recess in the larger room, and swing doors through the pantry give access to the kitchen which also opens onto the dining porch. The stairs lead up from one corner of the living room, with a coat closet at the side.

The interior view given here shows the effective handling of the woodwork of the living room, which is merely a natural use of structural parts such as door and window frames, posts, beams, etc. In front of the fireplace we have shown a long Craftsman settle with a table placed behind so that the lamplight will fall over the shoulder of anyone reading. A few pieces of willow furniture such as the armchair shown here will form a pleasant contrast to the oak furniture and add a lighter decorative note to the room.

Three good-sized bedrooms and bathroom are provided on the second floor, each opening out of the narrow L-shaped hall which leads down to the pleasant stair landing. This is

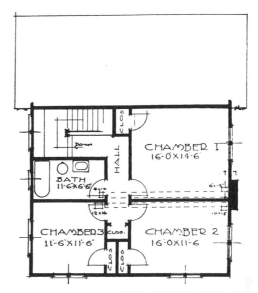

COTTAGE NO. 128: SECOND FLOOR PLAN.

lighted by two windows beneath which a long seat is built. Each bedroom has a closet and there is also a linen closet in the hall.

Although small, the cottage is one which lends itself to interesting furnishing, and with a little thoughtful planning of arrangement and color schemes can be made very homelike.

ONE CORNER OF LIVING ROOM IN COTTAGE NO. 128. THE CRAFTSMAN FIREPLACE-FURNACE OF TAPESTRY BRICK, THE LOW BOOKCASES ON EITHER SIDE, THE PLEASANT WINDOW GROUPS AND THE ARRANGEMENT OF CRAFTSMAN FURNITURE, MAKE THIS ROOM BOTH PRACTICAL AND HOMELIKE.

SMALL SHINGLED HOUSE WITH RIGHT USE OF STRUCTURAL FEATURES AND WOODWORK

WE have suggested the use of shingles for the walls of this simple little cottage because they seem the best adapted to the details of its construction. They should, however, be laid in double course, the top ones being well exposed and the under ones showing not much more than an inch below, giving an interesting effect of irregularity to the wall surface. All the lines of the framework are simple to a degree, but the plainness is relieved by the widely overhanging eaves and rafters of the roof, the well-proportioned

As the floor plans show, the arrangement of the interior is very convenient, the rooms being light and airy and fairly large, and the communication between them as simple as possible to facilitate the work of housekeeping. The entrance door leads directly into the living room, and the first thing one would see on entering would be the fireplace, which is built diagonally across the corner with a built-in seat between it and the landing of the staircase. This fireplace is made of rough red brick, with a wood mantelshelf set on a line

Published in The Craftsman, February, 1907.

SEVEN-ROOM SHINGLED HOUSE: NO. 46.

porch which is balanced by the extension at the rear, the heavy beams which run entirely around the walls and the effective grouping of the windows.

The roof of the porch projects two and a half feet, affording protection even in a driving storm. Also for protection all the exposed windows are capped by small shingled hoods. The eaves of the main roof project over the front for two and a half feet, and the weight is supported by purlins placed at the peak of the roof and at its connection with each of the side walls. This widely projecting roof gives a comfortable and homelike effect of shelter, an effect which is heightened by the way in which the little casement windows on the second story seem to hide under its wing.

with the wainscot. Three steps lead up to the small square landing from which the stairs go up to the second story. Bookcases are placed beneath the window in the opposite corner of the room.

The posts and panels of the wainscoted walls and the fireside seat, and the slight alcove effect of the front group of door and windows with their small square panes, make the room one of much structural interest. The hanging of Craftsman bracket lanterns from the posts above the seat, as shown in the illustration, suggests other possibilities for a useful and decorative arrangement of the various fittings and furnishings of the room.

An attractive feature of the dining room is the little recess in the back with its built-in china closet. Swing doors lead through the

VIEW IN LIVING ROOM OF HOUSE NO. 46, SHOWING CORNER HEARTH, BUILT-IN SEAT AND LOWER END OF STAIRWAY.

pantry, with its ice-box and cupboards, into the kitchen, which communicates with a small entry in the rear.

Upstairs there are three bedrooms and a bathroom. The two front rooms have square closets and in the back bedroom and the hall corner closets are provided.

If greater privacy were wanted downstairs, an ordinary partition and door might be used between dining room and living room instead of the post and panel construction. And if a fireplace nook were desired, the chimneypiece might be placed along the side wall at the left with the seat at right angles to the wall. This would form a comfortable little inglenook, and at the same time the high back of the seat would shield those about the hearth from any draft from the front door.

HOUSE NO. 46: FIRST FLOOR PLAN.

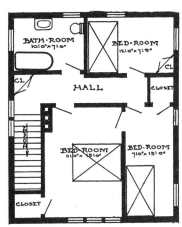

HOUSE NO. 46: SECOND FLOOR PLAN.

RUSTIC BUNGALOW WITH OPEN UPPER STORY

AS this dwelling is to be occupied for only a few weeks of the year, the most rigid economies must be observed in its construction, so that the first cost is not prohibitive and that the investment does not become a burden. The house is therefore planned to be built of stock material, such as can be purchased in any locality, and the simplest methods of construction are recommended. The exterior is of wood with Ruberoid roof, battened.

The plan is shown without foundation. In selecting a site for this bungalow care should be taken to secure a dry, well-drained surface, so that dampness will not rot the floor timbers, as the sills are to rest directly on posts

most delightfully to decoration in cool tones of a gray or green stain.

An abundance of windows have been provided for light and ventilation. Casements are used, being the least expensive to install, as well as giving the added charm of windows which can be thrown wide open. The broad entrance porch, with its balcony overhead, supported by hewn trees for posts, is most pleasing in effect. A living room, three bedrooms and a kitchen are provided on the first floor. No bath is shown because in a summer cottage running water is seldom available, the locality chosen being generally one where public bathing may be had in lake or surf. If,

Published in The Craftsman, March, 1911.

CRAFTSMAN SHINGLED BUNGALOW: NO. 109.

sunk in the ground. A large flat stone will form a good footing for the posts and will prevent the house from settling. Sawn shingles of cedar or cypress may be used for the exterior and may be left to weather. But for a few dollars the owner can himself add much to the beauty as well as to the life of the cottage by applying oil stain to the shingles, selecting harmonizing colors to blend with the colors of the roofing and the surrounding landscape.

The walls are constructed of 3 x 4 dressed spruce or hemlock studs, placed about five feet apart, and over these are nailed North Carolina sheathing boards with the dressed side exposed in the rooms. The overhead beams are left exposed, with the floor above forming the ceiling. This panel construction of side walls and ceiling is at once inexpensive and interesting; the whole interior being of wood, lends itself

however, the owner desires to go to that expense, another partition may be added and a bath placed between two of the bedrooms.

The fireplace, built of stone or brick, laid up with wide joints, will add to the rustic appearance of the interior and afford much comfort to those who have the leisure to spend a few weeks of the early fall in such a pleasant place. A door opens directly from the kitchen to the porch, so that meals may be served in the open.

Ample storage room is provided in the attic by partitioning off the spaces under the eaves to a height of about five feet. Both ends of the attic are left entirely open, and this space will accommodate a number of cots and form most delightful sleeping quarters.

This type of construction, with its provision for open air sleeping, is especially wel-

SUMMER BUNGALOW WITH OPEN UPPER STORY

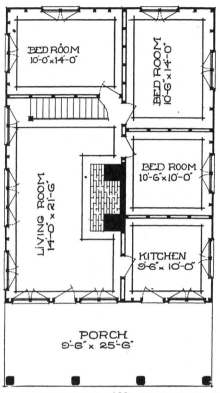

BUNGALOW NO. 109: FIRST FLOOR PLAN.

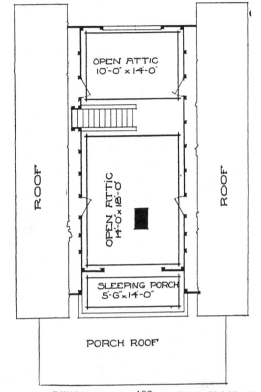

BUNGALOW NO. 109: SECOND FLOOR PLAN.

come now that people are coming more and more to realize the importance of healthful environment during sleeping as well as waking hours. Medical science has discovered that plenty of fresh air is one of the greatest preventives as well as cures for tuberculosis and many other diseases, and surely those of us who are in good health should welcome equally an opportunity to breathe the purest air during every one of the twenty-four hours. For tuberculosis patients or people at all liable to consumptive developments such a home as the one illustrated here would afford ample chance for the fresh air sleeping which has proved so efficacious.

In addition to the artistic possibilities of its interior this bungalow could be made very attractive outside, with rustic seats on the porch or at the side of the building. A rustic gateway like the one shown here would be a charming feature if the garden boundaries were defined. By using local materials but little expense would be involved, while the pleasure of such picturesque and friendly surroundings would quite compensate for the

labor. In any garden, in fact, rustic structures of this sort add a welcome note, and perhaps if we had more inviting seats and sheltering arbors about our homes we might be tempted oftener to work and play where there are flowers and sunlight and pure air.

SUGGESTION FOR A RUSTIC GATEWAY.

SUMMER BUNGALOW WITH OPEN ATTIC

Published in The Craftsman, March, 1911.   FIVE-ROOM BUNGALOW WITH SLEEPING BALCONIES: NO. 110.

THIS little summer cottage has the same general construction as No. 109, previously described. The exterior walls, however, are sheathed and battened, with gables shingled. Rough boards for these outside walls, undressed rafters, hewn posts and stone foundation combine to give enough of the rustic effect to make this house especially suited for a mountain camp. The living room being open to the rafters affords a delightful expanse of spacious walls and ceiling. The balcony is reached by a stairway from kitchen or porch, and the ends of the attic are thrown wide open for air, with the balcony extended out some four feet beyond the outside walls.

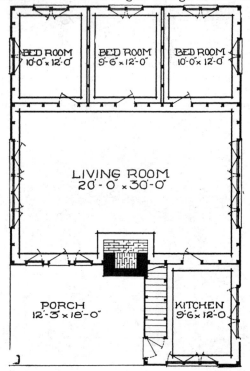

BUNGALOW NO. 110: FIRST FLOOR PLAN.

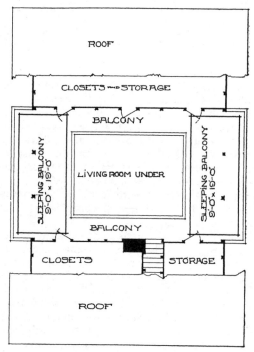

BUNGALOW NO. 110: SECOND FLOOR PLAN.

RUSTIC ONE-STORY BUNGALOW, WITH COMPACT INTERIOR AND COMFORTABLE FITTINGS

CONSTRUCTED entirely of dressed lumber, with rough stone for the foundation and chimney, with hewn posts, shingled walls and boarded gables, this bungalow has sufficient of the rustic character to harmonize with its surroundings of woods and mountain.

Casement windows are used, with small panes, and where the windows are not sufficiently sheltered by the roof they are hooded at the top by springing out a row of shingles. Upon the grouping of the windows depends much of the attraction of this very simple exterior.

more definite idea of the homelike effect of the open hearth and inviting fireside seats. The high wainscot, the paneled doors with the square lights in the upper portion, and the simple yet decorative construction of the seats, all are typical of a Craftsman interior. The details, of course, could be modified to suit the taste or convenience of the owner. For instance, the back of the seat on the left of the inglenook could be extended all the way up to the ceiling, if preferred, instead of only part way as shown in the sketch, or a curtain could be hung in the open space to shield those

Published in The Craftsman, May, 1911.

SIX-ROOM SHINGLED BUNGALOW: NO. 116

On entering the living room, the open shelves of books, the fireplace nook with comfortable cushioned seats, and the china closet and wide sideboard in the dining room present an interesting picture. The large groups of casement windows in the front wall and the group over the sideboard will flood the rooms with light and air. The general effect is one large commodious room with so much of the furniture built in that only a table and a few chairs are necessary to complete the furnishing.

The illustration on the next page shows the inglenook in the living room and gives one a

about the hearth from any possible draft and secure a greater sense of privacy. The color and design of the curtain would of course be chosen to harmonize with the cushions and other fittings of the nook, and carry out the general decorative scheme of the rooms. A copper bowl placed in the recess above the mantelshelf would be another welcome glint of color, and sconces could be fitted to the walls as shown in the drawing, or hanging lanterns suspended from the beam which runs across the nook. In fact, the task of furnishing and decorating the rooms will prove full of pleas-

RUSTIC BUNGALOW WITH COMFORTABLE INTERIOR

INGLENOOK WITH STONE CHIMNEYPIECE AND FIRESIDE SEATS IN LIVING ROOM OF RUSTIC BUNGALOW, NO. 116.

ant possibilities for those who take delight in making a home beautiful.

Especially interesting is the arrangement of bedrooms and bath, and the little hall is cur-

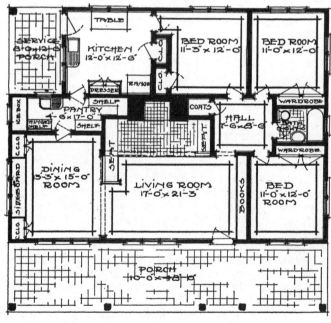

FLOOR PLAN OF RUSTIC BUNGALOW. NO. 116.

tained off from the living room by portières to insure more privacy. A door leading from the kitchen affords communication to the bedrooms without having to go through the dining and living rooms. The kitchen is well arranged with ample pantry and closet room and a small service porch. The pantry has swing doors between dining room and kitchen, and has ample shelf room, one of the shelves being hinged to afford more room when not in use. The kitchen has the usual dresser and a closet, and there is plenty of closet or wardrobe space in each of the bedrooms. A coat closet is also provided in the hall.

The floor plan could of course be modified in various ways to meet special requirements. For example, if two bedrooms were sufficient, the front bedroom could be used as a library or den, and made to open out of the living room instead of the hall. Or the partition might be omitted and the space included in the main room, in which case the bookshelves could be built elsewhere.

ONE-STORY SHINGLED CRAFTSMAN BUNGALOW FOR RURAL SURROUNDINGS

Published in The Craftsman November, 1908.

SHINGLED BUNGALOW: NO. 54.

THIS bungalow is intended for summer although it can be heated sufficiently for winter use if desired. The design is very simple and inexpensive. Shingles are used for the walls. The entrance is at the end, where a little recessed porch floored with red cement extends the whole width of the house. The weight of the gable is supported by four heavy log pillars. The foundation and chimney are of field stone and the floor is kept as near to the level of the ground as possible. An excavation of two feet clear is left under the building, but the exterior effect that is sought is that of the closest possible relation between the house and ground; therefore, from the porch one steps directly off onto the grass.

The interior arrangement is simple and compact, the stone fireplace being in the center. The living room is spacious and homelike, with ample cupboards, and with box couches which add materially to the sleeping accommodations. The kitchen is fitted with cupboards and drawers, and a long closet in the bedroom will be found useful.

Plenty of windows are provided so that the rooms are all light and airy. In fact the little cabin could be made both comfortable and picturesque, while the compactness of its arrangement and practical placing of the built-in furnishings would make the housework light, allowing ample time for outdoor life.

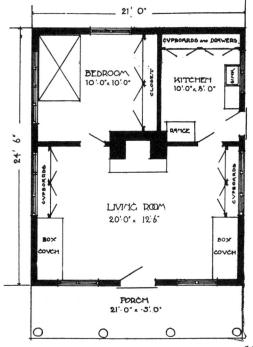

FLOOR PLAN OF BUNGALOW NO. 54.

TEN-ROOM HOUSE FOR TOWN OR COUNTRY LIFE

Published in The Craftsman, July, 1909.   TEN-ROOM HOUSE OF BOARDS AND SHINGLES: NO. 70.

THIS house is built on a foundation of field stone. The lower walls are covered with weather-boarding, and above this rived shingles are used, with vertical boards in the gable. The large living porch is at the side of the house, with glass doors opening from the dining room. It has a low parapet of stone, pillars of wood, floor of cement, and flower-boxes between the posts. The roof of the small entrance porch is also supported by wooden pillars, and wooden seats are built along the sides.

The entrance door leads through a small vestibule into a hall, the end of which is raised to form a landing from which the staircase goes up to the second story. A coat closet fills the space under the stairs.

On one side of the hall a wide opening leads to the living room with its open fireplace and wide built-in seats on each side, with case-

ment windows above. The opposite corners of the room are filled with bookshelves, making a very symmetrical arrangement and giving the room a homelike appearance even before

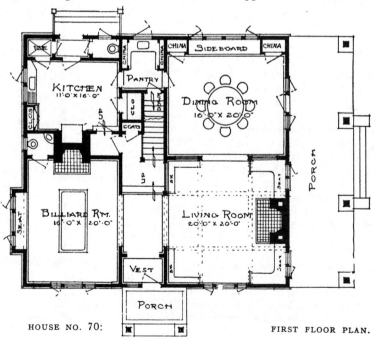

HOUSE NO. 70:   FIRST FLOOR PLAN.

TEN-ROOM HOUSE FOR TOWN OR COUNTRY LIFE

the rest of the furnishings have been moved in. Between the living room and dining room is a narrow partition of spindles. The entire end of the dining room is filled with a long built-in sideboard with casement windows set in the wall above, and china closets on each side. A door on the left leads to the pantry, which is fitted with shelves and sink and communicates with the kitchen. A door from the kitchen leads to the stair landing and thus gives ready access to the front door.

The billiard room is large and well lighted, and is fitted with a long window seat, an open fireplace and a small lavatory.

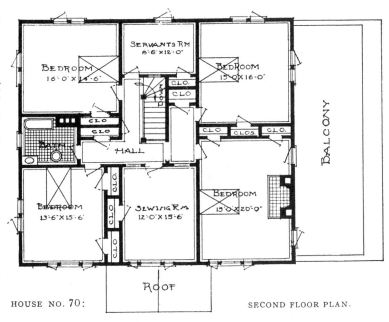

HOUSE NO. 70:   SECOND FLOOR PLAN.

CORNER OF DINING ROOM IN HOUSE NO. 70, WITH BUILT-IN SIDEBOARD AND CLOSETS, AND CASEMENT WINDOWS.

COMPACT TWO-STORY CRAFTSMAN HOUSE PLANNED FOR SLOPING SITE

Published in The Craftsman, September, 1910.

NINE-ROOM CRAFTSMAN HOUSE: NO. 98.

ALTHOUGH planned to fit a special site, this house would look equally well in any commanding position. The ground on which it is built includes two lots, the front one low and level and the second one rising in a curve. The rough stone parapet, with its massive irregular coping stones, rises several feet from the lawn below, affording ample room for a line of casement windows that give light to the billiard room which occupies the front of the basement.

On the walls the usual proportions of the clapboards and shingles are reversed, the clapboards being carried much higher than ordinary in order to emphasize the broad effect of the building. The grouping of the windows and the low pitch of the roof tend to increase this effect. From the pergola porch in front a recessed door leads directly into the large living hall. The sheltered position of the door makes a vestibule unnecessary. On each side is a convenient closet in which coats, overshoes, etc., may be kept. On entering, one is greeted at once by the hospitable welcome of the open fireplace with its wide tiled hearth, which occu-

pies the back of the hall. This fireplace really serves for dining and living room as well, for the divisions between the three rooms are so slight that the effect is practically that of one long, spacious apartment. The side wall of the living room on the right is filled by a window seat with built-in bookcases on each side of it. The front and rear walls of this room are broken by window groups, including a glass door leading out onto the corner porch at the back of the house. The dining room on the opposite side

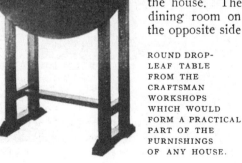

ROUND DROP-LEAF TABLE FROM THE CRAFTSMAN WORKSHOPS WHICH WOULD FORM A PRACTICAL PART OF THE FURNISHINGS OF ANY HOUSE.

FARMHOUSE PLANNED FOR COMFORTABLE HOME LIFE

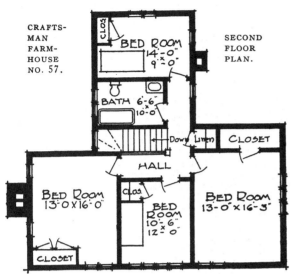

CRAFTS-MAN FARM-HOUSE NO. 57.

SECOND FLOOR PLAN.

The remaining space at this end of the living room is occupied by a fireplace nook. The brick chimneypiece is flush with the wall, and the mantel shelf above is set at the height of the picture rail that runs all around the room, giving an unbroken line, as the tops of the windows, doors and built-in cupboards all conform to it. The built-in seats at either side of the fireplace afford a comfortable lounging place, and the beam that extends across the entrance to the nook gives it a little sense of separation from the rest of the room. The stair landing is lighted with a window of simple design, preferably in amber or hammered antique glass, as either of these give a delightful mellowness to the light.

The kitchen is conveniently arranged with plenty of cupboards, a long window over the sink and unusually wide draining boards which are necessary in a farmhouse kitchen, where large vessels, milk tins and the like have to be washed. Above the draining boards on either side of the sink would be shelves for keeping pots and pans and various cooking utensils. The outside kitchen can be closed in for the winter, as a low wall is built around it and upon this wall could be placed a door, put in where the opening is shown. The laundry and heating apparatus are in the cellar.

Upstairs are four bedrooms. In the front bedroom on the left a window seat could be built in the recess beside the closet. The other rooms are also provided with closets, and shelves are placed in the closet in the hall.

LIVING ROOM IN CRAFTSMAN FARMHOUSE NO. 57, WITH GLIMPSE OF INGLENOOK, ENTRY AND STAIRCASE·

TYPICAL ONE-STORY CRAFTSMAN BUNGALOW SUIT-
ABLE FOR EITHER SUMMER OR ALL-YEAR USE

Published in The Craftsman, November, 1908.   ONE-STORY RUSTIC BUNGALOW: NO. 53.

ALTHOUGH so arranged that it can be easily heated to the point of comfort in the severest winter weather, this little bungalow is built primarily for a summer home. It is meant to stand in a small clearing made in the natural woodland, and is especially designed for such surroundings. It would be most desirable for those who wish to build an inexpensive summer or week-end bungalow for holiday or vacation use. Of course, the plans would serve perfectly well for a tiny cottage for two or three people to live in, but the design and general character of the building are not adapted to the ordinary town lot, and would be more effective in the country.

Wherever it is possible, local material should be used to give a close relation to the surroundings. Split field stone may be employed for foundation and chimneypiece, and if the site is woodland the thinning out of surrounding trees will furnish logs for the thick hewn pillars that support the porch roof. The unusual size of these pillars and the fact that they are merely peeled logs, hewn here and there to take off the more exaggerated irregularities, does more than any other feature to establish the quaint and "homely" individuality of this little

shelter in the woods. The porch and open-air dining room may be floored with red cement.

The walls are sheathed with boards. An interesting structural decoration is the truss of hewn timber in each gable. This truss projects a foot and a half from the face of the wall and not only gives added support to the roof, but forms a decorative feature that relieves the extreme simplicity of the construction.

The casement windows are all hung so that they will swing outward and are mostly small and set rather high in the wall. At the ends of the building these casements are protected by simple shutters, each made of two wide boards.

The roof may be shingled and colored ac-

FIREPLACE CORNER IN BUNGALOW NO. 53.

TWO-STORY HOUSE PLANNED FOR SLOPING SITE

of the hall has its side wall filled by a built-in sideboard flanked by china closets, so that both ends of the long open apartment are full of interest, and form a very practical as well as decorative part of the furnishings. From the dining room a swing door leads into the kitchen, which is fitted with all the necessary conveniences.

At the back of the square living hall is the landing of the staircase which runs up behind the chimneypiece to another landing, which also communicates with the kitchen stairs and from which the main staircase goes on up to the second story. The floor plans give a clear idea of the compactness with which the rooms are arranged and the sense of wide

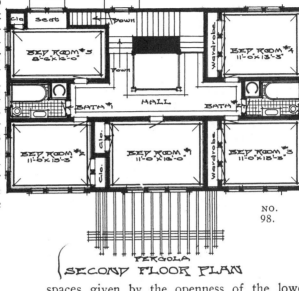

CRAFTSMAN HOUSE:

NO. 98.

SECOND FLOOR PLAN

spaces given by the openness of the lower story.

Five bedrooms and two bathrooms occupy the second floor, each room opening out of the central hall.

There is plenty of wardrobe space, and in one of the rear bedrooms a window seat is built into the recess formed by the corner closet and the wall of the kitchen staircase.

The illustrations of fittings from the Craftsman workshops shown on these pages are merely suggestions of the sort of furnishings which will be found most appropriate for this interior. They are simple in line, solid in construction, and the materials and workmanship that go into the making of them give them a certain dignity and beauty —qualities which must always belong to the ideal home.

DOME OF COPPER OR BRASS, WITH AMBER TINTED PANELS OF HAMMERED GLASS, TO BE USED IN LIBRARY OR OVER DINING TABLE.

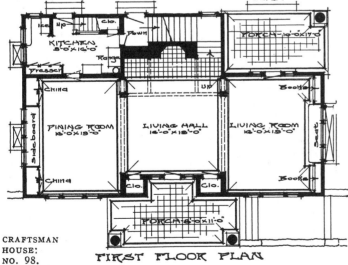

CRAFTSMAN HOUSE: NO. 98.

FIRST FLOOR PLAN

UMBRELLA STAND OF SIMPLE, PRACTICAL DESIGN: A USEFUL SUGGESTION FOR CITY OR COUNTRY HOUSE.

CRAFTSMAN FARMHOUSE PLANNED FOR COM-FORTABLE HOME LIFE

Published in The Craftsman, December, 1908.

SEVEN-ROOM FARMHOUSE WITH OUTSIDE KITCHEN: NO. 57

BELIEVING that no form of dwelling better repays the thought and care put upon it than the farmhouse, we give here a design for the kind of dwelling that is meant to furnish a pleasant, convenient and comfortable environment for farm life and farm work. This house is low, broad and hospitable looking in its proportions, and simple in design and construction. The walls are sheathed with clapboards and rest on a low foundation of field stone. The low shingled roof, the groups of casement windows and the long dormer add to the charm of the exterior.

The rooms are arranged with a view to making the work of the household as light as possible. The greater part of the lower floor is taken up by the large living room which practically includes the dining room, as the division between them is so slight. The front door opens into an entry or vestibule divided from the living room by a curtain. Provision is made in this entry for hanging up hats and coats and for keeping other outdoor belongings, such as umbrellas and overshoes.

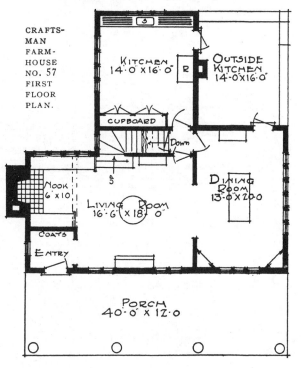

CRAFTS-MAN FARM-HOUSE NO. 57 FIRST FLOOR PLAN.

RUSTIC BUNGALOW FOR SUMMER OR ALL-YEAR USE

THE RECESSED OPEN-AIR DINING ROOM IN CRAFTSMAN COUNTRY BUNGALOW NO. 53: RUSTIC FURNISHINGS.

cording to the character of the location, which has much to do with deciding the color as well as the shape of the roof. One thing it is well to remember, that while a roof may be stained to a green, brown or gray tone, paint should be used if it is to be red, as the effect is much more satisfactory than when a red stain is tried.

Southern pine would be suitable for finishing the interior, and may be stained green or brown to harmonize with the color scheme of the furnishings.

The fireplace may be built of selected split field stone and fitted with a hood like that shown in the detail of the living room.

The interior arrangement is so convenient as to give the utmost space within the small compass. The living room leads into the open-air dining room or porch at the back, which can be left open in summer and glassed in for cold weather. There is plenty of cupboard and closet room, the kitchen being provided with shelves over which are casement windows overlooking the recessed porch. On each side of these shelves are built-in cupboards. A china closet is placed beside the living room fireplace, and small panes are used in its glass doors as in the other doors and windows of the room.

In addition to the living room, kitchen and bathroom, there are two bedrooms which occupy the other side of the plan. If only one bedroom were needed, the space of the front one could be included in the central room.

As suggested in the illustration of the open-air dining room shown above, rustic furnishings would be found very appropriate for this type of dwelling, and would harmonize with the rest of the construction. In fact, rustic furniture could be used not only on the recessed porch, but throughout the interior, if desired, especially if the bungalow were intended only for summer use. If it were used for a permanent all-year home, solid oak pieces would probably be preferred for the rooms, and very simple Craftsman fittings could be chosen, quite in keeping with the general character of the bungalow.

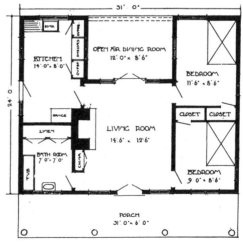

FLOOR PLAN OF BUNGALOW NO. 53.

ARCHITECTURAL DEVELOPMENT OF THE LOG CABIN IN AMERICA

WHAT is there about a log cabin that appeals to our imagination, that seems so alluring and full of the suggestion of romance? Is it not because the house of logs is a part of our heredity? It was a primitive home to man, a rudimentary sheltering of domestic life, a place of safety where love and friendship could be shut in and foe and danger shut out. The early homes of our Germanic ancestors were huts in the forest, sometimes built around a central tree which grew up through the roof and spread its sheltering branches over the dwelling. We came from the forest, and trees formed our home and our protection. And so today a house built of wood which has not been metamorphosed into board and shingle, but still bears the semblance of the tree, rouses in us the old instinctive feeling of kinship with the elemental world that is a natural heritage.

To us in America the log cabin seems a near friend. For many of us it was the home of our immediate ancestors, and it forms a vital part of the life of the white man in this continent. What a train of historical reminiscence the mere thought of the log cabin awakens: the landing of the first settlers, the unbroken wilderness of the primeval forests, the clearing of the ground, the building of the first homes. How great must have been the need of the comfort of the hearth and the strength of fellowship in that lonely and desperate struggle against the elements, the foe and starvation! Scattered far over this continent, moving northward, southward and westward, the log cabin has been the pioneer of civilization, the sign of the determination of the white man to face the unknown and to conquer all obsta-

cles. Viewed in this light, it seems of a certain poetic significance that Lincoln, one of the greatest of the nation's leaders, should have been born and reared in a log cabin.

Since the log house has played so important a part in our history its development into a definite and characteristic type of architecture might give us something national, something peculiarly American in suggestiveness. There are elements of intrinsic beauty in the simplicity of a house built on the log cabin idea. First, there is the bare beauty of the logs themselves with their long lines and firm curves. Then there is the open charm of the structural features which are not hidden under plaster and ornament, but are clearly revealed—a charm felt in Japanese architecture, which is, as Cram has said, "the perfect style in wood as Gothic is the perfect style in stone." The Japanese principle, "The wood shall be unadorned to show how beautiful is that of which the house is made," is true of the Craftsman development of the log house. For in most of our modern houses "ornament by its very prodigality becomes cheap and tawdry," and by contrast the quiet rhythmic monotone of the wall of logs fills one with the rustic peace of a secluded nook in the woods.

Of the distinction and charm of such a type the log house at Craftsman Farms is a proof, for it is a log cabin idealized. Some idea of its homelike beauty can be gathered from the views and floor plans given here. And in addition several smaller and simpler forms of this construction are shown—little log bungalows for summer or all-year use, in woods, or mountains, or by the shore.

THE LOG HOUSE BUILT AT CRAFTSMAN FARMS

Published in The Craftsman, November, 1911: Designed and Built by Gustav Stickley.

VIEW OF LOG HOUSE AT CRAFTSMAN FARMS, SHOWING ENCLOSED PORCH, FIFTY-TWO BY FOURTEEN FEET.

AS in the pioneer days, the space for this house had first to be cleared in the forest. The abundant chestnut trees were cut down and of them the house is built. The logs are hewn on two sides and peeled and the hewn sides laid together and chinked with cement mortar. The logs are stained the color of the bark.

A stone foundation runs under the whole building, including the wide veranda across the front of the house. The most practical piece of furniture here is a long combination bench and wood-box in which is kept the smaller wood for the fires.

From the veranda a wide door leads into the great living room with its fireplace at either end. The large hearths, which have special ventilating and heating appliances, are built of field stone gathered on the place and are topped with low-hanging hoods. Most of the available wall space is filled by bookcases. Above the bookcases and over the settles are windows with small diamond panes, and the light is softened to a mellow glow by casement curtains of burnt orange. The color scheme of the whole room reminds one of the forest— brown and green, with the glint of sunshine through the leaves, suggested by the gold of the windows and the gleam of copper in the

hearth-hoods, the door-latches and the vases and bowls on the bookcases and table.

The dining room runs parallel to the living room. Here also is a big ventilating hearth. These fireplaces heat the entire house with hot water and warm air.

Beyond the dining room is the kitchen, a large room, light and airy, painted white, with a large range. There are special appliances for convenience in washing dishes, etc.

The main bedrooms on the second floor are at the two ends of the house; one of them is furnished and decorated in yellow and seems aglow with sunshine; the other, a much larger room, is done in blue and gray with woodwork of dark gumwood. The walls are covered with gray Japanese grass-cloth, the hearth is of dull blue Grueby tiles with a brass hood, and the furniture is gray oak.

The illustrations give but an inadequate idea of the charm and comfort of the interior, its harmony with nature and its unity of the best of civilization with the best in cruder forms of life. Three views are given of the great living room—the first showing the big stone fire-place at one end with bookshelves at the side and Craftsman chairs and table grouped around the hearth. A second view, at the top of page 149, gives one some impression of the

THE LOG HOUSE AT CRAFTSMAN FARMS

SIDE VIEW OF LOG HOUSE AT CRAFTSMAN FARMS.

DETAIL IN ONE END OF THE LIVING ROOM, SHOWING CRAFTSMAN FURNITURE ABOUT THE BIG STONE FIREPLACE.

THE LOG HOUSE AT CRAFTSMAN FARMS

VIEW OF GREAT LIVING ROOM, WITH STAIRCASE AT THE LEFT AND STONE CHIMNEY AT THE FURTHER END.

DETAIL OF LIVING ROOM, WITH ENTRANCE INTO THE DINING ROOM: THE LOG CONSTRUCTION IS INTEREST-
INGLY SHOWN HERE.

THE LOG HOUSE AT CRAFTSMAN FARMS

ONE END OF THE DINING ROOM IN THE LOG HOUSE: THE FURNITURE IS FROM THE CRAFTSMAN WORKSHOPS.

SIDE OF DINING ROOM, SHOWING LONG CRAFTSMAN SIDEBOARD: THE LOGS IN THIS ROOM ARE FINISHED WITH A WOOD OIL WHICH GIVES A DELIGHTFUL MELLOW TONE AS THOUGH SUNLIGHT WERE POURING INTO THE ROOM.

ONE CORNER OF THE LARGE BEDROOM ON THE SECOND FLOOR OF THE LOG HOUSE, WITH ALCOVE FOR BED.

wide hospitable spaces of the interior, showing the long vista down the room with the other fireplace at the further end, the staircase on the left and the big glass doors opening onto the veranda at the right. The lower view on the same page shows a detail of the room, including the long table, the piano, and a glimpse through the curtained opening into the dining room beyond. Here again one feels the harmony of the carefully-designed furnishings with the more primitive dignity of the log construction. The remaining views show dining room and one of the bedrooms.

THE LOG HOUSE: FIRST FLOOR PLAN.

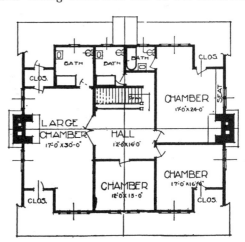

THE LOG HOUSE: SECOND FLOOR PLAN.

LOG COTTAGE FOR SUMMER CAMP OR PER-MANENT COUNTRY HOME

Published in The Craftsman, March, 1907.

CRAFTSMAN COTTAGE OF LOGS, WITH STONE FOUNDATION AND CHIMNEY, AND SHINGLED ROOF: THE TWO LONG PORCHES AND THE DINING PORCH AT THE REAR GIVE AMPLE ROOM FOR OUTDOOR LIVING: NO. 48.

INTERIOR VIEW IN COTTAGE NO. 48, SHOWING LIVING-ROOM INGLENOOK WITH STONE CHIMNEYPIECE AND BUILT-IN CORNER SEATS, AND DINING TABLE IN THE FOREGROUND: THE NATURAL USE OF THE LOGS AND DECORATIVE EFFECT RESULTING FROM PRACTICAL HANDLING OF STRUCTURAL FEATURES IS MOST HOMELIKE.

LOG COTTAGE FOR SUMMER CAMP OR PERMANENT HOME

ALTHOUGH this log bungalow is primarily intended for a summer home, it is so carefully planned and so well constructed that it could be used as a regular dwelling all the year round. While the lines of the building are simple to a degree, the proportions and details have all been so thoughtfully considered that with all this simplicity and freedom from pretense there is no suggestion of bareness or crudity. It is essentially a log cabin for woodland life, and looks just that; yet it is a warm, comfortable, roomy building, perfectly drained and ventilated, and if properly built ought to last for many generations.

There is a foundation of stone or cement, sufficiently high to secure good drainage and save the lower logs from decay. This foundation, however, is almost entirely concealed by terracing the soil up to the top of it, to the level of the porch floors. By this means perfect healthfulness is secured, and at the same time the wide, low cottage of logs appears to rest upon the ground in the most primitive way.

The logs used in building have the bark stripped off and are stained to a dull grayish brown that approaches as closely as possible the color of the bark. The removal of the bark prevents rotting, and the stain restores a color that harmonizes with the surroundings.

The wide porches afford plenty of room for outdoor living. One porch is recessed at the end to form a square dining porch, which opens into the kitchen and also into the big room which is a combined living room and indoor dining room.

The entry opening from the porch gives access on one side to the two bedrooms, and on the other leads by a wide opening into the main room. The walls and partitions are of logs and the ceiling is beamed with logs flattened on the upper side to support the floor above. The fireplace, like the chimney outside, is built of split stone, and is in a nook formed or suggested by the two logs placed one above the other across the ceiling logs, and by the two posts at the ends of the fireside seats.

The perspective view of the living room shows what a decorative effect results from this simple rustic treatment, and how entirely the furnish-ings are in keeping with the purpose and character of the log construction. There is a primitive, picturesque quality about the whole that would be lacking in a more formal interior, and the natural use of the logs seems to relate the rooms very closely to the exterior of the cottage and the woods and hills around.

The upper story may be arranged as the builder pleases. If intended for a permanent home, it can be divided into bedrooms and a bath, but for camp life in the woods a large single room may be left where things can be stored and cots put up or hammocks slung.

The expense of furnishing the bungalow would be somewhat reduced by the built-in fireside seats in the living room and the long seat which stretches beneath the windows in the opposite wall. These could be made with hinged tops, thus providing very useful storage space in addition to the large closet between the living room and bedroom, the kitchen cupboards and the space below the stairs.

If a larger bedroom were desired on the first floor, the entry shown in the plan might be omitted, including this space within the adjacent bedroom and using the door in the corner of the recessed dining porch as the entrance door. Or if only one bedroom were needed a room might be used as library.

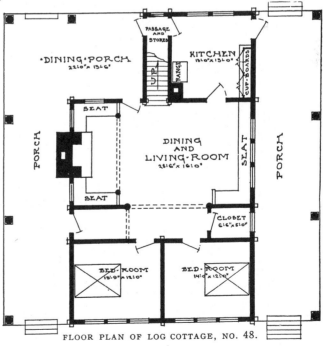

FLOOR PLAN OF LOG COTTAGE, NO. 48.

SMALL BUT COMFORTABLE LOG DWELLING

Published in The Craftsman, March, 1907.

LOG HOUSE WITH RUSTIC INTERIOR: NO. 49.

A HILLTOP or slight elevation is the site for which this little cottage was designed, and the ground is terraced to the level of the porch floors, concealing the foundation and seeming to connect the building more closely with the soil. The main roof and that of the porch are shingled, and the columns supporting the latter are thick peeled tree trunks, harmonizing with the peeled and stained logs of the walls. The chimneys are made of split stone. Flower-boxes at the upper windows give a little touch of grace and color that is

LIVING ROOM IN LOG HOUSE NO. 49, WITH UNIQUE CHIMNEYPIECE CONSTRUCTION AND RUSTIC FIRESIDE SEATS

SMALL BUT COMFORTABLE LOG DWELLING

unusually attractive against the brown background of logs. The porch is floored with red cement and the steps leading up to the house are of split stone laid in cement and smoothed off.

The central living room is simple in construction, but there is a dignity in the unbroken lines of the logs that is very effective. An interesting structural feature of the stone chimney-piece is the framing made by the ends of the logs forming the partition on each side of the bathroom, and the log that crosses the mantel-breast at the top, like a lintel. On either side of this fireplace is a large settle built of peeled saplings stained to the same color as the logs of the house. The supports for the seat cushions and the backs are made of ropes twisted and knotted around the frame of the settle. The seat cushions and pillows are of canvas or some such sturdy material in keeping with the rustic interior.

There are two downstairs sleeping rooms, one on each side of the bath. The upper story, which is left undivided, has plenty of light and ventilation, so that it could easily be partitioned into rooms if desired. Casement windows are used throughout, hooded where exposed to the weather. Dutch doors, V-jointed,

RUSTIC PERGOLA FITTED UP FOR OUTDOOR LIVING.

and with large strap hinges, are used for outside doors.

In this sort of cottage, where the porch is likely to be much in use for outdoor meals and as a cool, shady place for work, rest or play, rustic furniture would be as practical as it would be charming. A long seat, a few chairs and a table would serve all the purposes of usefulness and comfort, and would be in perfect harmony with the rest of the building, helping to carry out the rustic effect of the log construction. Or perhaps down by the water's edge or in some other pleasant spot a rustic pergola could be erected, like the one shown above, with vine-clad pillars and roof, inviting chairs, a little table for books or sewing or afternoon tea, and possibly a swinging seat suspended between two of the posts. Thus the hospitality of the log dwelling would be extended as far as possible into the nature world around it, luring one always from the shelter of the cottage into the fresh mountain air, while the unity of the log construction would link the little home more closely to the surrounding woods of which its walls were once a living part. In fact there are various possibilities for practical and picturesque constructions of this sort which ingenuity and skill could devise, at little labor and expense.

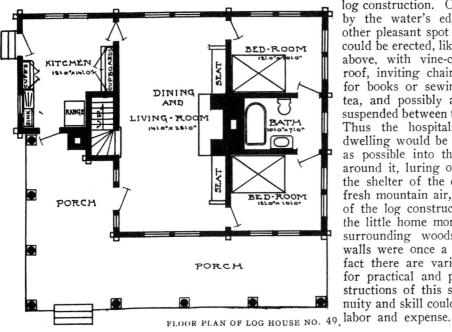

FLOOR PLAN OF LOG HOUSE NO. 49.

LITTLE WOOD COTTAGE ARRANGED FOR SIMPLE COUNTRY LIVING

Published in The Craftsman, March, 1907.

RUSTIC COTTAGE BUILT OF SLABS: NO. 50.

THIS cottage is built of slabs, and while not actually as massive as log construction, gives the same effect of primitive and rugged comfort. The slabs are peeled, nailed to the sheathing of the walls, and stained as nearly as possible to the color of bark. The proportions of the building are low and broad. The widely spreading roof is shingled, the porch columns are logs peeled and stained, and the foundation is concealed under the terrace. The front porch serves all the purposes of an outdoor living room, and the one in the rear is intended for a dining porch, whenever the weather permits.

In the living room every feature of the construction is frankly revealed, and this forms the chief element of decoration. The deep nook that divides the porches is the center of comfort and restfulness for the whole house. Bookshelves are built in on each side of the big fireplace of split stone, and there are two large box-seats made of peeled slabs. The nook has no ceiling, but extends up into a gable, separated by a railing from the attic.

Another fireplace is built in the rear wall of the living room, in this instance the placing of seats being left to the choice of the owner. This end of the room, being between the dining porch and the kitchen, is intended to

be used as an indoor dining room whenever the weather is not mild enough for meals to be carried out onto the porch. The front wall of the living room is filled by a group of three windows, and on the right are doors leading to the two bedrooms, in one of which is a long window seat. The kitchen is provided with ample shelf and storage room, and between the kitchen and bedroom walls the stairs lead up from the living room to the attic. This may be arranged as desired, either divided into several small bedrooms or left in one large room for storage purposes or to

SUGGESTION FOR A RUSTIC GATEWAY AND SEAT.

RUSTIC COTTAGE ARRANGED FOR SIMPLE COUNTRY LIVING

INTERIOR VIEW OF COTTAGE NO. 50, SHOWING SPACIOUS LIVING ROOM AND RECESSED FIREPLACE NOOK.

accommodate cots and hammocks when extra sleeping room is required.

The view of the living room and inglenook shown above suggests a satisfactory method of handling the structural features of the interior, the natural use of the woodwork being especially appropriate for this type of building. In fact, the arrangement of the bungalow, and the way in which the structure itself is made the basis of all decorative effect, are both an illustration and suggestion of how much can be accomplished by working along these practical, straightforward lines. While in this instance, of course, the design and scale of the cottage is of the most unpretentious, it embodies in its simple construction many of these characteristics which are typical of the Craftsman ideal home.

Rustic furniture for the porch would be serviceable and in keeping with the slab walls of the building, and the sketch of the rustic gateway, with its pergola roof draped with wistaria and the primitive charm of the little seat below, suggests an appropriate entrance to the garden, and may serve to suggest other vari-

ations on the same theme. A circular rustic seat, for instance, might be built around one of the neighboring trees.

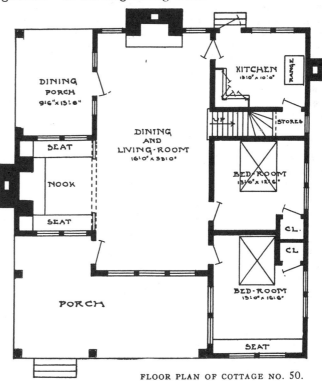

FLOOR PLAN OF COTTAGE NO. 50.

COMFORTABLE ONE-STORY BUNGALOW OF LOGS

ROUGH stone foundation, walls of log, and roof of colored Ruberoid are the materials used for this bungalow. The cement floor of the recessed entrance porch is extended beyond the house line as shown, and a log pergola is set on a cement floor at the rear of the building.

The floor plan has been worked out with an idea of economy of effort in housekeeping.

The entrance door opens directly from the porch into the living room, the deep recess

other has a comfortable built-in seat. The open bookshelves on the other side of the door to the pergola and the groups of high casements break up the wide expanse of wall space and form an interesting group of furnishings.

Both bedrooms are separated from the living room by a narrow hall, and the bath is located between the bedrooms—an arrangement combining convenience and privacy. Ample closet room is provided, and the groups of windows

Published in The Craftsman, May, 1911.

FIVE-ROOM LOG BUNGALOW: NO. 115.

sheltering it sufficiently to make a vestibule unnecessary. On either side of the door are two casement windows with small panes. In fact this style of window is used throughout the building, being more suitable for a rural dwelling than the double-hung type, and the small panes breaking up the surface of the walls and adding considerably to the interest of both the exterior of the bungalow and the rooms within.

The center of comfort and charm of the interior is of course the open fireplace which occupies the center of one of the living-room walls and uses the same chimney as the flue of the kitchen range just behind.

A coat closet is conveniently located on one side of the fireplace, while the space on the

are so situated as to allow cross ventilation.

On the opposite side of the house is the dining room, which, owing to the limitations of the floor plan, is separated from the main room more than is usual in a Craftsman interior. In the present instance, however, this arrangement may be found preferable, as it affords more opportunity for privacy and gives ready access between kitchen, pantry and dining room. Both the kitchen and pantry are arranged with the utmost convenience, with plenty of table and closet room and two sinks, and although neither room is large the very compactness of the arrangement makes for economy of housework. The dining room, like the bedroom at the opposite corner, has front and side window groups as well as smaller

COMFORTABLE ONE-STORY BUNGALOW OF LOGS

FIREPLACE CORNER OF LIVING ROOM IN BUNGALOW NO. 115, SHOWING CHIMNEYPIECE OF SPLIT FIELD STONE WITH RECESSED SHELF, AND INTERESTING USE OF WOOD FOR WALLS AND BUILT-IN FIRESIDE SEAT.

casements placed rather high in the wall over-looking the front recessed porch.

The little rear porch built under the main roof adjoining the kitchen may be glassed in winter and screened in summer, and will thus serve as an additional room for kitchen and laundry work.

The interior view given above shows the fireplace corner of the living room and gives a general idea of the appearance of the rest of the interior. The chimneypiece of split field stone, with the deeply recessed shelf, though simple in construction forms a very effective part of the structure, and emphasizes the hospitable air of the spacious room. The corner seat on the left, with its wainscoted back of wide V-jointed boards, could be made very comfortable with a few pillows, and the casement windows in the wall above as well as the small glass panes of the door that leads to the pergola porch at the rear, all help to make the room a pleasant, homelike place.

In this bungalow, as in most of the others shown, a few pieces of rustic furniture grouped about the porch would help to increase its

hospitality and comfort, and would insure the bringing of many little household tasks into the fresh air whenever the weather permitted. Seats could be placed on each side of the front porch beneath the casement windows, and rustic fittings could be used for the rear porch.

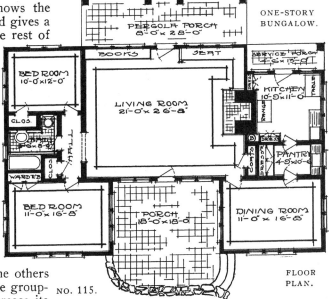

NO. 115.

PERMANENT SUMMER CAMP OF LOGS WITH TOP STORY ARRANGED FOR OUTDOOR SLEEPING

Published in The Craftsman, August, 1911.

PERMANENT SUMMER LOG CAMP: NO. 121.

WE have planned here a log building for a summer camp, so inexpensively and simply built that it can be closed with safety during the winter and easily put into livable order each spring.

The logs are placed upright and chinked with a mixture of one part Portland cement and three parts sand. This is a permanent chinking and will take a stain like the logs if desired. The main room, with fireplace and built-in seat, may be used as the dining room. The windows are casement, which are much cheaper than double-hung windows and can be easily removed and screens inserted for the

VIEW OF LIVING ROOM IN LOG CAMP, NO. 121, SHOWING STONE CHIMNEYPIECE AND BUILT-IN CORNER SEAT.

LOG CAMP WITH OPEN TOP STORY FOR OUTDOOR SLEEPING

ventilation of the rooms during the summer.

The main feature is the large open sleeping room upstairs which may be sheltered from wind or rain by duck curtains, and closed up entirely in winter by batten blinds. This sleeping room may be separated into as many small dressing rooms as desired by curtains run on wires or on wooden poles and drawn back when not needed to insure a free circulation of fresh air.

The illustration given here shows the rugged simplicity of the interior, which in spite of its rustic character, holds many possibilities for the making of a comfortable home. The irregular split field stone of the fireplace, with its broad opening and plain

SUGGESTION FOR A RUSTIC GARDEN SEAT.

shelf, the corner seat, the casement windows, with their small, square panes, and the sturdy construction of the logs and boards of walls and ceiling, all combine to form a picturesque background for whatever furnishings may be introduced. Rustic chairs and tables would, of course, harmonize perfectly with this type of construction, but plain oak pieces could be used if preferred, and willow would be both practical and appropriate. On the porch and beneath the trees about the building, rustic seats and benches and small tables would prove a welcome addition to the belongings of the camp, and would extend the boundaries of its comfort

NO. 121.

KITCHEN 10'-0"x17'-0"

RANGE   SHELVES

SEAT

UP

LIVING ROOM. 18'-0"x30'-0"

PERGOLA PORCH 10'-0"x32'-0"

SUMMER LOG CAMP.

FLOOR PLAN.

and hospitality. We are showing here sketches of a sheltered seat and arbor, which may serve to suggest other possibilities along the same lines. The putting up of such structures would be a delightful task for the boys of the party, who would no doubt welcome a chance to exert their ingenuity and muscles in such an effective way and prove their skill as builders and carpenters. In fact, a camp of this sort will be found to afford endless opportunities for the development of all those outdoor tasks and pastimes in which labor becomes a source of wholesome joy.

A DECORATIVE GRAPE ARBOR WITH FLOWERS PLANTED FROM POST TO POST

LOG BUNGALOW FOR SUMMER USE, WITH COVERED PORCH AND PARTIALLY OPEN SLEEPING ROOM

Published in The Craftsman, August, 1911.

SUMMER BUNGALOW OF LOGS NO. 122.

VERY like the one previously shown is this camp, both in purpose and general construction. Here, however, the logs are placed horizontally and a long porch is provided, covered, like the main roof, with Ruberoid. The stone fireplace and chimney add to the comfort and picturesqueness of the building, and the upper apartment, being open at both ends, provides an airy place to sleep.

From the porch a door leads into the large living room, and on each side of the door are groups of casement windows with small square panes. Similar windows are also placed in the opposite wall and on each side of the fireplace. In one corner is the staircase leading up to the big, airy room above. A wide opening from the living room leads into the kitchen, which is fitted with long shelves and a stove, and like the living room, has a door opening onto the porch and another door at

the rear. A closet is provided in the space beneath the stairs.

The interior view shows one corner of the living room with its stone chimneypiece and massive log construction. The heavy central

PERGOLA PORCH OF SPLIT STONE AND LOGS·

PART OF BIG LIVING ROOM IN LOG BUNGALOW NO. 122, SHOWING STONE CHIMNEYPIECE AND CASEMENT WINDOWS, AND EFFECT OF PRIMITIVE COMFORT RESULTING FROM THE WISE USE OF STRUCTURAL FEATURES.

log that runs across the ceiling is in reality two joined in the middle and supported by a post of hewn wood, like the pillars of the porch.

As to the porch itself, pergola construction could be used if preferred, with pillars of split stone, as suggested in the detail sketch, and another porch might be added at the rear of the bungalow if desired. In fact, like all the designs in this book, the plans and the construction may be modified to suit the special requirements of the owner.

The use of vines about the stone chimney and pillars of the porch will add greatly to the charm of the building, and make it even more definitely a part of its surroundings.

In this bungalow, as in the one previously described, box-seats can be built in around the rooms, providing useful storage space for the winter, and rustic chairs and tables, simple and easily made, will prove both an economical and harmonious form of furnishing.

With such a camp, hospitality can be extended indefinitely, for with a living room and kitchen, tent bed-

rooms, hammocks and sleeping bags will afford accommodations for week-end parties.

Since oxygen has proved such an important factor in the prevention and cure of disease, this bungalow, with its open upper story, would be just the thing for a consumptive patient or anyone whose health necessitated the greatest possible amount of fresh air, day and night. Its simplified interior would entail little work, leaving ample time for outdoor life.

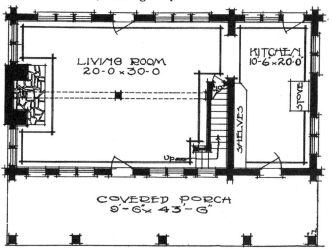

FLOOR PLAN OF LOG BUNGALOW: NO. 122.

CRAFTSMAN COUNTRY SCHOOLHOUSE OF LOGS

Published in The Craftsman, July, 1911.

CRAFTSMAN LOG SCHOOLHOUSE: NO. 119.

THE rural schoolhouse has in many instances grown into the poorest imitation of city educational institutions, in no way suited to the rural life and environment of farm boys and girls. In most cases as it exists today it not only does not fit them to understand, appreciate and make good in farm life, but actually creates a spirit of discontent with country existence and distaste for real work of any sort. This is a disaster not only to the community, but to the nation, to say nothing of the boys and girls.

America must, for progress' sake, have good country schools, suited to rural conditions. We must have townships that are successful without relation to cities, and people who are contented to dwell in the townships. How to bring this about is one of the most important economic questions of the times. It has seemed to us that something toward this end might be accomplished through the right kind of schools—schools that might become, as did the guildhalls of Mediæval times, the center of a widespread general activity and progress. Why make our schoolhouses such dull, uninviting spots that children must be driven into

them and parents never enter? Why not build schools which will develop the community spirit and definitely prepare the pupils for the kind of lives they are most likely to live? The school should suggest that work, if well done, is not drudgery, but one of the greatest factors in the betterment and uplifting of humanity.

Believing that what our country life needs so vitally is better social, economic and educational advantages, we are showing here two schoolhouses, each designed to be of service to every resident of the district where it is built.

The smaller schoolhouse. No. 119, is made of logs dressed on two sides so that they fit together—the inside and outside left round. The chinking is of cement mortar, which is permanent and takes a stain with the logs, if staining is desired.

The direction of the light is from casement windows at the back and left, and the teacher's desk is placed where full view is had of the two cloak rooms, which are provided with lavatories. Bookcases, closets and blackboards are arranged for in the main room. In rural schools all grades must be accommodated in

CRAFTSMAN COUNTRY SCHOOLHOUSE OF LOGS

CORNER IN SCHOOLHOUSE NO. 119, WITH FIREPLACE-FURNACE, BOOKCASES AND BLACKBOARD: THE ARRANGE-MENT OF STONE IN THE CHIMNEY AND MASSIVE EFFECT OF THE LOGS MAKE THIS AN INTERESTING INTERIOR.

one room, so low tables have been set in a bright corner for the little ones. Desk room is provided for forty-two students, and when lectures are given that interest the community at large the kindergarten table can be removed and extra chairs placed around the room, greatly increasing the seating capacity.

Both schoolhouses are planned to be heated and ventilated with a Craftsman fireplace-furnace, which is so simple in management that it can be taken care of by the children themselves. A great advantage of such heating is that fire can easily be kept over night so that the schoolroom will be warm in the morning.

The view of the interior shows the corner of the classroom in which the Craftsman fireplace-furnace is built. The recessed shelf and decorative placing of the irregular stones in the chimneypiece, and the massive effect of the logs make the interior very interesting from a structural standpoint, and the arrangement of the built-in bookcases, with their small glass panes, the casement windows, blackboards and closets, should prove practical and convenient.

Both this schoolhouse and the one on the next page are very simple in design, and could be enlarged to meet the special needs of the community. They suggest, however, what may be accomplished along these lines, and if they help to awaken keener interest in the important subject of rural education and to stimulate a desire for more practical, comfortable and beautiful country schools, they will have served their purpose.

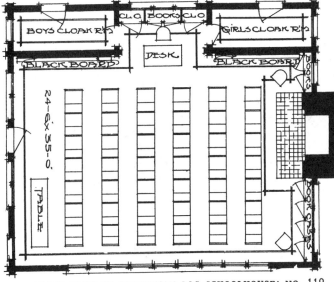

FLOOR PLAN OF CRAFTSMAN LOG SCHOOLHOUSE: NO. 119.

RURAL SHINGLED SCHOOLHOUSE PLANNED WITH CONNECTING WORKROOM

Published in The Craftsman, July, 1911.   RURAL SCHOOLHOUSE WITH CONNECTING WORKROOM: NO. 120.

ONE SIDE OF MAIN ROOM IN SCHOOLHOUSE NO. 120, WITH BRICK FIREPLACE-FURNACE AND BUILT-IN BOOKCASES.

RURAL SCHOOLHOUSE WITH CONNECTING WORKROOM

SHINGLES are used for this schoolhouse, for both roof and walls. Inside, the walls and ceiling are finished with plaster. The workroom is separated from the main room by folding doors, which can be thrown open to form a hall where lectures on scientific farming can be given, political meetings held, entertainments of a social nature enjoyed. This workroom is fitted with a fireplace of its own so that it can be used separately if desired. It may serve as a metal or woodworking shop, with the older boys in charge of the younger

FLOOR PLAN OF SHINGLED SCHOOLHOUSE: NO. 120.

ones at times. Or, it can be shut off from the main room while special instruction is given by visiting teachers to the advanced pupils. It can be used by the girls as a sewing room, and there are separate shelves or lockers on either side of the fireplace to hold the various materials which the children will require for their work.

Ample blackboard space is provided, as well as bookcases, which are behind glass and fitted with locks. The building-up of the library can be made the stimulus for much good work on the part of the students. They can sell the products of their handicraft in the workroom and purchase books with the proceeds, or use their studies in literature as basis for entertainments of various kinds. The older people of the district can also help collect books bearing on whatever subject will benefit the com-

munity at large in its various phases of activity.

The lighting of this building is from the back and left, so that the eyes of the pupils will not be put to needless strain, and the windows are casement, ample and attractive enough to satisfy the double purpose of use and ornament. There is desk room for fifty-six pupils, besides the kindergarten chairs at the low table, and the seating facilities can be greatly increased by extra chairs in the workroom when political and neighborhood meetings are held.

The study of botany should include practical demonstrations of flower-planting in the yard. A plot of ground can be set aside where wild flowers can be transplanted and cared for. Children can be taught to remove carefully a vigorous plant from among a colony of them where its loss will not be felt, and place it where its beauty will be fully enjoyed. They can study seed growth by growing garden flowers around their schoolhouse and thus learn also to beautify a place, a knowledge they will put to use in building their own homes later on.

The craftsmanship learned in the workroom can be put to various practical uses in the yard, so that all the pupils can have the pleasure of knowing they have helped to make the plot of ground set aside for them beautiful and serviceable. Classes in carpentry can be held in the yard, and fences built and gates made from designs of their own, perfected during the winter months in the school workroom, and demonstrations of practical forestry can be given when the flagpole is selected, felled, prepared and set up again.

In fact, a schoolhouse of this sort, while as simple and economic in design and construction as its rural location demands, should prove a very definite factor in the development of the community. We have merely suggested here a few of the ways in which the building and its facilities could be made of service to the pupils and their parents and friends, but other ways will no doubt suggest themselves with the increasing interest of the people in every department of their manual, mental and social life, and with their eagerness to keep in touch with the best of world progress.

CRAFTSMAN GARDENS FOR CRAFTSMAN HOMES

A CRAFTSMAN house should be surrounded by grounds that embody the Craftsman principles of utility, economy of effort and beauty. All these qualities it is possible for the average man to achieve in his garden by a little careful study and skilful planning. The majority of home owners today are people who must necessarily depend upon their own efforts for taking care of and beautifying their home grounds. As far as the men are concerned, they are as a rule workers in the city who could afford to give perhaps a part of Saturday and all day Sunday to any garden they had, with an occasional hour in the morning and the evening and holidays thrown in. This, of course, means that their gardens must be planned in such a way as to require the minimum amount of care and stand the maximum amount of neglect. In answer to the obvious question: "Since the time I could spend upon it is likely to be limited, could I really have much of a garden?" the answer is emphatically, "You can if you wish. You can have a most considerable garden of vegetables, flowers, fruit and berries that will quite fulfil the purposes of beauty and utility and give you a splendid outlet for your natural desire to grow things." The amount of ground you have is a ruling

factor, of course, in your plans, but even on the smallest suburban lot, say sixty by one hundred feet, perhaps less, a very satisfactory garden scheme can be worked out.

In order to illustrate practically just what can be done, we have taken four of our most popular designs for Craftsman houses and have made garden plans for them in which the most economical use of the surrounding land has been taken into consideration, and in which we have had regard also for beauty. In house number one we have taken a plot approximately seventy-five by one hundred feet and put on it a house that is about forty feet square, and we have pictured it as it would appear in the early spring. As will be noted, we have provided for a vegetable garden, a drying space, an orchard, a good-sized lawn and flower borders. In laying out the part devoted to vegetables we have suggested a large number of paths. These paths are almost a necessity. While they cut down the space, they make it possible for the home owner to hoe his vegetables without going up to his ankles in mud, and thus the garden is likely to get much more attention. The space as given does not seem large. It will, however, provide more vegetables than the average person would imagine, and would certainly grow sufficient of the staple vegetables to keep a family of four or five well supplied throughout the summer.

In choosing the vegetables you will plant, and, in fact, in considering the entire garden scheme, it is best to be careful not to plan for more than you can really take care of. Agree with yourself that you will be faithful to your garden; decide just how many hours you are sure you will be able to spend each week upon it, and err on the small side in making your estimate, rather than on the larger. Do not put into your vegetable garden things which will require a large amount of cultivating throughout the season, such as celery, which has to be banked up. Choose the standard things such as peas, beets, beans, green onions, carrots, spinach, radishes, limas, parsley, turnips, that practically can be had for the trouble of sowing, harvesting and a small amount of labor each week. Tomatoes, lettuce and asparagus require a little attention and should be added only after considerable thought. It is better not to have them than to have them come to nothing through neglect. You can have corn and squash and cabbage,

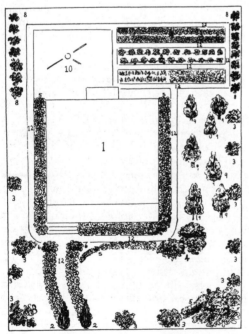

PLAN FOR PLANTING SPRING GARDEN: NO. 1.

CRAFTSMAN GARDENS FOR CRAFTSMAN HOMES

CRAFTSMAN HOUSE WITH SPRINGTIME GARDEN IN BLOOM: YELLOW PREDOMINATING: NO. 1.

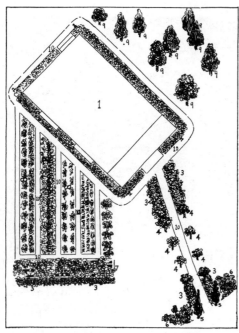

PLAN FOR PLANTING EARLY SUMMER GARDEN: NO. 2.

small fruits for the Craftsman garden are gooseberries and currants. These bushes ask practically no attention. Raspberries are possible, but they require cutting down each year. Blackberries should be avoided because they have a tendency to run wild. The plan provides, as can be seen, a good piece of lawn close to the house. It is best that this should be kept practically open and free from small flower beds or shrubs, as these are troublesome when the lawn is being mowed.

The character and color of the house itself must be very carefully taken into consideration in choosing and planting the flowers, shrubs and trees. It goes without saying that a house should have some trees about it; if there are any already on the ground, so much the better; if not, of course, they must be furnished. Trees of a very satisfactory size, quite large enough to be really impressive, can be bought from any nursery, and if the home owner can afford nothing else he should at the outset afford several good trees. Evergreens, such as cedars, spruces, firs and arborvitæ are most satisfactory because they decorate the grounds the year through. On the plan we have indicated a cedar tree at each side of the front gate. These grow quite tall and have a pyramidal shape that suits them especially for flanking the gateway. Maples grow rather quickly and one placed close to the house might be added to this plan, to take away any sense of bareness from the façade. Birches, because of their beautiful white bark, are decorative even in winter, and one ought to be included among the trees planted. Dwarf Japanese cut-leaf maples have a beautiful red foliage in spring and fall, and a place should be found for at least one where it will be seen against evergreens, if possible.

The flower garden should be planned with a view to its harmonizing in color with the house. The first illustrated is brown with a dark red roof. Success in making the colors of the flowers harmonize with the house is merely a matter of careful thought and planning. One can have from flowers almost as many colors as a painter can mix on his palette, and one can have them from early spring until late fall, and in the winter one can have shrubs with beautiful red, yellow or green branches. What are known as hardy herbaceous plants are the most popular ones now, and justly so. They are the best ones for a Craftsman garden because they mean the smallest amount of

and perhaps muskmelons and watermelons, too, if your space permits. If you wish to add potatoes you must be able to provide considerable land and time for them.

It is well to bear in mind that horticulture specialists are all the time studying to produce varieties of vegetables, fruits and flowers that will stand bad conditions and neglect and be free from pests. It is wise to get the catalogues of good seedsmen, read them carefully for suggestions, because they are usually reliable, and select those varieties of flowers and vegetables which are quoted as most hardy.

Fruit and some small berries can be included in the garden of a Craftsman house. Recently very satisfactory dwarf fruit trees have been developed. You can get apples, peaches, cherries, plums and nectarines. They grow to about six feet and are very compact of form, and produce for their size a large amount of perfect, good-flavored fruit. They are especially suited to a Craftsman garden because, though like all fruit trees they must be sprayed and pruned, these processes involve the smallest amount of labor and can be done from the ground instead of from ladders. In plan number one we have placed these trees on the south side of the house where they will get the largest amount of sun. The best

AN EARLY SUMMER CRAFTSMAN GARDEN IN ROSE, LAVENDER, BLUE AND WHITE: NO. 2.

trouble, and because they are likely to survive the largest amount of neglect. After they are once put out they stay in their places forever, and all they need is to be raked around with the hoe occasionally and to have their roots thinned out when they have begun to grow too thickly. Even when not in bloom they furnish decorative foliage to cover the bare earth. In planting the flowers make a careful selection so that you may have a succession of bloom and so that the colors of the flowers shall not clash with each other or clash with the house. Be careful not to put the magenta flowers against pink ones for example, or to have on the porch climbing roses that will not harmonize with the red of the roof, or purple against pink.

The suggestions we give for planting the garden of house number one will bring a general impression of a cheerful yellow all over the garden. In the garden scheme flowering shrubs must be included, and we have suggested here forsythia or golden bell as the most important shrub. To assist in giving the yellow effect we have included daffodils sprinkled thickly in the borders, also red and yellow tulips, yellow iris and yellow crocus. At each side of the steps we have placed a yellow peony. With these flowers in predominance an especially bright and sunny effect will be produced in the springtime. In the beds there will, of course, be other hardy annuals showing their foliage to fill in the bare spots. These will come out later, but they naturally also should be planted with an understanding of the combination of color they will make at their period of bloom, and its relation to the house. The plot surrounding this house is seventy-five by one hundred feet, room enough for a small garden.

House number two is built of grayish brown stone and brown shingles, and has a dull-green roof. The plot on which it is located is of slightly irregular shape, as plots usually are in the better class of properties. It is about one hundred and fifty by two hundred feet and slopes slightly up from the northeast to a level space, on the edge of which the house is placed, facing southeast in order to get the sunlight in the living room, dining room and main bedrooms.

In making the plan for the flower planting we have had in mind the general appearance of the place in early summer. These are the months when one can expect to get the best out of one's roses. A delightful rose for a Craftsman garden is the Japanese variety usually called rugosa, which seems to be proof against all floral ailments. It produces flowers somewhat like the wild rose, only larger and richer in color, and has a thick, somewhat lustrous foliage that makes it very satisfactory as a shrub as well as a flower. It is being constantly developed, and the newer proved varieties are sure to be satisfactory to the Craftsman gardener. It produces large red seed-pods that are extremely decorative in the fall. Rugosa roses can be planted freely among the shrubs. A climbing rose is always a cheerful decoration to a house. It softens the lines and gives shade if allowed to run over the porch. Some varieties of climbing roses bloom with an almost miraculous profusion. As the roof of the house is a dark green, we would suggest in this case a deep pink climbing rose. Standard roses are those that have been grafted to the top of a sturdy trunk, and usually stand two or three feet high, bushing out at the top. These can be planted at the edges of a walk, as we suggest in this plan. They have a note of formality that is not too strong to harmonize with a Craftsman house.

The choice of shrubs offered for this time

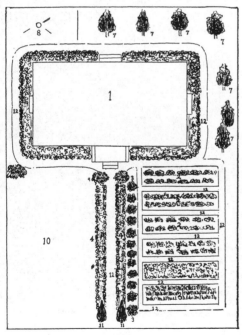

PLAN FOR PLANTING LATE SUMMER GARDEN: NO. 3.

A LATE SUMMER CRAFTSMAN GARDEN, WITH FLOWERS AND VEGETABLES SIDE BY SIDE   NO. 3.

CRAFTSMAN GARDENS FOR CRAFTSMAN HOMES

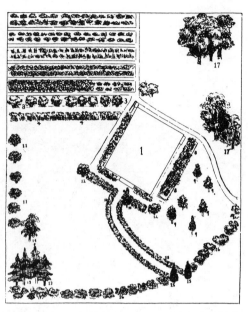

PLAN FOR PLANTING FALL GARDEN: NO. 4.

of the year is quite generous. We have in mind a scheme of coloring largely lavender and white. The key to this scheme will be set in shrubs by the lilacs which can be had in both white and lavender. There are Japanese snowballs, mock orange and spiræa for the note of white in the shrubs. Among the flowers, columbine, iris, forget-me-not and lily-of-the-valley will contribute to the general lavender and white effect, and will come in bloom in this period.

Grapes a Craftsman gardener can have without much trouble, and a grape arbor is included in the second plan. The vegetable garden is placed to the side and is screened from the road by the grape arbor, and gooseberry and currant bushes have been planted along another side to hide it partially from the main pathway to the house. If borders are placed on the lawn side of the arbor and the row of bushes the effect will be very satisfactory. There should also be borders in front of the house, and we have suggested that they run part of the way down the path from the house on both sides, and part of the way up from the gate on both sides, the standard roses serving to join the two effects of bloom. Poplar trees are of interesting shape, making slim pyramids, and are suitable to plant, as we have indicated in this plan, at the sides of the gateway. A low hedge of privet might be placed

at the edge of the lawn to separate it from the public roadway or sidewalk. Dwarf fruit trees would be effective on the slope at the east side of the house, and evergreens might be clustered behind the beds at the gateway and in the front corners of the plot. A maple tree and perhaps a birch might be planted close to the house.

An interesting arrangement of flowers for midsummer, that would harmonize with this house would be one emphasizing the blues and whites. This would make the garden seem cool during the hot July and August days when one prefers to have the red and yellow out of sight. The larkspurs, the campanulas or bell flowers, the aconitums or monkshoods, and the platycodons will make a good show of blue and white at this time. And among the shrubs deutzia and blue spiræa are in blossom.

Plan number three is made for the effect of late summer. One of the important features of this plan is the placing of the vegetable garden in front of the house. A properly kept vegetable garden is in its way as beautiful as a flower garden, and by treating it decoratively and letting it have here and there a few clumps of flowers, it can be made a very charming spot indeed. It will be in conformity with the Craftsman spirit that so essential a part of the home as the vegetable garden need not be hidden. In late summer this garden will have its vegetables well toward maturity, and if corn has been planted it will be showing its decorative foliage. As one method of marking the boundary of this vegetable garden we have placed gooseberry and currant bushes between it and the pathway to the house. The floral scheme consists of long borders at the edge of the path from the gate, and borders around the house. A few annuals, such as nasturtiums, poppies, asters and cosmos require so little attention that they can be used profusely in a Craftsman garden. This late summer plan calls for poppies at the front of the house. In the long borders beside the main walk the predominant flower is golden glow. Hollyhocks have been indicated in the beds at the side of the house. Unless somewhat protected from heavy winds, these are likely to be damaged, and so a sheltered location such as the one indicated is best. The plot for this garden is seventy-five by one hundred feet.

The substantial house we have chosen in

A BRILLIANT FALL CRAFTSMAN GARDEN, FOR LITTLE LABOR AND MONEY: TONE RED AND PURPLE: NO. 4.

this case is of cement with brownish yellow stone and a brown roof. The general effect of the flowers in the garden will harmonize well with this house, since the predominant colors are a warm yellow and white. Rose of Sharon is a good-sized shrub that blossoms in late summer. The white variety would be best for this planting. The house faces the north, and the dwarf fruit trees are placed to the south and west. The evergreens and other trees could be planted at the edges of the plot with the shrubs in between. An interesting arrangement would be to have little round box bushes flanking the gateway, and Rose of Sharon on each side of the pathway in front of the house.

The fourth garden plan contains suggestions for planting with fall effects in mind. Here again the house is on an irregularly shaped piece of property and on the brow of a slight slope. This piece of ground is about two hundred and twenty-five feet by one hundred and seventy-five feet, and the house is placed to face the northwest. The garden occupies ground to the northeast and is partly screened by gooseberry and currant bushes, before which is a flower border. In the front of the house are two borders with a path between, the one closest the house being filled with nasturtiums that keep up their bloom until frost, and the other devoted largely to red, white and yellow chrysanthemums. The path down to the gate is also fringed with nasturtiums.

One of the most beautiful fall flowers—an annual, by the way—is salvia. It is so wonderful in color that one can hardly afford to do without it, but it must be started indoors in March in "flats." Its color is so decided that it kills nearly everything else, and so should be very carefully handled. We have indicated salvia on one side of the house, where it will be seen almost alone and not clash with other flowers. Cosmos will last till frost and might be planted in the border shielding the vegetable garden, in some strong deep reds that would stand the proximity of the brilliant salvia. The grape arbor is placed to the southwest of the house, and the orchard of dwarf fruit trees on the slope to the southwest. What is known as Japanese barberry, that turns an exquisite deep red in the fall, makes a hedge of moderate height. This might be used to divide the lawn from the roadway. About the only shrub that can be

counted on at this time of the year is the hardy hydrangea, and we have suggested one placed at each end of the second border before the house. The Japanese cut-leaf maples have a gorgeous foliage in fall, and a good specimen tree of this would be effective near the house.

This is the time of the year when evergreens will be most useful, and a house to be occupied in the fall should have clumps of such trees planted about.

SCHEDULES OF PLANTING FOR EARLY SPRING GARDEN. 1.—House. 2.—Cedars. 3.—Shrubs: forsythia, spiræa, deutzia, etc. 4.—Banks of rose-bushes: Red, yellow and white rugosas. 5.—Border beds of hardy flowers: Daffodils, iris, crocus, tulips in bloom, backed by other flowers such as larkspur, columbine, phlox, bell flower. 6.—Peony bushes. 7.—Plots with vegetables. 8.—Gooseberry and currant bushes. 9.—Dwarf fruit trees in bloom. 10.—Drying ground. 11.—Lawn. 12.—Walks. (See page 168.)

SCHEDULE OF PLANTING FOR EARLY SUMMER GARDEN. 1.—House. 2.—Border: Lily-of-the-valley close to house, phlox. 3.—Border: Sweet-william, iris, phlox, etc. 4.—Standard rose-bushes. 5.—Poplars. 6.—Shrubs: Japanese snow-ball, mock-orange, spiræa, backed by small evergreens. 7.—Grape arbor. 8.—Vegetable garden. 9.—Dwarf fruit trees. 10.—Walks. 11.—Currant and gooseberry bushes. (See page 170.)

SCHEDULE OF PLANTING FOR LATE SUMMER GARDEN. 1.—House. 2.—Vegetable garden. 3.—Currant and gooseberry bushes. 4.—Borders with phlox and golden glow as main flower. 5.—Border with poppies. 6.—Borders with hollyhocks. 6a.—Lilies in the vegetable garden. 7.—Dwarf fruit trees. 8.—Drying yard. 9.—Rose of Sharon. 10.—Lawn. 11.—Pyramidal box bushes at gateway. 12.—Walks. (See page 172.)

SCHEDULE OF PLANTING FOR FALL GARDEN. 1.—House. 2.—Vegetable plot,—corn prominent. 3.—Currant and gooseberry bushes. 4.—Border with red and white cosmos. 5.—Border of salvia. 6.—Border of nasturtiums. 7.—Border with chrysanthemums: Red, white and yellow. 8.—Grape arbor. 9.—Dwarf fruit trees. 10.—Japanese cut-leaf maple. 11.—Shrubs. 12.—Hardy hydrangeas. 13.—Evergreens. 14.—Birch or pin oak. 15.—Pyramidal privets. 16.—Japanese barberry hedge. 17.—Old trees. (See page 174.)

PERGOLAS IN AMERICAN GARDENS

A DOUBLE PERGOLA, VINE-COVERED AND ROSE-GROWN: THE OVERHEAD POLES OF THE PERGOLA ARE OF CEDAR, AND THEIR RUSTIC EFFECT IS IN KEEPING WITH THE PLANTING SCHEME AND IN PLEASING CONTRAST TO THE FORMAL LINES OF THE HALF-TIMBER OF THE HOUSE FROM WHOSE PORCH THE PERGOLA STRETCHES FORTH.

WHATEVER connects a house with out of doors, whether vines or flowers, piazza or pergola, it is to be welcomed in the scheme of modern home-making. We need outdoor life in this country; we need it inherently, because it is the normal thing for all people, and we need it specifically as a nation, because we are an overwrought people, too eager about everything except peace and contentment. I wonder if anyone reading this article has ever in life received the following invitation, "Will you come and sit in my garden with me this afternoon?" I doubt it very much, at least in America. In England this would happen, or in Italy, and I think in Bavaria the people rest in their gardens at the close of the day and grow strong and peaceful with the odor of flowers about them, and the songs of birds. In a garden the silence teaches the restless spirit peace, and Nature broods over man and heals the wounds of the busy world. In essence a garden is a companion, a physician, a philosopher. It is equally the place for the happy, the sorrowing, for the successful, for the despondent.

And so here in America of all things we need gardens, and we must so plan our gardens that we shall live in them, and we must have in them our favorite flowers, long pathways of them, which lead us from gate to doorstep, and we must enter our gateway under fragrant bowers. We must build up arbors for our fruit, rustic shelter for our children, and above all these things our garden, which should be our outdoor home, must surely have a pergola, a living place outdoors that is beautiful in construction, that is draped in vines, that gives us green walls to live within, that has a ceiling of tangled leaves and flowers blowing in the wind, a glimpse of blue sky through open spaces and sunshine pouring over us when the leaves move.

PERGOLAS IN AMERICAN GARDENS

With a pergola in the garden you can no more escape living out of doors than you can avoid swimming in the sea if you happily chance to be living on the edge of the ocean. A pergola focuses your garden life. It is like a fireplace in a living room; it is the spirit of the outdoor environment held in one place to welcome you. It is essentially a place in which to rest, or to play or to do quiet domestic tasks; it is the outdoor home for children, for old folks, a spot in which to dream waking dreams or to sleep happily, or, best of all, for

on the other hand, as in one of the illustrations, it gracefully hides a group of unbeautiful farm buildings. It may lead to a beautiful garden or out to a wonderful view, or it may be the culmination of the garden scheme and furnish the only vista of which limited grounds are capable. It epitomizes modern outdoor life, and its beauty is through simplicity of construction and intimacy with Nature. A pergola inevitably means good simple lines of construction, beautified with vines, hidden with fruit or flowers, and with sunlight in splashes

SHOWING THE USE OF PERGOLAS TO HIDE IN A PICTURESQUE FASHION THE OUTBUILDINGS OF A FARM: THIS PICTURE IS A REPRODUCTION OF THE PERGOLAS AT THE STETSON FARMS, STERLINGTON, N. Y.

romance. For a pergola is a wonderfully inspiring spot in twilight, or when moonlit.

The outdoor living place is suited equally to any landscape or climate. It can be adjusted to any kind of architecture. It can be built directly with the house, a part of the architectural scheme, as in the original Italian pergolas, or it may be half-hidden at the end of a garden or creeping along the edge of the woods. It may convert a path into a cloister or a grape arbor into a summer house. It has many traditions but no formal rules.

It has been used as a triumphant architectural feature in a modern country house;

on the foliage, pillars, furniture and floor.

As we have already said, in construction a pergola may relate closely to the architecture of the house, or on the other hand it may suggest an ornamental addition of a later date and be developed in materials different from the house, or it may bear no relation whatever to the house construction. The adobe pergola is a fascinating feature of many of the Pacific Slope houses; yet one often sees the adobe house with a pergola or pergola porch of redwood, designed on straight lines with Japanese effect. In New England and on Long Island the pergola with brick sup-

PERGOLAS IN AMERICAN GARDENS

PERGOLA-PORCH FOR A COUNTRY HOUSE AT EAST HAMPTON, LONG ISLAND: THE PERGOLA PORCH IS RAPIDLY **TAKING** THE PLACE OF THE OLD-TIME PIAZZA.

PERGOLAS IN AMERICAN GARDENS

ports and wooden overhead beams is most usual, while out in New Jersey more often you find the pergola used in place of a porch, possibly a new feature of a quaint old house, and built of ordinary lumber, just as one would construct a trellis or a fruit arbor.

As a matter of fact, a pergola attached to the house is an ideal substitute for a piazza. This is especially true where there is the slightest tendency for the rooms to be somewhat dark, as it affords a decorative finish to the house, a charming resting place, a picturesque opportunity for vines, and yet permits all possible sunlight to reach the windows.

In one of the illustrations in this article the cement supports of the pergola are topped with rustic poles heavily draped with vines, and the effect is most picturesque. In fact, an entire rustic pergola is charming in an informal simple garden. It has, however, the drawback of not being as free from insects and dampness as the concrete structures.

As for the pergola "drapery," there is seemingly no limit to the beautiful things which the concrete or stone or brick columns will support. In the Far West some of the most beautiful pergolas are almost bowers of tea roses, intertwined with wistaria and monthly honeysuckle. In the East it is necessary to use the hardier roses, the Ramblers in different hues, white and red and pink. Wistaria is also one of the most attractive pergola vines when combined with others of the more hardy foliage and later bloom. It is difficult to get the monthly blooming honeysuckle in the East, but it proves most graceful as a pergola cov-

ering where it can be secured. Through the North, such vines as ivy, clematis and woodbine are all satisfactory, and nothing is more delightful than a pergola covered with grapevines, where the location and latitude are suitable, for the bloom of the grape is ineffable in the spring, the foliage is heavy through the summer and the fragrance and color of the fruit delicious in the fall. The delicately leaved jessamine with its sweet blossoms, the Allegheny vine, even more lace-like in foliage and graced by bells of white, the canary vine of yellow-orchid beauty, are unequaled for small, slender pergolas. The wild cucumber should be better known and appreciated, and also the bittersweet with its clusters of sweet white blossoms of springlike beauty, and its orange berries that break asunder at the first frost and reveal scarlet fruit which hang together, orange and scarlet, even when snow outlines twig and branch. The hop with its pale green pendant seed pods should be more in evidence in our garden as a decorative vine. The ornamental gourd is a quick-growing vine that can flourish verdantly while other vines are starting their slower climb, and its strange fruit can be put to a number of charming uses. The Dutchman's pipe is a vine whose curious flowers will repay cultivation.

It is always wise, in planning your garden, to plant about a pergola from two to four kinds of flower-bearing or fruit-bearing vines, so that each season will have its fragrance and color. It is also interesting to plant rows of shrubs at the foot of the supports and between the supports, that the whole structure may be more intimately connected with the ground.

Some pergolas are completely hidden by vines festooned from pillar to pillar; this is especially satisfactory in very hot climates. While others have vines twining only about the pillars with adequate protection overhead. This is by far the more classical and intrinsically beautiful method of treating a pergola. It has the disadvantage, however, of leaving the inner portion of the pergola a little less restful and homelike than when curtained by vines and shrubs.

For the newly built pergola there are many quick-growing vines which will give it a green and cheerful effect the first season,—morning-glo-

PERGOLA OF COBBLESTONES AND RUSTIC, WITH WISTARIA VINES.

PERGOLAS IN AMERICAN GARDENS

A PERGOLA-ARBOR, SHOWING AN INTERESTING APPLICATION OF THE PERGOLA IDEA TO AN OLD-FASHIONED GRAPE ARBOR, ESPECIALLY ADAPTED TO THE MORE SIMPLE TYPE OF COUNTRY ARCHITECTURE.

ries, scarlet runners, clematis, with castor beans at the entrance and geraniums at the sides and you have by July the effect of many years' growth.

Pergola gateways are attractive when bowered by flowering vines, and a driveway arched at the entrance with a simple pergola has charm hard to excel. A division or retaining wall can be redeemed from monotony by using it as one side of a pergola, constructing the pillars of brick if the wall is of brick, or of stone or concrete if the wall is of either of these materials. The rafters can be of rustic or square-hewn beams. Such treatment of a wall would have quite the spirit of cloister walks, and seats built in would heighten this monastic quality.

As to the materials to be used in construction of all pergolas, the resources of the immediate locality should be drawn upon in preference to all others. Stone piers built of cobble will be most suitable to one neighborhood, while split stone is better in another, and in some places it would be possible to have them

of whole field stone. Pillars of rough brick are decoratively valuable at times, terra cotta at others, cement at still others. They can be placed singly, in pairs or in groups to harmonize with the surrounding type of garden and house.

Turned wooden columns of classic design, either plain or fluted, are favorite supports for trellised roofs. Rustic pillars of cedar, fir, white pine, cypress, oak, madrone, redwood, with girders of the same wood a trifle small in size, are unequalled for informal gardens. Rustic is the most inexpensive material of which a pergola can be built, if it can be obtained with little cost of transportation, the square wooden supports coming next in order. Satisfactory combinations are sometimes devised, such as cement pillars and eucalyptus rafters and girders, stone supports with wooden rafters and trellis of various woods.

To preserve the true pergola form, to keep it from becoming an arbor, the trellis strips must not be put on horizontally between the pillars—this is the chief distinguishing note

PERGOLAS IN AMERICAN GARDENS

and must not be transgressed. Vines may be draped from pillar to pillar and not mar the purity of type, or trellis strips may be placed against the pillars, parallel with them, for vines to clamber upon, and purity of style be intact, but the horizontal feature must not appear upon the pergola—unless you want an arbor.

It is an excellent idea to plan a pergola with built-in seats at the sides and with rustic permanent tables, also with rough flooring for damp days. The joy of this garden feature is its livableness, to get the full satisfaction of which it must be a convenient homelike place for reading, sewing, afternoon tea, children's games. And of all things it should be the ideal spot for the writer or for the student, for working out of doors means working with health, and as a health-giving feature the properly constructed, properly draped pergola is second only to that other most wholesome development of modern building, the outdoor sleeping porch.

The pole pergola is a sort of pergola that is especially adapted to rustic surroundings, and many a restored cottage on abandoned farms has been made lovely by the introduction of such a feature, the poles having been cut from woodlot saplings. Even where all the materials had to be purchased,—cedar posts, plants, and the labor counted in—twelve or fifteen dollars, depending upon locality, would be fully sufficient to cover the whole cost.

The pergola-arbor illustrated on page one hundred and eighty-one is from the cottage of Mr. Frederick C. Keppel at Montrose, New York, designed by Edward Shepard Hewitt. For a pergola-arbor of this sort there could be no lovelier covering than the wild-grape, or the wild clematis, and, again, the kudzu vine, which comes to us from Japan and is found to be perfectly hardy everywhere, will, by reason of its extraordinarily rapid growth and luxuriant foliage of enormous rich green leaves, prove especially useful where a quick effect is desired.

The illustration on page one hundred and seventy-nine of a pergola porch on a country house at East Hampton, Long Island, exhibits another form of the pergola which requires far more restraint in planting, for it is intended that it should stand forth itself as an architectural feature; hence the vine-growth here will never be permitted completely to obscure the design of its support. The two great jars of terra-cotta add striking notes to the pergola and make this, in design, a successful house approach.

The pergola illustrated on page one hundred and seventy-eight is one connected with the outbuildings on the Stetson Farms, Sterlington, New York, designed by Alfred Hopkins. Here has been presented the problem of making the pergola serve, not only as a screen, but as a support for an overhead cartage rail which serves to facilitate the removal of stable litter expeditiously, neatly and hidden from observation. Ultimately the planting here will form a complete screen, summer and winter.

A PLEASANT VISTA OF APPROACH FORMED BY PERGOLA WITH RUSTIC ROOF SUPPORTED BY PILLARS OF CEMENT.

TWO BRICK BUNGALOWS WITH CYPRESS GABLES

Published in The Craftsman, February, 1912.

ROOMY ONE-STORY BRICK BUNGALOW: NO. 129.

BRICK is undoubtedly advancing in favor as a building material for houses. This is not only because people are demanding a more permanent form of home architecture, but because the wood supply of the country is becoming a matter for serious consideration, and some material must be found to take the place of wood, which is equally or even more satisfactory.

Brick nowadays is much more beautiful and durable than formerly. It shows significant signs of eventually superseding wood, at least in the exterior construction of houses, and is becoming a feature of interior finish as well. It is adapted to almost any style of building, whether large or small, furnishing a delightful note of color to any landscape, and carrying a distinct and pleasing individuality. Although the first expense of building a brick house is somewhat greater than that of a frame house, yet in the end it is decidedly the more economical, for after it is once finished it requires almost no additional expense to keep it in order, while a frame house requires constant repairing and painting. Is it not much more profitable to build better and repair less? Besides, there are other advantages. A brick house is more easily heated during the winter, and is far cooler in summer than a frame house.

Brick being practically fireproof, the rate of insurance is less, and being more durable the building does not deteriorate in value so quickly.

Perhaps one of the most notable things about modern brick is the way it is laid up, for the result is so much more interesting and beautiful than with the old-time method. The old brick was of a uniform red, laid up with a narrow white joint. This mortar was made of fine sand, cement and lime, and the joints were very narrow and pointed smooth. Sometimes these joints were painted a glaring white so there was no mistaking the regularity and perfection of the bond. But the modern brick is far removed from this, for the aim now is to avoid startling contrasts and pronounced colors. If the house is to be of red brick, they are used in many different harmonious tones; if of buff brick, they are in shades of old buff, golden brown and deep cream. These are placed in position about as they come, care being taken not to put together any two of a like tone. This gives an indescribable variety to the wall, an effect of great uniformity of tone, yet full of interest that is far superior to the monotonous solid red wall of old time.

The new mortar is made to produce a texture similar to that of the brick and is often

TWO BRICK BUNGALOWS WITH CYPRESS GABLES

one-third or one-half the thickness of the brick. This innovation is made practical by the improved method of the mixture. "Grit," sand, cement, lime and coloring matter are mixed according to an exact formula. The "grit" consists of small pebbles screened from sand in order to allow a perfect measuring of sand and "grit." The sand is coarse and sharp and is never taken from a beach, for in the spring the effervescing of salt water causes an unpleasant disfigurement of the wall.

We give one formula for mixing mortar, and it is hardly necessary to add that any for-

trowel, and the "raked out joint" made by cutting the joint back from the surface of the brick with the point of the trowel, a nail or a bit of wood. In both cases the mortar should show as much texture as the brick.

Believing, therefore, that there are great possibilities for durability and beauty in the modern use of brick, we have planned here two bungalows which embody several new ideas in brick construction. The use of brick in the interior as well as the exterior of these bungalows is of especial interest, and we are giving several drawings which show in detail

GLIMPSE OF LIVING ROOM, INGLENOOK AND DINING ROOM IN BUNGALOW NO. 129, SHOWING UNIQUE METHOD OF INTERIOR CONSTRUCTION INCLUDING THE USE OF BRICK, PLASTER AND WOOD FOR PARTITIONS AND WALLS.

mula used must be strictly adhered to throughout the building, so that no variation of shade mars the perfection:

"Grit"	3	parts
Sand	5	"
Cement	1	"
Lime Putty (hydrated lime)	½	"
Brown (paste)	⅓	"
Yellow (powder)	⅓	"
Black (paste)	1/50	"

The joints are finished in many ways, though the most frequently used are the "rough cut flush," made by allowing the mortar to ooze out beyond the surface of the brick and then cutting it off with a sharp, quick stroke of the

the great decorative effect obtained by this new method. Rough-surfaced, hard-baked brick, of several harmonious tones of red or brown, is to be used, which gives a rich sense of warm friendly color decidedly different from the old-time lifeless red.

In the exterior of these bungalows the brick has been combined with stone, relieved by wood in the upper story and by the ornamental as well as structural use of heavy beams. A detailed floor plan of the porch of the first house, No. 129, is given, showing how an interesting combination of concrete, brick and stone can be made. Dividing the floor space into three sections by the use of brick brings about a charming decorative effect, while the

TWO BRICK BUNGALOWS WITH CYPRESS GABLES

low stone balustrade gives a sense of seclusion and permits a note of color to appear in the form of flowers or ferns placed upon the low corner posts.

Formerly the brick walls of a house were laid up in an eight- or twelve-inch solid wall, and the plaster was put directly on the inside of the wall. A wall constructed in this way sweats, so it was found necessary to furr it, leaving an air space between the brick wall and the plaster.

The walls of these bungalows are made by erecting two four-inch walls, side by side, leaving a two-inch space between. These walls are tied together by metal tie straps inserted every few courses. This provides a good air space all around the house, giving perfect insulation from heat and cold, and at the same time it allows the use of fancy brick for the inside wall, which considerably lessens the expense of building. The cost of furring will be saved also, for the plaster can be put directly on the inside wall, as the air space will prevent condensation of moisture, or sweating. The partitions of these houses are of brick, the wall at the baseboard, side and head casings being eight inches thick, while the panels between are only four inches thick. These panels are plastered on both sides, leaving a reveal between the plastered panels and casings of

about one and one-quarter inches. Doors and windows are hung on jambs only, expensive frames and trim being thus saved. This treatment of the walls gives æsthetic quality to the whole interior.

The use of brick in the interior of a house not only lends it decorative charm and individuality, but is a source of economy. The in-

FLOOR PLAN OF ONE-STORY BRICK BUNGALOW: NO. 129.

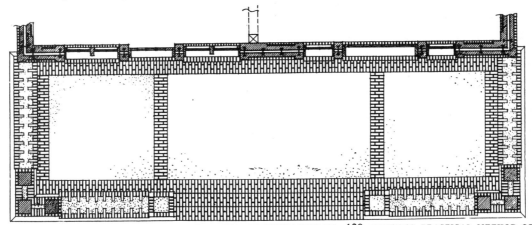

DETAIL FLOOR PLAN OF FRONT ENTRANCE PORCH OF BUNGALOW NO. 129, SHOWING PRACTICAL METHOD OF CONSTRUCTION, DECORATIVE USE OF BRICK AND CONCRETE, AND EFFECTIVE GROUPING OF CORNER POSTS.

TWO BRICK BUNGALOWS WITH CYPRESS GABLES

Published in The Craftsman, February, 1912.   BRICK BUNGALOW WITH PORCHES AND PERGOLA COURT: NO. 130.

terior wood finish of a house is always expensive, because it requires skilled labor, the best of materials, and cannot be done quickly.

The main walls only of these houses have been planned to be built of brick, but where partitions are only suggested—as between the living and dining rooms and inglenook of the first bungalow, No. 129—we have used the post and panel construction in wood. As the interior view shows, wooden ceiling beams mark the division between the rooms and run around the walls above the brick frieze; and the built-in seats and bookshelves of the nook, as well as the long window seat in the dining room, are all of wood, the seats being paneled with V-jointed boards. Not only does this use of woodwork add to the friendly quality of the interior, but it serves as a link between the structural features, built-in fittings and the rest of the furniture, while the combined effect of the brick, plaster and wood gives to the rooms an interesting sense of variety of textures and materials, and yet does not mar the underlying harmony of the whole.

The unity introduced into a room by a consistent color scheme is not, however, the only necessary element of harmony. Another factor is needed: namely, design. Now brick not only furnishes the uniformity of color requisite to carry out whatever tone harmony is desired, but it can also be laid in a pattern which will either emphasize the prevailing style of the room or else be in itself the suggestive or dominating note. Brick as now manufactured lends itself to various forms of design, for it comes in so many sizes that almost any geometric pattern can be carried out with it, and the finished frieze, support or arch will have almost the quality of a mosaic.

A frieze such as we have designed in these two bungalows, running around the whole room, has therefore the double interest of pleasing color and design. The interior view of bungalow No. 129 and the details given of the two fireplaces in the second bungalow, No. 130, illustrate the decorative results of this method of wall treatment. If the bricks are well chosen as to color and laid with good judgment and taste, they are most effective, and add to a room a rich note not unlike that of old tapestries. They can be laid in many patterns, intricate or simple, according to the

TWO BRICK BUNGALOWS WITH CYPRESS GABLES

PERGOLA COURT WITH CENTRAL FOUNTAIN IN BUNGALOW NO. 130: A MOST INVITING SPOT FOR OUTDOOR LIFE.

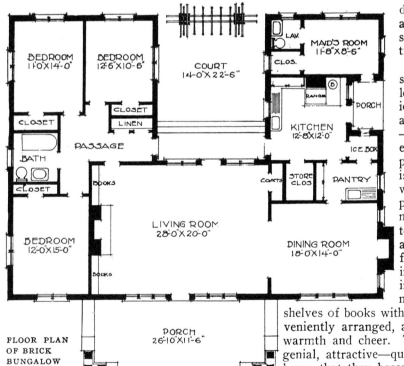

FLOOR PLAN OF BRICK BUNGALOW NO. 130.

desire of the owner. We are showing three simple styles that are both practical and pleasing.

In planning the floor space of the first bungalow, No. 129, convenience—always an important item in home building—was carefully considered, and a study of the plan will reveal how satisfactorily it has all been worked out. A roomy, pleasant, homelike atmosphere is noticed on entering the house, brought about partly by the view from the large living room into the bright sunny dining room, and the cozy nook by the fireplace with shelves of books within easy reach, lights conveniently arranged, and an open fire to give warmth and cheer. The whole effect is rich, genial, attractive—qualities so endearing in a home that they become another cause of desire for permanence.

TWO BRICK BUNGALOWS WITH CYPRESS GABLES

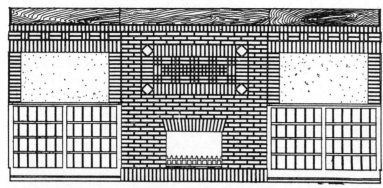

WALL IN LIVING ROOM OF BUNGALOW NO. 130, SHOWING USE OF BRICK IN CHIMNEYPIECE AND AROUND THE ROUGH PLASTER PANELS OVER THE BOOKCASES.

the warmth and cheerfulness of its welcome.

The placing of the bedrooms upon one side of the house and the kitchen and dining room upon the other is particularly happy, for each is thus practically shut off from the other. The pergola court with hanging vines and splashing fountain makes a delightful passageway between the two divisions. A small hall near the living room permits indirect entrance into the bedrooms, thus giving a desired sense of privacy. The kitchen is provided with a convenient and pleasant little porch, similar to the one in No. 129. And there is also a large ice-box, pantry, store closets, two sinks, with the maid's room within

Every convenience has been planned for the kitchen. The pantry, which is indispensable for serving and prevents the kitchen odors from entering the dining room, is fitted with a sink and a drain board on each side. Another sink and large drainboard are placed in the kitchen under the windows so that plenty of light can be had at this necessary working place. The range is within easy reach, a good-sized storeroom is provided, and even a cheerful kitchen porch, which serves the combined purpose of separating the maid's sleeping room from the kitchen, giving access to the refrigerator, and holding extra vegetables and different working accessories of the kitchen.

The bedrooms are shut off from the kitchen side of the house and the bath is placed conveniently. Not a particle of space is wasted in this plan, which includes living room, dining room, kitchen, maid's room, three other bedrooms, hall, bathroom, many closets and two porches, either of which is large enough for an outside living room in summer.

The floor plan of the second bungalow, No. 130, is if anything even more interesting than the first one. This gives a large living room with a dining room which is practically an extension of it. As one enters this room a direct view is had into the open pergola court, and also the fireplaces of both rooms can be seen, which gives a combined sense of home comfort and outdoor delight. The color of this room, brought about by the rich tones of the rough-surfaced brick, is especially restful, and the light from the fireplaces and from the windows that open onto the court add to

DINING-ROOM WALL IN BUNGALOW NO. 130, WITH PRACTICAL AND DECORATIVE BRICK CONSTRUCTION IN CHIMNEY, WALLS AND FRIEZE.

rect entrance into the bedrooms, thus giving a desired sense of privacy.

easy reach, yet separated by the porch. There is a similar number of rooms in each house, the court of one taking the place of the second porch of the other, but the arrangement of the given space is decidedly different in each bungalow; each one is attractive in an individual way to suit the needs or pleasures of different people, yet both are practical and homelike.

These bungalows have been designed especially for Eastern climates and are therefore fitted with Craftsman fireplace-furnaces which thoroughly heat and ventilate each building.

CONCRETE BUNGALOWS: ECONOMY OF CONSTRUCTION ATTAINED BY THE WAY THE FORMS ARE USED

I AM presenting here two Craftsman bungalows embodying a practical and economical idea in concrete construction. I believe that this new method, which is illustrated with perspective views and working drawings, will mean a reduction in cost and an increase in efficiency over the methods hitherto used, and so will be of interest to architects, builders and all who are considering the problem of building a home.

In order to make clear this new process of construction it may be well to explain briefly those usually employed. When concrete was first used it was found to be an ideal building material, indestructible and fireproof. The problem, however, was just *how* to use it to the best advantage. Solid concrete walls were built at first, but these had a serious disadvantage. Concrete is a good conductor of heat and cold and is affected by changes of temperature and varying atmospheric conditions. In winter, therefore, the cold air outside the house chilled the solid concrete walls, making the inner surface colder than the air within the rooms; whereupon the warm air within the house, coming in contact with the cool wall, was at once chilled, decreasing its moisture-holding capacity and causing the surplus moisture to condense upon the cool inner surface and run down the walls. This is what is known as sweating, and the dampness produced not only made the rooms chilly and unwholesome, but also stained and discolored the wall coverings and hangings.

Various methods were devised in an attempt to obviate this difficulty and to construct a solid concrete wall which would not sweat. Furring was used—that is to say, strips of wood were placed at intervals against the inner surface of the solid concrete wall, and lath and plaster were applied, the air space left between the concrete and the plaster serving as an insulation and thus preventing sweating. This construction, however, besides not being fireproof, involved the extra cost of wood and plaster, much time and labor, and so has never been considered quite satisfactory. Such a structure, moreover, is not ideal from an architectural standpoint, for it represents an attempt to remedy or cover up the defects of an unsatisfactory structure by imposing a superstructure not so durable.

At the present time one of the most widely used and efficient forms of concrete construction is the hollow concrete block. But even in this a serious objection is present, for although the hollow spaces extend vertically through the blocks at close intervals, and thus provide frequent air spaces between the inner and outer surfaces of the completed wall, the sides of the blocks which form the divisions between the holes still serve as a connection between the inner and outer surfaces of the wall, forming an occasional but nevertheless active conductor of heat and cold. The wall is thus only partially insulated, and sweating takes place to some extent wherever this solid connection occurs.

Concrete walls have also been made so as to include a continuous insulating air space, but these have either been cast in one piece or else expensive interchangeable metal forms have been used, and both methods, though efficient, have rendered the cost of construction high.

The only drawback to this last method being its expense, I have worked upon the theory that the most satisfactory form of concrete wall is one which can be cast with a continuous vertical air space, or other insulation, between two thicknesses of concrete, yet built

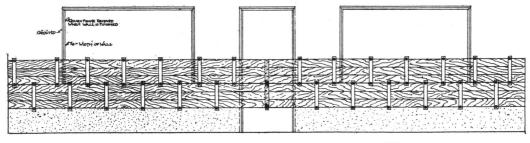

FIG. 1: ELEVATION OF FRONT OUTER WALL OF LIVING ROOM IN BUNGALOW NO. 131, IN PROCESS OF CONSTRUCTION, SHOWING DOOR AND WINDOW FRAMES SET IN WOODEN FORMS PREPARATORY TO FILLING IN CONCRETE.

ECONOMICAL CONCRETE CONSTRUCTION

Published in The Craftsman, March, 1912.

ONE-STORY CONCRETE BUNGALOW WITH SHINGLED GABLE AND RUBEROID ROOF: THE CONSTRUCTION IS ESPECIALLY ECONOMICAL OWING TO THE WAY IN WHICH THE WOODEN FORMS ARE USED IN CASTING THE CONCRETE WALLS (SEE WORKING DRAWINGS): NO. 131.

ECONOMICAL CONCRETE CONSTRUCTION

in such a way as to necessitate only the simplest, fewest and least expensive forms possible. I have decided, therefore, to use wooden forms, which cost much less than the metal ones and can be put up right on the building site by any carpenter, the forms being interchangeable, so that they may be used again and again as the wall is gradually built up, thus minimizing the number of forms required. I have also tried to devise reinforcing ties that would be sufficiently strong and yet as simple and economical as possible.

In designing the two bungalows which illustrate this new process, I have omitted the cellars because this permits a concrete foundation on which the concrete partitions of the house can be built. The omission of a cellar is a considerable saving of time, labor and materials, and if the bungalows are heated and ventilated by a Craftsman fireplace-furnace the only excavation needed would be for the ash-pit. If a different heating system is desired, however, with the furnace located in the cellar, a sufficient space can be excavated for this purpose, in which case, of course, the coal bin would be included in the cellar instead of being on the ground floor. But if the cellar is used the usual wooden partitions would be built instead of the solid concrete partitions shown in these bungalows, as the excavation would prevent the use of the concrete foundation needed as a base for the concrete walls.

With the form of concrete construction used here, a trench is dug for the base of the outside walls. This trench is made deep enough to carry the walls below frost level, and the foundation walls are built up to the height desired. The ground enclosed by these walls is leveled off, covered with a layer of cinders, and on top of this is poured a layer of concrete. Nailing strips, 2 x 2, to which the wood flooring of the house may be nailed, are placed in this concrete layer while it is still soft, and the concrete which fills the spaces between these strips is leveled off flush with the top of them. This hardens and forms an inexpensive, practical and sanitary foundation. The exterior concrete walls extending below frost level prevent any frost from penetrating beneath the floors of the bungalow; the bed of cinders forms an insulation by taking up any

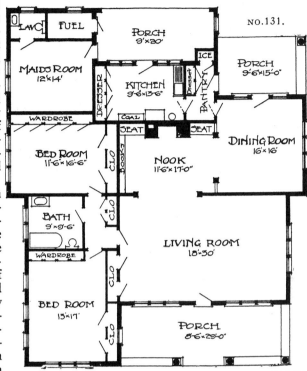

FLOOR PLAN OF CRAFTSMAN CONCRETE BUNGALOW.

moisture, and the concrete layer beneath the flooring gives the necessary base for the concrete partition walls of the interior.

The walls—which are preferably of cinder concrete—are cast in wooden forms. Each form consists of matched sheathing boards ⅞ inch thick and 5½ inches wide—known as the ordinary 6-inch sheathing boards—three of which are fitted together as shown to make each side of the form, which is thus 16½ inches deep. These three boards are then fastened together by wooden strips or cleats, D, nailed to the form at intervals of about 24 inches as shown in Figure 3, which represents part of two of the forms during the casting operation. Bolts are provided which extend through the cleats and sides of the form, each bolt head having two projections or pins, and a beveled washer, B, being inserted between the head of the bolt and the inner side of the form, as shown in Figure 2. The outer end of the bolt has the usual washer and nut which may be screwed up to secure the parts rigidly in place.

Three similarly joined boards are held in place opposite the first, to make the other side

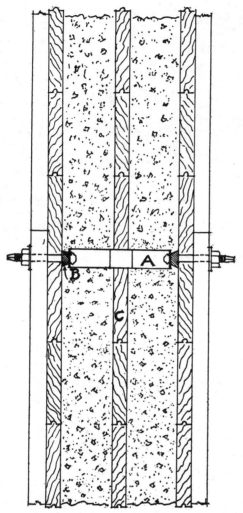

FIG. 2: VERTICAL SECTION THROUGH TWO OF THE WOODEN FORMS USED IN CONSTRUCTION OF BUNGALOWS NOS. 131 AND 132, SHOWING CENTRAL INSULATING BOARDS EMBEDDED IN CONCRETE AND HELD IN PLACE BY METAL REINFORCING TIE.

mum swelling point. Thus, when they are embedded in the concrete wall, they will shrink and become somewhat loose, leaving a slight air space on either side and so more completely insulating the concrete surfaces. Three of these boards are fitted together and temporarily fastened by means of wooden laths, and a saw notch is made in the edge of each outside board to receive the metal tie which is to hold the parts together. This reinforcing tie, A, which is 1½ inches wide and ⅛ inch thick. is bent in the center, as seen in the drawings, in order to hold the insulating boards in position and prevent any side motion of them during the casting operation. The ends of this tie are bent and provided with holes having opposite notches which register with projections or pins on the heads of the bolts. This allows the bolt heads of each wooden form to be passed through the holes in the ends of the metal ties; whereupon the bolts are given a part turn so that the projections will hold the tie in place, the nuts are screwed up tight and the two sides of the wooden form and the central insulating boards are thus held rigidly in position the required distance apart.

A sufficient number of wooden forms are constructed to allow them to be placed around the foundation of the house, in two rows, one above the other, and the upper row is fitted to the one below by means of the cleats as shown in Figures 1 and 3, with the central insulating boards and reinforcing ties in place as just described. The mixture of concrete is then poured in from above until it fills the spaces between the sides of the wooden forms and the central boards, and as the mixture is sufficiently liquid to spread and fill all the crevices, a solid wall is obtained.

This is left standing until it has set, after which the lower of the series of wooden forms is removed by simply loosening the nuts that hold the securing bolts, giving each bolt a slight turn to allow its head and projections to be withdrawn through the hole and notches in the bent end of the metal tie, and then pulling away bolts, inside washer and wooden forms from both sides of the concrete wall. This leaves a solid construction consisting of two thicknesses of concrete with the continuous insulating boards in the center, all held together rigidly by the metal reinforcing ties which are left embedded in the wall.

The holes left in the sides of the concrete by the removal of the inside washers are pointed

of the form, the two sides being 8 inches apart, with the central insulating boards, C, between and parallel with them. These are also sheathing boards, the same as those used for the sides of the form. These boards are selected because they are comparatively inexpensive and are always carried in stock, and by having the outside forms and the central insulating boards of corresponding sizes, the work of building up and casting the walls is greatly simplified. Before using these insulating boards they should be soaked in water for 24 hours, which will bring them to their maxi-

ECONOMICAL CONCRETE CONSTRUCTION

up with a trowel, and any ridges or unevenness caused by the joint or roughness of the boards are smoothed off with a wooden float. This gives an interesting sand finish to the concrete, and if a perfectly smooth finish is desired a steel trowel may be used and a skim coat applied.

Another series of central insulating boards, C, is then fitted above those of the second row, provided with metal reinforcing ties, A, with the bottom row of forms, just removed, fastened on either side of the central insulating boards, the cleats being always arranged in staggered relation as shown in the drawings. The bolts are then tightened and concrete is again poured into the molds around the walls of the house.

This process is repeated, one layer of concrete being cast each day, until the entire outer walls are completed. By estimating the amount of time and labor required for each daily operation, the exact number of men needed can be employed, putting the work on a most economical basis.

One of the most practical features of this construction is the simple way in which the doors and windows are set into the outside walls. In building up the forms and casting the successive layers of concrete around the house, wherever such an opening is needed, the rough frame of a door or window is placed inside the wooden forms, with the sides of the frame at right angles to the sides of the forms: see Figure 1. This frame, which consists of side and top boards, rests on the hardened concrete layer below, and is temporarily fastened to the forms to hold it in place while the wall is being cast. It is provided with vertical grooves, as shown in Figure 4, to insure its being locked firmly in the concrete. As this rough frame is only 4 inches wide and the wall is 8 inches wide, a temporary rough inner frame, 8 inches wide, is fastened to the 4-inch frame, thus closing the door or window opening during the casting operation. The concrete is then poured into

FIG. 3: VIEW OF PART OF TWO WOODEN FORMS DURING CASTING OPERATION, SHOWING ARRANGEMENT OF CLEATS, METAL TIES, INSULATING BOARDS AND CONCRETE.

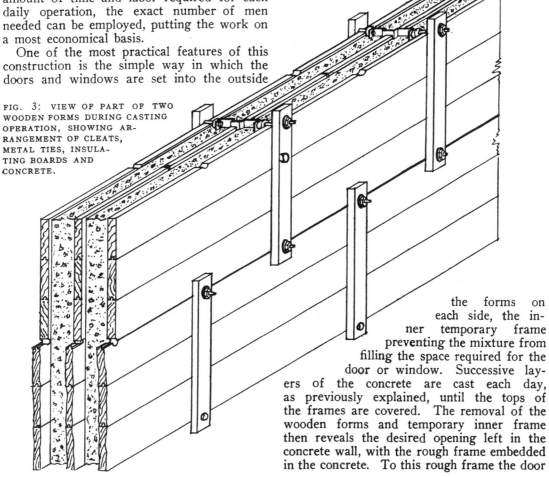

the forms on each side, the inner temporary frame preventing the mixture from filling the space required for the door or window. Successive layers of the concrete are cast each day, as previously explained, until the tops of the frames are covered. The removal of the wooden forms and temporary inner frame then reveals the desired opening left in the concrete wall, with the rough frame embedded in the concrete. To this rough frame the door

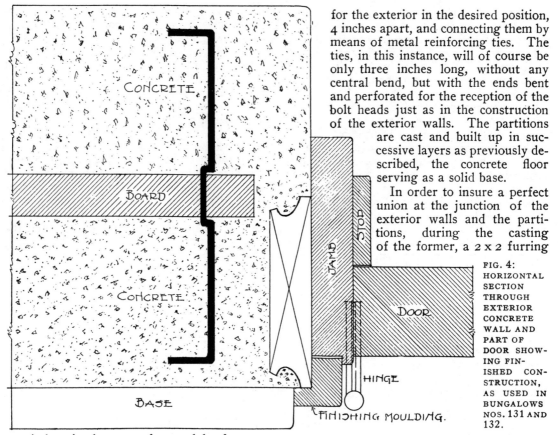

for the exterior in the desired position, 4 inches apart, and connecting them by means of metal reinforcing ties. The ties, in this instance, will of course be only three inches long, without any central bend, but with the ends bent and perforated for the reception of the bolt heads just as in the construction of the exterior walls. The partitions are cast and built up in successive layers as previously described, the concrete floor serving as a solid base.

In order to insure a perfect union at the junction of the exterior walls and the partitions, during the casting of the former, a 2 x 2 furring

FIG. 4: HORIZONTAL SECTION THROUGH EXTERIOR CONCRETE WALL AND PART OF DOOR SHOWING FINISHED CONSTRUCTION, AS USED IN BUNGALOWS NOS. 131 AND 132.

or window jambs may afterward be fastened, leaving a concrete reveal. When several windows are grouped together, making an extra wide opening in the wall, like those shown in Figure 1, the top of the opening is reinforced to center the load, and the frame is propped in the middle until the mullions are inserted, after which the prop may be removed.

From this description and the drawings it will be seen that the walls are cast in successive layers all around the house, unhindered by the door and window openings, which are thus provided for at the same time.

The interior or partition walls of the bungalow are somewhat different in construction, for the temperature on either side of them will be practically the same, no moisture will condense, and so no central insulation will be needed. For these partitions, therefore, solid concrete can be used. Each partition is 4 inches thick and is made by placing the wooden forms used

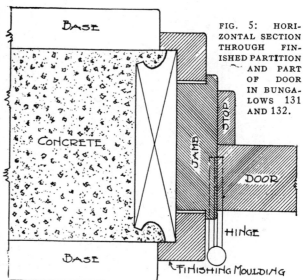

FIG. 5: HORIZONTAL SECTION THROUGH FINISHED PARTITION AND PART OF DOOR IN BUNGALOWS 131 AND 132.

strip is placed upright on the inner side, within the wooden form, at the point from which the partition wall is to extend. When the forms are removed this furring strip is also pulled away, leaving a vertical groove on the inner side of the concrete wall. Afterward, when the partition is being cast, the concrete poured into the wooden forms fills this vertical groove, hardens, and ties the outside and inside walls of the house firmly together. Thus when the whole has been cast, foundation, walls and partitions will form practically an integral construction.

Usually, in building a house, the interior trimming is one of the most expensive items, often representing one-fourth of the total building cost, for it involves both expensive materials and skilled carpentering. With the method of construction used here, however, this expense is reduced to a minimum.

In constructing the partitions of these bungalows, openings are left in the 4-inch concrete walls by inserting rough wooden frames within the wooden forms and casting the wall around them just as in the case of the exterior walls, the rough wooden frames serving as a foundation to which the door jambs are afterward fastened. In this instance, however, no temporary inner frame is needed, the walls and rough frames being the same width. This construction will be seen clearly by reference to Figure 5, which shows, in horizontal section, the concrete partition with baseboards on either side, the rough frame embedded in the concrete, the door jamb fastened to the rough frame and rabbeted to receive the finishing moldings, the rabbet being sufficiently deep to prevent any crack showing if the wood shrinks, and tight enough to insure a close fit between jamb and moldings. The

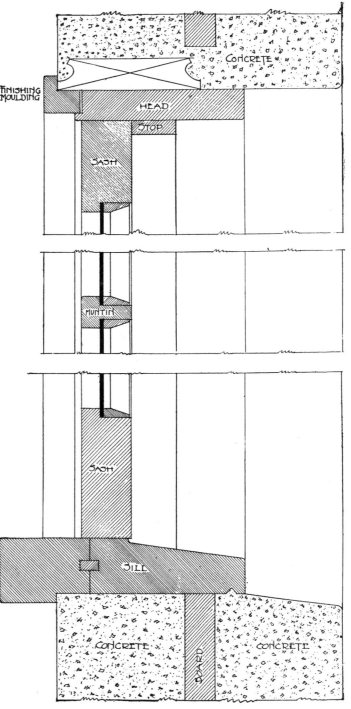

FIG. 6: VERTICAL SECTION THROUGH WINDOW IN CONCRETE CONSTRUCTION USED FOR BUNGALOWS NOS. 131 AND 132, SHOWING HOW THE VARIOUS PARTS ARE SET INTO THE OPENING IN THE CONCRETE WALL.

ECONOMICAL CONCRETE CONSTRUCTION

Published in The Craftsman, March, 1912.

ONE-STORY CONCRETE BUNGALOW SHOWING PRACTICAL AND DECORATIVE USE OF WOODEN BEAMS FOR PILLARS AND GABLE OF PORCH: THE ECONOMICAL FORM OF CONCRETE CONSTRUCTION USED HERE IS EXPLAINED IN DESCRIPTION AND WORKING DRAWINGS: NO. 132.

ECONOMICAL CONCRETE CONSTRUCTION

door stop is fastened to the jamb and the door is hung in the usual way. The edges of the rough frame will serve as "grounds" for the plasterer.

These parts and similar parts for the windows, constitute practically all the interior trimmings required, and the material can be got out in the mill and sent to the job already stained and finished, so that all which is needed is for the carpenter to miter the pieces at the corners and put them in place. In this way the whole interior can be trimmed at little labor and expense, compared with that usually incurred.

The gables of both bungalows are shingled, the roofs are of Ruberoid, and the chimneys, though shown of concrete, would be equally or possibly more satisfactory if of brick. In each case the rooms are all on one floor, as compact as possible and yet with a hospitable sense of openness in the arrangement of living and dining rooms, inglenook and porch spaces.

In bungalow No. 131 the entrance door leads from the recessed corner porch, with its concrete pillars, parapets and flower-boxes, directly into the spacious living room, made cheerful by three pleasant window groups and by the welcome vista of the inglenook at the farther end. From the dining room, through another wide opening, a glimpse is also had of this pleasant nook, with its open hearth, built-in bookshelves and fireside seats, so that both rooms share its comfort and friendliness. An interesting feature of the left-hand fireside seat is the fact that it may serve as a storage place for coal, which may be put in from the kitchen and taken out in the nook as needed for the fire.

From the dining room a door leads to the corner porch at the rear, where meals can be served in warm weather. Doors also lead from the dining room and porch to a small square passageway communicating with the kitchen and pantry. The kitchen in turn opens upon a recessed porch which will serve as an outside kitchen or laundry. Off one side of this porch is the coal bin and a door to the maid's room, which is provided with a lavatory. Two bedrooms, bathroom and ample closets occupy the rest of the floor plan, being shut off from the living room by a small hallway.

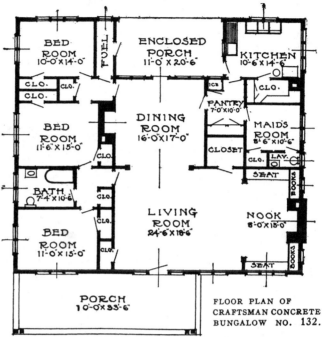

FLOOR PLAN OF CRAFTSMAN CONCRETE BUNGALOW NO. 132.

In bungalow No. 132 a somewhat different arrangement is shown. The large living room and dining room are planned with only a slight division between, so that upon entering from the front porch one has a vista through both rooms to the dining-room windows in the rear which overlook the enclosed porch. The inglenook occupies the whole right-hand end of the living room, and on each side of the chimneypiece are built-in bookcases and seats. A large closet is also provided, and a smaller closet is placed at the left of the entrance door for umbrellas, wraps, etc. A fireplace is also built in the dining room. In one corner of the plan are pantry, kitchen, maid's room and lavatory, with ample closet space and shelves. The kitchen communicates with the enclosed porch at the rear, which will serve as an open-air dining and living room, and on the opposite side of which is a place for fuel. Three bedrooms and bathroom are provided on this side of the bungalow, with plenty of closets both in the rooms and in the small hallways between them.

The compactness of both bungalows will minimize the household work, and either design would be suitable for those who do not wish to keep a maid, as the bedroom set aside for that purpose would serve equally well for one of the family.

THE CRAFTSMAN FIREPLACE: A COMPLETE HEATING AND VENTILATING SYSTEM

ON account of the number of inquiries that have been received in regard to the Craftsman fireplace-furnace, I have thought it advisable to publish another description and set of drawings, embodying several improvements over the form of fireplace originally shown. These improvements have simplified not only the construction of the heater but also the work of installing it.

As shown in Figures 1, 2 and 3, the heater body is made of large sheets of steel, welded together by special welding machinery into

VIEW OF CRAFTSMAN FIREPLACE OF TAPESTRY BRICK, WITH OPEN HEARTH AND ANDIRONS FOR BURNING WOOD.

THE CRAFTSMAN FIREPLACE

one piece of continuous metal, making leakage of gas, smoke or dust an impossibility. It is so constructed that each smoke compartment is self-cleaning; the smoke areas being vertical, there is no place for soot and moisture to collect. The heater is six feet high and four feet wide and weighs complete with grates and other iron parts needed in the construction about 1,000 pounds.

Grates for the burning of coal or coke are supplied with each heater. These consist of only three parts and are easily and quickly set in place. Figure 1 shows the removable metal hearth and grates in place for the burning of coal. The ashes sift through the grate into the ash pit, which is so large that it needs emptying only once a season. This also eliminates the objectionable feature of dust from the ashes escaping into the room. If it is desired to burn wood upon an open hearth, the metal hearth and grates are removed and the opening into the ash pit is covered by a metal plate on which andirons may be placed for burning wood, as shown in the photograph. Whether the fireplace is equipped with hearth and grates for the burning of coal, or is arranged with open hearth and andirons for the burning of wood, the impression given is at once satisfactory and permanent.

The heater is set on the floor level, and the installation consists in merely building a four-inch brick wall around it. This wall, carried up to the ceiling and roofed over, forms the warm air chamber above the furnace body. In one leg of the chimneypiece is set a smoke flue, shown by dotted lines in Figure 2, which is connected with the body of the heater. I furnish one section of this flue lining, having three holes: one which fits onto the flange around the smoke outlet of the heater, another which may be connected with a pipe from the kitchen range, and a third which opens by register into the room for the purpose of checking the coal fire, but which is

VERTICAL SECTION THROUGH CENTER OF CRAFTSMAN FIREPLACE.

kept closed when wood is burned. This flue starts at the bottom of the smoke outlet on the heater, shown in Figure 3, leaving the leg

THE CRAFTSMAN FIREPLACE

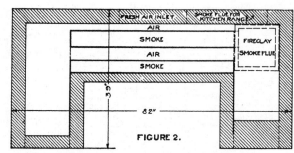

FIGURE 2.

SECTIONAL PLAN OF THE CRAFTSMAN FIREPLACE.

of the chimney below the flue free for the circulation of air.

Any mason can build the wall and make a correct installation. The cost of the brickwork complete with chimney is less than for the usual fireplace of equal size. About 3,000 brick are required where there is a cellar and the chimney is carried up two stories. At a cost of $10.00 per thousand for brick and an equal sum per thousand for sand, cement and labor, the entire cost of brickwork, including $5.00 for flue lining, would be about $65.00.

I have used the common hard-burned brick as a basis for the above figures; where the owner desires to make the fireplace of plaster, stone, Tapestry brick or tile, the additional cost will depend upon the material selected. Hard-burned brick laid up with a wide mortar joint will make a beautiful fireplace. There are no limitations as to the design of the chimneypiece, the only requirement being that the inside measurements are kept to those shown in Figure 2.

The Craftsman fireplace may be installed in houses already built, as well as in new ones, the work in each case requiring a new chimney and the cost being practically the same. Because of the universal favor of the open fire it seems best to make only a medium-sized heater, as many people would prefer to have two or even more fireplaces in different parts of the house. The piping of warm air to the various rooms is then a small factor of the cost, as the pipes will be few and short. These are to be furnished by the owner, since they are always in stock at the local hardware store and are inexpensive.

The operation of the heater itself is as follows: As shown in Figure 1 the smoke generated by the fire passes up through the smoke compartment, down behind the steel smoke wall to the bottom of the heater, then up through another smoke compartment to the smoke outlet flue shown in Figure 3, and out through the chimney.

During its passage the smoke heats the steel walls of the smoke compartments, which in turn heat the air in the air compartments, as will be seen by reference to Figures 1 and 2. The air is thus caused to rise and pass up into the warm air chamber. This action draws in outside air through the fresh air inlet, up through the air compartments into the warm air chamber. At the same time air is also being drawn in from the room through the registers at the base of the fireplace, up through the air compartments into the warm air chamber, where it mixes with the warmed fresh air from outside. The warmed air passes through the upper registers into rooms on the first floor and also through the air pipes to the upper rooms. These air pipes and registers are proportioned in size so that each one will deliver the proper amount of air to the various rooms.

The warm air, upon entering each of the upper rooms, being lightest, rises and spreads out in an even layer against the ceiling. This layer, as it cools, descends to the floor and passes out under the door, down the stairway opening to the lower floor. Part of this air is drawn into the fire and passes out through the chimney, and the rest is drawn into the lower registers. The circulation is rapid and positive, being accomplished, as seen, by gravitation, the heavier or colder air seeking the lowest level and the lighter or warmer air the highest. The heater thus maintains a constant circulation between the various rooms as well as a movement of the air within the rooms, making a given air supply go much farther than with other heating systems.

In this circulation, the air absorbs all impurities, and naturally the zone of the most vitiated air is nearest the floor. It is from this zone that the fireplace draws immense quantities of air and discharges it through the chimney. An adult vitiates from 2,500 to 3,000 cubic feet of air per hour. The fireplace is constructed to admit 20,-000 cubic feet of fresh air and discharge through the chimney the same amount of vitiated or used air per hour, thus making perfect ventilation for seven adults. In this way the air throughout the house is entirely replaced with fresh warmed air from outdoors every fifteen or twenty minutes. Doors and win-

THE CRAFTSMAN FIREPLACE

dows should be kept closed in order that the circulation of air may not be disturbed, for upon the proper circulation depends the efficient heating and ventilating of the house. Under these conditions there can be no drafts.

The danger of the fireplace smoking is entirely eliminated, as the smoke and air openings are properly proportioned and, being part of the steel body, do not depend upon the judgment of the mason. Moreover, it is not only impossible for back drafts to force smoke into the room, but sparks are prevented from escaping through the flue, thereby removing all danger of fire on the roof.

The conserving within the brick walls of all heat which has formerly been lost in the cellar; the circulating of volumes of air in contact with the large areas of smoke surface, thereby extracting practically all the heat from the smoke, and the radiation of heat direct into the room from the open fire, make the Craftsman fireplace a most efficient heating system. One fireplace will amply heat a seven-room house, with a consumption of from seven to ten tons of coal per year in a climate like that of our Central States. The exact amount of fuel consumed, however, depends largely upon the exposure, the number and size of the windows, and the construction of the house. Coal or coke will furnish a more even and steady heat both day and night than wood, but because of the slow combustion due to the down draft, wood may be used as a fuel with entire satisfaction from a standpoint of both economy and attention. Then, too, the wood fire is so much quicker than coal or coke in producing heat and so easily started that its use will be almost universal for fuel during the late fall and early spring.

The price of the steel heater complete with grates, registers and all metal parts (except the pipes needed to conduct warm air from the heater to rooms distant from it) amounts, with the freight, to $150.00. By combining this with the cost of the brickwork and the pipes one can easily install the heating plant complete inside of $250.00. The fireplace is sold only direct to users. I require the plans of each house in which it is to be installed, and from them I make and furnish free to the owner a heating layout which shows the location and size of warm air pipes and registers, and includes complete plans and instruc-

tions for the mason to use in building the brickwork. I guarantee the fireplace to heat and ventilate properly each house in which it is installed, and by making the heating plant myself and selling it direct to users, I am in a position to assume the entire responsibility of its giving satisfaction.

I am ready to make shipments of Craftsman fireplaces, and shall be glad to hear from all those who are considering the installation of

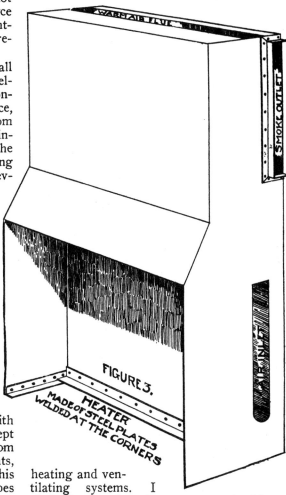

FIGURE 3.

heating and ventilating systems. I shall also be pleased to correspond with any readers who may wish further explanation of the construction of the heater and the manner of its operation.

CRAFTSMAN BUNGALOWS

How to Build a Bungalow

THE term "Bungalow" in the process of transplantation from the banks of the Ganges to the shores of Saranac Lake and other summer abiding places, has lost its significance in a large measure; the American bungalow being nothing more or less than a summer residence of extreme simplicity, of economic construction and intended for more or less primitive living. In too many instances the summer residence, in spite of the every appeal from the woods, the streams and the rocks for simplicity, is but an illy-designed suburban house taken bodily, in many instances, from architectural pattern books.

In response to many requests The Craftsman presents herewith various drawings in which it is intended to give a solution of the problem. The exterior presents a combination of materials easily obtainable in any locality, which may be put together by any man having the slightest knowledge of mason-work and carpentry. The building is constructed in the usual manner of the balloon framed houses, covered with sheathing tarred paper, over which are placed large pine, cedar, or red-wood shingles, as are most available in the locality in which the building is situated. It is purposed to stain these shingles a dull burnt sienna color, and the roof in a color technically known as silver-stain. This

ELEVATION OF FRONT

ELEVATION OF SIDE

sienna color, in a very short time, comes to look like an autumn oak leaf; and this, together with the rough stone of the large chimney, tends to tie the building to its surroundings and to give it the seeming of a growth rather than of a creation. It is a curious fact that the principles laid down by the late lamented Frederick Law Olmsted, relative to the coloration of buildings with regard to their surroundings,—principles so capable of demonstration and so obvious,—should meet with so little recognition; and that, instead of structures which seem to grow from the plain or the forest and become a part of the landscape, we have otherwise admirable architectural efforts that affront the sensitive eye; crying aloud in white lead and yellow ochre the blindness of the owner to even the A B C of decorative fitness. The large and spacious veranda, the simple forms of the roof, and the short distances between joints (eight feet, six inches) tend to give the construction an air of genuine homeliness: a quality in design much to be sought for and not always attained. It is, however, a subject for congratulation that the country side is no longer affronted with lean, narrow, two-story houses surmounted by mansard roofs, and situated on farms of anywhere from seventy-five to two hundred acres; the designers of these monstrosities seeming to have forgotten that the mansard roof was the result of the endeavor to evade the building laws of Paris, and equally seeming to be unconscious of the fact that the building laws on the average farm are not quite so stringent.

The interior is as simple as the outside, and while presenting no particular novelty of plan or construction, is deemed worthy of consideration. In order that the sylvan note may be retained equally as in the outside, the interior, as far as its color is concerned, aspires to harmonize with the dull but rich tones of autumnal oak leaves. This quality, which is only too often neglected, should be strongly insisted upon in all structures of this nature, as it is not easy of accomplishment to be in touch with Nature and at the same time to live in an environment of white and gold, accented with Louis XV. furniture.

The large general living room, with an ample fire-place and the bookcase for the few necessary volumes of summer reading, together with the other features indicated by the perspective drawing, gives it a certain distinction that is oftentimes lacking in erections of this class. The walls of this room are sheathed and covered with burlap of a dull olive yellow, while the exposed construction of the ceiling is stained a wet mossy green color, by a mixture, which, while inappropriate to side walls, seems on the ceiling, where it may not be handled, to serve the purpose better than anything else. Water color tempered with glycerine, —the glycerine never drying as oils would do,—in this instance serves the purpose very much better and gives to the color incorporated in it a suggestion of the woodland to be obtained in no other manner. The floor is of hard maple, and will receive a dark shade of brown, considerably lower in value than any other color in the room. The balance of the woodwork throughout the house is preferably of cypress; but should contingencies require, it may be of hemlock. The visible stone-work of the fireplace (if it can be obtained), will be of limestone that has weathered by exposure a

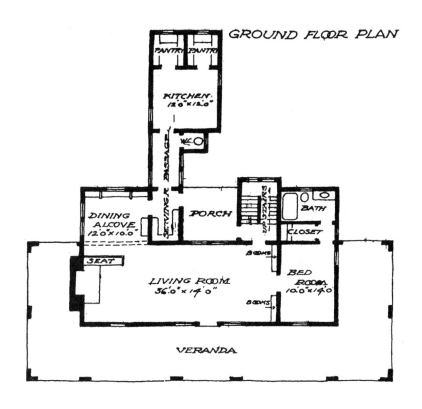

GROUND FLOOR PLAN

PANTRY PANTRY

KITCHEN
12'0"x12'0"

W.C.

SERVING PASSAGE

DINING
ALCOVE
12'0"x10'0"

PORCH

UP STAIRS

BATH

CLOSET

SEAT

LIVING ROOM
36'0"x14'0"

BOOKS

BED
ROOM
10'0"x14'0"

BOOKS

VERANDA

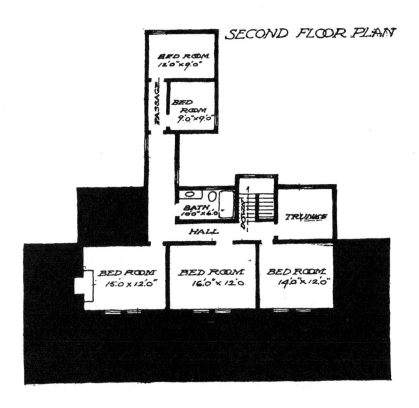

SECOND FLOOR PLAN

BED ROOM
12'0"x9'0"

BED
ROOM
9'0"x9'0"

PASSAGE

BATH
10'0"x6'0"

DOWN

TRUNKS

HALL

BED ROOM
15'0"x12'0"

BED ROOM
16'0"x12'0"

BED ROOM
14'0"x12'0"

sufficient length of time to give it that characteristic spongy look found in the strippings of limestone quarries. This treatment, if used with raked-out joints, is extremely effective and will harmonize admirably with the simplicity of the plans of the house, and, at the same time, give a strong masculine note. From the height of the top of the door to the underside of the ceiling extends a frieze in stencil, of conventional objects relating to primitive life, done in the same straight-forward manner as the balance of the structure. In this decoration the slightest attempt at anything beyond pure symbolism would result in disaster, as the building is essentially primitive in its general design, and equally so should be the decoration. This arrangement, together with window hangings of extreme simplicity, such as a figured creton in varying shades of pale yellow accented with dull red, should satisfactorily complete the room.

The dining-alcove, opening from this apartment, being a continuation of the living room, is treated in the same manner. The permanent fittings of the alcove consist of a primitive sideboard and a convenient and unobtrusive serving shelf.

The alcove, separated from the living room by the arch and two posts, as indicated in the drawing, is so arranged that it may be used either as a portion of the living room, or as a provision for guests, as a bedchamber. It is provided with a couch, which may serve as a bed, a chest of drawers, a pier glass and a writing desk; the pier glass facing the large fireplace in the living room and reflecting the same. The kitchen, and its accompanying offices, are, as this bungalow is intended for summer occupation only, semi-detached and only connected by means of a covered way, from which, except in inclement weather, the glass and sash are removed. For obvious reasons the cellarage for the kitchen is omitted and such storage as is desired is provided for on the ground floor. The bed rooms are moderately spacious and easy of ventilation. The treatment of the bed room, as far as material and color are concerned, is identical with that of the living room: viz., burlap side walls and stained construction of the ceiling; the former of olive green; the latter of moss green.

The sanitary arrangements of the bungalow consist of a single bath room on the second story, supplied with a tub and an earth closet, together with a lavatory on the ground floor; and the provisions for water are made by the wind-mill shown.

In connection with these drawings is a scheme which, for the usual site in which this bungalow would be built, seems adequate, proper, and tending to unite the structure to its surroundings without the usual abrupt transition from handicraft to Nature.

THE BUNGALOW'S FURNITURE

If, after having been built with great respect for harmony and appropriateness, the bungalow should be filled with the usual collection of badly designed and inadequate furniture, the *ensemble* would be distressing, and the thought involved in the structure of the building thrown away. The term furniture implies, *per se*, movable portions of the building, and, as such, should be conceived by the designer. Otherwise, nine times out of ten, an unpleasant sense of incongruity prevails. The importance of

Fireplace in living room

Alcove off of living room

unity between the furniture and the structure, in spite of the fact that every writer on the topic has insisted upon it, in the majority of instances is further from realization than it was in the Stone Age, when, by force of circumstances, harmony of manners, methods and materials was a necessity. It is not intended by this to suggest that we should return to that period, but to emphasize the fact that necessity involves simplicity and that simplicity is the key note of harmony. This furniture, while adapted with much precision to its various functions, is of almost primitive directness. It is done in oak with a pale olive Craftsman finish, and thus becomes an integral part of the bungalow.

Whatever hardware is used in connection with this furniture is of wrought-iron, in the "Russian finish," which falls into place very readily in the general scheme.

Great care has been taken in furnishing this bungalow to omit every article that is not absolutely essential to the comfort or the convenience of the occupants, it not being intended to make the building in a small way a cheap museum to be indifferently managed by an amateur curator, as is usually the case in urban residences and frequently happens in the summer cottage, to the great disturbance of the simple life.

A FOREST BUNGALOW

WORDS themselves, like the thoughts of which they are the winged messengers, modify their meaning, as they pass from mouth to mouth. Formerly, the name Bungalow, when pronounced, reflected in the minds of those who heard it pic-

Front elevation

tures of the East Indies. And to those who were unable to represent to themselves the suburbs of Bombay or Calcutta, the dictionaries offered the following definition:

"Bungalow,—a house or cottage of a single story, with a tiled or thatched roof."

Such definition is no longer adequate. The idea of the convenient little habitation has developed and extended during its passage to new countries. The single story and thatch, or tiles, are no longer the essentials of the Bungalow. Camps or cottages passing under this name, and in which the primitive type native to British India is wholly obscured, accent the Atlantic coast, the Adirondack forests, and the shores of the Saint

Lawrence. A structure of the later, more advanced type, as may be learned by reference to the accompanying illustrations, is now offered by The Craftsman, in response to the demands of the vacation period.

The Bungalow here presented in elevation, is designed to be set low, with the first floor at a level not exceeding eight inches above the surrounding grade.

The building is supported by rough piers of masonry extending below the frost line; while the pillars upholding the roof are tree trunks, still covered with their bark.

The structural timber employed is hemlock or spruce, rough from the mill; the frame being covered with matched boards, surfaced on

Side elevation

the inner side. This boarding may be overlaid on the outer side with building paper, in order to assure additional warmth, and the walls are lastly covered with split shingles, laid wide to the weather and left to acquire a natural stain. The large area of the roof with its dormers, is also covered by shingles; in this instance of the ordinary kind; brush-coated to a deep moss-green.

A Forest Bungalow

A FOREST BUNGALOW

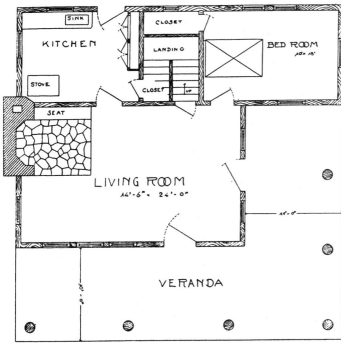

First floor plan

is left exposed with the intervening panels either stained to a warm brown, or hung with burlap, as desired. The ceiling is not covered: the exposed floor-joists of the second story thus giving it a beamed effect.

A cross-section at the rear of the building contains, at the right: a bedroom, ten by fifteen feet in size, with dependent closet; next, an ample space is devoted to the staircase which opens into the living room; while the large square remaining at the left of the rear cross-section, forms a well-ventilated, convenient kitchen, provided with a built-in cupboard, a sink with drain-board, and a second cupboard or closet made by utilizing the space beneath the stairs.

The batten doors can easily be made upon the site; the flooring of the veranda is of two-inch plank; the chimney is built of boulders gathered from the locality, with field stones used as binders to strengthen the masonry.

The space of the first floor is apportioned into a living room, a bed room and a kitchen.

The first of these rooms has dimensions of fourteen feet, six inches by twenty-four feet; one end being occupied by a fire-place large enough to contain a four foot log. The hearth is formed of large flat stones set in a bed of earth, and the floor of the room is laid in matched pine boards, six inches in width. The studding of the side walls

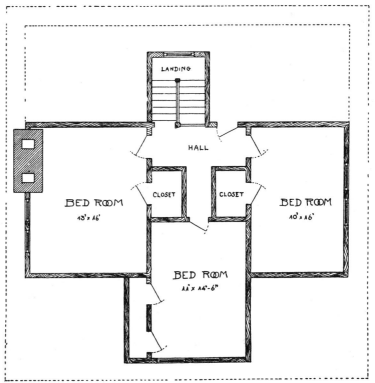

Second floor plan

The second floor contains three bedrooms, with storage room under the eaves at the rear of the building: this extension of space being in itself a proof that the Bungalow, in its later development, is a habitation much more convenient and agreeable than existed in its primitive form.

THE CALIFORNIA BUNGALOW: A STYLE OF ARCHITECTURE WHICH EXPRESSES THE INDIVIDUALITY AND FREEDOM CHARACTERISTIC OF OUR WESTERN COAST

WE have the pleasure of publishing in this issue of THE CRAFTSMAN some of the best examples that have come to us of the new American architecture, which as yet can hardly be considered a style so much as a series of individual plans adapted to climatic conditions and to the needs of daily living, and in harmony with the natural environment and contour of the landscape. In a country like our own, where all these requirements vary so widely, any one style would be altogether inadequate, but the new architecture that is so rapidly and steadily developing in America is rather a general expression of that spirit of individuality and freedom which is especially characteristic of this country. In the north and east, for example, a style of building is required which would be absolutely out of harmony with the life and surroundings to be found in the south and west, and in California,—especially in the southern part of the state,—conditions prevail which are found hardly anywhere else on the continent. For fully eight months in the year the constant sunshine, unbroken by clouds or storms and relieved only by an occasional fog drifting in from the ocean, permits a life that is practically all out-of-doors, or, at all events, maintains such a friendly relation with out-of-doors that the house seems more in the nature of a temporary shelter and resting place than a building designed to be lived in all the time and to afford constant protection from the elements.

The country out there is one of great restful spaces, with wide plains and low, rolling hills which lead up gradually to the stupendous mountain walls of the Sierra Nevada and the lesser but still imposing peaks of the Coast Range and the Sierra Madre. There are no thickets of slim saplings and green undergrowth, no little creeks and springs, and none of the somewhat aggressive picturesqueness found at every hand in the east; only huge grain fields, orchards and vineyards and wide stretches of sun-dried grass, scorched to a warm, tawny brown during the long rainless season that follows the brief winter of green grass and wild flowers. The colors, too, are differ-

"THE ADOBE WALLS, WHICH WERE FORMERLY BUILT FOR DEFENSE, ARE NOW MODIFIED INTO GARDEN WALLS, WHICH AFFORD COMPLETE SECLUSION.

A California House and Garden

Myron Hunt & Elmer Grey, Archt's.

"THERE ARE HALF-COVERED PORCHES (PERGOLAS)
THAT SUGGEST SHADE AND COOL, AND STILL
ALLOW THE SUN TO CARPET THE GROUND WITH
DAPPLED SHADOWS."

HOUSE & GARDEN for DR. GUY COCHRAN
MYRON HUNT & ELMER GREY,
ARCHITECTS, LOS ANGELES, CAL.

"THE GROUPING OF THE WINDOWS IS A FEATURE OF MARKED INDIVIDUALITY: THEY DO AWAY WITH THE SENSE OF BEING ENCLOSED WITHIN WALLS."

"IN A COUNTRY WITH THE CONTOUR AND COLOR-ING OF CALIFORNIA THERE CAN BE NO STYLE OF ARCHITECTURE SO HARMONIOUS AS THAT FOUNDED UPON THE OLD MISSION BUILDINGS."

THE CALIFORNIA BUNGALOW

ent. Our watery, gray-blue skies and the blue haze of the distance is replaced by burning sapphire overhead and an atmosphere so filled with the golden dust haze that all distance disappears in a mist of warm rosy violet.

In a country with the contour and coloring of Southern California there can be no style of architecture so harmonious as that founded directly upon the old Mission buildings, and no material that blends so beautifully with the colors about it as some modification of the old adobe or sun-dried brick, covered with creamy plaster. The old Mission padres knew what they were about, and in nothing that remains of their work is this knowledge more convincingly shown than in the plans of the old Mission buildings which were the forerunners of the modern adobe houses. Even the adobe walls, which were formerly erected for defence against hostile Indians outside the Mission grounds and the protection not only of the monks but of the Mission Indians who sought refuge within the enclosures, are now modified into garden walls which afford complete seclusion, if desired, by giving a garden close, filled with green grass and tropical foliage, which is almost a part of the house.

Messrs. Myron Hunt and Elmer Grey, the architects who designed the houses shown here, are pioneers in the development of the new American architecture. They both brought to their work in Southern California the energy and progressive spirit of the Middle West and the training of finished architects. Mr. Hunt went to Los Angeles from Chicago and Mr. Grey from Milwaukee, both in search of the improved health that is to be found in the mild and equable climate of Southern California, and in going out there both found the ideal conditions for the full development of a very unusual gift for designing simple and beautiful buildings, which are also remarkable examples of direct thought based on the fundamental principle of response to need. As Mr. Grey says:

"Many eastern people seem to consider that we have a distinctive style out here. If such a quality does exist in California architecture, it is not because our architects have striven to be unique in their designing, but because they have tried to eliminate from it all features not properly belonging to their climate and to their local conditions,—because they have tried to be simply natural. The California architect is not surrounded, as is the easterner, by a great mass of previously constructed buildings, constituting a dead weight of tradition from which it is difficult to break away; he is in a comparatively new country, the climate of which is radically different from other portions of the United States, and so in design he seeks suggestion, not from the work about him,—which is apt like his own to be more or less experimental,—nor from remote parts of the country which are very different from this; but from Italy, Spain or Mexico, where similar climatic conditions prevail. If he has a proper sense of the fitness of things he will not implant amid the semi-tropical foliage of California such architecture, for instance, as the Queen Anne or the Elizabethan. He may admire the English style greatly, and may have profited by some of its lessons, but if his designs show anything of this influence they will also express his loyalty to California and his desire not to place any foreign element in

THE CALIFORNIA BUNGALOW

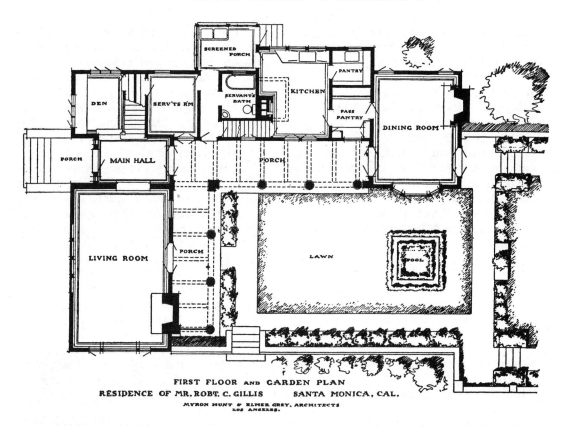

FIRST FLOOR AND GARDEN PLAN
RESIDENCE OF MR. ROBT. C. GILLIS   SANTA MONICA, CAL.
MYRON HUNT & ELMER GREY, ARCHITECTS
LOS ANGELES.

it that has not first been thoroughly naturalized. His respect for traditional architecture may be profound; but because he does not wish to see destroyed what little tradition his own part of the country may have, he feels bound to respect its peculiarities and to try to preserve its architectural integrity in his work."

The examples shown here amply illustrate the viewpoint held by Mr. Grey. They are almost all planned after the manner of the bungalow, a word which is generally used to convey the idea of a dwelling with its rooms all on the ground floor. Such a house, of course, is not well adapted to a cold climate, as it is difficult to heat easily and economically a number of rooms spread over the ground. In California this objection has no weight, as there is

no need of heating any house save by means of an occasional fireplace, and the bungalow there has the advantage of simplifying housekeeping and making its occupants feel a closer relationship to the great out-of-doors. The California bungalow does not, however, resemble the original East Indian dwelling of that name so closely as it does the old Mexican *hacienda* or ranch house, which was almost invariably built around three and sometimes four sides of a square or rectangular court. This style is called a *patio* house, and it makes a most delightful form of dwelling for Southern California. Such a house, of course, must be surrounded by trees and spacious grounds, as it would be entirely out of place in a city lot with high buildings around it, and

THE CALIFORNIA BUNGALOW

so again it conforms to the conditions of life in Southern California rather than to those of the east.

THE dwelling of Mr. Robert C. Gillis, although a decided modification of the *patio* house, is a characteristic example of a house intended for life in Southern California. The garden is enclosed within a wall which affords a sense of privacy from the street without giving any feeling of confinement or separation from the country all around. The living room opens directly upon the long porch, from which one again walks out almost on the same level onto the lawn. The only way to reach the dining room is through the porch which runs at right angles to that opening from the living room. The entrance to the house is on the opposite side from this porch, and one especially attractive feature of the plan is the long vista across the main hall and porch through the dining room and along the entire length of the gar-

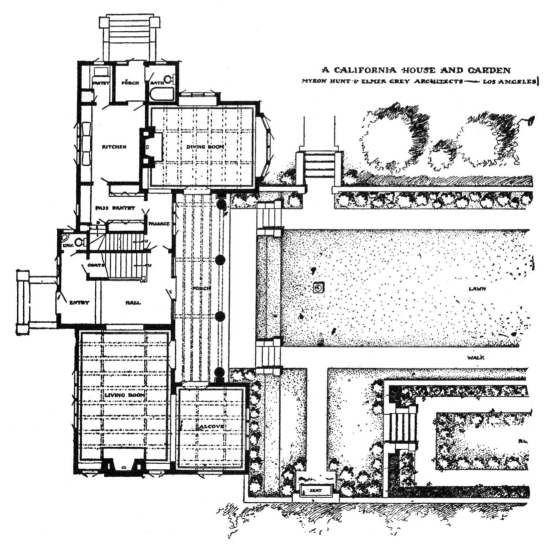

A CALIFORNIA HOUSE AND GARDEN
MYRON HUNT & ELMER GREY ARCHITECTS — LOS ANGELES

THE CALIFORNIA BUNGALOW

den. French windows are employed in the place of doors, so that nothing occurs to break the vista. The main bedrooms are all upstairs facing the court.

IN the design called "A California House and Garden," a still greater departure from the strict form of the *patio* house and a nearer approach to the more usual eastern planning is seen, yet the principal features of this house plainly show its adaptation to the California environment. The dining room is approached most easily from the living room by way of the covered porch, the small pas-

sage between the hall and the dining room being incorporated merely as an emergency thoroughfare to be used in inclement weather. Here again a delightful vista, through glass doors and windows across the porch and then down the length of the garden, is seen by anyone entering the hall. Both the living room and dining room face the garden, while the kitchen is placed upon the north side of the house facing the street, so that the main outlook is always upon the beauty and seclusion of the enclosure that is dedicated as the house itself to the family life. One feature of this

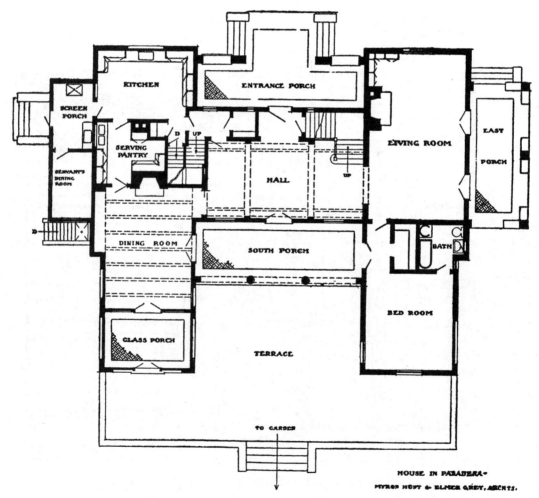

THE CALIFORNIA BUNGALOW

house that adds much to its attractive individuality is the grouping of the windows, which not only admit the greatest possible amount of air and sunshine, but form an admirable division of the wall space. The bedrooms are all upstairs facing the garden, which, of course, is the sunny side of the house.

THE chance to live out of doors Pasadena shows less of an enclosure within the walls of the house and a larger enclosed space out of doors, the whole plan of the garden being such that the house is merely the center of a well-balanced scheme.

The entrance porch is on the north side of the house, and directly across the large hall is the south porch which leads out to the broad terrace, from which steps go down into the garden. The living room opens upon the east porch and the dining room is a closed porch at the south side which connects directly with the terrace. All the bedrooms, save one, are upstairs, and a beautiful feature of the second story is the pergola covered with vines, which affords a charming outdoor sitting room that is shaded with green and yet cuts off very little light and no air from the bedrooms.

HOUSE FOR DR. GUY COCHRAN
LOS ANGELES CALIFORNIA
MYRON HUNT & ELMER GREY ARCHITECTS

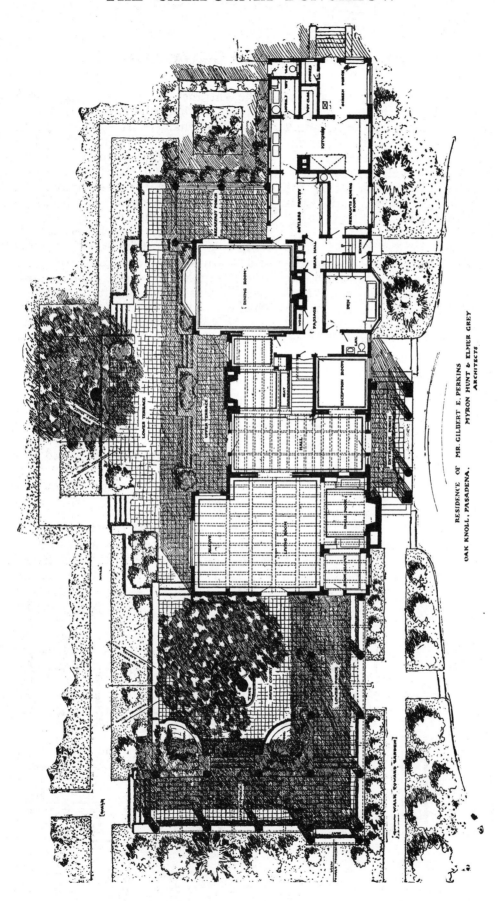

RESIDENCE OF MR. GILBERT E. PERKINS
OAK KNOLL, PASADENA. MYRON HUNT & ELMER GREY
ARCHITECTS

THE CALIFORNIA BUNGALOW

Porch and Terrace — The Gilbert E. Perkins Residence
Myron Hunt — Elmer Grey, Architects.

The beautiful lines and proportions of this house and its perfect suitability to its surroundings make it one of the best examples of the group.

PERHAPS the very best, though, is the house and garden designed for Dr. Guy Cochran, which is less distinctively Californian in design, but is nevertheless admirably adapted for the southern climate and outdoor life, and in itself is one of the most beautiful houses which has ever been reproduced in the pages of THE CRAFTSMAN. Here again the grouping of the windows is a feature of such marked individuality that it commands the attention with the first look at the house. The enormous windows from the living room, looking out upon the terrace and garden, give such a sense of relationship between the two that there is almost no feeling of being enclosed within walls. The French windows seen elsewhere give the same sense of direct communication with the garden from the dining room and the music room, and equally large casements placed just above look out from the upper rooms upon the green drapery of the two pergolas that shade the terrace. The long line of casements shown in the broad, low dormer that seems to grow out of the roof gives exactly the right balance to the great spread of glass below, and the lines of the roof itself are so friendly, gracious and inviting in their suggestion of comfort and shelter that they add the last touch of the feeling of inevitableness that is conveyed by the whole design. Here again the garden is almost a part of the house and is walled away from the street on one side and the cliff on the other.

ONLY a suggestion is given in the small line drawings made of "Oak Knoll," Mr. Gilbert Perkins' residence in Pasadena, but the large floor plan showing the way in which

THE CALIFORNIA BUNGALOW

the house and garden are laid out and connected so closely that they may almost be called interwoven, gives a better idea of the beauty of this place than the most elaborately detailed perspective. When reduced to its essential elements the plan is quite simple. The main rooms of the first story are the living room, hall, dining room and kitchen, as the little reception room and den are merely incidents and can hardly be included as important parts of the plan. The unusual and most delightful feature of this house is the system of paved terraces built around two spreading live oak trees. One of these oaks at the side of the house is completely surrounded by a covered porch, the square or court thus formed being paved with tile and made delightfully attractive by a semi-formal arrangement of paths and steps leading up to the higher portion of the porch. The other oak is situated in front of the house and also has terraces built all around it, thus making additional living space which receives the benefit of its shade. From both of these terraces a magnificent view of the San Gabriel valley and of the Sierra Madre mountains is obtained. Although the interior plan of this house is not so very different from many eastern houses, the system of terraces and porches and the means provided for ready access to all of these is well worth studying as a plan that is admirably adapted to Southern California, as it is most expressive both

of the country and of the sunny, leisurely outdoor life that under all normal conditions is lived there by everyone.

THE chance to live out of doors and yet enjoy the utmost comfort, even luxury, is what the California bungalow suggests, not only at a first glimpse, but after most careful investigation. The entire building is kept close to the ground; there are groups of windows that bring indoors the pleasure of blue sky, of purple hills or wide stretches of hazy prairie; there are vine-covered pergolas that suggest shade and cool, and still leave patches of blue overhead and allow the sun to carpet the ground with dappled shadows of leaves and beams. The house, the garden, the terrace, the patio, the open porch are all one domain, one shelter from the outside world. It is home in that big, fine sense of the word that leaves the horizon, not four walls, for the boundary lines.

And this dwelling, which at the first blush seems but a cross between an East Indian bungalow and a Mission adobe house, in reality proves to be the most genuine expression of American feeling in domestic architecture that has yet appeared. Built to suit the needs of one great section of our country, it has developed a beauty and a charm of its own. It is original because it is like the country it has grown out of; it is becoming a definite style because it has met a definite demand, and because it is genuine it will be permanent.

A SMALL BUNGALOW WORTH STUDYING

ABOUT three and a half miles from Pasadena is located a bungalow, here illustrated, designed and built by Mr. Louis B. Easton for Mr. C. C. Curtis. The house 44 feet x 32 feet, and barn 20 feet by 80 feet, together form a ranch house, and the barn, built in the form of an "L," makes a court at the back and adds mass to the combined structure. At the rear, and within easy view, stands Mt. Lowe with its observatory, and running down the mountain the inclined road of the Pacific Electric. The house has the lines of the old Mexican buildings of adobe, but differs from them in construction, being built of boards running up and down and heavily battened. Such a bungalow, carefully built, would be entirely practical for an all-the-year-round home in California, and, where one wishes to live the simple life, is much better adapted to winter use in this locality than the regulation small house.

The central living room, 20 feet x 23 feet, has a big fireplace with a high settle at one side, which serves a double purpose. The back of this settle faces the entrance door, thus helping to form a vestibule and making a convenient place for hanging wraps and coats, while at the same time it shelters the fireplace from the wind.

At the opposite side of the fireplace is a built-in bookcase nine feet in length, beyond which are a desk and typewriter desk, furnished with a long bench upon which, when at work, one may easily move from one to the other. A couple of magazine racks, a rough table and a few chairs complete the furnishings of this room. In the dining room are a built-in buffet, a round table and old splint chairs, which lend an air of homely comfort and cheer.

All lumber throughout the house is of rough redwood, smoothed with a steel brush. The ceilings are of 14-inch boards battened on the upper side, and these, as well as the boarding on the outside of the buildings, are the color of weathered driftwood. Beams and trim are finished in a dark brown tone, with which the burlap above the wainscot is in harmony.

Provision is made for hot and cold water, the plumbing is much better than that which is provided in the usual five-room house, and under all is a good cellar.

Facing west, the house fronts on a beautiful lawn, with a young orchard at the north and a rose garden at the south. The bungalow as a whole seems simply to have found lodgment at the foot of a great mountain, where it makes no pretense beyond that of offering shelter and comfort.

See page 534

A BUNGALOW NEAR PASADENA DESIGNED BY
LOUIS B. EASTON, WHICH HAS THE LINES OF
THE OLD MISSION HOUSE, THOUGH BUILT OF
BOARDS.

LOOKING FROM DINING ROOM THROUGH SIT-
TING ROOM TO BEDROOM, SHOWING INTEREST-
ING INTERIOR CONSTRUCTION.

See page 534

VIEW OF SITTING ROOM IN BUNGALOW
DESIGNED FOR MR. C. C. CURTIS.

INTERESTING TIMBER CONSTRUCTION IN A CALIFORNIA BUNGALOW

THE bungalow shown in the accompanying illustration was designed by Mr. C. W. Buchanan for Mr. Furrows of Pasadena, California. It is interesting to note how closely the graceful proportions and structural effects of this little dwelling suggest the simplicity of the wooden temples of the early Greeks.

The roof has a projection of three feet at the eaves, which makes the building appear lower than it is. The timbers that support it are exposed, which relieves the long edges of the slopes and gives the keynote of sturdiness to the whole structure. The house is covered with 8-inch clapboards one inch thick, and the heavy shadows cast by their overlapping edges maintain, even from a distance, the rugged aspect of the construction.

As the building has but one story, and no window is necessary above the porch, the raised lattice in the gable is purely decorative. It is built on a heavy crosspiece and six uprights and suggests the exposed timber construction found in the roof, the window-casings and the porch. This gives the decoration the added charm of consistency. Furthermore, the lattice completes a pleasing proportion of spaces on the front of the house. In merely a passing glance the eye is conscious of the harmony between the narrow cobblestone parapet, the broad shadow of the porch opening, the rough space of clapboarding and the darker area of the lattice. A similar proportion is found in the intervals between the exposed roof supports.

The sharp corners of the porch opening are blunted by two beams running diagonally from the box pillars that support the porch roof to the porch ceiling, and the general outline is softened by a rich curtain of vines. The porch is under the main roof so that the pillars covered with the same siding have the novel appearance of being a continuation of the front wall of the house. It has a concrete floor and is ceiled with narrow pine boards left in the natural color and varnished. The entire building is stained a moss green.

Within, the house is quite as attractive as without. The living room, dining room and the den, connected with the latter by sliding doors, are floored with selected Oregon pine stained to give the effect of Flemish oak. The ceilings are finished with plaster between the box beams, which are set four feet apart.

The fireplace in the living room is very simple; the hearth is of square tiles; the chimneypiece of red brick with a shelf of

PASADENA BUNGALOW:
FLOOR PLAN.

C. W. Buchanan, Architect

A CLAPBOARD BUNGALOW OF UNUSUALLY INTERESTING TIMBER CONSTRUCTION, THE HOME OF MR. FURROWS OF PASADENA.

PORCH OF THE BUNGALOW, SHOWING BOX PILLARS AND COBBLESTONE PARAPET.

SHOWING INTERESTING EFFECT OF DINING ROOM RAISED
SEVERAL FEET ABOVE LIVING ROOM FLOOR.

SIMPLE CONSTRUCTION OF FIREPLACE AT ONE END OF THE
LIVING ROOM.

thick pine board. The little casements on either side of the chimneypiece with built-in seats below add a great deal to the interest of that end of the room.

The dining room has the novelty of being raised a step or two above the living room. As is usual in such an arrangement, the length of the two rooms is emphasized. It is the more attractive in this case because the porch, a good-sized room in itself, opens directly into the living room. Thus a very pretty vista is got from either end. The dining room is made especially effective by the amount of woodwork in it, which gives it a character of its own and makes the necessary contrast to the room above which it is raised. It is wainscoted with V-jointed boards to the ceiling, which is rough plastered and tinted a golden brown. Except for the wainscoting in the dining room, the interior walls are all plastered and tinted. The sideboard, about ten feet in width, is built in and runs from floor to ceiling; the doors are of leaded glass. The glint of glass, as one looks into the room, is pleas-antly repeated by the doors of the book-cases, also built in and running between the square pillars on either side of the steps and the narrow partitions between the living room and dining room.

The arrangement of the rest of the house is given in plan and shows its delightful roominess and ample allowance for closets of every description. The kitchen and bathroom are finished with white enamel.

In view of the beauty and comfort of this little house, the tabulation of cost given below amounts to a surprisingly small total:

Lumber	$700.00
Carpenter Labor	660.00
Mill Work	350.00
Paint and Stain.........	250.00
Masonry and Plaster.....	422.00
Hardware	110.00
Electric Work	45.00
Tin and Galvanized Iron.	50.00
Plumbing	330.00
Total	$2917.00

SPLIT FIELD STONE AS A VALUABLE AID IN THE BUILDING OF ATTRACTIVE BUNGALOWS AND SMALL HOUSES: BY CHARLES ALMA BYERS

IN this group of six small houses the use of split field stone is especially worthy of notice. The splitting of natural stone brings into sight interesting markings and variegated colors in the rock which are not seen upon the faces that have been exposed to the action of the soil and the weather. This variety in the new surfaces, exposed by the splitting of the stone, makes them blend with almost any color in woodwork and gives a desirable ruggedness to the appearance of a house.

The use of split stones thus treated has been a fairly common custom in the chimneys and foundations of large houses, but there has been a very general feeling that such a heavy material would be quite out of place in a cottage or a bungalow. However, the increase in one-story houses called for an increasing supply and variation in the building materials. Cobblestones were effectively used and these paved the way for an attempt to utilize field stone. Naturally enough, this simple and informal style of architecture found an invaluable aid in the simply prepared masonry, which can be as effectively used inside as outside of the house. A chimneypiece of rough hewn stone fits with delightful appropriateness into a long, low living room, especially where the beams of the ceiling or other structural features are left exposed, and, as the illustrations show, the entire parapets of porches may be made of stone without seeming too heavy for the rest of the house.

The stone may be variously laid; sometimes the joints are trimmed although the faces are left rough, and it may also be laid with the joints following the natural formation of the pieces. In either case, since the faces are comparatively flat, the structural lines are left unbroken, which is not so in cases where the round heads of cobblestones are used. In the houses shown, we find two sorts of stone,—white limestone and two varieties of sandstone

one red and rather soft and the other a much harder variety of a deep cream color.

In the first house red sandstone is used, finished with trimmed joints. The heavy timbers are of Oregon pine and the siding of the house is cedar shingles. The woodwork is stained to a dark green, in the trimmings and in the supporting construction, which is exposed, it is so deep as to be almost black. The steps and the path are of red cement to match the stonework and the whole makes a rich and artistic color combination. The foundation is also of sandstone, but if this were seen, the house, which is naturally low, would lose too much in height; to obviate this a paneled wainscoting extends around the body of the house and covers all except a narrow strip of the foundation near the ground. The house was built for $3,200.

The second house uses the cream colored sandstone, the frames of the windows painted white to match. The joints of the stone are trimmed and the steps and walk are of cement colored to match. The timbers are rough and square sawn and the house is covered with weatherboarding of Oregon pine, stained to a deep brown. The house is a very low rambling structure containing six rooms, with a large porch, almost a room in itself. The cost of this house was $3,000.

The third house contains eight rooms and the cost is consequently somewhat greater. It was built for about $3,800. The stonework is of white limestone, finished with copings of cement. The pieces are irregular in contour but are carefully selected as to size and shape. The supports of the porch roof as well as the parapets are of the stone, and a stone pergola over the drive at the side of the house will make a most attractive entrance and frame to the garden in the rear when the vines which are planted about it grow up and cover it. The entire house, roof and walls are stained to an emerald green. The

A SMALL CALIFORNIA BUNGALOW COSTING $3,200, SHOWING THE USE OF RED SANDSTONE FOR PORCH PILLARS, PORCH FOUNDATION AND CHIMNEY.

A CLAPBOARD HOUSE WITH PORCH FOUNDATION AND CHIMNEY OF CREAM SANDSTONE AND TRIMMING OF CREAM WHITE: COST $3,000.

BUNGALOW COSTING $3,800, WITH WHITE LIMESTONE USED FOR FOUNDATION, PORCH AND PERGOLA: JAPANESE EFFECT IN WOODWORK.

BUNGALOW BUILT FOR $3,300: INTERESTING SIMPLE WOOD CONSTRUCTION, WITH FOUNDATION, PORCH AND PORCH PARAPET OF WHITE LIMESTONE.

$3,000 HOUSE OF WOOD AND STONE, SHOWING COLOR SCHEME OF BLUE-BLACK WOODWORK, WITH WHITE IN STONEWORK AND TRIMMING.

$2,800 CALIFORNIA COTTAGE WITH UNUSUAL WINDOW ARRANGEMENT IN THE ROOF AND WITH PICTURESQUE PORCH PILLARS AND CHIMNEY OF LIMESTONE.

USE OF SPLIT FIELD STONE IN BUILDING

trimmings about the windows are painted white to match the stonework.

In the fourth house the arrangement of the masonry suggests that of the first. This is, however, of white limestone and the joints are not trimmed. Here again we find shingled walls with the wooden paneling covering the foundations. The posts of the porch are very interesting,—a group of four square sawed beams of Oregon pine stand upon the cement coping that finishes the stone posts of the porch. All the woodwork in the house is stained a dark green, except the sashes of the windows, which are white. This house contains seven rooms and the building cost was $3,300.

The fifth house shows more masonry in its construction. Here a pergola continues the porch and extends over the side entrance, and high stone posts rise above the parapet to the eaves of the porch. The color scheme of this house is very peculiar, but nevertheless very attractive. The woodwork is of blue-black stain, and the trimmings are white, as is the limestone used in the masonry. This house was built for $3,000.

The last house of the group, although the smallest and least expensive, since it cost only $2,800, is one of the most interesting structurally. For so small a house it has a great many interesting variations, and yet does not appear crowded or over-decorated. The slant of the roof is very slight, but the house is saved from any appearance of flatness by the shallow dormer which is broken through at the center of the roof, through which light is let in at the top of the living room. Everywhere the timbers used in the construction are left exposed. The porch on the front of the house is largely protected by the main roof and at the side is covered by a pergola construction. The stonework is of white limestone, and the house is stained in two shades of dark green.

In each of the above cases, whatever the color of the house, the stone blends with the surrounding woodwork and adds a certain distinction and solidarity to the whole. With its aid the cottages seem to accomplish that happy position of being neither too dignified nor too insignificant and informal, a position at which it is hard for a small one-story house, not actually in the woods or mountains, to arrive. In most cases the masonry is repeated in the chimneypieces within, and the interior of these houses maintains the same dignified informality which characterizes them from without. Another point in favor of the use of split field stone of any variety is that usually it is so inexpensive. If it had to be quarried and transported to the builder the expense would be a different matter, but in rocky portions of the country when property is being cleared for building, oftentimes a man may find close at hand all the stone that he wants for the small trouble of splitting it.

Another advantage of using the stone native to the environment in the construction of a house is a certain appearance that the house gains of long familiarity with the setting, especially where much of the surrounding property is still left in its natural rugged condition. The use of the stone in the house establishes a link between the building and the country in which it is located that is not the less a powerful influence because it is not obvious. It is these subtle influences that bind a house with neighboring houses or with the landscape, into a pleasing unity that makes us find in some buildings an amount of charm entirely disproportionate to the actual beauty of design that they possess.

Of course, a house must have good structural lines, but it is the attention to matters like these, the taking time to decide correctly whether one style or another of architecture is best suited to the character of the landscape that adds much or takes much from what a house already possesses of beauty and charm.

SUMMER BUNGALOWS IN DELAWARE, DESIGN-ED TO AFFORD COMFORT IN LITTLE SPACE

THE originals of the five little bunga-lows illustrated in this article are standing in one of the most attrac-tive portions of the State of Dela-ware. With the exception of the two larger cottages they are for week-end use and were designed by the owners them-selves. The first is of rough pine boards stained brown with white trim. The obvi-ous simplicity of the body of the house is relieved by the rustic porch supports and the curving lines in the railing of twisted withes. The second is built on sloping ground against a charming background of leafy trees and thick underbrush. The body of it is plaster of a gray color; the chimney, which suggests a cozy fireplace within, is built of field stone. The top of the chimney shows an interesting variation in chimney build-ing; it is of plaster held together on the outside with sticks, after the fashion of a crow's nest. The roof and porch hood have not been painted but left to take the stain of the wind and weather, so that in the winter the house is as little noticeable against the bare gray trees as when it is half hidden with summer greenery. There is something delightfully suggestive in the furnishings of the porch; a table, a chair and a book rest. The table is a mere board, the chair is a most primitive support roughly made of boards and unfinished logs, but the book rest has a graceful series of Gothic arches carved upon its supports.

The third bungalow is covered with broad weather-boarding, the porch closed in by rustic trellis-like sides for vines, the roof is of tarred paper, the chimney inside and out of field stone roughly trimmed. Here in a more practical way we get the sense of completeness and comfort, of "much in little"; the little house with its owner pleasantly entertaining a friend on the porch, the vegetable garden in fine and flourishing condition, the pleasant sugges-tions of shadowy wooded walks to be had for the seeking, and in all probabilities a delightful neighbor near by.

The little cottage called "The Poplars" is perhaps the most picturesque and de-lightful of all. With the exception of the black tarred-paper roof, it is a soft, weather-stained gray. Meadow grass and the wild flowers brush up against its walls and the poplar trees lean over it from above. Soon the young sapling be-fore the porch will grow up and its branches droop around the entrance, so that the house will hardly be seen for the mass of green about it.

The last bungalow is set in the very midst of the woods. It is less roughly con-structed than the others. The beams are trimmed smooth and stained, and the broad porch is screened in so that the living space is practically divided into rooms and porch.

To the people who really love the life of the country and the woods, "to rough it," these little bungalows will unfold the many pleasures that they afford their owners. It is not necessary to have a large house and an elaborate menage to enjoy the country, indeed they are a drawback, a barrier of artificiality, a limitation upon freedom of thought and action. In the city our house is our refuge from noise and turmoil, our library a place for rest and quiet thought. In the country, the woods themselves are the securest cloisters, their clean, sweet aisles insuring perfect peace. The house is but a shelter from the storms, the store house against our material needs, the place where we sleep, although for that, most of us can say truthfully with the simple-hearted philosopher of Syria sleeping un-der the stars, "The pillow I like best is my right arm."

There can be no doubt in the minds of those who have followed the rather slow development of an architecture adapted to American country life that the bunga-low has furnished a most valuable source of inspiration. It was designed in the first place in Eastern countries for the life of intelligent busy people, whose ex-istence is a practical one and whose aim must of necessity be as simple as is con-

A DELAWARE BUN-
GALOW OF ROUGH
PINE BOARDS
STAINED BROWN
WITH WHITE TRIM:
NOTE THE SIMPLIC-
ITY OF CONSTRUC-
TION RELIEVED BY
RUSTIC PORCH SUP-
PORTS AND THE
RAILING OF TWISTED
WITHES: THE CASE-
MENT WINDOWS
ADD A DECORATIVE
TOUCH TO THE
WALLS OF THE
HOUSE, AND THEY
ARE PLACED HIGH
TO FLOOD THE LIT-
TLE ROOMS WITH
LIGHT: AN EXCEL-
LENT MODEL FOR
LOGS OR CEMENT
CONSTRUCTION.

SIDE VIEW OF THE
ABOVE BUNGALOW,
SHOWING THE USE
OF PORCH AS AN
OUTDOOR LIVING
ROOM AS WELL AS
AN ADDED PICTUR-
ESQUE QUALITY AS
TO THE GENERAL
APPEARANCE: THE
ROOF OF TARRED
PAPER IS AN IM-
PORTANT SUGGES-
TION FOR AN INEX-
PENSIVE BUNGA-
LOW: THE SIMPLIC-
ITY OF THE STYLE
OF ARCHITECTURE
WOULD HARMONIZE
CHARMINGLY WITH
ANY PRIMITIVE
SURROUNDINGS.

BUNGALOW OF GRAY
PLASTER WITH
SHINGLED ROOF AND
RUSTIC PORCH SUP-
PORTS: THE ROOF
AND PORCH HOOD
ARE NOT PAINTED,
BUT LEFT TO
WEATHER: THE
CHIMNEY OF FIELD
STONE IS A PICTUR-
ESQUE ADDITION TO
THE TINY COTTAGE:
FOR SO SMALL A
HOUSE THE WIN-
DOWS ARE EXCEP-
TIONALLY WELL
PLACED: THE
SLIGHT EXPENSE OF
BUILDING WOULD
MAKE THIS COT-
TAGE PRACTICABLE
FOR A COUNTRY
PLACE FOR WEEK-
ENDS ONLY.

THIS BUNGALOW IS COVERED WITH BROAD WEATHER-BOARDING: THE PORCH IS CLOSED IN WITH RUSTIC TRELLIS SIDES FOR VINES: THE CHIMNEY IS OF FIELD STONE ROUGHLY TRIMMED, AND TAR PAPER COVERS THE ROOF FOR WARMTH AND SECURITY FROM RAIN: A HOMELIKE NOTE IS GIVEN IN THE FLOURISHING VEGETABLE GARDEN AT ONE SIDE OF THE HOUSE AND THE NEAT LITTLE PATH DIVIDED IT FROM THE FLOWERS.

THIS COTTAGE IS CALLED "THE POPLARS" AND IS PICTURESQUELY SITUATED: MEADOW GRASS AND WILD FLOWERS BRUSH UP AGAINST THE WALLS AND THE POPLAR TREES LEAN OVER AND SHELTER IT FROM ABOVE: WITH THE EXCEPTION OF THE BLACK TAR-PAPER ROOF, THE LITTLE HOUSE IS A SOFT WEATHER-STAINED GRAY, WITH WHITE CASEMENT TRIMMINGS: AN ENCHANTING SPOT FOR WEEK-END VISITS.

CUDDLED BACK IN THE VERY HEART OF THE WOODS THIS BUNGALOW RESTS: IT IS A LITTLE LESS PRIMITIVE IN CONSTRUCTION THAN THE OTHERS: THE BEAMS ARE TRIMMED SMOOTH AND STAINED AND THE BROAD PORCH IS SCREENED IN SO THAT THE LIVING SPACE IS PRACTICALLY DIVIDED INTO ROOMS AND PORCH: IT SUGGESTS A LONGER RESTING TIME THAN A WEEK-END VISIT.

SUMMER BUNGALOWS IN DELAWARE

sistent with comfort and attractiveness. And although it has gone through many changes in the readjustment to Western ideas of comfort and beauty, fortunately it has not lost in the transition its original fundamental purposes of furnishing space without elaboration, beauty without extravagance and comfort for the least expenditure of time and money.

Of course, there is a wide range of variation shown in the evolution of the bungalow in this country. In some of the Adirondack camps it has grown into an elaborate structure, with a second story added and many sumptuous details of finish and ornament; while in the Delaware week-end or summertime buildings, illustrated in this article, it has diminished into something scarcely more than a shingled cabin, yet even here holding to the better idea of space and to the suggestion of outdoor living on the wide porches. For every bungalow is designed always with the view of outdoor living or else it is not a self-respecting bungalow.

The country homes in America which are essentially an outgrowth of the bungalow, and yet emphatically adapted to our ideas of home life, have grown almost into a definite type of native architecture, so completely have they responded to the realities of the life of the vast majority of American people and this type of architecture, which we almost think of as new, aims not only to provide space for the unencumbered existence which sensible people have grown to demand, but it is adding to its inherent picturesqueness every sort of sane material comfort. And in addition it is also bravely facing the servant problem by seeking to reduce the amount of housework without essentially lessening the actual beauty of the house interior; rather adding to it, in fact, by insisting that, for the first time in the history of our domestic architecture, we shall present right structural line and well thought out color schemes in the interior of our homes, and insisting upon simplicity with beauty.

A MOUNTAIN BUNGALOW WHOSE APPEARANCE OF CRUDE CONSTRUCTION IS THE RESULT OF SKILFUL DESIGN

GREENE and Greene, who are responsible for so much of the interesting domestic architecture of the Pacific coast, are also the architects of this unusual bungalow built in the foothills of the Sierra Madres. These hills form some of the most beautiful scenery of southern California; they are low and sharply defined, swinging up from the rich valleys where the cities and towns are built; their heights are perpetually wound about with scarfs of rose and purple mist, below which emerge the forests of cypress, cedar and redwood, stretching a mantle of ruddy brown foliage down to the very edges of the peaceful olive orchards that cover the low slopes of the hills with their shimmering gray-green crowns. The coloring is intense but not brilliant; the landscape is deep and restful, rugged with frequent masses of richly-toned stone.

The architects, as nearly as it is possible, have reflected the general character of the landscape in the bungalow that they have designed. It is, as the picture shows, low and rambling, the roof low-pitched, with broadly projecting eaves. The foundations and chimneys are of the rough stone; the timbers are all of Oregon pine left rough and undressed, and wherever it is possible in the construction they are left exposed. The siding is of broad boards set upright with the cracks battened down with two-inch straps. The color blends with the ruddy brown of the hills, and the stonework is repeated by the big boulders that are scattered here and there over the property.

One of the chief charms of the house is its roughness; it gives the impression of being a haphazard construction carelessly built to serve as a mountain shelter for vagrant travelers. The native stone that is used in the construction is left quite rough and its arrangement appears to be governed by chance. The chimney, for example, shown in the second illustration, seems hardly more than a great heap of rock, so gradually does it narrow above the unusually broad base. The broad gaps between the stones at the bottom are filled in with the tendrils of an ivy vine which is planted at its base, and in the autumn the red of the foliage, massed irregularly against the gray-brown rock and the deeper toned house form a startlingly beautiful bit of natural decoration.

The bungalow is designed so that it makes a shallow patio or court surrounded on three sides. This space, shaded by the house, is converted into a miniature flower garden, where rustic seats are placed and hammocks swing. The bungalow contains six rooms, two sleeping rooms, besides a living room, den, dining room and kitchen, and all save the kitchen open upon the patio by wide doors set with glass panes above a short panel of wood.

The interior of the house has the same rough character as the exterior. The walls, and the ceiling, following the shape of the roof, are of the same broad boards of Oregon pine, battened at their junctures, but they are more smoothly finished than upon the outside of the house, as also are the timbers and the tie beams. The whole is given the dark stain of weathered oak.

All the furniture possible, such as bookcases, seats, writing desks, the sideboard and so forth, are built into the house, and the use of the broad boards and battens is most effective in the cabinet work. The rest of the furniture has been made especially to match the woodwork. The pieces are heavy and designed after a most simple and primitive model. The rails and posts of the chairs and settles are straight pieces of board, the posts four by four, and the rails nearly two inches thick. All the rails are notched into their supports, the ends projecting beyond and held in place by wooden pins. This rough construction gives an appearance of great strength and ruggedness which is in keeping with the massive fireplaces that heat

A CALIFORNIA MOUNTAIN BUNGALOW

the living room and den. These fireplaces are built of field stone, with the same effect of rude construction as the chimney outside; the stones are kept in place by inserting the back parts only into cement, and the effect is of a pile of stones built up about the fire, rather than a carefully constructed chimneypiece. A heavy pine board, five by six inches thick, forms the lintel above the fire opening, which is unusually large and has a capacity for huge logs. Above the lintel another heavy board forms a shelf, the ends extending beyond the massive chimney. On the hearth at either side of the fire opening, two boulders project in a natural way from the rest of the stonework and form two delightful fireside seats.

A house of such unusual design cannot but be interesting in itself, and the fittings which have been chosen for it are entirely in keeping with the exterior. Fabrics of Indian manufacture, with their quaint designs and rich coloring, form the hangings for the rooms, and the house contains many lovely pieces of Indian pottery, and baskets and relics of the earlier Indians.

The American bungalow has, at present, more general interest than any other form of house. Whether its rough and rugged exterior and the primitive features of its construction result from the carefully planned effects of some skilful architect, as in the case of this mountain shelter, or from the crude workmanship of the amateur who, following out the instincts of his forbears, builds his own rambling, one-story shack, the bungalow has more individuality than any other sort of dwelling place.

The reason is, in a way, obvious. It is only slowly that architects are getting away from the idea that life is more than "a round of calls and cues" and understanding that the town home may have just as strong an individuality and freedom in its construction, even if it be of a different sort, as a country house. In the bungalow, which is admittedly the shelter of an informal and untrammelled mode of living, the builders have, so to speak, let themselves go, unleashed their fancy, and, restrained only to meet the actual needs of life, have produced a variety of charming and individual structures, ranging from small, week-end houses to two-story buildings for all year use, under the name of bungalow.

And modern Americans are getting farther away, every day, from the formal, prescribed methods of conducting their households and their lives, and consequently are approaching simplicity and spontaneity even in their town life. The former artificiality of living was reflected in the artificiality and formality of the house, inside and out, and even after it began to disappear in practical living, custom made us retain the spirit of it in our architecture. Following the lead of a few clear-sighted builders who saw this gradual change of conditions, the town houses recently built, although showing a solidity and reserve consistent with their surroundings, yet exhibit more character and interest than ever before. It is not too much to say that this period of architecture has responded generously to the influence of the simple, informal bungalow.

Greene & Greene, Architects.
See page 329.

A BUNGALOW BUILT IN THE FOOTHILLS OF THE SIERRA MADRES: THE FOUNDATION AND CHIMNEY ARE OF FIELD STONE, THE TIMBERS ARE UNDRESSED OREGON PINE.

THE CHIMNEY OF THE BUNGALOW BUILT BY GREENE & GREENE HAS
AN ESPECIALLY PICTURESQUE BEAUTY. IT SEEMS TO SPRING FROM
THE GROUND, YET IS AN INHERENT PART OF THE ARCHITECTURE.

BUNGALOW OWNED BY MR. E. A. WEBBER, OF LOS ANGELES: DESIGNED BY MR. ALFRED HEINEMAN.

AN EXAMPLE OF PROGRESSIVE ARCHITECTURE FROM THE PACIFIC COAST: BY HELEN LUKENS GAUT

SO many beautiful and unusual designs for houses come to us from the Pacific Coast, that it would almost seem as if the West were the only home of the new American architecture. It is perhaps natural that this should be so, for the true Westerner is a practical soul, and ever open to suggestions from any quarter which promise to increase his comfort and gratify his sense of beauty. Furthermore, the Californian has the courage of his convictions in building the kind of house that seems to him most suitable for the climate and surroundings of that part of the country. Therefore, he either builds it of concrete, in which case it takes naturally a form resembling that of the old missions; or he builds it of wood, and here we get the influence of the Orient, especially of Japan. This does not mean that both types of houses are not entirely modern and distinctively American, only that the same conditions which created the older forms of building have been met with equal directness in the new.

Therefore the bungalow shown here reminds one distinctly of the Japanese grouping of irregular roof lines, and also of the Japanese use of timbers. Yet there is hardly a feature which one could point out as being derived from the Japanese. The resemblance comes rather from the same appreciation of the decorative possibilities of wood as a building material, and of the modifications that present themselves naturally when the wood is combined with the rough cement blocks and pillars of a part of the construction. Both the shingles and the heavy timbers are of redwood, the rich red brown tone of the oiled wood contrasting pleasantly with the deep biscuit color of the concrete. The decorative use of wood is shown in marked degree in the fence which extends from the back of the house to the stable. The device of wide boards of alternate length, set close together and capped with a heavy square rail, is so simple that the individual effect of such a fence is amazing, and sets us to wondering why most of these high screening fences are so irredeemably ugly when it is such an easy matter to make them beautiful.

This bungalow, which was designed by Mr. Alfred Heineman, a Los Angeles architect, and is owned by Mr. E. A. Webber, of Los Angeles, shows the result of close sympathy and clear understanding between the architect and the owner. It contains eight rooms, with a bathroom, screen porch, large upper screen bedroom, front veranda, patio, cellar and furnace room, and being on one floor it naturally spreads over a fair amount of ground. It is not at all the sort of a building to be put up on a narrow city lot, for in addition to covering a reasonable area of ground itself, it absolutely demands to be set in an ample space of grass and shrubbery, or much of its charm would be hidden.

One of the most charming features of the house is that which marks it as belonging to a warm, sunshiny climate,—the patio on the south side. This is put to precisely the same use as it was in the old Spanish days; that is, much of the family life is carried on out there, the place being made charming with rough, comfortable furniture that can stand exposure to the weather, and with pots and hanging baskets of palms, ferns and flowering plants. A small open space between the pavement and wall of the house allows for a flower bed, so that all the plants are growing and healthy. At night the place is lighted with lanterns of hammered glass that hang in wrought-iron frames from the cross-beams of the pergola. The vines, which will ultimately

PATIO IN MR. WEBBER'S BUNGALOW.

clamber all over this pergola, have been planted so recently that they have barely reached to the top of the pillars, but when they attain their growth, as they will do within a marvelously short time, the last touch of beauty will have been added to this pleasant outdoor retreat. The admirable arrangement of the bungalow is clearly shown by the floor plan, but a more

LIVING ROOM, LOOKING INTO DEN.

vivid idea of the rooms and their relation to one another may be seen in the reproductions from photographs of the interior. Although this house is distinctly a bunga-

low, there is nothing crude about its finish or construction, either inside or out. The woodwork of the interior is all of redwood, finished so that the satiny surface and beautiful color effects are given their full value. The beams which span the ceilings of the living room, dining room and den are all boxed, as are the massive square posts that appear in the openings between the living room and den and also between the dining room and breakfast room.

A particularly charming effect is given by the arrangement of the tiled chimneypiece in the living room. This is low, broad and generous looking, and the bookcases on either side, with the leaded glass windows above, form a part of the structure which is treated as a whole and fills the entire end of the room. Leaded glass, in beautiful landscape designs and harmonious coloring, is used with admirable effect in the windows above the piano and fireplace, and also in the glass doors of the buffet and book-

LIVING ROOM, SHOWING FIREPLACE.

cases. The den, which forms a part of the living room, is treated in much the same way as the larger room, save that its walls are wholly paneled with wood, and in a recess at one side of the window is built a wall bed which can be let down when necessary, converting the room into an additional bedroom to be used when the house is full. The opening into the dining room is so wide that it also seems to be a part of the living room. The ceiling differs from that of the other room in that it runs up to a slight peak where a massive girder affords support for the cross - beams. The walls of this room are paneled with red-wood to the height of the plate rail, and the wall space above is covered with tapestry paper in a low-toned forest design. The large buffet is built in, and with the china closet above, extends to the ceiling.

Just off the dining room is a small breakfast room which, with its wide bay window, is hardly more than a very large window nook that is flooded with sunshine in the morning, and is a delightful place for breakfast. It is also used as a supplementary dining room when enter-

tainments are given. The same taste that ruled the building and decorating of this house also directed its furnishing, so that the furniture falls readily into place as a part of the whole scheme of things, and harmonizes completely with the woodwork and the whole style of construction. It is not often that one sees this because, although people may build an entirely new house, they usually go into it laden with possessions which are dear to them, but which can hardly be said to harmonize with the structural scheme of a modern bungalow. In this case, however, the furniture might have been chosen with a special reference to this house. Even the Turkish rugs, ordinarily so difficult to reconcile with the slightly rugged effect that usually prevails in a bungalow, are quite at home here, because the whole interior finish is so com-

DINING ROOM, SHOWING BUILT-IN SIDEBOARD.

plete and delicate that the house affords an admirable setting for Oriental rugs.

Plenty of outdoor sleeping accommodations are afforded because a screen porch opens from one of the bedrooms, and up-

PROGRESSIVE ARCHITECTURE IN THE WEST

stairs is a large screen room which gives ample accommodation to all who care to sleep out-of-doors. This upstairs screen room is not only a convenience, but its presence adds much to the exterior beauty of the house, as it gives an opportunity for a slight

into a sunroom by the addition of a glass roof and a front wall of glass in place of the pergola and pillars. With a southern exposure this would mean a delightful sunroom and conservatory, especially in winter,

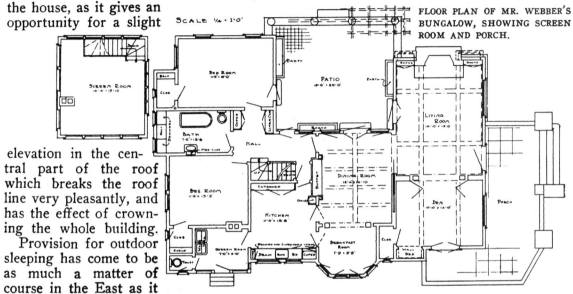

FLOOR PLAN OF MR. WEBBER'S BUNGALOW, SHOWING SCREEN ROOM AND PORCH.

elevation in the central part of the roof which breaks the roof line very pleasantly, and has the effect of crowning the whole building.

Provision for outdoor sleeping has come to be as much a matter of course in the East as it is in the West, and this screen room would be particularly well adapted to the Eastern climate, because the widely overhanging roof affords plenty of shelter even from driving storms. Also in an Eastern climate it might be advisable to transform the patio

as it would get all the sunshine there is and would also be sheltered from cold and wind by the walls of the house. If the glass roof gave too much light the open space could, of course, be roofed over in the ordinary way.

A CHARMING AND INEXPENSIVE COTTAGE IN THE BUNGALOW STYLE: BY HELEN LUKENS GAUT

HERE is yet another bungalow from the land of bungalows,—southern California. It was designed by Mr. Charles E. Shattuck, a Los Angeles architect, and was built in that city. It is a plan that may easily be adapted to the requirements of an Eastern climate, especially as it is carefully finished in every detail, being meant for a permanent dwelling instead of a summer camp or vacation home. Like most California houses it is built of wood, and the red brick used for the chimney and the pillars of the pergola blends well with the warm brown tones of the timbers and shingles.

The plan is admirable in the regard for convenience and comfort shown in the arrangement of the rooms, and in the economy of space that gives a larger amount of room than would seem possible within the limits of a small house. The house itself seems really larger than it is, because, being all on one floor, it is long and wide in proportion to its height, and the low-pitched, wide-eaved roof has a splendid straight sweep giving the effect as well as the actuality of shelter.

By a rather unusual arrangement, the big outside chimney is at the front of the house, and the entrance from the street to the recessed porch, which runs partly down the side, is at the corner. Beyond this there is a good-sized porte-cochère, sheltered by a pergola supported upon massive square brick pillars that taper slightly toward the top. Both roof and walls of the bungalow are covered with shingles, left unpainted so that they may take on the delightful tones of silvery gray and brown that only the

LOOKING THROUGH THE PERGOLA PORTE COCHERE.

weather can give. The foundation is entirely hidden by shrubs and flowers that grow close to the walls, and the woodbine that partially covers the chimney softens the severity of its straight lines. Between the pillars of the porte-cochère are heavy iron chains, which have been allowed to rust to a rich golden brown color, and be-

COTTAGE IN BUNGALOW STYLE

hind them a high lattice clothed with vines shelters the house from its next-door neighbor. The window frames are painted white, so that they form high lights in the general color scheme and repeat the white of the cement walk, steps and floor of the recessed porch.

LIVING ROOM, SHOWING INGLENOOK.

The interior of the bungalow is plastered throughout, and all the walls and ceilings are tinted in harmonizing tones of cream, brown and old gold. The woodwork, of which there is a great deal, is all brown, and the floors are of oak. The massive mantel of red-brown brick seems to center in itself the warmth of the whole color scheme. On the side of the living room opposite the fireplace is a deep alcove which was built and used by the original owner for installing a pipe organ,

but is now used for a cushioned recess. Bookcases with wooden doors extend across the entire end of the room, and a line of latticed windows fills the space between these cabinets and the plate rail that runs just below the plaster frieze. More bookcases with leaded glass doors extend up the side of the room to the corner of the recess. On either side of the fireplace are two large windows, so that the room is amply lighted.

A small hall with a built-in seat connects the living room with the dining room, and also with the rear hall which affords a means of communication to

DINING ROOM.

the bedrooms and the bath. The treatment of the dining room differs only in minor details from that of the living room. A high wainscot has panels of dark brown leather paper, divided with four-inch stiles set eighteen inches apart. This wainscot is topped with a wide plate rail, and the wall above is tinted to a soft tone of light buff. The ceiling, like that of the living room, is spanned with beams, and the plaster panels between are tinted to the same color as the walls. All the furniture in the dining room is of cedar,

LIVING ROOM, WITH GLIMPSE OF DINING ROOM. and was specially designed by

COTTAGE IN BUNGALOW STYLE

the owner to express his own ideas.

The two bedrooms, with the bathroom between and the screened sleeping porch, are at the rear of the house. A small room for the servant opens off the kitchen, which is equipped with all modern conveniences. As the bungalow was built, it would be suitable for any climate, as it has hot and cold water, electric lights, a good cellar, furnace and all the other comforts that are required in the East, but are more or less optional in the mild California climate. The approximate cost in Los Angeles, where the house was built, was, including fences, woodshed and cement walks, $3,500. It would probably cost more to build a bungalow of this size and design in any part of the East, as

DETAIL OF PERGOLA CONSTRUCTION.

the vicinity of Los Angeles than it is in the neighborhood of New York or Boston, for example. Of course, much would depend upon the attitude of the owner toward the work, as this materially affects the cost of building a dwelling. If he gave the matter his personal attention, hired his men in the most economical way, and saw to it that he obtained his building materials at the lowest possible cost, the price of the house would be considerably less than the estimate given by the average contractor. A great deal of difference also arises from the kind of materials used. If an expensive hardwood is chosen for the interior woodwork, the price goes up instantly. Fortunately, beautiful effects can be obtained by the right use of comparatively inexpensive native woods, and if the owner has sufficient skill in the treatment of wood to finish the woodwork of both exterior and interior himself, one considerable item of expense will be lopped off in the beginning. A house finished, like this one, in redwood costs comparatively little in California, where this beautiful wood is abundant, easily obtained and not at all expensive. If the house were built in the East, it might

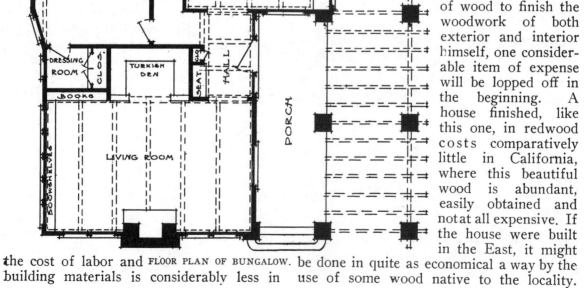

FLOOR PLAN OF BUNGALOW.

the cost of labor and building materials is considerably less in

be done in quite as economical a way by the use of some wood native to the locality.

A CALIFORNIA BUNGALOW TREATED IN JAPANESE STYLE: BY ARNOLD L. GESELL

THERE were a few things the builder of this bungalow was sure of from the start: It should be an outdoor house, suited to rural surroundings —light, open, airy, unplastered and unpapered. It should also be a long, low structure like the Mexican hut whose simple, comfortable, horizontal lines seem architecturally so harmonious with the landscape and atmosphere of our Western country.

MINIATURE OF BUNGALOW

MEXICAN HUT WHICH FURNISHED BUNGALOW SUGGESTION.

Another primary suggestion came from the beautiful tall eucalyptus tree (which often grows beside the Mexican hut). This tree is one of the characteristic features of southern California. Though a native of Australia, it thrives on the Pacific Coast almost as though indigenous to the soil, and promises to be one of the great resources of the State; dressed and polished, it rivals mahogany. Its clean pinkish-gray bark also adapts it to unfinished, rustic uses.

To begin with, we made rough sketches of a long, low house, with eucalyptus beams. An arts and crafts friend became interested

BUNGALOW WOODWORK IN JAPANESE STYLE

and suggested a clever way by which the walls of the house could be sturdily constructed of one-inch boards, overlapped in a manner to make unnecessary the use of flimsy battens.

We built a miniature house at the start. It is hard for the untrained mind to think in three dimensions, and the putting together of the house model suggested many possibilities which a struggle with pencil on a plane surface alone could never have done. This miniature took the place of architect's drawings. In fact, we did not use blue prints at all; we planned as we built, rather than the reverse. The fourteen corners of the house were first put up; then the placing of the long, spacious windows was determined, and the walls were literally built around the windows. The partitions were all located for the first time after the floor was down. The fireplace was planned the night before we were ready to use the stone. Much of the furniture was built into the

PYROGRAPHIC OUTFIT FOR TREATING WOOD.

house as we proceeded, and was adapted to its lines and angles. Everybody, even visitors, had a chance to give constructive suggestions. And so the house changed, grew and took shape under our combined hands.

From the road you can hardly see the embowered bungalow; but you catch glimpses of it through the large, leafy English walnut and the dark green orange trees. A prim brick walk leads past a little "public bird bath" and, under the wide-spreading walnut boughs, to the broad front door, or through the long rustic pergola built of unhewn eucalyptus tree trunks. At the further front corner is a eucalyptus stairway which takes you to a roof lookout where you can see stretches of lovely mountains. Not a board in the house was painted, varnished or stained; but every piece was literally charred and brushed on each exposed face and edge before it became a part either of the structure or the furniture. It was a laborious task, but not without recompense, for under this pyrographic treatment even the least interesting wood becomes beautiful, taking on a soft brown corrugated sheen.

Our method was as follows: Each board was placed on a rough easel; the hot blast of a plumber's double-mouthed torch was applied until the whole surface was distinctly charred. Merely scorching the wood to a cloudy brown is an easy matter; it is the charring to a crisp black which take patience—and brings the reward. The intense heat fashions the character of the wood; it burns the hard fiber a permanent strong dark brown and the soft fiber it

SHOWING METHOD OF CONSTRUCTION.

BUNGALOW WOODWORK IN JAPANESE STYLE

THE SECLUDED COURTYARD.

completely incinerates. When a board has been charred it looks no more promising than a slab which might have come from the ruins of a burned building; but under the plowing, biting attack of the stiff steel butcher's brush what transformation! A dozen hard strokes, and nature's hidden pattern emerges into beautiful relief. If you discount the hard work this brushing is most fascinating and interesting; the burning is especially so done in the quiet dark of the night.

After the boards were burned, brushed and sawed, the walls were reared, but without nails. First, the fourteen corners, each consisting of two upright boards at right angles; then long ribbons (6 inches wide) were strung horizontally from corner to corner. There are three pairs of these ribbons, one at the top, forming the roof plate, one in the middle and one at the bottom. The method of construction is shown in the illustration. (A door, built like the walls, has been taken from its hinges and laid on its side to show a sectional view.) The ribbons serve as binders for the wall boards (12 inches wide), which are placed upright with an overlap of 1½ inches. The alternate open spaces (9 inches wide) between

the wall boards and the ribbons are filled with "filler blocks" (shown dark in the picture). The whole is tightly bound together by 4-inch carriage bolts, inserted through the middle axis of each board to allow for shrinkage and expansion, without splitting.

This triple-bound, triple-bolted wall, with a gross diameter of 4 inches, makes a staunch support for the heavy eucalyptus beams, and has an individual beauty besides. The top and bottom ribbons, with their regularly recurring bolt heads, make a pleasing border for the interior of each room and for the exterior of the house. The upright boards alternate in such a manner that every wall, inside and out, forms a series of raised and sunken panels.

The back doorway is nothing more than a comfortable arch between a large orange and a large lemon tree. These two trees complete the enclosure of a secluded quadrangular court which is really a central room. The floor of this court is a soft red brick pavement; the roof is the azure California sky.

From the court you can peep into the kitchen. Sink, cooler, closet, bins are all within arm's reach, compactly contrived to save steps. And every piece of wood is

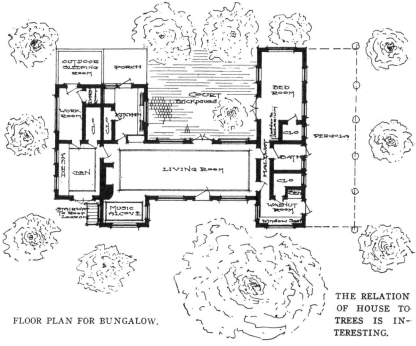

FLOOR PLAN FOR BUNGALOW.

THE RELATION OF HOUSE TO TREES IS INTERESTING.

BUNGALOW WOODWORK IN JAPANESE STYLE

pyrographed and brushed, so that in finish the kitchen is as attractive as any part of the house. Why shouldn't it be?

In the outdoor sleeping room the woodwork is not so impressive, for the walls are almost all screens—with a mesh wide enough to admit sweet air from orchard and mountains.

Adjoining the outdoor sleeping room is a workshop, with carpenter's bench and tools. Brushing aside a curtain made of the long pendant strings of eucalyptus acorns you enter the den. This looks like a workshop, too, with its long, wide desk built like a shelf along one whole side of the wall. The wood in the den has a darker tone, because though pyrographed in the same manner as the other wood, it was brushed *with* the grain instead of *crosswise*. Orange trees shade the windows on one side; on the other is the soft brown masonry of the fireplace, and a little stone wall. Through the lattice above the wall you may peep into the living room.

Returning to the court you pass through French doors into the bedroom. This room has a special charm. An orange tree, with its deep green leaves and golden fruit, presses close against the many-paned window at the end, giving an effect in color and design more wonderful than anything possible in stained-glass art. The room is built

FIREPLACE IN LIVING ROOM.

of California redwood, soft in texture and delicate in its pervading salmon hue. Gold-colored curtains add a little extra glory to the sunlight.

A hallway leads to a cozy room with a long seat and a generous window through which an English walnut tree almost forces its way. A wallbed is built into the closet of this room. By a peg ladder, constructed after the primitive log-cabin style, you can climb onto the sundeck. This deck is really nothing more than the "floored ceiling" of the closets and bath below. A big skylight overhead makes of it a solarium, which gathers precious sunshine in the cool weather.

From the sundeck one can peer down and through the eucalyptus beams and rafters into the long living room. This extensive room is the delight of the bungalow. It is literally bathed in sunlight. Through the sundeck windows at one end, through the chimney transom and skylight at the other, through the variegated panes of art glass in the eaves and through the long windows on either side, the sun comes in. In the cool but sunny weather which prevails through most of the California year, this big airy room is kept at a delightful natural warmth. When the weather is warmer a space two feet wide, extending the

CORNER OF LIVING ROOM.

BUNGALOW WOODWORK IN JAPANESE STYLE

whole length of the ridgepole, can be opened.

The ridgepole was a tall, straight eucalyptus tree, which it took two strong horses to drag. Unhewn and unspliced, it extends from the sundeck into the masonry of the fireplace, a distance of 36 feet. The rafters, crossbeams and ridgepole are all held together, like Solomon's temple, by stout wooden pegs. On one of the crossbeams sits an Arctic owl, on another the carved home of two cuckoos from the Black Forest.

The appointments of the living room are most simple. The double crotch of an orange tree with a redwood top serves as a table; the bookshelves with long curving sides are built in at the ends of windows and benches. The absence of excessive furniture is perhaps one reason why so many people can gather and chat with ease in this one room. It is easily converted into a banquet hall by swinging the long table from the crossbeams and drawing up the benches.

comfortable instead of a ponderous and stiff appearance. It makes a pretty stone-wall partition and at the same time an effective mantelpiece for vase, fruit and flowers. Through a grating made of beautiful burnt wood, you get glimpses of the adjoining den and of the green and gold orange groves beyond. It is especially interesting to note the relation of house to trees.

One feels in the description of this house, at once its individuality and its utility. It is especially suited to the needs of the people who planned and built it. It is arranged to satisfy their ideal of beauty and their idea of comfort. It is planned for plenty of air and sunlight, for outdoor life, and for the mental rest which comes from peaceful vistas and well-harmonized color.

All together it is not the kind of house these particular people could ever have bought finished. The ready-to-use house is built to sell, not use; it is an investment, not a dwelling place. You have got to be intimate with the construction of your house,

VIEW OF BUNGALOW HIDDEN IN WALNUT AND ORANGE TREES.

An alcove makes room for a couch and piano. The long window above the piano is far more alluring than a landscape painting, for it frames an ever-changing view of the distant mountain tops. The house holds many vistas, glimpses and cross-glimpses, and the eye wanders on many journeys through the transom windows, French doors and skylights.

The walls, the drapery, the benches, the carpet and the fireplace all are brown or fawn color.

One of the happiest features of the living room is the low lateral extension of the chimney. It gives the whole fireplace a

to have a sense of intimacy in the finished structure. No one can make a home for you, any more than a character can be developed for you, and the more of yourself that goes into the designing and building of the place in which you are going to live the more happiness you'll get out of living there.

This bungalow with Japanese finish is like a family friend to the owners. It expresses old theories, new points of view, hopes for the future and memories of the past, and incidentally is a message to others who wish to build, telling them to follow out the fundamental idea, not the floor plans, for their joy and peace of mind.

CALIFORNIA BUNGALOW WORTH STUDYING

BUNGALOW IN PASADENA, CAL., DESIGNED BY EDWARD E. SWEET.

A CALIFORNIA BUNGALOW OF STONE AND SHINGLE WORTH STUDYING, BOTH IN DESIGN AND INTERIOR FINISH

THAT it is wise to put new wine in new bottles cannot be doubted, and that it is the part of wisdom to put new architecture in new lands is also true. The West is not as yet put to the sad necessity of building houses in perpendicular form, "standing room only," on tip-toe to catch a bit of sun and air! They can assume a comfortable horizontal position, lounging at ease in the midst of gardens! The long low-sweeping line of roof of these charming bungalow-houses permits a beauty such as is often obtained in the "sheer" of a boat.

The accompanying photographs of a house built by Edward E. Sweet of Pasadena, California, at a cost of only $3,500.00 is an excellent type of the commodious, beautifully proportioned bungalows now becoming known as Californian—the new architecture of a new land. This building grows from a rock foundation quite as vegetation springs from the earth, the chimneys rising above it as large rocks occasionally lift their gray heads above the grass and flowers associated with them

DINING ROOM IN BUNGALOW.

in the lawns of Nature's making.

The use of shingles forms a distinct decorative note; the beams and cobbles are handled in a most interesting way; the windows are pleasant spots placed happily in the composition, and the roof completes the whole in a satisfactory manner. Nothing jars, but every feature unites in forming a house of exceptional beauty.

The arrangement of the interior is no less satisfying, combining comfort, convenience, privacy, simplicity, yet creating a luxurious sense of space. The large living room with its reading table within comfortable proximity to the fireplace, a smaller room joined in

BUNGALOW LIVING ROOM.

CALIFORNIA BUNGALOW WORTH STUDYING

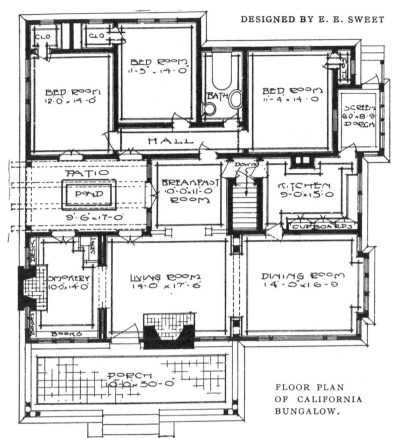

DESIGNED BY E. E. SWEET

FLOOR PLAN
OF CALIFORNIA
BUNGALOW.

easy access to the patio.

This patio provides another feature of great interest, in its endless possibilities for the enjoyment of outdoor teas, moonlight nights, flowers, vines, fountains, hammocks.

The picturesque use of beams throughout the whole house and the harmonious repetition of the curve of them at the windows appeals to one as a unifying note of exceptional charm. The built-in sideboard and china closets in the dining room show that compactness is a phase of beauty if rightly understood and used. The interior finish of woodwork, the method of lighting, the polished floors add their distinct characteristics to the general effect of substantiality and charm.

The color scheme of the exterior deserves especial consideration, for there are no sudden contrasts of positive color to disturb the eye. The concrete walk joins with the stone foundation, flows into it as one undivided tone. The green of the grass is caught again at the entrance palms and patio vines. The redwood beams and shingles are as one, and the glimpse of chimneys above the roof holds it all together with the foundation, binding the separate parts into a perfect whole.

social manner to the larger room, with no sense of lonesome separateness, yet giving certain seclusion to the smokers or perhaps the young students of the household, suggest hominess, joy of family life.

A large dining room for the formal dinner, a cozy breakfast room just off the patio where glimpse of a pond can be seen, where perhaps a fountain plays or waterlilies grow, provides perfect dining room facilities.

The three bedrooms at the rear give quiet seclusion to sleepers, are within convenient proximity to the bathroom and have

The type of architecture is eminently suitable to the land, for it is low like the foot-hills about it, broad and substantial.

A SECOND VIEW OF $3,500.00 CALIFORNIA BUNGALOW.

A CALIFORNIA BUNGALOW OF ORIGINALITY AND CHARM

A CALIFORNIA BUNGALOW OF ORIGINALITY AND CHARM

IT would be difficult for even a stranger, much less an acquaintance, to pass by this house without entering and making himself happily at home upon the cool wide porch! Its invitation is so evident, so genuine and irresistible that it seems to include the world at large as well as intimate friends. The soft green of the rugs and wicker chairs, the palms and ferns so excellently placed, the rich color of the wood, combine to weave a lure that is almost peremptory. The low railing around this porch is an interesting feature, forming a convenient receptacle for a magazine, book, workbasket or pot of flowers, as well as adding a cozy sense to what is essentially an outdoor living room. Everyone likes to sit on the railing around a porch, no matter how high, frail or uncomfortable it is, and this low, broad, substantial balustrade permits such treatment in comfort and safety. Such a simply constructed railing should be a joy to any housekeeper, for it is free from the obstructions found on most porch railings that make it difficult to keep the floor well swept.

The most distinctive feature of this charming Los Angeles bungalow is the roof, which the architect, Reginald Harris, has treated in the bold and original manner so suitable to California architecture. The immense overhang of it, the grace of its sweeping lines, the balance of one line with another, the composition of the whole, the management and arrangement of the upper and lower roof areas are distinctly original and decidedly beautiful and give an air of magnificence to a house that is really very simple and inexpensive. The house is a typical bungalow in the height of its ceilings, which are eight feet six inches downstairs and seven feet six inches upstairs, and the low, gradual, broad sweep of the roof lines keep the two-story house within conventionalized bungalow limits. The large copper lantern is in admirable keeping with the general style of breadth and grace, adding a note of welcome at night, throwing a soft, subdued light over every-

DETAIL OF THE PORCH SHOWING INTERESTING USE OF CONCRETE.

A CALIFORNIA BUNGALOW OF ORIGINALITY AND CHARM

thing. French windows opening from the dining room make it easy to move the table out on the porch, that the breakfast, luncheon or tea may be served there.

The interior of this home is simple, convenient and comfortable. Large windows and doors made of glass let in plenty of light and air and are so arranged that they make a decorative note in the general design of the exterior. The outside of this commodious house is of ordinary weather boarding with concrete pillars and chimney, and ruberoid roof.

The living-room walls and ceilings are finished in Oregon pine stained the soft green that can be so successfully obtained on this wood. In every room is to be found some useful built-in features. In the sitting room are bookcases, in the dining room a buffet, and cabinets in the kitchen, chests of drawers in the bedroom. Economy of space is thus obtained, a convenient place for everything is assured, and a decorative effect in each room is produced which is attractive and satisfying in every particular.

The walls and ceiling of the dining room are also finished in Oregon pine, with the exception of the frieze introduced above the plate rail. This frieze adds to the sense of outdoors given to the room by the large windows and glass doors, for it shows a bit of forest, just such a glimpse of trees and soft skies as would be seen through real windows. The frieze of trees, continuing from window to window, gives an apparent outdoor view without a break around the whole room, so that the dining table seems to be set at the edge of a forest glade, the real open windows giving a vista of sunny plains.

Another interesting feature of this house is the outdoor sleeping room, which is entered from the upper hall, through large French windows. These outdoor bedrooms have come to be as much a part of a Californian house plan as the kitchen, dining room or reception room, for whoever has once slept in the open air never willingly shuts himself up in the ordinary old-time bedroom again. Almost everyone in this favored clime has, through friend or hotel, been given an oppor-

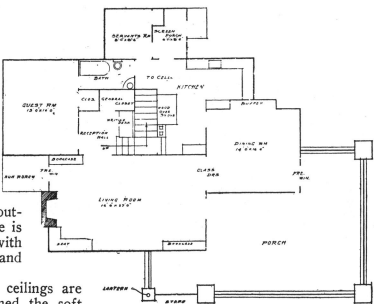

CALIFORNIA BUNGALOW: FIRST FLOOR PLAN.

tunity to sleep in one of these starlit rooms and at once the ambition to possess such a sweet, wholesome bedroom takes possession of the guest or traveler. So hardly a home is to be found without such a bedroom, either built especially for such purpose or else created as successfully as possible from some porch.

In this sleeping room a disappearing bed is installed which permits the room to be used as outdoor sitting or sewing room during the day, the bed itself forming a comfortable seat and convenient lounging place.

The bedrooms are all finished in white, which is a universally satisfactory way of finishing sleeping or dressing rooms because of the resultant lightness, freshness, cleanliness, airiness.

Nothing expensive has been installed in this house. It is just another of the many beautiful bungalows being constructed by home-makers and architects throughout the

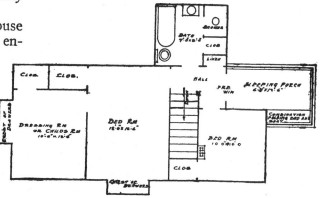

CALIFORNIA BUNGALOW: SECOND FLOOR PLAN.

A CALIFORNIA BUNGALOW OF ORIGINALITY AND CHARM

VIEW OF THE OUTDOOR LIVING ROOM.

West. The immense overhang of the roof creates the shade so much to be desired at midday in this sunny land, besides adding the distinct note of originality and beauty to the building. This bungalow, so simple, informal, comfortable, "homey" in every way, could be duplicated, considering the number of rooms it contains, for a price surprisingly low, because it is so free from unnecessary ornament or display.

The floor plan is well worth a careful study by anyone wishing to build a home where economy of space is to be a feature, for there is no waste of double partitions, no unnecessary hall space. The rooms fit together with the utmost ease, apparently, yet all home-builders know that this is the result of careful planning. All the measurements are broad and generous, like the entrance to the house itself, and also the passages from o n e room into another. The vistas from room to room, the charming use of glass doors from living room into dining room and the French door from the dining room onto the porch, give a sense of space, as of one great room barely walled f r o m the weather. The many windows and the sun-porch extension heighten this

sense of outdoor life. Certainly as much of the light, cheer and vigor of the out-of-doors is retained as is possible in any house.

The centering of stairways leading up to the bedrooms and down to the basement, with the s e v e r a l closets, is an excellent arrangement of great working convenience and an example of wise use of wall space —w h i c h simplifies building. This use of the inner walls for household convenience leaves the outer walls free for an abundance of large windows. Where there is not a window it is because there is a door leading to a porch. The kitchen porch is well placed for entry and usefulness generally.

In the second floor plan can be seen the same simple arrangement of rooms that distinguishes the first floor. The many closets and the built-in chests of drawers lead one to believe that the housekeeper must be a perfectly satisfied one, for certainly the rooms are amply provided with these necessities of order and convenience. The plan shows the sleeping porch with the bed which closes into a lounging couch or seat during the day, thus converting the sleeping porch of the night into an outdoor sitting room for use during the daylight hours.

CORNER OF OUTDOOR LIVING ROOM.

A CALIFORNIA BUNGALOW OF ORIGINALITY AND CHARM

It is hard to find more ideal conditions for the exercising of an architect's ingenuity and good taste than in this western land. The cost of construction is much less than in the East because the necessity of meeting the severity of winter is done away with. The problems of plumbing, lighting and heating are reduced to a minimum, so that an architect can devote the major part of his skill to creating beauty. Elsewhere these three problems sometimes d r i v e beauty of line into the background and they also demand so large a part of the price set aside for the construction of the home that there is little left to be devoted to the beauty without which a home is built in vain.

The West, or rather the people who are drawn to seek a home in the West, encourage simplicity of living. And simplicity of living permits simplicity of building. It also encourages originality in every direction, the builder's ideal being not to build as others have built, but to build as he himself desires. And when people dare to be true to themselves there is bound to be a great manifestation of originality. For it is

INDOOR LIVING ROOM LOOKING INTO DINING ROOM

the slavish obedience to custom or precedent that makes for monotony, and monotony leads to degeneration. A copy of a copy is the surest way in the world to lose the beauty that marked the original and that prompted the first copy. Just as no two people are alike in character, but each interesting in some especial direction, so no two homes would be alike, but each interesting and beautiful in a separate way if the builders of the houses would but exercise the individuality they find in themselves. Since the West encourages originality in every way and scoffs at the dulness that knows only how to imitate, the homes of its people, the office buildings, stores, bridges are marked by a freshness of design that furnishes one of the chief charms of the Pacific Coast. Every effort is made to have each new home different from all others, not that it may rival its friend and neighbor, but that the beauty of each and the civic beauty of the whole community may be enhanced. Imitation in architecture is not the "sincerest form of flattery"; it is a form of cheapening.

ONE CORNER OF DINING ROOM.

HOW I BUILT MY BUNGALOW: BY CHARLOTTE DYER

Illustrated by Helen Lukens Gaut.

FRONT VIEW OF CALIFORNIA BUNGALOW, SHOWING COVERED AND PERGOLA PORCH.

LIKE most young girls I built a "castle in the air" and waited for the "fairy prince." My "castle" was, a bungalow. I studied descriptions and illustrations of these pretty little houses far more earnestly that I did my Latin or the fashions, and waited. Of course, I knew I should never have a bungalow of my own until after the arrival of the "fairy prince." And at last, however, though even now it seems too good to be true, every wish is realized. My "castle," without a bump, a thump or a bruise, has settled gracefully to terra firma, and my "fairy prince" has come and has turned into a king, and we are, as the story books say, going to live happily ever after.

We started housekeeping in an apartment house, but we both hated such a life. Electric cars whizzed and rumbled in front of us, while a bull terrier and a poll parrot barked and shrieked at the back of us. We wanted to be quiet and alone, and almost at once we began looking for a ready-made bungalow into which we could move our bags and baggage, and in which we could turn our unrest into peace. We looked at scores of houses, and while we didn't feel we were especially hard to please, we couldn't find anything that just suited. We wanted a view of the mountains, and we knew we wouldn't be satisfied with anything else. Several friends said: "Why don't you buy the lot you want and design and build your own house?" I told them I couldn't do such a thing as design a house, that I knew absolutely nothing about building. I kept their suggestion in mind, however, and the more I thought about it, the more I thought that perhaps I could design my house. Whenever I passed a bungalow in course of construction, I looked over the foundation, framework, finish, etc., until I acquired a certain familiarity with house construction.

About this time I met a woman whose business was that of designing and building houses to sell. She was most proficient in her line, in fact, had made a small fortune in this work. She encouraged me to go ahead and build my bungalow, saying she would be glad to help me in any way. These talks with her gave me inspiration and courage, and very soon I began the actual planning and superintendence of our home. I decided not to engage an architect. I knew exactly what I wanted, and so often an architect will insist on incorporating his own ideas, and I wanted just us, my husband and myself, in the "thought" of our home. I wanted a bit of our personality driven in with every nail.

We now began lot hunting in earnest, and finally found one that pleased us im-

HOW I BUILT MY BUNGALOW

SIDE VIEW OF BUNGALOW.

mensely, for it had a long sweeping view of valley and mountains. This lot, however, was somewhat small, only 40 by 120 feet, and we had set our hearts on having one with at least sixty-feet frontage. On making inquiry we found that the adjoining lot was for sale, so we decided to buy both of them. After holding a "family" consultation, we made up our minds to build a long narrow bungalow on a part of one of the lots, leaving the balance to increase the size of the other lot, on which we intended to build later on. As neither of us had ever built before, we concluded

to call this first house our experiment, a sort of elementary schooling to fit us for building the next, which was to be, so we then thought, our real home. We planned to live in the "experiment" for a little while, then sell at an advance, or rent it. But that was at the beginning. Now that the Bungalow is finished and we are living in it, we have neither desire nor intention of giving it up. Scarce a week passes that some real-estate agent does not stop to inquire if the bungalow is for sale, and somehow I can't help feeling a bit indignant that anyone should suggest my giving it up. I watched it grow so lovingly, from the first thought and foundation stone, to the last timber and pot of paint, and I prize every board and shingle and nail in it as if they were piece and parcel of my very soul.

While there is nothing very technical in building a small bungalow, there are lots of little points to be considered, and lots to be avoided. The very first thing to do is to find an honest carpenter foreman, one, if possible, who has some understanding of drawing up plans

FIREPLACE CORNER IN BUNGALOW, SHOWING INTERESTING WALL TREATMENT AND FURNISHINGS.

HOW I BUILT MY BUNGALOW

and specifications. My architect friend sent out the right man to me with highest recommendations, and I immediately engaged him to draw up the plans at my suggestion, and to act as carpenter foreman on the job. Fortunately he was an excellent draughtsman.

During the previous month I had made as thorough a study of bungalow construction as I could. I always carried a rule and spent much time measuring the width of shakes and the number of inches they were laid to the weather, in fact I measured the heights and depths and widths of everything that interested me, and took particular note of building materials of all sorts, so that I was able to explain with a certain degree of accuracy, just what I wanted. I couldn't see any reason why plans and specifications should be drawn up, for I was to have the work done by the day, and intended to give it my personal supervision, but my friend advised me strongly to have them, so there could be no possible chance of confusion or misunderstanding with the workmen. She said I should sublet contracts for the plumbing and the masonry, the electric wiring and the roofing; in this case plans and specifications would be absolutely necessary to

THE LIBRARY END OF THE LIVING ROOM.

bind the contractors. When the plans were all ready, work began in earnest. My husband had urgent business affairs to look after at this time, and seeing how deeply interested I was, and feeling confidence in me, inexperienced though I was, he gave me entire charge of buying the materials and the superintendence of the building. At first I was a bit nervous and several times asked advice of my friend. After the first week, however, I gained independence and relied entirely on my own wits and judgment to carry me through safely. I employed four men, a working foreman at $4.00 a day, a carpenter at $3.50, a helper for $2.50, and a painter at $3.15, and just nine weeks after the first foundation stone was laid, the house was completed.

I felt that a bungalow to be harmonious, must have a low, flat roof, and the only difficulty I had with my foreman was in trying to convince him that a roof with a pitch of one to six would be practicable. But I had my way in this, as in all things, and the roof is quite satisfactory. Instead of shingles I had asbestos roofing, which is white and contrasts attractively with the

GLIMPSE OF DINING ROOM OUT OF LIVING ROOM.

HOW I BUILT MY BUNGALOW

dark walls. The eaves, which have a four-foot extension, are supported by heavy redwood timbers.

Fortunately, my men were most agreeable and willing; in fact, they seemed pleased with every suggestion. I had heard so much about workmen disliking to have a woman "hanging around," that I was, to be sure, happy in finding them so amiable. When I gave an order I stuck to it, and I guess the novelty of a woman who didn't change her mind every minute rather pleased them. I also guarded myself against being "fussy." My foreman often 'phoned for me to come out and explain just how I wanted this or that when he could have gone ahead and finished it up in his workmanlike way and I would never have known the difference. He would go into detail about the various ways of doing the inside finishing, and ask me which I preferred. He was a first-class carpenter; in fact, a cabinet maker, and it all sounded so "pretty" when he told me about it, that I had all the woodwork in the house mitered and finished in the most careful and approved style. Of course, this cost a lot of money, but I wanted my bungalow to be frank and strong and true, so I didn't skimp or economize in anything. I visited the house once a day, usually in the morning, so that I could outline the work for the day if it seemed necessary for me to do so. My husband went out twice a week.

The only real trouble or annoyance I had was with the man who was sent out to do the cobblestone work. He was a foreigner, very independent and very impudent, and two or three times my carpenters, hearing him "boss" me, threatened to throw him bodily off the premises. He insisted that the wall and porch supports ought to be of little stones laid smooth and even, while I insisted that they should be of large stones of irregular sizes laid in the mortar with ends and sides projecting outside the main plaster line. He paid no attention to my wishes, but went ahead, doing exactly as he pleased, mortaring the little round stones together like so many marbles. I realized if this continued the house would be ruined. The first day or two I was too proud to say anything to my husband about the matter. But after laying awake all night I "gave in" and cried out my trouble on his shoulder the next morning. He 'phoned to the contractor

who had taken the masonry work, asking him to discharge this troublesome man and get another. I lost no more sleep over the cobblestone proposition, for another and perfectly satisfactory workman was sent me. I was particularly anxious to have a large flat stone on which to put the house number, laid in the mortar in one of the porch pillars, and this man put aside quite a heap of boulders so that I might take my pick. It is such little considerations that make a woman eternally grateful to a workman.

All along the porch wall, and at the tops of the stone piers supporting the rustic porch timbers, I had the mason leave space for flowers, a trough six inches wide and sixteen inches deep. I think this arrangement much prettier, and certainly it is much neater than the ordinary wooden flower boxes, that invariably leak muddy water over the porch floor when the plants are irrigated. I decided on black pointing for the stone work. It brings out the shape and size of every stone, and somehow it gives more character to the masonry, especially where large boulders are used. I had the porch floor cemented and marked off in twenty-four inch blocks, while the ceiling was of narrow wood beading, varnished.

I deliberated quite a bit before settling upon what to use for the exterior walls, finally deciding that split redwood shakes would be best. These called for an inter-wall lining of heavy building paper. Without the latter the house would not be weatherproof. All window and door casings were made of finished lumber and painted green, while the shake walls were stained a corresponding shade. My painter advised two coats of this stain, which consists of paint and distillate mixed in equal quantities, so I bought the material and told him to go ahead. I have since learned, however, that one coat of stain is quite sufficient. By putting on two coats the painter doubled his time check, but I don't blame him. If I had as big a family to support as he has, I might also try to make my jobs elastic. At any rate my house is sufficiently puttied and painted to last for some time.

I had my heart set on a sleeping porch, so incorporated it in the plan. It consisted of a wood platform, 12 x 14, with a pergola roof, and was to be accessible from our bedroom by means of a double

HOW I BUILT MY BUNGALOW

French window. I asked a dealer for an estimate on the canvas for the walls of this sleeping porch. The roof was to be left open, so I could look up at the stars. His bid was $16 for canvas on rollers. This price seemed rather high. After looking about I decided to buy material and sew it and hang it myself. I bought twenty-seven yards of drilling at twelve and one-half cents a yard, the whole coming to a trifle over $3. I measured off breadths for each of the sides, sewed them, and fastened them to the timbers by means of rings sewed to the cloth, and hooks screwed into the wood. I did this so the curtains could be readily removed and laundered. Just now I am having a struggle to prevent the vines which have clambered up the sides, and which are most welcome there as sun screens, from covering the roof. It is such a delight to see the stars the last thing before going to sleep, and the blue sky the first thing upon opening my eyes in the morning.

Floors throughout the house are double. The first, or foundation floor is of six-inch tongue and groove Oregon pine. In living room and dining room the finish floor is of number one quarter-sawed oak, and in the other rooms the finish floor is of white maple. I should never have a maple floor in my kitchen again, for it absorbs the grease in such a way that spots are practically impossible to remove without taking the floor along with them. If building again I would have an ordinary pine floor in my kitchen and give it three or four coats of paint, or better still, cover it with white and green checked linoleum, which always looks clean, even when it is dirty. Adhering throughout to the idea that a bungalow should be low, my ceilings are only eight and one-half feet high. Doors are six feet six inches by thirty inches and are No. 1 grade.

I gave a great deal of time and thought to the interior finish and furnishing of the bungalow. I firmly believe that domestic harmony applies to the things in a house as well as to the people who live in it. An execrable color combination in a room is bound to make one feel out of humor. Furnishings should be harmonious, so that when one comes in tired, one will feel rested and comforted. I struggled and planned and matched things and samples, in an effort to bring about just such a restful result.

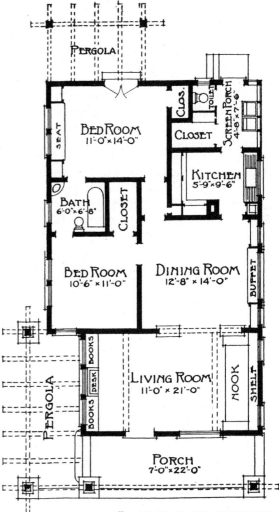

FLOOR PLAN OF BUNGALOW

My color scheme for the living room was brown, with here and there a dash of yellow, ruby and green. I selected two small art-glass windows to go above the mantelshelf on either side of the fireplace. In these were shades of yellow, green and ruby. I got small pieces of this glass from the factory where the windows were made, took them to a wall-paper store, and finally succeeded in finding a narrow frieze in which the colors exactly matched those of the glass. I studied out every little detail in just this same way, even to the glass in the copper and iron electric fixtures. In the living room, bookcases, desk, mantelshelf and buttresses are all four feet high. The paneling ends on the same line, while the square lattice windows are the same height from the floor. Between the paneling and the picture molding, excepting a six-inch space that is given up to the frieze, is a gold-brown wall paper. Above the picture molding, walls and ceiling are

HOW I BUILT MY BUNGALOW

covered with deep cream paper. Mantel and hearth are of eight-inch red brick tile, while the hood and twelve-inch facing under the mantelshelf are of hammered copper. I had considerable difficulty in finding tile the right shade. The first lot sent to the house had to be returned. I then went to the shop armed with a bit of copper and a piece of the brown wall-paper, and selected enough red-brown tile of uniform color that blended perfectly with my color scheme. All the woodwork in this room I had stained in imitation of Flemish oak. One arrangement that I find most convenient is that of having a wide, deep box seat on either side of the fireplace, one in which to keep wood, and the in which to keep kindling. They do not leak dirt like baskets, and they hold enough fuel to last a long time. Filling in one entire end of the living room under the lattice windows, is a built-in desk with a bookcase on either side, and now that we are living in the house, we make amusement for ourselves and friends by designating this end of the room as our "library," the central portion where the piano is, our "music room," and the other end as our "living" or "reception room." I fully intended having my foreman make all the furniture for this room, but after he had finished a table, a chair and a foot stool, I found the work, as well as the materials were proving unreasonably expensive, in fact the three pieces cost us $75.00, and while they were beautifully made and finished, I could get just as good in the shops for much less money. I selected a golden-brown bungalow net for the curtains in this room, a color matching exactly the wall-paper.

For our bedroom I chose white paper with white dots—an imitation of dotted swiss, also a cut-out frieze showing garlands of blue roses and green leaves. For the other bedroom I selected a striped paper in white and palest pink-gray. with a cut-out garland frieze of pink roses and green leaves. In both these rooms, as well as in the bath, I had the woodwork finished in white enamel. I planned a built-in arrangement for one side of my bedroom which proves a great blessing. Under the wide window is a roomy box seat with a lid. On either side of this, and fitting into the corners are buttresses thirty inches wide, two feet deep, and four feet high. These have shelves and doors.

In one of them I keep my big hats, in the other my shirt-waist boxes as they come home from the laundry.

I had my kitchen done in cream enamel, even to the furniture, which I bought in the shop unfinished, and had my painter finish it just as he finished the woodwork. For my sink casing, as well as for my drain board and molding board, I selected a cream wood stone. This is better looking, and far more serviceable than the white pine usually used for such purposes.

I had the dining-room woodwork finished to correspond with that of the living room. Under the high windows on the east side of the room is a built-in buffet with shelves and drawers. The color scheme in this room is Delft blue and cream. The furniture is all of white ash of special design. The chairs have woven reed seats.

All the electric fixtures in living room and dining room were made to order from my designs, and while they were somewhat expensive I feel repaid because they are "different."

COST ESTIMATE.

Building permit	$2.00
Water tap	9.00
Cement and stone work, including walks	381.00
Plumbing	190.00
Sewer connection	28.00
Electric wiring	22.00
Electric fixtures	95.00
Lumber	480.00
Doors and windows	116.00
Roofing	90.00
Plaster	75.00
Hardware	57.00
Paint, stain, etc.	90.00
Copper hood, etc., for mantel	30.00
Wall-paper	30.00
Wood stone drain board	12.00
Screens	23.00
Duplex window shades	11.00

LABOR.

Carpenters	540.00
Painter	92.00
Helper	148.00
Floor finisher	12.00
Total	$2,531.00

Since my bungalow has been completed I feel more and more that the building of one's own house is the great step toward reducing this American tendency of moving practically every spring.

A RANCH BUNGALOW EMBODYING MANY MODERN IDEAS: BY CHARLES ALMA BYERS

I T is the exception nowadays for us to build a house in town or suburbs without some, at least, of the modern time- and labor-saving conveniences. We plan for as many bathrooms as we can afford or the size of the family demands; sideboards, bookcases and seats are incorporated into the living room; linen drawers and clothes closets with mirrors set in the doors are planned for the bedrooms, and the kitchen equipment includes a built-in icebox, convenient sink and drainboard, and there must be a compact cabinet that will save time and steps for the housewife.

While these things are considered more or less essential for houses built in more populous sections, it is unusual to find any thought given to the conservation of energy in planning houses for the real country. As a rule, in building a farmhouse the main thing that is considered is the erection of a shelter from the elements, a place to eat in and sleep in, but not necessarily to live comfortably in. It is exceptional to find running water and bathroom facilities in farmhouses, for the drainage problem is one that has to be solved separately for each house, and for that reason is seldom considered at all.

We are accustomed to think sentimentally of the charm of the old-time country house, but when it is compared with the kind of house modern invention has made practical for us, its drawbacks stand out

A RANCH BUNGALOW: A. S. BARNES AND E. B. RUST, ARCHITECTS.

rather sharply and it becomes less alluring. When the daily round of work and discomfort, the wear of wasted energy are considered, it is small wonder that the youth of our country refuses to see the joys of living in houses that are insufficiently heated, at times badly ventilated, and planned with such lack of thought that it is necessary to take ten steps to do the work of one. Farmers' wives perhaps breathe less pure air than any other human beings, for it takes all day long to do the work of a family and, in this country, the work is all indoors. A walk in the fields or woods holds no allurement for feet that are ready to drop off with weariness, aching with the effort to keep up with the tide of work that never abates.

Life on a farm will never hold interest for those who work too indefatigably to realize its beauties, who never see the sunset because the bread must be baked, and who never hear the birds sing because the work in the pantry must not go unfinished. These conditions prevail to a great extent all over the country, and yet it is not impossible to incorporate modern conveniences in farm homes,—the time- and labor-saving (sometimes even life-saving) features that would make life less a round of drudgery for weary women. Here and there the more progressive of our country folk are demanding for themselves the benefits that the city house affords, and the ranch bungalow illustrated here shows a possibility in this direction. The house is located on a forty-acre ranch or farm, near Burbank, California,

A RANCH BUNGALOW

LIVING ROOM IN RANCH BUNGALOW.

pretentious environment. It is not a small house, as it is 75 feet 4 inches wide and 44 feet 4 inches deep. The front porch is 11 feet by 34 feet 6 inches. One end of the porch is continued into a *porte-cochère,* and the other end is enclosed by one wall of the den. Both the porch and the *porte-cochère* are of massive proportions, and, like the chimneys, walks, steps and porch flooring and parapet, are built of brick. The siding is of cedar shakes, spaced about six inches apart, and stained a soft brown. The roof is of shingles, painted white. There are many windows, mostly casement, and over the front entrance is a series of small dormer windows, set with panes of art glass.

The interior differs most markedly from the old-style farmhouse. There are numer-

and is the home of Mr. J. C. McConnell, a rancher who believes in modern ideas. The house follows decided California bungalow lines, and is modern in every respect. The style and finish, both inside and out, would make it entirely suitable for a city home, and it also deserves especial attention as an example of what can be accomplished in rural home building.

The exterior is particularly attractive,

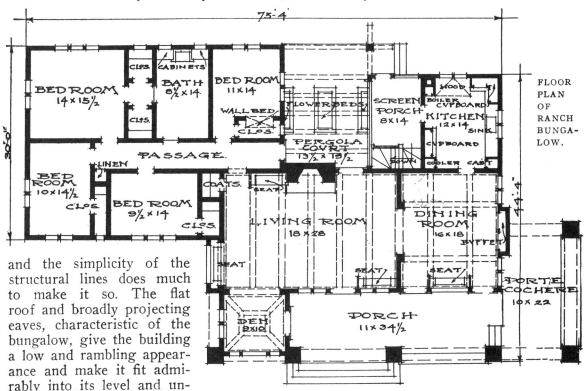

FLOOR PLAN OF RANCH BUNGALOW.

and the simplicity of the structural lines does much to make it so. The flat roof and broadly projecting eaves, characteristic of the bungalow, give the building a low and rambling appearance and make it fit admirably into its level and un-

A RANCH BUNGALOW

ous built-in features. In the living room there are three built-in corner seats and a large fireplace with a mantel of pressed brick; the dining room contains an attractive buffet and a comfortable window seat. There are four bedrooms in the house, each with a roomy closet and one with a built-in wall bed, and in the hall there is a convenient linen closet. The bathroom has convenient cabinets, as well as the usual bathroom fixtures, and is 14 feet by 8 feet 6 inches in size.

The kitchen contains ample cupboard space, a draught cooler, an instantaneous heater, a stationary hood for the kitchen range, a sink and a small storage closet. On the small screened porch adjoining the kitchen there are two stationary tubs for washing, and leading from this porch is a stairway to the basement.

Oak floors are used throughout the house, except in the kitchen, bathroom and screened kitchen porch. The ceilings of the living room, dining room and den are beamed, and the walls of these three rooms are paneled to a height of 5 feet, topped by a plate rail. The woodwork, which is of Oregon pine, is finished to resemble Flemish oak, and the furniture has been selected to match this finish. The upper portions of the walls and the ceilings are plastered and tinted a light buff. The woodwork of the bathroom, kitchen and bedrooms is of Oregon pine, enameled white, and the plastered portions of the walls in the bedrooms are tinted in delicate colors.

One of the most appreciated features in summer is the small pergola in the rear. This is a sort of court, 13½ feet by 19½ feet, enclosed on three sides, and is accessible from both the living room and the hall. It has a cement floor, into which have been sunken spaces for flower-beds. This pergola is furnished with a hammock and rustic chairs, and is an ideal retreat for outdoor lounging.

The house is substantially and warmly constructed throughout. It has a furnace, and is piped for water. The supply of water comes from an elevated tank, and a cesspool is provided for the run-off. The house, complete, represents an expenditure of $4,200, and it ought to be possible to duplicate it in almost any locality for approximately this amount. A. S. Barnes and E. B. Rust of Los Angeles, California, were the architects.

A BUNGALOW BUILT IN SPANISH STYLE

A MODERN CALIFORNIA HOUSE OF THE SPANISH TYPE: BY DELLA M. ECHOLS

A BUNGALOW BUILT IN SPANISH STYLE IN GLENDALE, CAL., THE HOME OF MRS. J. S. JONES.

TYPICAL of the comfort, ease and enjoyment of life that is supposed to be inherent in southern California and its bungalows, is the Spanish residence designed for Mrs. J. S. Jones by a local architect. It is built on one of the beautiful avenues of the suburban town of Glendale, a few miles north of Los Angeles, and is surrounded by wide-spreading pepper trees and other native shrubbery.

This type of dwelling is especially adapted to the southern climate, for all its rooms are spread out on the ground and so are in close touch with out of doors. Moreover, with no stairs to climb, the work of housekeeping is considerably lessened.

The exterior is of sawed shakes down to the water-table, below which are red brick in white mortar. The massive chimney is also of red brick in white mortar. Like all Spanish residences, the roof is flat with a wide overhang about 3½ feet in width, extending the entire distance around the house. This gives the building a much wider appearance and emphasizes the low bungalow effect.

A great deal of skill is shown in the ar-

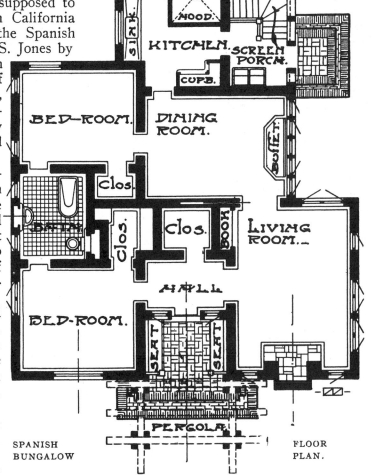

SPANISH BUNGALOW   FLOOR PLAN.

A BUNGALOW BUILT IN SPANISH STYLE

FIREPLACE CORNER OF LIVING ROOM IN SPANISH BUNGALOW, SHOWING INTERESTING WALL FINISH.

rangement of the rooms, the idea having been to get the maximum of comfort, convenience and beauty with a minimum of expense. This has been accomplished by a practical and very compact floor plan and by making interest of materials and structural proportions the basis of all decorative effect. There is no attempt at elaborate ornamentation; everything is simple, homelike, designed primarily for household comfort, beautiful because it is appropriate and worked out with artistic feeling.

LOOKING INTO DINING ROOM FROM LIVING ROOM.

A BUNGALOW BUILT IN SPANISH STYLE

From the pergola at the entrance one steps into a hall which separates the living room from the guest chamber. The house is trimmed in natural woods, unmarred by paint and varnish and finished so that one feels the interest and color of the grain. The wainscoting of channel boarding in hall, living room and dining room is 6 feet high. This not only adds to the friendliness and charm of the rooms, but is especially harmonious with the built-in furniture—bookcases, buffet, china closets, etc. These are all constructed on strong, simple lines, and in filling the various needs in a practical way add much to the structural decoration of the interior.

The central point in the living room is, of course, the fireplace, which is built of old gold brick. What a contrast is this "room to live in"—16 x 20 feet—to the cheerless, formal "parlor" of twenty-five years ago! The dining room beyond forms an extension of the living room, and with its combined buffet and china closets is especially convenient.

The kitchen is equipped with all modern conveniences, so that the work of the housewife is more of a pleasure than a drudgery. A very practical feature is the large built-in hood which comes down low over the stove in one corner of the room and carries off all smoke and cooking odors. The kitchen is as cheery in appearance as the other rooms, being all white enameled. A screen porch immediately off the kitchen contains the sanitary laundry trays and also the stairs leading down to the basement, where the furnace is placed.

The bedrooms no less than the living or day rooms are planned for health and restfulness. The windows and doors are arranged so as to provide the best possible lighting and ventilation, while leaving ample space for the beds and other furniture. Access from the bedrooms to the bathroom is easy, and these rooms are conveniently separated from the rest of the plan. The bathroom has a modern equipment, being finished with a tile floor, white enamel woodwork and nickel hardware.

There is one feature in home-building which every woman appreciates, and that is an abundance of clothes closets, particularly the kind that admits sufficient light and air. This plan makes ample provision for such closets. Another factor which adds materially to the beauty of the rooms and helps to lighten the work of keeping them clean, is the provision of hardwood floors. These do not add greatly to the cost, and are certainly worth while, for they permit the abolition of carpets and the use of rugs—both an æsthetic and a sanitary gain. The electric fixtures throughout were designed by the architect, and it is just such attention to detail and careful workmanship evinced in every room which helps to make this little home a place of unusual comfort and loveliness.

The total cost of construction was $2,600.00.

"THE BARNACLE": A LITTLE CALIFORNIA HOUSE MADE FROM A BARN.

THE BARNACLE: TRANSFORMING A BARN INTO A BUNGALOW: BY EUNICE T. GRAY

MY seaside cottage, the "Barnacle," is one of the most successful transformations that I have ever known. In the first place, my sister and I chose, as the site of our cottage, Carmel-by-the-Sea, California, a coast village of unusual beauty and charm. The lots were situated on a gentle seaward slope covered with the sweet smelling Southern wood, rich-hued manzanita bushes, scrub-oak and cascara; two giant Monterey pines with strangely twisted low lying limbs, stood on the seaward side of our lots and a group of smaller pines at the east.

The house completed, faces the east, and the dining-room and living-room windows look out upon beautiful Carmel Bay; the view from the southern windows is the full sweep of the chaparral-covered point between the bay and a small inlet into which the Carmel River flows. This river, in summer, is a placid low-running stream between banks of sycamore and willow; in the winter, fed by the rains and snows it is a roaring flood of mountain wash, rushing through the rich Carmel Valley to the sea. Beyond the river are the foothills, green and wooded, and sloping down to the coast in the long rocky point, called Lobas,

where the rarely beautiful, roseate, abalone shells with their pearly "blisters" are found.

From the upper windows looking eastward we catch a glimpse of the cross of the historic church of San Carlos Mission, founded nearly a century and a half ago.

But in the beginning there was no living room or dining room, for the house like its name began as a barn. It was built foursquare, a carriage house, horsestalls, barndoors and hayloft, painted red and set on the barest corner of the four lots. It cost the sum of eight hundred dollars.

The original barn was twenty-four feet square, built of California redwood, with a shingled gambrel roof, and outside finish of board and battens which we had painted dull red. The lower floor was divided through the center by a partition, which

SHOWING THE RUSTIC GATEWAY AND FENCE.

TRANSFORMING A BARN INTO A BUNGALOW

LIVING ROOM IN "THE BARNACLE."

The upper room was lighted by two east windows and a double dormer window to the south, glass doors opened onto a semi-enclosed west balcony from which we could witness the marvelous sunsets over the bay.

Before the barn was finished we had an opportunity to rent it as a residence to a carpenter who was at work in the neighborhood, so we decided to furnish it simply and comfortably for his family for the winter. We had couches, rugs, linoleum and curtains from our town house which were past their first freshness but still in good condition, these we had shipped down by freight; dishes and kitchen furnishings we bought at the village store; bedding and rag rugs we industriously made, to keep the house as homespun and old-timey as possible. A new stove in the "horse division," a cupboard built of boxes and a work table constituted the kitchen; the carpenter built shelves and a table in the west end, and called it the dining room. The carriage house was converted into a cozy, comfortable living room, with rag rugs, a couch and cushions, a large circular table, two rocking chairs and two low hickory chairs with rawhide seats.

We hung the sides of the upper room with flowered chintz, soft blue covered with roses, the space between this temporary wall and the sloping roof made two long airy closets. We furnished it with cots,

was made by covering the upright beams with heavy gray building paper, on the south side of which an enclosed staircase led to the loft above. Two windows, three feet high and two wide, faced west to the sea, and a door opened onto an uncovered west veranda. The north and south windows were long and narrow, three by one and one-half feet, placed in the exact center of opposite walls.

SOUTH VIEW OF "THE BARNACLE" SHOWING BAY WINDOW AND SECOND FLOOR DORMER.

TRANSFORMING A BARN INTO A BUNGALOW

hickory chairs, dressing-tables made of boxes, patchwork quilts and dull blue rugs. Altogether it was a most attractive room and the wonderful views from the windows were never forgotten by the numerous guests who later occupied the quaint airy chamber.

For two years the new barn, which never housed a hoof or a wheel, was used as a house. We entertained jolly house parties of four to ten in number and the year of the earthquake and fire in San Francisco we found it a safe and quiet refuge from the distress and disorder of the city. The third year we abandoned all idea of building the larger house under the pines and decided to convert the barn into a bungalow. A three-windowed bay was added to the south side, and the second floor balcony, which was found impracticable in stormy weather, was enclosed and made into a tiny bedroom.

The little village had not yet a sewerage system, so modern plumbing was out of the question for that year, at least, but a bathtub was installed in a curtained recess of the living room and a sink and drip-board in the kitchen. The walls of the first floor were wainscoted to within three feet of the ceiling with white pine, waxed and shellacked. The upper portion was covered with linen canvas, and a plate rail was built all around the room. The effect was very artistic and the house was unusually light and attractive. These improvements cost $90.

That summer we rented the "Barnacle" to vacationers through the entire season. They paid $1 a day, and all expressed themselves satisfied with the simple arrangements and comforts of the cottage.

The following fall I bought out my sister's interest in the Carmel cottage and made $300 worth of improvements. With this expenditure all traces of the original barn disappeared; the carriage-house entrance was replaced by pine paneling and three large windows. The "horse door," built in an upper and lower section, was taken out and a very proper door with a pane of glass

and a lock and key was hung in its place.

The old staircase was pulled out and built into the northeast corner, which was now, by the construction of a partition, the front hall; the west end formed a kitchen twelve by eighteen feet. The sink was placed under the long window, and a door was cut on the north side leading onto a covered platform which was used as a woodshed. The east end of the living room is now used as a dining room, and the crowning glory of this long, light room with its beautiful outlook, is a great red brick fireplace with a chimneyshelf and a crane, and a wide hearth and niches on either side for the Chinese bowls and candlesticks. The chimney is not enclosed but rises solidly to the ceiling directly in the center of the house. It has been, indeed, the heart of the house, and when a group of merry friends are gathered about the roaring fire,

"Oft died the words upon our lips,
  As suddenly. from out the fire
Built of the wreck of stranded ships,
  The flames would leap and then expire."

And in those little silent times we experienced true comradeship.

The second floor of the house has received due attention, a bathroom with modern plumbing is the prime improvement, a second dormer was thrown out on the north side and the room finished with pine and divided into three bedrooms.

The rose vines climb over the pergola, and a hardy group of eucalyptus trees rustle their gray-green leaves in the ocean breeze, golden poppies and wild lilac have wandered in from the roadside, and mingle their sweet wild beauty and fragrance with pink geranium and sweet alyssum.

While our architectural methods, as the foregoing account reveals, were certainly unorthodox and unique, both the exterior and interior of our bungalow proved practical and homelike. And perhaps the results illustrated here may inspire some other home-makers to work transformations of a similar nature.

A BUNGALOW OF RARE COMFORT

A PRACTICAL AND COMFORTABLE BUNGALOW BUILT BY A WESTERN ARCHITECT FOR HIS OWN HOME: BY CHARLES ALMA BYERS

WHEN an architect builds a home for himself it is naturally to be expected that he will create something "different" — something at least not stereotyped. In the first place, no one can interfere with his plans, and in the second place, he can avail himself of the opportunity to put into use many ideas that must have gradually accumulated in his mind. And while practically every architect will allow himself a certain degree of freedom, no matter what style of house he may design, one can expect even more in this way when a Western architect builds for himself a bungalow home.

The bungalow, as has often been stated in THE CRAFTSMAN, probably surpasses all other styles of architecture in its adaptability to individuality. It permits far greater freedom in construction, and makes possible the installation of many more built-in features. In fact, the built-in features of the bungalow have been developed in such interesting fashion and are so necessary a part of the structure that they are a distinct characteristic of this style of building. The bungalow is definitely designed for a home that is both attractive and inexpensive, and to meet these requisites it is essential that the interior be made

cozy and homelike without the use of a great deal of expensive furniture. It is here that built-in features are most helpful. They do much toward making the furniture list simple, and at the same time they make possible an interior scheme of furnishing that is harmonious in both color and finish. The immovable fittings of a house are usually built on plain, straight, structural lines, and it is comparatively easy to secure furniture constructed on the same principles and of a finish to match.

The bungalow shown in the accompanying reproductions is an excellent illustration of these facts. It is the home of Mr. E. B. Rust, an architect of Los Angeles, California. Mr. Rust has designed a large number of the bungalows of Southern California which are well known throughout that country, and naturally in his own home one might expect to find embodied some of his best ideas.

As seen from the outside the bungalow is characteristic of its type, but not particularly unusual. Even for the bungalow style it is rather plain and regular in contour, but has pleasing proportions, and, indeed, much of its charm is due to its simplicity. Incidentally, it is gratifying to realize that the age of bizarre architecture is surely passing; that we are being gradually educated into an appreciation of plain, simple and dignified houses

This bungalow has the usual low roof and broadly projecting eaves. The siding

A BUNGALOW OF RARE COMFORT

is of redwood shingles, as is also the roof and the masonry is of brick. There is a small front porch of well-proportioned lines, and in the rear is the customary screened porch, 6½ x 10 feet in size. The windows are almost all casement, a style that always seems especially suitable for a low-roofed house. The exterior color scheme is two shades of olive brown—a light olive stain for the siding and a darker shade of olive for the trim,—which, with the dull red of the brick, makes a most effective combination.

While the exterior is attractive, the interior shows the skill of the architect to a greater extent. He has given it special consideration. In studying the accompanying floor plan drawing, noting the numerous closets and built-in features and their arrangement, it becomes evident that Mrs. Rust also had considerable to do with their planning. There seems to be "a place for everything," and the location of the various features is so convenient that there could be little excuse for not having everything always in its proper place. And even with so much built-in furniture, a general feeling of simplicity is maintained—a fact which deserves particular mention.

The house contains five rooms, besides a sort of book alcove and the bathroom. The alcove is really a part of the living room, but is sufficiently secluded from the front entrance to give opportunity for the utmost privacy. This nook contains the fireplace, which occupies one corner, three

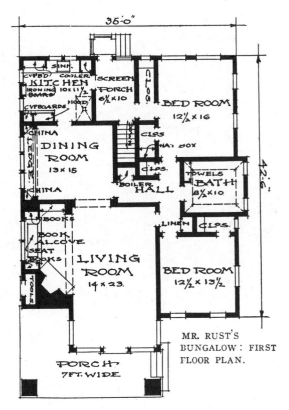

MR. RUST'S BUNGALOW: FIRST FLOOR PLAN.

built-in bookcases of excellent workmanship, and a long comfortable window-seat. The top of the seat is hinged so that it may be lifted as a lid and the box underneath serves as a receptacle for fuel. The fireplace is of brick covered with cement plaster, and the mantelshelf is of wood in plain design. The corner occupied by the fireplace has given an opportunity for a novel feature—a garden-tool closet, which is ac-

LIVING ROOM OF MR. RUST'S BUNGALOW, SHOWING END OF ALCOVE WITH BOOKSHELVES.

A BUNGALOW OF RARE COMFORT

LIVING ROOM, SHOWING THE OTHER END OF ALCOVE, FIREPLACE AND WINDOW SEAT.

cessible from the outside of the house.

A broad arch, hung with portières, connects the living room and dining room. A rather unusual buffet has been built into the latter. Beneath a series of three large casement windows there is a broad, low ledge, into which have been fitted three capacious drawers. At each end of this ledge, which also means at either side of the three windows, there is a corner china closet, the doors of which contain ten panes of plate glass and correspond in design with the windows.

The woodwork of the living room and dining room, including, of course, the alcove, is of California redwood, which has been waxed, and left in nearly its natural color. This is a very effective wood, and it is impossible to improve upon its color tones. The walls of both rooms are tinted a roseleaf green, and the ceilings which, except in the alcove, are plastered like the walls, are colored a light buff. The ceilings are vaulted, or slightly arched, for the purpose of aiding the indirect light-

ing scheme. The lighting fixtures are particularly interesting and in simplicity of design are quite in keeping with the interior finish and the other features. In the living room the principal fixtures are two large inverted domes of hammered brass suspended on chains, and in the dining room there is a single dome, similarly arranged, made of glass, covered with lacquered bamboo splints. These inverted domes, which hold the electric bulbs, reflect the light against the vaulted ceiling, where it is diffused to all parts of the room in equal strength. In the living room and alcove there are also, at convenient intervals, smaller lighting fixtures of the ordinary kind.

To many a housewife a study of the kitchen of this house will prove interesting. This room is finished in white enamel, and is most convenient in arrangement of built-in features. There are numerous cabinets

ONE END OF THE DINING ROOM, SHOWING BUILT-IN CHINA CLOSETS.

A BUNGALOW OF RARE COMFORT

A CORNER OF THE KITCHEN, SHOWING BUILT-IN
IRONING BOARD AND CONVENIENT CUPBOARDS.

and drawers, the usual sink, a hood for the range, a draught cooler, a built-in flour bin, a disappearing bread board, and an ironing board that folds up into its own special cabinet.

There is a roomy closet in each of the two bedrooms, and in the closet of the rear bedroom there is a built-in hat box. On the rear screened porch there is a large storage closet, and in the T-shaped hall that gives access to the bathroom from practically all parts of the house there are two more closets, as well as the boiler cabinet. The bathroom is finished in ivory enamel, and has mahogany towel and medicine cabinets. The woodwork of the hall and the two bedrooms is also enameled, the former in ivory and the latter white, and the walls and ceilings are plastered and tinted in delicate colors.

The house has a small basement, the stairway to which leads from the rear screened porch, and a basement furnace supplies additional heat when that afforded by the alcove fireplace is insufficient. Unlike California's first experiments in bungalow building, the house is strongly and warmly constructed and would be suitable for almost any locality, no matter how severe the winters might be.

Careful attention has been given not only to the more important structural features, but the minor details as well. The interior is satisfying and harmonious in both color and finish, even to the curtain and portière poles, which are made of the same material and with the same straight lines as the rest of the woodwork.

The house has ample ground space, and a few massive old trees that at one time practically monopolized the plot have been given a little pruning, and left to form the basis for a most delightful environment. Home-builders are gradually realizing that such monarchs as these do not grow quickly, and that as a rule it is advisable to plan the house in relation to the natural surroundings. Too often valuable trees are cut down in the mistaken idea that it is necessary to plan the grounds after the house is constructed instead of planning them first. When the house is completed before the grounds are planned and laid out, the builder often learns when it is too late that by the time the garden is mature the house is old and sometimes dilapidated.

HOME OF MR. AND MRS. W. S. JOHNSON, PASADENA, CALIFORNIA: LOUIS B. EASTON, ARCHITECT.

A CALIFORNIA BUNGALOW PLANNED FOR COMFORT: BY LAURA RINKLE JOHNSON

WHEN we purchased our little ranch of five acres on the outskirts of Pasadena, we were very decided as to the kind of house we did *not* wish to build for our home. The problem was to find an architect who would undertake the construction of a well-built, comfortable house, perfectly adapted to the grounds, the surroundings, and our tastes. After some investigation the right man was found in the person of Louis B. Easton.

We were especially fortunate in the location of our property, as in addition to three acres of fine orange trees, there were scattered over the place twelve magnificent live-oak trees of large proportions, some of them possibly three hundred years old. Another advantage was an excellent lawn, formerly used for a croquet ground, closed in on the south—toward the highway—and on the west, by a six-foot hedge of Australian pea-vine. The eastern side of the lawn was filled in with loquat and olive trees. The fourth side of the square was chosen for the location of our bungalow.

The plans decided upon were somewhat on the lines of a Mexican ranch house, adapted to meet the ideals of Craftsman construction, and to conform with the environment. The completed home, a long, low building with an overhanging roof that forms the porch covering, seems just as much a part of the landscape as the oak trees whose branches spread protectingly above the roof.

The materials used in building were Oregon pine and California redwood, the outside being covered with split shakes. These overlap each other eleven inches and the ends were left uneven as cut from the log. There are no "fake" beams or posts in the house, every stick of timber is just what it appears to be, and does just what it seems to be doing.

The porch—fifty feet in length—is an ideal outdoor sitting room. The floor is brick, easily cleaned, and cool on hot days. Four strong pine posts support the porch roof, on the under side of which the construction timbers are exposed. The entrance door of the bungalow we consider most craftsmanlike. In fact, Mr. Easton was so pleased with it when it was finished that he strongly objected to the "sacrilege" of a screen door that would conceal its beauty! However, we now have a screen door, but one especially built to harmonize with its setting.

The natural reddish hue of the redwood is preserved and intensified by a most in-

A CALIFORNIA BUNGALOW-COTTAGE

teresting process. Stiff wire brushes are used to scrape the wood, removing all the loose splinters and bringing out the grain of the wood in high relief. After this treatment the wood is either waxed or given a chemical wash, and the result is most unusual and effective. The metal work on the doors—hinges, latches, etc.—is of iron, copper plated, and was made by a blacksmith near by from designs drawn by Mr. Easton. Throughout the house, the primitive style of latch and handle is used on the doors; the locks consist of a pin of oak, whittled smooth and fastened to the door by a buckskin thong. The pin is thrust above the latch into a fastening on the door casing.

The porch leads into a hall formed by two partitions five and a half feet high, which separate it from the living room, and a wide opening between the partitions forms the entrance into the living room. A group

LIVING ROOM IN THE JOHNSON BUNGALOW, SHOW-ING INTERESTING INTERIOR FINISH AND FURNISH-INGS, ALSO HARMONIOUS FITTINGS.

of four casement windows, with small panes, lights the hall. At the eastern end of the hall is the dining room, and opposite, at the other end of the hall, is a bedroom.

The living room has the real home feeling; its low ceiling and paneled wall spaces, and most of all the spacious fireplace, seem to express our ideal of the spirit of hospitality and simple living. At the right of the entrance is a seat, the back of which is formed by the partition, at right angles to the fireplace. In the fireplace we have tried to express also the spirit of comfort and good cheer we want our home to typify. It is wide and deep, strongly built of red brick, with clinker brick as the only ornamentation; the mantel shelf is a slab of burl redwood, gnarled and knotted; and the hearth of brick is laid in herring-bone pattern.

The partition at the other side of the entrance to the living room offered opportunity for

DINING ROOM WITH GLIMPSE OF LIVING ROOM.

A CALIFORNIA BUNGALOW-COTTAGE

DELIGHTFULLY ARRANGED LIVING PORCH.

built-in bookshelves. Opposite the entrance is a group of five casement windows above a broad window seat. The walls here, as in the hall, dining room and sleeping rooms downstairs, are paneled with redwood of strongly marked grain. The space between the wainscoting and ceiling is covered with soft gray monk's cloth; neither plaster nor wallpaper is used in the house.

The ceilings throughout the lower floor carry heavy exposed beams of Oregon pine which convey the impression of great strength. A door leads from the living room into one of the bedrooms on the ground floor. This room is finished much like the living room, and has a door opening into the bathroom, which in turn opens into the bedroom at the end of the hall. Each sleeping room has French windows and a group of three casement windows, thus insuring an abundance of air and sunlight.

The chief feature of the dining room is the massive built-in buffet, and much charm is also given to the room by the French windows opening to the east, where we have a fine view of the snow-covered peak of "Old Baldy." The buffet stands between two doors, one leading into the kitchen and the other into the cellar, for, unlike the majority of California bungalows, this one has both a cellar and a furnace.

The kitchen is small, and absolutely no space is wasted. The convenient cupboards, air cooler and work table combine to make the culinary duties less irksome. The kitchen opens onto a large screened porch which is used as a breakfast room.

On the second floor (the stairway leads up from the kitchen) are the guest's room, the maid's room and a large trunk room. The sleeping rooms each contain a lavatory, and in the trunk room a small closet was partitioned off for a toilet. These rooms are finished in the same style as the rooms below, except for the walls, which, instead of being covered with monk's cloth, are paneled the entire height with redwood.

On the lawn, in front of the house, is

COURT BACK OF THE JOHNSON BUNGALOW WHICH FURNISHES OPPORTUNITY FOR SECLUDED OUTDOOR LIVING.

A CALIFORNIA BUNGALOW-COTTAGE

what we call a birds' pool, built from our own design. It is of brick, circular in form, and filled with clear water it affords an opportunity for our feathered friends to drink and bathe. They take naturally to it, and we spend many pleasant moments watching them. Around the pool are planted large elephant's ears and tall stalks of papyrus, and in the water blooms the water hyacinth.

Around the oak tree at the front of the house we laid a brick pavement, and from the porch we can look under the drooping branches of this oak to the nearby mountains.

The buildings at the rear form three sides of a court—a pergola connecting the screened porch with the garage, a small building conforming to the lines of the bungalow, in which are three rooms—a large one for the car, and two smaller ones—a study for the owner and a playroom for the small boy of the family. Extending from the garage is a small building with screened sides, containing a collection of foreign song birds.

Along the rear of the house are planted red geraniums, and roses will soon cover the pergola. A violet bed occupies a favored spot, begonias of various kinds are growing along the front of the aviary, and a banana tree is flourishing in the little court at the back of the house. On the east side we have rose bushes of many varieties and colors, and in a nook is a fern garden, most attractively set among rocks and half-decayed eucalyptus logs. The western exposure boasts a planting of Shasta daisies and climbing roses, and in this land of sunshine a very short time will suffice to produce luxuriant growth.

The electric fixtures of the house are of copper and are made from a design by Mr Easton, to harmonize with the decorative lines in the living room panels.

Our bungalow is livable, homelike, well built, inexpensive and beautiful, to our way of thinking—and more than this no one has a right to demand of a dwelling place.

The possibilities for securing ideal gardens seem greater in southern California than elsewhere, especially in the frostless belt that embraces Los Angeles and vicinity. No flowers have to be disturbed by being taken up for the winter as in the Middle West and East, thus plants attain a larger growth in a single year. The surrounding hills have many wild shrubs and flowering bushes which may be borrowed from them without any damage to their forestry, as some plants, such as the mountain laurels, often need to be thinned out, and these add much native beauty to the home garden, linking it, as it were, with its environment. Then the bungalow is a type of home which seems to come closer to nature than more pretentious buildings, and touches of rusticity are always in harmony with it, and create a feeling of oneness with the land.

A BACHELOR'S BUNGALOW

IF there is a style of bungalow that demands absolute comfort, stability and freedom from non-essentials, it is likely to be that designed for a bachelor. Indeed, the very mention of a bachelor's home in the country conjures up thoughts of freedom, physical comfort and an absence of mundane care. The accompanying plan for such a house emphasizes the intention of solidity in construction, sensibility in design and convenience in arrangements.

That the idea of solidity might be carried out in this bungalow it was constructed of brick, a material well suited to endure and to render the home cool in summer. "Tapestry" brick with wide, rough-cut flush joints face its walls, giving variety and the charm of color to the surface. The same treatment is carried out in the interior of the living room and in the large, welcome-giving fireplace. Again the idea of stability and convenience is presented by the tile floors and walls of both kitchen and bathroom, extending in the former case to a height of 6 feet and in the latter to 4 feet. Here then is nothing in interior wall finish to fade, to wear out or which cannot readily be kept clean and sanitary.

The door frames of all the exterior walls are white oak; other outside trim and shingles being of cypress.

DESIGNED BY H. A. HAWTHORNE.

PERSPECTIVE SKETCH OF BUNGALOW.

SECOND VIEW OF BUNGALOW.

Again the idea of stability is accentuated.

The plan of the house is found sensible in that it utilizes well every bit of valuable space, and in its apparent openness to the outer world. The large living room is open to the roof, affording a sense of space and freedom without which no home in the country lives up to its highest benefits. Moreover, this particular living room is made distinctive by its large open hearth, showing on either side an ample accommodation for books. Its woodwork, stained a walnut brown, harmonizes with the open-air impression of the house, blending well with the brighter colors of nature. The living room opens onto the dining-room porch, which is free to the sky and the sunlight. Should, however, the taste of the bachelor incline toward horticulture, it could be attractively covered, pergola-like, with vines. The pantry and kitchen are so situated as to make service to either the dining porch or the living room entirely simple.

One bedroom is on this ground floor and opens at one end into a commodious bathroom, and at the other onto a recessed porch which might serve delightfully for either an outdoor sleeping room or for an informal breakfast room. The upper half story provides two rooms and a bath, one of which would of necessity be used for a servant. A large cedar closet is in

A BACHELOR'S BUNGALOW

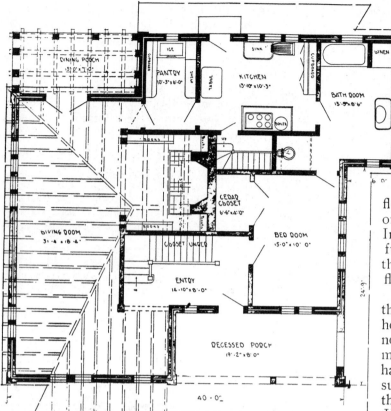

FLOOR PLAN OF BACHELOR'S BUNGALOW.

In this plan of a bachelor's bungalow, the call of the open air life is met. It gives no suggestion of restraint within walls except in places of necessity. Its atmosphere is one of simplicity and freedom. Just as it should be. The owner may have the scout's eye, but it is not for flecks of dust on the shelves or for tarnish on the silver. In his lair, he sees things of fuller meaning, and delights that there is nothing superfluous about.

Should he drop his pipe on the floor, its ashes burning a hole in the carpet, he barely notices the damage. Even it may be that he prefers to have no carpet; the floors are substantial—a rug here and there suits best his fancy. Holding this attitude, the entire furnishings of such a bungalow should be simple in the extreme, strong in outline. They should also be durable, since bachelors invariably expect full service from chairs, tables and other household objects. That furnishings are plain, however, does not in any sense mean that they are crude. They may be made harmonious with the scheme of the bungalow and pleasing as well to the eye. In fact a bachelor's bungalow gives him of all things needful, the opportunity to enjoy his own individuality.

the bedroom, and there is sensible accommodation for linen and household stores.

With the advent of cold weather, the bachelor owning such a home need not be driven cityward by an early cold snap or because the crows have flown over the cornfields with their farewell call! He may rest by his own fireside as late in the season as he chooses, since a Craftsman fireplace makes his home a real shelter from inclement weather. Here he can feel the cheer of warmth and home beside his welcome open fireplace throughout the autumn days. And he can equally well entertain friends over the holidays, knowing that the furnace is substantial and in order, and that it will keep his bungalow from feeling the nip of Jack Frost.

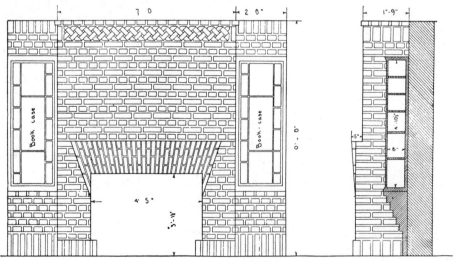

DETAIL OF CRAFTSMAN FIREPLACE IN LIVING ROOM.

SIX-ROOM BUNGALOW BUILT FOR COMFORT

A SIX-ROOM BUNGALOW: IN-EXPENSIVE, COMFORTABLE AND ATTRACTIVE: BY CHARLES ALMA BYERS

THE time seems now to have come when a man of comparatively meager financial supply need be no longer without a home, comfortable and artistic, in which to shelter himself and his family. The six-room bungalow herein illustrated is not only pleasant in its structural lines, but it affords ample space in which to move about, and is planned so as to make housekeeping as simple a matter as feasible. It was built at a cost of only $3,200.

It is distinctively a California bungalow, although of comparatively new interpretation. Its lines, those most suitable for a city home, are straight and regular, simple and dignified. The almost flat roof has at its eaves and gables a broad projection of nearly three feet, its sweep giving to the bungalow an appearance of much greater length and size than it actually possesses. The siding is of redwood shakes, showing about 12 inches of their length; the framing and finishing timbers of Oregon pine and the porch pillars and other masonry work of concrete. Cement forms the floor of the porch, the steps, as well as the paths about the house. The pillars, with their projecting copings, are of massive proportions and are responsible to an extent for the substantial look of this bungalow.

SIX-ROOM BUNGALOW BUILT FOR MR. J. S. CLARK IN LOS ANGELES: HAROLD BOWLES, ARCHITECT.

The arrangement of the front porch may be regarded as a strong point of the exterior. At one end it is enclosed with glass, converting it virtually into a small sunroom, the enclosure being created by a series of casement windows, each one capable of opening when a free circulation of air is desired. The unusual lighting device for the porch is noticed in a modernized Japanese lantern, set on a low pedestal-like pillar, standing at one side of the entrance steps.

The exterior of the house pleases by its apparent strength of construction and its attractiveness is heightened by its color scheme. The roof, a sort of asbestos composition, is white, as is also the concrete and cement work, while the siding and other woodwork are stained in rich brown, causing the whole structure to stand out effectively from the background of green afforded by a line of eucalyptus trees.

In its floor plan this bungalow is particularly commended on account of its convenience, its openness and its built-in furniture. Passing through the front door into the living room it is seen that a screened breakfast room lies beyond, so-called French doors intervening between the two rooms. At the left of the living room is placed the dining room, entered by way of sliding doors, while directly at its rear is a kitchen including as accessories a small pantry and the customary screened porch. At the right side of the living room are located two bedrooms, each with a good-sized

SIX-ROOM BUNGALOW BUILT FOR COMFORT

FIREPLACE CORNER OF LIVING ROOM.

Indeed, the coloring of the room has been commended as more than usually effective.

A large well built-in sideboard marks the dining room, also a commodious window-seat, the top of which is on hinges, in which instance it discloses an appreciable space for storing away various articles. Chocolate-colored leather is used to panel the room to a height of 4 feet, above which a rail is run for holding plates. The upper part of the walls and ceiling, likewise the floor and trim, have been subjected to the same treatment as those of the living room. An ingenious lighting of the room is contrived by art lights concealed in the four corners of the ceiling beams, besides the usual drop light is suspended from the center.

The den, while small, makes a direct appeal to members of the family caring for informality and absolute comfort. It is here that letters are written, there being a built-in desk in one corner, and books read, two bookcases showing against the

closet, a bathroom supplied with medicine chest and linen closet and the den, the latter connecting with the living room by a broad arch.

A feature not to be overlooked in this plan is the short hall which leads from the end of the living room and connects the two bedrooms with the bathroom. It can be shut off by means of a door so that this section of the bungalow has complete privacy.

Regarding the principal features of the living room, the fireplace first attracts attention since it is large and occupies a sort of Dutch nook in one corner of the room. Its hearth and mantel are of brown tile, while the shelf above is of wood, severe and plain in treatment. Small built-in seats at either end of the fireplace add much to its welcoming sentiment. The room is finished in slash-grain Oregon pine made to look like fumed oak. The floor is also of oak. To hold the room in harmony, the walls, which are of plaster, are tinted a light chocolate brown, the ceiling running off into a delicate buff.

THE DEN IN THE CALIFORNIA BUNGALOW.

SIX-ROOM BUNGALOW BUILT FOR COMFORT

ONE END OF DINING ROOM WITH BUILT-IN WINDOW-SEAT AND SIDEBOARD.

walls. The most unique feature of the den, however, is the so-called disappearing bed. This bit of furniture is concealed in the wall between the den and the enclosed end of the front porch, and is so arranged that it can be rolled either into the den or out on the porch. When not in use for sleeping it looks simply like an innocent couch, both from the porch side and that of the den. The finish of the den is similar to that of the living and dining rooms. French doors form for it the means of passing out onto the porch.

FLOOR PLAN OF MR. CLARK'S BUNGALOW.

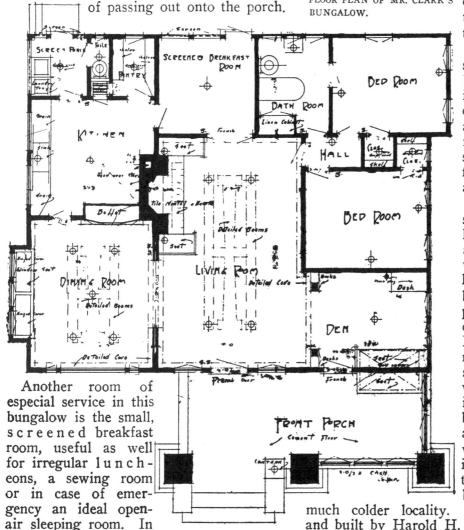

finish and trim it corresponds with the other mentioned rooms.

The kitchen, beside the usual cupboards and closets, is supplied with a draught cooler and a hood for the range. It has the same white enamel finish as the bath and bedrooms.

Although this six-room bungalow is located in a mild climate, where it cannot help but gain much benefit from its porches, its numerous windows and French doors, admitting floods of sunshine and warm, sweet air, it is equipped with a basement furnace, and is in every way so up-to-date in its arrangements that its plan should be feasible in a

Another room of especial service in this bungalow is the small, screened breakfast room, useful as well for irregular luncheons, a sewing room or in case of emergency an ideal open-air sleeping room. In much colder locality. It was designed and built by Harold H. Bowles, an architect of Los Angeles, California, who is authority for the statement that it could be duplicated in almost any part of the United States for from $3,000 to $3,400, its approximate cost in California. The house is the home of Mr. J. S. Clark.

VACATION BUNGALOWS THAT APPEAL BESIDES AS HOMES OF COMFORT AND REFRESHMENT

WITH the return of summer a longing slips into the heart of men and women alike to be on the wing, as it were, to fly away from the routine of life which occupies regularly the greater part of the year, and in some chosen spot of the earth to refresh themselves by Nature's companionability and to drink deeply of her soothing influences. And somewhere for the earnest man and woman there is waiting a spot, perchance by the sea, at the base of a hillside or near a running stream, where a shelter can be built for the vacation season of the year.

Many, however, are held back from even seeking the bit of earth likely to give them solace, simply because they think they cannot afford to build thereon a home. Their conception of a "cheap house" includes ugliness and inconvenience. Therefore they succumb to the tyranny of a summer boarding-house where the food is often not well cooked or nourishing and where beds are hard and unsympathetic. Later they return to their regular occupations, feeling that disappointment has marred their vacation time.

Probably the most satisfying summer outings are spent in snug little homes, informal places, or at least under a roof where all city-cramped faculties can have full play, for the men and the women who live restricted lives owing to the character of their various occupations above all things crave freedom in their summer outings.

THE CRAFTSMAN has proved that to build a bungalow snug, attractive and comfortable, in full view of the setting sun and where the air moves freely, is not as costly an undertaking as many people suppose. It can be made to come within the means of most home lovers with moderate salaries. If well done in the beginning, it then not only provides a shelter for the summer outing, but a home for all time, paying liberally for itself as time passes. It has always been the ideal of THE CRAFTSMAN to provide men and women of small incomes with homes in which their individuality might be truly expressed, where they

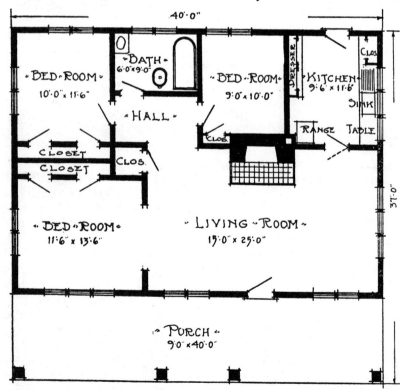

FLOOR PLAN OF CRAFTSMAN BUNGALOW NO. 161.

CRAFTSMAN VACATION BUNGALOWS

CRAFTSMAN SHINGLE BUNGALOW NO. 161: FIVE ROOMS, BATH AND LIVING PORCH.

might feel themselves in reality a part of their environment.

The two vacation bungalows presented this month by THE CRAFTSMAN make, even through their illustrations, a direct appeal to bachelors, bachelor maids and small families wishing to abide for a while close to the green things of the earth. These houses rest in so friendly a fashion on the ground that they seem to be a part of it. Both are very simple but dignified in character. About them is an air that would attract the interest of anyone seeking peace and joy close to Nature.

BUNGALOW No. 161, the larger of the two, can be built for from $1,500 to $2,000, not a large expenditure when one takes into consideration the completeness of the structure as a home, and the fact that it can be made habitable for the whole of the year should the owner desire.

Sometimes a member of a family may succumb for a time to ill health, when the possession of such a bungalow is of inestimable value. The patient can there regain his health economically in comparison with the charges made at various resorts and sanitariums.

The exterior of this bungalow is covered with shingles. The porch having supports of hewn posts which carry out the idea of harmony with Nature. The roof can be of some sheet composition such as Ruberoid, its slant being hardly sufficient for the use of shingles. When well colored, perhaps by a combination of brown shingles and a green roof, or one of red where a brighter touch is desired, this home appears to fit into the landscape as completely as though it were Nature's own handiwork.

The arrangement of the interior shows this vacation home to be planned so that no space is wasted. From the porch, stretching the full length of the building, one steps directly into the living room with its spacious fireplace opposite the door of entrance. The room is well lighted by the double casements on each side of the door, and by a group of three on the right, so that it will have as much fresh air and sunshine as possible. And as this room and the porch will naturally be the most popular portions of the bungalow, they should be considered in deciding its placing. The best exposure will probably be facing south, giving the living room and porch the eastern, southern and western sunlight.

The living room is a good-sized place— 15 by 25 feet—and its size seems increased by the wide openings into the bedrooms on the left and the hall in the rear. If the owner preferred, of course, one or both of these openings might be closed by an ordinary partition and door, or by portières. The east end of the living room can well be used for an informal dining room whenever the inclemency of the weather forbids eating on the porch.

The kitchen directly behind this section of the living room is fitted up along its light east side with a table, sink and drainboard and a closet. The range in the corner of the room uses the substantial chimney for its flue. China closets add to the completeness of the equipment.

This floor plan provides for three bedrooms, each one furnished with a closet, and there is also a large closet in one corner of the living room convenient for coats, or for golf sticks, tennis rackets, fishing tackle, etc. Perhaps only two bedrooms may be necessary, in which case the one opening from the living room may be turned into a study, office, music room or studio, according to the inclination of the home-builder. The two bedrooms in the rear and the bathroom between them open out of the hall, resulting in a certain amount of seclusion for this part of the house, and shutting off at will the living-room section.

More space or more elements of comfort could hardly be gained in a plan of these dimensions. The rooms are well lighted by good-sized windows and the circulation of air is untrammeled.

BUNGALOW No. 162 is considerably smaller than the first one illustrated this month, yet as practical. The cost of its construction need not exceed $1,200. It is built of shingles, field stone and hewn posts, and its roof is sufficiently sloped to permit of the use of shingles, should they be preferred to composition sheet roofing.

As in the first bungalow, the door opens directly from the porch into the living room, and on each side are double casements, while a group of three casements lights the right-hand wall and a single casement is placed on each side of the fireplace opposite. This will ensure plenty of air and sunlight, especially if the bungalow is built, as it probably will be, facing south. While this bungalow occupies less space than the one previously described, its living room is even larger than the first, being 16 by 29 feet. The arrangement of the open fireplace and built-in seats on each side results in considerable structural interest at this end of the room and gives the place an air of comfort and hospitality. We would suggest that these seats be made with hinged lids, for the storage space beneath will be particularly welcome in such a small home.

The rear of the floor plan is occupied by

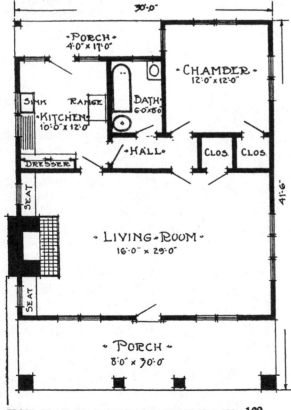

FLOOR PLAN OF CRAFTSMAN BUNGALOW NO. 162.

CRAFTSMAN VACATION BUNGALOW NO. 162: THREE ROOMS AND LIVING PORCH.

the kitchen, bathroom and bedroom, each of which opens out of a small hall, which gives the necessary privacy that is so often lacking in bungalow life. The kitchen is equipped with built-in dresser, sink and drainboard beneath the left-hand windows, with the range opposite where it will get plenty of light from the windows at the back. A door opens onto the small porch, where many of the kitchen tasks may be done in the open air.

The bedroom in the corner will prove particularly comfortable during the summer, for it has windows on three sides that will provide for plenty of cross-ventilation. A good-sized closet is built here next to the one which opens out of the living room.

With thoughts of the spring and early summer wild flowers growing spontaneously about these vacation houses and the asters and golden rods of autumn adding later to their brilliancy, it is hoped that they

will suggest to many ideals of comfortable home life filled with the joy of outdoor living and tranquillity.

In the illustrations of these two bungalows, it will be noticed, we have suggested the use of rustic garden furniture, and in the first sketch is shown a boat-landing with a rustic railing. Other practical suggestions along these lines will be found in an article on page 349, which includes illustrations of various forms of rustic construction—settles and chairs, garden tables, summer houses and pergolas, simple and at the same time decorative in design. Not only do such features invite one to spend as much time as possible in the open air, but they may prove a very effective means of making the little bungalows seem at home among rugged woodland surroundings.

CRAFTSMAN HOUSES BUILT FOR "OUTDOOR" LIVING

THE CRAFTSMAN, in showing in this outdoor number four plans of houses instead of the customary two, does so because it wishes to share with its readers the conviction that the desirable country house of the present is the one that brings the open country nearest to the fireside. This idea is also typified by the two extra plans given this month on pages 322 and 324, which may prove especially serviceable at this season of the year.

For a long time THE CRAFTSMAN has felt that too close and unbroken a home enclosure is not good for the general health of family life, and that all forms of interior stuffiness should be abolished. Moreover, to the fact of living in rooms through which air cannot circulate freely is due, THE CRAFTSMAN thinks, much of the lack of fiber and the physical weaknesses of many people. A superabundance of hangings, innumerable sofa cushions, thick carpets and deep-cushioned seats deprive the individual of the

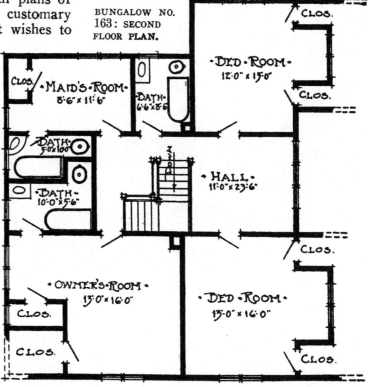

BUNGALOW NO. 163: SECOND FLOOR PLAN.

power to resist the inroads of illness. In succumbing to their influence he forgets his own force. The thinking mind realizes that to live in the open as much as possible is beneficial not only to the body but to the mind, the two together working toward the inevitable weal or woe of humanity.

In planning the two houses shown here, the idea has been to arrange the interiors compactly and economically, and to provide a generous amount of airy, sunlit space while keeping the houses as roomy as possible; in other words, to provide open rooms that have prac-

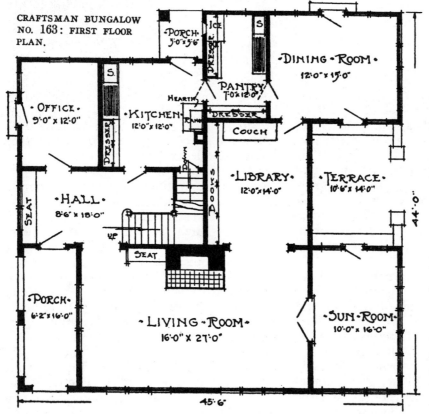

CRAFTSMAN BUNGALOW NO. 163: FIRST FLOOR PLAN.

Gustav Stickley, Architect.

CRAFTSMAN BUNGALOW (TWO-FLOORS) NO. 163: BUILT
TO BRING ALL THE SUN AND AIR POSSIBLE INDOORS.

Gustav Stickley, Architect.

CRAFTSMAN BUNGALOW NO. 164: THE SPECIAL FEATURES
ARE A SUNROOM, LIVING PORCH AND SLEEPING PORCH.

tically the value of porches and yet are a permanent part of the living area.

HOUSE No. 163, a two-floor structure of cement with a roof of asbestos shingles, while presenting an exterior different from most Craftsman houses, has lost neither simplicity nor dignity; it has nevertheless gained considerably in power to open up freely to the outside air, and to draw within its shelter the beauty and freshness of the garden.

The lower walls of this house are made up largely of casement windows, which can be thrown open readily to flood the interior with sunlight and air. The windows of the sunroom can be completely removed during the warm weather and their place taken by screens. This generous amount of windows and the way in which they are grouped together is one of the most interesting and unique features of the exterior. Moreover, they give the house an appearance of close relationship with nature, so that even indoors one will not feel shut away from the odor of flowers and the sweet smell of the earth.

In order to emphasize this wholesome idea of opening a house well to the out-of-doors, we have illustrated the east side of this dwelling, the morning sun bathing it early and working gradually around to the south, where it suffuses the sunroom, living room and entrance porch.

This porch can be better seen in the plan than in the perspective view. From it one steps into a hall lighted by double casements, beneath which the long window-seat is built. The woodwork of the staircase, which turns up to the right, may be made an attractive part of this hallway, and if it seems advisable to have a coat closet here one might be built in the corner between the stairs and kitchen. The arrangement of the hall will be found particularly convenient, as it shuts off the kitchen from the main living portion of the house. It also insures privacy for the room which we have marked "office," and which may, of course, be put to whatever use is most desirable for some busy member of the family.

From the hall one passes into the living room, which will prove an unusually light and cheerful place, with its many windows, its open fireplace and built-in seat, around which the furnishings will naturally be grouped. From this room two glass doors give access to the sunroom.

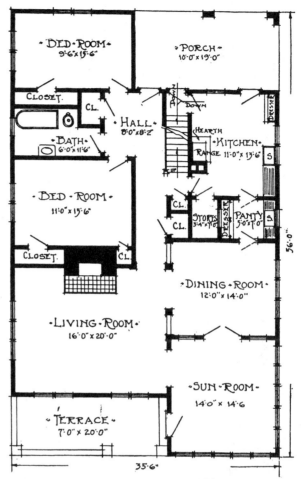

CRAFTSMAN BUNGALOW NO. 164: FLOOR PLAN.

This sunroom should naturally hold no furniture or floor covering likely to be damaged by a whimsical shower or by a rough wind driving the leaves from the trees through its open spaces. It depends, moreover, upon the inclination of the owner whether or no the glass windows, with the passing of cold weather, are replaced by screens or blinds, also a good deal upon the location of the house. If situated in a section of the country free from mosquitoes, Japanese blinds would be preferable, as they can be lifted up when not needed for shade, leaving no hindrance to the entrance of air. In this sunroom, away from office, entrance porch, hall and their traffic, one may find secluded comfort and shelter. Flowers, vines, and other plants could be grown in this room, making it almost into a conservatory.

From the sunroom one steps through a glass door flanked by windows down onto the terrace, which, while sheltered by the walls of the house, is open overhead. This terrace is raised a little above the garden level, and an additional air of coziness is

CRAFTSMAN BUNGALOWS BUILT FOR "OUTDOOR" LIVING

given by low cement parapets and posts. The latter offer just the places for pots of flowers—nasturtiums would give rich patches of color—while in the corners of the terrace against the walls, tall potted shrubs might be set. The terrace floor might be of cement, unless a note of warmth and variety were preferred in the shape of red brick tiles.

Overlooking the terrace are the windows of the library, which opens out of the living room, and in this light pleasant place we have indicated bookshelves lining the long wall and a couch against the shorter partition.

Nearby is the dining room, which is built practically like the sunroom, with its walls almost entirely of windows and glass doors opening to the terrace and garden. In winter this room will be glassed in, while in summer screens may take the place of windows, converting it into an outdoor dining room or porch.

A good-sized pantry with two dressers, sink and ice-box separates the dining room from the kitchen and the latter connects with a small porch from which the ice-box may be filled.

The second floor plan will be found especially convenient. There is a large central hall lighted by three windows overlooking the terrace; the two bedrooms on this side of the house are irregular in shape on account of the dormer construction, and on each side of the dormers are closets beneath the slope of the main roof. These dormer alcoves can be made very inviting by the building of window-seats. For these two bedrooms a bathroom is provided at the head of the stairs, while the rest of the second floor is taken up by the owner's room with its two large closets and private bath, and the maid's room and bath.

IN order to carry out properly the scheme of House No. 164, it should be built facing the south, for this will insure plenty of sunlight for the many windows of dining room, sunroom and living room. While this house is very different in layout from its predecessor, all the rooms being on one floor, the same principles are used in the general construction and arrangement of the sunroom.

The lower part of the building is of brick, the upper part and chimneys finished with stucco, while the roof is covered with asbestos shingles. This combination gives variety of texture and lends itself to an interesting color scheme. By way of contrast with the red brickwork, asbestos shingles of a soft green might be chosen; brown woodwork would look well with the natural-colored stucco, while a lighter note might be added by painting the door and window sash white.

The charm of this house is its nearness to the garden and its homelike coziness. The terrace offers the means of entrance and is enclosed by a low parapet topped by boxes in which flowers are planted. These and the flower-boxes at the sunroom windows bring the garden and house into such intimate companionship that one hardly knows where one leaves off and the other begins. To keep these boxes filled with flowers that show bloom during the months that the house is occupied, flowers rich in color and alluring in fragrance, at once becomes a delightful occupation for one member of the family. When the house is lived in throughout the year, as will most likely occur, the plants of summer's gay bloom can be replaced in the autumn by evergreens able to stand cold, harsh weather and to lift themselves in their cheerful dress of green above the whiteness of the snow. It is at this season that the glass windows, on which the sun shines freely, warm the room with an electrifying glow obtainable from no other source.

A couple of steps from the terrace lead up to the sunroom, which, if made cheerful with plants and comfortable with willow furniture, will prove an entrance at once unique and inviting. A wide opening leads to the living room, which is lighted by casement windows and warmed by an open fireplace, and on the right, separated by post-and-panel construction, the dining room is found. From this room glass doors with windows on each side lead to the sunroom, and as there is also a group of three casements on the right it will prove an unusually light and interesting place for the serving of meals.

Behind the dining room are the pantry and kitchen, the latter opening on to a large sheltered porch at the rear, where many of the kitchen tasks may be done during the warm weather. If this porch is surrounded by a parapet it could even be used for sleeping purposes, as it is convenient to the bedrooms and bath. The attic may be used for storage or it may be finished off as a maid's bedroom.

MORE CRAFTSMAN BUNGA-LOWS FOR COUNTRY AND SUBURBAN HOME-BUILDERS

AS the months go by we are having more and more requests for simple bungalow designs—five- and six-room homes, suitable for suburban or country surroundings, with the kind of plans that will combine homelike comfort with economy of construction. And especially these prospective home-builders want all their rooms on one floor, so that one maid can do the work easily; while in many cases the arrangement must be so simple that the housewife can dispense with outside help altogether.

We have already designed and published in THE CRAFTSMAN a great many bungalows along these practical lines, but there seems almost no limit to the possibilities of variety in bungalow planning — not variety merely for its own sake,

but to meet different local conditions and different family needs. And so, realizing that the more designs we publish, the more helpful we can be in aiding our friends to select or work out their own ideal plans, we are presenting two more this month.

If we have overestimated the popularity of the one-story bungalow, and many of

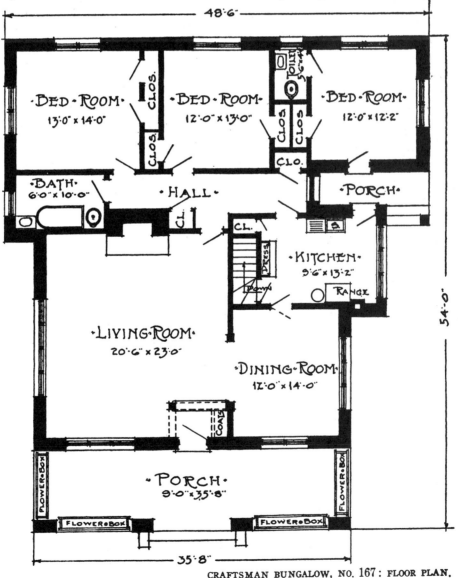

CRAFTSMAN BUNGALOW, NO. 167: FLOOR PLAN.

Gustav Stickley, Architect.

SIX-ROOM CRAFTSMAN BUNGALOW OF FIELD STONE, WITH LONG PORCH AND COMPACT HOMELIKE INTERIOR: NO. 167.

Gustav Stickley, Architect.

FIVE-ROOM CRAFTSMAN BUNGALOW OF STONE AND SHIN-
GLES, PLANNED FOR SIMPLE HOUSEKEEPING: NO. 168.

our readers are interested in other types, we shall be only too glad to hear from them personally, so that in future we may work up other plans that will be useful to them. For the more closely we get in touch and the more familiar we become with the needs and ideals of those whom our magazine reaches, the better able we shall be to help them through its pages in molding those ideals into realities.

The bungalows illustrated here are planned for country spots and will look equally well among the woods or mountains, beside a lake or stream, or near the shore. They may be built for summer homes and furnished with a few simple, durable belongings, or they may be built and furnished to live in all the year round. Probably most people will prefer to use them for permanent homes, as they are roomy and well equipped, planned for the greatest possible family comfort both for indoor and outdoor living.

While especially adapted, as we have said, to a more or less rural environment, many home-builders whose occupations make it necessary for them to be within easy reach of the city, may prefer to build these bungalows on suburban lots. And in this case we would lay emphasis upon the need of care in choosing the location; for such low, simple dwellings as those we have pictured here will not appear to advantage unless the houses around them are very similar in style. Needless to add, the more garden space there is, and the more rugged and irregular the ground, the greater possibility of achieving picturesque results.

The plan of the first bungalow, No. 167, was worked out for one of our clients who

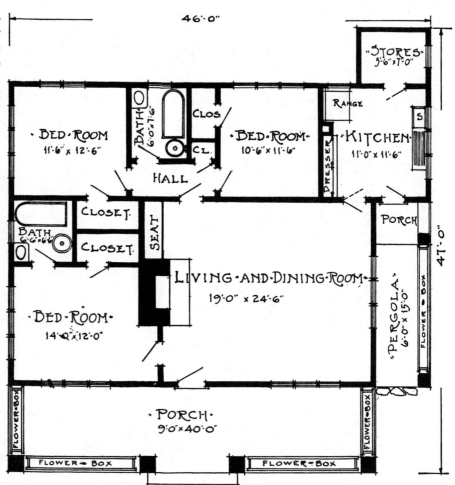

FLOOR PLAN: CRAFTSMAN BUNGALOW NO. 168.

wanted us to design him a summer home. There is plenty of field stone where he intends to build, and as he is particularly fond of this material he decided to use it as much as possible in the construction. Accordingly, we have shown stone walls and stone pillars for the porch, with shingles in the gables and roof.

If others wish to build from this design and field stone does not happen to be available in their locality, brick, concrete or shingles may be used instead. If built of brick, either brick or wood pillars would be most appropriate for the porch; if of concrete, square concrete posts or turned wood columns would be in keeping; and if of shingles, hewn log posts would add to the rustic air. In any case, we would suggest that the gables be of different material from the main walls, to give a little variety and to emphasize the low effect of the exterior.

The porch floors are of cement, and we have indicated wooden flower-boxes between the pillars, as they will give a little privacy and will help to link the house and garden together.

BUNGALOWS WITH LARGE LIVING ROOMS

From the front porch one steps into a small vestibule which provides a place for coats and screens the rooms from draughts from the front door. The living room is well lighted by groups of small-paned casements on two sides, and there is plenty of room for comfortable chairs and settles to be grouped about the open fireplace at the farther end.

A wide opening on the right leads to the dining room, which, although only 12 by 14 feet, will be quite large enough for a family of three or four people and their guests.

The kitchen is just behind, with the cellar stairs on the left beside the built-in dresser, and a broom closet in the corner. The sink and range are not far from the windows, and a door at the rear leads out onto the small porch from which the maid's bedroom opens. The latter is large and well lighted by windows on two sides, and in addition to the closet there is a private toilet. This arrangement separates the service portion of the bungalow from the rest, giving the maid her own little home, as it were, secluded from the family rooms.

It will also be noticed that the arrangement of this narrow porch permits the placing of a window in the right-hand end of the long hall which separates the family bedrooms and bathroom from the rest of the plan.

As the space beneath the roof is merely ventilated by louvres in the gables and is not intended to be used for storage, we have provided as many closets as possible —two small closets in the hall, two in the middle bedroom and a single long one in the room on the left.

It would be a good plan to install a Craftsman fireplace in the living room of this bungalow, for this would keep the rooms at a comfortable temperature during much of the spring and fall without lighting the cellar furnace.

THE second bungalow, No. 168, is not quite as large as the first, and is entirely different in arrangement and construction. We have shown the walls covered with shingles, the roof with composition sheet roofing, while field stone is used for the foundation and end pillars of the front porch, as well as for the chimneys. For the pillars on each side of the entrance, however, we have used wood, for this forms an intermediate link between the textures of the rough stonework and smooth roof. Wood pillars are also used for the

pergola porch at the side. As in the preceding bungalow, we have indicated flower-boxes between the pillars, set on the cement floor.

The entrance door opens directly into the big main room, which is living and dining room combined. A coat closet may be provided across the right-hand corner, and if the owner prefers to have the entrance nearer to the closet and farther from the fireplace, the arrangement of the front windows and door may be reversed.

A fireside seat is built in on one side of the chimneypiece, and this end of the room will naturally be furnished as a general living room, while the dining table and sideboard will be placed over toward the right, near the kitchen.

The pergola porch at the side will be a convenient place for outdoor meals, for it is accessible from the kitchen. The latter has windows at the side and rear, which ensure plenty of light at the range and sink; a long dresser is built on the left, and there is a large closet for stores at the back, lighted by a window on the side.

If the owner wishes to build this bungalow with a cellar, the right-hand portion of the plan may be excavated and the kitchen rearranged to make room for the stairs. In this case the laundry may be in the cellar; otherwise, wash trays may be placed in the kitchen, or the closet at the back, which we have marked "stores" may be used as a laundry and a door arranged to open directly into the back garden.

The bedrooms should prove especially convenient, for they afford that privacy which is so desirable in a one-story home. The owner's room, large and light, with its private bathroom and big closet, opens out of the living room, while the two other bedrooms are separated from the rest of the plan by a small hall.

The bungalow, as it stands now, would be suitable for a small family, where the mistress wished to do her own work; but it could be readily adapted to accommodate a maid by making the right-hand rear bedroom open from the kitchen instead of the hall.

IN building the two bungalows which we have shown here, the question of the exterior color scheme will naturally be an important one and will depend on the nature of the landscape or neighboring houses and the owner's taste. If the first bungalow is built of field stone, as we have shown, the varied tones of the stone will give interest of color and texture to the walls and porch, which may be brightened by light green flower-boxes, door and window trim and white sash. A deep moss-green in the gables and reddish brown for the shingles of the roof will be in keeping, especially if the building is set among woodland surroundings.

The second bungalow will probably look well if the shingled walls are stained light golden brown and the roof is olive green. The trim and flower-boxes may also be green and the sash cream or white.

THE EVOLUTION OF A HILLSIDE HOME: RAYMOND RIORDON'S INDIANA BUNGALOW

UCCESSFUL home-building implies something more than the selection of a desirable site, the drawing of suitable working plans and the erection of a practical construction. It implies a sympathetic use of building materials, an understanding of that harmony which should exist between the house and its environment, between the exterior construction and the interior finish and furnishing, between the character of the house and the characters of those who are to live in it. And perhaps more important than all, it implies a genuine home-seeking, home-loving spirit. For the factor that determines the architectural, and one might almost say spiritual, success of such an undertaking is the vision that guides the architect's pencil and the builder's tool, the ideal that inspires the home-maker in the working out of his plans, from the general scheme down to the smallest detail. The house he is building is the house of his hopes and dreams, probably the fruit of long years of work and study and contemplation; its erection means the fulfilment of a long-cherished plan; it is to be a home for his soul as well as for his body, a little corner of the world that is essentially his own. This vision, this ideal is the "north star" which guides the successful home-builder safely into his desired haven.

It is just such hopes and dreams, you feel, that must have inspired the planning and building of the house shown here—the home of Mr. Raymond Riordon, Superintendent of the Interlaken School at Rolling Prairie, Indiana. Whether you view it from the lake, the garden or the clover-covered hillside, or whether you step inside its sheltered porch and hospitable rooms, you feel instinctively that it is a real home, planned by those who knew by heart the country, the materials and the needs of the people who were to live therein, and who had studied out, thoughtfully and lovingly, how to make the building fulfil those needs in the wisest and most beautiful way.

Seldom have we encountered a more interesting example of utility and beauty combined, and seldom have we seen a house that was more at home among its surroundings. Nestling there snugly against the gently sloping shore, with the log schoolhouse, dormitory and other school and farm buildings clustered around it, the hill of white clover and the young apple orchard nearby, this brick and clapboard bungalow raises its many-windowed walls, shingled roof and sturdy chimney, an embodiment of architectural peace.

THE CRAFTSMAN HOME OF RAYMOND RIORDON, SUPERINTENDENT
OF THE INTERLAKEN SCHOOL AT ROLLING PRAIRIE, INDIANA

ONE END OF THE LIVING PORCH IN MR. RIORDON'S HOME, WITH A GLIMPSE OF THE SLEEPING PORCH BEYOND.

A CORNER OF THE SHELTERED SLEEPING PORCH IN MR. RIORDON'S HOME OPENING FROM ONE OF THE BEDROOMS.

FIREPLACE NOOK IN THE LIVING ROOM OF
MR. RIORDON'S BUNGALOW.

A CORNER OF ONE OF THE BEDROOMS, WITH
SUN AND AIR THE FIRST CONSIDERATION.

CRAFTSMAN BUNGALOWS   521

IN WORKING OUT HIS OWN PLANS FROM THE ORIGINAL CRAFTSMAN DESIGN, MR. RIORDON INCLUDED THE LONG SPACIOUS "ATTIC" LIVING ROOM, TWO VIEWS OF WHICH ARE SHOWN ABOVE.

AN INDIANA HOME ON CRAFTSMAN LINES

Behind the house an excavation has been made and a red brick court built with a retaining wall eight feet high, edged with cement flower-boxes and broken by an entrance of brick steps leading down to the kitchen door. Above the kitchen steps is a pergola, and the projection overhead, seen in the photographs, is a rainwater box with a pipe leading to the kitchen basin. This rainwater box contains a steam coil which keeps it warm in winter and free from frost—one of the many instances of practical forethought in which this home abounds. In addition to this, the kitchen is piped, of course, for hot and cold water.

In front of the house is a flower-bed which was planted with a thousand tulips—and one can easily imagine what color glory their bloom must have lent this woodland spot. When their reign was over, the bulbs were taken out and heliotrope planted in their stead to form another link in the garden's circling chain of color and fragrance.

On one side, facing the faculty house, the hill was planted with crabapple and cherry trees, while on the slight slope from the wall to the brick court, vivid peonies bob out in all colors, ready for the picking. In the shadow of the slope and sheltered by these lordly neighbors, modest lilies-of-the-valley raise their white blossoms among the green; toward the ice-house stand the friendly hydrangeas, ready to follow the tulips, peonies and geraniums with their lavish bloom.

On the lake side, the steeper slope is closely planted with flowering currant, spirea, buckthorn, syringa, and here and there a cluster of bright tiger lilies flashes on the eye. A winding path leads to the boat house, where canoe, rowboat and sailboat nestle on runners ready to slide out for pleasure or for rescue.

The rear of the house is massed with shrubs and cherry trees, and here one finds the rose garden, where hundreds of varicolored blossoms scent the air and add to the beauty of the hill.

And all this gardening was done, all this expanse of plant life propagated, protected and cared for, by boys —mostly by one little boy of twelve!

THAT brings us to the most delightful feature of this lakeside bungalow—the fact that it is not only the home of the superintendent, but also a club house for the boys and teachers of the school community of a hundred and seventy people. And surely, this bungalow is an ideal gathering place for the inmates of such a school — a school that aims to develop body and mind in wholesome harmony.

Turning to the plans and illustrations, we find that the design was adapted from a certain five-room, stone and shingle Craftsman bungalow, published about three years ago in THE CRAFTSMAN Magazine. And it is interesting to note how carefully and at the same time with

AN INDIANA HOME ON CRAFTSMAN LINES

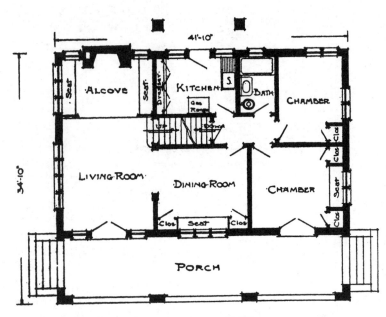

MR. RIORDON'S BUNGALOW: FIRST FLOOR PLAN.

what pleasing originality the owner and his assistant architect, George W. Maher of Chicago, have adapted the Craftsman plan to meet the special needs of individual and site.

The main floor plan of "Number Ninety-three" was carried out practically as we had drawn it, and to it were added a basement and second story. The changes in the elevation and the detail on the second floor were drawn by Mr. Maher from specifications which Mr. Riordon furnished, and between them they have certainly managed to achieve an unusual and satisfying result.

The front entrance is through the long porch which extends across the entire front of the building and is divided into a "sitting porch" and a sleeping porch, the former opening into the big living room, the latter into one of the bedrooms. Some idea of the substantial comfort and cheerfulness of the arrangement can be gathered from the photographs which Mr. Riordon has sent; for as he remarks in his letter to us, "Photographer Koch has made his lenses do effective work."

Stepping from the porch into the living room, one is greeted by the welcome sight of a big, comfortable fireplace nook, where built-in seats and bookshelves with curtained windows above add to the interest of the rough brick chimneypiece and tiled hearth.

The dining room with its wide opening is nearby, so that it seems almost a part of the large main room, and its wide windows frame a generous view of the lovely countryside.

The rest of the floor comprises a small hallway which serves to shut off the kitchen from the dining room and also separates the two bedrooms and bath from the rest of the house.

The woodwork of the interior is especially interesting, for its simple construction and mellow finish evince the real craftsman spirit, filling the rooms with an atmosphere of peace and dignity that reminds one of the quiet forests from which the timber came. Oak flooring is used

AN INDIANA HOME ON CRAFTSMAN LINES

throughout, and oak is also the finish of the living room. Downstairs all the rest is birch, upstairs yellow pine.

AND now we come to the "attic." We put it in "quotes" because the word loses, or rather outgrows, its usual meaning when applied to such a room as the one pictured here. No dingy, cobwebbed place is this, tucked away beneath the rafters and breathing that strange, musty odor which shrouded in mystery the attic that our childhood knew. No—the term has acquired a new meaning, now that we have seen the photographs of Mr. Riordon's bungalow home. For this is an attic of distinction, comfort and charm.

You climb the staircase that leads up beside the fireplace nook, and find yourself in the center of a long, well lighted room with simple and inviting furnishings—long cushioned seats beneath the curtained windows, willow armchairs and roomy settles, handy tables and shelves where books and magazines lie temptingly about, and best of all an open fireplace, with andirons upon the hearth and faggots that need only a match to start a crackling blaze. The rugs upon the polished oak floor, the shelved closets built against the walls beneath the sloping roof, the lamps for table, wall and ceiling which at nightfall shed their soft mellow glow about the room — all these things contribute to the general air of comfort and loveliness.

The room is large enough for sixty-five boys to enjoy its hospitable spaces, lounge around among the seats and cushions, bury themselves in books, indulge in rest or study, serious debate or idle chat as the spirit moves them. And one cannot help thinking how jolly and companionable it all must be, what a spirit of comradeship such hours must bring to teachers and students alike. Unconsciously one remembers the inscription above the chimneypiece downstairs, *To Teach Boys to Live*"—and after all, to what finer purpose could any man dedicate his home?

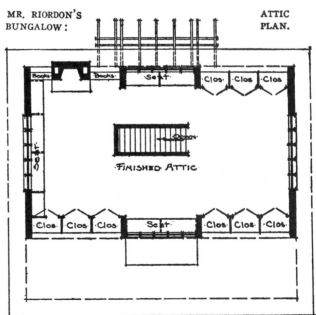

MR. RIORDON'S BUNGALOW: ATTIC PLAN.

A WESTERN BUNGALOW IN
WHICH ECONOMY AND BEAUTY MEET:
BY H. L. GAUT

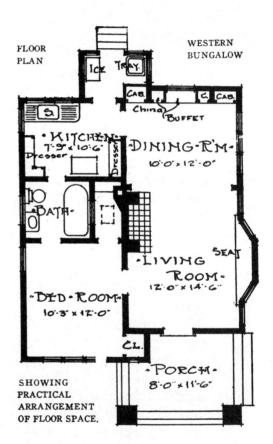

WESTERN BUNGALOW

SHOWING PRACTICAL ARRANGEMENT OF FLOOR SPACE.

THERE seems no end to the variety that an architect can get out of that apparently simple combination—four rooms and a bath. At any rate, the designer of the California bungalow shown below seems able to achieve originality with each small home that he undertakes, and undoubtedly his success is due to the fact that he works out the plans in close sympathy with the needs of the owner and with due respect to the limitations of the site. And in striving thus for the greatest possible amount of practical comfort within a restricted space and income, he gains an unusually picturesque and satisfying result.

In this low-roofed, many-windowed little home we find much that is charming. The simple and effective use of cobblestones, concrete and wood has made a very attractive entrance, and the addition of ferns on the posts and in the window-boxes has added to the friendly air. The floor plan is full of thought for the convenience of those who live and work there, and the arrangement of the woodwork, built-in

A WELL PLANNED BUNGALOW

A BUNGALOW SHOWING INTERESTING COMBINATION OF WOOD, STONE AND CEMENT.

fittings and other structural features suggests how much substantial beauty can be embodied in even so inexpensive a dwelling.

One of the most interesting points about this bungalow is the grouping of the windows in the right-hand wall of the living and dining rooms. As a glance at the plan and exterior will show, this wall is practically of glass, so that plenty of light and air is insured for the interior. The bay window of the living room is made doubly inviting by the building-in of a seat, and one can imagine how readily both rooms must lend themselves to simple and artistic furnishing.

The fireplace of course is an important feature, and as it is built in the center of the left-hand wall, its warmth and cheery glow can be enjoyed from both rooms; besides, the division between them is so slight that the effect is of one long room extending the depth of the bungalow.

The layout of the kitchen and bedroom on the left with the bathroom between and accessible from both, is especially compact and utilizes the given space to the best advantage.

DETAIL OF BUNGALOW REVEALING EXCELLENT ROOF LINES.

A CRAFTSMAN BUNGALOW WHOSE OWNER WAS HIS OWN ARCHITECT

BUNGALOW AT GRANDVILLE, MICHIGAN, THE HOME OF MR. WILLIAM F. FREEMAN, PLANNED ALONG CRAFTSMAN LINES BY THE OWNER, WHO WAS HIS OWN ARCHITECT, SUPERINTENDED THE BUILDING AND DID MUCH OF THE ACTUAL WORK HIMSELF.

OUR mail is full of pleasant surprises, and not the least delightful among them recently was the unwrapping of the bungalow photographs which are reproduced here. For although we receive many pictures of houses, Craftsman and otherwise, from all parts of the country, few of them have proved more charming than this little Michigan home. Therefore, knowing that every successful house holds innumerable suggestions for other builders, we decided to share the views in question with our readers.

Perhaps the best way to describe the building of this bungalow is to let its owner, Mr. William F. Freeman, tell the story in his own words, which he did very simply and clearly in his letter to us.

"Here," he said, "are some Kodak pictures of a bungalow I have built for myself—not from any particular Craftsman plan, but from ideas gained through reading your magazine. We first determined what our requirements were, made a list of them, and then started to plan around them. I made my own drawings, and while they were somewhat crude, the carpenters had little trouble in grasping my ideas.

"The bungalow contains a living room, dining room, two sleeping rooms, bath-room, kitchen, pantry, coat room and entrance hall on the main floor. There is a large attic, which will be divided into three rooms later. The good-sized basement contains a water-heating system and a gas-engine-driven water system. I did all the plumbing and electric wiring, drove my own well, installed the water system and also the water-heating system. In this, however, I had to have the assistance of a steam fitter, as the weather was getting cold and we had to hustle it in, which we did in six days. The other work was done during evenings and holidays, extending over the whole summer.

"We built a shack for a kitchen and slept in a tent that we might be on the ground and watch the builders—for the bungalow was put up by day labor. Considering that we did not have the services of an architect, we think ourselves lucky in getting the results we have, and we feel greatly indebted to THE CRAFTSMAN for many ideas.

"We find the bungalow a very convenient place in which to live and work, and when we finish our grading, planting and the many other things that remain to be done, we believe it will be a thoroughly successful home."

There is something curiously stimulat-

BUILT HIS OWN CRAFTSMAN HOUSE

A VISTA THROUGH THE BUNGALOW INTERIOR, SHOW-ING THE USE OF POST-AND-PANEL CONSTRUCTION AND SMALL-PANED WINDOWS.

ing, inspiring even, in the sort of thing that this home-maker has accomplished. It re-minds one of the spirit of the old pioneer, the feeling of adventure which is really at the root of all constructive work, although we have most of us lost sight of it in our ready-made civilization. Many of us would like to do just what Mr. Freeman has achieved; but we are afraid to trust our own skill and judgment. We feel the need of professional architects, contractors and builders. It is so much easier to turn things over to others than to work them out for ourselves.

Of course, this is necessary to a great extent, for most of us have no time to give such an undertaking the study and atten-tion it demands. We cannot compete with experts who have years of specialized train-ing behind them. But when a man *can* work out his own plans, hire his own labor, pitch his tent right there on the ground to see that the work is done as he wants it done, and even take off his coat, roll up his shirt sleeves and do a good deal of it himself—he will find that the re-sults amply repay those efforts. And not the least of his benefits will be the joy he has tasted in tackling the work at first hand, coping successfully with difficulties and molding gradually into tan-gible shape the home of his heart's desire.

Besides, an experience of this kind has a definite technical as well as spiritual value, and is by no means to be despised as a factor in

the development of skill as well as character. The man who has the brains and ingenuity to do his own plumbing and electric wiring, to paint his own porch and stain his own interior trim, may well be proud of his achievement, for it shows that civilization has not robbed him of manual dexterity and that he is not ashamed to dig and plant in his own little Eden in order later to reap the fruits and gather the blossoms of his toil. We all know the charm of an inglenook and the comfort of our "ain fire-side"; but how many of us know the pleasure of sitting beside a chimney-piece that we ourselves have built?

The exterior of the building, with its simple lines, its use of rough stone in the chimney and pillars of the entrance porch, the low roof lines, overhanging eaves, and long dormer, all show the same simplicity and frankness which characterize Crafts-man designs.

Indoors, too, one finds the same practical and attractive use of structural features, such as the inglenook with brick chimney-piece, built-in bookshelves, high windows above, and plain wood settles on either side.

Certainly Mr. Freeman has the happy faculty of culling from many designs the principles and features which please him, and applying them to his own needs in a natural and serviceable way. For in this little bungalow one feels no sense of "patch-work architecture." Its most evident qual-ity is that of repose. And planted there in the woodland landscape, it seems the very embodiment of homelike peace.

INGLENOOK IN THE FREEMAN HOME, WITH BRICK FIREPLACE, BUILT-IN BOOKSHELVES AND SEATS.

A NEW ZEALAND BUNGALOW THAT SHOWS THE TRUE CRAFTSMAN'S ART

"IF a craftsman is to be successful he must base his efforts on essential principles. He can only be sure of himself after years of study and deep seeking. In other words, he must discover the relation of art to human life. With this rock for his foundation, he may speak, through the medium of wood and brick and stone, the truths that have come to him."

There is much wisdom in this simple statement of a craftsman's creed, and it is lent all the more weight because it comes from the pen and heart of one who has sought to embody its meaning in concrete form. It is the expression of a successful architect, a man who has himself thought and studied much, who plans and builds not only with due consideration for those who are to occupy his dwelling, but also in keen sympathy with the materials beneath his hand. He respects the individuality of each—and incidentally, in doing so, expresses his own.

The result, as the accompanying photographs show, is a building of sturdy charm, stamped, in spite of its simplicity—perhaps because of it—with a certain rare distinction that one does not meet in every bungalow. It is quaint, but not eccentric; unique, but not affected; fashioned with frank intention of material comfort, yet imbued with an atmosphere that is far from materialistic. For the spirit of home is there—the brooding quiet, the sheltering friendliness that comes with simple walls and solid woodwork, pleasant windows that gather air and sunlight, and furnishings that invite to sociability and rest.

The fact that this architect, Mr. J. W. Chapman Taylor, is a New Zealander, and the bungalow in question was designed and built by him for a family in New Plymouth, New Zealand, gives an additional interest to these illustrations, for it shows how wide and all-pervading is the architectural *zeitgeist* of today. This new home-building spirit, with its yearning for comfort, for simplicity and beauty, for sincere and earnest craftsmanship, is by no means limited to America and the countries of the Old World, but is stretching out into other continents and colonies and inspiring pioneers beyond other seas. It is infusing into a craft which modern industrial methods have commercialized, somewhat of the old-time ideals that guided the builders and artists and cabinetmakers of long ago. It is forsaking the cult of the machine-made and the gaudy, and hailing the rebirth of a half-forgotten art.

One cannot glance at these pictures of "Plas Mawr," this New Zealand bungalow, without feeling an echo of the home-ideals and the enthusiasm that must have gone into its conception and making.

NEW ZEALAND HOUSE IN CRAFTSMAN STYLE

Even the exterior, with its plain, light-reflecting walls, its casement windows nestling beneath the eaves, its broad sheltered entrance and sloping roof, suggests the unpretentious comfort and the artistic restraint one finds within. And the neat, inviting grounds with their well kept lawn, cobblestone wall with pergola above the walk, and fernery at the farther end, all hold a promise of vine-clad loveliness. For the house, one must remember, is a new one, and the garden has not yet had time to soften with foliage and blossoms the boundary line between art and nature.

IT is interesting to read the architect's description of this bungalow and see how he adjusted plans and materials to meet the needs of owner and site. The lot, it seems, was a triangular one, with its long side to the street, and the "motor house" and boundary wall were already built of river boulders laid in cement when the planning of the house was begun. The space being limited, the problem was to place the house so that while the rooms had sun and view the remaining ground would be left as much as possible in one broad piece.

The material chosen for the walls was ordinary building brick laid as smoothly as possible on the inside and roughcast outside to keep out the damp. The roof was covered with green slates, a few purple ones being introduced here and there to vary the color and surface—a plan that had already been adopted in the "motor house," and the repetition of which brought the two into harmony. Under the roof a large attic room was provided, twenty-eight feet long and twelve feet wide, with cupboards and a built-in window-seat to add to its convenience.

The ceilings were plastered between the beams, and the surface worked to a suitable texture with a brush while the plaster was still wet. The whole interior was distempered white, forming a pleasant contrast with the rich dark-colored jarrah wood of the trim, which was oiled and waxed. Concrete flags were used for the floor, laid on dry sand with cement-pointed joints, and small red tiles were set at the corners to give a brighter note. The floor was well waxed so that it would be pleasant to the tread and easy to keep clean.

For the structural timber work and the furniture, both movable and fixed, the jarrah wood was adze-hewn, mortised and tenoned together and fastened with wood pins, the heads of which project slightly, giving a decorative touch while adding to the effect of strength. In fact, the furniture is constructed on the lines followed by the old wagon-builders of England. It is strong, comfortable, with a certain primitive art that comes of itself when simple tools

"PLAS MAWR," A MODERN BUNGALOW OF UNUSUAL CHARM DESIGNED AND BUILT BY J. W. CHAPMAN TAYLOR, ARCHITECT, FOR MRS. C. H. BURGESS, NEW PLYMOUTH, NEW ZEALAND.

LIVING ROOM AND INGLENOOK WITH CRAFTSMAN FIREPLACE IN THE NEW ZEALAND BUNGALOW: A PLACE OF UNPRETENTIOUS CHARM THAT SHOWS IN EVERY DETAIL THE TOUCH OF SYMPATHETIC ARCHITECT AND CABINETMAKER.

A GLIMPSE INTO THE DINING RECESS OF "PLAS MAWR," REVEALING THE SIMPLE BEAUTY OF THE ADZE-HEWN WOODWORK AND THE RESTFUL ATMOSPHERE THAT PERVADES THE HOMELIKE ROOMS.

A BEDROOM CORNER IN THE BUNGALOW, WHERE CHINTZ CURTAINS ARE USED WITH PICTURESQUE EFFECT: THE CASEMENT WINDOWS AND CURTAINED DOORS ADD TO THE DECORATIVE INTEREST OF THIS DAINTY INTERIOR.

NEW ZEALAND HOUSE IN CRAFTSMAN STYLE

and human handiwork are employed. On seeing it one instinctively contrasts it with the modern machine-made type; for although the machine, by performing many mechanical operations such as the cutting of mortises, boring of holes or making of joints, can relieve the cabinetmaker of much labor, it can never form a substitute for the hand and spirit of the worker.

Realizing this, the maker of the woodwork and furniture for this bungalow, instead of using the planing machine to smoothe the surface of his wood, chose the more primitive adze, which gives to the surface a look of unevenness that lends individuality and charm. It brings out, moreover, the knotty, irregular nature of the wood, its odd little twists of grain, all those intimate, inherent qualities that remind one of the tree of which it was originally a part. As the architect of this bungalow has fancifully put it, "Even though our beams come to us mill-sawn, there is a better and more beautiful beam inside the sawn one; and it is this that the adzeman reveals when he hews away those parts which the blind machinery has left overlaying the beauty of the tree—just as the sculptor releases with his chisel the statue reposing in the marble block."

This principle, as Mr. Taylor reminds us, applies to all materials, from brick to jewels, and it was kept in mind during the designing and making of every detail of "Plas Mawr." Each part bears the impress of an individual hand, from the white-washed walls to the pottery on the mantelpiece.

It is particularly interesting—to us, at least—to discover in this bungalow many evidences of its owner's study of Craftsman designs. The post-and-panel construction between the rooms that lends such airy spaciousness to the interior; the frank treatment of each structural feature; the solid proportions and plain yet satisfying lines of the furniture; the elimination of unnecessary trim or ornament, and finally the Craftsman fireplace that strikes such a home-like note in the living-room inglenook—all reflect in their own fashion the source from which they were drawn.

Whichever way one turns something original and delightful greets one, whether it be the touch of brick in the window sills, the cushioned seats built around the walls of the dining recess, the chintz curtains and lamp-topped posts of the bedroom or the flower-filled vases that brighten table and shelf.

Yet with all the art that has been woven into this bungalow interior, there is no displeasing self-consciousness, no straining after the unusual or extreme. Whatever is unique and surprising seems rather the result of spontaneous enthusiasm and natural feeling for picturesqueness, ready sympathy with the materials, eagerness to make even the commonest detail a thing of loveliness.

THE COTTAGE-BUNGALOW

COTTAGE-BUNGALOW: A NEW DEVELOPMENT IN INTIMATE HOME ARCHITECTURE: PHOTOGRAPHS BY HELEN LUKENS GAUT

THE cottage-bungalow is the newest development in the small American home. We are presenting in this article two designs for this most interesting and intimate variety of domestic architecture. As is the case in many very practical ideas in modern building, these houses have been built in California, yet in spite of their perfect adaptability to the climate there, they furnish us throughout the eastern section of America a most valuable inspiration for home-making. The California architect, Sylvanus B. Marston, has, as examination of these floor plans shows, been able to combine the best points of the simple, old-fashioned cottage and the more elaborate and modern bungalow idea.

In working out this interesting and successful experiment—which may have been quite an unconscious one on the part of its originator—Mr. Marston has chosen from each style those characteristics which are most in keeping with modern American ideas of home comfort, health and beauty. He has retained the simple, sturdy, democratic air of the cottage, with its suggestion of solid indoor comfort and wholesome living; at the same time he has combined with it the airy porches, the ample living rooms, friendly firesides and craftsmanlike woodwork and fittings of the bungalow. And while placing most of the rooms on the ground floor to save unnecessary housework and stair-climbing, he has also utilized the space beneath the roof for sheltered open-air sleeping.

The result is a new type of intimate home architecture which is likely to prove wide in its appeal. And as it is capable of endless modification to meet the diverse tastes and requirements of different families, and the demands of varying climates and environments, the cottage-bungalow should prove a fresh inspiration for the home-builders of our land.

Two examples of this style of dwelling are illustrated here, both of them revealing a practical and sympathetic treatment of design and plan. They bring together, in an original and delightful way, the most desirable traits of the cottage and the bungalow. Neither word alone would accurately describe them; their qualities can only be expressed by employing both. The low long roof lines, the wide eaves, the placing of the main rooms on the ground floor, would seem to assign the buildings to the bungalow category. Yet the construction of the walls, porch pillars and

COTTAGE-BUNGALOW IN PASADENA, CALIFORNIA: A NEW TYPE OF DOMESTIC ARCHITECTURE WHICH COMBINES MANY PRACTICAL AND CHARMING FEATURES: COST OF CONSTRUCTION $4,000: SYLVANUS B. MARSTON, THE ARCHITECT, HAS ACHIEVED HERE AN UNUSUALLY SATISFYING EXTERIOR AS WELL AS PLAN.

THE COTTAGE-BUNGALOW

pergola are suggestive of Colonial cottages. But whichever influence predominates, they are certainly satisfactory "hybrids," and will be found worth studying, for they have been arranged and built for real comfort, pleasure and durability. Their compact simple layout, moreover, will appeal to housewives who wish to dispense with the services of a maid.

THE cost of construction of the first cottage-bungalow was $4,000. Its walls are of pearl-gray siding with white trim; the chimneys are dark red brick, and the roof is covered with moss-green shingles. The ventilators in the roof, the heavy barge-board molding at the eaves, the curved group of small-paned windows at the front, and the inviting recess of the porch

room is especially attractive with its open fireplace and small windows on either side, while a seat fills the curve of the bow window, flanked by built-in bookcases. In the dining room, buffet and china closets extend across one wall with windows above.

The arrangement of pantry, kitchen and screen porch is unusually practical, for the space is utilized to the best possible advantage, and is shut off from the rest of the plan. A small hall off the pass pantry gives access to cellar and attic stairs, and in this hall a coat and a broom closet are provided. The long hall at the left communicates with the three bedrooms and bath, which are thus separated from the remainder of the house. One of these bedrooms has a door onto the screen porch, however, so that it may be used for a maid, if necessary.

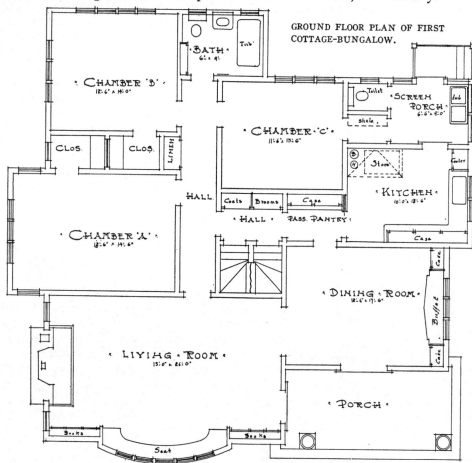

GROUND FLOOR PLAN OF FIRST COTTAGE-BUNGALOW.

are all interesting structural items. A decorative note is added by the wooden frame for vines on each side of the window group.

The building is 45 by 46 feet in area. The plan shows a very convenient arrangement of living and dining rooms, which open from the front porch. The former

Although one would hardly guess it from the front view, there is considerable space beneath the roof of this cottage-bungalow, which is lighted by windows in the gables and in the rear roof. In the latter, moreover, is an extension which makes full head room possible. This gives space for a large screen porch and dressing room up-

THE COTTAGE-BUNGALOW

SIMPLE YET DECORATIVE EXTERIOR, AND COMPACT, HOMELIKE ARRANGEMENT WITHIN, MAKE THIS COTTAGE-BUNGALOW IN PASADENA WORTH STUDYING: COST OF CONSTRUCTION $3,500: SYLVANUS B. MARSTON, ARCHITECT: THE ARCHED ENTRANCE AND PERGOLA-ROOFED PORCH ARE PARTICULARLY INTERESTING.

stairs, increasing considerably the sleeping accommodations and value of the house without adding much to its cost.

THE second house required even less outlay—$3,500—for it is somewhat smaller, having only two bedrooms on the ground floor. And while the style of the building reminds one of the first, it is quite different in plan. The exterior is provided in this case with a long porch across the front, the central part roofed and arched gracefully to shelter and emphasize the entrance, and the space on each side being of open pergola construction.

This cottage is 43 by 40 feet, with 14 by 16 cellar and concrete foundation. Heat is furnished by fireplace and furnace. The outside walls are of resawed redwood siding, painted dove gray, and the trim is white. Out-swinging lattice windows are used, and the entrance door, with its long narrow windows, is heavily cased, with curving bracketed top following the lines of the hood. The interior woodwork is of straight-grain Oregon pine, kitchen and bath being all in white with hard plastered walls and enameled woodwork.

The living room is large, with pleasant window groups and open fireplace, and the dining room with its built-in buffet and china cabinets is separated from the other room merely by bookcases and posts. In this cottage-bungalow no pass pantry is provided, but a small hall separates the kitchen from the front of the house. A screen porch with laundry tubs is built beyond. The two bedrooms and bathroom are also shut off from the other rooms by a hallway from which the cellar and attic stairs ascend. Upstairs are two sleeping porches and a dressing room, all built under the rear raised roof.

These cottage-bungalows furnish, moreover, interesting examples of that significant feature of modern home-making—the architectural solution of the servant problem. For many years we have been growing more democratic in our ways of building as well as in our manner of living. American women have been coming to feel that a large house and several servants are luxuries that have a superficial rather than a genuine value. Many have begun to discard elaboration for simplicity, to prefer a small, comfortable home to a large preten-

THE COTTAGE-BUNGALOW

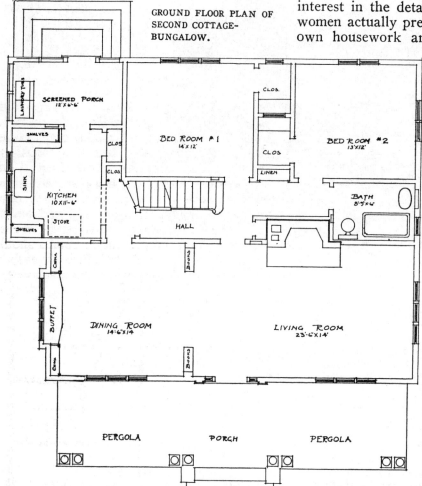

GROUND FLOOR PLAN OF
SECOND COTTAGE-
BUNGALOW.

interest in the details of the home. Some women actually prefer to do much of their own housework and cooking. The difficulty, too, of procuring competent helpers and the higher cost of living has brought increased interest in domestic channels.

These things, naturally, are gradually being reflected in our architecture. Homes are being planned to meet the new conditions. The wide popularity of the bungalow and cottage types is evidence of the growing desire for the small, intimate, compactly planned home. Elimination of all needless halls, passages and stairways, to save the housewife's steps; the simplifying of all the woodwork and fittings to make dusting and cleaning as light as possible; the building of many furnishings, such as sideboards, china closets, bookcases and seats, as integral parts of the interior to reduce sweeping and moving to a minimum—all these features are part of the general and wisely democratic trend.

tious one, and to plan their hospitality on an informal instead of a formal scale. This change of attitude toward essential things has naturally brought about a simplification in household management, a more personal

COMFORT AND ECONOMY COMBINED IN SMALL CRAFTSMAN HOMES

ONE of the greatest charms of most old-fashioned dwellings—Colonial homes, for instance, or English farm or manor houses—lay in the generous size of their rooms, especially the main or living room. They were built in the days of large families, and before the concentrative energies of modern civilization had made men measure real estate by the square foot instead of by the acre. Today, many of our home-builders, particularly in the suburbs of the larger cities, find themselves confronted with the problem of obtaining the utmost modern comfort in a moderate-priced house on a narrow lot—and it sometimes needs considerable ingenuity to devise a plan which will utilize the available space to the best possible advantage.

One difficulty in planning a small cottage or bungalow is to provide a sufficient number of rooms in the limited area given, and yet prevent the interior from seeming cramped and small. It is desirable that a feeling of openness should be insured above all for the living and dining rooms, since this part of the house is sure to be the most used. A practical and pleasant way to accomplish this is to have the two rooms communicating with each other, with a wide opening between them. In the Craftsman bungalow and cottage which we are showing this month, we have introduced a variation of this

method which may offer a timely suggestion to those of our readers who are planning homes. We have made the division between the rooms even less than usual, so that they have substantially the effect of one long room. A study of the plans will show just how this has been done in each case, and will reveal a compact and economical use of space throughout the rest of the interiors. The arrangement of rooms should make the housework comparatively easy.

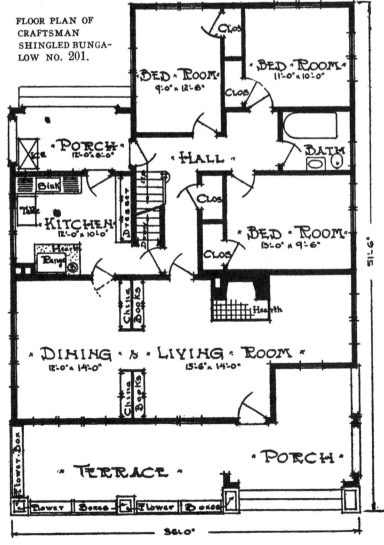

FLOOR PLAN OF CRAFTSMAN SHINGLED BUNGALOW NO. 201.

Gustav Stickley, Architect.

CRAFTSMAN SHINGLED BUNGALOW NO. 201: THIS SIMPLE, COMFORTABLE HOME
HAS BEEN PLANNED TO MEET THE NEEDS OF A SMALL FAMILY, AND COULD BE
BUILT ON A NARROW SUBURBAN LOT: THE ATTIC SPACE MIGHT BE FINISHED
OFF FOR MAID'S ROOM, GUEST CHAMBER OR NURSERY, AS DESIRED.

Gustav Stickley, Architect.

THIS TWO-STORY CRAFTSMAN HOUSE, NO. 202, IS BUILT WITH THE LOWER WALLS OF STUCCO, AND SHINGLES IN THE GABLES AND ROOF: THE FLOOR PLANS, ON THE OPPOSITE PAGE, SHOW AN UNUSUALLY COMPACT AND ECONOMICAL ARRANGEMENT OF THE INTERIOR.

COMFORT AND ECONOMY IN SMALL HOMES

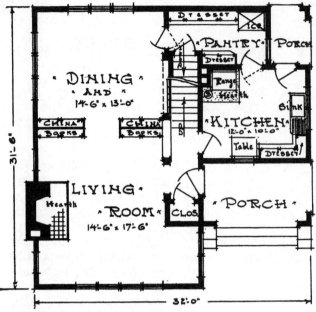

CRAFTSMAN CONCRETE AND SHINGLE BUNGALOW NO. 202: FIRST FLOOR PLAN.

THE first design that we are presenting here is a bungalow, No. 201, planned for a small family of moderate means who wish to combine real home comfort with simplified household arrangements. The building is particularly suitable for the suburbs, and being only 36 feet wide could easily be placed on a 50 foot lot without crowding too close to possible neighbors.

The shingled walls and roof have been kept fairly low, both for economy of construction and to emphasize the homelike air of the exterior. Rough stone is used for the foundation and chimneys, to give a note of variety in texture and coloring, although brick would accomplish the same result if stone did not happen to be available in the locality where the bungalow was built.

The entrance is especially inviting, for one steps up onto a sheltered porch, one corner of which is cosily protected from winds by the walls of the living room. The parapet on the right, and the arrangement of pillars and roof, make it possible to enclose the space by screens in summer or glass in winter. A terrace extending across the rest of the front also provides a pleasant space for open-air life, separated a little from the garden by the low stone wall and flower-boxes between the small brick posts —a device which makes the outlook from the dining and living room windows very pleasing. Brick has also been used above the stone steps of the porch.

As the roof of the porch shelters the front door, no vestibule is provided, so that

you step directly into the living room and are greeted by the welcome sight of the big open fireplace with its tiled hearth. At the right of this is a sort of alcove off the main room, with two casements overlooking the garden at the right and another on the recessed porch. The rear wall of this alcove provides an appropriate place for the piano, while the music cabinet could stand either beside the chimneypiece or in the front corner.

As we have indicated on the plan, this room and the dining room are practically one, for the division between them consists merely of low cabinets, with shelves for books on one side, and for china on the other. The dining end of the room has a group of three casements in the front and side walls, and as there is no projecting porch roof except at the entrance corner, the place will be light and sunny, especially if the bungalow is built facing south. If the owner prefers to have the entrance at the left-hand side, and the morning sun in the dining room and kitchen, this can be attained by simply reversing the plan. Another modification, which some people might desire, and which would probably be necessary in a cold climate, is the utilization of the recessed corner of the front porch for a hall or vestibule. In this case, of course, the entrance door would be arranged here instead of where indicated at present.

The idea being to keep the bungalow as simple and economical as possible, no pass pantry has been provided; the kitchen,

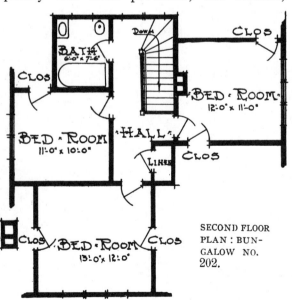

SECOND FLOOR PLAN: BUNGALOW NO. 202.

COMFORT AND ECONOMY IN SMALL HOMES

though only 12 by 10 feet, is quite large enough for a dwelling of this size, and the range, dresser, sink and work-table are well-lighted and convenient. The ice-box is on the service porch, which is so constructed that it can be screened or glassed in, according to the season.

In the center of the bungalow is a hall which affords convenient communication between the front and rear, and separates the sleeping rooms from the living portion of the house. From this hall, also, descend the cellar stairs, with those to the attic just above, and a closet for coats or linen against the opposite wall. If the three bedrooms and bath on this floor did not afford sufficient accommodation, the space beneath the roof, which is lighted by windows in the gables, could be finished off and used for maid's room, guest chamber or nursery, according to the family needs.

THE second design, No. 202, shows a two-story cottage, with the lower walls of stucco, and shingles in the gables and gambrel roof. If built with the living room facing south or east, plenty of sunlight will be insured for this room and the dining room. The entrance is well sheltered by the angle of the walls, and the living room is further protected from draughts by the small passage or hall, with its coat closet, which is arranged here. This hall also gives access to the stairs, and permits one to answer the front door bell from the kitchen without passing through the other rooms.

The same type of combined living and dining room is shown here as in the preceding house, and the arrangement of the groups of casement windows and open fireplace adds to the decorative interest as well as comfort of the place. The staircase is partially screened from the dining room by a grille and from the living room by a half-height partition with a shelf for ferns or pottery, giving an opportunity for an effective use of the structural woodwork. A pass pantry with two built-in dressers and an icebox forms the communication between dining room and kitchen, and from this pantry the cellar stairs descend beneath the main flight. In the kitchen, the sink and work-table are placed beneath windows, and a dresser is built into the corner between. A small recessed porch is provided at the rear.

The second floor has been planned so as to obtain three bedrooms with full-height ceilings, and plenty of closet space is provided beneath the slope of the roof. There is also a linen closet in the hall.

TWO THOUSAND DOLLARS FOR A SIMPLE HOME

WHAT TWO THOUSAND DOLLARS WILL ACCOMPLISH IN BUILDING A COMFORTABLE HOME: BY CHARLES ALMA BYERS

Photographs by the Author.

IT has often been declared that an attractive house need not cost any more than an unattractive one. This seems especially true of the bungalow, for there is no type of building that lends itself more easily to economical and at the same time beautiful construction. Our California architects, particularly, have proved this in their many successful designs. They seem instinctively to appreciate the decorative possibilities of their materials. In the exteriors they use brick and stone, cement, shingles and timbers, always in a way that brings out the natural beauties of texture, coloring and form. And in the design and finish of interior woodwork and structural features, they work along equally simple and artistic lines. In the arrangement of the rooms, too, they evince a delightful originality without being at all eccentric, and by solving each problem from an individual standpoint they manage to achieve a remarkably distinctive and homelike result. And all this they accomplish at a surprisingly reasonable outlay.

The home-builder, therefore, who seeks economy as well as comfort, finds it worth while to study California bungalow plans,

THE BUNGALOW HOME OF MR. R. H. DREW, LOS ANGELES, CALIFORNIA, DESIGNED BY E. B. RUST, ARCHITECT, AND COSTING ONLY $2,000.

and the one presented here serves as an excellent illustration of the principles that underlie most of the buildings of this general type.

This charming little five-room home cost only $2,000 to erect, and when one notes its many admirable points one wonders how it could have been built for such a comparatively small sum; for it is not only pleasing in appearance, both outside and within, but also substantially constructed and well equipped.

In style it has all the characteristics of the Western bungalow—a roof that is almost flat, wide eaves, rough sturdy timbers, and generous window groups. The outside walls are shingled, and the masonry work is of brick and cement, while a white composition is used for the roof. The main woodwork of the exterior is stained a dark brown, with white trim, and these, together with the red brick, white cement and white roofing, produce an interesting color scheme.

There is a small front porch and a pergola on one side, both of which have cement steps and flooring. In the rear is the usual screened porch with its stationary wash tubs.

The interior is very compact and cozy in its arrangement. The living room, in front, contains a chimneypiece of old-gold brick, with a built-in bookcase on one side and a seat on the other. The top of this seat is

TWO THOUSAND DOLLARS FOR A SIMPLE HOME

CORNER OF DINING ROOM IN THE DREW BUNGALOW, SHOWING PANELED WALLS AND SIMPLE BUILT-IN BUFFET: THERE IS JUST THE SORT OF HOME ATMOSPHERE ONE WOULD EXPECT IN A BUNGALOW OF THIS TYPE.

hinged so that the space underneath may be used as the fuel receptacle. The woodwork, which is of Oregon pine, is given a finish like Flemish oak, and the walls are covered with a paper of soft brown. In this room as well as in the dining room and small library, the flooring is of polished oak.

The dining room opens from the living room and has glass doors leading into the side pergola, in addition to the group of four windows on the right. An attractive and convenient buffet is built at one end, as shown in the photograph. The walls are paneled to a height about four feet six inches, along the top of which is a narrow plate rail. The paper used in this room is olive green, but the woodwork is finished like that of the living room.

There are two bedrooms of ample dimensions, between which the bathroom is placed, and a small hall separates them from the rest of the house. The woodwork in these rooms and in the hall is enameled white, and the walls in the two sleeping rooms have paper of moiré pattern in delicate shades.

The kitchen possesses an unusually complete and practical arrangement of cupboards and other fittings and is of convenient size for a home of this kind. Behind the kitchen is a little breakfast room with a built-in cupboard. White enamel is used for the woodwork of both these rooms, also for the kitchen walls.

As indicated by the view of the dining room, the interior of this bungalow is very simple and homelike. The furnishings are few, but well chosen and the whole arrangement is such as to make the household work light.

The bungalow is the home of Mr. R. H. Drew, of Los Angeles, California, and was designed by E. B. Rust, an architect of that city. Costing but $2,000 in Los Angeles, it should be duplicated for approximately that sum in almost any locality. It does not possess a furnace, however, and this would be needed in other climates. But a furnace for a building of this size should cost less than a hundred dollars—not counting the excavation, which would naturally vary according to local conditions.

Being only 28 feet wide, the bungalow is particularly suitable for a narrow lot, and for this reason as well as for the convenience of its arrangement and economy of its construction, the plan merits careful consideration from those who contemplate the erection of an inexpensive home.

To those who expect to build on a corner lot, and need a design of this simple, economical type, the plan would also appeal, for it could be placed with the living room and porch fronting one street, and the dining room windows overlooking the other, with the bedrooms at the rear for quiet and privacy. If it seemed preferable, in

TWO THOUSAND DOLLARS FOR A SIMPLE HOME

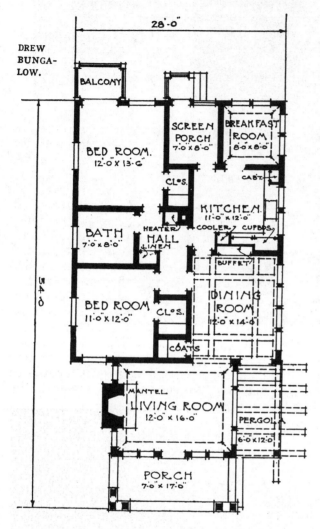

DREW BUNGA-LOW.

BALCONY

BED ROOM.
12'-0" X 13'-6"

SCREEN PORCH
7'-0" X 8'-0"

BREAKFAST ROOM
8'-0" X 8'-0"

CL'S.

CAB'T.

BATH
7'-0" X 8'-0"

HEATER

HALL

LINEN

KITCHEN.
11'-0" X 12'-0"

COOLER. CUPB'DS.

BED ROOM.
11'-0" X 12'-0"

CL'S.

BUFFET

DINING ROOM.
12'-0" X 14'-0"

COATS

MANTEL

LIVING ROOM.
12'-0" X 16'-0"

PERGOLA
6'-0" X 12'-0"

PORCH
7'-0" X 17'-0"

28'-0"

54'-0"

FLOOR PLAN.

such a case, to screen the kitchen and breakfast room more effectually from the street, the pergola which is now indicated in the corner could be projected and extended along the dining room, kitchen and breakfast room wall. This would increase the outdoor living space, screen the bungalow better from the view of passersby, and add considerably to its architectural interest. In order to avoid darkening the kitchen windows, the planting of vines might be omitted at this point.

For a wide but shallow lot, the plan would also be practical, in which case also the pergola arrangement just suggested would be desirable across the front—which is now the side.

Needless to say, a home of this character is equally suited in design, construction and interior arrangement to an Eastern as to a Western site. Indeed, the influence of California architecture is quite noticeable among our modern Eastern bungalows.

"BRIARWOOD": A HILLSIDE HOME AMONG THE TREES

THERE are few sites that lend themselves to home-building with more readiness and charm than a wooded hillside. This is partly because the sloping ground gives an opportunity for that irregularity of architectural contour which is so apt to result in a picturesque air, and partly because the trees, especially if they are evergreens, form a warm, friendly background against which the house seems to nestle, while the foliage and branches in the foreground help to break the lines of the building and give its newness a fairly mellow look.

We are presenting here an unusually attractive little country home of this character, owned by two business women—Dr. Alle Smith and Sue Dorris—and designed by the former. "Briarwood" is the name of this inviting retreat—so-called from the abundance of sweetbriar that grows all around. And the simple design and finish of the building, both inside and out, are quite in keeping with its woodland name.

The winding steps form a pleasant link between hill and home, the porch and balcony offer plenty of space for outdoor living, and the general shape of the cottage with its dormered roof, suggests the simple comfort to be found within. The balcony was especially built to afford an elevated outdoor vantage point from which could be enjoyed the wonderful view presented by

HILLSIDE BUNGALOW OWNED BY TWO BUSINESS WOMEN, DR. ALLE SMITH AND SUE DORRIS: THE BUNGALOW, WHICH WAS DESIGNED BY DR. SMITH, COST ONLY $2,200.

"BRIARWOOD," A HILLSIDE HOME

the landscape around the front of the house. And behind the building is a concrete retaining wall, beyond which is the kitchen garden. This wall is covered, in season, with nasturtiums, which give a bright spot of color to the scene.

The outside of the bungalow is covered with rough rustic shingles, stained a driftwood gray, and for the inside trim is used fir of comparatively fine grain, which is given a warm gray stain. The inside walls are tinted the same tone, and the ceilings are a rich cream color. These neutral shades form an excellent background for the hangings, which are blue gray with colored borders in Japanese design. The contrasting colors needed to brighten the rooms are furnished by the Turkish rugs, pottery, Maxfield Parrish pictures and other decorative features. The two photographs of the interior give a general idea of the simplicity with which the place is furnished. There is no crowding of pieces, and everything is planned for use, durability and comfort, the decorative effects being mainly the outcome of homelike arrangement and harmonious design.

The most interesting feature of the living room is, of course, the fireplace, which is built of tiles made by the owners under the instruction of Miss Olive Newcomb, now teacher in the Los Angeles schools. The clay of which these tiles were made was found less than half a mile from the site of the bungalow, so that they literally add a bit of "local color" to the room. They are lightly tinted in harmony with the color scheme of the interior, and on each side, as seen in the picture, is inlaid a panel picture done in clay, made from a camera view taken by Sue Dorris. Above the mantel is a motto in tiles—"East, West, Home's Best"—which completes this much-admired chimneypiece.

But perhaps the most important thing about the fireplace is the fact that it is so constructed as to heat not only the living room but other rooms besides—for, according to the opinion of the two enterprising women who own this charming home, the heating system was much too vital a matter to be disposed of in the usual casual way, by leaving it in the hands of an outsider, however expert. They devised, therefore a system of coils which carry water from the fireplace to the radiators in the various rooms, and then to a reserve tank. There are three radiators in this system—one in the dining room, one in the first-floor bedroom, and another in the dressing room upstairs. The bath is also connected with the fireplace and range, so that there is always plenty of hot water to be had.

"BRIARWOOD," A HILLSIDE HOME

Those who are contemplating the building of a country bungalow may find many helpful suggestions in the two floor plans shown with this article. The main entrance is from the sheltered recessed porch into the long living room with its fireplace, bookshelves and corner seat. Beyond, through the arch, is the dining room with a built-in

A CORNER OF THE CHEERFUL DINING ROOM: A BUILT-IN BUFFET EXTENDS BENEATH THE FARTHER WINDOW.

FLOOR PLAN OF "BRIARWOOD," DESIGNED BY A BUSINESS WOMAN.

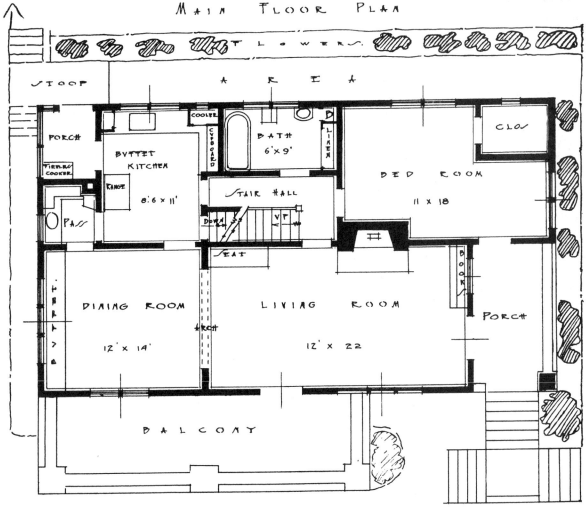

"BRIARWOOD," A HILLSIDE HOME

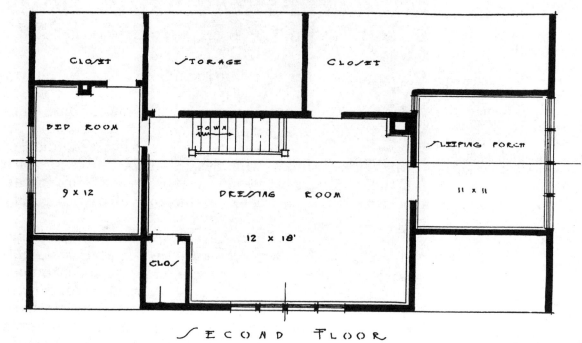

SECOND FLOOR

SECOND FLOOR PLAN OF "BRIARWOOD."

buffet occupying the farther end beneath the windows. A small pass pantry leads to the kitchen, which can also be reached through another door, and from one corner of the kitchen the cellar stairs descend beneath the main flight. A glassed-in service porch is provided at the rear, and here is placed the fireless cooker.

The rest of the first floor plan is occupied by the bathroom and bedroom, both opening from the stair hall, while on the floor above is a large dressing room, on one side of which is a bedroom and on the other a sheltered sleeping porch open at one end. The rest of the space beneath the room is utilized for closets and storage.

The cost of construction of this bungalow was $2,200—surely a very reasonable amount for such a comfortable home.

THE "COLONIAL BUNGALOW:" A NEW AND CHARMING VARIATION IN HOME ARCHITECTURE: BY CHARLES ALMA BYERS

Photographs by the Author

THE bungalow, since its introduction into this country a few years ago, by way of California, has enjoyed greater popularity than any other type of home. For it has fulfilled in a simple, homelike and usually inexpensive way the needs of a growing number of American families who desired comfortable modern homes that were roomy, compact and convenient, suited to a democratic mode of existence, and provided with plenty of space of sheltered outdoor life.

While retaining these general characteristics, however, the bungalow has always been more or less influenced by other styles of architecture, and in consequence has been passing through a continuous evolution away from its early American prototype, becoming more and more adapted to the requirements of the country as a whole. Originally it was in this country planned for Southern California only, where the climate is mild throughout the year. But even in this land of perpetual summer, the leading bungalow architects have gradually come to realize the desirability of possessing a durably and warmly constructed home—a home, at least, of far better construction than was the bungalow in the beginning. Hence the more substantial modern developments in this field both in the East and West.

The newest variation of the bungalow type is a combination of the original design with the Colonial cottage, and the result has come to be known as the "Colonial bungalow." It includes the most admirable features of the two styles in a particularly charming manner, and is adaptable to almost any locality. Like the bungalow, it is but one story in height and presents a rather low and rambling appearance. On the other hand, it adheres to the cottage characteristics in that its roof is shingled and its outside walls are covered with resawed weather-boarding, which is painted instead of stained. In pitch of roof and projection of eaves it strikes a happy medium between the two styles, and in structural lines in general it retains an almost equal number of the characteristics of each of the original models. Instead, however, of possessing any suggestion of the usual rustic air of the old-time bungalow, it is of extremely dignified Colonial appearance, and of substantial and warm construction. The arrangement and finish of the interior show a marked leaning toward those of the average bungalow, rather than the Colonial style, which means greater convenience and comfort.

THE "COLONIAL BUNGALOW"

THE accompanying illustrations reveal a particularly successful example of this new style of home, and will be found worth studying by those who contemplate building along these general lines. The house has a frontage of thirty-nine feet and a depth of forty-seven. The siding and all the finishing timbers are painted white, the shingled roof is moss green, and the exposed masonry work is of bluish-red brick. The combination of colors is particularly effective, and the simple mahogany-finished front door gives a touch of contrast that emphasizes the entrance in a pleasant, hospitable manner. Over this door is a slight canopy-like projection, the rest of the front porch being practically an uncovered terrace.

This terrace, as well as the walk and steps leading to it, is of brick, and along the outer edge are placed four garden urns containing dwarfed shrubs, which add an attractive note to the bungalow. There are four French windows in the front wall and three in the wall next to the side street, and those that do not open upon the front terrace are provided with small brick landings that serve also to break up the line of the foundation and link the bungalow with the surrounding grounds. A rather massive outside chimney of brick is a prominent feature of one corner, and it is to the excellence of the masonry throughout that much of the charm of the exterior is due. Every detail, however, has received the most careful attention, even to the arrangement of suitable awnings over the windows.

An especially admirable outside feature of this home is the small court or patio in the rear. Enclosed on three sides, this court provides an excellent outdoor retreat entirely shut off from the view of passersby, and at the same time it receives an unhindered circulation of fresh air. It is floored with cement, and overhead are a few pergola beams which, covered with vines, afford a pleasant shelter from the sun and add considerably to the charm of the court. One French window opens from a rear bedroom into this inviting enclosure, and three others lead from the dining room, the rear wall of which is thus practically of glass.

AS the floor plan shows, the arrangement of the interior is both homelike and convenient. Folding glass doors form the only division between the living room and dining room, and by throwing these wide open the two may be converted into virtually one large room. In the living room is an open fireplace with facing and hearth of chocolate-colored tile, and in the dining room is a charmingly designed and well-built buffet with a china closet at either end. These two rooms have quarter-sawed oak floors, and the woodwork, which is of straight-grain pine, is given a fumed oak

"COLONIAL BUNGALOW" IN LOS ANGELES, THE HOME OF MARION R. GRAY, DESIGNED BY HAROLD BOWLES, ARCHITECT, AND BUILT AT A TOTAL COST OF THIRTY-FIVE HUNDRED DOLLARS.

DETAIL SHOWING THE PERGOLA-COVERED COURT IN THE REAR OF THE COLONIAL BUNGALOW, WITH FRENCH WINDOWS OPENING FROM THE DINING ROOM: A CHARMING PLACE FOR SERVING MEALS AND FOR GENERAL OUTDOOR LIVING.

FIREPLACE CORNER IN LIVING ROOM OF COLONIAL BUNGALOW SHOWING TILED MANTEL, SIMPLE SUBSTANTIAL FURNISHINGS AND TASTEFUL CRETONNE DRAPERIES AT THE LONG WINDOWS.

THE DINING ROOM OF THE BUNGALOW, WITH ITS BUILT-IN SIDEBOARD AND CHINA CLOSETS, EXCELLENT IN BOTH DESIGN AND WORKMANSHIP.

THE "COLONIAL BUNGALOW"

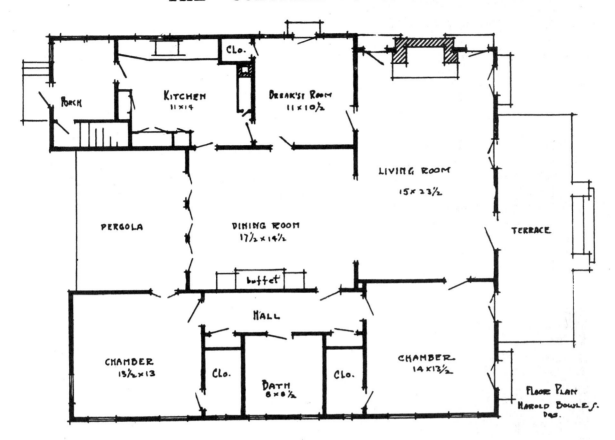

finish. The walls of the dining room are finished with a leatherette wainscot reaching to the usual plate shelf, and the walls above, as in the living room, are papered. The lighting fixtures consist of inverted domes, and the drapery used for the several French windows is yellow-flowered cretonne. The furnishings are simple, substantial and homelike.

On one side of the house, shut away from the living and dining rooms, are the bedrooms and bath. Each of the bedrooms has a roomy closet lighted by a small window, and in the hall that connects these rooms with the bathroom are two small linen closets. The bathroom is finished with a tile wainscot, and the walls of the bedrooms are papered. The woodwork in all of these rooms, as well as in the connecting hall, is enameled white.

The kitchen, which is on the opposite side of the bungalow, possesses all of the usual conveniences, including cupboards, cabinets, drawers, a draught cooler and a hood for the range; and

the finish here also is white enamel. In the rear of the kitchen is the customary screened porch, and between the kitchen and the living room is located the breakfast room, with white enamel woodwork and decorations in delft blue. This room would be equally appropriate for den, library or maid's room.

Under the rear of the house is a basement, eleven by fourteen feet, which is walled and floored with concrete. A hot-air furnace located here furnishes heat to the rooms when required. The stairway to this basement descends from the screened porch behind the kitchen.

This charming and practical little "Colonial bungalow" is located in Los Angeles, California, and is the home of Marion R. Gray. It was designed and built by Harold Bowles, an architect of that city, and represents a total cost of thirty-five hundred dollars. For approximately this sum it should be satisfactorily duplicated in almost any locality.

MAKING THE BUNGALOW EXTERNALLY ATTRACTIVE: BY M. ROBERTS CONOVER

THOUGH the name bungalow comes from India and belongs properly to a one story building consisting of a central large hall with smaller rooms opening from it and a wide covered porch all around to protect from tropical suns, it has come to be quite generally applied in America to almost any small country house. A country house of a story and a half or even two stories if it has a large porch across one or more sides of it is now, though technically incorrect, referred to as a bungalow. In India the name is given to even very large and imposing houses of stone or brick, almost equaling a palace in rank if but one story in height, to government rest houses and to army quarters providing they are but the one story height.

So many of our little country houses are called bungalows that the name has come to be endeared to us. It conjures a comfortable, well shaped little house in the midst of a garden, shaded by trees, with the perfume of flowers floating in through open windows.

It is not difficult to make this picture a reality. The planting of a few vines to give it relation to the garden, a shrub or so at the corners to soften sharp angles and break too severe lines and a tree to give play of light and shade over the house will bring it about. There is a wide list of vines, annuals, perennials, shrubs and ornamental trees from which one may make choice, but several things should be borne in mind; chief of these is the winter aspect of the bungalow. Summer sees to it that it is attractive from April to November, but we must look to it that it is beautiful the rest of the time. There are evergreen shrubs such as pines, cedars, spruces, retinosporas, cypresses that can be had tall or round, dwarfed or large and of many shades of green, and there are the broad leaved shrubs such as

azaleas, laurels, rhododendrons, etc., that in addition to keeping green all winter put forth gorgeous blossoms in the spring and early summer. Many trees are as beautiful in winter as in summer, because of their delicate tracery of branches. Some shrubs have brightly colored stems which after the leaves have fallen give a grateful sense of color. Others like barberries and viburnums have bright berries; so with a little study winter beauty can easily be provided.

For summer planting color harmony must be considered when the main planting of perennials has been decided upon. Then the annuals can be varied with each season. Some of the most ornamental trees are those which bear fruit. Fruit trees in the front yard are not considered proper by some, but no tree takes on a more picturesque form than an old apple or cherry tree. The accompanying photographs hold helpful suggestions for bringing about external beauty of country cottages.

The first photograph shows a bungalow built to give a view of the Raritan Bay through the porch, so that a picture of the bay and sky is had as one approaches the house, which is built on a side hill. The back portion does not resemble a bungalow so much as the front, for it is on a level with the ground. This porch extends around the two sides of this house and forms the main living room of the family during the summer.

The second photograph illustrates the charm of roof and porch lines broken by

BUNGALOW BUILT TO GIVE VIEW OF THE RARITAN BAY FROM THE PORCH.

INTERESTING BUNGALOW ARCHITECTURE

the use of a gable. The large tree makes a pleasant play of sunshine and shadow across the house and the large porch suggests a cozy comfortable outdoor room.

The charm of the vine-clad cottage is shown in the third photograph. This cottage is completely covered with Boston ivy. The effect is cool and bowerlike. We can imagine the beauty of color of this house in the fall.

In the fourth photograph an example of planting to cover a basement made conspicuous by the slope of land is given. From the street this house is apparently a one story bungalow. The problem was to cover the necessary and useful basement at the back

BUNGALOW WITH A LARGE PORCH USED FOR OUTDOOR SITTING ROOM.

of the house formed by the lay of the land. As may be seen it was effectively solved by a planting of blossoming shrubs. The vine against the chimney carries the line on up most gracefully and the trees bear promise of welcome fruit.

The fifth picture shows a bungalow enclosed with boards which are allowed to project log-cabin fashion at the corners. The small windmill is a novel feature for a bungalow. The vines across the front of it make a graceful curtain to shut out too strong rays of the sun. The very simple rustic pergola leading to the front door gives promise of a beautiful walk when the vines have had a chance to cover them.

The last photograph shows how a roof line may be softened in imitation of the old thatched roofs of English cottages. The hedge and the winter trees give promise of summer beauty. An evergreen at either side of the steps and a planting of large leaved evergreens at the corner of the

COOL AND BOWER-LIKE EFFECT OF BUNGALOW COVERED WITH VINES.

INTERESTING BUNGALOW ARCHITECTURE

house would have added warmth to this cottage through the long winter.

The economical aspect of artistic building has been commented upon in the most convincing way by Maurice B. Adams. He says, "The artistic aspect of country-side architecture naturally appeals to the majority of readers far more directly than any discussion on financial matters would do, however appropriate and necessary others will consider such a question of ways and means. These last-named essentials frequently induce some to believe that ugly, crude, or tasteless buildings are necessarily cheaper, or that picturesque, convenient, and architecturally well-proportioned buildings must relatively be more costly. This is not true. There is such a thing in building as 'cheap and nasty,' which in plain

INTERESTING EXAMPLE OF PLANTING TO COVER A CONSPICUOUS BASEMENT.

terms reads 'dear at any price.' Indifferent construction and poor materials will without a doubt incur perpetual expense in the upkeep which bad work always renders unavoidable. There is only one reliable way of minimizing the ultimate cost of maintenance, and if this does mean a larger initial outlay, the advantage of a wise investment is thereby ensured. This self-evident commonplace might perhaps have demanded an apology but for the fact that people are continually endeavoring to obtain what they term 'cheap building work,' and with this end in view are induced to put their faith in the so-called 'practical man,' who, however efficient he may be otherwise, unblushingly gives the most con-

GALOW ENCLOSED WITH BOARDS WHICH ARE ALLOWED TO PROJECT LOG-CABIN FASHION AT THE CORNERS.

INTERESTING BUNGALOW ARCHITECTURE

THE ROOF LINE OF THIS BUNGALOW IS MADE IN IMITATION OF THATCHED ROOFED ENGLISH COTTAGES.

clusive evidence as to his entire inability to produce well-contrived, properly-built, homely, or tasteful houses. The speculating builder is no doubt often exceedingly clever, and in an ingenious fashion knows how to cater for the public, occasionally providing quite a remarkable amount of accommodation, of a kind, for a strictly modest rental; and he also quite understands to what extent a degree of pretentiousness attracts the popular fancy. He builds to sell, and in common with all speculating investments when he realizes, the profits are large. No architect can compete on these lines with such builders, and he need not attempt to do so. In the long run there can remain no question as to which kind of building pays the owner best. An unqualified designer not only fails to obtain a homely character and graceful simplicity in his work, but he seldom if ever employs his materials economically, scamp as he may; and buildings carried out in this fashion will cost the building owner much more than if he had given his commission to a good architect. Even assuming that the money outlay in either instance be the same, and that in structural stability there is not much difference, it cannot be pretended that the results in any sense are identical, even though the areas of the rooms correspond.

"The main essentials consist of the charm of artistic fitness by which alone a building can be harmonized with its site and surroundings, making it as it were part of the ground on which it stands, restful and unobtrusive, comfortable and suitable. These are the qualities which alone can impart interest and give durable pleasure. Such qualities do not depend so much upon money expenditure as upon an application of thought and good taste. They exist quite apart from elaborateness of detail, and are mostly obtained by avoiding all ornamental excrescences, which ill accord with the environment of the hedgerow and the coppice. Picturesqueness comes of simplicity of form, and belongs to good proportion producing pleasant groupings, giving graceful sky-lines, and casting telling shadows, so essential for contrast and color."

We might add that the picturesqueness that comes of simplicity does not come from the simplicity that is uncouthness, plainness, an unthought-out, unadorned crude thing. True simplicity, the highest attainment of art, approaches the divine. Simplicity does not mean a half formed, ignorant construction, but something so fine, pure and superior that it stands apart from the ordinary as a flower stands apart from common weeds.

A STORY OF HOME-MAKING

(Illustrated by photographs of a house designed by J. S. Long, and built by the Long Building Co.)

WHEN one enters upon the pleasant adventure of home making, all sorts of exciting things begin to happen, as is quite to be expected with adventures. The most carefully laid plans fail utterly and better ones arise in their stead, disappointment over the result of some detail is soon forgotten in success beyond all hope of another one. But unlike Stevenson's joy of the road that was so much greater than the "arriving," the quest of the home, joyous though it is, cannot compare with the quiet hours of peace and contentment after the home is finished and one looks upon his work and sees that it is good. It is good to sit upon one's own vine-covered porch and contemplate the many perfections of the hard won achievement, to enjoy in retrospect the paths of difficulty and of pleasure over which the adventure led.

The story of home making ought to be as interesting as any other tale of adventure, of travels in a new land or even of love, for every home story is the best kind of a love story. A house is much like a composite picture—designers, carpenters, masons, plumbers, brick, mortar, steel and wood, furniture and furnishings of silk, cotton, linen, glassware,

HOUSE ALONG CRAFTSMAN LINES, DESIGNED AND BUILT BY THE LONG BUILDING CO., SEATTLE.

tin and silver have all influenced the character of the finished house, left some weak or strong, beautiful or ugly impress of themselves upon the final picture. Houses are recorders of experience, vouchers of taste or the lack of it. A man's thumb-prints upon paper have no more convicting a variation of individuality than the house he elects to build upon the lot of his choice. The bumps and depressions of a man's head are no more an indication of his character than the windows, porches, roof and doors of his house— were there some new species of phrenologist to interpret them. The preference of Georgian, Colonial, Dutch, English, Craftsman or the many other styles are as

LIVING ROOM SHOWING FIREPLACE NOOK IN THIS SAME HOUSE.

A STORY OF HOME-MAKING

DINING ROOM OF THE HOUSE DESIGNED BY THE LONG BUILDING CO.

the house, an excellent view of Mount Ranier can be obtained and from the front porch Lake Washington and the Cascades may be seen. With such superb triumphs of nature as neighbors, it would seem sacrilege to intrude a too ornate, artificial, flippantly designed house. The site demands an unobtrusive, respectful, harmonious structure with windows and porches, permitting the beauty of nature to be enjoyed in the ever changing aspects of morning and evening light. A certain reverent simple dignity of architecture is fitting.

Within, this house was ordered for comfort and convenience of housekeeping. A study of the floor plans reveals that thought

indicative of temperament as the choice of one's clothing.

Every mail brings us some pleasant report of homes built along Craftsman lines, because there was something in them that found echo in the hearts of the builders, some note of sympathy, some expression of practicality, some demand for honesty.

Mr. J. S. Long has recently sent us the floor plans and photographs of a bungalow designed by him, one, as he says, "in distinctly Craftsman style." This house, though designed especially for a corner lot, can just as well be built on any 60 foot lot.

The following detailed description will certainly be appreciated by prospective builders who desire a house of this size. It is of cedar shingles laid two, three and seven inches to the weather and all exterior trim with the exception of window and door panes is of selected rough fir. The main body of the house is stained a light brown, the rough trim a little darker. The roof is black; window and door frames, sash and lattice on rear porch are pure white; with this rustic texture and color, cobblestones are undoubtedly the most effective material of which a chimney could be made. Concrete would have made too extreme a contrast, dark clinker-brick might have been used, but the cobblestones, especially since a few stones appear in the garden, seem perfectly appropriate. Vines will in time add to the rustic naturalness of the whole effect.

From the pergola porch at the side of

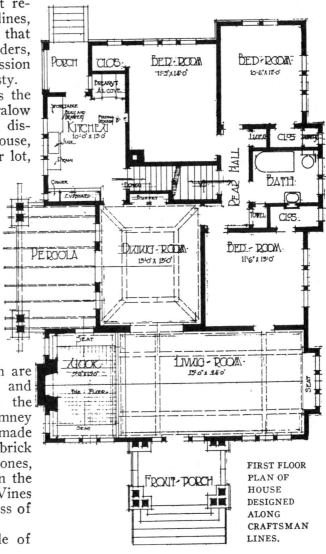

FIRST FLOOR PLAN OF HOUSE DESIGNED ALONG CRAFTSMAN LINES.

A STORY OF HOME-MAKING

PULLMAN DINING ALCOVE, FOLDING IRONING BOARD CLOSET SHOWN BY THE GAS STOVE.

dining room is beamed and paneled and a buffet built in the side nearest the kitchen. The woodwork gives a soft warm glow to the room. Absence of all gingerbread work gives it a pleasant, modest dignity.

But it is in the kitchen that the greatest ingenuity has been displayed. This room is what the Long Building Company, architects and builders, declare to be a "strictly cabinet" kitchen throughout, that is, it is arranged to save unnecessary steps, planned with every thought for the minimizing of labor, with every care for convenience, with the ideal of intensive housekeeping always in mind. Everything has been placed within easy reach for the work at hand; a stairway leads directly from the kitchen to

has been taken to make the interior seem as open and roomy as possible, to save steps in the kitchen, to get bedrooms and baths conveniently related. How many home ideas have been incorporated within the compass of that small home! The vine-wreathed porch for pleasing entrance, the cozy fireplace flanked by shelves of books, the sunny dining room with pergola hard by that can be incorporated with it in one glorious room simply by opening wide the glass doors, the outdoor pergola that can be sitting room or breakfast room as needed, the kitchen, with all that heart can desire in the way of cupboards, spacious bedrooms, large attic storage place and healthful sleeping porch, all go toward the making of a most delightful and convenient home.

The living room and tile fireplace-nook together make a room 33 feet in length. By raising the "cozy nook" up from the main room by two steps a little sense of privacy or of importance was given it. On either side of this reading or conversation corner are seats hinged so that they provide convenient storage space. The cove pointed granite fireplace extends to the ceiling. Opposite this rest end of the room is a bay window with a built-in seat. The walls are paneled and the ceiling is beamed. All the woodwork here and in the dining room has been stained a mission brown and the walls kalsomined to a creamy tint that suitably corresponds with it. The

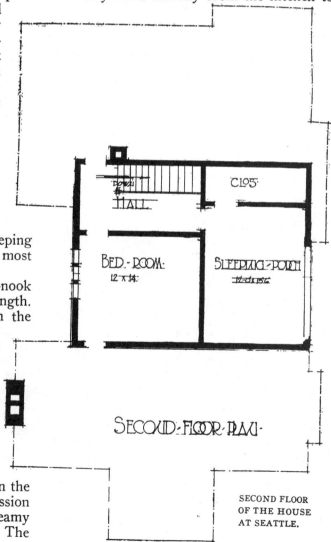

SECOND FLOOR
OF THE HOUSE
AT SEATTLE.

the large cement basement in which are located the coal bins, fruit room and laundry. There are a number of clever built-in features, such as a folding ironing board, flour bins, coolers, drawers, work table and cupboards, the latter being located in the wall nearest the dining room. One of the most practical features is the "Pullman" breakfast alcove. Every home maker who prepares her own meals will appreciate the saving of labor which such an alcove provides. It saves many a trip in and out of the dining room, with first the dishes and the food, with many return trips to the kitchen, after the meal is over and the putting in order of the dining room. Such an arrangement is a great labor saver, and with its flower shelf and cozy relation to the attractive kitchen it certainly is a pleasant place in which to have breakfast. Everyone likes a kitchen if it is well ordered. Under a home-loving woman's efficient management it is often the pleasantest room in the house, a room where every member of the family so loves to congregate that they get "underfoot" in most obstructive way.

Three bedrooms, each with ample, well lighted closets, and a bath, are provided on the first floor, while an additional bedroom and large sleeping porch are located upstairs. All these rooms are finished in enameled old ivory. It will be observed that there is an abundance of light in each room and also a window in each closet. For a house of this size there is little left to be desired in the way of cheerful home comfort; but the best thing about it all is the amazingly low cost of its building. The figures which we give below seem to cover a great deal of good material and work for very little money. We are publishing the full cost of this fine little home just as a proof of what can be done under skilled planning, management and careful oversight: Excavating, $45; concrete walls, $230; concrete floor, $110; brick, $150; tile, $50; lumber and mill work, $900; hardwood, $90; hardware, $85; sheet metal, $25; plastering $185; plumbing, $200; sewer, $45; carpenter work, $500; electric light wiring, $70; furnace heat, $140; painting, $175; miscellaneous, $50; ground, $300; total, $3,350. These figures of course represent what can be done in the West and not in the East. However, though some items would be greater in the East, some others would be less.

A CHARMING SIMPLE BUNGALOW WITH PALATIAL FURNISHINGS: BY CHARLES ALMA BYERS

Photographs by Lenwood Abbott.

A CHARMING bungalow home in Southern California embowered in flowers and greenery throughout the year is outlined, sometimes bathed in purple haze, against a wall of mountains. In the valley below it is always summer, but the peaks of the mountain wall often wear a crown of snow. Near the bungalow grow stately eucalypti and straggly oaks, the bungalow itself is low and rambling, and from whatever point it is viewed it conveys a most picturesque impression.

And even more interesting, but in a different way, is its interior. Ordinarily one thinks of the bungalow as a type of home adaptable only to the tastes of the family of moderate means. But the bungalow we are showing in this article is the home of a millionaire, and its interior is palatial in its furnishings and decorations. There are rare old pieces of furniture, antique mirrors, paintings by old masters, and rich rugs and draperies from many lands, while among the collection of books are found volumes of almost priceless value. Certainly one would rarely ever find a home of more elegance.

THE OPEN END OF THE PATIO IS SCREENED BY A ROW OF BAY TREES. HOME OF JOHN P. CUDAHY, ESQ.

Structurally, this bungalow is an excellent representation of the popular bungalow home of California. It is designed to enclose an open court or *patio,* on three sides. In the main it is but a single story high, but one of the wings possesses a low second-floor addition. The shingled roof is of comparatively slight pitch and has wide overhangs in the eaves and gables. The walls of the first-floor portion are of creamy white stucco over building tile, while the walls of the upper part are covered with redwood shakes. The woodwork is stained a soft brown color, which contrasts strikingly with the creamy stucco, and produces a very attractive color scheme.

Perhaps the most generally admired feature of the bungalow, structurally, is the *patio.* It is roomy and airy, and with decorative lattice work covering the walls. It is floored with dark red brick, and overhead it is entirely unprotected, save for the wide projections of the roof. A row of bay trees screens it on the open side, and from one of the rear corners a tall picturesque old eucalyptus grows right up through the flooring. To even more closely link this *patio* with the extensive garden plot which surrounds the house, a number of palms and ferns spring from aptly placed fern boxes and jardinieres of rare old terra cotta from Venice. Much

A SIMPLE BUNGALOW, RICHLY FURNISHED

of the floor space is carpeted with weatherproof rugs, and wicker chairs and tables furnish it.

Besides this *patio* there is a pergola-veranda along the side of one of the wings. This is likewise paved with brick, and pergola beams are the only covering. A low perpendicular-boarded parapet, coped with a continuous flower box, forms the outside enclosure, and into the space open two sets of French doors, making it another convenient and inviting retreat.

ENTERING the house through this pergola, one is ushered directly into the immense drawing room, which is over forty feet in length. To maintain the bungalow appearance here, the rafters and braces are exposed, but in every other respect one might imagine that he had stepped into a palace. Papal velvet hangings of deep red are at the doors and windows, and the Papal lamps of copper are swung by chains from the old Saxon crown design; the highbacked chairs, the carved tables of English oak and the wonderful old screen from a French chateau combine to give the impression of England in the time of King Richard the Lion Hearted. This old early English idea is still further emphasized by the antique church bench which has been cushioned in velvet, the odd fender rail in front of the fireplace, and by the pictures and

BUNGALOW IN PASADENA, CALIFORNIA, DESIGNED FOR JOHN P. CUDAHY, ESQ., MYRON HUNT, ARCHITECT.

antique mirrors which grace the walls. Oriental rugs cover the floor, and in the center is a square of rich red, like the velvet hangings at the doors and windows. Along a portion of one of the side walls is an immense case full of books—plain books in wonderful bindings and wonderful books in plain bindings. Many of them are very old and rare, among them a set of Shakespeare printed in 1830.

At right angles to the long drawing room is the dining room, with only the velvet hangings intervening, and here again one gets a fine sense of perspective, for it is fifty-five feet from one end of the dining room across the end of the drawing room. The walls of this room are in old blue, gold and copper tones, and the velvet hangings are of Gobelin blue; the furniture is Jacobean with the high-backed chairs cushioned in blue.

The music room is reminiscent of France, with its pale gold covered walls, its hangings of soft champagne tone. There is a fireplace in one corner of the room, and before it is a French firescreen. The mahogany chairs are covered in embroidered gold brocade, and the lighting fixture is a chandelier of carved wood from Florence, which has been treated with dull gold.

Adjoining the music room is a boudoir,

A SIMPLE BUNGALOW, RICHLY FURNISHED

which is finished in delicate shades of pink and rose. Pink satin covers the walls, and in one corner is a huge pink covered couch. The chairs are covered in rose, as is a small sewing table.

The house also contains a children's sunny nursery, a den, and sleeping porch.

PATIO WITH LATTICE WORK COVERING WALLS, FLOORED WITH DARK RED BRICK.

This unusual bungalow is located in Pasadena, California, and is the home of Mr. and Mrs. John P. Cudahy. It was designed by Myron Hunt, a well known California architect.

DRAWING ROOM OF THE CUDAHY HOME SHOWING SHELVES FILLED WITH RARE OLD BOOKS.